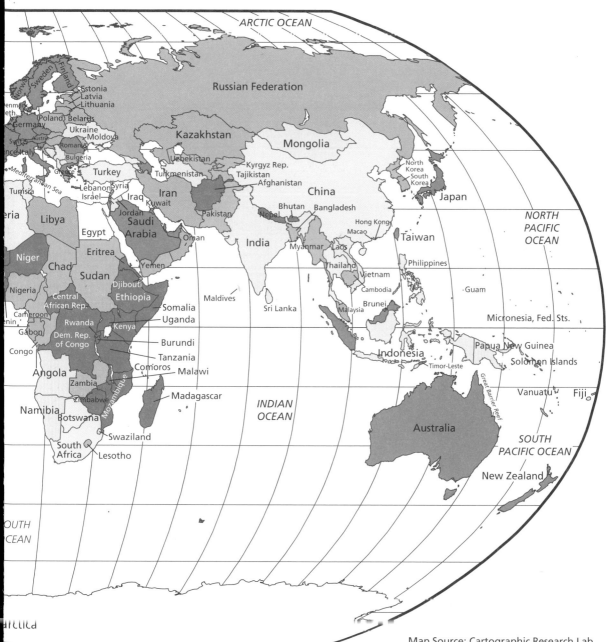

Map Source: Cartographic Research Lab,
University of Alabama

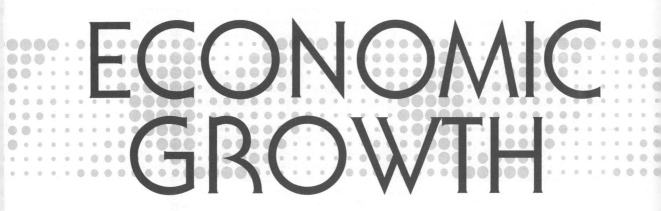

ECONOMIC GROWTH

THIRD EDITION

DAVID N. WEIL

BROWN UNIVERSITY

PEARSON

Boston   Columbus   Indianapolis   New York   San Francisco   Upper Saddle River
Amsterdam   Cape Town   Dubai   London   Madrid   Milan   Munich   Paris   Montréal   Toronto
Delhi   Mexico City   São Paulo   Sydney   Hong Kong   Seoul   Singapore   Taipei   Tokyo

Editor in Chief: Donna Battista
AVP/Executive Editor: David Alexander
Senior Editorial Project Manager: Lindsey Sloan
Editorial Assistant: Emily Brodeur
Director of Marketing: Maggie Moylan
Executive Marketing Manager: Lori DeShazo
Marketing Assistant: Kim Lovato
Senior Managing Editor: Nancy H. Fenton
Senior Production Project Manager: Kathryn Dinovo
Senior Manufacturing Buyer: Carol Melville
Cover Designer: Jonathan Boylan

Manager, Visual Research: Rachel Youdelman
Photo Researcher: Jorgensen Fernandez
Manager, Rights and Permissions: Michael Joyce
Permissions Specialist, Project Manager: Jill C. Dougan
Media Director: Susan Schoenberg
Executive Media Producer: Melissa Honig
Supplements Editors: Alison Eusden and Kathryn Dinovo
Full-Service Project Management: Integra
Printer/Binder: Edwards Brothers Malloy
Cover Printer: Lehigh-Phoenix Color/Hagerstown
Text Font: 11/13, MinionPro

Cover photos: Vintage photo of print shop, ChipPix/Shutterstock; close-up of gears from old mechanism, Tischenko Irina/Shutterstock; machine for writing (typewriter), Jocic/Dreamstime; detail of steam machine valve, Zanico/Dreamstime; green bananas, Anan Kaewkhammul/Shutterstock; Kerala, South India, March 10, 2011, farmer treats rice field buffaloes, Vladj55/Shutterstock; cargo container ship, Egd/Shutterstock; overloaded truck on highway, Rajasthan, India, Paul Prescott/Shutterstock; a bunch of network cables in a data center, Supri Suharjoto/Shutterstock; big old noria (water wheel) on the river in Hama, Syria, Valery Shanin/Shutterstock.

Credits and acknowledgments borrowed from other sources and reproduced, with permission, in this textbook appear on the appropriate page within text or on page 556.

Many of the designations by manufacturers and sellers to distinguish their products are claimed as trademarks. Where those designations appear in this book, and the publisher was aware of a trademark claim, the designations have been printed in initial caps or all caps.

Library of Congress Cataloging-in-Publication Data
Weil, David N.
  Economic growth / David N. Weil.—3rd ed.
    p. cm.
  ISBN-13: 978-0-321-79573-1
  ISBN-10: 0-321-79573-3
  1. Economic development. I. Title.
HD82.W37 2013
338.9—dc23
                          2012016784

10 9 8 7 6 5 4 3

ISBN 10:   0-321-79573-3
ISBN 13: 978-0-321-79573-1

To Rachel

BRIEF CONTENTS

Contents v
Preface xi
About the Author xx

CHAPTER 1   THE FACTS TO BE EXPLAINED 1

CHAPTER 2   A FRAMEWORK FOR ANALYSIS 29

CHAPTER 3   PHYSICAL CAPITAL 48

CHAPTER 4   POPULATION AND ECONOMIC GROWTH 82

CHAPTER 5   FUTURE POPULATION TRENDS 121

CHAPTER 6   HUMAN CAPITAL 150

CHAPTER 7   MEASURING PRODUCTIVITY 179

CHAPTER 8   THE ROLE OF TECHNOLOGY IN GROWTH 201

CHAPTER 9   THE CUTTING EDGE OF TECHNOLOGY 238

CHAPTER 10   EFFICIENCY 268

CHAPTER 11   GROWTH IN THE OPEN ECONOMY 298

CHAPTER 12   GOVERNMENT 330

CHAPTER 13   INCOME INEQUALITY 363

CHAPTER 14   CULTURE 399

CHAPTER 15   GEOGRAPHY, CLIMATE, AND NATURAL RESOURCES 432

CHAPTER 16   RESOURCES AND THE ENVIRONMENT AT THE GLOBAL LEVEL 463

CHAPTER 17   WHAT WE HAVE LEARNED AND WHERE WE ARE HEADED 503

CONTENTS

Preface   xi
About the Author   xx

CHAPTER 1
THE FACTS TO BE EXPLAINED   1

1.1   Differences in the Level of
      Income among Countries   3
      BOX: Total GDP versus GDP per Capita   6

1.2   Differences in the Rate of
      Income Growth among
      Countries   8
      Growth's Effect on the Level of Income   8
      BOX: Working with Growth Rates   10
      Growth during Recent Decades   13
      BOX: Growth versus Business Cycles   13
      Growth since 1820   14
      Growth before 1820   17
      BOX: Income Inequality between and within
      Countries   18
      BOX: Economic Growth as Seen from Outer
      Space   20

1.3   Conclusion   22
      APPENDIX Measuring and Comparing GDP Using
      Purchasing Power Parity   25

CHAPTER 2
A FRAMEWORK FOR ANALYSIS   29

2.1   The Economics of Sylvania and
      Freedonia: A Parable   29

2.2   From Parable to Practice   33
      The Production Function   34
      From Income Levels to Growth Rates   36

2.3   What Can We Learn from
      Data?   37
      Scatter Plots and Correlations   38

      BOX: Randomized Controlled Trials   42
      BOX: Learning from Historical Data   44

2.4   Conclusion   44

CHAPTER 3
PHYSICAL CAPITAL   48

3.1   The Nature of Capital   49

3.2   Capital's Role in Production   51
      Using a Production Function to Analyze Capital's
      Role   51
      BOX: Capital's Share of National
      Income   54
      Factor Payments and Factor Shares   54

3.3   The Solow Model   56
      Determination of Capital per Worker   56
      BOX: The Rise and Fall of Capital   58
      BOX: Measuring Change over Time   59
      Steady States   59
      BOX: Steady State: A Noneconomic
      Example   61
      The Solow Model as a Theory of Income
      Differences   63
      The Solow Model as a Theory of Relative Growth
      Rates   66

3.4   The Relationship between
      Investment and Saving   68
      Explaining the Saving Rate: Exogenous versus
      Endogenous Factors   70
      The Effect of Income on Saving   71
      BOX: Government Policy and the
      Saving Rate   72

3.5   Conclusion   74
      BOX: The Rise and Fall of Capital Revisited   75
      APPENDIX Further Exploration of the Cobb-Douglas
      Production Function and the Speed of Convergence
      in the Solow Model   79

CHAPTER 4

POPULATION AND ECONOMIC GROWTH 82

4.1 Population and Output over the Long Run 84

Population over the Long Run 84

The Malthusian Model 85

BOX: The Power of Population 85

The Breakdown of the Malthusian Model 90

4.2 Population Growth in the Solow Model 93

Population Growth and Capital Dilution 93

A Quantitative Analysis 95

4.3 Explaining Population Growth 97

Mortality Transition 98

Fertility Transition 100

The Interaction of Fertility and Mortality 102

4.4 Explaining the Fertility Transition 105

Reduced Fertility: The Means 105

BOX: Family-Planning Programs and Their Effects 108

Reduced Fertility: The Motives 109

4.5 Conclusion 113

APPENDIX A More Formal Description of the Total Fertility Rate, Life Expectancy, and Net Rate of Reproduction 117

CHAPTER 5

FUTURE POPULATION TRENDS 121

5.1 Forecasting Population 122

Forecasting Mortality 124

Forecasting Fertility 125

BOX: AIDS in Africa 126

BOX: The Tempo Effect 129

Demographic Momentum 132

Population in the Very Long Run 133

BOX: How Many People Can the Earth Support? 134

5.2 The Economic Consequences of Demographic Change 136

The Slowdown in Population Growth 136

Population Aging 138

Redrawing the World Map 143

BOX: Going for the Gold 145

5.3 Conclusion 146

CHAPTER 6

HUMAN CAPITAL 150

6.1 Human Capital in the Form of Health 151

The Effect of Health Differences on Income 151

Modeling the Interaction of Health and Income 154

BOX: Health and Income per Capita: Two Views 156

6.2 Human Capital in the Form of Education 158

Changes in the Level of Education 159

BOX: The Economic Effects of Malaria 160

Education and Wages 161

Human Capital's Share of Wages 163

BOX: The College Premium in the United States 164

6.3 How Much of the Variation in Income across Countries Does Education Explain? 169

A Quantitative Analysis of the Impact of Schooling Differences among Countries 169

6.4 Conclusion 176

BOX: Human Perfectability and the Growth Slowdown 177

CHAPTER 7

MEASURING PRODUCTIVITY 179

7.1 Productivity in the Production Function 180

7.2 Differences in the Level of Productivity among Countries 182

Measuring Productivity Differences among Countries 183

The Contribution of Productivity to Income Differences among Countries 187

BOX: Problems with Measuring Capital—and Their Implications for Measuring Productivity 188

7.3 Differences in the Growth Rate of Productivity among Countries 192

Measuring Countries' Productivity Growth 192

The Contribution of Productivity to Growth Differences among Countries 194

7.4 Conclusion 196

BOX: A Tale of Two Cities 197

CHAPTER 8

THE ROLE OF TECHNOLOGY IN GROWTH 201

8.1 The Nature of Technological Progress 202

Technology Creation 202

Transfer of Technology 203

Determinants of R&D Spending 204

8.2 Patents and Other Forms of Intellectual Property Protection 206

Problems with the Patent System 208

Alternatives to Patents 210

8.3 Modeling the Relationship between Technology Creation and Growth 211

One-Country Model 211

Two-Country Model 215

BOX: International Technology Transfer 216

8.4 Barriers to International Technology Transfer 223

Appropriate Technology 224

Tacit Knowledge 227

BOX: Embodied Technological Progress and Leapfrogging 228

8.5 Conclusion 229

MATHEMATICAL APPENDIX Incorporating Technological Progress into the Solow Model 233

CHAPTER 9

THE CUTTING EDGE OF TECHNOLOGY 238

9.1 The Pace of Technological Change 239

Technological Progress before the 18th Century 239

BOX: Some Milestones of Technological Progress 240

The Industrial Revolution 243

Technological Progress since the Industrial Revolution 246

9.2 The Technology Production Function 248

BOX: General-Purpose Technologies 249

The Relationship between Technology Level and the Speed of Technological Progress 250

BOX: Science and Technology 251

Decreasing Returns to Scale in Technology Production 252

Implications for the Future of Technological Progress 253

BOX: Where Is the Cutting Edge of Technology? 254

9.3 Differential Technological Progress 256

Differential Technological Progress: Two Theoretical Examples 257

Technological Progress in the Real World: Goods versus Services 258

Technological Progress in the Real World: Information Technology 259

BOX: Predicting Technological Progress 260

9.4 Conclusion 262

MATHEMATICAL APPENDIX An Improved Version of
the Technology Production Function 266

CHAPTER 10
EFFICIENCY 268

10.1 Decomposing Productivity into
Technology and Efficiency 269

Analyzing Cross-Country Data 270

10.2 Differences in Efficiency:
Case Studies 273

Central Planning in the Soviet Union 273

Textiles in 1910 274

Differences in Productivity within an Industry 276

Subsurface Coal Mining in the United States,
1949–1994 278

10.3 Types of Inefficiency 280

Unproductive Activities 280

Idle Resources 281

Misallocation of Factors among Sectors 282

Misallocation of Factors among Firms 288

Technology Blocking 289

BOX: Finance and Growth 290

10.4 Conclusion 294

CHAPTER 11
GROWTH IN THE OPEN
ECONOMY 298

11.1 Autarky versus Openness 298

Measuring Output in an Open Economy 300

Globalization: The Facts 300

Globalization: The Causes 302

BOX: Tariffs, Quotas, and Other Trade
Restrictions 305

11.2 The Effect of Openness on
Economic Growth 306

Growth in Open versus Closed
Economies 307

How Changes in Openness Affect
Growth 308

The Effect of Geographical Barriers to
Trade 310

11.3 Openness and Factor
Accumulation 311

Growth with Capital Mobility 312

Assessing the Free-Capital-Flow
Model 314

11.4 Openness and Productivity 316

Trade as a Form of Technology 317

BOX: The Rise and Fall of Consolidated
Alchemy 318

Openness and Technological
Progress 319

Openness and Efficiency 320

11.5 Opposition to Openness 322

BOX: Anti-Globalization 324

11.6 Conclusion 326

CHAPTER 12
GOVERNMENT 330

12.1 Defining Government's Proper
Role in the Economy 333

The Case for Government Intervention
in the Economy 333

The Case against Government Intervention
in the Economy 335

Swings of the Pendulum 336

12.2 How Government Affects
Growth 337

Rule of Law 337

Taxation, Efficiency, and the Size of
Government 339

Planning and Other Industrial
Policies 343

BOX: The Other Path 344

BOX: Planning Is Not Always a Failure 345

Civil Conflict 346

12.3 Why Governments Do Things That
Are Bad for Growth 348

Some Other Goal 348

Corruption and Kleptocracy 349

Self-Preservation 350

BOX: Government Regulation: Helping Hand
or Grabbing Hand? 352

12.4 Why Poor Countries Have Bad
Governments 353
  Causation Running from Income to Government
    Quality 354
  BOX: Democracy and Economic Growth 356
  Causation Running from Government Quality to
    Income 358

12.5 Conclusion 359

CHAPTER 13
INCOME INEQUALITY 363

13.1 Income Inequality:
The Facts 364
  Using the Gini Coefficient to Measure Income
    Inequality 365
  The Kuznets Hypothesis 368
  BOX: Is Growth Good for the Poor? 371

13.2 Sources of Income Inequality 373
  Explaining the Recent Rise in Income
    Inequality 378

13.3 Effect of Income Inequality on
Economic Growth 380
  Effect on the Accumulation of Physical
    Capital 380
  Effect on the Accumulation of Human
    Capital 381
  Income Inequality, Income Redistribution, and
    Efficiency 384
  Sociopolitical Unrest in Response to Income
    Inequality 388
  Empirical Evidence 389

13.4 Beyond Income Distribution:
Economic Mobility 392

13.5 Conclusion 396

CHAPTER 14
CULTURE 399

14.1 The Effect of Culture on Economic
Growth 400
  Openness to New Ideas 400
  Hard Work 402

Saving for the Future 403
Trust 404
BOX: What Parking Tickets Say about Culture 405
BOX: Pitfalls of Cultural Explanations for Economic
Growth 407
Social Capital 408
BOX: Importance of Social Capital at the Village
Level 410
Social Capability 411
BOX: Changes in Appropriate Culture 414

14.2 What Determines Culture? 416
  Climate and Natural Resources 416
  Cultural Homogeneity and Social Capital 417
  Population Density and Social Capability 420

14.3 Cultural Change 422
  BOX: Determinants of Cooperation: An
    Experimental Approach 423
  Economic Growth and Cultural Change 424
  Government Policy and Cultural Change 425
  Media and Cultural Change 427

14.4 Conclusion 428

CHAPTER 15
GEOGRAPHY, CLIMATE, AND
NATURAL RESOURCES 432

15.1 Geography 433
  Location, Trade, and Growth 434
  BOX: Guns, Germs, and Geography 436
  Geographic Concentration and Spillovers 438
  Geography's Effect on Government 438

15.2 Climate 442
  Climate and Agricultural Productivity 444
  Climate and Disease 446
  Climate and Human Effort 449

15.3 Natural Resources 450
  The Relationship between Natural Resources
    and Growth 450
  Explanations for the Resource Curse 453

15.4 Conclusion 458
  BOX: Resources and Early Industrial Development:
    The Case of Coal 460

CHAPTER 16

RESOURCES AND THE ENVIRONMENT AT THE GLOBAL LEVEL 463

16.1 Natural Resource Concepts 464

Nonrenewable Resources 464

Renewable Resources 467

Property Rights over Resources 469

Resources and Production 471

16.2 Incorporating Natural Resources into the Analysis of Economic Growth 473

BOX: Resource Disasters 474

Revising National Accounts 476

Resource Prices 478

BOX: The Bet 482

Why Resource Limitations Do Not Prevent Economic Growth 482

BOX: Resource-Saving Technologies 486

16.3 Growth and the Environment 486

The Environmental Kuznets Curve 488

BOX: The Environmental Kuznets Curve in London 490

Global Warming 492

16.4 Conclusion 496

APPENDIX Technological Improvement versus Resource Depletion 500

CHAPTER 17

WHAT WE HAVE LEARNED AND WHERE WE ARE HEADED 503

17.1 What We Have Learned 503

Factor Accumulation 503

Productivity 504

Fundamentals 506

17.2 What the Future Holds 507

BOX: Will Growth Make Us Happy? 508

What Will Happen to the World Income Distribution? 511

Will Technological Progress Continue Apace? 511

What Is the Future of World Demographics? 512

Will Global Economic Integration Continue? 512

Will Shortages of Natural Resources Constrain Economic Growth? 513

17.3 A Final Thought 513

References 514

Glossary 530

Index 536

Credits 556

NEW TO THIS EDITION

The world economy is evolving rapidly, as is research in the field of economic growth. I have updated the textbook to reflect changes in both dimensions.

- There has been a massive updating of data used throughout the book. Data on gross domestic product (GDP) is now from the Penn World Tables, version 7.0. The period of analysis on which I focus in the first seven chapters of the book is now 1975–2009 (the period was 1960–2000 in the first edition and 1970–2005 in the second edition). Data on human capital, mobility, inequality, and many other variables have been updated by using new or more current sources. Additionally many other historical time series have been extended for additional years.

- Material on randomized controlled trials (RCTs) has been inserted systematically throughout the book, starting with a discussion of RCTs in the context of inference in Chapter 2 and then followed up with examples of the use of RCTs in research in Chapters 4 and 6, as well as discussion of RCTs in several end-of-chapter problems.

- A new section (in Chapter 12) discusses civil violence and its relationship to growth.

- A new section (in Chapter 8) examines patents and other forms of intellectual property protection.

- The discussion of the Easterlin paradox (Chapter 17) has been completely revised to reflect the conclusions from new research.

- New data has been added on intergenerational mobility in the United States, comparisons of mobility across countries, and differing perceptions of mobility.

- New research on the role of media in affecting social capital and cultural attitudes toward fertility and women is presented in Chapter 14.

- New material has been added on government-owned banks, peak oil, natural resource prices, how the correlation of firm productivity with size varies across countries, and the Extractive Industries Transparency Initiative, as well as a new figure on global temperatures.

In addition to these larger additions, there are dozens of other places throughout the book where new research findings are brought to bear as part of the narrative. Innumerable bits of information that appear throughout the text have been updated. Recent events, such as the great recession of the late 2000s, have been incorporated as well.

ECONOMIC GROWTH AS A FIELD OF STUDY

Economic growth is a compelling topic. You cannot read the newspaper or travel to other parts of the world without wondering why differences in standards of living among countries are so large. You cannot help but marvel at how more than a billion people in China are leaping out of poverty within a generation, whereas the incomes of hundreds of millions of others elsewhere in the world have stagnated. It is impossible not to wonder whether our grandchildren will be as rich compared to us as we are compared to our grandparents.

Economists have been thinking about these issues for a long time. The puzzle of why some countries are economically more successful than others is right there in the title of Adam Smith's *Inquiry into the Nature and Causes of the Wealth of Nations* (1776). The questions of why some countries are rich and others poor, and why some countries grow quickly and others slowly, never disappeared as a part of economic investigation, but in the period after World War II, they were divided among several different fields. The formal theory of economic growth became part of macroeconomics; the study of poor countries became the field of economic development; productivity growth was part of industrial organization; and the study of how the currently wealthy countries came to be that way was subsumed in economic history.

Over the past three decades, economic growth has reemerged as an independent field. To see how rapidly the field has expanded, look at the figure on page xiii, which shows how frequently the phrase *economic growth* has appeared in the titles or abstracts of journal articles in the Econlit database from 1981 to 2010. Over that period, the frequency has grown sixfold. This rise in the number of journal articles has been matched by a rise in graduate courses on the topic and by a rise in the number of researchers working in the area. A generation of Ph.D. economists now works on economic growth as a field in its own right rather than as a piece of some other field.

The melding of disparate lines of research into the single field of economic growth has been one of the most exciting intellectual developments in economics over the past three decades. But there has been more than a rearrangement of intellectual cargo. New theoretical tools, new data, and new insights have been brought to bear on the old questions of why some countries are richer than others and why some countries grow more quickly than others. Of particular importance has been the application of new data that put empirical flesh on a skeleton built of both old and new theories.

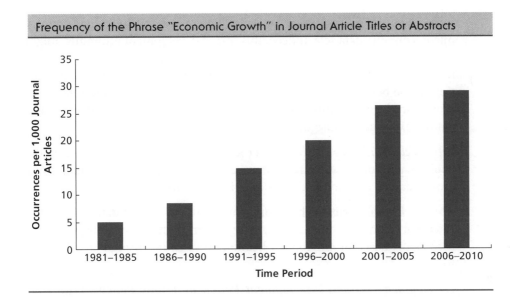

Frequency of the Phrase "Economic Growth" in Journal Article Titles or Abstracts

GOALS AND INTENDED AUDIENCE

This book is my attempt to synthesize the burgeoning literature in economic growth. Recent research has produced a vast quantity of new examples, data sets, and analytic perspectives. The organization of this new material into a coherent intellectual structure not only makes it easier for students to assimilate but also suggests new avenues for future research.

Beyond synthesizing a wide range of literature, I have sought to present research on economic growth in a form easily accessible to a broad audience. The book requires no more background than a course in principles of economics and uses no calculus in the main body of the text. (However, mathematical chapter appendixes and a series of advanced modules available for download from the Web site allow for a more rigorous presentation for teachers who are so inclined.) The book is optimally suited for the following courses:

- ***An Undergraduate Course in Economic Growth*** Many faculty whose research centers on growth have not been able to teach an undergraduate course in their area of interest because they have been reluctant to undertake all the work necessary to translate professional level research for an undergraduate audience. Now they can.

- ***An Undergraduate Course in Economic Development*** Many development economists will find that this textbook fits perfectly with their perspective, including standard models and results that are drawn from single-country microeconomic data sets. Indeed, this sort of development economist might find that the current book better matches his or her perspective than do textbooks that have "Economic Development" in their titles. This third edition of the book moves a step closer to the current trend in development economics by integrating discussion of randomized controlled trials and natural experiments into the text.

- **Advanced Macroeconomics**   Macroeconomists might want to use the book as part of an Advanced Macroeconomics course that would cover growth as well as other research topics in macroeconomics.

- **Applied Econometrics**   The book, along with the online data set and the extensive online Lab Exercises by Ann Owen of Hamilton College, can be used as the basis for an Applied Econometrics course using either Stata or Excel.

- **Development Studies, Development Policy, or Public Policy**   With suitable supplements, the book is appropriate as part of a broader course in development studies, development policy, or public policy at the undergraduate or M.A. level.

- **Ph.D. Courses**   For Ph.D.-level courses in economic growth, economic development, and macroeconomics, this book can serve as a quick, broad introduction to the literature and key issues. It also provides a coherent framework in which students as well as professors can locate their own research.

CONTENT AND ORGANIZATION

Following the first part's two introductory chapters, which describe the facts to be explained and define the book's approach, there are three substantive parts:

- **Factor Accumulation (Chapters 3–6)**
  These chapters examine physical capital, human capital (including both education and health), and population growth and explore the degree to which income variation among countries can be explained by variations in factor accumulation, as well as the determinants of factor accumulation itself. They heavily emphasize quantitative analysis of the role of factors of production in determining output.

- **Productivity (Chapters 7–11)**
  These chapters begin with a development accounting exercise in Chapter 7, showing the importance of variations in the level and growth rate of productivity in explaining cross-country differences in the level and growth rate of income. Chapters 8 and 9 then analyze technology, the former looking

primarily at cross-country differences in the level of technology and the latter focusing on the determinants of progress at the cutting edge of technology. The last two chapters, 10 and 11, examine how institutions and openness to the world economy affect the efficiency with which the economy operates.

- *Fundamentals (Chapters 12–16)*
  These five chapters probe into the deeper determinants that underlie differences in factor accumulation and productivity among countries. Included here are government, income inequality, culture, geography, climate, and natural resources.

This approach of beginning with proximate determinants of income variation and then digging down to see what deeper factors explain these proximate determinants enables undergraduates to assimilate a good deal of information and analysis while retaining a clear structure in their minds. The approach also (not coincidentally) replicates the way in which the field of economic growth has evolved over the past 30 years: Growth economists have shifted their focus from factor accumulation to technology to nontechnological aspects of productivity, and finally to searching for the deeper factors that underlie all of the more proximate determinants of growth.

ALTERNATIVE SYLLABI

Teachers with an interest in the more formal aspects of growth theory might want to skip some or all of the chapters on fundamentals in the last third of the book. They also might want to focus more on the chapter appendixes, as well as the more advanced mathematical modules available on the Web site.

Teachers with a particular interest in development policy will find the Fundamentals chapters of the book, along with components of the Productivity chapters (particularly Chapters 10 and 11, respectively, on efficiency and openness) to be most important. They might want to cover Chapters 3 and 7–9 quickly.

Teachers looking to cut out technical material can excise one or both of the following blocks of material without compromising the structure of the book as a whole: (1) the Solow model and its quantitative implications: all of Chapters 3 and 7, along with Section 4.2, the first part of Section 5.2, and Section 6.3; (2) formal models of technological progress and spillovers: Section 8.3 and all of Chapter 9.

Chapter 5, on future population trends, stands largely on its own and can be skipped without a loss of continuity. Chapter 16, on resources and environment at the world level, is also something of a stand-alone chapter and can be omitted.

Many faculty might want to proceed slowly, giving their students empirical assignments using the data analysis facility on the Web site and the Lab Exercises by Ann Owen as well as the many data sources with links on the Web site.

KEY FEATURES

- ***Rich Data***   Data from a large cross-section of countries, on attributes ranging from desired fertility to disease environment to rule of law to income inequality, are used to motivate and illustrate the models presented in the book. In addition, extensive use is made of results drawn from household and village-level data, including randomized trials and natural experiments.

- ***Robust Theoretical Framework***   A simple yet robust theoretical framework helps students to conceptualize how the different factors that affect growth fit together as part of the overall story.

- ***Quantitative Orientation***   Throughout the text, students are shown how to go beyond thinking, "Does x affect growth?" to ask, "*How much* does x affect growth?"

- ***Up-to-Date Content***   The text includes the latest research in this rapidly developing field. The data in the tables and figures are the most recent available.

PEDAGOGICAL AIDS

- Chapter 2 lays out the book's structure in the form of a vivid parable. Chapter introductions remind students of the book's overall organization.

- Numerous special-topic boxes in each chapter present self-contained examples or discussions of research.

- Several mathematical chapter appendixes provide more rigorous derivations and extensions of material in the book.

- Each chapter ends with Key Terms, Questions for Review, and Problems. Special icons in the margin identify problems requiring a computer or calculator ▦ and those requiring calculus $\int dy/dx$.

- A Glossary at the end of the book defines all the Key Terms and provides handy page references.

ADDITIONAL RESOURCES AVAILABLE ONLINE

The Web site that accompanies this book, www.pearsonhighered.com/weil, has a number of features to enrich students' experience of the course. These features include a Data Plotter, Lab Exercises written by Ann Owen of Hamilton College, Further Readings, Web Links, and PowerPoint Slides containing all figures and tables in the text.

For instructors only, an online *Instructor's Solutions Manual* accompanies the text. Written by author David N. Weil, the online *Instructor's Solutions Manual* contains the solutions for all the problems in the text. This new edition of the instructor's manual will include additional problems for professors to assign, as well as their solutions. It is available for download on the Instructor's Resource Center, www.pearsonhighered.com/irc.

ACKNOWLEDGMENTS

I had a lot of help in writing this book. Colleagues at Brown, notably Oded Galor, Peter Howitt, Ross Levine, Louis Putterman, Herschel Grossman, Enrico Spolaore, Vernon Henderson, Andrew Foster, Toby Page, and Susan Short, were generous with their time and insight. I also received extremely useful input from colleagues elsewhere, including Victor Lavy, Joram Mayshar, Omer Moav, and Avi Simchon (all of Hebrew University), Philippe Aghion (Harvard University), Elise Brezis (Bar Ilan University), Yaakov Khazanov (Ben Gurion University), Jong-Wha Lee (Korea University), Kevin O'Rourke (Trinity College, Dublin), Steve Parente (University of Illinois), Michael Spagat (Royal Holloway University of London), Joakim Stymne, and Chris Weber (Seattle University). Greg Mankiw taught me how to do economic research and served as a model for textbook writing. Several generations of Brown graduate students were drafted as research assistants, reviewers, or both, including Areendam Chanda, Sebnem Kalemli-Ozcan, James Feyrer, Lennart Erickson, Michal Jerzmanowski, Phil Garner, Chad Demarest, Jeff Brown, Malhar Nabar, Adrienne Lucas, Doug Park, Alaka Holla, Ishani Tewari, Joshua Wilde, Isabel Tecu, Momotazur Rahman, and Adam Storeygard. I benefited from the labor of a series of undergraduate research assistants, including Thomas Benson, Susan Gunasti, Nick Advani, Saranga Sangakkara, Nathan Marcus, Khang Nguyen, Gauri Kartini Shastry, Ameya Balsekar, Jessica Yonzon, Jeffrey Kang, and Mary Bryce Millet. Students at Brown, Harvard, and Hebrew universities had the dubious pleasure of seeing me teach this material out of early drafts. In putting together the third edition, I was aided by the superlative team of Fatima Aqeel, Martin Fiszbein, Evan Friedman, and Daniel Prinz.

I also received crucial input from the following reviewers who provided detailed comments:

Daron Acemoglu, *Massachusetts Institute of Technology*
Marcellus Andrews, *Columbia University*
Susanto Basu, *Boston College*
Charles Bischoff, *Binghamton University*
Henning Bohn, *University of California, Santa Barbara*
Patrick Coe, *Carleton University*
Steve Colt, *University of Alaska, Anchorage*
Brad DeLong, *University of California, Berkeley*

Eric Fisher, *California Polytechnic State University*
Terry Fitzgerald, *Federal Reserve Bank of Minneapolis*
Gerhard Glomm, *Indiana University*
Jonathan Haughton, *Suffolk University*
Harvey James, *University of Missouri, Columbia*
Louis D. Johnston, *College of Saint Benedict, St. John's University*
Barry Jones, *Binghamton University*
Garett Jones, *George Mason University*
John Keating, *University of Kansas*
Louise Keely, *University of Wisconsin, Madison*
Peter Klenow, *Stanford University*
Steve Knack, *The World Bank*
Gregory A. Krohn, *Bucknell University*
Jong-Wha Lee, *Korea University*
Ross Levine, *University of California, Berkeley*
Bernard Malamud, *University of Nevada, Las Vegas*
Jenny Minier, *University of Kentucky*
Olivier Morand, *University of Connecticut, Storrs*
Malhar Nabar, *Wellesley College*
Ann Owen, *Hamilton College*
Chris Papageorgiou, *International Monetary Fund*
Pietro Peretto, *Duke University*
Diego Restuccia, *University of Toronto*
James Robinson, *Harvard University*
David Romer, *University of California, Berkeley*
William Seyfried, *Rollins College*
Peter Solar, *Vesalius College*
Kevin Sylwester, *Southern Illinois University, Carbondale*
Robert Tamura, *Clemson University*
John Tang, *Australia National University*
Jonathan Temple, *University of Bristol*
Akila Weerapana, *Wellesley College*
Larry Westphal, *Swarthmore College*
Mark Wright, *University of California, Los Angeles*
Randall Wright, *University of Wisconsin*
Darrell Young, *University of Texas, Austin*
Lester A. Zeager, *East Carolina University*

Beyond these specific people who provided direct input, I also owe a general debt of gratitude to the large group of scholars working on growth. Over the past

25 years, I have been privileged to do my research in an area where (as Alfred Marshall wrote) "good work is rightly appreciated, invention and improvements... have their merits promptly discussed: If one man starts a new idea, it is taken up by others and combined with suggestions of their own; and thus it becomes the source of further new ideas." Many of the ideas presented in this book are distilled from the informal haze that circulates in the air of conferences and seminars. The National Bureau of Economic Research deserves special mention as the location of so many illuminating gatherings.

I am also indebted to several teachers (and their students) who enthusiastically used drafts of the manuscript as the basis for their courses. The reaction of those actively teaching and learning from the material provided unique "from-the-trenches" input that helped me improve the presentation in many ways. I thank Shankha Chakraborty (University of Oregon), Patrick Coe (Carleton University), Terry Fitzgerald (Federal Reserve Bank of Minneapolis), Barry Jones (Binghamton University), Ann Owen (Hamilton College), Peter Solar (Vesalius College), and Robert Tamura (Clemson University).

Working with the people at my publisher has been a great experience. I continue to be grateful to those who worked with me on the first edition. Many thanks to my editors Sylvia Mallory and Jane Tufts, Denise Clinton, Nancy Fenton in production, Gina Hagen Kolenda for the design, Melissa Honig for the Web site, and Heather Johnson at Elm Street Publishing Services. For the second edition, there was another great team headed by my editor Noel Seibert. Kathryn Dinovo oversaw the production process that time around, Emily Friel at Elm Street Publishing Services gave the second edition a wonderful design, and Kim Nichols at Elm Street Publishing Services handled production tasks. For the third edition, I'd like to thank Lindsey Loan, my editorial project manager, and Kathryn Dinovo for her management of the production process. I'd also like to thank Kristin Jobe at Integra (formerly Elm Street Publishing Services).

My deepest thanks go to my wife and colleague, Rachel Friedberg. It was Rachel who first encouraged me to produce something beyond the standard output of journal articles. She contributed to every stage of this project, but readers of the book should particularly thank her for the pages of showy technique and pointless diversions that they do *not* see as a result of her comments. More important from my perspective, Rachel built with me a happy marriage and household and also gave birth to our three children during the five years that it took me to gestate this one book.

–D.N.W.

ABOUT THE AUTHOR

David N. Weil is the James and Merryl Tisch Professor of Economics at Brown University and a Research Associate of the National Bureau of Economic Research and Brown's Population Studies and Training Center. He received his B.A. in History from Brown in 1982 and his Ph.D. in Economics from Harvard in 1990. He has written widely on various aspects of economic growth, including cross-country empirics, accumulation of human and physical capital, appropriate technology, fertility, migration, habit formation, health, and the use of satellite data to measure income, as well as on such nongrowth topics as demographic economics, Social Security, monetary policy, and portfolio allocation. He has held visiting faculty positions at Harvard University and Hebrew University. He is coeditor of the *Journal of Development Economics* and codirector of the NBER project on the Causes of African Development Successes.

CHAPTER 1

THE FACTS TO BE EXPLAINED

We live in a world of rich and poor. The 7 billion people who inhabit the earth exist under a vast range of economic circumstances. In the developing countries, 925 million people do not have enough food to eat, 884 million do not have access to safe drinking water, and 2.5 billion have no access to sanitation. Roughly 5,000 children under the age of five die every day from diseases caused by contaminated water. At the other extreme, among the industrialized countries, diseases caused by too much food have replaced those caused by too little as a major health problem. Life expectancy at birth is 76 years among the 2.1 billion people living in countries classified by the United Nations (UN) as having high human development, 69 years for the 3.6 billion people living in countries with medium human development, and 56 years for the 1.1 billion in countries with a low level of human development.[1]

> Science is built up of facts, as a house is with stones. But a collection of facts is no more a science than a heap of stones is a house.
>
> —Henri Poincaré

Even when we look beyond these life-and-death matters, the differences in people's living standards are striking. In 2008 there were 687 passenger cars for every 1,000 people in Australia. The corresponding figure for Bangladesh was 2. Sub-Saharan Africa, with 11% of the world's population, accounted for 2.3% of world electricity use in 2003. The United States, with 4.6% of the world's population, accounted for 26%. The fifth of the world that lives in the richest countries receives 60% of the world income. The World Bank estimates that 1.1 billion people survive on incomes of less than one dollar per day, and 2.6 billion live on less than two dollars per day.[2]

These differences among countries pose a mystery. Why are some countries so rich and others so poor? Does it have to be this way? Are there factors that we can point to (and perhaps change) that lead to these enormous gaps? Does the enjoyment of the rich somehow depend on the continued suffering of the poor?

[1] United Nations (2010), http://www.wfp.org/hunger; http://www.unicef.org/wash/, http://www.unicef.org/wash/, http://www.unep.org/Documents.Multilingual/Default.asp?DocumentID=617&ArticleID=6505&l=en.
[2] United Nations (2006).

When we look at how countries have developed over time, a second set of mysteries emerges. Comparing wealthy countries today to their own history, there is once again an immense difference in living standards. A Japanese baby born in 1880 had a life expectancy of 35 years; today life expectancy in Japan is 83 years. In Great Britain, the average height of men rose 9.1 centimeters (3.6 inches) between 1775 and 1975 as a result of better nutrition. In 1958, a worker in the United States earning the average wage had to labor 333 hours to buy a refrigerator; today a worker can earn enough to buy a better product in one-fifth as much time. Since the late 19th century, the fraction of their income that Americans spend on recreation has tripled, while the fraction spent on food has fallen by two-thirds.[3]

This growth in material wealth has been accompanied by a sharp reduction in the amount of work that people have to do. In the United States in 1870, the average workweek was 61 hours, and the concept of retirement in old age was almost unheard of. Today the average workweek is 34 hours, and the typical worker can expect to experience a decade of leisure in retirement.[4]

Even countries that today are relatively poor enjoy living standards that, prior to the last 100 years, were without precedent anywhere. Egypt, Indonesia, and Brazil currently have higher life expectancy than did members of the British nobility at the beginning of the 20th century. For most of human history, something as simple as a reading light at night was a luxury reserved for the very wealthy. Today, 79% of the world's population has access to electricity at home.[5] The fraction of the world's population with income of less than one dollar per day fell by half between 1981 and 2002. In China alone, the number of people with income of less than one dollar per day fell by 200 million during this period.[6]

For most of the world, the last half-century has seen an unprecedented rise in living standards. In the richest countries, this rise has been going on for more than a century, leading to the impression that economic circumstances should always be getting better. But what is the source of this growth?

When we compare growth in different countries, more questions emerge. Some countries have grown along largely parallel tracks. For example, Britain and France have had roughly comparable living standards for centuries. Some countries, such as Argentina—which was one of the wealthiest countries in the world at the beginning of the 20th century—have failed to keep up with the pack. Others, such as Japan, were for a long time far poorer than the world's leaders but then experienced great bursts of growth and caught up. In the

---

[3]Costa (2000), Federal Reserve Bank of Dallas (1997).
[4]Cox and Alm (1999).
[5]Baumol and Blinder (1997), http://www.iea.org/weo/electricity.asp
[6]World Bank (2002).

post–World War II era, these explosions of miraculous growth became increasingly dramatic, with countries such as South Korea making the transition from pauper to industrial power in a single generation. Still other countries have thus far been immune to the contagion of growth and have remained desperately poor. The average African household, for example, consumed 20% less in 1998 than it did 25 years previously. What differences among countries have led to these divergent experiences?

A final question raised by these observations of growth is: Where is this all leading? Will the richest countries in the world continue to grow richer, so that our grandchildren will look back in amazement at the primitive circumstances in which we lived? Will the poor countries continue to trail far behind the richest ones, or will the gaps between rich and poor close? In the face of declining stocks of natural resources, some observers have argued that even the richest countries will have to cut back on their consumption. Will limitations on resources make it impossible for the four-fifths of the world's population still living in relative poverty to catch up? Or will new technologies allow the human race to leave behind the state of want that has been its lot for almost all of history?

This book is an attempt to grapple with the questions of why countries differ in their standards of living and why countries grow richer or fail to grow richer over time. The rest of this chapter lays out in greater detail the scope of the facts to be explained. We first look at differences among countries in their *levels* of income and then examine national differences in the *growth rate* of income. As we will see, there is a close link between these two measures: Countries that are rich today are precisely those that have grown quickly and for a longer period of time in the past.

1.1 DIFFERENCES IN THE LEVEL OF INCOME AMONG COUNTRIES

We begin by examining differences in economic status among countries. Our focus will be on **gross domestic product (GDP),** which is a measure of the value of all of the goods and services produced in a country in a year. GDP can be calculated as either the value of the output produced in a country or equivalently as the total income, in the form of wages, rents, interest, and profits, earned in a country. GDP is thus also known as *output* or *national income*, and these terms are used as synonyms for GDP throughout this book.

Using GDP to measure a country's well-being is not without its problems. Many aspects of economic well-being are not measured by GDP, and there are serious conceptual and practical problems in measuring and comparing GDP across countries or in a single country over time. Despite these drawbacks, however, GDP remains a rough-and-ready measure of standard of living. Where possible, we

A typical Malian family with their possessions.

will flesh out data on GDP with other measures of economic well-being. Still, the gaps among countries' living standards are so large that even an inexact measure brings them into focus.

In comparing income among countries, one issue we face is how to deal with their different currencies. Similarly, in examining income within a single country over time we face the issue of fluctuations in the price level. This book will express data (GDP and other economic measures) in terms of a common unit of currency—U.S. dollars for the year 2005. To convert amounts from other years and countries, we use a set of artificially constructed factors called **purchasing power parity (PPP)** exchange rates.[7] The appendix to this chapter presents a more extensive discussion of how PPP exchange rates are calculated and how they affect comparisons of GDP among countries.

The differences in income among countries are enormous—so large that they can be difficult to comprehend. One useful image, suggested by the

---

[7]Data on GDP and PPP exchange rates are from Heston, Summers, and Aten (2011).

A typical English family with their possessions.

economist Jan Pen, is to think of the people of the world marching by in a parade. Each person's height is proportional to average income in his country, with the average height of all the marchers in the parade being six feet (1.82 meters). You are observing the parade from a reviewing stand, and the parade takes exactly an hour to pass by you. Marchers in the parade proceed at a steady pace, so that after 15 minutes, for example, one-quarter of the people in the world will have passed by. People march by in order of their height, starting with the shortest.

What does the parade look like? For almost all of the time, it is a parade of dwarfs. The first seven minutes are primarily made up of countries from sub-Saharan Africa with heights less than one foot (29 centimeters). Starting in the 13th minute, India passes by, taking up almost 10 1/2 minutes, with marchers 23 inches (59 centimeters) tall. China arrives on roughly the half-hour mark, with marchers 55 inches (1.40 meters), taking 12 minutes to pass. At the 45-minute mark, one sees marchers from Turkey, who have almost exactly the world average height. During the last 15 minutes of the parade, the height of the marchers escalates frighteningly. Nine-foot (2.78-meter) marchers from Croatia pass in the 50th minute and 18-footers (5.51-meter) from Japan in the 52nd minute. Japan is followed by roughly 3 minutes of Western European countries in the 19- to

TOTAL GDP VERSUS GDP PER CAPITA

Much of this book is concerned with what makes countries rich. But *rich* is not always easy to define. One could look at a country's total income or at income per capita. In many ways, income per capita is the more natural measure. The total GDPs of Mexico and Canada are roughly equal ($1,291 billion in Mexico, $1,213 billion in Canada). But we think of Mexico (GDP per capita of $11,629) as being a middle-income country and Canada (GDP per capita of $36,209) as being rich. Certainly most of us would rather live in a country that was "rich" in per capita terms but "poor" in its level of total output than in a country that was "rich" in the sense of having many people, each with a low income.

But depending on what we are interested in, GDP per capita is not always the correct measure to use. The ruler of a country might care about how much tax can be collected and so might be concerned about the total size of national income, not income per capita. Similarly, if we are interested in how large an army can be raised, then total population might be more relevant than total income. Table 1.1 shows the world's top 11 countries in the year 2009 according to three different measures: GDP per capita, total GDP, and population.

Differences among countries in income per capita pose more of a mystery than differences in total GDP. Some countries have high total GDP simply because they have many people. But we have a lot more trouble explaining why some countries are rich in per capita terms and others are not. (And, as we will see in Chapter 4, the relationship between income per capita and the size of the population is complex.)

TABLE 1.1

Top 11 Countries in Year 2009 According to Three Different Measures

Rank	Highest GDP per Capita		Largest Economies		Most Populous Countries	
	Country	GDP per Capita ($)	Country	Total GDP ($ trillions)	Country	Population (millions)
1	Qatar	159,469	United States	12.62	China	1,320
2	Luxembourg	84,525	China	10.08	India	1,160
3	United Arab Emirates	52,946	Japan	3.81	United States	307
4	Bermuda	52,090	India	3.76	Indonesia	240
5	Macao	51,057	Germany	2.66	Brazil	199
6	Norway	49,945	United Kingdom	2.07	Pakistan	181
7	Singapore	47,373	Russia	2.05	Bangladesh	154
8	Kuwait	46,639	France	1.98	Nigeria	149
9	Brunei	46,229	Italy	1.68	Russia	140
10	Australia	41,304	Brazil	1.62	Japan	127
11	United States	41,099	Mexico	1.29	Mexico	111

24-foot range (5.6–7.3 meters), and then by the United States, at 24.8 feet (7.51 meters), which also takes almost 3 minutes. The end of the parade is made up of a few wealthy industrialized countries (Australia, Singapore, and Norway), together taking about 15 seconds, as well as a set of very small, very wealthy countries (including Luxembourg, United Arab Emirates, Kuwait, and Qatar) with heights ranging from 32 to 95 feet (9.7–29 meters), but which pass by in a matter of a second or two.

Figure 1.1 examines these same data; in fact, it looks exactly like the parade just described as viewed from a distance (for visual clarity, Qatar is excluded from the picture). The vertical axis plots countries' levels of income per capita, and the horizontal axis measures the fraction of the world population that has marched by. The figure shows that the world average level of income per capita is $9,909 (this corresponds to six feet in the parade example). The figure also makes clear how unevenly income is distributed. The 20% of world population that lives in the richest countries receives 60% of world income.

FIGURE 1.1

The Parade of World Income

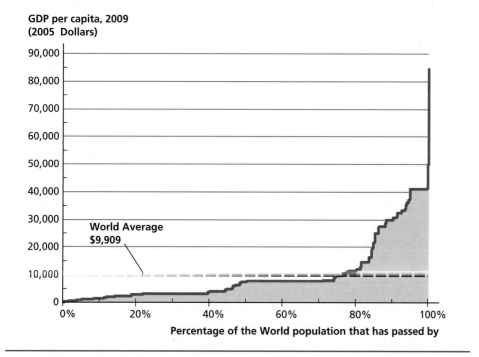

Source: Heston, Summers, and Aten (2011).

One problem with Figure 1.1 is that because the richest countries are so much richer than the rest of the world, the figure tends to obscure differences among the poorer countries. From the perspective of the United States (GDP per capita of $41,099), the differences among Iran (GDP per capita of $10,624), Moldova ($2,493), and Ethiopia ($684) might not seem enormous. We would be tempted to call the United States "rich" and the other three countries "poor." But looking more closely, we can see that in terms of ratios, Iran is just as much richer than Moldova (a factor of four) as it is poorer than the United States. Similarly, Moldova is just as much richer than Ethiopia (again, a factor of four) as it is poorer than Iran. What had seemed like a monolithic block of poor countries is actually more dissimilar than similar.

1.2 DIFFERENCES IN THE RATE OF INCOME GROWTH AMONG COUNTRIES

Figure 1.1 examined the *level* of income in different countries. These data raise the question: Why are some countries so much richer than others? A second sort of measure that we will want to examine is countries' *growth rates* of income (i.e., how quickly their income per capita is rising). Growth is important because a country that grows faster will move to a higher level of income over time.

Growth's Effect on the Level of Income

Figure 1.2 shows the level of income per capita in the United States going back to 1870, the first year for which there are reliable data.[8] The most striking message of this graph is just how much better off people are today! The pattern resembles the parade of dwarfs and giants that we see in comparing income across countries—only now the citizens of the 1870s are the dwarfs, and those of today are the giants. GDP per capita in 2009 was 12.3 times as large as GDP per capita in 1870. This massive increase in income is a testament to the power of compound growth. The average growth rate of GDP per capita over this period was 1.8% per year. Such a change is hardly noticeable from one year to the next. But compounded over 139 years, the effect has been dramatic.

When we look at data on income over long periods of time, it is often useful to use a ratio scale (see "Working with Growth Rates"). Figure 1.4 uses a ratio scale to examine the same data as we examined in Figure 1.2: GDP per capita in the United States. In Figure 1.4, note how regular the process of growth appears when viewed over such a long horizon. The year-to-year fluctuations in output that grab newspaper headlines are certainly visible in the picture, but growth is remarkably predictable. For example, a forecast made in 1929 simply by drawing a trend

---

[8]Maddison (1995).

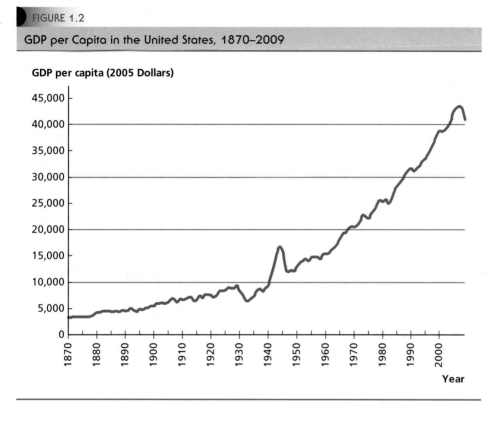

FIGURE 1.2

GDP per Capita in the United States, 1870–2009

GDP per capita (2005 Dollars)

line through the data up to that year would come within a small margin (15%) of accurately forecasting output per capita 80 years later.

The experience of the United States over this period explains the way that Americans have come to think about growth. Presidential candidates ask, "Are you better off than you were four years ago?" implying that getting better off all the time is the natural state of affairs. It turns out, however, that the experience of constant, trendlike growth in the United States since 1870 is almost unique in world history. If we look at other countries or at longer periods of time, such regularity disappears.

Figure 1.5 looks at long-term growth in three countries—the United States, the United Kingdom, and Japan—once again using a ratio scale.[9] The data raise a number of interesting points. Over the 139 years between 1870 and 2009, the United Kingdom grew at an average rate of 1.5% per year, compared with 1.8% per year in the United States. But this small difference in growth had a large effect over time: In 1870 the United Kingdom was 31% richer in per capita terms than the United States; by 2009, it was 19% poorer.

---

[9]Maddison (1995).

WORKING WITH GROWTH RATES

Suppose we observe some economic quantity X in two adjacent years. The growth rate of X is the change in X from the first year to the second, divided by the value of X in the first year. Let t designate the first year and $t + 1$ designate the second. Mathematically, if we call the observations X_t and X_{t+1}, the growth rate g is given by this equation:

$$g = \frac{X_{t+1} - X_t}{X_t}.$$

For example, if $X_t = 100$ and $X_{t+1} = 105$, then the annual growth rate is

$$g = \frac{105 - 100}{100} = 5/100 = 0.05 = 5\%.$$

We can modify this formula to find an average rate of growth over several years. First rewrite the formula for the growth rate as follows:

$$X_{t+1} = X_t \times (1 + g).$$

Now consider the case where X grows at the same rate, g, for two years in a row. Rewrite the equation to apply to years $t + 1$ and $t + 2$, then substitute for X_{t+1} from the same equation:

$$\begin{aligned} X_{t+2} &= X_{t+1} \times (1 + g) \\ &= [X_t \times (1 + g)] \times (1 + g) \\ &= X_t \times (1 + g)^2. \end{aligned}$$

Similarly, if something grows at rate g for n years, we can write

$$X_{t+n} = X_t \times (1 + g)^n.$$

Suppose now that X_t and X_{t+n} are known. We can rearrange our previous equation, solving for g to obtain the average growth rate (technically, this is the geometric average growth rate) over this time:

$$g = \left(\frac{X_{t+n}}{X_t} \right)^{1/n} - 1.$$

For example if we observe $X_t = 100$ and $X_{t+20} = 200$, then the average rate of growth is

$$\begin{aligned} g &= \left(\frac{200}{100} \right)^{1/20} - 1 \\ &= 1.035 - 1 = 0.035 = 3.5\%. \end{aligned}$$

To graph data on variables that grow over time, it is often useful to employ a ratio scale (also called a *logarithmic scale*). On a **ratio scale,** equal spaces on the vertical axis correspond to equal *proportional* differences in the variable being graphed. For example, the vertical gap between $X = 1$ and $X = 10$ is the same as the vertical gap between $X = 10$ and $X = 100$. (By contrast, on the more common **linear scale,** equal spaces on the vertical axis correspond to equal differences in the variable

The most dramatic part of the picture is the data on Japan. The first thing that is striking is just how poor Japan was relative to the other two countries. In 1885 (the year in which the Japanese data begin), Japan's income was almost exactly one-quarter of U.S. income. Over the next half-century, Japan grew slightly faster than the United States, but even as late as 1939, Japanese income was only 35% of U.S. income. After World War II, however, there was a qualitative change in Japanese growth. Some of this fast growth represented a recovery from the ravages of the war, but by the 1960s, Japan had surpassed its prewar trend and continued being graphed.) On a ratio scale, a quantity growing at a constant rate plotted over time will yield a straight line. Figure 1.3 shows an example of how a ratio scale changes our perspective. Both panels consider some quantity X that starts with a value of 1 in the year 0 and grows at a rate of 3% per year for 200 years. The upper panel uses a linear scale, and the lower panel uses a ratio scale.

A useful mathematical approximation for dealing with growth rates is the **rule of 72**. The "rule" is a formula for estimating the amount of time it takes something growing at a given rate to double:

$$\text{doubling time} \approx \frac{72}{g},$$

where g is the percentage annual growth. For example, if something is growing at 2% per year, then it will double in approximately 36 years.

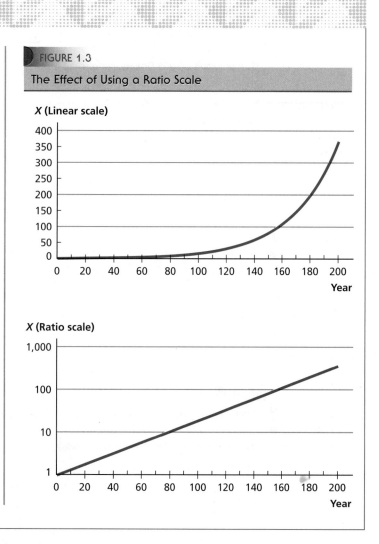

FIGURE 1.3

The Effect of Using a Ratio Scale

to grow rapidly. Between 1950 and 1990, the average growth rate of income was 5.9% per year in Japan versus 2.1% per year in the United States. By 1990, Japanese income per capita was 85% of the U.S. level.

Given the trend in Japanese growth in the postwar period, it seemed to many observers in the late 1980s that Japan would certainly surpass the United States in income per capita around the year 2000 and that, in a few decades more, Japan would have left the United States far behind. Such thoughts generated pride on one side of the Pacific and panic on the other, exemplified in books like *A Japan*

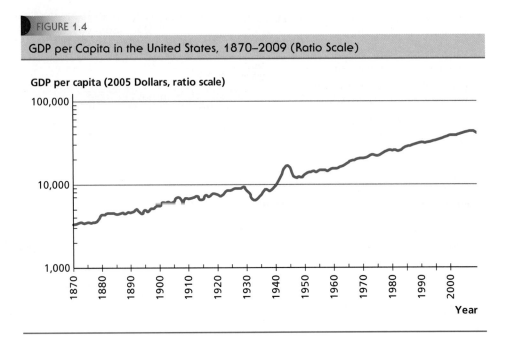

▶ FIGURE 1.4

GDP per Capita in the United States, 1870–2009 (Ratio Scale)

▶ FIGURE 1.5

GDP per Capita in the United States, the United Kingdom, and Japan, 1870–2009

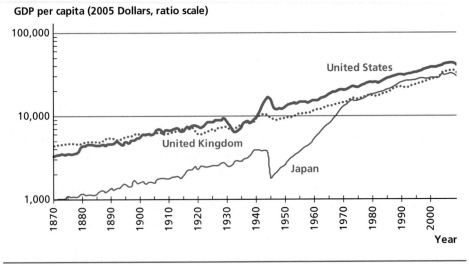

Source: Maddison (1995), Heston, Summers, And Aten (2011).

That Can Say No (1989) by Shintaroi Ishihara, a conservative politician who argued that Japan had amassed enough economic power to assert independence from the United States, and the novel *Rising Sun* (1992) by Michael Crichton, in which Japanese corporations and criminals extend their influence over Los Angeles. But as the figure shows, Japanese growth slowed as Japan approached the level of U.S. income—and the decade that followed the bursting of the asset bubble in the early 1990s was disastrous for the Japanese economy (see box "Growth versus Business Cycles").

Growth during Recent Decades

Like income levels, income growth rates vary among countries. To give a sense of the variety of growth experiences, Figure 1.6 examines data from a sample of 156 countries over the period 1975–2009. The data cover almost all of the

▶ GROWTH VERSUS BUSINESS CYCLES

Growth, in the distinction drawn by economists, is defined to be a long-run phenomenon. The state of the economy fluctuates on an annual or even monthly basis. Yet we find it useful to separate these short-run fluctuations, which are called business cycles, from longer-term trends that span decades. Figure 1.5 clearly shows such distinctions. In the United States, long-run (or trend) growth was relatively constant, and such events as the Great Depression, the boom in output during World War II, and the recessions of 1974, 1982, and 2008 stand out as deviations from the trend. In Japan, there were clearly two changes in trend growth: one at the end of World War II, when growth quickened, and the other in 1973, when growth slowed down.

Although it is relatively easy to separate trend growth from business cycles when we are looking at historical data, it is much more difficult to figure out what is going on in real time. For example, even now it is not clear whether the period of slow growth that began in Japan

in the 1990s is the result of a long recession—that is, a transitory deviation from the long-run trend—or the beginning of a new era of lower long-run growth.

Short-run fluctuations in output attract the most attention in the press. We read about the growth of GDP over the last quarter, unemployment over the last month, or the stock market over the last 15 minutes. Long-run movements are much less newsworthy—indeed, because it may take a decade to figure out that a trend growth rate has changed, it would be hard to say much about it even once a year. But over time it is the long-run trend that determines how rich a country is. If reporters had to summarize the history of the U.S. economy in the 20th century, the headline would not tell the number of recessions or expansions but would say, "Growth of Income per Capita Averages 1.8% per Year."

Comparing countries makes it easier to focus on growth and its long-run effects. The United States during a recession is still a whole lot richer than India during a boom year.

world's population. Each country is categorized according to its average annual growth rate of income per capita. The chart shows the number of countries that fall into each group, along with several examples of countries in the group. For example, Canada's growth rate over this period was 1.6% per year, so it is one of the 29 countries that fall into the category of growth rates between 1.5% and 2.0% per year.

Figure 1.6 demonstrates how large the variation in growth rates has been. At the top of the chart are the well-known "growth miracles." At the bottom are "growth disasters," among them Nicaragua, Somalia, and Zimbabwe, where income per capita actually fell over this period. The average growth rate of the countries in the figure (weighted by their populations in 2009) was 3.3% per year. Notice that the 1.8% annual growth rate of U.S. income over the period 1870–2009—which produced a 12.3-fold increase in income per capita—would have fallen roughly in the middle of the distribution of growth rates shown in Figure 1.6.

Just as growth in a single country compounds over time to result in a large increase in income, differences in average growth rates between two countries will translate over time into differences in countries' relative levels of income. For example, in 1960, South Korea and the Philippines had roughly equal levels of income per capita ($1,782 and $1,314, respectively), but over the next five decades, their growth rates differed dramatically. South Korea was one of the East Asian miracle economies, growing at an average rate of 5.5% per year. The Philippines grew at an average rate of 1.6% per year—a slow rate by world standards but certainly not disastrous. By 2009, however, this difference in growth rates had been translated into an enormous difference in the two countries' levels of income: $25,034 in South Korea and $2,838 in the Philippines. Although South Korea started off poorer, it was almost nine times richer than the Philippines by the end of the period. (The two countries make a particularly interesting case study because, as of the 1960s, many development economists considered the Philippines more likely to succeed economically.)[10]

Growth since 1820

The data in Figure 1.6 cover only the 34-year period ending in 2009. Data similar to this are available for most of the world going back to 1960. Before that year, however, the data are sketchier, both because governments collected less information and because the locations of some borders shifted as a result of conquest and decolonization. To deal with the problems in looking at earlier data, economists

---

[10]Lucas (1993), Easterly (1995).

FIGURE 1.6

The Distribution of Growth Rates, 1975–2009

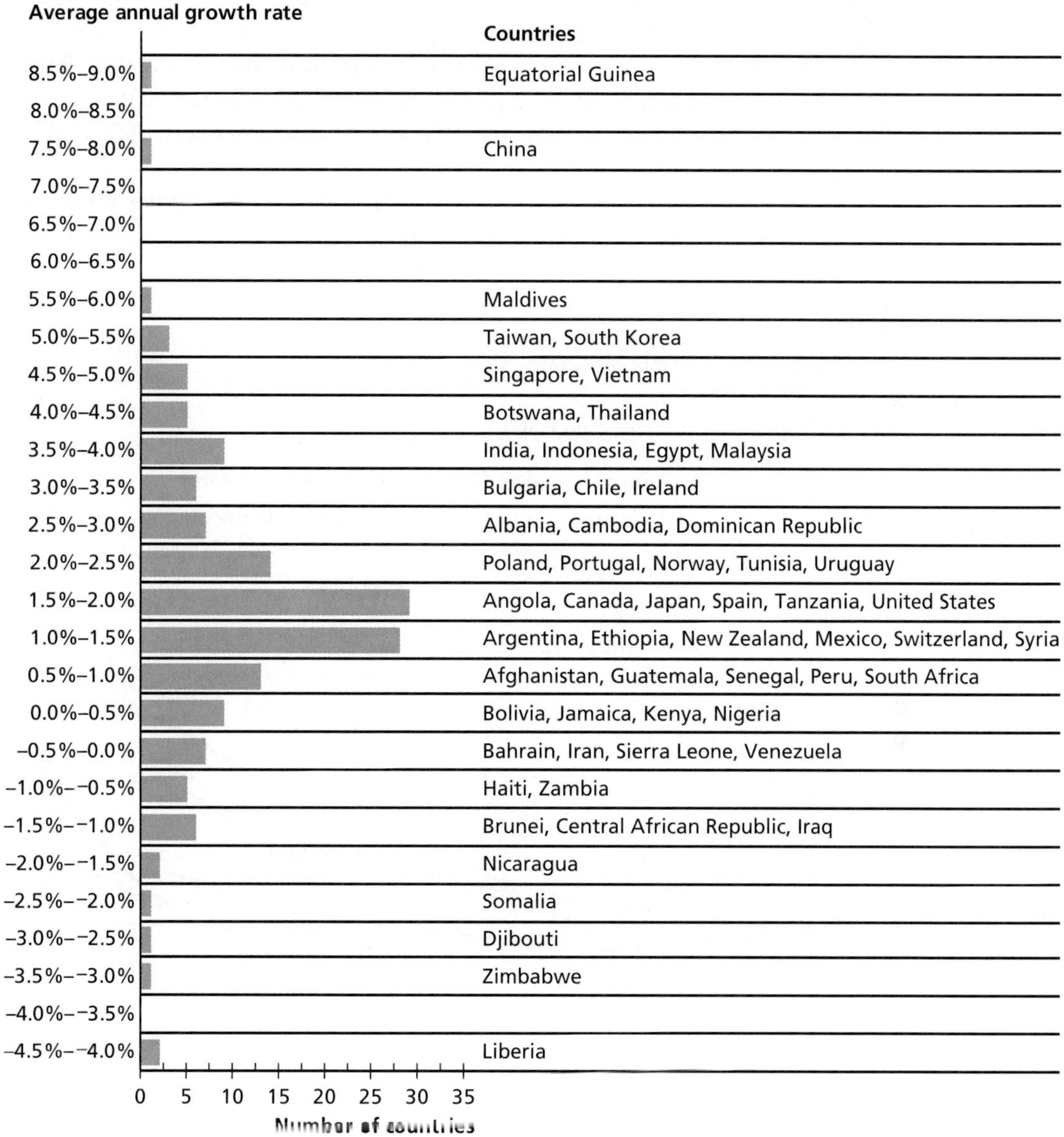

Average annual growth rate

Growth rate	Number of countries	Countries
8.5%–9.0%		Equatorial Guinea
8.0%–8.5%		
7.5%–8.0%		China
7.0%–7.5%		
6.5%–7.0%		
6.0%–6.5%		
5.5%–6.0%		Maldives
5.0%–5.5%		Taiwan, South Korea
4.5%–5.0%		Singapore, Vietnam
4.0%–4.5%		Botswana, Thailand
3.5%–4.0%		India, Indonesia, Egypt, Malaysia
3.0%–3.5%		Bulgaria, Chile, Ireland
2.5%–3.0%		Albania, Cambodia, Dominican Republic
2.0%–2.5%		Poland, Portugal, Norway, Tunisia, Uruguay
1.5%–2.0%		Angola, Canada, Japan, Spain, Tanzania, United States
1.0%–1.5%		Argentina, Ethiopia, New Zealand, Mexico, Switzerland, Syria
0.5%–1.0%		Afghanistan, Guatemala, Senegal, Peru, South Africa
0.0%–0.5%		Bolivia, Jamaica, Kenya, Nigeria
−0.5%–0.0%		Bahrain, Iran, Sierra Leone, Venezuela
−1.0%–−0.5%		Haiti, Zambia
−1.5%–−1.0%		Brunei, Central African Republic, Iraq
−2.0%–−1.5%		Nicaragua
−2.5%–−2.0%		Somalia
−3.0%–−2.5%		Djibouti
−3.5%–−3.0%		Zimbabwe
−4.0%–−3.5%		
−4.5%–−4.0%		Liberia

Number of countries: 0 5 10 15 20 25 30 35

Source: Heston, Summers, and Aten (2011).

examine data on groups of countries—some composed of a single country, some of a number of relatively similar countries. Figure 1.7 shows data on GDP per capita over the period 1820–2008 for 10 such country groups that together encompass the entire world.[11] To give a sense of the groups' sizes, the figure also shows the population of each country group in 2009.

As the figure shows, the pace of growth worldwide has accelerated. Between 1820 and 1870, average GDP per capita in the world grew at a rate of 0.5% per year. Between 1870 and 1950, the pace was 1.1% per year, and between 1950 and 2008, the pace was 2.2% per year.

Figure 1.7 also shows that over this 188-year period, the gap has widened between the rich and the poor. In 1820 the richest part of the world had income per

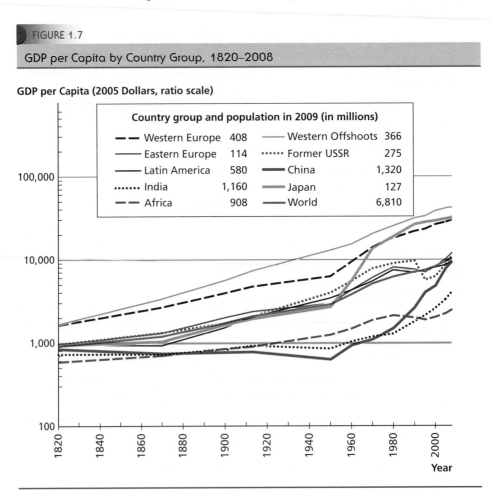

FIGURE 1.7

GDP per Capita by Country Group, 1820–2008

GDP per Capita (2005 Dollars, ratio scale)

Sources: Maddison (2008), Heston, Summers, and Aten (2011).

---

[11]Maddison (2001), Heston, Summers, and Aten (2011).

capita that was three times as large as income per capita in the poorest part of the world. By 2008 the ratio of income per capita in the richest part of the world to income per capita in the poorest part of the world was 17 to 1.

We can also see in Figure 1.7 the changing relative positions of country groups. Japan overtook Eastern Europe, Latin America, the former Soviet Union, and Western Europe over the course of the 20th century. The Western offshoots (the United States, Canada, Australia, and New Zealand) were slightly poorer than Western Europe in 1820 but had twice Western Europe's income in 1950. China, the poorest part of the world in 1950, had more than twice the level of GDP per capita of India and Africa by 2008.

Growth before 1820

Before 1820 the data are even sparser. Forming an estimate of the standard of living and comparing it among countries requires combining historical records, reports from travelers such as Marco Polo (a Venetian who traveled to China in the 13th century) and the Spanish conquistadors (the first Europeans to see the Aztec Empire in what is now Mexico), and even the examination of skeletal remains. But what information is available allows us to draw several conclusions.

First, growth was glacially slow. Economist Angus Maddison estimates that the growth of average GDP per capita in the world was 0.07% (seven one-hundredths of one percent) per year over the period 1700–1820 and 0.04% per year over the period 1500–1700. Even in Western Europe, which during 1500–1820 ascended to world dominance, average growth was only 0.14% per year. (China is now growing at about 7% per year; so it is doing in a year what Western Europe did every 50 years!) Going back even further in time, there is little evidence that living standards had any trend growth at all before 1500.

The lack of trend growth does not mean that living standards were constant. Quite the contrary, the preindustrial economy was characterized by year-to-year fluctuations (often driven by harvest conditions) and by longer-term cycles, sometimes lasting hundreds of years. Economist John Maynard Keynes described the situation this way:

> From the earliest times of which we have record—back, say to two thousand years before Christ—down to the beginning of the eighteenth century, there was no very great change in the standard of life of the average man living in the civilised centres of the earth. Ups and downs certainly. Visitations of plague, famine and war. Golden intervals. But no progressive, violent change. Some periods perhaps 50 per cent better than others—at the utmost 100 per cent better—in the four thousand years which ended (say) in A.D.1700.[12]

---

[12]Keynes (1930).

INCOME INEQUALITY BETWEEN AND WITHIN COUNTRIES

In this book we are primarily concerned with differences among countries in their average levels of income. Thus, when we examined the parade of world income, we assumed that everyone in a given country had income equal to that country's average. But, of course, differences among countries are not the only source of inequality. In every country, some people are better off and some are worse off than average. Thus income inequality in the world is a result of both *within-country* income inequality and *between-country* inequality.

These two sources of inequality suggest a natural question: Which is more important? Figure 1.8 presents data that point to the answer. The figure shows a measure of overall world inequality over the period 1820–1992, along with a breakdown of overall inequality into the part resulting from between-country variation and the part resulting from within-country variation.[*]

The specific measure of inequality used is called the *mean logarithmic deviation.*[†]

There are three noteworthy findings in Figure 1.8. First, although inequality has increased since 1820, most of that increase took place before World War II. The rise in inequality between 1820 and 1950 was seven times as large

as the rise between 1950 and 1992. Following 1980, world inequality declined.

A second important point in Figure 1.8 is that in the world today, between-country inequality is the most important source of inequality. Specifically, between-country inequality explains 60% of overall world inequality.

Finally, even though between-country inequality dominates today, it has not always done so. Quite the contrary: in 1820, within-country inequality accounted for 87% of world inequality. Over the period examined in Figure 1.8, within-country inequality was roughly constant, but between-country inequality increased substantially. This increase in inequality among countries also appears in Figure 1.7.

For the period since 1992, data that is consistent with previous measures are not available. However available evidence seems to show a very sharp decline in world inequality over the last two decades, bringing inequality down to near its level at the beginning of the 20th century. The change came entirely through a decline in between-country inequality, with little change in the average level of within-country inequality.[‡]

Even though between-country inequality accounts for the majority of world inequality

A second aspect of this period is that income differences among countries were very small by modern standards; there was even less inequality among countries than in 1820. Economic historian Paul Bairoch estimates that differences in standards of living between the richest and poorest parts of the world were only a factor of 1.5 or 2.0. He further estimates that standards of living were roughly equivalent in Rome in the 1st century A.D., the Arab caliphates in the 10th, China in the 11th, India in the 17th, and Europe at the beginning of the 18th century.[13]

---

[13]Bairoch (1993).

today (and growth In between-country inequality accounts for all of the growth of world inequality since 1820), we cannot forget about within-country inequality. As Figure 1.8 shows, such inequality also is an important determinant of variation in world income. Furthermore, the degree of income inequality within a country may itself be an important determinant of that country's economic success, and thus may affect the average level of income. Chapter 13 will explore this issue in depth. Finally, when we consider what aspect of their income people *care* most about, it may well be that where they stand

relative to the people in their own country (those with whom they compare themselves) is more important than where their country stands relative to other countries. This is a point we will return to in Chapter 17.

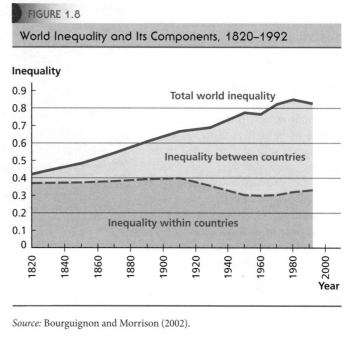

FIGURE 1.8

World Inequality and Its Components, 1820–1992

Source: Bourguignon and Morrison (2002).

* Bourguignon and Morrison (2002).

†Mathematical Note: The mean logarithmic deviation is defined as

$$\frac{1}{n} \sum_{i=1}^{n} \ln\left(\frac{\bar{x}}{x_i}\right),$$

where $\bar{x}$ is the mean value of x and n is the number of observations.

‡ Bourguignon (2011).

Finally, just as in the period after 1820, there were significant changes before 1820 in countries' ranking in the distribution of income. An observer looking over the earth in the 15th century would have been more impressed with the vast colonial empires of the Ottomans, Incas, and Aztecs than with the achievements of Western Europeans.[14] Among the European colonies in the Western Hemisphere, the richest in 1790 was Haiti, which is now one of the poorest countries in the world.

The most dramatic story of relative economic decline is that of China. Between the 8th and 12th centuries, China experienced a burst of economic

---

[14]Fernandez-Armesto (1995).

ECONOMIC GROWTH AS SEEN FROM OUTER SPACE

Economists studying economic growth rely heavily on estimates of GDP, which are produced by national statistical offices (such as the Bureau of Economic Analysis in the United States) as well as by various international agencies. In addition to many well-known conceptual problems with GDP, there are more mundane problems with this data. The surveys and administrative records from which GDP estimates are constructed are prone to all sorts of errors. Some economic activity (i.e., the black market) is deliberately hidden, whereas in other cases officials simply fail to notice it. Sometimes data from a small sample of productive units is used to estimate output for large sectors of the economy. Governments occasionally engage in deliberate falsification. During times of political turmoil, data collection can cease all together. Further, errors can creep in via the PPP adjustments that are discussed in the appendix to this chapter.

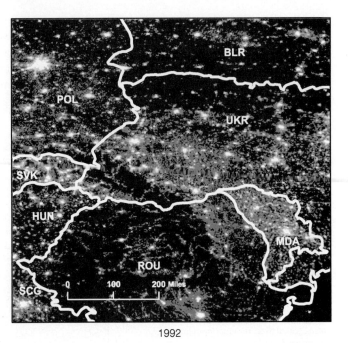

1992

Eastern Europe in 1992 as seen from orbit.

For these reasons, it is useful to check measured GDP against other sources of data, when they are available. One unconventional form of data is the amount of light that is visible at night from outer space. Light leaks into space from houses, workplaces, cars, and other places where people are active at night. Not surprisingly, richer countries tend to produce more light. Of course the relationship between economic activity and light produced is inexact, and some economic activities, such as flaring

growth that brought it to a level of commercial and industrial development unparalleled elsewhere until the end of the 18th century. This period saw the invention of gunpowder, printing, and a water-powered spinning wheel; the use of coal in smelting iron; and the digging of canals and building of locks that, together with rivers, formed a 30,000-mile (48,280-kilometer) network of navigable waterways.[15]

---

[15]Pomeranz (2000), Kelly (1997).

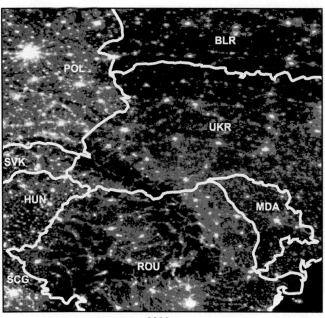

2002

Eastern Europe in 2002 as seen from orbit.

The accompanying pictures show two views of Eastern Europe taken 10 years apart, in 1992 and 2002. This was a period of remarkable change in the region, following the dissolution of the Communist economic bloc and the Soviet Union in 1991. Traditional economic relationships were disrupted, opening new opportunities for some countries (particularly those close to Western Europe) and causing widespread economic decline in others.

These changes are visible in the pattern of nighttime lights, which confirm evidence from conventionally measured GDP. The greatest increase in light intensity was in Poland (GDP growth of 4.2% per year), followed by Hungary (growth of 3.4% per year) and Romania (2.5% per year). In Ukraine (where GDP growth was roughly zero over this period) there is a noticeable dimming of nighttime lights. There is much more extreme dimming in Moldova, where GDP per capita shrank at an annual rate of 1.2% over this period.

of natural gas from oil wells, the use of bright lights to fish for squid at night, and forest fires set to clear land for agriculture, produce an inordinate amount of light compared to their economic value (experts in the field have learned to adjust the data to eliminate some of these factors).*

*Henderson, Storeygard, and Weil (2012).

China had also started out on the same path of world exploration that Europe was to follow in later centuries. In the early 15th century the Chinese admiral Zheng He undertook voyages of exploration as far as the east coast of Africa. Despite this impressive beginning, the Chinese economy stagnated. While Europe industrialized and spread its influence over the rest of the world, China became increasingly insular. Europe's standard of living surpassed that of China sometime around 1750, and by time of the Opium Wars in the middle of the 19th century, China found itself defenseless before the onslaught of an industrialized Europe.

One of Zheng He's ships compared to one of Christopher Columbus's ships.

1.3 CONCLUSION

Economists have been thinking about why some countries are rich and some are poor at least since Adam Smith published *An Inquiry into the Nature and Causes of the Wealth of Nations* in 1776. The subsequent two centuries have seen an explosion of economic growth unlike anything in the previous history of the world. Having changed barely at all for 2,000 years, the standard of living among the countries that are now the world's richest was utterly transformed. In the richest countries, income per capita today is at least 10 times as large as it was 200 years ago.

But the growth of income has been uneven. Among the countries that started growing first, including parts of Western Europe and such offshoots as the United States and Canada, relatively slow growth, compounding over almost two centuries, was responsible for the change in living standards. Other countries, such as Japan, started growing later but then grew more quickly than the early starters and caught up in terms of income by the end of the 20th century.

After World War II, the average rate of growth of world income increased, as the contagion of growth spread to much of the planet. Seventy-two percent of the world's population lives in countries where income per capita at least doubled between 1960 and 2000, and 27% lives in countries where income per capita increased more than fourfold. Even during this period, however, some parts of the world failed to grow. In many countries, particularly in sub-Saharan Africa, income per capita fell over this 40-year period.

The uneven distribution of growth among countries has led to a vast widening in the income gaps between rich and poor countries. Indeed, differences among countries in their standards of living today dwarf those that inspired Smith's inquiry. This between-country inequality is now more important than within-country inequality as a contributor to overall world inequality.

The unequal distribution of income among countries is arguably the most important economic fact in the world today. This high level of inequality influences developments in international relations, the environment, and health. The most important implication of the gap between rich and poor countries is that it suggests a potential for alleviating poverty. The fact that so many countries have emerged from poverty—from the United States starting in the early 19th century to South Korea starting in the 1950s—is a hopeful sign for the billions of people who remain needy. Indeed, despite all of the economic problems in the world today, we are living through the greatest period of poverty alleviation in the history of the planet.

For economists, the gaps between rich and poor countries, and the divergent experiences of countries that grew quickly and those that stagnated, present a set of puzzles. What factors determined which countries prospered? Can we point to specific economic policies? Are there specific country characteristics that determine economic fate? Is prosperity just the result of luck? As the Nobel Prize–winning economist Robert Lucas wrote, "The consequences for human welfare involved in questions like these are simply staggering: Once one starts to think about them, it is hard to think about anything else."[16]

KEY TERMS

gross domestic product (GDP) **3**	ratio scale **10**	rule of 72 **11**
purchasing power parity (PPP) **4**	linear scale **10**	

QUESTIONS FOR REVIEW

1. What is the magnitude of income differences between the richest and poorest countries in the world today?

2. What is the magnitude of income differences between the world's richest countries today and their own income per capita 200 years ago?

3. In what cases is GDP per capita the best measure of a country's income? In what cases is total GDP the best measure?

4. How does the average growth rate of income per capita in the world since 1960 compare with growth in the previous century? How

---

[16]Lucas (1988).

did growth in the 19th century compare with growth in the previous centuries?

5. What is the relative importance of within-country inequality and between-country inequality in explaining total world income inequality? How has the relative importance changed over time? Why?

PROBLEMS

1. How would using a ratio scale (rather than a linear scale) affect Figure 1.1?

2. How fast would a country have to be growing to double its output in nine years? You should answer this question using the rule of 72, *not* a calculator.

3. Suppose that in a particular country, GDP per capita was $1,000 in 1900 and $4,000 in 1948. Using the rule of 72 (*not* a calculator), approximate the annual growth rate of GDP per capita.

4. Suppose that the entire population of the world consists of four people, divided into two countries of two people each. The following table shows data on their income and nationality. Based on this table, which is the more important source of world inequality: between-country inequality or within-country inequality?

Person	Nationality	Income
Alfred	Country A	1,000
Bob	Country B	2,000
Carol	Country B	3,000
Doris	Country A	4,000

5. In 1900 GDP per capita in Japan (measured in year 2005 dollars) was $1,617. In 2000 it was $29,639. Calculate the growth rate of income per capita in Japan over this period. Now suppose that Japan grows at the same rate for the century following 2000. What will Japanese GDP per capita be in the year 2100?

6. In 2009 GDP per capita in the United States was $41,099, whereas GDP per capita in Sri Lanka was $4,034. Suppose that income per capita in the United States has been growing at a constant rate of 1.8% per year. (Figure 1.4 shows that this is roughly true.) Calculate the year in which income per capita in the United States was equal to year 2009 income per capita in Sri Lanka.

7. Between 1975 and 2009, China's GDP per capita grew at an average rate of 7.9% per year whereas GDP per capita in the United States grew at an average rate of 1.8%. In 2009, U.S. GDP per capita was $41,099 and Chinese GDP per capita was $7,634. Assuming that the two countries continue to grow at these rates, in what year will China overtake the United States in terms of GDP per capita?

For additional exploration and practice using the Online Data Plotter and data sets, please visit www.pearsonhighered.com/weil.

MEASURING AND COMPARING GDP USING PURCHASING POWER PARITY

Gross domestic product (GDP) is the value of all goods and services produced in an economy in a year (excluding *intermediate goods*, which are used in the production of *final goods*). In principle, calculating GDP just involves counting up all of the goods and services produced (for example, 2 million tons of coal), multiplying each by the appropriate price ($100 per ton), and adding them together. Performing this calculation for the United States in 2009, we learn that GDP was $12.6 trillion, or $41,099 per capita. Although these are certainly interesting numbers in and of themselves, most of the questions we want to address have to do with comparisons of GDP (or GDP per capita)—for example, between two countries or within the same country at different points in time. To make these comparisons, we need some way of converting our different measures of GDP (which might be in yen or in 1927 dollars) into the same units.

The problem of comparing quantities of dollars measured at two points in time is a familiar one in macroeconomics. We know that inflation erodes the quantity of real goods and services that can be purchased with a dollar. You may be familiar with the idea of constructing a *price index* such as the consumer price index (CPI) or the GDP deflator, which can be used to compare dollar quantities at two different points in time.

When it comes to comparing GDP in different countries, each with its own currency, it would at first seem that we do not have to go through the difficulty of creating a price index—that we could just use the exchange rate. Indeed, every day, we can look up the exchange rate between the dollar and any other currency. Two observations hint at the potential trouble with this sort of comparison, however. First, market exchange rates fluctuate daily, often by a large amount. The yen might appreciate relative to the dollar by 10% in a given week. If we were using this exchange rate to compare GDP per capita in the two countries, we would have to conclude that the average Japanese resident had become 10% richer relative to the average American, even though the amount of output produced in the two countries had not changed.

The second problem with market exchange rates is somewhat more subtle. It arises from the interaction of two facts. The first fact is that the price of goods traded in international markets, relative to goods that are not traded, tends to be much higher in poor countries than in rich countries. The second fact is that exchange rates tend to be such that the price of traded goods will be the same when these prices are converted to a common currency at the market exchange rate. (This second fact, often called the *law of one price*, is a simple result of the possibility of arbitrage.) Travelers to developing countries notice right away that locally produced goods, such as restaurant meals and haircuts, are dirt cheap to a visitor who has dollars to spend, but internationally traded goods (or goods that have a large traded component, such as airplane tickets) are not particular bargains.

As a result of the interaction of these two forces, comparisons of GDP at market exchange rates systematically understate the relative income of developing countries. A simple example demonstrates this point. Table 1.2 considers two economies, each of which produces two goods: televisions, which are traded, and haircuts, which are not. Richland produces four times as many televisions per capita as Poorland, and also four times as many haircuts. Logically, the measure of GDP that we use for comparison should tell us that per capita output in Richland is four times as high as in Poorland. The fourth and fifth columns of the table show the prices of televisions and haircuts in the two countries. These prices are measured in units of the local currencies (the Richland dollar and the Poorland dollar). Notice that the price ratio of traded to nontraded goods in Poorland (10 to 1) is twice as high as the ratio in Richland (10 to 2). The last column shows GDP per capita in the two countries, also calculated in units of the local currency.

Suppose we want to compare GDP in the two countries. Because televisions are traded, we expect that the exchange rate will be such that the prices of televisions will be the same when converted into a common currency. Thus, the exchange rate will be one Poorland dollar to one Richland dollar. If we use this exchange rate to convert Poorland's GDP into the currency of Richland, we will conclude that GDP per capita in Poorland is one-sixth the level in Richland. The difference in the ratio of prices of traded and nontraded goods leads to an understatement of the relative income of Poorland.

TABLE 1.2

Production and Prices in Richland and Poorland

Country	Production of Televisions per Capita	Production of Haircuts per Capita	Price of Televisions in Local Currency	Price of Haircuts in Local Currency	GDP per Capita in Local Currency
Richland	4	40	10	2	120
Poorland	1	10	10	1	20

	TABLE 1.3

The Effect of Using PPP on Comparisons of GDP

Country	GDP per Capita in 2009 Using Market Exchange Rates (dollars)	GDP per Capita in 2009 Using PPP Exchange Rates (dollars)
United States	41,099	41,099
Japan	36,651	30,008
Germany	36,702	32,488
Argentina	6,519	11,961
Mexico	7,257	11,629
India	1,041	3,239

To get around this problem, economists have constructed a set of artificial exchange rates, called *purchasing power parity (PPP) exchange rates*, which are based on the prices of a standardized basket of goods and services (both traded and nontraded). In the example of Richland and Poorland, a natural basket of goods to use would be 1 television and 10 haircuts (because this is the ratio in which these products are consumed worldwide). Such a basket would have a price of 30 dollars in Richland and 20 dollars in Poorland. The prices of the basket in the two countries suggest a PPP exchange rate of two Poorland dollars for every three Richland dollars. Using this exchange rate, Poorland's GDP per capita (20 Poorland dollars) would be worth 30 Richland dollars—and we would conclude (correctly) that, on the basis of PPP exchange rates, Poorland's GDP per capita was one-quarter of Richland's.

Throughout this book we will use PPP exchange rates in making comparisons among countries. Table 1.3 shows the effect of switching from market exchange rates to PPP exchange rates for a typical set of countries.

As the table shows, Japan's currency was overvalued relative to PPP. Using market exchange rates, Japanese GDP per capita is 89% of the U.S. level, whereas using PPP exchange rates, Japanese GDP per capita is only 73% of the U.S. level. India, as is typical for developing countries, had market exchange rate that was severely undervalued relative to PPP. Switching to PPP raises GDP per capita relative to the United States by a factor of three.

PPP exchange rates are useful for comparing quantities other than GDP. For example, journalistic reports of conditions in developing countries will often translate the average wage of a worker into U.S. dollars using the market exchange rate. Using a PPP exchange rate instead would yield a different, more accurate picture.

PROBLEMS

A.1. The number of people worldwide living on less than one dollar per day can be calculated using either market exchange rates or PPP exchange rates. Which will be larger? Explain why.

A.2. Suppose that there are only two goods produced in the world: computers, which are traded internationally, and ice cream, which is not. The following table shows information on the production and prices of computers and ice cream in two countries:

Country	Computers Produced per Capita	Ice Cream Produced per Capita	Price of Computers in Local Currency	Price of Ice Cream in Local Currency
Richland	12	4	2	4
Poorland	3	1	1	1

a. Calculate the level of GDP per capita in each country, measured in its own currency.

b. Calculate the market exchange rate between the currencies of the two countries.

c. What is the ratio of GDP per capita in Richland to GDP per capita in Poorland, using the market exchange rate?

d. Calculate the PPP exchange rate between the two currencies.

e. What is the ratio of GDP per capita in Richland to GDP per capita in Poorland, using the PPP exchange rate?

For additional exploration and practice using the Online Data Plotter and data sets, please visit www.pearsonhighered.com/weil.

2

A FRAMEWORK FOR ANALYSIS

Explaining why some countries are rich and some are poor will require us to weigh the importance of many different factors. Before setting out on such a challenging project, it will be helpful to have a vision of what we are aiming for. Section 2.1 of this chapter presents a parable meant to shape such a vision.

This parable does *not* provide the final answer to our question. Rather, it shows what an answer could look like. In real life, the data are not so easy to come by, and the numbers never work out so cleanly. More significantly, the world of the parable is pared down in the interest of clarity. The parable ignores many of the factors that will concern us later in the book. Eventually, these factors will fit into the framework we are putting together. But for now, it is easier to think about the framework without worrying about these other factors. In Section 2.2 we consider how the parable relates to the more fully developed model in the rest of the book. And in the last section we examine how economists use data to test and quantitatively analyze the theories they construct.

2.1 THE ECONOMICS OF SYLVANIA AND FREEDONIA: A PARABLE

Imagine yourself as the president of a prestigious economic consulting firm. You have been hired by the king of the country of Sylvania to answer a simple question: Why is Sylvania so much poorer than its neighbor, the Republic of Freedonia?

Having assembled a crack staff (who will do all of the real work), and armed with the vast resources of the National Office of Statistical Research, you set to work. Your first task is to figure out just how big the gap is between the two countries. You carefully measure the value of all the goods and services produced in each country (i.e., gross domestic product [GDP]). You find that GDP in Freedonia is eight times as large as GDP in Sylvania. A quick check of the two countries' censuses shows that they have almost exactly the same population, so you conclude that the important differences between them must be on a per-capita basis: Freedonia's level of GDP per capita is eight times that of Sylvania.

Now that the dimensions of the problem are clear, you look for explanations. You send your staff out to examine conditions in the two countries, and they make an interesting observation. In both countries, goods and services are produced using two inputs. One of these inputs is the labor of workers. The other is the tools that the workers have at their disposal: machines, vehicles, buildings, and other pieces of equipment that are collectively called **capital.** Your staff notices that, on average, each worker in Freedonia has much more capital to work with than his or her counterpart in Sylvania. Further, in both countries, the more capital that a worker has to work with, the more output the worker produces.

These observations suggest that differences in the capital available to each worker could explain the difference in income between Freedonia and Sylvania. But what is the source of this difference in capital per worker? Your staff has one possible answer: They observe that the quantity of **investment**—that is, the goods and services devoted to the production of new capital rather than consumed—in Freedonia is much higher than in Sylvania. Indeed, your staff calculates that each year Freedonia invests 32 times as much as Sylvania.

Using basic economics, you know that the investment in new capital taking place in each country must represent saving by the citizens in that country. The fact that Freedonia saves more than Sylvania is really not such a mystery, because Freedonia is, after all, a much wealthier country. But looking at the numbers, you see that Freedonia saves a higher *fraction* of its income than does Sylvania: Its investment is 32 times as high, whereas its income is only eight times as high. Therefore, its investment rate (the fraction of its income that it invests) must be four times as high.

You think you may have found the smoking gun. Perhaps the entire difference in income between Freedonia and Sylvania is solely a result of this difference in thrift: Sylvania saves (and invests) a lower fraction of its income than does its neighbor. Because its investment rate is lower, its capital per worker is lower, and so is its total income.

To evaluate this theory, you pose the following question to your staff: "Suppose that the only difference between Freedonia and Sylvania is that Freedonia invests four times as much of its income each year as Sylvania. What difference in income can be expected to result from this difference in investment rates?" Your staff labors long and hard on this issue. Their answer is that the difference in investment can explain some, but not all, of the difference in income between the two countries. Specifically, if the two countries differed by a factor of four in their investment rates and there were no other differences between them, then they would differ by a factor of two in their levels of income. (Like any good staff, yours shields you from the messy details of this calculation. But in Chapter 3 we will learn how they did it.) Because the two countries differ in their income by a factor of eight, most of the difference in income—a factor of four—is not explained by differing rates of investment. This residual difference, says your staff, is not a result of how much capital each country has but rather the **productivity**—that is, the amount of output produced with each unit of capital.

Clearly, productivity is important. But what determines productivity? Why is Freedonia's productivity so much higher than Sylvania's? To tackle this question, you convene your entire staff for a brainstorming session. One staff member suggests that perhaps the reason a given amount of capital per worker in Sylvania produces so much less than in Freedonia is that Sylvania is backward in its **technology**—the available knowledge about how inputs can be combined to produce output. After all, she says, technological progress should enable a country to produce more output with the same amount of inputs. You decide to pursue the idea and have your staff conduct a survey of the state of technology in the two countries. They reach a startling conclusion: Sylvania is roughly 35 years behind Freedonia technologically. That is, the technologies used in Sylvania today are the same ones that were used in Freedonia 35 years ago, on average.

To see whether this technological gap can explain the difference in productivity between the two countries, you ask your staff, "How much less output would be produced in Freedonia today if workers were using the same technology that they used 35 years ago?" Your staff comes back with an answer: Given the rate at which technology has been improving in Freedonia, the country would produce roughly half as much output as it actually does if it were using 35-year-old technology. Put another way: Over the last 35 years, the level of technology has doubled. (Once again, your staff does not trouble you with the details of how they came to this conclusion. But Chapters 7 and 10 will look into how they reached it.)

So, of the difference in productivity of a factor of four, half (a factor of two) is the result of technology. What about the rest? Your staff says that in observing the two countries closely, they discern a pattern: In addition to having more capital and better technology, Freedonia simply seems to have its act together. People work harder at their jobs, the quality of their products is higher, and less time is wasted than in Sylvania. Even comparing factories that use the same amount of capital per worker and the same technology, those in Freedonia produce more output.

Your staff calls this slippery but nonetheless significant attribute **efficiency**: how the available technology and inputs into production are actually used in producing output. Differences in productivity between the two countries that cannot be explained by differences in technology, they say, can well be explained by efficiency. Your staff suggests a simple "decomposition" of productivity into two pieces: Productivity is equal to technology multiplied by efficiency. Because productivity differs between Freedonia and Sylvania by a factor of four and technology differs by a factor of two, efficiency must also differ by a factor of two.

Synthesizing your staff's research, you write a report explaining that Sylvania's relative poverty has three sources: a lower rate of investment (leading to a lower quantity of capital), inferior technology, and lower efficiency. Each of these problems contributes a factor of two to Sylvania's relative poverty. If any one of these problems could be eliminated, Sylvania would be one-fourth as rich as its neighbor; if two could be eliminated, it would be half as rich; and if all three problems could be eliminated, Sylvania would be just as rich as Freedonia.

You present your report to the king at a lavish state banquet. Although the king thanks you graciously, he is not fully pleased. You have told him what is wrong, but you have not told him the *source* of the problem. "It is as if you have told me that the royal horse failed to win a race because he had weak muscles and a sore hoof. But you have not told me the source of these problems: for example, a poor diet, too much training, or bad breeding. I want to know the deeper causes of my country's problems."

So, once again, you and your staff sit and brainstorm. What are the deeper, underlying factors—the **fundamentals**—that make Sylvania so much poorer than Freedonia? Your previous research told you how these deeper factors will be expressed: in a lower saving rate, which leads to less capital accumulation; in a failure to develop new technologies as quickly as other countries; and in inefficient use of the capital and technologies that are available. But what are the factors themselves?

To get to the bottom of this question, you embark on a broad program of research, measuring possible fundamentals in a large number of countries and seeing how they correlate with saving, technology, and efficiency. You sift through an array of possibilities. Perhaps the countries have differences in culture (e.g., in thriftiness or in the effort that people put into their work). Perhaps the two countries' economic policies (taxes, tariffs, and regulations) are the explanation. Maybe differences in geography (natural resources, climate, or proximity to world markets) are to blame for Sylvania's relative poverty.

Sorting out these possible fundamentals is a delicate business, but luck is on your side. It happens that on many of the possible fundamental dimensions, Sylvania and Freedonia are the same (e.g., the two countries have the same climate). Thus, these factors cannot be sources of the difference in income between the two countries. On other dimensions the two countries do differ (e.g., the side of the road on which cars drive), but your statistical analysis shows that these factors do not explain differences in income among countries. There is only one measure in which the two countries differ that also turns out to be an important explanation of income differences among countries.

Having sent your staff safely out of the country, you compose a second report for the king, explaining your findings.

"The root cause of Sylvania's relative poverty," you write, "is its form of government. Compared to Freedonia's democracy, the monarchy of Sylvania exacts a high price on the country's economic development. Residents of Sylvania are a naturally thrifty people, but they are reluctant to save their money and accumulate capital because at any time the king may expropriate their wealth. In Freedonia, by contrast, property is protected, and the citizens know they will be able to enjoy the fruits of their thrift. In Freedonia clever inventors are paid well to create new productive technologies, whereas Sylvania's equally talented scientists spend their efforts creating new weapons for the king's endless, petty wars. Finally, in Sylvania the most reliable route to wealth and status is to win the king's favor, and this is where the best efforts of the most capable men and women are directed. In Freedonia, by contrast, the route to success is through concrete accomplishment—doing your job well. This explains why things run so much more efficiently in Freedonia.

"Thus, all of the sources of Sylvania's relative poverty that we identified in our first report—accumulation of capital, technological backwardness, and inefficiency—can be traced back to the single root cause of monarchy."

You deliver the report and make a hasty exit. Racing toward the border, pursued by a troop of the palace guard, you reflect that perhaps your effort and insight would be better rewarded in a country like Freedonia.

2.2 FROM PARABLE TO PRACTICE

The parable of Sylvania and Freedonia is not meant to be taken literally. In particular, a country's form of government (monarchy, democracy, or something else) is only one of the fundamental determinants of income that we will consider in this book. Rather, the parable is intended to guide our thinking about the determinants of economic growth by showing how one can analyze and weigh the relative importance of different factors that lead to differences in incomes among countries. There are three key ideas from the parable that we will carry with us throughout the book:

- We can distinguish between two specific things that can make a country richer: the accumulation of inputs into production versus the productivity with which those inputs are used. In the parable, the only input into production other than labor was capital, but we will see that there are other inputs as well.

- We can further break down differences in productivity among countries into two components: differences in technology and differences in efficiency. Technology can be discussed in terms of research and development, dissemination of knowledge, and scientific advancement. Efficiency relates to the organization of the economy, institutions, and so on.

- We can learn much by looking beyond the immediate determinants of a country's income to examine what fundamental or deeper characteristics shape these. We can think of the distinction as one between proximate and ultimate factors affecting growth. (A **proximate cause** is an event that is immediately responsible for causing some observed result. An **ultimate cause** is something that affects an observed result through a chain of intermediate events.)

Each of these key ideas is at the center of one part of the book. Part II focuses on how countries differ in their accumulation of inputs into production. Part III is concerned with productivity and its components, technology, and efficiency. Finally, Part IV looks at potential fundamental factors that explain differences among countries in all of the things that are examined in Parts II and III.

In the rest of this section, we briefly consider how we can carry over the first of the basic ideas just listed into more formal economic analysis, and how we can use the analysis of differences in countries' *levels* of income—the subject of the parable—to understand differences in *growth rates* as well.

The Production Function

The parable of Freedonia and Sylvania introduced the idea that countries can differ in their income per capita for two reasons: because they differ in their accumulation of inputs used in producing output or because they differ in the productivity with which those inputs are used. In the parable, there was only one input to production other than labor: capital. As we will see in Part II, capital is just one of several inputs into production that a country can accumulate. Collectively, these inputs are referred to as **factors of production.**

Throughout this textbook, we use a production function to express the relationship between factors of production and the quantity of output produced. In microeconomics, a **production function** is a mathematical description of how the inputs a firm uses are transformed into its output. We will use the same idea here, although now the output we will consider is the output of an entire country.

Figure 2.1 shows an example of a production function. The horizontal axis is labeled *Factors of production per worker* to show that we could be

FIGURE 2.1

The Production Function

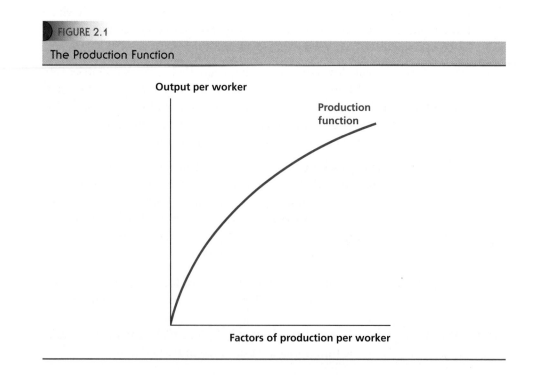

considering any particular factor of production or all of them taken together. The vertical axis measures output per worker. The production function slopes upward, illustrating that a country with more factors of production is able to produce more output. The production function also becomes flatter as the quantity of factors of production per worker increases, for reasons that we will explore in Chapter 3.

Considering the production function in this general form allows us to raise an issue we will pursue throughout the book: To what extent are differences in income among countries the result of differences in their accumulation of factors of production, and to what extent are differences in income the result of differences in the production function itself? Figure 2.2 considers the case of two countries, designated 1 and 2. Output per capita in Country 1, y_1, is higher than output per worker in Country 2, y_2. Each of the three panels of the figure shows a possible explanation for why the two countries differ in output. In panel (a), the two countries have the same production function, but Country 1 has a higher level of factors of production per worker, and thus higher output. In panel (b), the two countries have the same quantities of factors of production, but the production function of Country 1 lies above that of Country 2; so for any quantity of factors of production, Country 1 produces more output than Country 2. In other words, Country 1

FIGURE 2.2

Possible Sources of Differences in Output per Worker

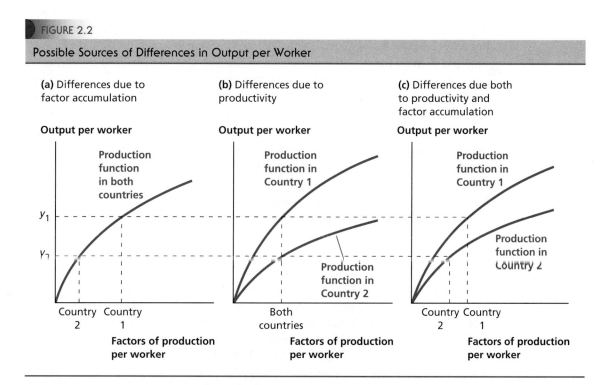

has higher productivity than Country 2. In panel (c), Country 1 has more factors of production and higher productivity than Country 2. Chapter 7 will use this analytic approach to determine how much of the variation in income among real countries is the result of varying accumulation of factors of production and how much is the result of varying productivity.

From Income Levels to Growth Rates

The parable of Freedonia and Sylvania was about differences between countries' *levels* of income. But as we saw in Chapter 1, many of the interesting facts in the data are about differences in *growth rates* among countries. How can we use the framework introduced in the parable to examine variations in the rate of economic growth?

The answer is that we will have to introduce into our analysis the idea of gradual adjustment to a new equilibrium level of output. To be concrete, let's go back to the simple world of Freedonia and Sylvania, where there was only one fundamental source of income differences, the form of government. In this example, Sylvania's monarchy was responsible for the difference in the two countries' incomes (a factor of eight).

Now suppose that the king of Sylvania is deposed and the monarchy is replaced with democracy. After the Sylvanian revolution, the two countries will have the same fundamentals. Our simple story of the determinants of output would lead us to expect Sylvania to produce the same level of output per capita as Freedonia, but we would not really expect the Sylvanian economy to catch up right away. Why not? For a start, some of the difference in income stemmed from a difference in the countries' capital stocks, which was a result of Sylvania's low saving rate. When the monarchy is deposed, Sylvania's saving rate will rise, but it will take time for Sylvania to accumulate as much capital as Freedonia. Similarly, another contributor to Sylvania's relative poverty was that Sylvania's monarchy had held back the acquisition of cutting-edge technologies from abroad. With the monarchy gone, Sylvania will catch up technologically with its neighbor, but not overnight. There will be a period of many years in which Freedonia remains the technological leader, even if by an ever-smaller margin.

This gradual adjustment of levels of income can be the basis for a story about growth rates. Because nothing has changed in Freedonia, it will continue to grow at the same rate as it did before the revolution in Sylvania. But Sylvania's catching up will be reflected in faster growth of income. Indeed, Sylvania will continue to grow faster than Freedonia until it has caught up.

At first, this rapid growth may seem surprising. Economists are always advising countries to undertake this or that policy because it will make them grow faster. Here, however, we have a case in which two countries have the same policy (democracy), but one country is growing faster. Furthermore, this fast growth seems to be a reward for having had a bad policy in the past.

The explanation is that Sylvania *is* paying the price for its past bad policy in the form of a lower level of income. Over time, however, as it remains a democracy, the damage done by that past bad policy fades away. And this fading away takes the form of rapid growth.

Generalizing from this example, we can easily turn our model of the determinants of income levels into a model of the determinants of income growth. Specifically, if two countries are the same in their fundamentals (or, more generally, if we would expect them to have equal levels of income based on their fundamentals), we can expect the country with a lower level of income to grow faster. One reason could be that the poorer country has income below the level we would expect, given its fundamentals (e.g., Sylvania right after the revolution). Or the richer country could have income above the level we expect from its fundamentals (e.g., if the democracy in Freedonia were replaced by a monarchy).

This analysis makes it clear why discussions of policies to affect economic growth can often be confusing. For example, when Bill Clinton announced early in his presidency his intention to "grow the economy," one potential target for his efforts was the painfully low U.S. saving rate. The Clinton administration asked economists how an increase in saving would affect economic growth. The correct answer would have been that an increase in saving would raise the growth rate of output in the years immediately after it took place, but eventually the growth rate would return to its baseline level (i.e., the level in the absence of an increase in saving). However, even though growth would be the same in the long run, the *level* of output would be higher than it would have been had saving not increased. Any politician would have lost interest long before the end of that answer.

2.3 WHAT CAN WE LEARN FROM DATA?

Economics advances our understanding of the world through a combination of theoretical reasoning and the examination of data. Economic theories are often stated in the form of **economic models,** which are simplified representations of reality that can be used to analyze how economic variables are determined, how a change in one variable will affect others, and so on. For example, the familiar model of supply and demand is used to analyze how the price of a good and the quantity purchased are determined. We can use the model of supply and demand to answer questions such as, "What happens to the quantity of bread consumed if the price of flour rises?" We can also use the supply-and-demand model to examine the effects of economic policies such as taxes and price ceilings.

One use of data is in testing economic theories. In the case of supply and demand, the theory is simple enough and has been well enough tested that there is little doubt about its validity. Other theories, however, are subject to active debate. By comparing a theory's predictions with what the data show, we can assess the accuracy of the theory.

Economists also use data in assigning magnitudes to the different parts of an economic model. This method is called *quantitative analysis*. Going back to supply and demand, we know from theory alone that an increase in the price of bread will lead to a decrease in the quantity of bread demanded. But knowing how large a decrease in quantity will result from a particular increase in price—that is, how steeply the demand curve slopes—requires going to the data. Similarly, if we want to evaluate the quantitative effects of a particular policy (e.g., how much revenue will be collected by a particular tax), we will need to examine data. Without this sort of quantitative analysis, theory is often useless.

For these reasons, economists are voracious consumers of data. But economists are also aware of many of the difficulties in using data to learn the things they want to know.

One problem is that economists never have enough good data. Many of the things economists would like to know about are not measured. For example, many economic theories are based on the idea of maximizing happiness, or *utility*, as it is called in economists' jargon. But an individual's happiness cannot be observed directly. In other cases, the things we want to know about are measured only inaccurately, as with a survey question that might ask, "How much did your household spend on food last week?" In looking at data from numerous countries, as this book frequently does, there is the additional problem that countries collect information in different forms. Finally, in some cases, the official agencies that collect statistics have a particular bias, which is expressed in the supposedly neutral numbers they report.

Another problem is that the data economists have at their disposal are almost always *observational,* in contrast to *experimental*. That is, economists can observe the world around them but usually cannot do controlled experiments in the way that biologists, chemists, and physicists can. This often makes it difficult for economists to figure out what is causing what.

Scatter Plots and Correlations

Economists often examine data by using a scatter plot. In a **scatter plot,** each observation (e.g., each country) is represented by a single point. One **variable** (i.e., a characteristic of the observation that we are examining) is measured along the horizontal axis, and one variable is measured along the vertical axis. A scatter plot allows us to see the overall relationship between two variables, as well as which observations are consistent with that overall relationship and which fall outside the usual relationship. The observations that are inconsistent are called **outliers.**

Figures 2.3 and 2.4 give examples of scatter plots, taken from later chapters of the book. Figure 2.3 shows a strong positive relationship between a country's latitude (i.e., its distance from the equator) and its level of GDP per capita.

Relationship between Latitude and Income per Capita

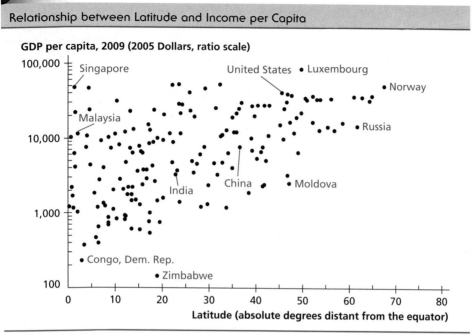

GDP per capita, 2009 (2005 Dollars, ratio scale)

Latitude (absolute degrees distant from the equator)

Relationship between Income per Capita and Population Growth

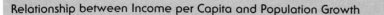

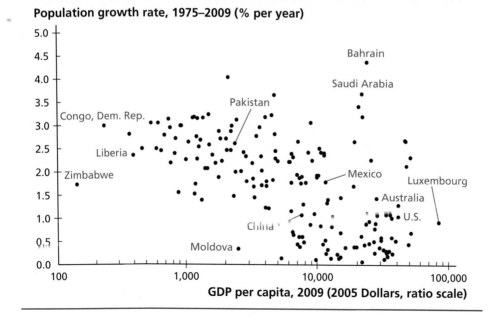

Population growth rate, 1975–2009 (% per year)

GDP per capita, 2009 (2005 Dollars, ratio scale)

Figure 2.4 shows a negative relationship between GDP per capita and a country's population growth rate. In Figure 2.3, the observation for Singapore (close to the equator but rich) is an example of an outlier.

One of our fundamental tools will be to look at the correlation between variables. **Correlation** describes the degree to which two variables tend to move together. Two variables are positively correlated if high values of one tend to be associated with high values of the other. They are negatively correlated if high values of one variable tend to be associated with low values of the other. For example, the number of hours that a student studies per week is positively correlated with his or her grade point average.

The degree of correlation between two variables is measured by the **correlation coefficient,** which is a number between –1 and 1. A correlation coefficient of 1 indicates perfect positive correlation; a correlation coefficient of –1 indicates perfect negative correlation. A value of 0 indicates that there is no tendency for the two quantities to vary together.[1] In Figures 2.3 and 2.4, the correlation coefficients are 0.52 and −0.42, respectively (note that these correlations are calculated using the logarithm of GDP per capita).

Examining the correlation between two variables is often a useful starting point for thinking about how they are related. But correlations have to be interpreted with care. Consider a positive correlation between two variables, X and Y. There are three possible explanations (which are not mutually exclusive) for the correlation that we observe in the data:

1. X causes Y. Variable X affects variable Y, so that if it were possible to change variable X, variable Y would change as well. For example, in cities where it rains a lot (X), people tend to own more umbrellas (Y). Causation running from X to Y may be direct, as in the example of rain and umbrellas, or it may operate through a chain of intermediate causal links. For example, a country's average temperature is correlated with the incidence of malaria, not because warm air causes the disease (as used to be thought) but because mosquitoes that carry the malaria parasite are more active in warm climates.

2. Y causes X. One might *think* that X causes Y when in fact the opposite is true. This situation is called **reverse causation.** For example, we could observe that the average number of neckties owned by residents of a country is positively correlated with income per capita. A naive person (or a representative of

---

[1]Mathematical Note: The formula for the correlation coefficient is

$$\frac{\Sigma(X - \bar{X})(Y - \bar{Y})}{\sqrt{\Sigma(X - \bar{X})^2}\sqrt{\Sigma(Y - \bar{Y})^2}}$$

where $\bar{X}$ is the mean of X and $\bar{Y}$ is the mean of Y.

the necktie industry) might interpret this finding as evidence that having more neckties causes income to be higher. A more reasonable interpretation is that neckties have no effect on income and that the correlation results from the fact that people in richer countries have more money to waste on uncomfortable clothes.

It is also perfectly possible that causation runs in both directions. For example, the amount of time a golf player spends practicing is positively correlated with the results he or she achieves. (Tiger Woods is said to practice four or five hours per day.) This correlation results from two facts: Practice improves a player's game, and naturally talented players have more incentive to practice.

In scatter plots, if we know that X causes Y and not vice versa, it is traditional to plot X on the horizontal axis and Y on the vertical. However, plotting a variable on the horizontal axis does not *prove* that it causes the other variable. In the cases where causation runs in both directions or where the direction of causation is not known, it is arbitrary which variable is plotted on the horizontal and which on the vertical axis.

3. There is no direct causal relationship between X and Y, but some third variable, Z, causes both X and Y. This third variable (Z) is known as an **omitted variable.** To give an example, the number of shark attacks taking place on a given day is positively correlated with the amount of ice cream consumed. It is pretty clear that ice-cream consumption does not cause shark attacks and vice versa. Rather, both ice-cream consumption and shark attacks are caused by the weather. On hot days, people are more likely to go swimming in the ocean and also more likely to eat ice cream.

Statisticians have devised many ways of dealing with the problems of interpreting correlations. In the case of omitted variables, the technique of *multiple regression* (taught in many econometrics classes) provides a way of separating out the effects of third variables from the relationship between the two variables of interest. There are also a number of techniques for teasing out causation (whether X causes Y, Y causes X, or both) from correlation. One of the most useful, which also is taught in many econometrics classes, is called *instrumental variables*. Although this book will not be using these statistical techniques directly, much of the literature from which we draw has applied them. In some cases, causation can be disentangled from correlation through experiments—that is, varying X and seeing if that causes changes in Y (see box "Randomized Controlled Trials.") Beyond these techniques, economic theory and common sense also have to be brought to bear in interpreting data.

The difficulties in learning about causation from observational data—summarized in the aphorism "Correlation does not imply causation"—are formidable. Yet if causation is what we are interested in learning about, correlation is often a good place to start looking.

RANDOMIZED CONTROLLED TRIALS

In recent years, economists have increasingly been deploying the powerful tool of randomized controlled trials (RCTs) to understand relationships among the variables they study and to craft policies.* RCTs in economics are modeled on the techniques that have long been used in medicine to assess the efficacy of new treatments. Economic RCTs usually involve considering a "treatment" (such as a subsidy, informational campaign, access to a program, etc.) that is randomly assigned to a group of individuals or villages, while another group that receives no treatment serves as a comparison or "control." Researchers then compare the average outcomes of treatment and control groups. Alternatively, several different treatments can be tested simultaneously, with each being assigned to a randomly chosen part of the relevant population.

There are several advantages to using RCTs. Most significantly, RCTs can solve the problem of teasing out causation from correlation that is discussed in the text. Because who gets which treatment is random, there is no danger that the treatment is correlated with omitted variables or subject to reverse causation. That means that if we observe groups that received different treatments having different outcomes, we can be sure that the treatment has had a causal impact. A second advantage of RCTs is that they allow for small-scale testing and refining of program designs that, if successful, can later be scaled up to have a large-scale impact.

RCTs are at their most effective in comparing different policies, all of which in principle will accomplish good things. Consider the problem of improving schooling. In many developing countries, schools are plagued by shortages of textbooks, teaching materials, and teachers. Further, many students have high rates of absenteeism because of illness. We would expect that the policies of supplying more textbooks or teaching materials, hiring more teachers, or addressing children's health needs would all raise student performance. But which policy is most cost-effective?

The way to answer this question is to conduct an RCT: randomly choose some villages to get one treatment (say, more textbooks), some villages to get a different treatment (say, deworming medicines, to address a common cause of absenteeism), and perhaps a third group to get no intervention at all. Assess student achievement before and after the interventions, and see where it rises the most (an RCT in Kenya found that deworming was by far the most cost-effective intervention.)[†]

RCTs like this have been used to examine the best way to encourage parents to have their children immunized, methods for reducing corruption in government road-building projects, and the effect of microfinance on prosperity at the level of neighborhoods, among many other topics.

RCTs can also be used to probe the underlying determinants of economic behavior. Different theories about why people behave in certain ways (e.g., what determines how many children they have or how much money they save) imply that people will respond in different ways when their environment changes. Researchers can use RCTs to vary the environment people face in one dimension at a time to test different theories. For example, one study tested the theory that limited access to credit was reducing the productivity of small firms in Kenya. Some firms were randomly chosen to receive loans, and their performance was compared to a control group that did not receive this treatment.

Although RCTs are excellent tools for answering some questions that economists face, they are far from a universal solution. One problem with RCTs is the issue of "external validity," that is, whether a treatment that works in one setting (e.g., a particular region) will work in other places. A more serious problem is that there are sharp limits on the kinds of hypotheses that can be tested using RCTs. Economic policies that affect an entire country, rather than just a single family or village, are hard to assess using RCTs. Examples of policies like these include protectionist trade policy (discussed in Chapter 11) and regulation of financial markets (Chapter 10). Further, because they focus on the effect of a treatment on the treated individual, RCT analyses may miss out on important effects. For example, an RCT can show that providing an individual with more schooling raises his or her earnings, but it does not show whether these higher earnings represent an addition to the total level of earnings in the economy or simply the treated individual displacing some nontreated person in a high-wage job.[‡]

RCTs are also not informative when one is considering deep factors that affect the level of development of the economy as a whole (i.e., "fundamentals" in the language of this chapter). For example, as discussed in Chapter 12,

economists spend a lot of time thinking about the role that different characteristics of government, such as the level or corruption or the extent of democracy, play in affecting economic growth. Answering this question with an RCT would require randomly dividing countries into different groups, then assigning one group to have corrupt governments and the other group to have honest governments, which is a practical impossibility. Similarly, issues such as the role of culture (Chapter 14), colonial history (Chapter 12), or geographical factors (Chapter 15) are areas in which it is difficult to learn anything using RCTs because there is no way for economists to manipulate the "treatment."

Believers in the RCT methodology have answers to many of these points, however. Although it is true that RCTs may never reveal the fundamental roots of economic underdevelopment, knowing these deep roots is of more academic than practical value anyway. Further, although it is true that there are some areas of policy making (e.g., trade policy) in which RCTs are uninformative, these are often areas in which policy is made for political reasons, and so even if economists knew the truth of what policy was best, it would not affect what actually got done. It is precisely in the areas in which there are policy choices to be made and in which those who make them might listen to what economists have learned that RCTs are most informative.

[*]Banerjee and Duflo (2011)
[†]Kremer and Miguel (2004).
[‡]Acemoglu (2010).

LEARNING FROM HISTORICAL DATA

Much of the data in this book are **cross-sectional data**—that is, observations of different units (e.g., countries or people) at a single point in time. An alternative to using cross-sectional data is to examine how economic variables change over time, either a period of decades or longer expanses of history. Historical data are particularly useful for thinking about why countries differ in their levels of income today because, as we saw in the last chapter, much of the variation in income today has its roots in the last 200 years of economic growth.

Although history can be revealing, it is also difficult to interpret. One problem in interpreting historical data (as with any other data) is that when two things happened at the same time, we do not know which event caused which, or even whether they were causally related at all. An additional problem with historical data is that, for many questions we are interested in, history effectively provides only one data point. Specifically, we are often interested in why something happened one way and not another—for example, why Europe developed before China or why England led the Industrial Revolution.

Economic historian Robert Fogel won the Nobel Prize in part for showing that one of the "obvious" lessons of history—that railroads were an essential cause of economic growth in the United States in the 19th century—was in fact a fallacy. Historians had been convinced of railroads' centrality in U.S. economic growth by the fact that over the course of the century, railroads became the dominant means of transporting agricultural commodities and manufactured goods around the country. But Fogel showed that railroads' dominance in transport did not prove that they were essential. Considering a "counterfactual" world in which railroads were not invented, Fogel demonstrated that the country's network of navigable waterways and canals, the growth of which was choked off by the railroads, could have done almost as good a job of handling the transport needs of the growing economy. Figure 2.5 shows Fogel's map of a water transport network that could have substituted for most railroads in existence in 1890.*

Because history happened only once, it is hard to eliminate completely the effect of luck. The history of movable type provides an example of the effect that luck can have on economic development. The introduction of movable type in Europe by Johannes Gutenberg in 1453 had profound economic and social effects on the continent's development. Interestingly, however, printing with movable type had been invented in China some 600 years before Gutenberg but did not take off in the way it did in Europe. Why was printing less popular in China than in Europe? One important reason is that written Chinese, which relies on thousands of pictographic characters, is much harder to set in type than are European languages, which use small alphabets. It is conceivable that this piece of luck, rather than the social and political

2.4 CONCLUSION

This chapter has presented a general framework for thinking about how differences in income among countries are determined. The parable of Freedonia and Sylvania introduced the three themes that are central to our approach. First, differences in income per capita among countries can be broken down into a piece factors that interest historians, is the most important explanation for the divergent fates of the two regions.

The bottom line is that, like any other data, history has to be interpreted with caution.

Historical experience can add to the weight of evidence for or against a particular theory. But it is rare indeed that "history proves" anything.

*Fogel (1964).

FIGURE 2.5

Fogel's Map of a Potential Water Transport Network for 1890

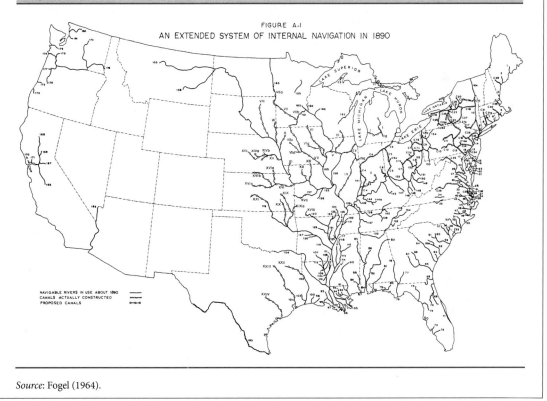

FIGURE A-I
AN EXTENDED SYSTEM OF INTERNAL NAVIGATION IN 1890

Source: Fogel (1964).

---

attributable to the accumulation of factors of production and a piece attributable to the productivity with which those factors of production are used. Second, productivity differences among countries can themselves be decomposed in part as a result of differences in technology and in part as a result of differences in efficiency. Third, beyond an examination of the proximate factors that determine income differences (factor accumulation, technology, and efficiency), a full understanding of economic growth requires an examination of the fundamental factors that determine the proximate causes.

These three themes will form the framework for the rest of the book. The next four chapters examine the accumulation of factors of production in detail, asking why factor accumulation differs among countries and how much of the variation in income per capita can be explained by differences in factor accumulation. Part III examines productivity differences among countries, as well as productivity's components, technology and efficiency. Finally, Part IV looks at a set of fundamental factors and traces their links to the proximate determinants of output differences among countries.

KEY TERMS

capital 30	ultimate cause 33	outlier 38
investment 30	factors of production 34	correlation 40
productivity 31	production	correlation
technology 31	function 34	coefficient 40
efficiency 31	economic model 37	reverse causation 40
fundamentals 32	scatter plot 38	omitted variable 41
proximate cause 33	variable 38	cross-sectional data 44

QUESTIONS FOR REVIEW

1. What is the difference between productivity and factor accumulation as forces that contribute to differences in income among countries?

2. What is the relationship among productivity, technology, and efficiency?

3. What is the distinction between *proximate* and *ultimate* determinants of a country's income per capita?

4. What is a production function? What are factors of production?

5. What are the obstacles to using data on correlation to infer causation?

6. How do randomized controlled trials overcome some of the problems in inferring causality from data?

PROBLEMS

1. Give an example of a possible proximate cause for low GDP per capita.

2. Give an example of a possible fundamental cause for low GDP per capita.

3. Draw a graph, analogous to those in Figure 2.2, showing how two countries can have the same level of output per capita but different levels of factor accumulation and productivity.

4. Country A and Country B have the same exact fundamentals, but Country A is twice as rich as Country B. Which country would you expect to have higher growth in the short run?

How will their growth rates compare in the long run?

5. Give an example of something that is correlated with GDP per capita where it is clear a priori that causation runs from GDP to that measure and not in the other direction.

6. A study finds that there is a strong correlation between being overweight and suffering a heart attack. Does this prove that being overweight causes heart attacks? Tell a story in which the correlation is the result of reverse causation. Tell a story in which the correlation is the result of an omitted variable.

7. For each of the following scenarios, discuss what statistical problem might make the inference incorrect:

   a. People who vote for right-wing political parties tend to live longer than those who vote for left-wing parties. Therefore, being a political conservative is good for you.

   b. People in hospitals are generally less healthy than those outside of hospitals. Therefore, it is best to avoid hospitals.

8. For each of the following pairs of variables, give your best guess (and an explanation) of whether the variables have a positive, negative, or roughly zero correlation in a cross-section of countries:

   a. GDP per capita and the number of books printed per capita

   b. GDP per capita and the fraction of the population suffering from malnutrition

   c. Fraction of the population that wears eyeglasses and life expectancy

   d. Number of automobiles per capita and number of letters in the country's name

9. A pharmaceutical company has created a new drug that it believes will help students learn more effectively. Describe how you would construct a randomized controlled trial on your college campus to assess this theory. Be as specific as possible regarding how you would recruit subjects, conduct the experiment, assess outcomes, and so on. Discuss some of the logistical and ethical obstacles you might face in conducting this trial. What problems might arise in your drawing a general conclusion about the efficacy of the drug from the trial you describe?

For additional exploration and practice using the Online Data Plotter and data sets, please visit http://www.pearsonhighered.com/weil/.

CHAPTER 3

PHYSICAL CAPITAL

It is not a bad definition of *man* to describe him as a *tool-making animal*. His earliest contrivances to support uncivilized life were tools of the simplest and rudest construction. His latest achievements in the substitution of machinery, not merely for the skill of the human hand, but for the relief of the human intellect, are founded on the use of tools of a still higher order.

—Charles Babbage[1]

The economist's name for tools—the physical objects that extend our ability or do work for us—is **capital.** Capital includes not only the machines that sit in factories, but also the buildings in which we work, infrastructure such as roads and ports, vehicles that we use for transporting goods and raw materials, and even computers on which professors compose textbooks. Performing almost any job requires the use of capital, and for most jobs, the worker who has more or better capital to work with will be able to produce more output.

Because workers with more capital can produce more output, differences in the quantity of capital are a natural explanation to consider for the differences we observe in income among countries. In 2009 the average U.S. worker had $201,618 worth of capital to work with. In Mexico in that year, the capital per worker was $66,081, and in India, it was only $17,918.[2] Figure 3.1 looks at the relationship between the amount of capital per worker and the level of GDP per worker for many countries. The close relationship between these two variables is striking. The huge differences in the amount of capital available to workers are an obvious explanation for the large differences in output among these countries. But as the discussion in Chapter 2 made clear, we will need to analyze the problem more carefully before we can conclude that the United States is richer than Mexico or India because it has more capital.

This chapter presents a capital-based theory of why countries differ in their levels of income. Such a simple model cannot explain all of the phenomena we observe, but it is instructive to see how far the model can take us. Many of the concepts introduced in this capital-based model will be useful later on when we

---

[1]Babbage (1851).
[2]Calculations based on Heston et al. (2010).

GDP and Capital per Worker, 2009

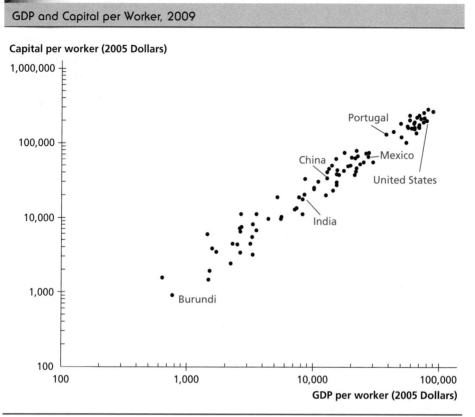

Source: Calculations based on Heston et al. (2010).

consider further complexities. Examining this model will also give us a chance to apply in a simple environment some mathematical techniques we will use later in the book.

3.1 THE NATURE OF CAPITAL

For the purposes of understanding the capital-based theory of income differences, we need to consider five key characteristics of capital: It is productive; it is produced; its use is limited; it can earn a return; and it wears out. Let's consider each characteristic in more detail.

Capital is productive; using it raises the amount of output that a worker can produce. We explore this property extensively in the next section.

Capital is something that has itself been produced; it has been built or created. The process of producing capital is called **investment.** The fact that capital is produced distinguishes it from a natural resource (such as a piece of land), which also allows a worker to produce more output but is not itself produced. Because it is produced, capital requires the sacrifice of some consumption. That is, the resources used to create a piece of capital could have been used for something else. A modern economy spends a large fraction of output on building new pieces of capital. For example, in 2009 the United States spent $2.1 trillion, or 16.6% of its gross domestic product (GDP), on investment. A country that lowers its investment, for whatever reason, will have more resources left over to spend on consumption.

The decision to build capital might be made privately (in the case of a piece of productive equipment) or by the government (in the case of a piece of infra-structure such as a road). In either case, corresponding to the creation of a piece of capital is an act of investment: the spending of resources on the creation of capital. Investment, in turn, has to correspond to an act of saving. Someone who had control over resources and could have spent them on consumption today has instead used them to build a piece of capital that will be employed in future production.

Capital is *rival* in its use. This is a fancy way of saying that only a limited number of people can use a given piece of capital at one time. In the simplest case—say, a hammer—only one person at a time can use a piece of capital. Other kinds of capital, including roads, can be used by a large but finite number of people at the same time.

Saying that rivalry in its use is one of the characteristics of capital may seem trivial because it is hard to think of many productive tools that *can* be used by an ar-bitrary number of people at once. However, such tools do exist, in the form of ideas. Like capital, ideas can make a worker more productive. And ideas share with capital the important property that they are the product of investment. In the case of ideas, this investment is called research and development. But ideas differ from capital in that, once an idea is created, an infinite number of people can use it at the same time. (Chapter 8 will discuss this property of ideas at much greater length.)

Because capital is productive and its use is limited, it is often able to earn a re-turn. If using a certain piece of capital will make a worker more productive, then the worker will be willing to pay to use it. In the case of a tool, the worker may act alone to invest in it, buying the tool and then keeping the higher wages earned by using it. In other cases, workers will rent a piece of capital. For example, taxi drivers may rent a cab for a shift. In the case of a more complex economic activity such as building cars, a large quantity of capital (a factory) may be used by thousands of workers. In this case, the workers do not buy or rent capital. Instead, the owners of the capital hire workers, and the profits that remain after the workers are paid are the return to the owners of the capital.

The return that capital earns is often the incentive for its creation. If you decide not to consume some of your income this year and instead invest it in the capital of some corporation, you do so in the hope of earning payments for the use of your capital in future years. Not all capital is privately owned, however. Infrastructure such as roads and ports is usually built and owned by governments.

Finally, capital wears out. The economic term for this wearing-out process is **depreciation.** Using a piece of capital usually causes it to wear down a little. Even when use itself does not cause wear, capital will depreciate simply because of the passage of time: It will rust or rot or get damaged by weather. Depreciation is a routine part of economic life, and no one would buy a piece of capital without taking it into account. A large fraction of the investment that takes place in the economy serves only to replace capital that has depreciated.

3.2 CAPITAL'S ROLE IN PRODUCTION

The first distinguishing characteristic of capital is that it is productive: It enables workers to produce more output. This section examines the relationship between capital and output more formally, to lay the mathematical foundation for a capital-based theory of why countries differ in their levels of income.

Using a Production Function to Analyze Capital's Role

We analyze capital's role in production using the concept of a production function. Recall from Chapter 2 that a production function expresses the relationship between inputs (i.e., factors of production) and the amount of output produced. For simplicity, we consider the case in which there are only two inputs into production: capital, symbolized by K, and labor, symbolized by L. Letting Y symbolize the quantity of output, we can write the following production function:

$$Y = F(K, L).$$

Two assumptions about this production function should be familiar from basic microeconomics. First, we assume that the production function has **constant returns to scale.** In other words, if we multiply the quantities of each input by some factor, the quantity of output will increase by that same factor. For example, if we double the quantity of each input, we will double the quantity of output. Mathematically, this assumption implies that

$$F(zK, zL) = zF(K, L),$$

where z is any positive constant.

Instead of examining the quantity of *total* output in a country, it is frequently more interesting to look at the quantity of output *per worker*.[3] The fact that the production function has constant returns to scale implies that the quantity of

---

[3]Notice that output per worker and output per capita are not the same thing because not every person in a country is a worker. Our analysis of capital accumulation in this chapter will be conducted in terms of output per worker, even though the data presented in Chapter 1, which motivated our analysis, were in terms of output per capita. If the ratio of workers to total population were the same in every country, then differences among countries in output per worker would be proportional to differences in output per capita. Chapter 5 will discuss how the ratio of workers to total population might differ among countries or might change over time.

output per worker will depend only on the quantity of capital per worker. We see this result by starting with the production function, $Y = F(K, L)$, and then multiplying both inputs by the factor $1/L$:

$$\left(\frac{1}{L}\right)Y = \left(\frac{1}{L}\right)F(K, L) = F\left(\frac{K}{L}, \frac{L}{L}\right) = F\left(\frac{K}{L}, 1\right).$$

The term $1/L$ plays the same role that the constant z played when we defined constant returns to scale.

Defining $k = K/L$ as the quantity of capital per worker and $y = Y/L$ as the quantity of output per worker, we can rewrite this expression as

$$y = F(k,1).$$

In other words, output per worker is a function only of capital per worker. Finally, because the second term in this per-worker production function does not change, we can ignore this part of the production function and write the per-worker production function as

$$y = f(k).$$

A second assumption about the production function is that it displays diminishing marginal product. The **marginal product** of a particular input is the extra output produced when one more unit of the input is used in production. For example, the marginal product of capital is the increase in output that results from adding one more unit of capital, or equivalently the amount that output per worker rises if one additional unit of capital per worker is used in production. Mathematically, the marginal product of capital (MPK) is given by the following equation:[4]

$$\text{MPK} = f(k + 1) - f(k).$$

The assumption of **diminishing marginal product** says that if we keep adding units of a single input (holding the quantities of any other inputs fixed), then the quantity of new output that each new unit of input produces will be smaller than that added by the previous unit of the input. Figure 3.2 illustrates diminishing marginal product. The horizontal axis shows the quantity of capital per worker, and the vertical axis shows the quantity of output per worker. The marginal product of capital is the slope of this function: the quantity of extra output per worker that results from using one more unit of capital per worker as an input.

It is often helpful to use a specific functional form for the production function. Throughout this book we will use a **Cobb-Douglas production function.** This production function does a good job of fitting data on inputs and outputs. The Cobb-Douglas production function is

$$F(K, L) = AK^{\alpha}L^{1-\alpha}.$$

---

[4]Mathematical Note: Using calculus, the marginal product of capital is the derivative of the production function with respect to capital: $MPK = \partial F(K,L)/\partial K$ or, in per-worker terms, $MPK = df(k)/dk$.

FIGURE 3.2

A Production Function with Diminishing Marginal Product of Capital

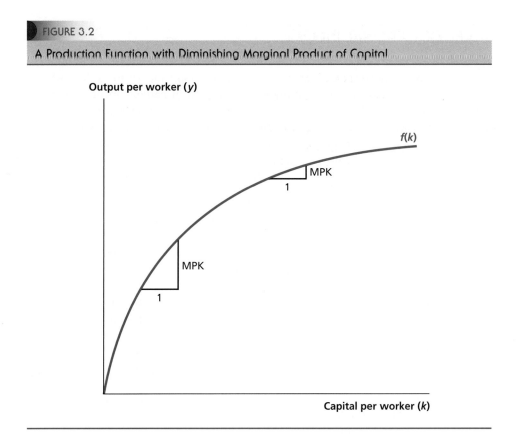

The parameter A can be thought of as measuring productivity: For given quantities of capital, K, and labor, L, a country with bigger A will produce more output. The parameter α (the Greek letter alpha), which is assumed to have a value between 0 and 1, determines exactly how capital and labor combine to produce output. We will discuss how economists estimate the value of α (see box "Capital's Share of National Income").

To write the Cobb-Douglas production function in per-worker terms, multiply both inputs and output by $1/L$:

$$y = \frac{Y}{L} = \frac{F(K, L)}{L} = F\left(\frac{K}{L}, \frac{L}{L}\right) = A\left(\frac{K}{L}\right)^{\alpha}\left(\frac{L}{L}\right)^{1-\alpha} = Ak^{\alpha}.$$

Restating the solution, we have an expression for per-worker production:

$$y = Ak^{\alpha}.$$

The appendix to this chapter presents a more detailed mathematical analysis of the Cobb-Douglas production function.

> ## CAPITAL'S SHARE OF NATIONAL INCOME
>
> The share of national income earned by holders of capital is one of the crucial pieces of data that economists examine in studying economic growth. Knowing capital's share of national income will tell us the value of the key parameter α if the production function is of the Cobb-Douglas form.
>
> Figure 3.3 shows data on capital's share of national income for a sample of 53 countries.* The average share in this sample is 0.35, or almost exactly one-third. Most countries' capital shares lie fairly near this average, although there are some significant exceptions. For example, in Botswana and Ecuador capital's share of income is estimated to be 0.55, whereas in Greece it is estimated to be only 0.21. It is also interesting to note that there is no systematic relationship between capital's share of national income and the level of GDP per capita; countries that are rich do not tend to have either higher or lower capital shares than countries that are poor. (In the United States capital's share of national income has ranged between 0.25 and 0.35 since 1935.)[†]
>
> There is no good theory to explain why the share of capital in national income differs among countries as shown in Figure 3.3. One distinct possibility is that this is a case of measurement error. It could be that the *true* value of capital's share is the same in every country but that the available measurements contain a good deal of "noise" that makes capital's share appear to vary. A piece of evidence in favor of this theory is that there tends to be much less variation in the measured share of capital in national income among rich countries (which tend to have better data) than among poor countries.
>
> Based on these results, we will use a value of 1/3 as our estimate of α throughout this book. Given the messiness of the data, it is unlikely that this estimate is exactly right, but it can serve as a good approximation.
>
> *Bernanke and Gürkaynak (2002), table 10 and note 18.
> [†]Gollin (2002).

Factor Payments and Factor Shares

Much as the return earned by capital motivates the investment that creates capital, the return earned by labor (i.e., the wage) motivates people to supply their labor to the economy. Later on, in considering other factors of production, we will see that they earn returns as well. Observations about these factor returns often are useful for assigning values to parameters of the production function such as α.

Recall from your previous economics courses that in a competitive economy, factors of production will be paid their marginal products. To see why, consider the problem that a firm faces in deciding how much of a given factor of production to employ. For example, think about a firm that is deciding how many workers it should have on its payroll. Hiring one more worker will produce extra output equal to the marginal product of labor, or MPL (indeed, this is the definition of the marginal product of labor). If the wage were lower than the MPL, the firm

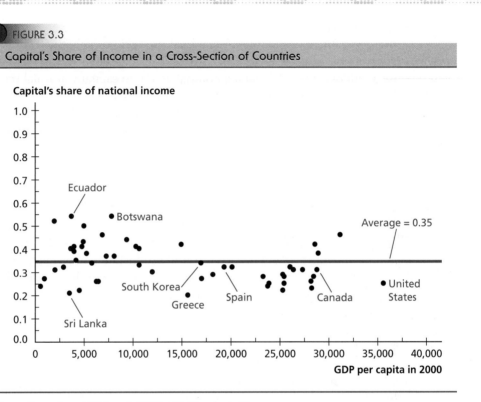

FIGURE 3.3

Capital's Share of Income in a Cross-Section of Countries

Source: Bernanke and Gürkaynak (2002), table 10 and note 18.

would want to hire more workers because each worker would earn the firm more than he or she costs. But because there are diminishing returns to labor, each time a new worker is hired, the MPL will fall, and eventually the MPL will be equal to the wage—at which point the firm would not want to hire any more workers. Similarly, if the wage were above the MPL, then the firm would want to eliminate workers until the MPL and the wage were equal. Thus, in choosing their optimal quantity of labor, firms will set the MPL equal to the wage. Similarly, the marginal product of capital will equal the "rental rate" of capital (i.e., the cost of renting one unit of capital for one unit of time).

In a Cobb-Douglas production function, there is a neat relationship between factor payments and the parameters of the production function. The Cobb-Douglas production function is

$$Y = AK^{\alpha}L^{1-\alpha}.$$

In the appendix, we show that the marginal product of capital for this production function is

$$\text{MPK} = \alpha A K^{\alpha-1} L^{1-\alpha}.$$

In a competitive economy, the marginal product of capital will equal the rental rate per unit of capital—in other words, the amount firms are willing to pay to use a unit of capital. The *total* amount paid out to capital will equal the rental rate per unit of capital multiplied by the total quantity of capital, that is, MPK × K. **Capital's share of income** is the fraction of national income (Y) that is paid out as rent on capital. Mathematically, the capital share is given by this expression:

$$\text{Capital's share of income} = \frac{\text{MPK} \times K}{Y} = \frac{\alpha A K^{\alpha} L^{1-\alpha}}{A K^{\alpha} L^{1-\alpha}} = \alpha.$$

A similar calculation shows that labor's share is equal to $1 - \alpha$. This result says that even though the quantities of capital and labor in the economy may vary, changes in the rental rate of capital and wage rate will be such that the shares of national income paid out to each factor of production will be unaffected.

This result is important because it tells us we can estimate the value of α just by looking at capital's share of national income. This number is generally estimated to be close to 1/3, and this is the value we will use.

3.3 THE SOLOW MODEL

With a production function that tells us how labor and capital are transformed into output, we can look at a simple model of economic growth that will illustrate the importance of physical capital in explaining differences among countries in their levels of income per capita. The model we examine is called the Solow model, after Nobel Prize–winning economist Robert Solow, who created it in 1956. The Solow model is simple because it focuses on a single dimension along which countries may differ from each other or along which a single country may change over time: namely, the amount of physical capital that each worker has to work with. Because the production function tells us the relationship between capital per worker and output per worker, the only remaining piece of the model to add is a description of how capital per worker is determined.

Determination of Capital per Worker

In this version of the Solow model, we assume that the quantity of labor input, L, is constant over time. We also assume that the production function itself does not change over time; in other words, there is no improvement in productivity. In the case of the Cobb-Douglas production function, this is the same as assuming that the parameter A in the production function is constant. Thus, all of the action in the Solow model comes from the accumulation of capital, which is governed by two forces: investment (the building of new capital) and depreciation (the wearing out of old capital). Later chapters will extend this simple Solow model to allow for changes in the quantity of labor input (Chapter 4), additional factors of production (Chapter 6), and changes in productivity (Part III).

At any point in time, the change in the capital stock is the difference between the amount of investment and the amount of depreciation. If I represents the quantity of investment and D represents the quantity of depreciation, then the change in the capital stock is represented as

$$\Delta K = I - D.$$

Again, it is useful to look at capital accumulation in per-worker terms. Let i and d be the quantities of investment and depreciation per worker. The equation for the accumulation of capital can now be written as follows:

$$\Delta k = i - d.$$

To go further, we must consider how the quantities of investment and depreciation are determined. In the case of investment, we assume that a constant fraction of output is invested. We denote this fraction γ (the Greek letter gamma). This assumption is represented in per-worker terms by the following equation:

$$i = \gamma y.$$

We will return to the question of how investment is determined later in this chapter. For now we treat γ as a constant. In the case of depreciation, we assume that a constant fraction of the capital stock depreciates each period. Denote this fraction δ (the Greek lowercase letter delta):

$$d = \delta k.$$

Combining the three preceding equations, we can write a new equation for the evolution of capital per worker:

$$\Delta k = \gamma y - \delta k.$$

Finally, given that the level of output per worker, y, is a function of the level of capital per worker, k, we can rewrite this equation as

$$\Delta k = \gamma f(k) - \delta k. \tag{3.1}$$

To see how to use this equation, apply it to a concrete example. Suppose that in the year 2010, the quantity of capital per worker in a certain country was equal to 100, the quantity of output per worker—that is, $f(k)$—equaled 50, the fraction of output invested was 20%, and the depreciation rate was 5%. Plug these numbers into the equation:

$$\Delta k = 0.20 \times 50 - 0.05 \times 100 = 10 - 5 = 5.$$

THE RISE AND FALL OF CAPITAL

Our analysis of growth in this chapter is conducted in a setting with only two factors of production: capital and labor. We take this approach both because it is simple—it is easiest to start with two factors and to add more later—and because today capital and labor are the two most important factors of production.

Before the 19th century, however, the most important factor of production other than labor was not capital but land. We can most easily see the changing balance of importance between land and capital by looking at how the value of these two factors has changed. Because both capital and land can be bought and sold, they have an easily observable value. Together, ownership of land and ownership of capital constitute the largest components of wealth. (There are other components of total wealth, such as ownership of houses, gold, or valuables, but these are less important.)

As Table 3.1 shows, the fraction of total wealth held in the form of land has declined dramatically in the United Kingdom over the last three centuries. This decline in land as a fraction of total wealth presumably mirrors a decline in payments to landowners relative to payments to capital owners. This change demonstrates the growing importance of capital as a factor of production.*

Why did capital replace land as a key input into production? The most important reason was changes in technology. The Industrial Revolution (beginning in roughly 1760) saw the invention of new technologies, such as the steam engine, that made capital immensely more productive. Similarly, advances in agricultural technology have allowed other inputs, such as chemical fertilizers, to substitute for land. Accompanying these technological changes, there has been a shift in the composition of

TABLE 3.1

Agricultural Land as a Fraction of Total Wealth in the United Kingdom

1688	64%
1798	55%
1885	18%
1927	4%
1958	3%

output, away from food (which requires land to produce) and toward goods that are produced using capital.

Is the rise of capital as a factor of production a permanent feature of economic growth? Not necessarily. Some observers have discerned the rise of a "postindustrial" economy in the most developed countries, where knowledge and skills are taking the place of physical capital as the key inputs into production. If the archetypical laborer of the 1950s worked in a factory filled with big pieces of machinery, the archetype in the 2010s uses no more capital than a laptop computer. In Chapter 6 we introduce the notion of *human capital* as an additional factor of production that includes the skills that are an increasingly important input into production.

Other observers have argued that the reduced importance of land (or natural resources more generally) as the most important factor of production is a temporary phenomenon. In the view of these pessimists, shortages of natural resources will mean that the fraction of national income paid to natural resource holders will rise over time. Chapters 15 and 16 will examine the role of natural resources in production.

*Deane and Cole (1969), Revell (1967).

> ## MEASURING CHANGE OVER TIME
>
> This book is largely concerned with how things change over time—mostly how they grow, but occasionally how they shrink. There are two ways to measure how something changes over time. The first method is to look at how much it changes between one year and the next. We call this measure the **difference,** symbolized with the Greek character Δ (uppercase delta). If x_t is the quantity of something at time t, and x_{t+1} is the quantity at time $t + 1$, then we denote the difference in x between these two periods as Δx_t:
>
> $$\Delta x_t = x_{t+1} - x_t.$$
>
> For example, the population of the United States on July 1, 2009, was 306,656,290; one year later it was 309,050,816. If we use L to symbolize population, then we have
>
> $$\Delta L_{2009} = L_{2010} - L_{2009}$$
>
> $$= 309,050,816 - 306,656,290$$
>
> $$= 2,394,526.$$
>
> In other words, the population increased by slightly less than 3 million people.
>
> It is often more natural to measure how quickly something is changing by looking at its growth rate. The **growth rate** expresses the change in a variable relative to its initial value. Expressed mathematically it is the difference (change over time) divided by the starting value. This book denotes growth rates by putting
>
> a "hat" (^) over the variable. Returning to the example of population, we calculate the growth rate as follows:
>
> $$\hat{L}_{2009} = \frac{L_{2010} - L_{2009}}{L_{2009}}$$
>
> $$= \frac{2,394,526}{306,656,290} \approx .0078$$
>
> $$= 0.78\%.$$
>
> In other words, population grew by 0.78% over the course of the year. More generally, for any variable x, the difference in x and the growth rate of x are related by this equation: *
>
> $$\hat{x} = \frac{\Delta x}{x}.$$
>
> *Mathematical Note: Readers who know calculus may be familiar with an alternative way of measuring rates of change. Rather than looking at the change in some variable over a discrete amount of time (the difference), we can measure the change in a variable continuously—that is, we can look at the *derivative with respect to time*. This book uses derivatives with respect to time only in some mathematical notes and appendixes. We symbolize these derivatives by putting a dot on top of a variable:
>
> $$\dot{x} = \frac{dx}{dt}.$$
>
> The relationship between the rate of growth and the derivative with respect to time is
>
> $$\hat{x} = \frac{\dot{x}}{x}.$$

Thus, the change in the capital stock per worker was equal to 5 units. The quantity of capital per worker in 2011 was 5 units more than 100, or 105.

Steady States

Equation 3.1 describes how capital evolves over time. According to the equation, if investment, $\gamma f(k)$, is larger than depreciation, δk, then the change in the capital stock, Δk, will be positive—that is, the capital stock will be growing. On the other hand, if $\gamma f(k)$ is less than δk, then the capital stock will be shrinking. If $\gamma f(k)$ is equal to δk—in other words, if the quantity of investment equals the quantity of depreciation—then the capital stock will not change at all.

Figure 3.4 analyzes Equation 3.1 graphically. The figure plots the two parts of the right-hand side of the equation—that is, $\gamma f(k)$, which represents investment, and δk, which represents depreciation. To serve as a reference, the figure also plots $f(k)$, the production function. The level of capital at which the lines representing investment and depreciation intersect is called the steady-state capital stock. It is labeled k^{ss} in the figure. If an economy has capital equal to k^{ss}, then the amount of capital per worker will not change over time—thus the name **steady state.**

What if the capital stock is not equal to the steady-state level? The figure shows that over time, the capital stock will move toward the steady state. For example, if the level of capital is below the steady state, then it is clear from the figure that $\gamma f(k)$, the quantity of investment, is greater than δk, the quantity of depreciation. In this case, the capital stock will grow, as we can also see from Equation 3.1.

▶ FIGURE 3.4

The Steady State of the Solow Model

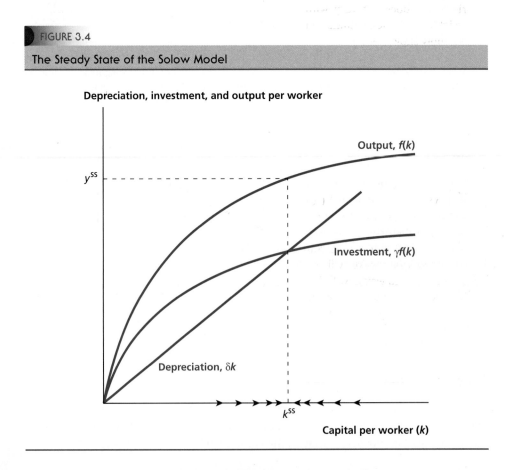

Depreciation, investment, and output per worker

y^{ss}

Output, $f(k)$

Investment, $\gamma f(k)$

Depreciation, δk

k^{ss}

Capital per worker (k)

STEADY STATE: A NONECONOMIC EXAMPLE

To help cement the idea of a steady state, consider an example from outside economics: the relationship between the amount of food a person consumes and how much he or she weighs. It is well known that a person who consumes more calories than he or she expends (or "burns") will gain weight, whereas a person who consumes fewer calories than he or she expends will lose weight.

In Figure 3.5, the vertical axis measures a person's daily calorie expenditure and consumption, and the horizontal axis measures the person's weight. We assume that calorie intake does not vary with weight, so calorie consumption is simply shown as a horizontal line. Calorie expenditure, however, rises with weight because a heavier person uses more energy than a light person in the course of daily physical activity. Thus, the line representing calorie expenditure slopes upward.

The figure shows that there will be a steady-state level of weight at the point where these two curves intersect. If a person starts off at less than this weight, calorie intake will exceed usage, and weight will rise. If a person starts off at more than the steady-state weight, calorie intake will be lower than usage, and weight will fall.

Figure 3.5 also shows what factors influence a person's steady-state weight. Raising food intake will shift up the line representing calories consumed and will thus raise steady-state weight. Similarly, a change in lifestyle or environment that causes an upward shift of the curve representing calories burned at any weight will lower steady-state weight.

FIGURE 3.5

Determination of Steady-State Weight

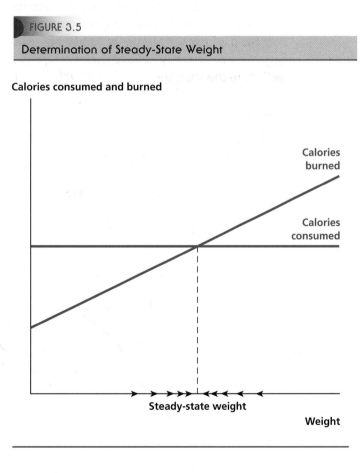

Calories consumed and burned

Calories burned

Calories consumed

Steady-state weight

Weight

Similarly, if the capital stock is greater than the steady-state level, depreciation will be greater than investment, and the capital stock will shrink over time. The steady state in this case is said to be *stable*: If the economy starts out with any capital stock other than k^{ss}, over time the capital stock will move toward k^{ss}.

Looking again at Figure 3.4, we see that there is a steady-state level of output, y^{ss}, that is associated with steady-state capital stock, k^{ss}. An economy that has capital below k^{ss} will have output below y^{ss}. Similarly, in an economy with any level of output other than y^{ss}, output will move toward y^{ss} over time.

We can also use this diagram to analyze how different aspects of the economy affect the steady-state level of output. Consider a change in γ, the fraction of output invested. Figure 3.6 shows the effect of increasing γ from γ_1 to γ_2. The $\gamma f(k)$ curve shifts upward, as do the steady-state levels of capital and output. Similarly, an increase in δ, the rate of depreciation, would make the δk curve steeper, leading to lower steady-state levels for capital and output.

FIGURE 3.6

Effect of Increasing the Investment Rate on the Steady State

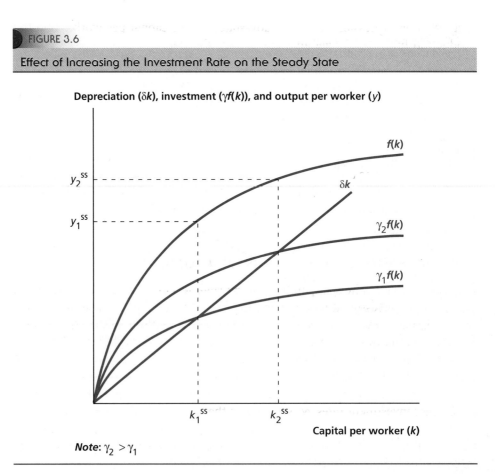

Depreciation (δk), investment ($\gamma f(k)$), and output per worker (y)

$f(k)$

δk

$\gamma_2 f(k)$

$\gamma_1 f(k)$

y_2^{ss}

y_1^{ss}

k_1^{ss}

k_2^{ss}

Capital per worker (k)

Note: $\gamma_2 > \gamma_1$

Using the Cobb-Douglas production function, $y = Ak^\alpha$, we can be more formal in our analysis. Equation 3.1 can be rewritten as

$$\Delta k = \gamma A k^\alpha - \delta k. \tag{3.2}$$

Finding the steady state simply entails finding a value of capital, k^{ss}, for which Equation 3.2 is equal to zero,

$$0 = \gamma A (k^{ss})^\alpha - \delta k^{ss},$$

which implies that

$$\gamma A (k^{ss})^\alpha = \delta k^{ss}.$$

To solve this expression for k^{ss}, first divide both sides by $(k^{ss})^\alpha$ and by δ. Then raise both sides to the power $1/(1 - \alpha)$:

$$k^{ss} = \left(\frac{\gamma A}{\delta} \right)^{1/(1-\alpha)}.$$

Plugging this expression for the steady-state level of capital per worker into the production function, we get an expression of the steady-state level of output per worker:

$$y^{ss} = A(k^{ss})^\alpha = A^{1/1-\alpha} \left(\frac{\gamma}{\delta} \right)^{\alpha/(1-\alpha)}. \tag{3.3}$$

This equation confirms the result shown in Figure 3.6 that raising the rate of investment will raise the steady-state level of output per worker. Raising γ will raise the numerator of the last term in this equation, so it will raise the steady-state level of output per worker. Similarly, raising the rate of depreciation, δ, will raise the denominator of the same term and will therefore lower y^{ss}.

The Solow Model as a Theory of Income Differences

Equation 3.3 shows how a country's steady-state level of output per worker will depend on its investment rate. If a country has a higher rate of investment, it will have a higher steady-state level of output. Thus, we may think of the Solow model as a *theory of income differences*. Naturally, we should ask how well this theory fits the data. That is, how do actual differences in income among countries compare with the differences predicted by the Solow model?

For simplicity, consider the case where the *only* differences among countries are in their investment rates, γ. We assume that countries have the same levels of productivity, A, and the same rates of depreciation, δ. We also assume that countries are all at their steady-state levels of income per worker, although we will later explore what happens when this assumption is relaxed.

Consider two countries, which we denote i and j. Let γ_i be the rate of investment in Country i and γ_j be the rate of investment in Country j. Their steady-state levels of output per worker are given by the equations

$$y_i^{ss} = A^{1/(1-\alpha)} \left(\frac{\gamma_i}{\delta} \right)^{\alpha/(1-\alpha)}$$

and

$$y_j^{ss} = A^{1/(1-\alpha)} \left(\frac{\gamma_j}{\delta} \right)^{\alpha/(1-\alpha)}.$$

Dividing the first of these equations by the second expresses the ratio of income per worker in Country i to income per worker in Country j:

$$\frac{y_i^{ss}}{y_j^{ss}} = \left(\frac{\gamma_i}{\gamma_j} \right)^{\alpha/(1-\alpha)}.$$

Notice that the terms A and δ have dropped out because both of these parameters were assumed to be the same in the two countries.

We can now make quantitative predictions from our theory. For example, let's suppose that Country i has an investment rate of 20% and Country j has an investment rate of 5%. We use the value of $\alpha = 1/3$, so $\alpha/(1 - \alpha) = 1/2$. Substitute the values of investment into the preceding equation:

$$\frac{y_i^{ss}}{y_j^{ss}} = \left(\frac{0.20}{0.05} \right)^{1/2} = 4^{1/2} = 2.$$

Thus, the Solow model predicts that the level of income per worker in Country i would be twice the level of Country j.

Figure 3.7 shows the results of applying this technique to data from a broad sample of countries. The horizontal axis shows the predicted ratio of income per worker in each country to income per worker in the United States, based on the data on investment rates (specifically, the average ratio of investment to GDP over the period 1975–2009). On the vertical axis are plotted the *actual* ratios of income per worker in each country to income per worker in the United States. If the Solow model worked perfectly, we would expect the data points in Figure 3.7 to lie along a straight line with a slope of 45 degrees; the actual ratio of every country's income per worker to income per worker in the United States would be the same as the ratio predicted by the model. By contrast, if the Solow model had no ability to explain why income differs among countries, no pattern would be visible in this comparison of predicted and actual ratios.

Overall, Figure 3.7 shows that there is some relationship between actual and predicted income, but not a strong one. The correlation of the two series is only 0.17 (although the correlation is 0.35 between the logarithms of the two series).

FIGURE 3.7

Predicted versus Actual GDP per Worker

Actual GDP per worker relative to the United States

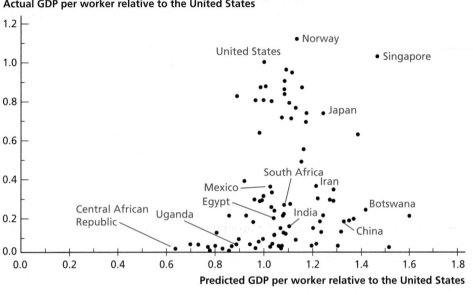

Source: Author's calculations using data from Heston, Summers, and Aten (2011).

Several countries such as China and Botswana are in the lower right portion of the graph, indicating that they are predicted to be relatively rich but are in fact relatively poor. The United States occupies an unusual position in the figure: according to the model, about half the countries in the sample should have GDP per capita higher than the United States, but in the actual data, only two countries do, Norway and Singapore. Overall, the differences in income among countries that the model predicts tend to be smaller than the actual differences that we observe in the data. For example, the country with the lowest predicted income is the Central African Republic, which is predicted to have 63% of the level of the United States. In the actual data, the figure is 1.9% of the U.S. level.

    What are we to make of the imperfect match between the predictions of the Solow model and the actual data on income per worker? For a start, we know there are other influences on countries' income that we have left out of this analysis (or else we would not need the rest of this book!). Specifically, later chapters show how the quantity of capital is determined not only by the level of investment but also by the rate of population growth (Chapter 4), introduce factors of production in addition to physical capital (Chapter 6), and allow for differences in productivity among countries (Chapter 7). Because we have not yet taken account of these factors, we would not expect the model to fit perfectly.

Beyond these reasons for the imperfect fit in Figure 3.7, a previously mentioned reason is that countries might not be in their steady states. Our analysis of the Solow model showed that over time, countries will gradually move *toward* their steady states, not that they will necessarily have reached their steady states at any particular point in time. There are several reasons a country might not be near its steady state at any given time. For example, if part of a country's capital stock were destroyed in a war, it would have a level of capital (and thus output) below its eventual steady state. Similarly, a country might have been at its steady state but then changed its investment rate. The country would then gradually move from its former steady state to its new one, but at the time that we observed it, the country might still be quite far from its new steady state.

In addition to explaining why the Solow model might not fit the data perfectly, the gap between countries' actual levels of income and their steady states can help us use the model to think about differences in the growth rates of income among countries. This is the subject to which we now turn.

The Solow Model as a Theory of Relative Growth Rates

Chapter 1 showed that there are large differences in growth rates among countries. A goal of any growth model should be to explain these differences. Can the Solow model provide an explanation?

The first thing to note is that the Solow model, in the form presented here, will not provide a *complete* explanation of growth rates. The reason is that once a country reaches its steady state, there is no longer any growth! Hence the Solow model will fail to explain growth over long periods of time, during which countries should have reached their steady states. Later in the book we will examine models (some of them extensions of the Solow model) that do explain long-term growth.

Despite this failing of the Solow model, we can still ask whether the model has something to say about *relative* growth rates—that is, why some countries grow faster than others. Here the model has useful predictions.

The key to using the Solow model to examine relative growth rates is to think about countries that are not in the steady state. Because any country that has a constant rate of investment will eventually reach a steady state in which the growth rate of output per worker is zero, all of the growth that we observe in this model will be *transitional*—that is, it will occur during the transition to a steady state. For example, a country with a level of output per worker below the steady state (the result of having a below-steady-state level of capital per worker) will have a growing capital stock and thus a growing level of output. Similarly, a country with output above the steady state will have a falling level of output.

The appendix to this chapter shows that the further below its steady state a country is, the faster it will grow. A country that is far below its steady state will grow very quickly, but as the country approaches the steady state, growth will slow down, approaching zero as the country approaches its steady state. Similarly, if a country has a capital stock far above its steady-state level, its capital stock will shrink rapidly, and this rate of shrinkage will approach zero as the country's capital stock approaches the steady state. We use the term **convergence toward the steady state** to describe this process by which a country's per-worker output will grow or shrink from some initial position toward the steady-state level determined by the investment rate.

Referring to the noneconomic example presented in the box on page 61 may make the intuition for convergence clearer. Consider a man who is currently at his steady-state weight. Suppose he reduces his calorie consumption. This reduction will be represented by a shift downward in the horizontal line in Figure 3.5. The moment calorie consumption falls, the steady-state weight also will fall. But the man's actual weight will not fall right away. Instead, his actual weight will gradually fall because he burns more calories each day than he consumes. As the man's weight falls, however, the number of calories he burns each day also will fall. Thus, the speed with which he loses weight will fall over time, and eventually he will stop losing weight altogether when he reaches the new steady state.

Returning to economic applications, the notion of convergence toward the steady state is the basis for three interesting predictions:

- *If two countries have the same rate of investment but different levels of income, the country with lower income will have higher growth.*

  Because their investment rates are the same, the two countries will have the same steady-state levels of income. If the richer country has income below this steady state, then the poorer country will have income that is even further below the steady state and will grow faster. Conversely, if the poorer country has income that is above the steady state, then the richer country will have income that is even further above the steady state, so the negative effect of moving toward the steady state will be greater in the richer country. Finally, if the poor country has income below the steady state and the rich country has income above the steady state, the movement toward the steady state will have a positive effect on the poor country's growth and a negative effect on the rich country's growth.

- *If two countries have the same level of income but different rates of investment, then the* country *with a higher rate of investment will have higher growth.*

  Of the two countries, the one with a higher rate of investment will have the higher steady-state level of output. If both countries are below their steady states, the country with higher investment will necessarily be *further* below its steady state and so will grow faster. Similarly, if both countries are above their steady states, then the country with low investment will be further above its steady state, so the negative effect on growth of being above steady state will be more pronounced. And if the high-investment country is below its steady state whereas the low-investment country is above its steady state, the high-investment country will grow faster.

- *A country that raises its level of investment will experience an increase in its rate of income growth.*

If the country was initially at its steady-state level of income, then the increase in investment will raise the steady state. Because income will now be below the steady state, growth will rise. If the country was initially at a level of income below its steady state, the increase in investment will mean it is further below the steady state, so, once again, growth will rise. Finally, if the country was initially at a level of income above its steady state, the increase in investment will mean that income is not as far above steady state or (if the rise in investment is large enough) that income is now at or below the steady state. In any of these cases, the growth rate of income will rise.

These predictions will hold true only if there are no other differences among countries, either in their levels of productivity, A, or in any of the other determinants of steady states that we will consider later in the book. However, the same general pattern of predictions arises from the Solow model when we do account for these other determinants of steady-state income. For example, Chapter 6 will show that the amount of effort that a country devotes to educating its workers functions in much the same manner as the investment rate does in determining the steady-state level of income. Thus, the Solow model predicts that if two countries differ in their levels of spending on education but are similar in other respects (and have equal levels of income), then the country with higher educational spending will grow more quickly. Similarly, the Solow model predicts that a country that suddenly raises its level of spending on education will experience rapid growth as it moves toward its new steady-state level of income.[5]

3.4 THE RELATIONSHIP BETWEEN INVESTMENT AND SAVING

The previous exercises show that the Solow model, though far from perfect, partially answers the questions of why some countries are rich and others are poor, and why some countries grow quickly and others grow slowly. But the answer that the model supplies—that differences in investment rates lead to different steady states—really just pushes the original question back another level. We are left asking why investment rates differ. This is the question to which we now turn.

Previously, this chapter explained that every act of investment corresponds to an act of saving. That is, building capital requires the use of resources that could otherwise have been used for something else. The entity (a person, family, or government) that uses its resources for building capital has forgone the opportunity to consume

---

[5]For a test of the Solow model's predictions about relative growth rates of countries, see Mankiw, Romer, and Weil (1992).

but in return has become the owner of a productive piece of capital. If we want to ask why investment rates differ among countries, we therefore should think about saving. Perhaps investment rates differ among countries because their saving rates differ. This explanation, however, has a potential problem: Although every act of investment corresponds to an act of saving, it is not true that the amount of investment in a given *country* corresponds to the amount of saving in that country. Why? Because investment can cross national boundaries. For example, a worker in the United States can choose to invest in a piece of capital in Brazil.

Thus, our investigation of why investment rates differ among countries will have two components. First, we investigate how and why saving rates differ among countries. Second, we explore whether the amount of investment in a country is related to that country's saving, or whether international flows of capital make the amount of saving in a given country irrelevant (or not very relevant) in determining the amount of investment there.

The second of these components—the analysis of flows of investment among countries—is taken up in Chapter 11. There we find that although international flows of investment can be important at times, the most significant determinant of a country's investment rate is indeed its own saving rate. In analyzing saving rates, as we do in the rest of this section, we can think of the saving rate as having the same effect on output, via the Solow model, that the investment rate has.

Figure 3.8 shows the relationship between saving rates and income per capita in a sample of 188 countries. The countries are ranked according to their income per capita in 2009, and the average saving rate is calculated for each decile (the poorest 10%, the next poorest 10%, and so on). The main point from this figure is

FIGURE 3.8

Saving Rate by Decile of Income per Capita

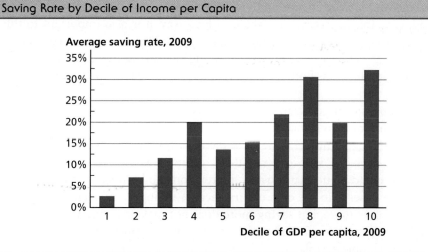

that there is a strong relationship between saving and income per capita. This relationship should not be a surprise, given two other findings: first, the Solow model's prediction that countries with high investment rates have higher levels of income, and second, the finding presented in Chapter 11 that countries' rates of investment are closely related to their rates of saving. So we are left with the question: What determines saving rates?

Explaining the Saving Rate: Exogenous versus Endogenous Factors

Economists distinguish between two types of variables in economic models. **Endogenous variables** are those that are determined within the model. **Exogenous variables** are those that are taken as given when we analyze a model—that is, they are determined outside the model. For example, when we apply the model of supply and demand to the market for bread, the price of bread and the quantity of bread purchased are endogenous variables, whereas factors that shift the supply-and-demand curves, such as the prices of flour and butter, are exogenous variables.

One possible approach to the differences in saving rates among countries is to think of saving as an exogenous variable. Under this interpretation, countries differ in saving rates for reasons that are unrelated to their levels of income per capita. These differences in saving lead to differences in investment rates, which lead in turn, via the Solow model, to differences in the level of income per capita.

If this approach is to help us understand differences in income among countries, however, we need to think about why saving rates differ. In Part IV of this book, we will do just that. There, many of the "fundamental" determinants of economic growth that we will consider have their primary effect on growth by affecting saving rates. Government policy (Chapter 12), income inequality (Chapter 13), culture (Chapter 14), and geography (Chapter 15) will all be examined with an eye toward their possible influence on the saving rate.

Although this approach can take us a long way, it is also important to think about how saving may be affected by income itself. That is, we must consider the possibility that saving is endogenous. Treating the saving rate as an endogenous variable has implications both for how we interpret the data and for how we model growth.

If we allow saving to be an endogenous variable, then the strong relationship between saving rates and income shown in Figure 3.8 is no longer usable as evidence that the Solow model is right. Someone who did not believe in the Solow model (e.g., someone who did not think capital was an important input into production) could argue that most of the relationship between output and saving rates that we observe in the data occurs because saving is endogenous: Countries that are rich save more, but saving more does not make a country rich. This difficulty in interpretation should make us cautious in concluding that the Solow model is the complete explanation for the relationship between saving and growth.

Nonetheless, most economists remain convinced that saving and capital accumulation play a significant role in growth.

Making saving endogenous also has implications for how countries will behave in terms of their growth rates and saving rates. We now examine these implications.

The Effect of Income on Saving

One natural explanation for the low rate of saving in poor countries (as illustrated in Figure 3.8) is that people there simply "can't afford to save." In economic terms, this interpretation says that people in poor countries are living at the margin of subsistence, so they cannot afford to reduce their present consumption to save for the future. Although this argument is plausible for the poorest countries in the world, it fails for even slightly richer countries. If residents of Uganda (average income per capita $1,152) cannot afford to save because they are on the margin of subsistence, then the same argument cannot be made about the residents of Pakistan (average income per capita $2,353) because they should be far above the subsistence level.

A variant on this argument focuses not on the constraints that poor people face (i.e., they can not afford to save) but rather on their voluntary choices. The idea is that the decision to save rather than to consume represents a choice between current and future satisfaction, so a person who does not care much about the future will not save. And in turn, according to this theory, being poor makes a person care less about the future. George Orwell nicely summarized this idea when he wrote in *Down and Out in Paris and London* that poverty "annihilates the future."

Whether for these reasons or others, it makes intuitive sense to many people that being poor lowers a person's saving rate, and similarly that poor countries will naturally have lower saving rates than rich countries. What are the implications of this effect for the Solow model? To examine this issue, we will assume that there are no flows of investment among countries, so that in every country, the investment rate is equal to the saving rate. Defining s as the fraction of output that is saved and γ as the fraction of output that is invested, this assumption implies that $s = \gamma$.

The saving rate, in turn, will be taken to depend on the level of income. We first consider the case where saving depends on income in an extreme fashion. Suppose there are two possible rates of saving: s_1, which is low, and s_2, which is high. If income per worker is below some level y^*, then the saving rate will be s_1. If income per worker is greater than or equal to y^*, then the saving rate will be s_2. In the form of an equation,

$$\gamma = s_1 \quad \text{if } y < y^*$$

$$= s_2 \quad \text{if } y \geq y^*.$$

GOVERNMENT POLICY AND THE SAVING RATE

The Solow model provides an explanation for why countries with higher saving rates should have higher levels of income per capita. Government policies that raise the saving rate can thus be a tool to raise the level of national income.

The most direct means by which a government can raise the national saving rate is by using its own budget. The national saving rate has two components: private saving, which is done by households and corporations, and government saving, which is the difference between what the government collects in taxes and what it spends. Budget deficits, which represent negative saving on the part of the government, reduce the national saving rate and thus reduce investment and economic growth.

Governments can also influence the private saving rates by a number of means. One of the most important is in setting up national old-age pension plans. Programs such as Social Security in the United States, in which benefits to the elderly are primarily funded by taxes on those who are currently working, do not generate saving (and thus investment). By contrast, programs in which individuals fund their own retirement by saving during their working years generate a large quantity of capital. During the early 1980s, Chile set up such a "funded" pension system, requiring workers to deposit a fraction of their earnings in an account with a private pension company. Partly as a result of this program, Chile's private saving rate, which had been near zero at the beginning of the 1980s, climbed to 17% by 1991. The success of the Chilean program led Argentina, Bolivia, Colombia, Mexico, Peru, and Uruguay to adopt similar plans in the 1990s.*

A more extreme version of this kind of pro-saving policy was implemented in Singapore. Starting in the 1950s, workers were required to contribute part of their wages to a "central provident fund," which could be used to finance not only retirement but also medical expenditures and the purchase of housing. The government determined the required contribution rate, which reached a high of 40% of a worker's salary in the early 1980s. This forced saving policy was an important determinant of Singapore's phenomenally high saving rate.

Not all pro-saving policies are so coercive, however. The Japanese government, for example, has relied on persuasion to get its citizens to raise their saving rates voluntarily. The government's Campaign to Encourage Diligence and Thrift (1924–1926) featured pro-saving messages on posters on trains and in temples, and in newspaper advertisements, motion pictures, radio broadcasts, and even at rallies. Following World War II, the Central Council for Savings Promotion launched a further series of pro-saving publicity campaigns. Included were programs to educate children about the importance of saving, and the creation of special banks for children within their schools. Japan has had one of the highest saving rates in the world since World War II, although sorting out the extent to which this high saving was as a result of government persuasion is not easy.[†]

*James (1998).
[†]Garon (1998).

Figure 3.9 illustrates what can happen in such a situation. It analyzes the same diagram that we used previously for finding the steady state of the Solow model (Figure 3.4). Specifically, it graphs the two terms on the right-hand side of the equation for the change in capital (Equation 3.1):

$$\Delta k = \gamma f(k) - \delta k. \tag{3.1}$$

FIGURE 3.9

Solow Model with Saving Dependent on Income Level

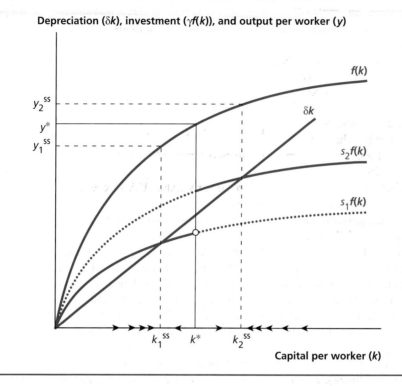

Depreciation (δk), investment ($\gamma f(k)$), and output per worker (y)

What is new in Figure 3.9 is a jump in the line representing $\gamma f(k)$. To see why, notice that corresponding to the level of income y^* that determines whether a country has a low or high saving rate, there is a level of capital below which saving will be low and above which saving will be high. This level of capital, k^*, can be determined from the production function. If capital is less than k^*, output will be less than y^*, so the saving rate will be s_1. Similarly, if capital is greater than or equal to k^*, output will be greater than or equal to y^* and saving will be s_2.

If the saving rate were always s_1, the steady state of the economy would occur at the level of capital labeled k_1^{ss}; if the saving rate were always s_2, the steady state would occur at the level of capital labeled k_2^{ss}. Notice that the level of capital at which saving switches from low to high, k^*, falls between k_1^{ss} and k_2^{ss}. This means that if the level of capital per worker is below k^*, the saving rate will be s_1, and the economy will move toward the steady state k_1^{ss}. But if the capital stock is above k^*, then the saving rate will be s_2 and the economy will move toward the steady state k_2^{ss}. In other words, there are *two* possible steady states in this economy, and a country will gravitate toward one or the other depending on its initial level of capital.

Figure 3.9 captures the idea that two countries could be completely identical in terms of the underlying determinants of their incomes but still end up with different levels of income per capita in the steady state. A country at the lower steady state can be viewed as being "trapped" there: Its level of income per capita is low because its saving rate is low, and its saving rate is low because its income per capita is low. This is an example of a more general phenomenon known as **multiple steady states,** in which a country's initial position determines which of several possible steady states it will move toward. Economists actively debate the extent to which multiple steady states can explain differences in income among countries. If multiple steady states are important, then differences in income per capita among countries do not necessarily arise because of "fundamental" differences among countries but rather because of self-reinforcing behavior: Being rich leads a country to behave in a manner that keeps it rich, whereas being poor leads a country to behave in a way that keeps it poor.

In Figure 3.9, the dependence of saving on the level of income is quite stark. An alternative story would be that the saving rate rises gradually as the level of income rises, rather than jumping up suddenly at a particular level of income as it does in this figure. In this case, it is still possible that there will be multiple steady states in the economy, but it is also possible that there will be only a single steady state. If there is only one steady state, however, the fact that saving rises with the level of income still has an important implication: The process of convergence toward the steady state will be slow. To see why, consider the case of a country that starts off with income (and thus capital) that is below the steady state. Previously, this chapter showed that in the Solow model with a constant investment rate, such a country will experience rapid growth at first but slower growth as the capital stock nears its steady-state level. In the case in which saving is endogenous, however, a country with income below its steady state will also have a low saving rate, and this low saving rate will reduce the rate of growth. The net result will be that the transitional growth that occurs along the path to the steady state will take place over a longer period of time than it would in the case in which the saving rate was constant.

3.5 CONCLUSION

In this chapter we have examined the role of physical capital in economic growth. The chapter has shown that the Solow model, based around capital accumulation, explains some of the differences in per-worker income across countries and also throws some light on differences among countries' growth rates.

But our analysis pointed out several big deficiencies in the Solow model. As an explanation for differences in income among countries, the model is incomplete. One reason is that it assumes that the only source of differences in income per worker across countries is differences in their per-worker capital stock, ignoring differences in other factors of production or in the production function by which

► THE RISE AND FALL OF CAPITAL REVISITED

To classical economists such as David Ricardo (1772–1823) and Thomas Malthus (1766–1834), the most important factor of production other than labor was not capital but land. There was good reason for this focus, for at the time these economists wrote, land was a much more important form of wealth than capital. With the advent of the Industrial Revolution in Europe, however, capital came to play a much more important role in the economy, and economists followed along.

The belief that the accumulation of capital is the key to economic growth reached its high-water mark after World War II. W. Arthur Lewis, who would later win the Nobel Prize, wrote in 1954, "The central problem of the theory of economic development is to understand the process by which a community that was saving and investing 4 to 5 percent of its national income…converts itself into an economy where voluntary saving is running at about 12 to 13 percent. This is the central problem because the central fact of economic development is rapid capital accumulation."[*] Prominent economist W. W. Rostow, in his influential description of the stages of economic growth, similarly defined an increase in the investment rate as a necessary part of the "take off" to sustained growth.

The apparent economic success of the Soviet Union (which we now know to have been something of an illusion) also contributed to the view that capital accumulation was the key to economic growth. In his famous economics textbook, Paul Samuelson, although noting the inefficiencies of the Soviet system, argued that it would nonetheless succeed in producing growth simply because of the "decision to cut down ruthlessly on current consumption in order to enlarge the flow of capital formation and economic development."

Economists' views on capital's role in producing growth in turn influenced the policies that developing countries and international agencies followed in attempting to promote economic development. In the decades after World War II, developing countries were advised to focus on raising their investment rates, and international aid was targeted toward helping poor countries acquire more capital.

These policies are now largely viewed as having failed. In almost all cases, injections of capital failed to produce significant growth in developing countries. The former Soviet Union itself, with its rusting, useless factories, has provided one of the most persuasive counterarguments to economists who focus exclusively on capital accumulation. Between 1960 and 1989, the Soviet Union devoted 29% of GDP to investment; in the United States, the comparable figure was 21%. Postmortem analyses of the Soviet Union have come to the conclusion that the massive accumulation of capital was accompanied by almost no growth in productivity—and that this failure of productivity growth doomed the economy to eventual stagnation.

In recent decades economists have discarded the view of development with capital accumulation as its centerpiece. They have paid more attention to factors such as education, technological change, and the structure of economic institutions. The downgrading of capital from its central position in development thinking does not mean that it is not important; rather, economists now see capital accumulation as just one of many aspects of economic growth.[†]

---

[*]Lewis (1954).
[†]Easterly and Fischer (1995), King and Levine (1994).

these factors are combined. Also, even restricting our focus to differences in capital among countries, the Solow model tells us that differences in investment rates are important but does not say anything about the source of these differences in investment rates. Still another drawback of the model is that it does not model long-run growth because in the steady state of the model, countries do not grow at all.

Later chapters will address all of these problems. These chapters will expand the Solow model to accommodate additional factors of production, differences in the production function among countries, and technological change over time. The discussion will draw on many of the ideas established using this simple version of the Solow model, such as convergence toward a steady state.

*No Long Run growth in Solow model bc * Steady state

KEY TERMS

capital   48
investment   49
depreciation   51
constant returns
  to scale   51
marginal product   52
diminishing marginal
  product   52

Cobb-Douglas production
  function   52
capital's share of
  income   56
difference (in a
  variable)   59
growth rate   59
steady state   60

convergence toward the
  steady state   67
endogenous
  variable   70
exogenous variable   70
multiple steady
  states   74

QUESTIONS FOR REVIEW

1. Why is capital a natural suspect when we consider differences in income per capita among countries?

2. What is the evidence in favor of the theory that differences in income among countries are the result of differences in investment rates? What is the evidence against this theory?

3. What is the effect of an increase in the investment rate on the level of steady-state output per worker in the Solow model? What is the effect of an increase in the investment rate on the growth rate of output per worker in the model?

4. How does the issue of whether saving rates are endogenous or exogenous affect our interpretation of how well the Solow model explains income differences among countries?

5. Why can a country not grow forever solely by accumulating more capital?

PROBLEMS

1. Explain whether or not each of the following is physical capital:
   a. A delivery truck
   b. Milk
   c. Farmland
   d. The Pythagorean Theorem

2. A country is described by the Solow model, with a production function of $y = k^{1/2}$. Suppose that k

is equal to 400. The fraction of output invested is 50%. The depreciation rate is 5%. Is the country at its steady-state level of output per worker, above the steady state, or below the steady state? Show how you reached your conclusion.

3. Describe in words and with a diagram an example of a steady state from outside of economics, similar to the one discussed in the box on page 61.

4. In Country 1 the rate of investment is 5%, and in Country 2 it is 20%. The two countries have the same levels of productivity, A, and the same rate of depreciation, δ. Assuming that the value of α is 1/3, what is the ratio of steady-state output per worker in Country 1 to steady-state output per worker in Country 2? What would the ratio be if the value of α were 2/3?

5. The following tables show data on investment rates and output per worker for three pairs of countries. For each country pair, calculate the ratio of GDP per worker in steady state that is predicted by the Solow model, assuming that all countries have the same values of A and δ and that the value of α is 1/3. Then calculate the actual ratio of GDP per worker for each pair of countries. For which pairs of countries does the Solow model do a good job of predicting relative income? For which pairs does the Solow model do a poor job?

a.

Country	Investment Rate (Average 1975–2009)	Output per Worker in 2009
Thailand	35.2%	$13,279
Bolivia	12.6%	$8,202

b.

Country	Investment Rate (Average 1975–2009)	Output per Worker in 2009
Nigeria	6.4%	$6,064
Turkey	16.3%	$29,699

c.

Country	Investment Rate (Average 1975–2009)	Output per Worker in 2009
Japan	29.9%	$57,929
New Zealand	18.6%	$49,837

6. Country X and Country Y have the same level of output per worker. They also have the same values for the rate of depreciation, δ, and the measure of productivity, A. In Country X output per worker is growing, whereas in Country Y it is falling. What can you say about the two countries' rates of investment?

7. In a country the production function is $y = k^{1/2}$. The fraction of output invested, γ, is 0.25. The depreciation rate, δ, is 0.05.

   a. What are the steady-state levels of capital per worker, k, and output per worker, y?

b. In year 1, the level of capital per worker is 16. In a table such as the following one, show how capital and output change over time (the beginning is filled in as a demonstration). Continue this table up to year 8.

Year	Capital k	Output $y = k^{1/2}$	Investment γy	Depreciation δk	Change in Capital Stock $\gamma y - \delta k$
1	16	4	1	0.8	0.2
2	16.2				

c. Calculate the growth rate of output between years 1 and 2.

d. Calculate the growth rate of output between years 7 and 8.

e. Comparing your answers from parts c and d, what can you conclude about the speed of output growth as a country approaches its steady state?

8. Consider an economy in which the amount of $\int dy/dx$ investment is equal to the amount of saving (i.e., the economy is closed to international flows of capital). Any output that is not saved is consumed. The production function is $y = Ak^\alpha$. Find the value of γ, the fraction of income that is invested, that will maximize the steady-state level of consumption per worker. (This is called the "golden rule" level of investment.)

9. In a country, output is produced with labor and physical capital. The production function in per-worker terms is $y = k^{1/2}$. The depreciation rate is 2%. The investment rate (γ) is determined as follows:

$$\gamma = 0.20 \quad \text{if} \quad y \leq 10$$
$$\gamma = 0.40 \quad \text{if} \quad y > 10$$

Draw a diagram showing the steady state(s) of this model. Calculate the values of any steady state levels of k and y. Also, indicate on the diagram and describe briefly in words how the levels of y and k behave outside of the steady state. Comment briefly on the stability of the steady state(s).

For additional exploration and practice using the Online Data Plotter and data sets, please visit www.pearsonhighered.com/weil.

FURTHER EXPLORATION OF THE COBB-DOUGLAS PRODUCTION FUNCTION AND THE SPEED OF CONVERGENCE IN THE SOLOW MODEL

The Cobb-Douglas production function is

$$Y = F(K, L) = AK^\alpha L^{1-\alpha},$$

where K is capital, L is labor, A is a measure of productivity, and α is between 0 and 1.

We begin by confirming that this production function has the properties of constant returns to scale and diminishing marginal product that we assumed in the text. To test for constant returns to scale, we multiply the quantities of capital and labor by some factor, z, and then confirm that this will raise the quantity of output by the same factor:

$$F(zK, zL) = A(zK)^\alpha (zL)^{1-\alpha} = z^{\alpha+1-\alpha}AK^\alpha L^{1-\alpha} = zF(K, L).$$

The marginal product of capital (MPK) is the derivative of output with respect to capital:

$$\text{MPK} = \frac{\partial Y}{\partial K} = \alpha AK^{\alpha-1}L^{1-\alpha}$$

To check for diminishing marginal product, we again take the derivative with respect to capital:

$$\frac{\partial \text{MPK}}{\partial K} = (\alpha - 1)\alpha AK^{\alpha-2}L^{1-\alpha} < 0.$$

This derivative is negative, indicating that the MPK will fall as the quantity of capital rises—in other words, there is diminishing marginal product.

Using the Cobb-Douglas production function, we can also conduct a more complete analysis of a country's growth rate when it is not at the steady state. We

79

start with the equation for the change in the level of capital per worker over time, Equation 3.2, which we repeat here,

$$\Delta k = \gamma A k^\alpha - \delta k, \qquad (3.2)$$

where k is capital per worker. The growth rate of capital, $\hat{k}$, is equal to the change in capital, Δk, divided by the level of capital. Thus, we can divide both sides of Equation 3.2 by the level of capital to derive an equation for the growth rate of capital:

$$\hat{k} = \frac{\Delta k}{k} = \gamma A k^{\alpha-1} - \delta.$$

Figure 3.10 graphs the two terms on the right-hand side of this equation. The equation says the growth rate of capital will be positive if the first term, $\gamma A k^{\alpha-1}$, is larger than the second term, δ. This clearly occurs on the left side of the figure, for low values of k. Conversely, for high values of k, the second term will be larger than the first, and $\hat{k}$ will be negative—in other words, the capital stock will be shrinking.

FIGURE 3.10

Speed of Convergence to the Steady State

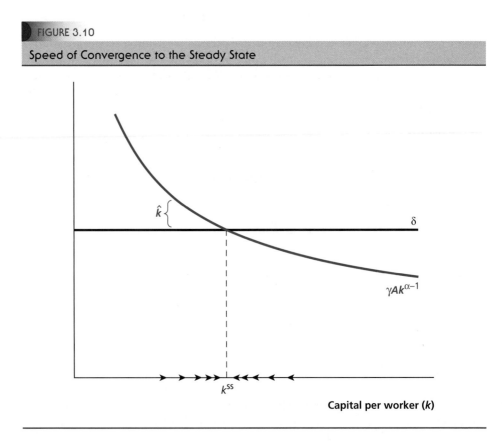

Where the two lines cross, the growth rate of capital will be zero. This will be the steady state. Notice that the condition for the steady state implied by this analysis, specifically that $\gamma A(k^{ss})^{\alpha-1} = \delta$, is the same as the one derived in the text, $\gamma A(k^{ss})^{\alpha} = \delta(k^{ss})$. To see this, multiply both sides of the first expression by k^{ss}.

The usefulness of this new way of looking at the model is that it tells something about the speed with which an economy approaches the steady state. Because the growth rate of capital is proportional to the distance between the curve representing $\gamma A k^{\alpha-1}$ and the line representing δ, this figure makes clear that the growth rate of capital is larger, the further below its steady state a country is. Similarly, if a country has capital per worker above its steady-state level, the capital stock will shrink at a faster rate, the further above the steady state the country is. As the level of capital per worker gets nearer to its steady-state level, the distance between the curves representing $\gamma A k^{\alpha-1}$ and δ narrows, and the growth rate of capital per worker approaches zero.

*expanding
Solow Model's
factors of production:*

POPULATION AND ECONOMIC GROWTH

With every mouth
God sends a pair
of hands.

—An old saying

This adage provides a good starting point for thinking about the impact of population on economic growth. It makes the point that changes in population affect both the consumption needs of an economy (the number of mouths) and the productive capacity of the economy (the number of hands). If the only thing used to produce output was labor, then the interaction of population and economic growth would not be very interesting: Twice as many people would mean twice as much output, so the size of the population would not affect output per capita. If, however, there are inputs to production other than labor, then adding one person adds one mouth and one pair of hands but no more of the other factors. In per-capita terms, more people will result in less of everything else.

This simple observation is the basis for including population in models that attempt to explain income per capita. As we will see, population can be a determinant of income in two different ways. In some contexts the *size* of the population is important, whereas in others the *growth rate* is important. Specifically, when we think about the interaction of population with some fixed natural resource, the important aspect is the size of the population. Holding other factors constant, a country with a lot of people relative to the amount of resources will be poorer. But when we think about the interaction of population with a producible input such as capital, then the relevant aspect is the growth rate of population.

Of course, over time, the speed with which a population grows is what determines how many people there are. But the words *over time* make a big difference. Countries can have slow population growth and a large population relative to their resources. Or they can have rapid population growth but a population that is small relative to their resources. Japan and Chad present examples of these two cases. Between 1975 and 2009, Japan's population grew at a rate of only 0.37% per year, but population density in 2009 was 917 people per square mile (354 people per square kilometer), among the highest in the world. In Chad, population growth over the same period was 2.68% per year, but in 2009, population density was only 21 people per square mile (8.1 people per square kilometer).

As Figure 4.1 shows, there is a strong negative correlation between income per capita and the growth rate of population. Although this negative correlation is easy to see in the data, fully understanding it is difficult. Recalling the discussion of causation in Chapter 2, the data in Figure 4.1 may be evidence that rapid population growth causes a country to be poor, that something about being poor leads to rapid population growth, or that causality runs in both directions. It is even possible that population growth and income per capita are not directly related at all; some other factor may affect both income per capita and population growth.

In the first section of this chapter, we look at the historical relationship between population and economic growth. We see how economic forces kept population growth in close check for most of human history but that the relationship between population and the economy has changed radically in the last two centuries. In the second section we consider how population growth can be incorporated into the Solow model discussed in Chapter 3. We also conduct a quantitative exercise to ask how large the income differences caused by population growth should be. We next examine the two determinants of population growth: mortality and fertility. In the final section we look more closely at economic explanations of why fertility falls as countries get richer.

FIGURE 4.1

Relationship Between Income per Capita and Population Growth

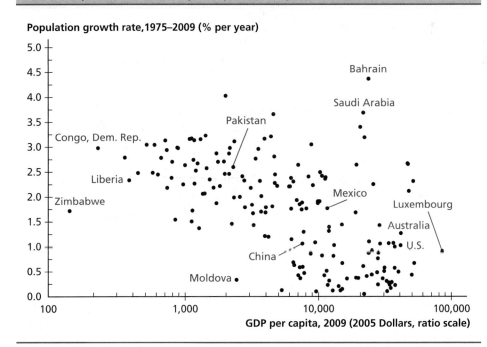

Source: Heston et.al. (2011).

4.1 POPULATION AND OUTPUT OVER THE LONG RUN

The last 200 years have been an extraordinary time in human history. As we saw in Chapter 1, only in the last two centuries have living standards anywhere in the world begun to show significant improvement. And as we will see in this chapter, a similar change occurred in the nature of population growth.

Most of this book is concerned with the current period of rapid change. For a complete understanding, however, it is helpful to get a running start by looking at how population and output interacted for most of human history.

Population over the Long Run

Figure 4.2 shows the size of the human population going back to 10,000 B.C. For most of history, the world's population was sparse in comparison with today's 7 billion. As late as A.D. 1000, for example, fewer humans walked the earth than now live in the United States.

Another striking aspect of the figure is how slowly the population grew for most of human history. Between 10,000 B.C. and the beginning of the first century

> FIGURE 4.2

World Population, 10,000 B.C. to A.D. 2010

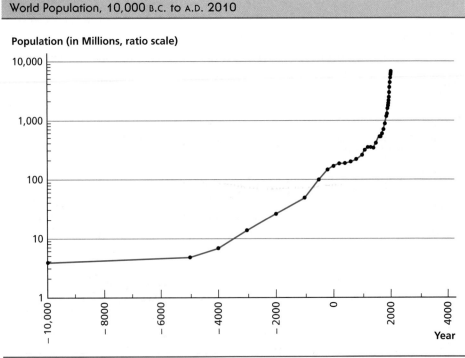

Source: Kremer (1993).

A.D., the average growth rate of the world's population was only 0.04% per year—in other words, population increased by 1% every 25 years. In the next 1,800 years, population grew at an average rate of 0.09% per year—high in comparison with what had come before, but minuscule in today's terms. As the figure shows, only in the last 200 years has the growth rate of population taken off: World population growth averaged 0.6% in the 19th century, 0.9% in the first half of the 20th century, and 1.8% over the second half of the 20th century. *. . . increasing rates . . .*

Thus, persistent population growth at a rate beyond a glacial crawl is a relatively new phenomenon. Exploring why population growth has behaved this way over the long run will give us insight into what determines population growth and why it differs among countries today.

The Malthusian Model

The explanation for the historical constancy of population was most famously elucidated by Thomas Malthus (1766–1834), an English parson whose *Essay on the Principle of Population* was published in 1798. Malthus began with the observation that, given the right circumstances, humans can breed at a prodigious rate (see box "The Power of Population"). The force that limited human population in the face of this potential fertility was simply the limited quantity of available resources—in particular, land. The

---

► THE POWER OF POPULATION

The group that demographers use as the best example of humans' ability to breed quickly is the Hutterites, a communally oriented Christian sect that migrated from Russia to the Dakotas and Canada in the 1870s. The Hutterite lifestyle was almost perfectly designed for maximum fertility. Women married young, and for religious reasons, couples never practiced birth control. The sect's early weaning of babies eliminated the effect of breast-feeding in reducing fertility. Further, unlike high-fertility populations in the developing world today, the Hutterites were well nourished and healthy. Their mortality rates were no different from those of the U.S. population as a whole.

The results of this high-fertility lifestyle were dramatic. The median Hutterite woman bore 10.4 children by the age of 45. One colony grew from 215 people in 1880 to 5,450 in 1960, without any outsiders moving in. The average growth rate over this period was 4.1%, roughly a doubling every 17 years. Although some countries in the developing world currently have population growth rates this high, none have kept up such growth for nearly as long.

Another example of the ability of human populations to expand in the presence of adequate resources—and of the power of compound growth—is the French Canadians, who arrived in Quebec in the 17th century. The 3,380 pioneers who migrated from France before 1680 grew, with little additional immigration, to a population of 2.5 million by 1950. Of the population in 1950, 68% of the gene pool was attributable to the initial settlers.*

*Larsen and Vaupel (1993), Livi-Bacci (1997).

smaller the population relative to the available land, the better off people would be. The better off people were, the faster population would grow. As the population grew, however, the amount of land available for each person would fall, and people would become poorer. This poverty would in turn limit population growth. Eventually society would reach a level of income commensurate with constant population.

Described this way, Malthus's model sounds purely biological. But Malthus observed that there is a crucial difference between humans and other forms of life:

> Among plants and animals the view of the subject is simple. They are all impelled by a powerful instinct to the increase of their species; and this instinct is interrupted by no reasoning, or doubts about providing for their offspring. Where ever therefore there is liberty, the power of increase is exerted; and the superabundant effects are repressed afterwards by want of room and nourishment, which is common to animals and plants; and among animals, by becoming prey of others.[1]

In the case of humans, however, there is a second consideration:

> Impelled to the increase of his species by an equally powerful instinct, reason interrupts his career, and asks him whether he may or not bring beings into the world, for whom he cannot provide the means of subsistence.... Will he not lower his rank in life? Will he not subject himself to greater difficulties than he at present feels? Will he not be obliged to labour harder? And if he has a large family, will his utmost exertions enable him to support them? May he not see his offspring in rags and misery, and clamoring for bread that he cannot give them?[2]

Thus, Malthus argued, although animals and plants were limited in their multiplication only by limitations on resources, humans were subject to a second sort of limitation: the deliberate reduction of fertility to prevent poverty. Malthus called the first of these mechanisms the "positive check" and the second, the one unique to humans, the "preventive check." Because humans could apply a preventive check, they were not fated to live in the same dire circumstances as animals. But when this check failed, the positive check was waiting in the wings.

Figure 4.3 is a graphical representation of the Malthusian model. Panel (a) of the figure shows the relationship between income per capita on the horizontal axis and the size of the population on the vertical axis. The effect of population size on the standard of living is represented by the downward-sloping line. Panel (b) graphs income per capita on the horizontal axis and population growth on the vertical axis. The upward-sloping line in panel (b) shows that higher income will raise the growth rate of population.

To use this diagram, consider starting with a given level of population, such as that represented by point A in panel (a). The panel shows how this population will translate into a level of income per capita. Reading down to panel (b),

---

[1] Malthus (1798), Ch. 2.
[2] Malthus (1798), Ch. 2.

▶ FIGURE 4.3

The Malthusian Model

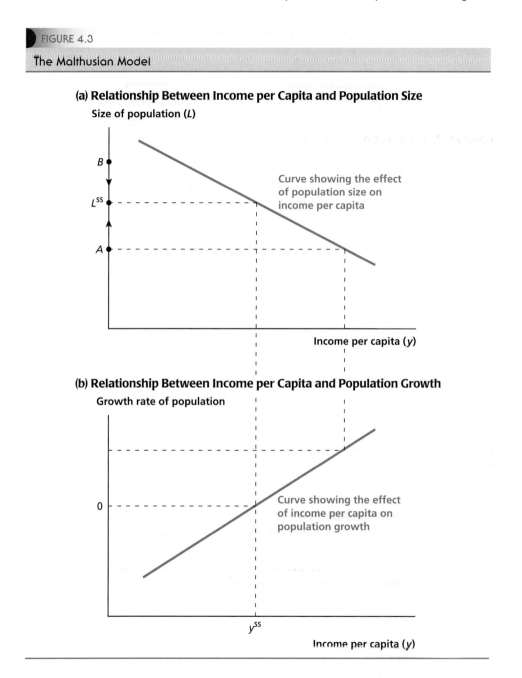

(a) Relationship Between Income per Capita and Population Size

Size of population (*L*)

Curve showing the effect of population size on income per capita

Income per capita (*y*)

(b) Relationship Between Income per Capita and Population Growth

Growth rate of population

Curve showing the effect of income per capita on population growth

y^{ss}

Income per capita (*y*)

we can then see how this level of income per capita translates into a growth rate of population—and thus how the level of population will change over time. For example, the size of population represented by point *A* implies a high level of income per capita and positive population growth. If population starts out at point *A*, it will grow over time (i.e., move up along the vertical axis in panel [a]).

Similarly, if population starts out at the level designated by point *B*, income per capita will be low, and population growth will be negative—that is, population will get smaller over time. These movements in population are symbolized by the arrows along the vertical axis in panel (a).

As the figure shows, there is a steady-state level of income per capita, y^{ss}, that is consistent with zero population growth. There is a corresponding steady-state population size, L^{ss}. If the population is smaller than L^{ss}, income per capita will be above y^{ss}, so the population will be growing. Conversely, if the population is above L^{ss}, then the population will be shrinking. Thus, the steady state is stable: No matter what a country's initial level of population, it will end up at the steady state.

We can use this diagram to analyze how changes in the environment or in behavior will influence income and population in the Malthusian model. Consider first how improvements in the productive environment will affect the standard of living. Suppose there is some advance in productivity—for example, the introduction of irrigation or the arrival of a new crop—that raises the quantity of food that can be grown on a given amount of land. Or suppose that new land (without people) is discovered. Such a change is represented by a shift outward in the relationship between population size and income per capita, as shown in panel (a) of Figure 4.4. At any given level of population, income per capita will be higher. The relationship between population growth and the level of income per capita, shown in panel (b), would not change.

The immediate effect of this improvement in the productive environment will be to raise living standards, just as we would expect. But over time, people who are better off will produce more children, and the larger number of people will dilute the benefits of the new technology or land. Population will continue to grow until the standard of living has returned to its old level (i.e., the level commensurate with zero population growth). In the new steady state of the economy, there will be a larger population, but the level of income per capita will not have changed. Better technology or more land, then, will *not* lead to healthier, happier people, just to more of them.

This implication of the Malthusian model—that countries with higher productivity will not have higher living standards but only more people—accords well with the data available from economic history. The slow pace of population growth over most of human history, shown in Figure 4.2, seems to match an equally slow rate of technological progress, both of which took place against a backdrop of roughly constant standards of living. When we compare different countries at the same point in time, the prediction of the model also seems to hold true. In A.D. 1000, China was the most technologically advanced country in the world, but because of its high population density, the Chinese people lived just as close to the margin of subsistence as technologically backward Europe. Another good example of this mechanism at work occurred when the potato, a plant native to the Americas, was introduced into Ireland. A field of potatoes could feed two or three times as many people as a similar field of grain, so the

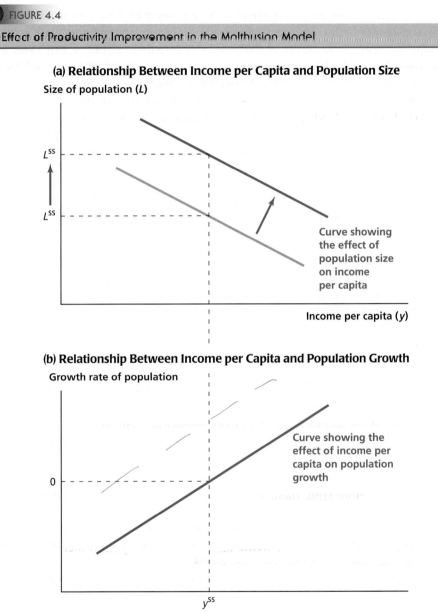

FIGURE 4.4

Effect of Productivity Improvement in the Malthusian Model

(a) Relationship Between Income per Capita and Population Size

Size of population (*L*)

L^{ss}

L^{ss}

Curve showing the effect of population size on income per capita

Income per capita (*y*)

(b) Relationship Between Income per Capita and Population Growth

Growth rate of population

0

Curve showing the effect of income per capita on population growth

y^{ss}

Income per capita (*y*)

potato resulted in a significant rise in Ireland's agricultural productivity. In the century after 1750, as the potato became the primary Irish staple, the population of the island tripled. Just as Malthus would have predicted, this rise in population resulted in little improvement in the standard of living.

If the Malthusian model predicts that improvements in productivity will not make people better off, then what will? Malthus's answer was that "moral restraint" in preventing births is the only way in which a society can raise its standard of living. Such a change is represented in panel (b) of Figure 4.5 by a downward shift in the curve relating population growth to income per capita. At any given level of income, population growth will be lower. In this scenario, the curve relating income to population size is unchanged. As the figure shows, a country that adopted a policy of moral restraint would have a lower steady-state population but a higher steady-state level of income per capita. Malthus explains it this way:

> In an endeavor to raise the proportion of the quantity of provisions to the number of consumers in any country, our attention would naturally be first directed to the increasing of the absolute quantity of provisions; but finding that, as fast as we did this, the number of consumers more than kept pace with it, and that with all our exertions we were still as far as ever behind, we should be convinced that our efforts directed only in this way would never succeed.... Finding, therefore, that from the laws of nature we could not proportion food to the population, our next attempt should naturally be to proportion the population to the food.[3]

The Breakdown of the Malthusian Model

The Malthusian model clearly does not apply to the world today. Evidence that the model has broken down comes from living standards. The Malthusian model predicts that standards of living will remain constant over time, even in the face of technological progress. This was roughly true for most of human history, but over the last two centuries, living standards in much of the world have risen dramatically. We can also see the breakdown of the Malthusian model in the relationship between income per capita and population growth. One of the key pieces of the Malthusian model is that higher income raises the growth rate of population. But Figure 4.1, contrary to what Malthus would have predicted, shows that the relationship between these two measures is negative: The richest countries in the world have the *lowest* rates of population growth.

Ironically, it was at roughly the time when Malthus wrote—the beginning of the 19th century—that the Malthusian model began to collapse. The changes affected the two key aspects of the Malthusian model: first, that the fixed supply of land means higher population will lead to declines in the standard of living, and second, that population will grow whenever income per capita is high enough. Over the last two centuries, both of these mechanisms have greatly weakened.

First consider the effect of population size on income per capita. The simple fact is that although population has grown enormously over the last two centuries,

---

[3]Malthus (1826), Book 4, Ch. 3.

FIGURE 4.5

FIGURE 4.5

Effect of "Moral Restraint" in the Malthusian Model

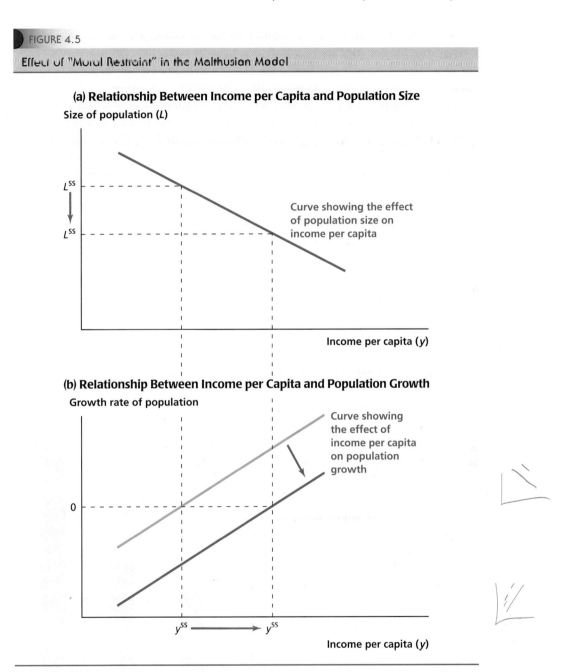

(a) Relationship Between Income per Capita and Population Size

Size of population (*L*)

Curve showing the effect of population size on income per capita

Income per capita (*y*)

(b) Relationship Between Income per Capita and Population Growth

Growth rate of population

Curve showing the effect of income per capita on population growth

Income per capita (*y*)

this increase has not prevented income per capita from rising as well. Growth in income has been possible because technological progress has been rapid enough to compensate for falling levels of natural resources per capita. We will consider the details of this process later in the book.

This chapter focuses on the weakening of the other part of the Malthusian mechanism: the dependence of population growth on the level of income per capita. Why have improvements in the standard of living *not* led to large increases in population growth, as Malthus would have expected?

Figure 4.6 shows the growth rates of output per capita and population in Western Europe, which is where the Malthusian model first broke down. As the figure indicates, the link between income and population growth was not severed all at once. Rather, as Europe got richer, its population grew at an unprecedented pace. Population had grown at an average rate of only 0.2% per year for the 200 years before 1700. Between 1700 and 1820, it grew at 0.4% per year, and between 1820 and 1870, at 0.7% per year. Still, economic growth outstripped population growth, and income per capita continued to rise. Then, in the late 19th century came a puzzling phenomenon: As the growth of income accelerated, population growth began to fall. And when we look forward from the present over the next several decades, the departure from the Malthusian model is even more dramatic because for many countries in Western Europe, population growth is projected to be negative! Clearly the Malthusian relationship between income and population growth is no longer operative.

FIGURE 4.6

Breakdown of the Malthusian Model in Western Europe

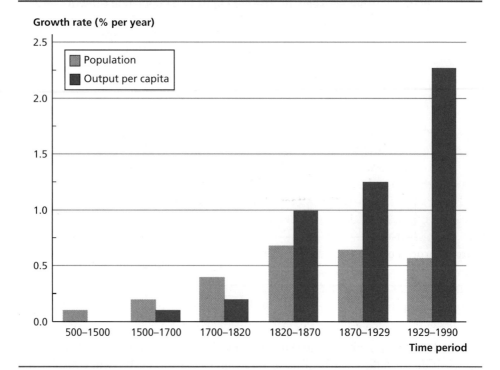

Source: Galor and Weil (2000).

This same pattern—economic growth initially leading to a period of rising population growth but later to a decline—has been repeated in many other parts of the world. Understanding this phenomenon is the subject of the second half of this chapter. But first we look at another channel by which population affects the level of income per capita: the effect of population growth on the quantity of capital per worker.

4.2 POPULATION GROWTH IN THE SOLOW MODEL

In the Malthusian model, the size of the population feeds back to affect the level of income per capita. This Malthusian mechanism kept the size of population and the level of income per capita relatively constant for most of human history. But as we just noted, in the last two centuries, the Malthusian mechanism has broken down as population growth and income per capita have risen to levels never before seen in history.

Does the fact that the Malthusian model no longer works mean that population has no effect on income per capita? The answer to this question is no, for two reasons. First, the Malthusian mechanism by which higher population will mean a shortage of resources such as land is still an important factor determining countries' income, even though it does not play the dominant role that it did historically. Second, there is a completely different channel, beyond the one that Malthus examined, by which population affects income per capita. This second channel runs via the effect of population on capital, the factor of production that we studied in Chapter 3. Further, where the Malthusian model focused on the *size* of the population, this second channel operates through the *growth rate* of the population. This second channel by which population growth affects income per capita is best understood by extending the Solow model, presented in Chapter 3.

Population Growth and Capital Dilution

To see how the growth rate of population interacts with the quantity of capital to affect income per capita, consider what happens in a country in which population is growing rapidly. If the quantity of capital in the country did not change, then population growth would result in less capital being available for each worker.[4] This negative effect of population growth on capital per worker is called **capital dilution.** The decline in the amount of capital per worker, for the reasons discussed in Chapter 3, would lead to a decline in the amount of output produced per worker. Alternatively, a country in which population is growing rapidly could maintain a constant level of capital per worker, but only by investing a large fraction of its output in building new capital.

An in-depth look at the effect of capital dilution requires a model of how capital affects output. Luckily, we already have one: the Solow model. In the version of

---

[4]We are assuming for now that the growth rate of the population is the same as the growth rate of the labor force. Chapter 5 explores what happens when this is not the case.

the Solow model presented in Chapter 3, there are two sources of change in capital per worker: investment (the building of new capital) and depreciation (the wearing out of old capital). The equation that describes the change in the quantity of capital per worker over time (Equation 3.1) is

$$\Delta k = \gamma f(k) - \delta k,$$

where γ is the fraction of output invested, δ is the rate of depreciation, $f(k)$ is the production function, and Δk is the change in the level of capital per worker.

We now want to incorporate capital dilution into this equation. As a concrete example, let's consider an economy in which the number of workers is rising at a rate of 1% per year and in which there is no depreciation of capital. If we wanted to keep the level of capital per worker constant in the face of this labor force growth, the quantity of investment would have to be large enough to supply each new worker with as much capital as each existing worker has to work with, so investment would have to equal 1% of the capital stock. Alternatively, if there were no investment in the face of this growth of the labor force, then the quantity of capital per worker would decline at a rate of 1% per year. Generalizing from this example and defining n as the growth rate of the labor force, we can write an equation for the change in the amount of capital per worker:[5]

$$\Delta k = \gamma f(k) - \delta k - nk = \gamma f(k) - (n + \delta)k.$$

Notice that dilution resulting from the arrival of new workers operates in exactly the same manner as depreciation.

Once we modify the equation for capital accumulation to take into account the effect of capital dilution, the rest of the Solow model is straightforward. The condition for a steady state is that the change in the capital stock, Δk, is equal to zero. This implies that

$$\gamma f(k) = (n + \delta)k.$$

We can show the determination of the steady state in a figure exactly like Figure 3.4, except that instead of a line with slope δ, there will be a line with slope $(n + \delta)$, as shown in Figure 4.7. Raising the rate of population growth rotates the curve representing $(n + \delta)k$ counterclockwise and leads to a lower steady-state level of output. Thus, the Solow model, modified to include population growth, provides a potential explanation for why countries with high population growth rates are poorer than countries with low population growth rates. Specifically, higher population growth dilutes the per-worker capital stock more quickly and so lowers the steady-state level of output per worker.

---

[5]Mathematical Note: We can derive the equivalent of this equation in continuous time by using calculus:

$$\dot{k} = \frac{dk}{dt} = \frac{d\left(\frac{K}{L}\right)}{dt} = \frac{L\frac{dK}{dt} - K\frac{dL}{dt}}{L^2} = \frac{\dot{K}}{L} - k\frac{\dot{L}}{L} = \frac{\gamma Y - \delta K}{L} - k\frac{\dot{L}}{L} = \gamma y - \delta k - nk.$$

Note that the definition of the labor force growth rate, n, is $n = \dot{L}/L$.

FIGURE 4.7

The Solow Model Incorporating Population Growth

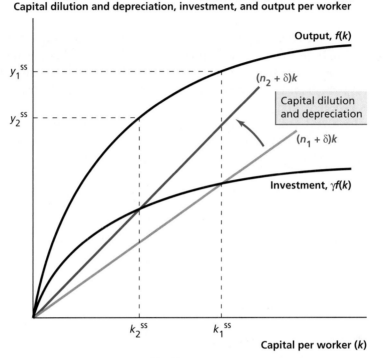

The figure shows how raising the population growth rate from n_1 to n_2 affects the steady-state level of capital per worker (k) and the steady-state level of output per worker (y).

A Quantitative Analysis

As we did in Chapter 3, we can go further, asking *how large* the Solow model predicts the effect of population growth on steady-state income will be. As in the last chapter, we assume that the production function takes the Cobb-Douglas form, which in per-worker terms is

$$f(k) = Ak^{\alpha}, \quad \text{← output per worker} \dots$$

where the parameter A measures productivity. The condition for the steady state is thus

$$\gamma Ak^{\alpha} = (n + \delta)k. \quad \text{→} \quad y^*$$

This equation can be solved to give the steady-state level of capital per worker, k^{ss}:

$$k^{ss} = \left(\frac{\gamma A}{n + \delta} \right)^{1/(1-\alpha)}.$$

Finally, substituting k^{ss} into the production function gives the steady-state level of output per worker, y^{ss}:

$$y^{ss} = A(k^{ss})^\alpha = A^{1/(1-\alpha)}\left(\frac{\gamma}{n+\delta}\right)^{\alpha/(1-\alpha)}.$$

To calculate the effect of population growth on the steady-state level of output per worker, suppose that we are comparing two countries that are the same in every dimension except their population growth rates. Thus, they have the same values for A (which measures productivity), γ (which measures the fraction of output that is invested), and δ (which measures depreciation). We call the countries i and j, and let n_i and n_j denote their growth rates of population (we continue to assume that population and labor force grow at the same rate). The equations for the steady-state levels of output per worker in the two countries are:

$$y_i^{ss} = A^{1/(1-\alpha)}\left(\frac{\gamma}{n_i+\delta}\right)^{\alpha/(1-\alpha)},$$

$$y_j^{ss} = A^{1/(1-\alpha)}\left(\frac{\gamma}{n_j+\delta}\right)^{\alpha/(1-\alpha)}.$$

To get an expression for the ratio of steady-state income in Country i to steady-state income in Country j, we divide the first of these expressions by the second:

$$\frac{y_i^{ss}}{y_j^{ss}} = \left(\frac{n_j+\delta}{n_i+\delta}\right)^{\alpha/(1-\alpha)}.$$

To implement this calculation, we need values for the rate of depreciation, δ, population growth in each country, n_i and n_j, and the exponent on capital in the production function, α. For the rate of depreciation, we will use the value 5%. For the rates of population growth, we pick values that span the rates that we observe in the data: $n_i = 0\%$ and $n_j = 4\%$. For the value of α, we use 1/3, for the reasons discussed in Chapter 3. The ratio of income per capita in the steady state is given by substituting these numbers into the previous equation:

$$\frac{y_i^{ss}}{y_j^{ss}} = \left(\frac{0.04+0.05}{0.00+0.05}\right)^{1/2} \approx 1.34.$$

Thus, our calculation says that the country with zero population growth (Country i) would have income per worker 34% higher than the country with 4% population growth (Country j).

This is a small difference in comparison to the large differences in income per capita that are associated with differences in population growth according to Figure 4.1. Notice, however, that this calculation is sensitive to the value of α. Suppose (for reasons that will be made clear in Chapter 6) that we use a value of

$\alpha = 2/3$. In this case, the ratio of steady-state income in the two countries will be 3.24—that is, Country i will be more than three times as well off as Country j.

This difference in income per capita—a factor of 3.24—is still not as large as the differences between the high- and low-population-growth countries in Figure 4.1. Nonetheless, the differences explained by population growth are potentially significant. Further, we would not expect this factor alone to explain all of the differences in income that we observe. We already saw in Chapter 3 that differences in investment rates between countries can partially explain differences in income, and we will see in later chapters that there are other factors as well.

In sum, the Solow model, extended to incorporate population growth, explains how higher population growth can lower income per capita through the channel of capital dilution. As such, this extended Solow model can partly account for the negative correlation between income per capita and population growth shown in Figure 4.1. But just as the simple Solow model of Chapter 3, which focused on the effects of investment, left open the question of why countries differ in the fraction of their output that they invest, this extended Solow model leaves unanswered the question of why countries differ in their population growth rates. This is the issue to which we now turn.

4.3 EXPLAINING POPULATION GROWTH

The Malthusian and Solow models both address the issue of how population affects the level of income per capita. The Malthusian model has an additional component that is lacking in the Solow model, however: The Malthusian model also explains how the size of the population is determined. Using the terminology introduced in Chapter 3, we say that the Malthusian model treats population as an endogenous variable—something determined within the model. By contrast, the Solow model treats population growth as exogenous (determined outside the model).

As we have seen, the Malthusian model provided a good explanation for both income and population until the last two centuries, but since that time, the Malthusian model of population has broken down. We also saw, in our quantitative analysis of the Solow model, that differences among countries in the growth rate of population can explain some (but not all) of the differences in income among countries. In the rest of this chapter, we explore the origin of these differences in population growth rates.

A useful framework for organizing our thinking about population growth is the idea of **demographic transition**—the process by which a country's demographic (population) characteristics are transformed as it develops. In this section we will see that the changes in population growth result from the interaction of changing patterns of death and birth—that is, a **mortality transition** and a **fertility transition.** The process of demographic transition is largely complete in the richest countries in the world but is still ongoing in much of the developing world. The incompleteness of the demographic transition—specifically, the fact that mortality rates have fallen faster than fertility rates—is the primary explanation for high population growth in much of the developing world.

Mortality Transition

The decline in the prevalence of death over the last two centuries has been one of the most remarkable transformations in human history. Living in a society in which most children can expect to live long, healthy lives makes it difficult for us to understand the precariousness with which life was viewed for most of human history, and by most of the world as recently as half a century ago.

Demographers measure mortality by calculating **life expectancy at birth,** which is the average number of years that a newborn baby can be expected to live. For example, in a country where all newborns lived to age 40 and then died, life expectancy at birth would be 40 years. Similarly, in a country where half of all newborns died immediately and the other half died at age 80, life expectancy at birth also would be 40. The appendix to this chapter contains a more extensive discussion of how life expectancy and other demographic measures are defined and measured.

Figure 4.8 illustrates how life expectancy has evolved in a number of de-veloped countries. The data go back to the middle of the 18th century and

FIGURE 4.8

Life Expectancy in Developed Countries

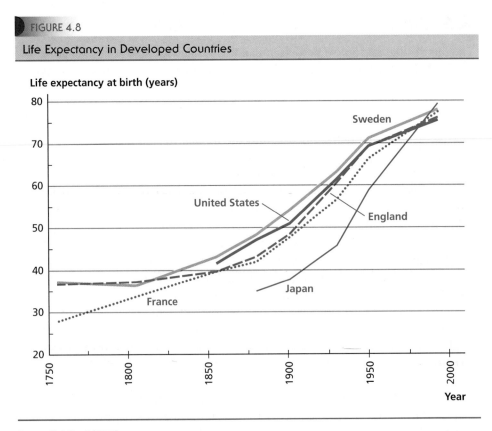

Source: Livi-Bacci (1997).

show a two-century-long period of improvement in mortality. As with income per capita, the available historical evidence indicates that there was little or no improvement in life expectancy before the 18th century, even in the most advanced countries.

For the set of developing countries in Figure 4.9, the data also indicate an improvement in life expectancy. In comparing Figures 4.8 and 4.9, note that the mortality transition in the developing world has been much more rapid than in the developed world. To give an example, in India life expectancy at birth increased from 26.9 years in 1930 to 55.6 years in 1980. In France a roughly comparable change took more than three times as long: Life expectancy at birth was 27.9 years in 1755 and reached 56.7 years only in 1930.

In addition to its speed, the crucial characteristic of the mortality transition in the developing world is its occurrence at a level of income per capita far below income in the rich countries when they went through a similar transition. For example, India achieved a life expectancy of 55.6 years in 1980 with income per capita of $1,239 (in 2000 dollars). By contrast, France achieved a life expectancy of 56.7 years in 1930 with income per capita of $4,998 (also in 2000 dollars).

▶ FIGURE 4.9

Life Expectancy in Developing Countries

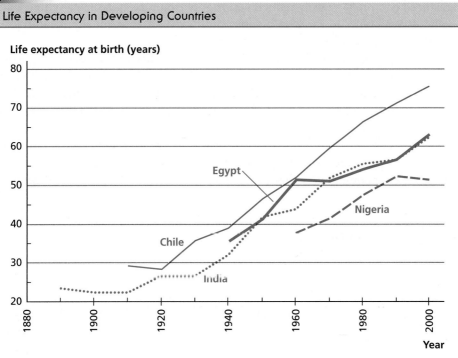

Year

Source: Kalemli-Ozcan (2002).

Explaining the Mortality Transition. Reduced mortality has resulted from three forces. First, there have been improvements in the standard of living, most notably in the quantity and quality of food consumed. Preindustrial populations were often so chronically malnourished that people died from diseases that would not be serious problems among a better-fed population. As people became richer, they were less hungry and thus more resistant to disease. In addition to better food, other advances in living standards, such as improvements in housing and more frequent washing of clothes, reduced the toll taken by disease. A second factor in lowering mortality has been improvements in public health measures such as the securing of clean water and food and the draining of mosquito-infested swamps. A third force in lowering mortality has been the role of medical treatments in curing diseases.

In the countries that experienced economic development first, these three improvements in mortality took place more or less one at a time—first better nutrition and living standards, then improved public health measures, and then medical advances. The economic historian Robert Fogel concluded that improvements in nutritional status appear to explain about 90% of the decline in mortality rates in England and France between 1775 and 1875, but much less of the decline in mortality that took place thereafter.[6] The second half of the 19th century saw the creation of modern sewage and water supply systems in the cities of the most advanced countries, sharply reducing mortality from diseases such as cholera and typhoid fever. Only in the 20th century did medical treatment significantly contribute to improvements in life expectancy.

The explanation for the rapid declines in mortality in the developing world is exactly that many of the advances that accumulated slowly in the rich countries arrived in the developing world almost all at once. Governments and nongovernmental organizations rapidly imported public health techniques and modern medicine in the years before and after World War II. This difference in the sources of mortality improvement also explains why developing countries achieved improvements in longevity at much lower levels of income per capita than the income levels that prevailed when mortality fell in the developed world.

Fertility Transition

Demographers measure fertility by constructing an indicator called the **total fertility rate (TFR)**, the number of children that a woman would have if she lived through all of her childbearing years and experienced the current age-specific fertility rates at each age. For example, if women aged 20–39 gave birth to an average of 0.2 children per year, and women outside this age group did not have any

---

[6]Fogel (1997).

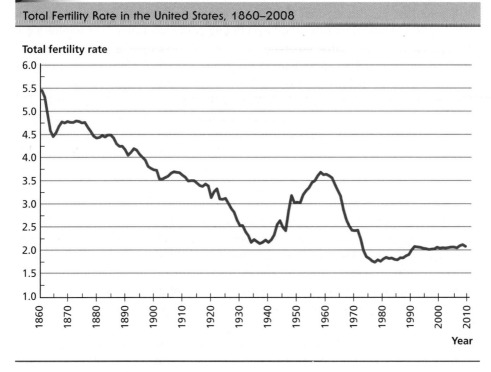

FIGURE 4.10

Total Fertility Rate in the United States, 1860–2008

Sources: Coale and Zelnik (1963), Wade (1989).

children, then the total fertility rate would equal 4 (that is, 20 years multiplied by 0.2 children per year). See this chapter's appendix for a longer discussion of how TFR is defined.

For an example of the fertility transition in the developed world, consider Figure 4.10, which shows the TFR in the United States since 1860. Fertility has fallen dramatically over the last 140 years, from more than five children per woman to roughly two. But unlike the case of mortality, the change in fertility has not been a smooth trend. Rather, there is a visible, temporary interruption in the downward trend of fertility: the baby boom of 1946 to 1964. This same pattern—particularly low fertility during the Great Depression and World War II, followed by a postwar burst of fertility—occurred throughout the developed world.

As in the case of mortality, the change in fertility in the developing world has been compressed into much less time than the fertility transition in the most developed countries. (For data on fertility change, see Table 5.1 in the next chapter.) For example, the movement from a TFR of five to a TFR of three took 63 years in the United States (from 1862 to 1925); in Indonesia the same change in the TFR occurred over only 15 years, between 1975 and 1990.

The Interaction of Fertility and Mortality

In Figure 4.10, we can see that the total fertility rate in the United States used to be roughly as high as that in many developing countries today (see Figure 5.4 in the next chapter). The same was true in Europe; for example, in the 18th century, England, France, and Spain all had TFRs greater than five. How is it that population growth rates in Europe and the United States never approached the levels seen in the developing world today? We find the answer by recalling that the TFR expresses the number of children that a woman would have *if* she lived through all of her childbearing years. In historical populations, only a fraction of women were so lucky. Many never made it to maturity, and many more died during their fertile years, often in childbirth. Thus, to understand population growth, we have to look at the interaction of fertility and mortality.

A measure that combines the effects of fertility and mortality in determining population growth is the net rate of reproduction. The **net rate of reproduction (NRR)** is defined as the number of *daughters* that each girl who is born can be expected to give birth to, assuming that she goes through her life with the mortality and fertility of the current population (once again, see the appendix for a more formal definition). For example, suppose that half of all girls die in infancy and the other half live through their childbearing years, that women who live through their childbearing years give birth to an average of 4 children, and that half of all births are girls. The NRR will be 1, because 1/2 probability of having any children × 4 children × 1/2 children being girls = 1 expected number of daughters. Another way to think about the NRR is to consider it the factor by which the number of girls in each generation will increase. An NRR of 1 is consistent with population being constant—that is, zero population growth. An NRR of 2 means that the number of girls, and thus the population as a whole, will double every generation.

The NRR provides a way to see the important role that a decline in mortality can play in population growth. As an example, suppose that we are examining a country in which, as was typical in many preindustrial societies, half of girls never lived to reach their reproductive years. Now imagine that mortality was somehow reduced so that all women survived their reproductive years. The NRR would double! If this population was exactly reproducing itself before the reduction in mortality (NRR of 1), then after the change, it would double every generation, without any change in fertility.

As a real-world example, Figure 4.11 shows the interaction of mortality and fertility changes in determining the NRR in Sweden, whose experience is fairly typical. Panel (a) shows the TFR; panel (b), life expectancy at birth; and panel (c), the NRR. As the figure illustrates, the NRR rose well above 1 in response to the initial decline in mortality. There followed a long period (roughly a century) during which the NRR remained higher than 1 while both fertility and mortality fell. Finally, by the middle of the 20th century, improvements in mortality had lost their power to affect the NRR (because almost all girls were surviving through their fertile years), and further reductions in fertility translated into a reduction in the NRR.

FIGURE 4.11

Fertility, Mortality, and the Net Rate of Reproduction in Sweden

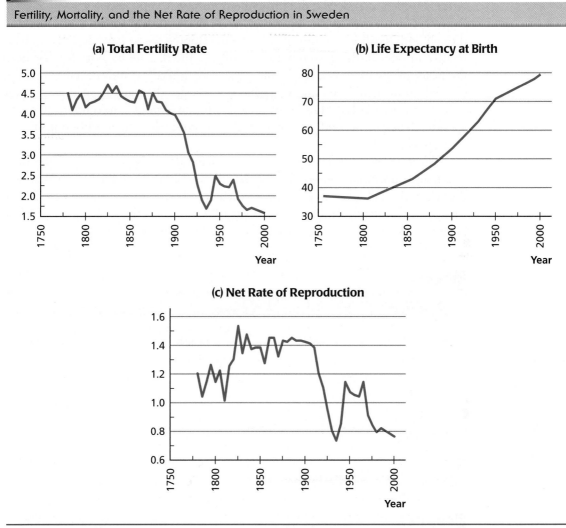

Sources: Keyfitz and Flieger (1968, 1990), Livi-Bacci (1997).

In these data we can also see how different levels of fertility and mortality can combine to produce the same level of the NRR. The NRR was almost exactly the same in three different years: in 1780 (when it was 1.21), 1915 (when it was 1.21), and 1965 (when it was 1.15). But the underlying levels of fertility and mortality were different. In 1780 the TFR was 4.54, and life expectancy was 36.9. In 1915 the TFR was 3.08, and life expectancy was 58.6. And in 1965 the TFR was 2.41, and life expectancy was 73.7.

Thus, we can see the increase in the NRR above 1 for a sustained period of time as a result of the mismatch in timing between the mortality and fertility reductions. This century-long process led to a large multiplication of the population in Sweden, as indeed it did throughout Europe.

What about the developing world? Here there are two salient facts. First, although both fertility and mortality in the developing world have declined quickly relative to rates in the currently rich countries, the decline in mortality has been the faster of the two. As a result, the gap between fertility and mortality that has opened up in the developing world has been larger than any experienced in the rich countries. The NRR (and thus the growth rate of population) has been correspondingly larger. Second, in many developing countries, the fertility transition is far from complete.

As examples, consider the experience of India and Nigeria, two of the most populous countries in the world today. In India, as shown in Table 4.1, the dramatic decline in the TFR over 45 years was sufficient to hold NRR constant in the face of rising life expectancy, and then to reduce NRR almost to the replacement level. In Nigeria, according to the data in Table 4.2, the TFR was roughly constant for several

TABLE 4.1

Demographic Data for India

Period	Total Fertility Rate	Life Expectancy at Birth	Net Rate of Reproduction
1955–1960	5.92	42.6	1.75
1965–1970	5.69	48.0	1.87
1975–1980	4.83	52.9	1.73
1985–1990	4.15	57.4	1.61
1995–2000	3.45	62.1	1.43
2000–2005	2.73	64.2	1.17

Source: United Nations Population Division (2010).

TABLE 4.2

Demographic Data for Nigeria

Period	Total Fertility Rate	Life Expectancy at Birth	Net Rate of Reproduction
1955–1960	6.90	38.2	1.97
1965–1970	6.90	42.0	2.12
1975–1980	6.90	46.1	2.28
1985–1990	6.70	50.2	2.38
1995–2000	5.92	52.5	2.20
2000–2005	5.61	50.3	2.00

Source: United Nations Population Division (2010).

decades whereas life expectancy rose, causing an increase in the NRR, which has only been reversed recently. Note that for both countries, the data start in the middle of the demographic transition. Even in 1955, the NRR in both countries was at the level found in Europe at the peak of population growth in the late 19th century.

4.4 EXPLAINING THE FERTILITY TRANSITION

Explaining the mortality transition is relatively easy for economists. As people grew richer, they consumed more of the things, such as food and housing, that enabled them to live longer. And because most people want to live a long, healthy life, societies adopted new techniques for reducing disease when those techniques became available. Explaining the fertility transition, by contrast, is difficult. Like good health and long life, children are generally considered desirable. Why, then, as a country gets richer, do its citizens choose to have *fewer* children?

Economic theory has a lot to say about how many children people will want and how the optimal number will change over the course of economic development. But children are not like most other goods that economics considers, in that people may not always have the number of children they want. Thus, in considering fertility transition, we must also look at people's ability to control the number of their offspring.

Reduced Fertility: The Means

Malthus took it as fundamental that unless "passion between the sexes" could be suppressed, the human race was doomed to breed itself into poverty. Since well before Malthus's time, however, people have been attempting to avoid producing children without forgoing their passions. The oldest written reference to birth control, the Kahun Medical Papyrus (c. 1850 B.C.), gives recipes for three vaginal suppositories, including one based on crocodile feces and fermented dough. The Bible mentions (and condemns) the use of withdrawal to avoid conception. And ancient Greek medical texts discuss contraceptive potions, barriers, and suppositories, as well as the rhythm method and techniques for abortion.

A number of cultures have also practiced infanticide to control family size. The Greeks "exposed" (i.e., left outdoors to die) children who were the products of rape or adulterous unions, and they may also have used the technique to limit the number of children. One ancient Greek writer commented, "Even a poor man will bring up a son, but even a rich man will expose a daughter."[7] The abandonment of children continued in Europe into the 19th century and was perhaps encouraged by the Catholic Church's policy of taking in foundlings—almost all of whom then succumbed to illness while under the church's care.[8]

---

[7]McLaren (1990), Riddle (1992).
[8]Kertzer (1993).

In Northern Europe before the Industrial Revolution, a pattern of relatively late marriage (the only birth-control method that Malthus approved of) served to reduce fertility. The median age at first marriage in 17th-century Britain was 28 for men and 27 for women. And in many cultures, a long period of breast-feeding has suppressed fertility. For example, in Indonesia in 1999, the median duration of breast-feeding was 24 months; one estimate is that if the duration of breast-feeding were to fall by half, the total fertility rate would rise by 37%.[9]

Over the last two centuries, the technology of fertility control has improved markedly. Condoms, which had existed for thousands of years, were improved in quality and fell in price after the invention of vulcanized rubber in 1844. The cervical cap was invented in 1838, the diaphragm in 1882, and the intrauterine device (IUD) in 1909. The contraceptive pill, now the most widely used form of contraception in the United States, became available in the 1960s.

Accompanying these technological changes, there has been a dramatic shift in the attitudes of society, and particularly government, toward fertility control. When U.S. birth-control pioneer Margaret Sanger (1879–1966) opened the first family-planning clinic in the United States in 1916, she was promptly arrested on obscenity charges. Theodore Roosevelt said, "The woman who flinches from childbirth stands on par with the soldier who drops his rifle and runs in battle." Only in 1965, with the Supreme Court's decision in *Griswold* v. *Connecticut*, were anti-contraception laws in the United States ruled unconstitutional. Many European countries maintained policies that were actively hostile toward birth control through much of the 20th century.

In the developing world, the post–World War II period has seen greatly increased concern about the consequences of rapid population growth, as well as the growth of policies designed to encourage fertility restriction. By 1990, 85% of the people in the developing world lived in countries in which the government considered the rate of fertility too high.[10]

Does the increased availability of contraceptives explain the fertility transition? In Europe, the answer is certainly no because the major decline in fertility took place before modern contraception became widely available. For example, in 1910, in the midst of a major drop in British fertility, only 16% of couples are estimated to have been using mechanical means of contraception such as condoms and diaphragms.[11]

In the developing world, the post–World War II decline in fertility did coincide with an increased use of birth control. Between the early 1960s and 2011, the rate of contraceptive prevalence—that is, the fraction of married couples aged 15–49 who are practicing some form of contraception—in the developing world

---

[9]Berg and Brems (1989), Population Reference Bureau (1999).
[10]Bongaarts (1994).
[11]McClaren (1990).

rose from 9% to 61%.[12] But this fact does not prove that the increased availability of contraceptives caused fertility decline. Fertility could have fallen even if contraception had not been available, as in Europe.

To test the importance of access to contraception in affecting fertility, a randomized controlled trial was conducted in the district of Matlab in Bangladesh over the period 1977–1996[13]; 141 villages were studied. In half of the villages, all married women received biweekly visits from community health workers, who consulted the women regarding their contraceptive needs, encouraged them to use contraception, and supplied free contraceptive products. Women in the control group of villages also had free access to contraception at government health centers, but for many women, the time involved in traveling to a clinic and the need to be accompanied by a family member when traveling outside the family compound imposed significant costs. Although fertility fell rapidly in both treatment and control villages over the study period (as it did throughout Bangladesh), treatment villages had fertility that averaged 15% lower than the control group—showing that access to contraception is potentially a significant part of the story of fertility decline. Other studies of the effects of family-planning programs, which made contraception available, have found that such programs explain between 10% and 40% of the decline in fertility in the developing world.[14] The rest of the decline is explained by changes in *desired* fertility—that is, in the number of children that families want to have. (See the box, "Family-Planning Programs and Their Effects.")

Figure 4.12 shows the relationship between actual fertility and desired fertility for a cross-section of developing countries, using data from the 1970s and 1980s. Desired fertility is measured based on surveys in each country asking women their ideal family size. If desired fertility were always equal to actual fertility, then all of the data points would lie along the 45-degree line shown in the figure. In fact, almost all of the data points lie above the 45-degree line, indicating that actual fertility is higher than desired fertility.

What is striking about the figure is that, for almost all of the countries, the two measures are fairly close. In a few countries, actual fertility is significantly higher than desired fertility—for example, in Bolivia (where the gap is 2 children), Pakistan (1.7 children), and Togo (1.5 children). But on average the difference is only 0.86 children per woman, and for the countries with the highest fertility, the gap is even smaller.[15]

Further evidence that differences in fertility among countries are not primarily the result of the availability of contraception comes from surveys that ask women directly about their desires. A woman is defined as having an "unmet need" for

---

[12]Sadik (1991), United Nations (2011).
[13]Joshi and Schultz (2007).
[14]Keyfitz (1989).
[15]Pritchett (1994).

FAMILY-PLANNING PROGRAMS AND THEIR EFFECTS

The most effective example of a fertility reduction program, although at the cost of significant restrictions on human rights, is China's "one-child" policy, initiated in 1979. Under the policy, couples who agreed to have only one child received higher wages, as well as preferential treatment in housing, and those who had too many children were sometimes assessed a "social obligation fee" to offset the burden they imposed on society. The duty of couples to enforce family planning was even incorporated into the Chinese constitution. The policy had a dramatic effect: The TFR fell from 5.99 in 1965–1970 to 1.76 in 1995. By 2000, when the policy was relaxed, it is estimated to have resulted in the birth of 70 million only-children.

In India, the government used similarly drastic measures for a short time during the 1970s. Forcible sterilizations were carried out on people, who were sometimes literally snatched off the street and who afterward received a transistor radio as a "reward" for their participation. In 1976 alone, more than 8 million people were sterilized. Extremely unpopular, the program was quickly halted.

In contrast to these heavy-handed approaches, most family-planning programs in the developing world have relied on education and persuasion. In Mexico the government has incessantly broadcast the jingle "Small Families Live Better" on television since 1974. In India a campaign to encourage families to have two children used the slogan "We Two and Our Two" and was later replaced by a campaign for one-child families, using the catchphrase "We Two Ours One."

Indonesia in the 1970s and 1980s undertook a particularly broad program, with 40,000 village centers distributing free contraceptives and educational materials. The government promoted birth control relentlessly: The back of the five-rupiah coin displayed a two-child family with the message "Family Planning: The Way to Prosperity," and the national family-planning jingle played whenever a train passed a railway crossing. At five o'clock every afternoon, sirens went off around the country to remind women to take their birth-control pills. The number of couples practicing birth control rose from 400,000 in 1972 to 18.6 million in 1989, and over the same period, the TFR fell from 5.6 to 3.4 children per woman.*

Not all developing countries have encouraged fertility reduction, however, and some have even worked against it. In Ethiopia, for example, successive governments have opposed family planning, initially for religious reasons and later because such programs risked being perceived as an attempt to limit the growth of one ethnic group at the expense of another. Between 1975 and 1995, the country's TFR rose from 5.2 to 7.4.[†]

How effective are government programs in reducing fertility? Researchers do not agree on the answer. Some estimate that government programs have only a trivial effect, but others say that such programs explain as much as 40% of the reduction in fertility that took place between the 1960s and the 1990s. Believers in the efficacy of government programs claim that a strong family-planning program will reduce the TFR by roughly one child per woman.

*Keyfitz (1989).
[†]Berhanu and Hogan (1997).

FIGURE 4.12

Desired Fertility versus Total Fertility Rate in Developing Countries

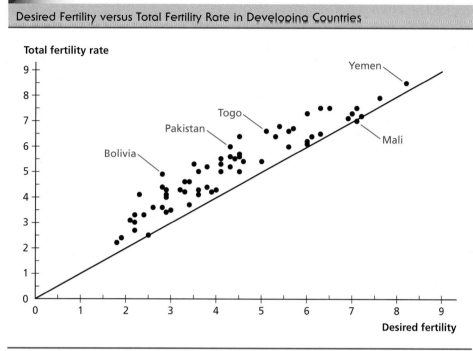

contraception if she is biologically capable of becoming pregnant, wants no more children within the next two years, and is using neither traditional nor modern contraception. Women who are currently pregnant or have just given birth are considered to have an unmet need for contraception if they report that their pregnancy was unintended. By this definition, only 17 percent of women in developing countries who were married or in a consensual union reported an unmet need in 2002. Thus, providing contraception to all women who wanted it in developing countries would reduce fertility by 17% at most.

The data on unmet need, along with Figure 4.12, suggest that the biggest contributor to differences in fertility is not women's ability to achieve their desired fertility, but rather desired fertility itself. Thus, if we want to understand why fertility falls as countries grow, we should focus on why desired fertility falls. In other words, we should look at how economic growth changes the environment that families face in such a way that they want fewer children.

Reduced Fertility: The Motives

The idea that economic growth is the best way to reduce fertility was famously summarized at a United Nations (UN) conference in 1974 in the phrase "development is the best contraceptive." What is it about development that leads to lower fertility? In this section we discuss four possible channels.

The Effect of Mortality Reduction. Section 4.3 showed that the growth rate of population is determined by the interaction of fertility and mortality. We also learned that economic growth is generally accompanied by declines in both fertility and mortality. One reasonable hypothesis is that the decline in mortality is in fact *causing* the decline in fertility.

The starting point for understanding this effect is the observation that families care not about the number of children who are born but about the number who survive to adulthood—and often particularly about whether they produce a surviving son. As mortality falls, it becomes possible for families to produce the same number of surviving adults with lower fertility.

As was the case in Sweden (as shown in Figure 4.11), the typical pattern is for declines in mortality to precede declines in fertility, leading to a long period of time in which the NRR is above 1. One explanation for this pattern is that it takes parents some time to recognize that mortality has fallen and consequently to adjust their fertility.

It is also possible for a decline in mortality to produce a more than offsetting decline in fertility—that is, for mortality decline to lower the NRR. The reason is that when mortality is high, parents have even more children than is necessary, on average, to produce the number of survivors they want. The extra children are a form of insurance against the riskiness of survival. A drop in mortality rates eliminates the need for this extra fertility.

An example can make this point more concretely. Suppose that all couples would like to have one surviving son. Suppose further that the probability of a child's surviving into adulthood is only 50%. A couple that had two sons would, on average, see one survive into adulthood. But in such a case, there would still be a significant chance (one in four) that neither son would make it to adulthood. Couples might well view this risk as unacceptable and so continue having children until they had three sons. In that case, the chance that none would survive to adulthood would fall to one in eight. If all couples had three sons—and thus six children on average—the average number of surviving children would be three, and the NRR would be 1.5.

Now consider what happens in this case when mortality falls to the point where all children will survive until adulthood. Couples will continue having children until they have one son (on average, two children). Because both children will survive to adulthood, the NRR will be 1. A decline in mortality therefore will have produced a more than compensating decline in fertility.

Income and Substitution Effects. Before probing further into why fertility falls as income rises, we should consider the opposite question: Why does fertility not *rise* as income rises? The logic for such an effect seems simple: People value children just as they value other "goods" on which they spend resources. As people become wealthier, they consume more of most other goods (so-called *normal goods*). The same should be true with respect to their desire for children.

The fault with this logic is that it ignores a second effect of income growth, which is that it raises the *price* of children. One of the things that children demand most is their parents' time, and when a country's income rises, the opportunity cost of that time—in other words, the wage that a parent could earn if he or she were not taking care of children—also rises. Thus, economic growth has two effects on the demand for children that should be familiar from microeconomics:

- An *income effect*—When you are richer you can afford more of everything.

- A *substitution effect*—When your wage is higher, children are relatively more expensive.

Whether the income or substitution effect dominates—that is, whether economic growth raises or lowers desired fertility—depends on the exact nature of households' preferences for children versus the other things that they could buy with their money.

The substitution effect results from the fact that as wages rise, the cost of spending time on raising children rises as well. Thus, an increase in wages raises household income and the price of children at the same rate. Furthermore, there is a phenomenon that amplifies this substitution effect over the course of economic development: Not only do wages rise in general, but the *relative* wages of women, who tend to do most child-rearing, also rise. For example, in the United States between 1890 and 1988, full-time earnings of women rose from 46% of men's earnings to 67% of men's earnings. This rise in women's relative wages causes the price of children—that is, the opportunity cost of women's time—to rise even faster than household income. This effect provides a further reason why fertility will fall with economic growth.[16]

The effect of women's relative wages on fertility has been reinforced by—and has in turn reinforced—the education of women. In a society where women will spend most of their adulthood tending to children, there is less economic motivation to provide girls with an education. As women spend more of their time working (and can earn fair wages for that work), the incentive to provide girls with education rises. Women who were educated as girls will in turn earn higher wages and thus face a higher opportunity cost of bearing children. Educated women are also more likely to know how to control fertility and to see a benefit in such control. Fertility surveys conducted in Latin America in the 1970s found that women with seven or more years of education had a total fertility rate of 3.2, whereas women with one to three years of schooling had a total fertility rate of 6.2.[17]

---

[16]Galor and Weil (1996).
[17]Shultz (1997), Table 3.

Resource Flows between Parents and Children. As a country develops, the economic benefits of children tend to fall while the cost of raising children rises. In developing countries, children can be productive at a young age, for example by doing simple tasks around the farm. A study of a village in Bangladesh in the 1970s concluded that a boy could begin paying his own way—that is, producing enough to compensate his family for the costs of feeding and sheltering him—by age 12. A historical example from Europe makes a similar point. In the 19th century, the French government paid families to take in abandoned children, with the scale of payments falling as children got older. Until 1852, the government took no responsibility for children over 12, on the assumption that such children could pay their own way.[18] In developed countries, by contrast, the period of time during which children do not work is much longer. Moreover, costs for education can continue well into the third decade of the child's life.

In developing countries, children also often provide for their parents in old age. Typically, no other sources of old-age support are available, so producing children (especially sons) becomes an economic necessity. In developed countries, by contrast, financial markets are sufficiently well developed that people can save for their old age. Further, although the young generation provides support for the elderly through government programs such as Social Security in the United States, this support is not provided by one's own children. Thus, the incentive for an individual family to produce children is reduced.

This change in the relative costs and benefits of children is clearly part of the explanation for the decline in desired fertility as a country develops. But it is not a complete explanation, for two reasons. First, it is clear that parents do not value children solely in economic terms. If they did, people in developed countries today would never have any children. Second, the costs of children have to be explained themselves. Parents today spend much more on their children than past generations, but to a large extent this spending is voluntary—that is, the spending is well beyond what ensures their children's survival. Thus, we really must consider why parents spend more today, a question to which we now turn.

Quality-Quantity Trade-offs. Parents hope that the resources they devote to rearing and educating their children will have payoffs in terms of better health, higher earnings later in life, and the general well-being of their children. We can think of these expenditures, beyond the minimum necessary for survival, as investments in the *quality* of the child. Parents may value child quality for a number of reasons. In cases where they are relying on their children for support in old age, children who are healthier or better educated, and thus likelier to earn high wages, will be better providers. In cases where children do not support their parents in old age, parents may be made happier by their children's happiness, so they still have an incentive to spend money on child quality.

---

[18]Cain (1977), Fuchs (1984).

Using this perspective, we can think of the decline in fertility that takes place over the course of economic development as a change in the mix of quality and quantity that parents are purchasing. The question is: What is it about economic growth that makes parents alter the mix of quality and quantity they choose?

We have already seen one important way in which economic growth changes the choice between quality and quantity: Growth is associated with a decline in mortality. In an environment in which many children will die before adulthood, parents will be reluctant to spend too much on the care or education of a single child. Instead, they will have many children and spread out their risk, much as investors diversify their portfolios by buying a number of different assets. In an environment in which survival to adulthood is almost assured, parents will be secure in concentrating their resources on only a few children.

A second channel by which economic growth induces parents to invest more in the quality of their children is by increasing the benefits that this quality produces. Specifically, growth is associated with an increase in the value of education, giving parents an increased incentive to educate their children. As we will see in Chapter 6, parents' choice to invest more in each of their children has important implications. Children who receive more education and better health care will be more productive workers as adults, and this increase in the quality of workers is an important contributor to economic growth.

4.5 CONCLUSION

In this chapter we have examined both how population affects economic growth and how population growth is itself determined. The Malthusian and Solow models provide two ways of analyzing how population affects growth. These models differ from each other in three respects. First, where the Malthusian model focuses on the interaction of population with a natural resource such as land, the Solow model focuses on how population interacts with capital. Second, where the Malthusian model concentrates on the effect of the *size* of the population on the income level, the Solow model concentrates on the effect of population *growth* on the income level. Third, in the Malthusian model, income and population are endogenously determined, whereas in the Solow model, the growth rate of population is taken as exogenous.

The Malthusian and Solow models are linked to other aspects of our study of economic growth. The Solow model presented in this chapter is an extension of the simpler version of the same model presented in Chapter 3. And in upcoming chapters we examine other aspects of the Solow model and further consider its ability to fit the data on cross-country differences in income. As to the Malthusian model's focus on the interaction between population and natural resources, Chapters 15 and 16 return to the more general question of how natural resources affect economic growth.

With the Malthusian and Solow models as our motivation, we investigated the determinants of population growth. The most important point to take from this analysis is the extent to which population is in rapid flux. The process of demographic transition—the reduction in both mortality and fertility that accompanies economic growth—which took roughly a century in the developed countries, is now occurring at greatly accelerated speed in the developing world.

Because the demographic transition in the developing world is incomplete, we do not know how it will end. Most important, it is difficult to forecast with any confidence whether population growth in the developing world will stabilize near zero. We return to this issue in the next chapter, where we also take up the question of whether population growth in the developed countries could potentially fall well below zero.

KEY TERMS

capital dilution **93**
demographic
　transition **97**

mortality transition **97**
fertility transition **97**
life expectancy at birth **98**

total fertility rate (TFR) **100**
net rate of
　reproduction (NRR) **102**

QUESTIONS FOR REVIEW

1. What two key mechanisms are at work in the Malthusian model? How do they lead to a steady-state level of population and income per capita?

2. How will changing the level of productivity in an economy affect income per capita in the Malthusian model?

3. How is population growth incorporated into the Solow model? Why does the model predict that countries with higher population growth rates will have lower steady-state income per capita?

4. What is a demographic transition?

5. How do fertility and mortality interact to determine the net rate of reproduction?

6. What are the possible channels through which economic growth leads to a reduction in fertility?

7. In *The Wealth of Nations* (1776), Adam Smith wrote, "The most decisive mark of the prosperity of any country is the increase in the number of its inhabitants." How would Smith's view have to be revised today? How would you explain the change to Smith?

PROBLEMS

1. Modern *Homo sapiens* emerged roughly 100,000 years ago. Assuming that originally there were just two *Homo sapiens* and that today there are 7 billion, what has the average growth rate of the population been?

2. For each of the following scenarios, use the graphical depiction of the Malthusian model to illustrate what happens to a country's

population size and per-capita income in the short run and in the long run.

   a. Scientists discover a new strain of wheat that can produce twice as much grain per acre.

   b. A war kills half of the population.

   c. A volcanic eruption kills half the people and destroys half the land.

3. Consider the Malthusian model, as shown in Figure 4.3. Suppose that the economy is in steady state when suddenly there is change in cultural attitudes toward parenthood. For a given income, people now want to have more children than they formerly had. Draw a graph showing the growth rate of population over time.

4. How would you use a randomized controlled trial (see box in Chapter 2) to assess the importance of "quality-quantity tradeoffs" in determining how much parents invest in their children? Can you think of a "natural experiment" that allows for similar inference without so many ethical problems?

5. Suppose that there are two countries, X and Y, that differ in both their rates of investment and their population growth rates. In Country X, investment is 20% of GDP and the population grows at 0% per year. In Country Y, investment is 5% of GDP, and the population grows at 4% per year. The two countries have the same levels of productivity, A. In both countries, the rate of depreciation, δ, is 5%. Use the Solow model to calculate the ratio of their steady-state levels of income per capita, assuming that $\alpha = 1/3$.

6. Consider the Solow model with population growth, as presented in the text. Assume that population can grow at two different rates n_1 and n_2, where $n_1 > n_2$. The population growth rate depends on the level of output per capita (and therefore the level of capital per capita). Specifically, population grows at rate n_1 when $k < \bar{k}$ and slows down to rate n_2 when $k \geq \bar{k}$.

   Draw a diagram for this model. Assume that $(n_1 + \delta)\bar{k} > \gamma f(\bar{k})$ and that $(n_2 + \delta)\bar{k} < \gamma f(\bar{k})$. Explain what the diagram says about the steady state of the model.

7. Suppose that two countries, A and B, have the same rates of investment and depreciation, the same levels of productivity, and the same levels of output per worker. They differ, however, in their rates of population growth. The growth rate of population in Country A is greater than in Country B. According to the Solow model, which country should have a higher growth rate of output per worker? Explain your answer. (Hint: It may be helpful to look back at pp. 66–68)

8. Suppose that in a country one-third of all females born die in infancy, one-third die at age 30, and one-third live to age 60. Women bear one child at age 25, one child at age 28, one child at age 32, and one child at age 35. One-half of children are girls.

   a. Compute the TFR and the NRR.

   b. Suppose that mortality is reduced so that there is no infant mortality. Half of all women die at age 30 and half at age 60. Compute the NRR.

   c. Suppose now that age-specific fertility changes, so that women have (on average) one-half child at ages 25, 28, 32, and 35. Compute the TFR and the NRR.

9. Consider the following Malthusian model. Suppose that the relationship between income per capita (y) and the growth rate of the population ($\hat{L}$) is given by the equation:

$$\hat{L} = y - 100.$$

   Suppose that output is produced using labor and land, according to the equation

$$Y = L^{1/2} X^{1/2},$$

   where X is the quantity of land. Assume that $X = 1{,}000{,}000$.

   a. Draw a graph with y on the horizontal axis and $\hat{L}$ on the vertical axis, showing the relationship between income per capita and population growth.

   b. Derive the relationship between population, L, and income per capita, y. (Hint: Remember that $y = Y/L$.) Sketch this relationship on a graph with L on the vertical axis and y on the horizontal axis.

   c. Use the equations you have derived to compute the steady-state values of L and y.

10. Consider a Malthusian model in which the equa-
    tion that relates the population growth rate to
    income per capita is

$$\hat{L} = \frac{y - 100}{100}.$$

Let X be the total quantity of land in the
economy, which is fixed. Let x be the quantity
of land per capita. The function that relates land
per capita and income per capita is

$$y = Ax,$$

where A is a measure of productivity.

a. Suppose that A is constant. What will
   the steady-state level of income per
   capita be?

b. Now suppose that A grows at a rate of 10%
   per year (that is, $\hat{A} = 0.1$). What will be the
   steady-state level of income per capita?
   Explain what is going on.

For additional exploration and practice using the Online Data Plotter and data sets, please visit
www.pearsonhighered.com/weil.

A MORE FORMAL DESCRIPTION OF THE TOTAL FERTILITY RATE, LIFE EXPECTANCY, AND NET RATE OF REPRODUCTION

This appendix presents more formal definitions of the demographic measures introduced in Section 4.3.

Demographers study mortality by constructing a **survivorship function,** which shows the probability that a person will be alive at different ages. The survivorship function starts at a value of 1 (i.e., 100% chance of still being alive) at the moment of birth and declines to reach a value of 0 at the maximum possible age.

Figure 4.13 shows how the survivorship function for women in Sweden has changed over the last 200 years. The reduction in mortality has been dramatic. In 1780 a newborn girl had roughly a 51% chance of living to age 40; two centuries later the chance was 98%. The highest mortality in preindustrial societies occurred in infancy and childhood. In 1780 there was an 18% chance that a newborn would die in her first year of life, and a 31% chance that she would die before age 5. It is at these young ages that the greatest improvements in mortality have taken place. But improvements have occurred at other ages as well. For example, the probability that a 20-year-old would survive to age 70 more than doubled, from 37% to 83%, between 1780 and 1980.

We can use the survivorship function to calculate a convenient summary measure of mortality: life expectancy at birth, which is the average number of years that a newborn baby can be expected to live. Mathematically, we define life expectancy at birth as the sum of the probability that a person will be alive at each possible age. Let $\pi(i)$ be the probability that a person will still be alive at age i—in other words, the survivorship function—and let T be the oldest possible age. Life expectancy at birth is then

$$\text{Life expectancy at birth} = \sum_{i=0}^{T} \pi(i).$$

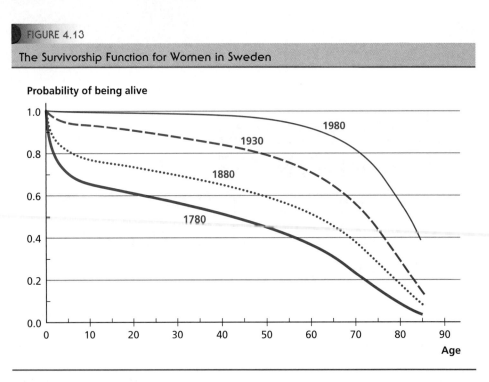

FIGURE 4.13

The Survivorship Function for Women in Sweden

Source: Keyfitz and Flieger (1968, 1990).

Life expectancy at birth can also be thought about graphically as the area under the survivorship function. For the Swedish data depicted in Figure 4.13, life expectancy at birth rose from 38.5 years in 1780 to 79.0 years in 1980.

Demographers measure fertility by examining the **age-specific fertility rate,** which is the average number of children that women of a given age will bear in a given year. Figure 4.14 shows examples of age-specific fertility for the United States and for Nigeria in 1999. In the United States, 25-year-old women gave birth to an average of 0.12 children in 1999. In Nigeria, women in the same age group gave birth to an average of 0.26 children.

The total fertility rate (TFR) is the number of children that a woman would have if she lived through all of her childbearing years and experienced the current age-specific fertility rates at each age. Mathematically, the TFR and the age-specific fertility rate, which we denote as $F(i)$, are related according to the following equation:

$$TFR = \sum_{i=0}^{T} F(i).$$

Graphically, the TFR is the area under the curve denoting age-specific fertility. In the data used for Figure 4.14, the total fertility rate in the United States was 2.1, and in Nigeria it was 6.0.

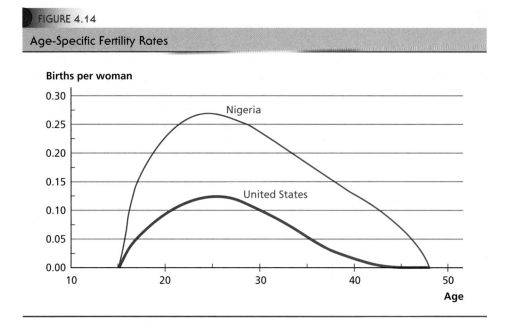

FIGURE 4.14

Age-Specific Fertility Rates

We now have the tools required to examine the interaction of fertility and mortality. The survivorship function, $\pi(i)$, tells us the probability that a person will still be alive at age i. The age-specific fertility rate, $F(i)$, indicates the number of children that will be born to a woman at age i. Combining these two, we can calculate the expected number of children that a newborn girl will produce at each age. For example, if the probability that a woman will live to age 25 is 50%, and the expected number of children that will be borne by a 25-year-old woman is 0.2, then the expected number of children that a newborn girl will have at age 25 is 0.1. Adding up these expected children for all possible childbearing ages, we can calculate the expected number of children that a newborn girl will produce over her life.

Finally, in examining population growth, it will be more convenient to focus on the number of *girls* that each newborn girl will produce over the course of her life. Call β the fraction of live births that are girls. This fraction is naturally slightly less than 50%. However, in several countries the use of selective abortion by families eager to produce sons has lowered this number significantly. In China, for example, only 47% of births in 2006 were girls. The net rate of reproduction (NRR) is defined as the number of daughters that each girl who is born can be expected to give birth to. In algebraic form,

$$NRR = \beta \sum_{i=0}^{T} \pi(i)F(i).$$

KEY TERMS

survivorship function   **117**   age-specific fertility rate   **118**

PROBLEMS

A.1. Consider the survivorship function and age-specific fertility functions depicted in the figure below.

   a. Calculate life expectancy at birth.

   b. Calculate the TFR.

   c. Calculate the NRR, assuming that half of children are girls.

A.2. Country X and Country Y have the same survivorship function. They also have the same TFRs. However, Country X has a NRR of 2, whereas in Country Y the NRR is only 1. Explain how this could happen by graphing possible age-specific fertility and survivorship functions in the two countries.

(a) Survivorship Function

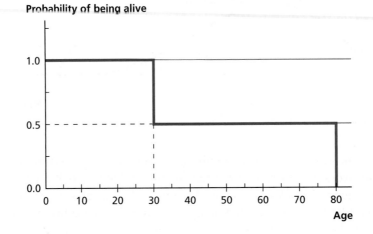

(b) Age-Specific Fertility Rate

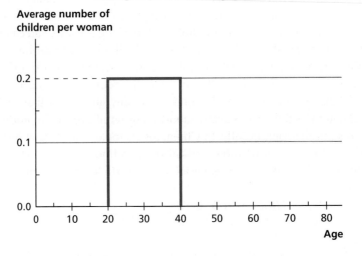

For additional exploration and practice using the Online Data Plotter and data sets, please visit www.pearsonhighered.com/weil.

FUTURE POPULATION TRENDS

We saw in Chapter 4 that population growth plays a crucial role in determining a country's level of income per capita. Countries with populations that are large relative to their natural resources will be poorer, for the reasons Malthus explained. And countries with populations that are growing rapidly will be poorer because of the effect of capital dilution that we analyzed using the Solow model. We also saw, in our discussion of the causes of fertility reduction, that lower fertility tends to be associated with an increase in the amount that parents invest in their children—and we will see in Chapter 6 that this extra investment in children is also a cause of economic growth. In this chapter we consider additional ways in which population affects a country's economic situation beyond those we examined in Chapter 4. Specifically, the age structure of the population—that is, the fraction of the population in different age groups—can significantly affect a country's level of income per capita.

In addition to these effects of a country's population on its economic growth, a set of links from population to growth functions at the level of the world as a whole rather than at the level of the individual country. As we will see in Chapters 15 and 16, a country can cope with a lack of natural resources by importing them. But when we think of population and natural resources for the world as a whole, trade cannot ease constraints on resources. Thus, even though the size of a country's population may not be relevant for the amount of natural resources available to each person in that country, the size of the *world's* population will definitely be relevant. World population will also be important when we consider world-scale environmental problems such as global warming. As the

> Indeed it is certain, it is clear to see, that the earth itself is currently more cultivated and developed than in earlier times. Now all places are accessible, all are documented, all are full of business....Everywhere there is a dwelling, everywhere a multitude, everywhere a government, everywhere there is life. The greatest evidence of the large number of people: we are burdensome to the world, the resources are scarcely adequate to us; and our needs straiten us and complaints are everywhere while already nature does not sustain us. Truly, pestilence and hunger and war and flood must be considered as a remedy for nations, like a pruning back of the human race becoming excessive in numbers.
>
> —Quintus Septimus Florens Tertullianus (*De Anima*, circa A.D. 200)

quotation at the beginning of this chapter makes clear, the question of how many people the world can support has long been a focus of scholarly inquiry.

For all of these reasons, the future course of economic development will depend on what happens with population. Of course, population growth has importance that goes well beyond its impact on economic growth. In thinking about the future of population, we are thinking about *people*: how many of them there will be, where they will live, and so forth. In looking at the future of population, we are probing into the most fundamental aspect of our planet's future.

We begin in this chapter by examining forecasts of future population and some assumptions that underlie them. We will see that much about population growth is predictable. We can make fairly accurate guesses about population growth over the next 20 or even 50 years. As we look further into the future, the picture becomes increasingly hazy, however. The biggest uncertainty surrounds the future of fertility, both in the richest countries, where it is now extremely low, and in the poorest countries, where it is still very high.

In the second half of the chapter, we take up the economic effects of the population changes that can be safely predicted. In the more developed countries, the fraction of the population made up of nonworking elderly will rise significantly, imposing an economic burden. Many developing countries, by contrast, will receive a "demographic gift" as population growth slows and the fraction of the population made up of children falls. There will also be a redistribution of the world's population away from the currently developed countries, in which population growth is slow, toward poorer countries, in which population growth is rapid.

5.1 FORECASTING POPULATION

In 1957, the demographers of the United Nations (UN) forecast that in 2000 the population of the world would be 6.28 billion.[1] The forecast was too high by only 220 million people, or 3.6 percent. Such accuracy over a horizon of 43 years, during which time the world population more than doubled, is remarkable. Although some of the success of the forecast may be attributable to good luck, it demonstrates the power of the tools that demographers have at their disposal. Certainly it would be hard to point to a long-range *economic* forecast that was nearly as accurate.

Figure 5.1 shows the level of world population over the last 160 years, along with a UN forecast for the next 140 years. According to the UN, we are entering a period of slowing population growth. After growing at a rate of 1.8% per year between 1950 and 2000, world population is expected to grow at a rate of 0.8% between 2000 and 2050 and 0.2% between 2050 and 2100. Looking even further into the future (which is obviously extremely speculative), the UN forecasts that world population will stabilize at just under 11 billion sometime around the year 2200.[2]

---

[1]Lee (1990).
[2]United Nations Population Division (2000).

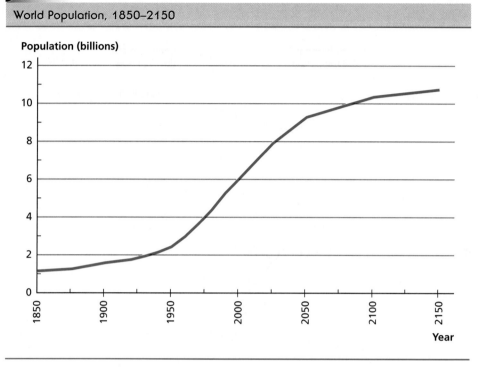

FIGURE 5.1

World Population, 1850–2150

Population (billions)

Source: United Nations Population Division (2000).

The tools that are used in making this sort of long-range population forecast are the age-specific survivorship function (which describes the probability that a person of a given age will not die over the next year) and the age-specific fertility function (which describes the probability that a woman of a given age will bear a child over the next year). These two functions are described in detail in the appendix to Chapter 4. Figure 5.2 shows how these pieces are combined to make a population forecast. The starting point is a breakdown of the population into the number of people of each age in a particular year. To forecast population in the next year, we begin by "aging" the population, making an adjustment for mortality. In the example in Figure 5.2, we determine the number of 21-year-olds in 2001 by starting with the number of 20-year-olds in 2000 and then adjusting for the fact that some will have died over the course of the year. This information on the likelihood of survival is contained in the survivorship function. We can use the same calculation to determine the number of people in all other age groups, with one exception: those aged *zero* in the year 2001—that is, the number born during the year. To get this number, we apply the age-specific fertility rate to the number of women in each age group in the year 2000. Finally, summing up the number of

FIGURE 5.2

Population Forecasting

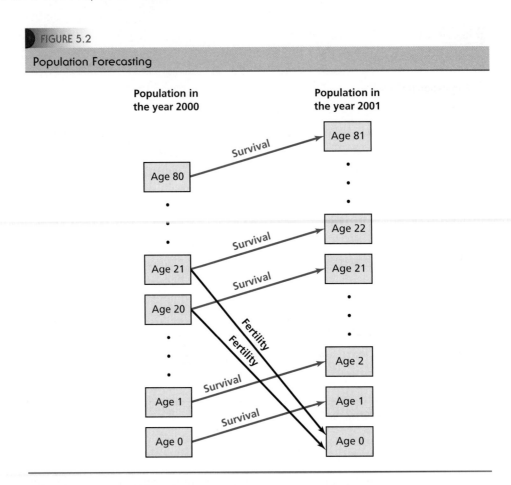

people of each age in 2001 gives the total population in that year. By carrying this process forward year by year, we can forecast the population far into the future. (To forecast the population of a particular country or region, we must also account for immigration and emigration).

The difficulty with forecasting using this method is in projecting how mortality and fertility will change in the future. We now look more closely at forecasts of future mortality and fertility.

Forecasting Mortality

An important lesson from Chapter 4 was that changes in mortality have been just as important as changes in fertility in determining population growth in the past. The reason is that, until recent improvements in life expectancy, the probability that a newborn girl would live through her childbearing years was far below 100%. Improvements in mortality thus significantly raised the net rate of reproduction (NRR). In forecasting future changes in population growth, how-ever, mortality changes are likely to have much less effect, for a simple reason: the fraction of girls living through their childbearing years is already so close to 100%. In the United States, a newborn girl has a 97% chance of living to age 45, and even in a developing country like India, the probability is 82%. Thus, poten-tial improvements in life expectancy will have a negligible effect on the NRR in the developed countries and a fairly small effect in even the poorest countries. However, reductions in life expectancy, such as those from AIDS, will reduce the NRR (see box "AIDS in Africa").

Changes in mortality do have another effect on the size of population, which is simply that if the number of births does not change but people live longer, then more people will be alive at any given time. Even in countries where there is minimal scope for further improvement in the mortality of women in their child-bearing years, this sort of improvement in the mortality at older ages will still be relevant.

Although improvement in old-age mortality is extremely difficult to predict, it is also quantitatively less important than changes in fertility in determining popu-lation growth. For example, in the United States, girls' life expectancy at birth is expected to rise from 78.9 to 82.1 over the period 1990–2020. A change in mortal-ity of this size, if it had no effect on the number of births, would increase the size of the population by only 4.0% (3.2 years gained divided by 78.9 years life expec-tancy) over the 30-year period.

Forecasting Fertility

Forecasts of fertility are often made relative to **replacement fertility**—the level of fertility that is consistent with a constant population size in the long run. Even in the most developed countries, there is some mortality before women's childbear-ing years, and slightly more boys are born than girls. Therefore, the total fertility rate (TFR) consistent with zero population growth is higher than 2.0. In the most developed countries, the replacement level of fertility is roughly 2.1 children per woman. In the developing world, where mortality is higher, replacement fertility is somewhat higher, although improvements in mortality rates in the recent decades mean that it is not much higher.

The most important question to be addressed by long-term fertility forecasts is whether fertility will be near the replacement level—in other words, will the growth rate of population be near zero? As we will see, this question has different connotations in the rich countries and the poor countries. In making its popula-tion forecasts, the UN predicted that in all of the countries in the world, the TFR would move from its current level toward replacement fertility over the next 50 years—specifically, that in almost all countries the TFR would be exactly 2.1 by the year 2050. For many developing countries, such an outcome would mean a sharp fall in fertility; for many rich countries, it would mean a significant rise in fertility.

AIDS IN AFRICA

The scope of the worldwide AIDS epidemic is staggering. In the year 2009, there were an estimated 33.3 million people infected with HIV, the virus that causes AIDS, and some 1.8 million deaths were attributable to the disease. In 2009, there were some 2.6 million new infections, down from a high of 3.2 million in 1997.[3]

More than 90 percent of the people infected with HIV live in developing countries. Sub-Saharan Africa alone accounts for two thirds of world cases. In this region 5% of the adults are now infected with HIV. Among the most severely afflicted countries are Botswana (25% of adults), Zimbabwe (18%), South Africa (17%), and Zambia (14%).

The impact of AIDS is clearly visible in population statistics. In the worst-afflicted countries, life expectancy at birth has fallen by more than 15 years since the outbreak of the epidemic. In Botswana, the worst-hit country, the growth rate of population fell from near 4% in the late 1970s to 1.3% in 2010.

Beyond the costs in terms of suffering and death of those infected and the grief of survivors, what are the economic effects of AIDS? The negative effects of the disease on growth run primarily through the human input into production. Workers who are HIV-positive cannot supply as much labor as those who are disease-free. A study of tea pickers in Kenya found that workers who are HIV-positive earned only 84% as much as healthy workers even two years before the infected workers had to leave the labor force entirely. In many countries, infection rates are particularly high among the educated, urbanized classes. In Zambia in 1994, for example, people with 10 or more years of schooling had three times the HIV infection rate of people with 4 or fewer years, and the infection rate in cities (28.2%) was more than twice that in the countryside (12.9%). Thus, the epidemic is destroying scarce human capital. Because most of those who have been stricken with AIDS were in their most productive years, the rising death toll has led to social disruption on a large scale. Children's education has taken second place to parents' medical expenses. One study in Cote d'Ivoire found that families with a member sick from AIDS halved

Fertility in the Rich Countries. The average TFR in the Organisation for Economic Co-operation and Development (OECD) group of wealthy nations in 2009 was 1.74 children per woman. But within this group there was broad variation. The United States, with a TFR of 2.05, was at the high end of the range. At the other extreme were countries with fertility far below the replacement rate: Italy (1.41), Spain (1.40), Japan (1.37), Germany (1.36), and South Korea (1.28). In the absence of large-scale immigration, these low fertility rates will translate into shrinking populations. For example, Japan's population is forecast to fall from 127 million in 2009 to 90 million in 2055, a decline of 29 percent.[4] Low fertility will also raise the average age of the population, a point to which we return in Section 5.2.

Strikingly low fertility in many of the developed countries has been an increasing source of agitation among politicians and journalists, with many observers

---

[3]UNAIDS (2010).
[4]Kaneko et al. (2008).

their spending on children's education. The epidemic has also left behind a large number of orphans, who often do not receive the same educational investment as other children.

A potential offset to these negative economic effects of HIV/AIDS has been the decrease in population growth as a result of the disease. Beyond purely biological effects (higher death rates and infected women's reduced ability to bear children), HIV further lowers population growth by encouraging the use of condoms, which also serve as contraception. In countries where physical capital and land are scarce and where there is a high ratio of children to working-age adults, a decline in fertility can have a large positive effect on income.

Calculating the overall economic effect of HIV/AIDS is difficult. One study by the World Bank concluded that the disease reduced the growth rate of gross domestic product (GDP) per capita in Africa by 0.5% per year. However, in a controversial series of papers, economist Alwyn Young argues that HIV will *raise* income per capita in sub-Saharan Africa over the next several decades. Young calculates that the extra resources generated by higher economic growth as a result of HIV are more than sufficient to pay for good care for those who suffer from the disease.*

Although the death toll from AIDS has already been horrifying, a strong possibility exists that the epidemic is just beginning. Spread of the infection continues unabated in many countries. And although recent advances in treatment have dramatically raised the survival rate for patients with HIV in rich countries, these therapies may be too expensive to significantly affect AIDS mortality in the developing world. In response to the spread of the disease, the UN recently lowered its projection for world population in the year 2050 by 300 million people, representing the cumulative effect of deaths and children never born because of the disease.

*Fox et al. (2004), Young (2005, 2007), Wehrwein (1999/2000), Fylkesnes (1997).

taking the view that there is something obviously sick about a society that is not reproducing itself. "The developed world," asserted one pundit, "is in the process of committing collective suicide."[5]

At the bottom of these discussions is the question of whether there is anything natural about fertility being at the replacement level. The short answer is no. As we saw in Chapter 4, the Malthusian model explains why population growth is near zero in an environment in which increases in population lower the standard of living beyond the subsistence level and in which the level of productivity is relatively constant. But in the rich countries today, neither of these conditions holds true, so the Malthusian mechanism no longer anchors the economy at zero population growth. In Chapter 4 we saw that there were numerous mechanisms by which economic growth has reduced the incentive to have children—by raising the costs

---

[5]Drucker (1997).

of children relative to their economic benefits, for example. We also saw that even if children are a net cost in economic terms, they still provide "utility" to parents, so parents continue to have them. But nothing in this cost-and-benefit calculation says that the average parent will want to have 2.1 children.

The fact that fertility has fallen below the replacement level does not necessarily mean that it will stay there, however. People's preferences may change, and governments may increase the incentives to have children. (However, in some of the lowest-fertility countries of Europe, these incentives—in the form of subsidized day care and free schooling through the university level—are already quite generous.) More important, it is possible that the currently low levels of fertility being observed are something of a statistical illusion (see box "The Tempo Effect").

The difficulty in forecasting fertility becomes clear when we examine how past forecasts have fared. For example, Figure 5.3 shows the actual TFR in Japan along with forecasts made at various points in time. As the country's TFR fell over the course of the last four decades, demographers consistently forecast that it would soon begin rising back toward the replacement rate and were just as consistently wrong. Demographers in the United States have not fared much better. They failed to predict both the post–World War II baby boom and the "baby bust" that followed it (see Figure 4.10). In 1964, for example, 4 million babies were born in the

▶ FIGURE 5.3

Total Fertility Rate in Japan: Actual versus Forecast

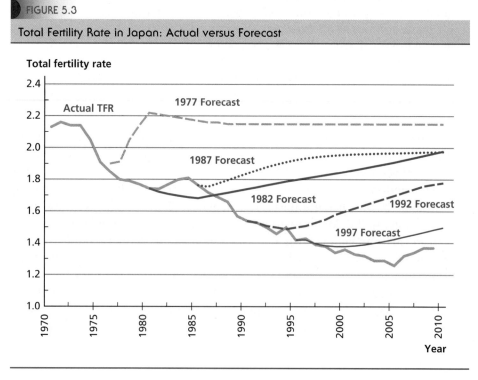

Source: Yashiro (1998).

THE TEMPO EFFECT

The dramatically low levels of fertility in many advanced countries are a great source of concern. A TFR of 1.3 as seen in South Korea today, if it remains unchanged, implies that the population will fall by roughly one-third per generation. However, a closer look at the numbers reveals that a low TFR does not necessarily imply that women are having fewer children. The source of the confusion is the effect that a rise in the average age of childbirth can have on the measured TFR. This is called the **tempo effect.**

We can use a simplified example to illustrate the tempo effect. Suppose that in a given country, every woman decided in the same year that she would delay all of her childbearing by one year. That is, at age 22, she would have the children that she originally planned to have at age 21; at age 23, she would have the children that she originally planned to have at age 22; and so forth. A woman who was just turning 22 at the time of this decision would have already had whatever children she had originally planned to have at age 21, so she would have no children at all during the following year. Then, at age 23, she would have the children that she initially had planned to have at age 22. Thus, in the year after women had made this decision to delay childbearing, *no* children would be born; the TFR would be zero. In the following year, however, the TFR would return to its level before the delay in childbearing.

A demographer looking at the data on the TFR from this country during the year following the decision to delay might conclude that women had decided to stop having babies. But this interpretation would be incorrect. Eventually, every woman would have the same number of babies that she would have had previously.

We can generalize from this example to derive a simple rule relating delays in childbearing to reductions in the measured TFR: A delay of x% of a year in childbearing will reduce the TFR by x% of its original level. Thus, for example, in a country where the TFR would be 2.0 in the absence of delay, a delay of 10% of a year in childbearing would reduce the TFR to 1.8.

When we consider the data on TFR in the wealthy countries, the natural question is whether this sort of delay in childbearing can explain the reduction in TFR below the replacement level that has been observed in the data. It is certainly true that in most of the developed world, the age of childbearing is rising. In the United Kingdom, for example, the average age of first childbirth rose almost three years, from 23.5 to 26.3, over the period 1970–1995. One study found that over the period 1985–1989, the tempo effect reduced TFR in the industrial countries by an average of 0.25 births per woman. In some cases, such as France, where the tempo effect accounted for 0.4 births per woman, adjusting for the tempo effect was enough to reverse the finding that TFR was below the replacement rate.[*]

Exactly how much of the decline in TFR in the most developed countries is explained by the tempo effect is a question that demographers cannot answer until all of the women now in their childbearing years have completed that period of life. But in Japan and other countries where fertility has been well below the replacement level for more than two decades, it is likely that the tempo effect accounts for only a small part of the fertility reduction.

[*]Bongaarts (2001).

United States, and the Census Bureau forecast that in 10 years, total annual births would reach 5 million.[6] In fact, only 3.2 million babies were born in 1974.

Fertility in Poor Countries.   In the world's poorest countries, the departure from the zero-population-growth equilibrium described by the Malthusian model is only a few decades old. As we saw in Chapter 4, rapid declines in mortality, combined with much slower reductions in fertility, have led most developing countries to experience high rates of population growth—far higher than were ever experienced in the currently developed countries. The future course of population in the developing world will depend on how quickly fertility declines continue in these countries.

In recent decades, the data show an uneven decline in fertility rates. Table 5.1 shows the size of the population in 2004 and a comparison of total fertility rates in 1970–1975 and 2000–2005 for the developing world as a whole, as well as a breakdown by region. For the developing world as a whole, the TFR has fallen from 5.5 children per woman to 2.9. In China, fertility has sunk below the replacement rate, whereas in sub-Saharan Africa, fertility has dropped only slightly. And in South Asia, fertility has steeply declined but remains far above the replacement level.

As mentioned in the discussion of Figure 5.1, the assumption underlying the UN's population estimates is that fertility in the developing world will decline to the point where most countries are at the replacement rate by 2050. To demonstrate the importance of this assumption, the UN reran its forecasts, allowing for a variety of other possible paths of fertility. At the most extreme, it considered the case in which fertility rates in each region remained at their current levels.

TABLE 5.1

Fertility in the Developing World

	2004 Population (millions)	Total Fertility Rate, 1970–1975	Total Fertility Rate, 2000–2005
All developing countries	5093.60	5.50	2.90
Sub-Saharan Africa	689.6	6.80	5.50
Arab States	310.50	6.70	3.70
East Asia & Pacific excluding China	636.10	5.45	3.19
China	1307.99	4.90	1.70
South Asia excluding India	441.00	6.21	3.94
India	1087.12	5.40	3.10
Latin America and the Caribbean	548.30	5.10	2.60

Source: United Nations Development Program (2007).

---

[6]Mankiw and Weil (1989).

In comparison with the baseline scenario, under which world population would reach 9.4 billion in 2050 and 10.4 billion in 2100, the constant-fertility scenario predicts a population of 14.9 billion in 2050 and 57.1 billion by 2100! In this constant-fertility scenario, the population of Africa alone would soar to more than 30 billion by 2100. As a more modest departure from the baseline forecast, the UN demographers considered the case in which fertility in developing countries continues to fall but does not go all the way to replacement. They assumed that fertility stabilizes at one-half child per woman above the replacement rate. In this scenario, the population of the world reaches 11.1 billion in 2050 and 17.5 billion in 2100.[7] This analysis of alternative scenarios reveals just how much is riding on small differences in future fertility.

To see why we might be skeptical of the UN's baseline fertility assumptions, let's look at the relationship between levels of income per capita and the TFR, as shown in Figure 5.4. Now let's consider what the UN's assumptions imply for a country like Nigeria, Africa's most populous country, with a population of 149 million in 2009. Nigeria's TFR in 2009 was 5.6, and the UN forecasts that it will reach 2.1 in 2050.

> **FIGURE 5.4**

> **Income per Capita versus Total Fertility Rate**

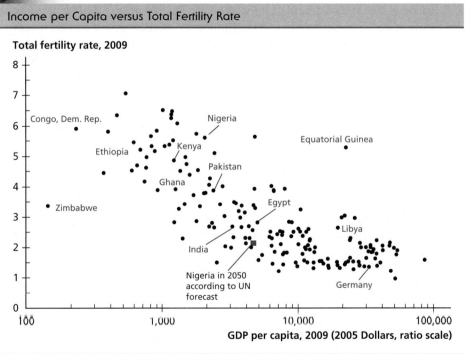

Sources: Heston, Summers, and Aten (2011), *World Development Indicators* database.

---

[7]United Nations Population Division (1998a).

Nigeria's level of GDP per capita in 2009 was $2,034. If Nigeria's income per capita grew at a reasonable rate of 2% per year starting in 2009, it would reach $4,581 in 2050. Yet Figure 5.4 shows that countries with income per capita near this level currently tend to have TFRs in the neighborhood of 3.0. In other words, the UN is assuming that Nigeria, as well as many other poor countries, will achieve replacement fertility at a level of income far lower than most countries had when they reached replacement fertility in the past. There is certainly no reason to think that such an outcome is impossible because the income level at which countries have been achieving replacement fertility has indeed been falling over time. It is also possible that Nigeria's income per capita will grow faster than 2% over this period. But such an analysis at least points out the tentative (and perhaps somewhat optimistic) nature of the UN's forecast.

Demographic Momentum

In Chapter 4 we saw that a country that achieves a NRR of 1—in other words, each girl that is born produces one daughter—will eventually have a population growth rate of zero. However, the word *eventually* is important. A country with an NRR of 1 will *not* necessarily have a population growth rate of zero right away. The reason is that the number of children born depends on two things: the rate at which women are having babies and the number of women who are in their reproductive years. If the number of women in their reproductive years rises, then the number of babies born also will rise, even if the rate at which women are having babies stays constant. This phenomenon is known as **demographic momentum.**

To see the importance of demographic momentum, consider a country with high fertility and rapid population growth. The number of children born each year will increase rapidly. As a result of this rising number of births, there will be many more people in young age groups than in older age groups—for example, there will be more newborn babies than 40-year-olds. Now suppose that the fertility rate falls suddenly to the level that would be consistent with an NRR of 1. Initially the number of babies born each year will decline because each woman in her reproductive years will be having fewer children. But over time the number of babies born will rise, for the simple reason that the number of women in their reproductive years will continue to rise. Only after several generations will the effect of this demographic momentum wear off, at which point the growth rate of population will be zero.

Demographic momentum tends to be highest in the countries in which fertility is highest. Thus, in these countries, population growth in the future will be high for two reasons: the TFR is high to begin with, and even if the TFR were to fall, demographic momentum would keep population growth high. Although a steep drop in the TFR in these countries is always possible, nothing short of a catastrophic increase in mortality, massive emigration, or a reduction in the TFR far below the replacement level will prevent demographic momentum from doing its work.

A useful measure of the extent of demographic momentum is the fraction of the population under age 15. Countries with a large fraction of the population in this age group are almost guaranteed to have rising population for the next several decades because of the increase in the number of women in their childbearing years. Currently, 47 countries, including 36 in Africa, have at least 40% of their population under age 15. In the United States, by comparison, the fraction of the population under age 15 is only 20%; in Japan it is 13%.

Because of demographic momentum, much of the future growth of population is almost inevitable. The UN calculates that if all couples had begun to bear children at the replacement fertility level in 1995, demographic momentum would have nonetheless carried the overall size of the world population to 8.4 billion by 2050 and to 9.5 billion before it finally stabilized in 2150. In India the 2009 population of 1.16 billion would still grow to 1.4 billion by 2050 if fertility had reached replacement in 1995.

Although demographic momentum tells us much about population growth in the next several decades, its importance diminishes when we look further into the future. Over the very long run, the most important determinant of population growth will be fertility, about which we have little theoretical basis for speculating.

Population in the Very Long Run

Figure 5.5 reproduces what economist W. W. Rostow calls "the great spike" in world population. The left half of the figure shows what we have already seen in Chapter 4: The growth rate of population was almost exactly zero for most of

FIGURE 5.5

The Great Spike in World Population Growth

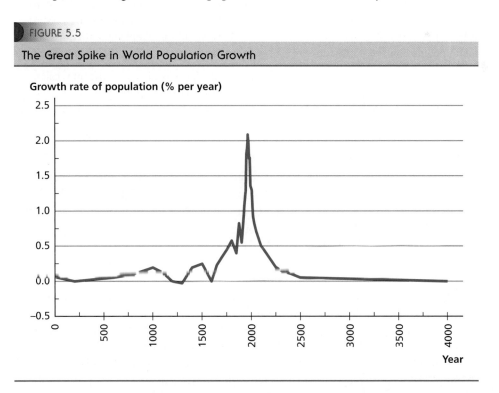

Growth rate of population (% per year)

HOW MANY PEOPLE CAN THE EARTH SUPPORT?

In 1968 biologist Paul Ehrlich published a book called *The Population Bomb*, describing the dangers of overpopulation.* In Ehrlich's view, the population at that time (roughly 3.5 billion) was already larger than the planet could sustainably support. Ehrlich predicted imminent mass starvation and ecological disaster as a result of overpopulation, not only in developing countries but in the industrialized world as well.

The subsequent 44 years have not fulfilled Ehrlich's predictions. Although fertility has fallen in most countries, there has not nearly been the kind of stringent reduction that Ehrlich thought necessary to stave off disaster. The earth's population has doubled since 1968, yet standards of living have risen in most of the world, and the kind of environmental meltdown he envisioned has failed to come about.

Ehrlich's analysis was part of a long tradition in which economists, demographers, scientists, and others have grappled with the question: How many people can the earth support? Some examples:

- In 1679 Antoni van Leeuwenhoek (the inventor of the microscope) calculated that if all the land in the world could support a population as dense as that of the Netherlands, the planet's maximum population was 13.4 billion.

- In 1931 H. G. Wells wrote that the world population at that time (1.9 billion) might have "passed the security point and [might] be greater than it should be for a prosperous sustained biological equilibrium." He added, "No doubt the earth could carry, at a bare level of subsistence, for a few dismal decades, an enormously greater population of degraded human beings than 1,900 million. Some authorities go as high as 7,000 million. But who wants that?"[†]

- An article published in *Scientific American* in 1976 examined potential agricultural yields from all the different types of soils and climates on the planet. The article concluded that the earth could support a population of 40 billion people on a diet of 2,500 calories per day.

- In 1998 the Worldwatch Institute calculated the maximum population that could be reached to be 11 billion: "Exceeding

human history, and it soared to unprecedented heights over the two centuries after the Industrial Revolution, peaking around 1970. The right half of the figure is much more speculative, of course. Rostow has assumed that the 200 years after the population growth peak will see a roughly symmetric reduction in population growth back toward zero. Viewed over the long span of history, this episode of population growth will indeed appear as a spike.[8] But how confident should we be about this pattern?

The argument against the persistence of high population growth far into the future comes from the observation of the power of compounding. To take a simple example, if population were to continue to grow at a rate of 1% per year (which

---

[8]Rostow (1998).

this level would likely trigger declines or implosions of population through famine, disease, war, etc."[‡]

Demographer Joel Cohen collected 65 estimates, published between 1679 and 1994, of how many people the earth can support. They ranged from fewer than a billion to more than a trillion.[§] In discussing these forecasts, Cohen makes three important points:

First, how many people the earth can support depends on what standard of living those people will have. The earth can support more people in small houses than in big ones; more vegetarians than meat eaters; more people with a Chinese standard of living than a U.S. one. It is therefore illogical to ask how many people the earth can support without asking at what standard of living.

Second, there is the issue of sustainability. Perhaps a high population can be supported only by using up stocks of natural resources. It is therefore possible that even though the planet supports 7 billion people now, it would not be able to support such a number in the long run. We return to this issue in Chapter 16.

Finally, there is the question of what level of technology we are considering. The current world population of 7 billion certainly could not have been sustained at a subsistence level, let alone at its current level, using the technologies that existed 200 years ago. Indeed, the Malthusian model implies that the population that existed at that time (900 million) was roughly the maximum that could be sustained at a subsistence level. Similarly, the size of the population that can be supported 200 or even 20 years from now will depend on future technological progress.

For these reasons, the question "How many people can the earth support?" is poorly posed, and we should not even try to answer it. However, the broader issue that this question tries to address—how important will limitations on resources be for growth?—is extremely relevant.

*Ehrlich (1968).
[†]Wells (1931), p. 190.
[‡]Worldwatch Institute (1998).
[§]Cohen (1995).

is below its current growth rate), it would reach roughly 45 billion by the year 2200 and 1 trillion by 2512. Such an outcome strikes many people as impossible, although given the great uncertainty involved in long-run forecasting, one should never be too confident (also see box "How Many People Can the Earth Support?").

It is surely possible that instead of the "great spike," future historians will talk about the "great step" in population growth: from zero to a permanently higher level.

It is also possible that Rostow's prediction of future population growth could be wrong in the other direction: He forecasts that population growth will return to zero. What if it falls below zero? Having had 200 years of rising population, couldn't humanity have an equally long period of falling population? Many of the most developed countries are already forecast to have falling populations, and it is certainly not impossible that the developing world might follow them. In this case, future historians perhaps would talk not about the "great spike" in population growth but instead about the "great zigzag."

This uncertainty about the future level of population stands in stark contrast to the near constancy of population for most of human history, as depicted on the left side of Figure 4.2. We saw in Chapter 4 the explanation for that near constancy: The Malthusian model of population implied that the size of the population would increase until the level of income fell to the point of zero population growth. But we also found that, starting around 200 years ago in the most developed countries, the Malthusian model no longer applied. Income has risen far above the level that would constrain population from growing. And the Malthusian relationship by which higher income automatically led to higher population growth has been overturned.

The bottom line is that, once we are in a world where the Malthusian model no longer applies, we know extremely little about the long-term path of population. Although we can be fairly confident about the path of population over the next few decades, maybe even up to a century, the more distant future is almost completely mysterious.

5.2 THE ECONOMIC CONSEQUENCES OF DEMOGRAPHIC CHANGE

To analyze the effect of demographic change on economic growth, we begin by looking at how the slowdown in the growth rate of population will affect output, using the techniques developed in Chapter 4. We then examine some additional economic implications of the predictable changes in population. Given the uncertainty of forecasts over the very long horizon, we limit ourselves to the next 50 years.

The Slowdown in Population Growth

As we have seen, the growth of world population over the period 2000–2050 (0.9% per year) is forecast to be only half as rapid as over the previous 50 years (1.8% per year). Table 5.2 shows the change in growth rates for three groups of countries as defined by the UN: more developed (North America, Europe, Japan, Australia,

TABLE 5.2

Average Annual Growth Rates of Population by Country Group

	1950–2000	2000–2050
More Developed	0.8%	0.0%
Less Developed	2.1%	0.8%
Least Developed	2.4%	2.1%

and New Zealand), least developed (the 48 poorest countries in the world), and less developed (everything in between). The decline in growth will be most extreme in the group of less developed countries, where the growth rate will fall by almost two-thirds. There will also be a large reduction in population growth, all the way to zero, among the richest countries. Among the least developed countries, population growth will fall only slightly, owing to the combination of high fertility and demographic momentum.

We can examine the economic effects of these changes in population growth by applying the Solow model, extended to accommodate population, as introduced in Chapter 4. Recall that rapid population growth lowers the level of output per worker because adding more workers lowers the amount of capital at each worker's disposal. This effect is called capital dilution. In Chapter 4, we derived an equation showing the ratio of steady-state income per worker in two countries that had different growth rates of population but were the same in every other respect. The equation is

$$\frac{y_i^{ss}}{y_j^{ss}} = \left(\frac{n_j + \delta}{n_i + \delta} \right)^{\alpha/(1-\alpha)},$$

where i and j denote the two countries, n_i and n_j are their growth rates of population, y_i and y_j are their levels of income per worker, and δ is the rate of depreciation. The parameter α is the exponent on capital in the Cobb-Douglas production function.

We can apply this same formula to look at the effects of slowing population growth, but instead of interpreting the formula to show how income per worker differs between two countries, we now interpret it to show how income per worker compares at two points in time within a single country (or within a group of countries). To be specific, consider the case of the less developed group of countries, whose population growth rate is forecast to fall from 2.1% to 0.8%. To compute how much this change would affect output per worker, we substitute these values into the preceding equation—specifically, we set the growth rate of population in Country i to be 0.8% and in Country j to be 2.1%. As in Chapter 4, we use values of 0.05 for δ and 1/3 for α:

$$\frac{y_i^{ss}}{y_j^{ss}} = \left(\frac{0.021 + 0.05}{0.008 + 0.05} \right)^{1/2} \approx 1.11.$$

This result says that the slowdown in population growth in the less developed countries would raise output per worker by 11% in steady state.

Recall from Chapter 4, however, that this calculation is sensitive to the value of α that is used. In Chapter 4 we redid the calculation using a value of $\alpha = 2/3$, Following that same path in this case, the calculation becomes

$$\frac{y_i^{ss}}{y_j^{ss}} = \left(\frac{0.021 + 0.05}{0.008 + 0.05} \right)^{2} \approx 1.50.$$

In this case, the slowing of population growth in the less developed countries will raise income per worker by 50%.

Thus, a slowdown in population growth, by reducing the effect of capital dilution, will raise the pace of economic growth. However, even as population growth slows, the *level* of population will continue to rise. There are forecast to be an additional 3 billion people on the planet by the year 2050, with most of this growth concentrated in the poorest countries. The natural way to think about how this larger population will affect economic outcomes is by using the model of Malthus: More people will lead to fewer natural resources per capita and thus to a negative effect on the level of output per capita. We return to this issue in Chapter 16.

Population Aging

One of the most important ongoing demographic changes is the aging of the world's population. Over the period 2000–2050, the median age of the global population is forecast to rise by almost 10 years, from 26.5 to 36.2 years. This aging results from both declining mortality and declining fertility. Of these two effects, the decline in mortality is the more straightforward—if each person lives to an older age, then it is obvious that the average age of the population will be greater. The effect of fertility on population aging is more subtle. Reductions in the fertility rate lead to slower population growth, and by lowering the ratio of people born recently to people born further back in the past, a reduction in fertility causes an increase in the average age of the population.

Figure 5.6 shows how the age structure of the population changes over the century between 1950 and 2050.[9] Data are presented for the three groups of countries discussed with regard to Table 5.2. For each group of countries, the population is broken into three age categories: children (ages 0–14), working age (15–64), and elderly (65 and older).

As the figure shows, throughout the world there is an ongoing decline in the fraction of population made up of children and an increase in the fraction made up of the elderly. But the timing of this restructuring differs among the groups of countries. In the more developed countries, the fraction of the population made up of children has already fallen significantly and is forecast to fall only slightly more over the next 50 years. But the fraction of the population that is elderly is rising dramatically, so that by 2050, there will be 1.7 times as many elderly people as children. In the less developed countries, the period 2000–2010 will see both a decline in the fraction of the population made up of children and a rise in the fraction made of the elderly, but even by 2050, children will still outnumber the elderly. In the least developed countries, children remained a large fraction of the population in the year 2000 (43%), but the forecast is for a rapid decline in this fraction over the following 50 years. In the least developed countries, the elderly

---

[9]United Nations Population Division (1998b).

FIGURE 5.6

Changes in the Age Structure of the Population, 1950–2050

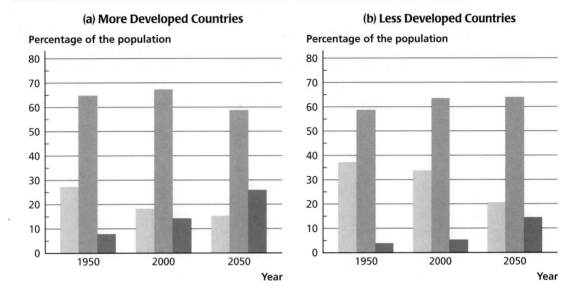

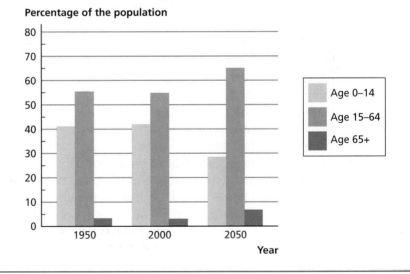

(a) More Developed Countries

(b) Less Developed Countries

(c) Least Developed Countries

Age 0–14
Age 15–64
Age 65+

Source: United Nations (2002).

fraction of the population is minuscule today and by 2050 will still be only 7%—the same as the fraction of elderly in the more developed countries in 1950.

To see why population aging is relevant for economic growth, let's return to a distinction we first made in Chapter 3: the difference between *GDP per worker* and *GDP per capita*. When we think about how productive a country is, it is often natural to focus on GDP per worker. However, when we ask how well off a country is, the more relevant measure is the amount of output that is available for *every person* in the economy—that is, GDP per capita.

To understand how these two measures relate, we start with their definitions:

$$\text{GDP per worker} = \frac{\text{GDP}}{\text{number of workers}},$$

$$\text{GDP per capita} = \frac{\text{GDP}}{\text{total population}}.$$

Combining these two equations and rearranging, we get

$$\text{GDP per capita} = \text{GDP per worker} \times \left(\frac{\text{number of workers}}{\text{total population}} \right). \qquad \textbf{(5.1)}$$

This equation highlights two reasons that countries might differ in their levels of GDP per capita: either they differ in their levels of GDP per worker, or they differ in their ratios of workers to total population.

One of the important determinants of a country's ratio of workers to population is its demographic situation. Because children and elderly people have low rates of labor force participation, the fraction of the population that works is greatly influenced by the fraction of the population that is of working age. (Of course, there is no hard-and-fast definition of *working age*. As we saw in Chapter 4, in many developing countries, children make a significant economic contribution. And the extent to which elderly people remain in the labor force also varies from country to country. Nonetheless, within a given country, a shift of population into or out of the middle part of the age range will affect the fraction of the total population that is working.) As Figure 5.6 makes clear, the population aging that is currently taking place will have significant effects on the fraction of the population that is of working age. Among the most developed countries, the fraction of the population aged 15–64 is forecast to fall from 67% to 59% over the period 2000–2050 as working-age adults move into old age. Among the least developed countries, the working-age fraction of the population is forecast to rise from 54% to 65%.

Figure 5.7 shows the working-age fraction of the population in the United States over the period 1950–2050.[10] The working-age fraction fell in the 1950s as

---

[10]Data are from the U.S. Bureau of Census International Database. In the rest of this section, working age is defined as ages 20–64.

> FIGURE 5.7

Working-Age Fraction of the U.S. Population, 1950–2050

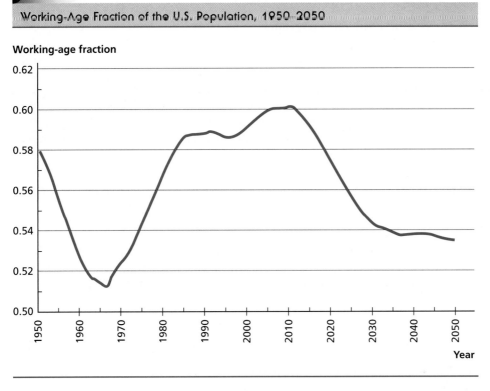

Working-age fraction

Source: U.S. Census International Database.

the postwar baby boom raised the fraction of the population made up of children. It then rose over the period 1965–1985 as these baby boomers entered the labor force and is forecast to fall again over the period 2010–2030 as these same baby boomers retire.

To compute the effect that a change in the fraction of working-age people will have on the growth rate of income per capita, we can transform Equation 5.1 into a version using growth rates.[11] We assume that the fraction of the population

---

[11]Mathematical Note: Define y^{cap} as income per capita, y^{wrk} as income per worker, and w as the fraction of the population that is of working age. Using these symbols, Equation 5.1 can be written as

$$y^{\text{cap}} = y^{\text{wrk}} \times w.$$

Taking logarithms and differentiating this expression with respect to time, we get

$$\hat{y}^{\text{cap}} = \hat{y}^{\text{wrk}} + \hat{w},$$

which is the expression in the text.

that works grows at the same rate as the fraction of the population that is of working age:

growth rate of GDP per capita

$\quad$ = growth rate of GDP per worker

$\quad\quad$ + growth rate of working-age fraction of population.$\qquad$(5.2)

As an example of how to use this equation, consider the coming decline in the fraction of the working-age population in the United States. Over the period 2010–2030, this fraction is forecast to fall from 0.60 to 0.54. The annual growth rate of the working-age fraction will be:

$$growth\ rate\ of\ the\ working\text{-}age\ fraction = \left(\frac{0.54}{0.60}\right)^{1/20} - 1 \approx -0.005 = -0.5\%.$$

Thus, using Equation 5.2, we see that demographic change will reduce the growth rate of GDP per capita in the United States by 0.5% per year. Similarly, over the period 1965–1985, when the working-age fraction rose from 0.51 to 0.59, demographic change *raised* the growth rate of GDP per capita by 0.7% per year.

Table 5.3 shows similar calculations for several other countries and time periods. In general, the most developed countries, in which fertility reduction took place earliest, have already been through a period in which the working-age fraction rose, and in the next several decades will be facing a declining working-age fraction. In many developing countries, declining fertility over the last several decades is still producing a rise in the fraction of the population that is of working age. In many cases, this "demographic gift" can have a large impact on economic growth. For example, in Bangladesh the growth of the working-age fraction will increase the growth rate of GDP per capita by

TABLE 5.3

Some Cases of Population Aging

Country	Time Period	Percentage of Population Aged 20–64 in the First Year	Percentage of Population Aged 20–64 in the Last Year	Effect of Aging on Growth of Income per Capita (% per Year)
Japan	2000–2020	62.3	54.9	–0.6
Malaysia	1980–2010	45.9	54.1	0.6
Mexico	1985–2015	42.7	57.7	1.0
Thailand	1990–2010	55.2	62.3	0.6
Turkey	1990–2010	49.2	63.2	0.8
Bangladesh	2000–2020	47.1	59.8	1.2

Source: U.S. Bureau of Census International Database.

1.2% per year over the period 2000–2020. Of course, these countries will also someday have to deal with the consequences of a larger elderly population, but that day is as much as half a century away. Finally, in many countries in which fertility is still high, declining fertility promises a boost to growth of GDP per capita sometime in the future.[12]

In addition to its effects on GDP per capita, population aging may change the nature of society itself. Teenagers and young adults account for the vast majority of criminals, for example, so as society ages, crime rates may fall. But young people also account for much of a society's dynamism. French demographer Alfred Sauvy has characterized a population that has stopped growing as one of "old people ruminating over old ideas in old housing."

Redrawing the World Map

One of the most significant demographic phenomena over the last several centuries—and in all likelihood over the next century as well—is the shift in how the population of the world is distributed among countries. Figure 5.8 shows the

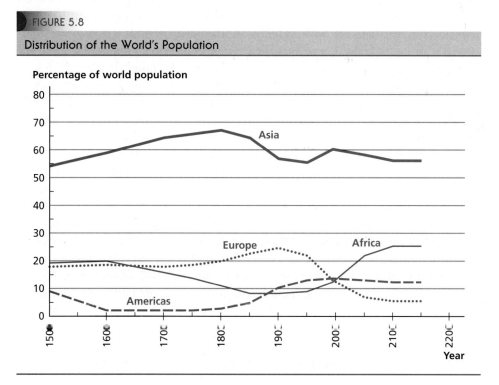

FIGURE 5.8

Distribution of the World's Population

Sources: Livi-Bacci (1997), United Nations Population Division (2000).

---

[12]Bloom and Williamson (1998).

fraction of the world's population living in each of four geographic areas: Asia, Africa, the Americas, and Europe. The figure reveals important changes in relative population sizes. Through the middle of the 17th century, Europe and Africa had roughly equal populations. In the following 250 years, however, Europe experienced a takeoff in both income and population size (see Figure 4.6), whereas population in Africa was stagnant. By 1900 Europe's population was almost three times as large as Africa's. The subsequent century saw a reversal of the trends in population, as fertility fell in Europe and life expectancy (and thus the NRR) rose in Africa. By the year 2000, the two continents were once again equal in size. By 2050 Africa is projected to be three times as populous as Europe. (The forecast on which this calculation is based is the one discussed in Section 5.1, in which fertility rates in both Europe and Africa move toward the replacement level by 2050. Alternatively, if fertility in the two areas remains constant at its current levels, with Europe below replacement fertility and Africa far above it, then by 2050 Africa's population will be more than five times as large as Europe's.)

The population of the Americas fell dramatically with the catastrophe of European "discovery." Only with massive immigration and economic growth in the 19th century did the population of the Americas rise to significance as a share of the world as a whole. By contrast, Asia's share of world population has been roughly constant, between 54% and 67%, for the entire period.

In addition to these intercontinental redistributions of population, there will also be changes in countries' relative populations. As noted in Section 5.1, in many of the most developed countries, the prospect is for shrinking populations. By contrast, in a number of developing countries, the combination of slowly falling fertility and demographic momentum almost guarantees a massive increase in population. To give a specific example, in 1950 the population of what is now Pakistan (40 million) was less than half the size of Japan's (84 million). By 2000 Pakistan's population was the slightly larger of the two (141 million versus 127 million). In 2050 the populations are forecast to differ by a factor of three (344 million in Pakistan versus 109 million in Japan). Shifts in relative population sizes of this magnitude are bound to have immense political and economic ramifications.

Another important aspect of these population shifts is that the countries expected to have the most population growth are also the poorest. Thus, the fraction of the population that will live in countries that are now rich will fall over time. The UN forecasts that the share of world population living in the currently more developed regions will decrease from 20% to 13% between 2000 and 2050, whereas the fraction living in the currently least developed countries will increase from 11% to 20%.

As shown in Table 5.4, this redistribution of the population can have an important effect on the growth rate of average income in the world.[13] Using data

---

[13]United Nations Population Division (2000), United Nations Development Program (2002). Data on GDP per capita at purchasing power parity (PPP) are from a different source from those used elsewhere in the book and so do not match precisely.

TABLE 5.4

The Composition Effect

	2000			2050			Growth Rate of GDP per Capita, 2000–2050
	Population (Millions)	Total GDP ($ Billions)	GDP per Capita ($)	Population (Millions)	Total GDP ($ Billions)	GDP per Capita ($)	
More Developed	1,191	23,921	20,084	1,181	63,845	54,060	2.00%
Less Developed	4,207	17,601	4,184	6,312	71,077	11,261	2.00%
Least Developed	658	800	1,216	1,830	5,990	3,273	2.00%
World	6,056	42,322	6,988	9,323	140,912	15,114	1.55%

Sources: United Nations Population Division (2000), United Nations Development Program (2002).

GOING FOR THE GOLD

Changes in relative population sizes among countries will have numerous effects on international relations. One area in which it is possible to measure the outcome of international competition is the Olympics.

Both high income per capita and high population should raise a country's medal count. Rich countries earn more medals because their citizens have more time to devote to athletics, better facilities for training, and generally better health. High-population countries win more medals because in a larger population there are likely to be more superior athletes.

Economists Andrew Bernard and Meghan Busse analyzed data on how many medals different countries won to assess the relative roles of population and income per capita.* They found that both factors were important, with population edging out per-capita income by a small margin. Specifically, they found that doubling a country's population will raise its share of Olympic medals by 1.1%, whereas doubling a country's level of income per capita will raise its share of Olympic medals by 1.0%. Because these two effects are so similar in size, a reasonable approximation is that a country's *total* GDP—that is, the product of GDP per capita multiplied by total population—is most important for winning a lot of medals.

Applying these findings to projections of future population implies a major redistribution in the shares of medals that different countries win. If the relative incomes of countries are constant and only their shares of world population change, then the share of world GDP produced in the currently developed countries will fall from 57% to 45% between 2000 and 2050 (see Table 5.4). In this case, we would expect a roughly commensurate drop in these countries' share of Olympic medals.

Amplifying this effect will be two other factors. First, as we've seen, the countries with slowly growing populations will also see a shift in population toward more elderly people—a group that does not win many Olympic medals. Thus, while Pakistan will have three times as many people as Japan in 2050, it is also forecast to have more than four times as many 20-year-olds. Second, there is a good possibility that in addition to this redistribution of population, poorer countries will catch up economically— that is, their income per capita will grow faster than that of rich countries. This income growth would also increase their share of Olympic medals.

*Bernard and Busse (2004).

from the UN, the table divides the world into three groups of countries. The second and fifth columns show the populations of these country groups in 2000 and 2050. The other two columns on the left side of the table show total GDP and the average level of GDP per capita in these groups in 2000. We consider a simple scenario for economic growth: Suppose that between 2000 and 2050, income per capita grows at a rate of 2% per year in every country in the world. It might seem at first as if this assumption would imply that the growth rate of *average* income in the world would also be 2%—but this is not the case. Comparing average income per capita in 2050 and 2000 under this scenario yields a growth rate of only 1.55%. The reason that the average level of GDP per capita in the world does not grow as quickly as the average in each country is that the balance of population is shifting toward poorer countries. This effect of population redistribution reducing the average growth rate of income in the world is called the **composition effect.**

The fact that the fraction of the world's population living in *currently* rich countries will fall does not mean that the fraction of the world's population living in rich countries will fall. The reason is that more countries are *becoming* rich over time. Thus, the overall balance between rich people and poor people in the world depends on which force is more powerful: the higher population growth rates of poor countries or the income growth that takes place in these poor countries.

5.3 CONCLUSION

Demographic forces work slowly but inexorably. Thus, peering several decades into the future, we can be confident about some demographic predictions in a way that we can't be confident about more standard economic forecasts. We can be fairly certain, for example, that the population of the world as a whole will grow to about 9.4 billion by the year 2050, that the growth rate of world population will slow down, that the balance of world population will shift away from the currently developed countries, and that the population of the developed world will age significantly.

As we gaze further into the future, however, the demographic picture becomes increasingly hazy. The two greatest areas of uncertainty are associated with fertility: Will fertility in the developing world fall to the replacement level? Will fertility in the rich countries rise to the replacement level? The shape of the world economy (as well as much else) hinges on these questions.

The changes in population forecast to take place over the next half-century will have both positive and negative effects on economic growth. Slower population growth will provide a boost to economic growth by reducing the need to provide new capital to new entrants into the labor force. In many of the most developed countries, the next several decades will see an increase in the fraction of the population made up of elderly people and a consequent reduction in the fraction made up of working-age people. This aging of the population will slow the growth rate of income per capita. In contrast to this "graying" of the most developed countries, in countries that have recently reduced fertility, the population is "maturing" in a manner that is economically beneficial—that is, the fraction of the population that is composed of children is falling, and the fraction made up of working-age adults is rising.

Among the poorest countries, demographic momentum will ensure that population continues to grow rapidly for the next several decades, even under the assumption that fertility rates will decline significantly. In these countries, the beneficial effects of low population growth and a smaller fraction of the population made up of children are at least two or three decades away. These countries will also see a large multiplication in population size over the next decades, which may affect growth by reducing the quantities of natural resources available per capita.

In two later chapters, we investigate questions that are intimately bound up with population growth. In Chapter 9 we trace the evolution of technology at the world level. Here the link to population is that a world of more people will have more brains to come up with new ideas, and thus more technological progress. In Chapter 16 we look at the relationship between the world's stock of natural resources and economic growth. Obviously, the standard of living that the finite base of resources on our planet can support depends on the number of people who will be enjoying that standard of living.

KEY TERMS

replacement fertility **125**	demographic	composition
tempo effect **129**	momentum **132**	effect **146**

QUESTIONS FOR REVIEW

1. How did the change in mortality affect population growth in the past? Why will its effect be different in the future?

2. What reasons are there to expect that fertility in the developed countries will or will not move toward the replacement level?

3. What is demographic momentum? What does it imply about how changes in fertility rates will affect future population growth?

4. Why will population aging over the next several decades have different economic effects in developed and developing countries?

5. Why does a reduction in fertility lead to a "demographic gift"? Why does this demographic gift eventually disappear?

PROBLEMS

1. The following table shows data from the country of Fantasia. Fantasians live for a maximum of five years. Another peculiarity of the country is that there are no men—the population is made up entirely of women (who are nonetheless able to reproduce). Using these data, calculate the population of Fantasia in the year 2001.

Age (as of Last Birthday)	Population in 2000	Fertility (Children per Woman)	Probability of Surviving to the Next Age
0	100	0.0	1.0
1	100	0.8	1.0
2	100	0.8	1.0
3	100	0.0	0.5
4	100	0.0	0.0

2. What is your forecast of the *growth rate* of the world population in the year 2200? Specifically, will it be roughly zero, greater than zero, or less than zero? Defend your answer using as many facts, economic theories, and so on, as possible.

3. Suppose that starting in the year 2010, Japan and Kenya had the same TFRs. How would their population growth rates compare? Why would they differ?

4. Using data from Table 5.2, calculate how much the change in population growth between the period 1950–2000 and 2000–2050 would affect the steady-state level of output per worker in the Solow model for the most developed countries.

5. Suppose that a country has the following female age structure in the year 2005:

Age	Population (millions)
0–20	60
21–40	40
41–60	20

Half of women die at age 40 and half live to age 60. Starting in the year 2005, each woman has exactly one daughter at age 20. What does the age structure of the female population look like in the year 2025? In 2045? In 2065?

6. Suppose that in a particular country, the TFR fell to zero and remained there. Also suppose that there was no immigration or emigration. Draw a graph showing how the fraction of the population that was working age would change over time. Immediately following the fertility reduction, would the working-age fraction rise or fall? How long would this trend continue? After how many years would the working-age fraction reach its maximum? Its minimum?

7. In 1950, 57.9% of the population in the United States was of working age. In 1965, only 51.2% of the population was of working age. Calculate the effect of this change in demographics on the annual growth rate of GDP per capita.

8. "Because of low fertility, the population of our country is aging. The large number of elderly, in comparison to the working-age population, is lowering our standard of living. The best way to remedy this situation is to raise fertility." Comment on this statement. Is it correct in the long run? In the short run?

9. Suppose that the world has only two countries. The following table gives data on their populations and GDP per capita. It also shows the growth rates of population and GDP. The growth rates of population and GDP per capita in each country never change.

   a. What will the growth rate of world population be in the year 2000? Following 2000, will the growth rate of world population rise or fall? Explain why. Draw a graph showing the growth rate of world population starting in 2000 and continuing into the future. Toward what growth rate does world population move in the long run?

b. Draw a similar graph showing the growth rate of total world GDP.

c. Draw a similar graph showing the growth rate of average GDP per capita in the world.

Country	Population in 2000	GDP per Capita in 2000	Growth Rate of Population (% per Year)	Growth Rate of GDP per Capita (% per Year)
Country A	1,000,000	1,000	0	2
Country B	1,000,000	1,000	2	0

For additional exploration and practice using the Online Data Plotter and data sets, please visit www.pearsonhighered.com/weil.

CHAPTER 6

HUMAN CAPITAL

> Give a man a fish, and you feed him for a day. Teach a man to fish, and you feed him for a lifetime.
>
> —Chinese proverb

So far, we have treated labor, the human input into production, as constant across countries and over time. But in fact, the quality of labor that a person supplies can vary enormously. A worker can be weak or strong, ill or healthy, ignorant or educated. In day-to-day experience, we see that people who have better labor to supply—those who are particularly smart or who can work tirelessly—are able to earn higher wages. The same has been true for stronger people for much of history, although it is rarely true in developed countries today. (But physical attributes do still matter: A study of workers in the United States and Canada found that those judged to have above-average looks earned 12% more than similarly qualified workers who were judged to have below-average looks.[1])

In this chapter we explore the idea that differences in the quality of workers are one explanation for differences in income among countries. We would not expect differences in labor quality to explain *all* of the differences in income that we see around us (as we have already laid out some other reasons why incomes differ, and we know more are to follow); but we want to look into how large a contribution to these differences labor quality makes.

The qualities of labor on which we focus go by the collective name **human capital** because they share several important qualities with physical capital. First, as with physical capital, we focus on qualities of people that are *productive*—that is, characteristics that enable them to produce more output. Second, we concentrate on the qualities that are *produced*, just as we said that a key aspect of physical capital is that it is itself produced. We will see that investment in human capital production is a major expense for an economy. Third, just like physical capital, human capital earns a return. The manner in which a return is earned differs between the two, however. Human capital earns a return by giving the worker who owns it a higher wage, and only does so while he or she is working, whereas physical capital can earn its return while its owner is relaxing at the beach. Finally, just like physical capital, human capital depreciates.

---

[1] Hamermesh and Biddle (1994).

6.1 HUMAN CAPITAL IN THE FORM OF HEALTH

As a country develops economically, the health of its population improves. This improvement in health is direct evidence that people are leading better lives. In other words, health is something that people value for itself. But health also has a productive side: Healthier people can work harder and longer; they can also think more clearly. Healthier students can learn better. Thus, better health in a country will raise its level of income. It is this productive aspect of health—that is, health as a form of human capital—that we now explore.

The Effect of Health Differences on Income

As countries develop, their people get bigger. The average height of men in Great Britain rose by 9.1 centimeters (3.6 inches) between 1775 and 1975. Similarly, in 1855 two-thirds of young Dutch men were shorter than 168 centimeters (5 feet, 6 inches), but today the figure has fallen to 2%. These changes are purely attributable to changes in environment because the genetic makeup of these populations has changed very little.[2]

As with many of the changes that we examine in this book, the change in physical stature in many developing countries has paralleled the shift in the developed countries, except that it started later and has proceeded more rapidly. For example, the average height of South Korean men in their 20s rose 5 centimeters (2 inches) between 1962 and 1995.

The principal explanation for these improvements in height is better nutrition. In Great Britain daily calorie intake per adult male rose from 2,944 in 1780 to 3,701 in 1980. Similarly, in South Korea daily calorie consumption per adult male rose from 2,214 to 3,183 between 1962 and 1995.[3] Height serves as a good indicator of malnutrition, particularly malnutrition experienced in utero and during the first years of life. Shortness is a biological adaptation to a low food supply because short people require fewer calories to get by.

People stunted by malnutrition are also less healthy. More significantly, the same malnutrition that causes shortness is also reflected in lower abilities as a worker. (Shortness does not always indicate malnutrition or poor health—it also reflects a person's genetic predisposition. In the United States, where most adults were well nourished as children, there is little relationship between a man's height and his wages; specifically, a 1% difference in height is associated with a 1% difference in wages. In Brazil, where malnutrition is extensive, a 1% difference in height is associated with a 7.7% difference in wages.[4])

---

[2]Fogel (1997).
[3]Data on height and calorie consumption in Korea are from Sohn (2000).
[4]Strauss and Thomas (1998).

Economic historian Robert Fogel has attempted to quantify the contribution of improved nutrition to economic growth in the United Kingdom in the two centuries between 1780 and 1980. Improved nutrition raised output by two means: first, by bringing people into the labor force who would otherwise have been too weak to work at all, and second, by allowing the people who were working to work harder. Fogel calculated that in 1780 the poorest 20% of adults in the United Kingdom were so badly nourished that they did not have the energy for even one hour of manual labor per day. By 1980, this sort of malnutrition had been completely eliminated, and all adults were nourished well enough to work. This change by itself would have increased the amount of output per adult by a factor of 1.25. Among adults who were working, Fogel calculated that the increase in caloric intake allowed a 56% increase in the amount of labor input that could be provided. Putting these two effects together, better nutrition raised output by a factor of 1.25 × 1.56 = 1.95. Spread over 200 years, this was an increase of 0.33% per year. Given that the actual growth of income per capita in the United Kingdom over this period was 1.15% per year, improved nutrition can be seen as having produced slightly less than one-third of the overall growth in income.

Although Fogel's work focuses on the effect of nutrition on the ability to do physical work, there is also an effect on mental capacity. This was shown in a randomized controlled trial conducted in Guatemala over the period 1969–1977. Pairs of similar villages were identified. From each pair, one village was randomly assigned to receive a treatment of a daily food supplement distributed freely to the entire population. The supplement was a high-protein energy drink known as *atole*. The control villages also received daily supplement, but this was simply a fruit flavored drink with no protein and one-third the calories of *atole*. Subsequently, researchers followed up adults who had been children in the treatment and control villages at the time of the experiment. They found that those who had grown up in the treated villages scored significantly higher on tests of reading as well as nonverbal cognition, and also had completed more schooling on average.[5]

In developed countries today, most people are well nourished. But in much of the developing world, malnutrition is still pervasive. Figure 6.1 shows the relationship between gross domestic product (GDP) per capita and the number of calories available for consumption per day. The richest countries have calorie supplies of between 3,000 and 3,500 per day; in the poorest countries, daily calorie supplies average less than 2,000. The levels of nutrition shown in this figure understate the true extent of malnutrition in a number of countries because they are national averages and do not take account of inequalities in food distribution within countries. For example, in Latin America the richest 20% of the population has per-capita food consumption that is 50% larger than that of the poorest 20% of

---

[5]Maluccio et al. (2008).

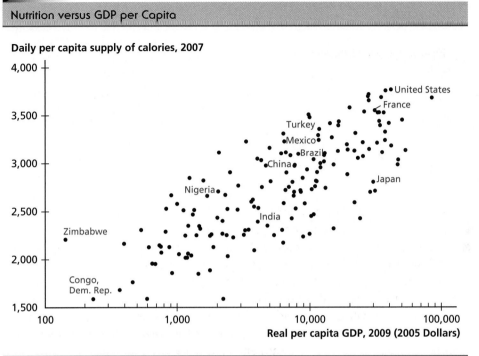

FIGURE 6.1

Nutrition versus GDP per Capita

Daily per capita supply of calories, 2007

Sources: FAOSTAT database, Heston, Summers, and Aten (2011).

the population.[6] Thus, even in countries with enough food on average, the poorest part of the population is malnourished. Worldwide, some 925 million do not have enough food to eat.

These differences in nutrition are paralleled by differences in health. One way of measuring the average level of health in a country is by looking at life expectancy at birth. Figure 6.2 shows a strong relationship between life expectancy and GDP per capita. Most of the poorest countries in the world have a life expectancy below 60 years, whereas among the richest countries, life expectancy ranges between 75 and 82 years. Other measures of health paint a similar picture. For example, the fraction of nonpregnant women who are anemic averages 48% for the poorest quarter of countries but only 18% for the richest quarter of countries.[7]

These data establish that there are large variations in health between rich and poor countries and that these differences can contribute to differences in income between the two groups. We now turn to the question of where these health differences originate.

[6]Rosen and Shapouri (2001).
[7]Shastry and Weil (2003).

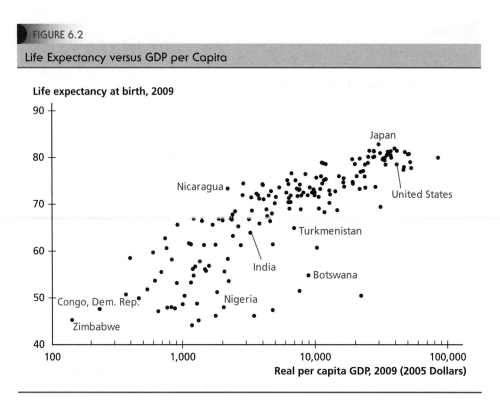

FIGURE 6.2

Life Expectancy versus GDP per Capita

Sources: Heston, Summers, and Aten (2011), *World Development Indicators* database.

Modeling the Interaction of Health and Income

In the previous section we saw that improvements in nutrition, by allowing workers to function more effectively, have contributed significantly to increases in income per capita. But this is only part of the story. Better nutrition is not only a contributor to, but also a *result of*, higher income because people in wealthier countries can afford more and better food.

What is true for nutrition is true for health more generally. People who are richer can afford better inputs into health, such as vaccines, clean water, and safe working conditions. Among the rich countries of the Organisation for Economic Co-operation and Development (OECD), there are an average of 2.2 doctors per thousand people; in the developing world, the average is 0.8; and in sub-Saharan Africa, the average is only 0.3.[8] And healthier people are better workers. Thus, for understanding the relationship between health and income, it is important to realize that both are endogenous variables. (Recall from Chapter 3 that we defined an

---

[8]United Nations Development Program (2000).

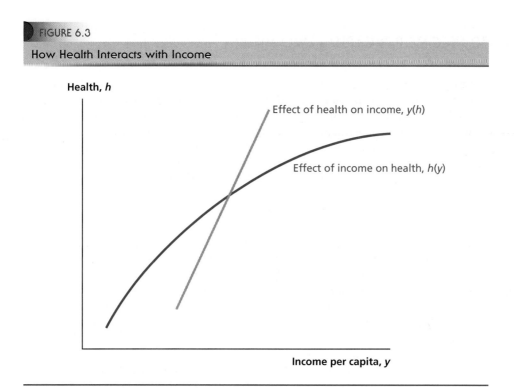

FIGURE 6.3

How Health Interacts with Income

Health, *h*

Effect of health on income, *y(h)*

Effect of income on health, *h(y)*

Income per capita, *y*

endogenous variable as one determined within an economic model, in contrast to an exogenous variable, which is taken as given when we analyze a model.)

Figure 6.3 illustrates the interaction of health and income. The horizontal axis measures income per capita, *y*, and the vertical axis measures the health of workers, which we denote as *h*. The curve labeled *y(h)* shows the impact of health on the level of income per capita. For higher values of *h*, workers are able to produce more output, so the curve is upward sloping. The second curve, *h(y)*, shows the impact of income per capita on health. This curve also is upward sloping, showing that higher income improves health. But notice that this curve flattens out at high levels of income. This flattening captures the idea that the beneficial effects of income on health are more pronounced at lower levels of income.

The intersection of the two curves in Figure 6.3 will determine the equilibrium levels of income and health. To see the implications of the model, consider a change in income that is unrelated to health. That is, suppose that for some exogenous reason—for example, an improvement in productive technology—workers of any given health level can now produce more output. As shown in Figure 6.5, such a change will shift the *y(h)* curve to the right. If there were no change in workers' health, the increase in output would match the increase in productivity. This effect is shown as the movement from point *A* to point *B* in Figure 6.5. However, as the figure makes clear, this is not the end of the story. The rise in output will improve

HEALTH AND INCOME PER CAPITA: TWO VIEWS

Poor countries have populations that are unhealthy in comparison to those of rich countries. There is also little doubt that raising income in a given country will improve its level of health and that improving health in a country will raise its level of income. The question that is left open in this analysis is: What is the primary source of differences in both income and health between rich and poor countries? Specifically, do the forces driving these differences come primarily from the side of health or from the side of income?

We can lay out this issue more formally using a diagram like the ones we have just examined. Consider two countries, A and B. Country A is both healthier and richer than Country B. In each of the two panels of Figure 6.4, points A and B represent these "data" about the two countries. What we cannot observe directly are the $h(y)$ and $y(h)$ functions that determine these points. Different combinations of these two functions could explain the data that we observe.

Panel (a), "The Health View," assumes that all differences between the countries have their roots in the countries' health environments—that is, in things other than income that also affect health (e.g., the presence or absence of tropical diseases). The health environment is summarized in the $h(y)$ function. We have assumed that this function in Country A, labeled $h_A(y)$, is higher than the corresponding function in Country B, $h_B(y)$. So at any given level of income, Country A has better health than Country B. By contrast, the two countries are assumed to have the same $y(h)$ function, so that for a given level of health, the two countries have the same level of income. In equilibrium, the two countries have different levels of income, however, because of their different health environments.

Panel (b), "The Income View," assumes the opposite: that all differences between the countries have their roots in aspects of production that are unrelated to health—for example, in physical capital accumulation or technology. At any given level of health, Country A produces more output than Country B. Thus the function $y_A(h)$ lies to the right of $y_B(h)$. In this case, we assume that the two countries have the same $h(y)$ function, so that for a given level of income, the two countries have the same level of health. As in the first panel, in equilibrium, the countries differ in both health and income.

As the two panels make clear, differences in either $h(y)$ or $y(h)$ are sufficient to explain the observed differences in both health and income between the countries. Either story is logically consistent in the sense that it could fit the data on how income and health differ among countries. To sort out which story is correct, we would have to look for additional data.

The two possibilities portrayed in Figure 6.4 are obviously extreme. Almost all economists would agree that in the real world, differences in income among countries are explained by differences in *both* the $y(h)$ and $h(y)$ curves. The issue that is hotly debated is which channel is relatively

workers' health, and this improved health will feed back to produce an additional increase in output. Thus, there will be a "multiplier" effect by which an initial increase in productivity will produce a larger increase in output. This is shown as the movement from point B to point C in Figure 6.5.

We can similarly use this model to think about the effects of exogenous health improvements such as those resulting from the introduction of a new vaccine or medicine. Such an improvement will shift the $h(y)$ curve upward—in other words, at any given level of income, workers will be healthier. Just like an improvement more important. One school of thought holds that almost all of the relative ill health in poor countries is a result of their being poor. In other words, if these countries were to raise their level of income per capita to the level of rich countries, they would also have the same level of health as rich countries. The other school of thought holds that there are large differences in the health environment between rich and poor countries that would persist even if the two groups of countries had the same levels of income per capita. Under this view, the poor health environment in poor countries is a *cause* of their low levels of income.[*]

In Chapter 15, we return to the subject of differences in health among countries as we explore the role of geography in affecting the health environment.

[*]Acemoglu, Johnson, and Robinson (2001); McArthur and Sachs (2001).

FIGURE 6.4

Health and Income per Capita: Two Views

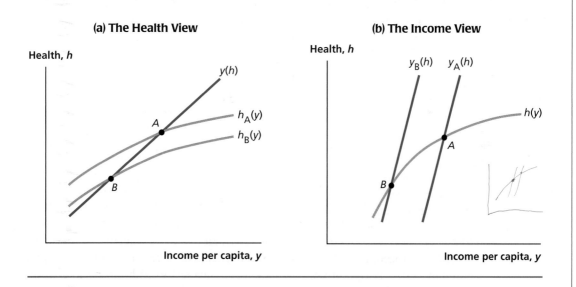

(a) The Health View

(b) The Income View

in productivity, this sort of exogenous improvement in health will produce a multiplier effect: Healthier workers will produce more output, and the higher level of output will allow for better nutrition, further improving health.

These exogenous improvements in health became especially significant in the 20th century. Many of the advances that have reduced mortality have also led to better health in general. For example, in the U.S. South before World War I, the hookworm parasite, which causes anemia, exhaustion, and stunted physical and mental growth, played a significant role in holding back economic development.

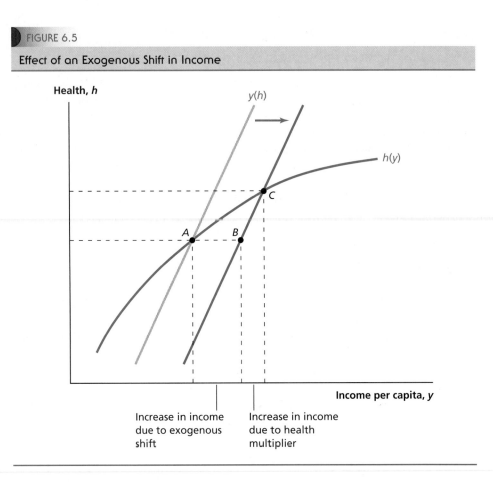

FIGURE 6.5

Effect of an Exogenous Shift in Income

Health, *h*

y(h)

h(y)

C

A   *B*

Income per capita, *y*

Increase in income due to exogenous shift

Increase in income due to health multiplier

Called the "germ of laziness" by one contemporary journalist, hookworm infected as much as 42% of the southern population in 1910, and it was estimated that sufferers from the disease earned only half as much as healthy workers. Following intensive public health efforts, the prevalence of the disease decreased markedly by the 1930s.[9] In many parts of the world, the control of malaria, which was greatly aided by the invention of the pesticide DDT during World War II, had a similarly dramatic effect on productivity.

6.2 HUMAN CAPITAL IN THE FORM OF EDUCATION

People work with their minds as well as their bodies. Indeed, in developed economies, intellectual ability is far more important than physical ability in determining a person's wage. For this reason, investment that improves a person's intellect—in other words, education—has become the most important form of investment in human capital.

---

[9]Ettling (1981).

Changes in the Level of Education

Education levels differ markedly among countries. Table 6.1 shows how the education level of the adult population has changed between 1975 and 2010 for three groups of countries: developing (122 countries), advanced (24 countries), and the United States (which is also included in the set of advanced countries). In 2010, 20.8% of the adult population in the developing world had no education at all. Among the advanced countries, the comparable figure was 2.5%; in the United States, it was only 0.4%. At the other end of the spectrum, only 5.3% of the adult population of the developing world had completed higher education (i.e., college), compared with 16.6% for the advanced countries and 20.0% for the United States.

Table 6.1 also points to a large increase in the number of years of schooling over the period for which these data are available. In the developing countries, education of the adult population increased by 3.5 years, whereas in the advanced countries, it increased by 3.0 years. Given the initially low levels of education in the developing world in 1975, the *percentage* increases in education were especially large. The average number of years of schooling and the fraction of adults that had finished primary school more than doubled. Even more remarkably, the fraction that had completed secondary school quadrupled, and the fraction that had completed higher education increased by a factor of 3.5.

Education is an investment in building human capital. And like investments in physical capital, it can be costly. In 2010 the U.S. government spent $675 billion on education, and private individuals spent another $236 billion.[10] Total educational spending came to 6.2% of GDP. But measuring spending this way greatly understates the true cost of educational investment. The reason is that in addition to the obvious

TABLE 6.1

Changes in the Level of Education, 1975–2010

			Percentage of the Adult Population with			
		Average Years of Schooling	No Schooling	Complete Primary Education	Complete Secondary Education	Complete Higher Education
Developing Countries	1975	3.2	47.4	32.9	8.1	1.6
	2010	6.7	20.8	68.8	31.5	5.3
Advanced Countries	1975	8.0	6.2	78.8	34.9	8.0
	2010	11.0	2.5	94.0	63.9	16.6
United States	1975	11.4	1.3	94.1	71.1	16.1
	2010	12.4	0.4	98.8	85.4	20.0

Source: Barro and Lee (2010). Data for population 25+.

---

[10]U.S. National Income and Product Accounts, Tables 2.4.5 and 3.17.

THE ECONOMIC EFFECTS OF MALARIA

Malaria is one of the great scourges of the world. In 2010 it was estimated to have caused some 216 million episodes of illness and 655,000 deaths, with this burden concentrated in poor, tropical countries. In April 2000, heads of state and other leading figures from 44 African nations convened in Abuja, Nigeria, to initiate a major effort to combat malaria. The declaration that emerged from the Abuja conference was quite explicit in discussing malaria's economic effects: "Malaria has slowed economic growth in African countries by 1.3% per year. As a result of the compounded effect over 35 years, the GDP level for African countries is now up to 32% lower than it would have been in the absence of malaria."

The humanitarian benefits of controlling malaria are enormous. But are the economic benefits really so large? Economists are far from agreement on this issue. Comparing the performance of countries with high versus low rates of malaria, or those that saw large reductions in the rate of disease to those that did not, many economists, most prominently Jeffrey Sachs of Columbia University's Earth Institute, have concluded that the economic effects of malaria are indeed large. (It was research by Sachs that was the source of the 1.3% growth effect cited in the Abuja declaration.) However, comparisons like this are subject to the sort of omitted variable bias discussed in Chapter 2. Countries with high rates of malaria may have other characteristics (for example, a climate that lowers agricultural productivity) that lead to low income. Similarly, the fact that a country was able to eradicate malaria may be evidence of some other good characteristic (e.g., effective institutions) that leads to high growth, rather than growth being the result of eradication *per se*. For these reasons, many economists are skeptical of Sachs's findings. One recent cross-country analysis that tried to isolate the effects of mortality reductions (result of malaria eradication as well as other health advances) by looking at the spread of medical technology in the decades after World War II found that increases in life expectancy had *no* effect on GDP per capita.*

Medical evidence suggests that the most important effects of malaria on worker productivity are associated with exposure in infancy and early childhood, as well as in utero. Young children account for the vast majority of severe malaria cases as well as deaths from the disease. By the time they are adolescents, most residents

costs of education—teachers' salaries, buildings, and textbooks—there is a more subtle expense: the opportunity cost that students pay in the form of wages they forgo while getting educated. One estimate is that the opportunity cost of forgone wages is roughly equal to all other educational spending in the United States—put another way, half of the cost of education is opportunity cost.[11] Doubling the figure for government and private spending to account for opportunity cost, we find that the total cost of investment in education was 12.4% of U.S. GDP in 2010. Coincidentally, that is exactly equal to the percentage of U.S. GDP that was invested in physical capital in 2010. More generally, this comparison makes the point that investments in the two types of capital, physical and human, are of similar magnitude.

---

[11]Kendrick (1976).

of high-malaria regions have developed some immunity. But malaria in childhood can damage an adult's human capital through several channels. The malaria parasite interferes with fetal nutrition and also causes preterm deliveries, both of which lower birth weight, which in turn affects cognitive development. Severe cases of the disease can also lead directly to brain damage. Among older children, lethargy resulting from anemia, as well as school absences as a result of malaria episodes, interfere with accumulation of human capital.

Historical studies have recently confirmed the medical evidence on the long-run effects of childhood malaria. Between 1940 and 1960, a massive international campaign using the newly discovered weapon of DDT largely eliminated malaria from an area that was home to one-fifth of the world's population. In Colombia, for example, the case rate for malaria was reduced by two-thirds between 1957 and 1961. In the Indian state of Uttar Pradesh, annual malaria deaths fell from 140,000 in 1952 to below 20,000 in 1963. Comparing children born just before and just after this disease reduction provides a "natural experiment" for examining malaria's long-run effects.

The findings from these studies show that childhood malaria has a large impact. For example, in India, malaria eradication raised literacy and primary school completion by 12 percentage points. In the worst-affected regions of Sri Lanka, malaria eradication raised the average amount of schooling per child by 2.4 years. In Brazil, Colombia, and Mexico, adults who suffered malaria in their early lives had productivity equal to half that of those who did not.[†]

Although suggesting that malaria may indeed have important economic effects, these studies also raise a caveat about the timing of the economic benefits of controlling the disease. If the main channel through which malaria affects the economy is indeed the human capital of children who are exposed to the disease, then controlling malaria will not result in a more productive labor force (and thus higher output) until the current adult population is replaced with people born after disease controls are introduced—a process that will not start at all for two decades and will not be completed for another four decades.

[*]Acemoglu and Johnson (2007), Gallup and Sachs (2001).
[†]Bleakley (2007), Lucas (2007). Cutler et al. (2007).

The increase in education around the world shown in Table 6.1 represents a large rise in the resources invested in producing human capital. In the United States, for example, government spending on education as a percentage of GDP rose by a factor of five over the course of the 20th century. In many developing countries, rapid population growth has caused a large fraction of the population to be of school age, so the burden of education spending is particularly large.

Education and Wages

Human capital in the form of education has many similarities to physical capital: Both require investment to create, and once created, both have economic value. We previously observed that physical capital earns a return—that is, firms or workers are willing to pay to use a piece of physical capital because doing so allows them to produce more output. If we want to see how productive a piece of physical capital is, we can simply measure how much of a return it commands in the market. In the case of human capital from education, however, calculating returns is more complicated because human capital is always attached to its owner. We cannot separate part of a person's education from the rest of his body and see how much it rents for. This fact makes measuring the return to human capital harder than is the case for physical capital.

To get around this problem, economists infer the returns to human capital from data on people's wages. The fact that people who have higher levels of education earn higher wages can be taken as evidence that the market values their human capital. We define the **return to education** as the increase in wages that a worker would receive if he or she had one more year of schooling. To be specific, suppose that we found the return to a particular year of schooling—say, seventh grade—to be 10%. This finding implies that if we compared two otherwise identical workers, one of whom had a sixth-grade education and one of whom had a seventh-grade education, we would expect the more educated worker to earn 1.10 times as much as the less educated worker.

Figure 6.6 shows an example of the relationship between wages and schooling, based on data drawn from both developing and developed countries. The returns to education on which the chart is based are 13.4% per year for the first four years of schooling (grades 1–4), 10.1% per year for the next four years (grades 5–8), and 6.8% per year for education beyond eight years.[12] (The fact that earlier years of schooling have higher returns is not surprising because these are the years in which the most important skills, notably reading and writing, are taught.) To understand the figure, start with the case of a worker with one year of schooling. Because the rate of return to first grade is 13.4%, such a worker will earn 1.134 times as much as a worker with no schooling. Similarly, a worker with two years of schooling will earn 1.134 times as much as a worker with one year of schooling, or 1.134^2 times as much as a worker with no schooling. Extending this logic, a worker with four years of schooling will earn 1.134^4 times as much as a worker with no schooling. Now consider the case of a worker with five years of schooling. Such a worker would earn 1.101 times as much as a worker with four years of schooling because the rate of return to the fifth year of schooling is 10.1%. This implies that the worker with five years of schooling will earn $1.101 \times 1.134^4 = 1.82$ times as much as a worker with no schooling. Carrying on in this fashion, we can calculate, for a worker with any number of years of schooling, his or her wage relative to that of a worker with no schooling. These are the numbers that are graphed in the figure.

---

[12]Hall and Jones (1999).

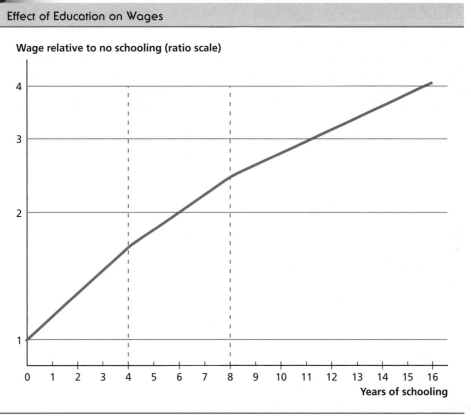

FIGURE 6.6

Effect of Education on Wages

Human Capital's Share of Wages

When we examined physical capital in Chapter 3, we measured physical capital's share of national income, which is the fraction of GDP that is paid to owners of physical capital in return for its use. The number that we calculated for physical capital's share of GDP was one-third. The part of GDP that is not paid to owners of physical capital—that is, the other two-thirds of output—is paid to labor.

Now that we have introduced the idea of human capital, we can investigate how much of the payment to labor represents payment to the human capital that workers possess and how much represents a payment for "raw labor," that is, what workers would have earned if they did not possess any human capital. Unfortunately, when one receives a paycheck, the two items are not listed separately! Our analysis of the relationship between education and wages provides the tools to accomplish this task. (Because we lack similar data on the relationship between health and wages, we focus only on human capital from education.)

Let's start with the case of an individual worker. Suppose that this worker has five years of education. In the discussion of Figure 6.6, we calculated that

THE COLLEGE PREMIUM IN THE UNITED STATES

The rates of return to schooling depicted in Figure 6.6 are averages for a large number of countries. In fact, the rate of return to schooling varies significantly from country to country and within a given country over time. For example, the return to education is generally higher in poor countries than in rich countries, reflecting the fact that skilled workers are scarcer in poor countries and thus earn higher relative wages.

What happens when we apply this same logic to a single country over time? Figure 6.7 shows the educational composition of the labor force in the United States from 1940 to 2008. Clearly there has been a significant rise in the fraction of labor input supplied by educated workers. College-educated workers have become far less scarce over this period. Our logic would imply that there should have been a resulting decline in the return to a college education over this period.

One way to measure the return to a college education is the **college premium,** which is the ratio of the wages of workers with college education to those with a high-school degree. Figure 6.8 depicts the college premium from 1940 to 2008. As the figure shows, the return to a college education

fell in the 1970s. In his book *The Overeducated American* (1976), economist Richard Freeman argued that this decline in the relative wage of college-educated workers was a result of their growing supply and that the college premium would only continue to decline as college degrees became more common. But then, starting around 1980, the college premium began shooting up. By 2008, the college premium was one

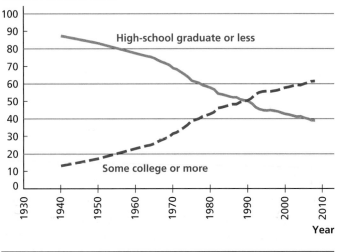

FIGURE 6.7

Share of Hours Worked by Education Level, 1940–2008

Share of Hours Worked

Sources: Autor, Katz, and Krueger (1998), Autor, Katz, and Kearney (2008), Acemoglu and Autor (forthcoming).

the wage of such a worker would be $1.134^4 \times 1.101 = 1.82$ times as large as the wage of an otherwise similar worker who had no education. The extra wage earned as a result of having received five years of schooling is the return to the human capital created by that education. For example, if the worker with no education earned $1.00 and the worker with five years of education earned $1.82, then we could think of $0.82 as being the part of the wage resulting from human capital and the remaining $1.00 as being the part resulting from and a half times as large as it had been in 1940, even though the fraction of hours worked by people with some education beyond high school had risen from 13% to 61%.

The explanation for this phenomenon is that some factor other than the increase in the number of college-educated workers affected the wage premium received by more educated workers. That is, compensating for the increase in the supply of college-educated workers, there was also an increase in demand for them.

The source of this increase in demand for educated workers (which was seen not only in the United States but throughout the developed world) remains a mystery. There are two prominent theories. The first is that the shift resulted from the opening up of economies to international trade. According to this view, because the world as a whole has a far lower percentage of educated workers than the United States, the opening of trade effectively made educated U.S. workers scarcer.

The second theory used to explain the increase in the wage premium for college-educated workers is that technological change over the last several decades has been "skill-biased." In other words, technology has made educated workers relatively more productive than their less-educated peers. Specifically, it is argued, the introduction of computers into the workplace allowed highly educated workers to increase their production greatly. The new technology had little effect on the output of less-educated workers and in some cases replaced them entirely.

FIGURE 6.8

Ratio of College Wages to High-School Wages

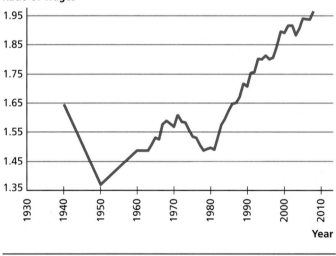

Sources: Autor, Katz, and Krueger (1998), Autor, Katz, and Kearney (2008), Acemoglu and Autor (2010).

raw labor. The fraction of the wages attributed to human capital would be $0.82/1.82 = 45\%$, whereas the other 55% of the wage would be the part attributable to raw labor. For a worker with fewer than five years of education, the fraction of her wage resulting from human capital from education would be smaller than 45%. For a worker with more than five years of education, the fraction would be greater than 45%. Given data on the educational attainment of the entire labor force, we can conduct a similar calculation for each worker and then

> TABLE 6.2

Breakdown of the Population by Schooling and Wages

			Percentage of the Population	
Highest Level of Education	Years of Schooling	Wage Relative to No Schooling	Developing Countries	Advanced Countries
No Schooling	0	1.00	20.8	2.5
Incomplete Primary	4	1.65	10.4	3.4
Complete Primary	8	2.43	18.0	12.3
Incomplete Secondary	10	2.77	19.3	17.8
Complete Secondary	12	3.16	23.2	37.4
Incomplete Higher	14	3.61	2.9	9.9
Complete Higher	16	4.11	5.0	16.6

Source: Barro and Lee (2010).

sum up to find the fraction of wages in the economy as a whole that represents returns to human capital from education.[13]

Table 6.2 shows the data required to perform such calculations for two groups of countries, developing and advanced. The population is divided into seven educational groups, ranging from no schooling through complete higher education. The second column of the table shows the number of years of education associated with each level of schooling. People who have some primary education but have not completed their primary schooling are assumed to have 4 years of schooling, those with incomplete secondary schooling are assumed to have 10 years of education, and those with incomplete higher education are assumed to have 14 years of education. The third column shows the wage of people in each educational category relative to the wage of workers with no schooling. These wages are calculated using the same methodology as in Figure 6.6. The final two columns of the table show the breakdown of the adult population by educational categories for the two groups of countries, developing and advanced.

Figures 6.9 (for developing countries) and 6.10 (for advanced countries) illustrate graphically how the numbers in Table 6.2 are combined to form an estimate of the fraction of wages that represents a return to human capital. The solid line in each figure shows the wages of workers with different levels of education. These wages are all measured relative to the wage of workers with no education. The dashed horizontal lines show the wage of workers with no education. For any given level of education, then, the distance between the solid line and the dashed line is the part of the wage that is the result of human capital. The entire area

---

[13]Pritchett (2001).

FIGURE 6.9

Share of Human Capital in Wages in Developing Countries

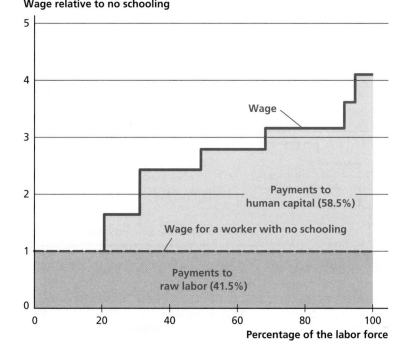

between the solid line and the dashed line then represents the total wages paid to human capital. Similarly, the area underneath the dashed line is the wages paid to raw labor. And the sum of these two areas—that is, the entire area under the solid line—represents the total amount of wages paid in the economy.

Dividing the part of wages as a result of human capital by the total amount of wages paid gives the share of wages paid to human capital. In the developing countries, this share is 59%, and in the advanced countries, it is 68%. Once we know human capital's share of wages, it is simple to calculate human capital's share of national income. Specifically, because wages are two-thirds of national income, we multiply human capital's share of wages by two-thirds. For the developing countries, this calculation yields human capital's share of national income as 40%, and for advanced countries, it yields 45%.

These numbers say that even in the developing world, the share of national income that flows to human capital is greater than the share earned by physical capital, and this is even more so in developed countries. In other words, throughout the world, workers are in effect "capitalists" in the sense that they are earning a return to their own previous investments in human capital. As

FIGURE 6.10

Share of Human Capital in Wages in Advanced Countries

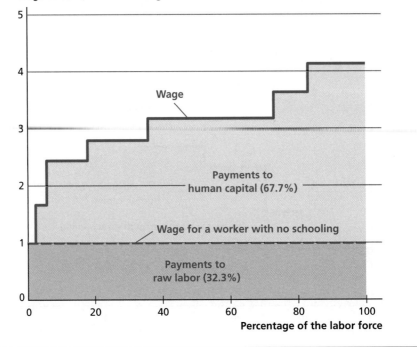

the level of education increases around the world, this mixing of "worker" and "capitalist" will continue. Some economists have argued this rising importance of human capital is what actually drove the decline of class politics in much of the world: When workers and capitalists are one and the same, the idea of class struggle makes less sense.[14]

These data on the share of national income that is earned by human capital can also shed light on some of our previous analysis using the Solow model. The ability of the Solow model to explain cross-country differences in income depends on the value of the exponent on capital in the Cobb-Douglas production function, α. In Chapter 3, we examined data on the share of national income that was earned by physical capital and found that one-third seemed to be a good average, which implied that α should also be 1/3. But in Chapter 4 we found that using a value of $\alpha = 2/3$ made the model fit the data better, in the sense of explaining differences in income between low- and high-population-growth countries, than using a value of $\alpha = 1/3$. Similarly, homework problem 4 in Chapter 3 showed that

---

[14]Galor and Moav (2006).

a larger value of α means that differences in investment rates among countries will have a larger effect on steady-state output per worker.

We can now explain why it is appropriate to use a value of α larger than physical capital's share of national income. The key idea is that we should take a broader view of what is meant by *capital*. If we include both human and physical capital in our definition, then the share of national income earned by capital is higher than two-thirds throughout the world. Thus, if we were to analyze the Solow model as we did in Chapters 3–5, in which the only factors of production were capital and labor, it would indeed be reasonable to assume that capital's share of national income was at least two-thirds and similarly to assume that the exponent on capital in the Cobb-Douglas production function, α, was at least 2/3.

6.3 HOW MUCH OF THE VARIATION IN INCOME ACROSS COUNTRIES DOES EDUCATION EXPLAIN?

Having found big differences in countries' levels of human capital, we now consider the extent to which such differences can explain differences in income per capita among countries. We focus on the effect of human capital as a result of schooling (rather than improved health) because this is the most important measure of human capital and also the only one for which we can get consistent data.

A Quantitative Analysis of the Impact of Schooling Differences among Countries

As shown by the scatter plot in Figure 6.11, the relationship between average years of schooling in a country and the level of income per capita is strong. But this observation alone does not tell us how much of the difference in income is *caused* by the difference in education. After all, it is also true that countries that are richer can afford to spend more on education. Even if education had no effect whatsoever on income, we would expect to see a positive relationship like the one depicted in the figure.

To get a quantitative measure of the effect of education differences on income differences, we conduct an exercise similar to Chapter 3's assessment of the effect of differences in investment rates and Chapters 4 and 5's assessment of the effect of population growth. In this case, we ask how much two countries that differ in their schooling but not in any other aspect of their factor accumulation (such as investment rate or population growth) will differ in their levels of income per capita.

We start with the same Cobb-Douglas production function as we used in Chapters 3–5. However, rather than supposing that each worker supplies one unit of labor, as in previous chapters, we now assume that countries differ in the amount of labor input that each worker supplies. We use the symbol h to denote

> FIGURE 6.11

Average Years of Schooling versus GDP per Capita

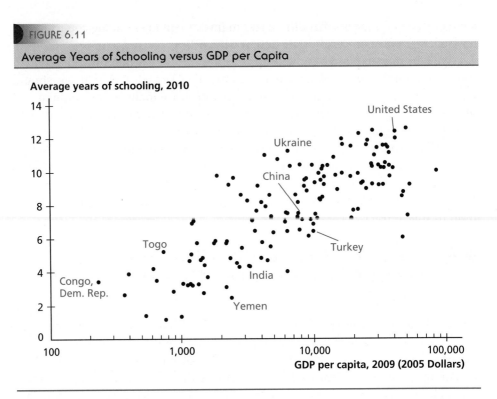

Sources: Barro and Lee (2010), Heston, Summers, and Aten (2011).

the amount of labor input per worker, and we will show how h is related to schooling. We assume that all workers in a country are the same, so that if L is the number of workers, total labor input in the country is hL. Incorporating this notion, the production function becomes

$$Y = AK^{\alpha}(hL)^{1-\alpha},$$

where A is a measure of productivity and K is capital.

It is useful to rewrite the production function by moving the measure of labor input per worker outside of the parentheses:

$$Y = h^{1-\alpha}AK^{\alpha}L^{1-\alpha}.$$

Notice that this is the same as the production function that we used in Chapters 3–5, except that the term A has been replaced by the term $h^{1-\alpha}A$. In Chapter 4 we derived the equation for the steady-state level of output per worker for a country that has an investment rate of γ, a population growth rate of n, and a depreciation rate of δ:

$$y^{ss} = A^{1/(1-\alpha)}\left(\frac{\gamma}{n+\delta}\right)^{\alpha/(1-\alpha)}.$$

Allowing for variation in the amount of labor input per worker, then, we can re-place the term A in this equation with the term $h^{1-\alpha}A$. Thus, the steady-state level of output per worker is.[15]

$$y^{ss} = (h^{1-\alpha}A)^{1/(1-\alpha)}\left(\frac{\gamma}{n+\delta}\right)^{\alpha/(1-\alpha)}$$

$$= h \times \left[A^{1/(1-\alpha)}\left(\frac{\gamma}{n+\delta}\right)^{\alpha/(1-\alpha)}\right].$$

This equation makes clear that the steady-state level of output is directly propor-tional to h, the measure of labor input per worker.

To determine how large a difference in output can be produced by variations in labor input per worker, we consider the case of two countries with the same val-ues for A, γ, and n but different values for h. Calling the countries i and j, we can write the ratio of their steady-state levels of output as:

$$\frac{y_i^{ss}}{y_j^{ss}} = \frac{h_i \times \left[A^{1/(1-\alpha)}\left(\frac{\gamma}{n+\delta}\right)^{\alpha/(1-\alpha)}\right]}{h_j \times \left[A^{1/(1-\alpha)}\left(\frac{\gamma}{n+\delta}\right)^{\alpha/(1-\alpha)}\right]} = \frac{h_i}{h_j}. \tag{6.1}$$

This equation says that if there are no other differences between the countries, the ratio of output per worker in steady state will just be equal to the ratio of labor input per worker. If the value of h is twice as big in Country i as in Country j, then steady-state output per worker will also be twice as big in Country i.

To determine the degree to which schooling differences explain differences in income per capita, we need only to investigate the relationship between our mea-sure of labor input per worker, h, and the amount of schooling in a country. To do so, we can go back to our analysis of the relationship between a person's wages and his level of schooling. We saw that the return to education is 13.4% for the first four years, 10.1% for the next four years, and 6.8% for schooling beyond eighth grade (these are the numbers depicted in Figure 6.6). In other words, a person with one year of schooling earns 1.134 times as much as a person with no school-ing, and so on. One way to interpret this finding is that a person with one year of schooling supplies 1.134 times as many units of labor as a person with no school-ing, and that each of these units of labor is then paid a fixed amount. Under this interpretation, the wage that a worker earns is simply proportional to his amount of labor input, h.

---

[15]Students with more patience can start with the production function and follow the steps of Chapter 4 to get the same result.

We can now use the data on average years of schooling to make quantitative predictions about the importance of educational differences for differences in income per capita among countries. Specifically, for each country we use its average level of schooling to construct a measure of h relative to a country with no schooling. According to Equation 6.1, if two countries differed only in their schooling, then their steady-state levels of income per worker would be proportional to their levels of h.

To be more concrete, let's consider a comparison of two countries. Let Country j have average schooling of 2 years and Country i have average schooling of 12 years. Call h_0 the level of labor input per worker in a country with *no* schooling. The level of labor input in Country j is:

$$h_j = 1.134^2 \times h_0 = 1.29 \times h_0.$$

The level of labor input in Country i is:

$$h_i = 1.134^4 \times 1.101^4 \times 1.068^4 \times h_0 = 3.16 \times h_0.$$

Using Equation 6.1 gives us a ratio of steady-state income in the two countries:

$$\frac{y_i^{ss}}{y_j^{ss}} = \frac{h_i}{h_j} = \frac{3.16 \times h_0}{1.29 \times h_0} = 2.47.$$

Figure 6.12 shows the result of applying this analysis to a large group of countries. We calculate the predicted ratio of income per worker in each country to income per worker in the United States based on the data on average schooling. These predicted values are plotted on the horizontal axis. On the vertical axis is plotted the *actual* ratio of income per worker in each country to income per worker in the United States. If differences in schooling explained all of the differences in income among countries, the data points in Figure 6.12 would lie along a straight line with a slope of 45 degrees; the actual ratio of every country's income per worker to income per worker in the United States would be the same as the ratio predicted by the model. If schooling differences had no ability to explain why income differs among countries, by contrast, no pattern would be visible when we compared the predicted and actual ratios of income.

According to the data plotted in Figure 6.12, variation in education explains some, but not all, of the variation in income per worker among countries. The poorer a country is predicted to be on the basis of its average schooling, the poorer it generally is. There are interesting outliers in the picture. Based on the measure of human capital, Singapore should be the 37th richest country in the sample; in fact it is the 2nd richest. Conversely, China and the Philippines are both predicted to be much richer in comparison to the rest of the world than they actually are. The other interesting aspect of the figure is that differences in income that are

FIGURE 6.12

Predicted versus Actual GDP per Worker

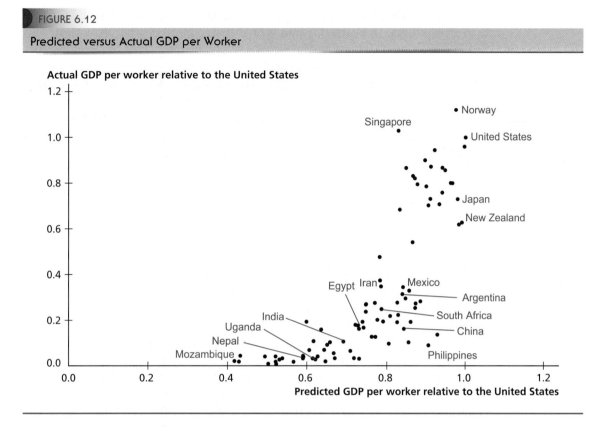

predicted on the basis of schooling data tend to be smaller than actual differences in income among countries. For example, based on schooling differences, the poorest country in the sample should be Mozambique, with income per capita equal to 43% of the United States. In fact, Mozambique has income per capita of only 1.9% of the United States.

It is interesting to compare Figure 6.12 with Figure 3.7, which conducted a similar exercise to look at the effects of differences in investment in physical capital among countries. Most important, in both figures the single factor that is being considered explains some, but not all, of the differences in income among countries. For example, using data on investment in physical capital, Uganda is predicted to have 80% of the income per worker of the United States. Using data on schooling, it is predicted to have 61% of the income per worker of the United States. Combining these two factors, Uganda would have income per worker equal to 0.80 × 0.61 = 49% of the income of the United States. Thus, using information about both human and physical capital takes us closer to fitting the actual data on income per worker, although this exercise still does not get us all the way, because Uganda's income per worker actually equals only 3.3% of U.S. income per worker. Similarly, the errors made in predicting where countries will fall in the world income distribution in the two exercises tend to offset each other. For example, in Figure 6.12, Mexico is predicted to be 7% richer than Iran, whereas in Figure 3.7, Iran is predicted to be 18% richer than Mexico. In fact, the two countries have roughly equal levels of income. These observations suggest that combining data on human and physical capital will allow us to do a better job of predicting which countries will be rich and which will be poor than looking at only one factor at a time. We pursue this project in Chapter 7.

Before we conclude our examination of the ability of human capital to explain differences in income among countries, it is worth considering some of the ways in which our exercise might be missing important aspects of the data. Here we examine two possibilities.

The Quality of Schooling. Our analysis of the impact of educational differences among countries has been based on data on the average number of years of schooling in each country. Implicitly, we have assumed that the quality of schooling does not vary among countries. Is such an assumption warranted?

We can measure the quality of schooling by looking at the inputs into education, such as teachers and textbooks, and the output from education—that is, what students know. In the case of inputs to education, there is clear evidence that richer countries are able to supply more. In 2005, the student-to-teacher ratio in primary schools in high-income countries was 16; among low-income countries it was 42, and in sub-Saharan Africa it was 48. In addition, teachers in developing countries are not as well trained as in the developed world. In Mozambique, for example, 70% of the teachers in grades 1–5 themselves have only seven years of schooling. And in many developing countries, textbooks are so scarce that students have to share them. Finally, as we saw previously in this chapter, widespread health problems in poor countries mean that students are able to learn less in a year of school than are students in rich countries.[16]

With respect to the output of education—what students learn—one measure is how well students perform on tests. Figure 6.13 shows the relationship between income per capita and student performance on a series of standardized math and science tests. Not surprisingly, students in rich countries tend to do better, although there are two interesting exceptions to the general trend: the United States, which has relatively low test scores for a rich country, and China, which has extremely high scores for a poor country (however, unlike most countries, where the tests were administered to a representative sample of students, tests in China were given only in Shanghai, the most economically dynamic city in the country.)

Overall, the evidence suggests that richer countries have not only *more* schooling than poor countries but also *better* schooling. Because of this difference in quality, the measure of human capital that we used—the differences in the number of years of education—will understate the true difference in the level of human capital of workers in those countries.

---

[16]UNESCO (1999, 2000), World Bank (2007a).

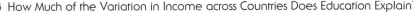

FIGURE 6.13

Student Test Scores versus GDP per Capita

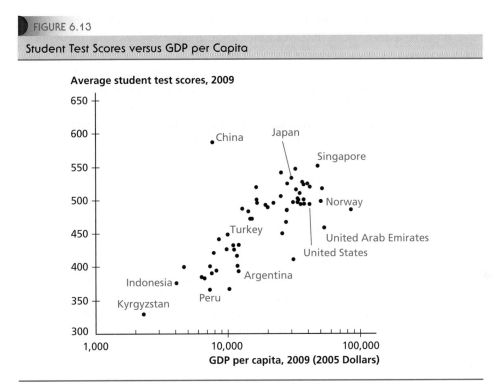

Source: PISA (2009).

Externalities. An important way in which human capital differs from physical capital is in the area of externalities. An **externality** is an incidental effect of some economic activity for which no compensation is provided. In the case of education, many economists believe that there are big externalities: that is, giving one person more education raises not only her own output but the output of those around her as well. For example, educated farmers are generally the first in an area to adopt new technologies (high-yielding seed varieties, new fertilizers, and so on), but these innovations are then copied by less-educated friends and neighbors. Thus, one person's education can raise the production of many. A study in Ethiopia found that the direct benefit received by a person who got an education was smaller than the total externality benefit of education, that is, the sum of benefits received by everyone else in the village. Put another way, more than half of the benefit of an individual's going to school for another year accrued to people other than the person attending school.[17] In developed countries, where education is more widespread, we would not expect externalities of

---

[17]Weir and Knight (2000).

this sort to be so significant. But there are other ways in which education can have positive externalities. For example, a more-educated population is more likely to have an honest and efficient government.

Positive externalities from human capital are one explanation for why governments often get involved in producing human capital (in the form of public education or mandatory schooling). Left on their own, people do not take into account the full social benefit of an education when they decide how much education to obtain for themselves or their children, so the amount they choose will be lower than what would be socially optimal.

The existence of externalities from education affects our calculation of the importance of human capital for explaining income differences among countries. In assessing the relationship between schooling and human capital, we looked only at the *private* return to education. That is, our starting point was the amount that a year of education raises an individual's wages. But if much of the contribution of an individual's human capital toward national income is not reflected in that person's own wages, then this private return to education will understate the true increase in human capital as a result of an extra year of schooling. If we were to redo our calculations, assuming a higher return to education, we would find that human capital played a larger role in explaining differences in income among countries.

6.4 CONCLUSION

In this chapter we have explored the improvements in the quality of labor that economists group together under the name *human capital*. In many ways, the accumulation of human capital and the impact of human capital on production are closely analogous to the situation with physical capital. Spending on education, which produces human capital, is similar to the investment spending that produces physical capital. Both human and physical capital are inputs into production—indeed, their shares of national income are roughly equal. Finally, differences in the accumulation of human capital among countries seem to be part of the explanation for why some countries are rich and some poor, just as was the case with the accumulation of physical capital.

Although human and physical capital have many similarities, there are also important differences between the two. The only reason for investing in physical capital is economic: Were it not for the returns that physical capital earns, no one would want to own any. By contrast, people value human capital in the form of health primarily for noneconomic reasons. The fact that being in good health makes a person more productive is of secondary importance when we make decisions about our own or our children's health. Decisions to invest in human capital through education are economic but only partly so. People value education both as a means toward higher income and as a way of enriching their intellectual and spiritual lives.

HUMAN PERFECTABILITY AND THE GROWTH SLOWDOWN

As this chapter has stressed, an important difference between human capital and physical capital is that the former is "installed" in its owner whereas the latter exists independently of its owner. As a consequence, there is no limit on the amount of physical capital that a single person can own. But for human capital, such a limit does exist. A person can only be so healthy or have so much education. Thus, there is no reason that the amount of physical capital each worker has to work with will not continue to grow over the next century as quickly as it has grown over the last, but we might worry that the limits on human capital accumulation are coming within sight.

In the case of health, the last century has seen great improvements, as measured by height and life expectancy, in the most developed countries. But most scholars agree that these improvements will not continue into the future. In the richest countries, almost everyone is now well enough nourished to attain his or her biological maximum height. Life expectancy in the United States rose from 51 years in 1900 to 77 years in 2000. It is unlikely to rise by an equal amount (to 103 years!) over the next century. The great health triumphs of the late 19th and 20th centuries—improvements

in sanitation, widespread vaccination, and the introduction of antibiotics—are unlikely to be matched in the future.

With respect to education, too, there is good reason to believe that the rate at which human capital is being accumulated in the richest countries will slow down in the future. The average level of education in the advanced countries increased by 1.8 years over the period 1960–1980 but by only 0.9 years over the period 1980–2000. Even without this evidence of a slowdown, one would suspect that education cannot go on increasing forever—if for no other reason, people have to work sometime before they die of old age.

For these reasons, then, the rise in human capital, which has been one of the major sources of economic growth over the last century, will contribute less to growth over the next century. This change will not bring an end to economic growth itself, however, because other sources of growth, such as technological change (discussed in Chapters 8 and 9), will remain in place. But the decline in the growth of human capital could well mean a decline in the overall growth rate.*

*Jones (2002).

KEY TERMS

| human capital **150** | college premium **164** | externality **175** |
| return to education **162** | | |

QUESTIONS FOR REVIEW

1. In what ways is human capital similar to physical capital? In what ways are the two different?

2. Why is health considered an element of human capital? How does human capital in the form of health differ from human capital in the form of education?

3. What does it mean to say that health and income are simultaneously determined?

4. What is the return to education?

5. How can we use data on the return to education to estimate how differences in education among countries contribute to differences in income among countries?

6. Why and how might education have externality effects?

PROBLEMS

1. Suppose that an effective vaccine against malaria were invented. Using Figure 6.3, describe the vaccine's effect on both health and income.

2. Country A and Country B differ in their intrinsic health environments. Specifically, for a given level of income per capita, workers in Country A will be healthier than workers in Country B. Suppose we observe that the two countries have the same level of income per capita, but people in Country A are healthier than people in Country B. What can we conclude about the aspects of production *not* related to health in the two countries? Explain, using a diagram.

3. In our discussion of education and wages, we assumed that education raises a worker's wage by increasing the amount of output he or she can produce. Suppose that we instead believe that more-educated workers earn higher wages for reasons that have nothing to do with their productivity. For example, suppose that educated and uneducated workers both produce the same amount of output, but that educated workers earn more because they can steal part of what the uneducated produce. If this were true, how would it affect the analysis of education differences among countries in Section 6.3?

4. What fraction of wages is the result of human capital for a worker who has nine years of education?

5. The highest levels of education among the adult (age 25 and over) population in the United States in 2010 were no schooling, 0.4%; partial primary, 0.8%; complete primary, 1.9%; incomplete secondary, 6.7%; complete secondary, 36.2%; incomplete higher, 22.4%; and complete higher, 31.6%. Using the method on p. 162, calculate the fraction of wages that represented return to human capital.

6. Suppose that we are comparing two countries, i and j, that are similar in every respect except the education of their population. In Country i, all adults have 10 years of schooling. In Country j, all adults have 4 years of schooling. Calculate the ratio of output per worker in steady state in the two countries.

7. In a certain country, everyone in the labor force in the year 2000 had 12 years of education. In 1900 everyone in the labor force had 2 years of education. What was the average *annual* growth in income per worker that was due to the increase in education?

8. Recall the discussion of education externalities in Section 6.3. Can you think of an externality (positive or negative) associated with health?

9. Countries A and B have the same rates of investment, population growth, and depreciation. They also have the same levels of income per capita. Country A has a higher rate of growth than does Country B. According to the Solow model, which country has higher investment in human capital? Explain your answer.

For additional exploration and practice using the Online Data Plotter and data sets, please visit http://www.pearsonhighered.com/weil/.

MEASURING PRODUCTIVITY

Imagine a contest in which two students are each presented with identical boxes full of tools and big piles of lumber. The students have eight hours to build as many widgets as they can. At the end of the contest, one student has built 10 widgets and the other 20. What explains the difference? Clearly it was not in the tools that the students had at their disposal because these were identical. Rather, the difference was in how effectively they used their tools. This is the idea of productivity.

Eliminate all other factors, and the one which remains must be the truth.

— Sherlock Holmes

In the widget-making contest, the difference in productivity might be the result of one student's superior knowledge of carpentry, his or her better way of organizing production, or simply his or her higher level of energy. In applying this idea to countries, the relevant tools are the factors of production that we have studied in preceding chapters. **Productivity** is the effectiveness with which factors of production are converted into output.

In the last four chapters we have looked at the accumulation of factors of production. We have seen that countries vary in their rates of investment in physical capital and in their populations' levels of human capital. We have also seen that countries vary in their rates of population growth, which is relevant for factor accumulation because of capital dilution. In each chapter, as we examined a particular aspect of factor accumulation, we related it to the question of why countries differ in their levels of income per capita. For example, we saw that, theoretically, a country with a lower rate of investment in physical capital should be poorer, and we saw empirically that indeed, such countries tend to be poorer than countries with high rates of investment. Similarly, countries with low rates of population growth tend to be richer than countries with high population growth, and countries with high levels of education tend to be richer than countries with less education. Each of these aspects of factor accumulation, in isolation, can explain some of the variation in income per capita among countries.

Given that each aspect of factor accumulation accounts for *some* of the variation in output per capita among countries, a question naturally arises: Taken together, do the different aspects of factor accumulation explain *all* of the variation among countries? The answer to this question, as we will see in this chapter, is no.

179

Specifically, we will find that countries differ in their output not only because they accumulate different quantities of factors of production, but also because they vary in the effectiveness with which they combine these factors of production to produce output—that is, in their productivity. Thus, to explain differences in income among countries, we must study productivity as well as factor accumulation.

We begin the chapter by discussing the nature of productivity and how it is measured. We then address four questions about productivity:

1. How much does productivity differ among countries?

2. How much of the variation in income per capita among countries is explained by productivity differences?

3. How much does productivity *growth* differ among countries?

4. How much of the variation in growth rates among countries is explained by variation in productivity growth, and how much by variation in factor accumulation?

To answer these questions, we use two techniques, called *development accounting* and *growth accounting*. Before introducing these techniques, we review the role of productivity in the production function.

7.1 PRODUCTIVITY IN THE PRODUCTION FUNCTION

Chapter 2 introduced the idea of a *production function*, which relates the quantities of factors of production in an economy and the level of output produced. In subsequent chapters, we considered specific factors of production, such as physical capital and human capital. As we begin our analysis of productivity, however, it is useful to go back to thinking about factors of production in general rather than in specific.

Figure 7.1 repeats an example of a production function we first encountered in Chapter 2, in which we show factors of production per worker on the horizontal axis and the quantity of output per worker on the vertical axis. The figure considers the case of two countries, labeled 1 and 2. We observe that output per worker in Country 1, designated y_1, is greater than output per worker in Country 2, designated y_2. Each of the three panels of the figure shows a possible explanation for why the two countries differ in output per worker. In panel (a), the two countries have the same production function, but Country 1 has a higher level of factors of production per worker, and thus higher output. In panel (b), the two countries have the same quantities of factors of production, but Country 1 is more productive—that is, its production function is above that for Country 2. Panel (c) makes the point that a difference in output per worker does not have to be the result of either factor accumulation or productivity alone; it could result from both. In this panel, Country 1 has both a better production function and more factors of production than Country 2.

FIGURE 7.1

Possible Sources of Differences in Output per Worker

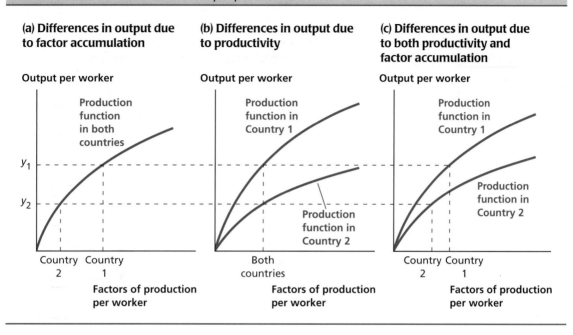

(a) Differences in output due to factor accumulation

(b) Differences in output due to productivity

(c) Differences in output due to both productivity and factor accumulation

With Figure 7.1 as background, we can now bring in data from real countries. The difference between looking at Figure 7.1 and looking at real-world data is that, in the real world, we do not necessarily see what the production function looks like. Instead, we see only data on output and factor accumulation. Our task is to infer something about productivity from these data.

Figure 7.2 shows some cases where it is—or is not—possible to determine which of two countries has higher productivity based only on these data. Panel (a) of the figure shows a case where two countries have the same level of factor accumulation, but Country 1 has a higher level of output. In this case, we can infer that Country 1 has a higher level of productivity than Country 2 because our definition of productivity is the effectiveness with which factors of production are converted into output. The second panel of the figure looks at a case in which two countries have the same level of output but different levels of factor accumulation. Specifically, Country 1 has greater factor accumulation than Country 2. In this case, we can infer that Country 2 must have higher productivity. Because more factors of production will always lead to higher output, if Country 2 had the same quantity of factors of production as Country 1, it clearly would produce more output per worker.

The third panel of Figure 7.2 presents a more complicated case. Here Country 1 has both higher output and more factors of production than Country 2. In this

FIGURE 7.2

Inferring Productivity from Data on Output and Factor Accumulation

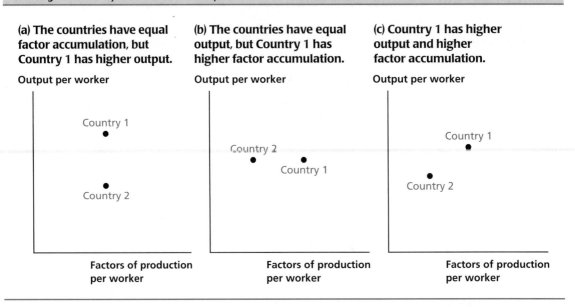

(a) The countries have equal factor accumulation, but Country 1 has higher output.

Output per worker

Country 1

Country 2

Factors of production per worker

(b) The countries have equal output, but Country 1 has higher factor accumulation.

Output per worker

Country 2

Country 1

Factors of production per worker

(c) Country 1 has higher output and higher factor accumulation.

Output per worker

Country 1

Country 2

Factors of production per worker

case, without more information, we cannot say which country has higher productivity. For example, the two countries might have equal productivity, as in Figure 7.1(a), or Country 1 might have higher productivity, as in Figure 7.1(c). It is even possible that Country 2 has higher productivity. To make progress in a case like this—which unfortunately corresponds to most of the data we see in the real world—we must bring to bear more information about the production function, as we now proceed to do.

7.2 DIFFERENCES IN THE LEVEL OF PRODUCTIVITY AMONG COUNTRIES

The discussion in Section 7.1 shows that comparing productivity among countries is problematic if the only information at our disposal is the countries' levels of output and factor accumulation. In this section we solve this problem by using the information about production functions that we developed in Chapters 3–6. Specifically, we will be able to determine which of two countries has higher productivity even in a case like the one illustrated in panel (c) of Figure 7.2, where one country has both higher output and higher factor accumulation than the other. We will also be able to make two other improvements over the graphical approach of Figure 7.2. First, we will be able to go beyond the general case in which we measure factors of production on the horizontal axis and instead use real data on physical capital and human capital. Second, we will go beyond the question of which country has higher productivity and examine *by how much* productivity differs. In other words, we will be able to look *quantitatively* at productivity gaps among countries. With quantitative measures of productivity differences, we will also be able to determine how much of the variation among countries' income per capita is explained by the variations in productivity and how much is explained by the accumulation of factors of production.

Measuring Productivity Differences among Countries

In Chapter 6, we examined the production function incorporating both human capital and physical capital. The production function is:

$$Y = AK^\alpha(hL)^{1-\alpha},$$

where Y is total output, A is a measure of productivity, K is the quantity of physical capital, L is the number of workers, h is the quantity of human capital per worker, and α is a number between zero and one. Dividing both sides of this equation by L gives the production function in per-worker terms:

$$y = Ak^\alpha h^{1-\alpha},$$

where y is output per worker and k is physical capital per worker.

Physical capital and human capital are the two factors of production used as inputs in this production function. It is useful to combine them into a single aggregate called "factors of production," which is then used in producing output. In other words, we can write:

$$\text{factors of production} = k^\alpha h^{1-\alpha}.$$

Then we can think of the production function as being:

$$\text{output} = \text{productivity} \times \text{factors of production}.$$

To compare productivity in two countries, we start by writing the production function separately for each country. For example, if the two countries we are looking at are called Country 1 and Country 2, then their production functions are:

$$y_1 = A_1 k_1^\alpha h_1^{1-\alpha},$$

and

$$y_2 = A_2 k_2^\alpha h_2^{1-\alpha}.$$

Stating our comparison as a ratio, we divide the first equation by the second:

$$\frac{y_1}{y_2} = \left(\frac{A_1}{A_2}\right)\left(\frac{k_1^\alpha h_1^{1-\alpha}}{k_2^\alpha h_2^{1-\alpha}}\right). \tag{7.1}$$

We can interpret this expression as follows. The term on the left side of the equation is the ratio of output per worker in Country 1 to output per worker in Country 2. The first term on the right side is the ratio of productivity in Country 1 to productivity in Country 2. If the two countries were identical in their factor accumulation—that is, if they had equal levels of human and physical capital—then the ratio of output in the two countries would be the same as this ratio of productivity. The second term on the right side of the equation is the ratio of inputs from factors of production. We can think of this term as representing what the ratio of output in Country 1 to output in Country 2 would be if the two countries had the same level of productivity—that is, if the only difference in their output were the result of differences in factor accumulation. The actual ratio of income in the two countries will be the product of the ratio of productivity in the two countries and the ratio of factor accumulation in the two countries:

ratio of output = ratio of productivity × ratio of factors of production.

This equation makes concrete the idea in Section 7.1 that countries can differ in their levels of output because of differences in productivity, factor accumulation, or both.

The equation also gives us a method for measuring productivity differences. Two of the three pieces of this equation are directly observable: output and factor accumulation in the various countries. We cannot measure productivity directly, but we can use the equation to measure it indirectly. We need only to rearrange the equation this way:

ratio of productivity = ratio of output/ratio of factors of production.

Now the two terms on the right side are measurable. For example, suppose we observe that two countries differ in their output by a factor of six (that is, the ratio of output in the richer country to output in the poorer country is six). If we know that they differ in their factor accumulation by a factor of two, then we can use the preceding equation to conclude that they differ in their productivity by a factor of three.

This expression says that, in determining the productivity difference between two countries, we look at their levels of output and levels of factor accumulation. The larger the ratio of output in the two countries, the larger a productivity gap we would infer. Conversely, the larger the gap in the accumulation of factors, the *smaller* the productivity gap we would infer. In other words, the larger the difference in output between two countries that is explained by differences in factor accumulation, the less reason there is to conclude that a difference in productivity is the source of differences in income between the two countries.

We similarly rearrange Equation 7.1 to get an expression that shows how the ratio of productivity in two countries depends on the ratio of output and the quantities of physical and human capital:

$$\frac{A_1}{A_2} = \frac{\left(\dfrac{y_1}{y_2}\right)}{\left(\dfrac{k_1^{\alpha} h_1^{1-\alpha}}{k_2^{\alpha} h_2^{1-\alpha}}\right)} . \tag{7.2}$$

This technique for breaking down differences in income into the part that is accounted for by differences in productivity and the part accounted for by differences in factor accumulation is called **development accounting.**

Before examining real data, let's consider a simple example of how development accounting can be used to analyze productivity differences among countries. Table 7.1 presents data on the relative levels of output and factor accumulation in Country 1 and Country 2. Country 1's output per worker is 24 times as large as that of Country 2, its capital per worker is 27 times as large, and its human capital per worker is 8 times as large. Substituting these numbers in Equation 7.2 and using our standard value of $\alpha = 1/3$, we get:

$$\frac{A_1}{A_2} = \frac{\left(\dfrac{24}{1}\right)}{\left(\dfrac{27^{1/3} \times 8^{2/3}}{1^{1/3} \times 1^{2/3}}\right)} = \frac{24}{\left(\dfrac{3 \times 4}{1}\right)} = 2.$$

In other words, productivity in Country 1 is twice as high as productivity in Country 2.

We now conduct this same exercise using real data on y, k, and h. Table 7.2 presents the results for a few representative countries (the data are for 2009). The second column shows the ratio of output per worker in each country to output per worker in the United States. The third and fourth columns give values of physical and human capital, again relative to the United States. The fifth column calculates the value of combined factors of production, that is, $k^{1/3}h^{2/3}$. Finally, the last column shows the value of productivity, A, relative to the United States.

▶ TABLE 7.1

Data Used to Analyze Productivity in Country 1 and Country 2

	Output per Worker, y	Physical Capital per Worker, k	Human Capital per Worker, h
Country 1	24	27	8
Country 2	1	1	1

▶ TABLE 7.2

Development Accounting					
Country	Output per Worker, y	Physical Capital per Worker, k	Human Capital per Worker, h	Factors of Production, $k^{1/3}h^{2/3}$	Productivity, A
United States	1.00	1.00	1.00	1.00	1.00
Norway	1.12	1.32	0.98	1.08	1.04
United Kingdom	0.82	0.68	0.87	0.80	1.03
Canada	0.80	0.81	0.96	0.91	0.88
Japan	0.73	1.16	0.98	1.04	0.70
South Korea	0.62	0.92	0.98	0.96	0.64
Turkey	0.37	0.28	0.78	0.55	0.68
Mexico	0.35	0.33	0.84	0.61	0.56
Brazil	0.20	0.19	0.78	0.48	0.42
India	0.10	0.089	0.66	0.34	0.31
Kenya	0.032	0.022	0.73	0.23	0.14
Malawi	0.018	0.029	0.57	0.21	0.087

Sources: Output per worker: Heston, Summers, and Aten (2011); physical capital: author's calculations; human capital: Barro and Lee (2010). The data set used here and in Section 7.3 is composed of data for 90 countries for which consistent data are available for 1975 and 2009.

The table tells a number of interesting stories. First, there are surprisingly large differences in the level of productivity, A, among countries. For example, the value of A in South Korea is only 64% of the value in the United States. In other words, if the United States and South Korea had the same levels of physical capital and human capital per worker, then the United States would produce 1.5 times as much output per worker. Moving farther down the table, we find even larger productivity differences: a given amount of human capital and physical capital would produce more than three times as much in the United States as in India and seven times as much in the United States as in Kenya.

The table also captures interesting variations in countries' relative strengths and weaknesses. For example, Japan has a significantly higher level of physical capital per worker and almost the same level of human capital per worker as the United States. In terms of factor accumulation, Japan is better off. But comparing productivity, we find that Japan is at only 70% of the U.S. level and thus is significantly poorer than the United States. Canada and the United Kingdom have almost equal levels of output per worker, but although Canada relies heavily on factor accumulation, the United Kingdom has higher productivity. Kenya and Malawi have roughly equal levels of factor accumulation, but Kenya is 61% more productive and thus has much higher income per capita.

The large productivity differences that this procedure measures are one of the most important findings of economists studying growth in recent years.[1] Much of the rest of this book will be devoted to thinking about these productivity differences: both how they determine income differences among countries and where the productivity differences themselves come from. Thus, before going on, it is worth thinking about whether there are any problems in the measurements themselves. That is, are we confident that the productivity differences derived by this procedure are correct?

If there is a deficiency with these productivity measures, it probably results from problems in measuring factors of production. The reason is simple: Productivity is the part of differences in output that is "left over" when differences in factors of production are accounted for. If we do not properly measure factors of production, then we will not properly account for their effect on differences in income among countries. As a result, the differences in output that are attributed to productivity also will be incorrect.

Different problems arise in the measurement of physical and human capital. The problems with measuring physical capital are discussed in the box "Problems with Measuring Capital." In the case of human capital, we considered some of the measurement problems in Chapter 6. As in that chapter, the calculations here use data on the number of years of education of adults to construct a measure of the amount of human capital per worker in each country. We do not measure the *quality* of schooling. Countries with higher average levels of schooling also tend to have better schools. As a result, the measure of h that we use understates the variation in the amount of human capital per worker—that is, differences in human capital between rich and poor countries are actually larger than those that we measure. Because we understate the variation in human capital, we understate the role of factor accumulation in explaining output differences and overstate the role of productivity differences.

How serious are these problems in measuring factors of production and the resulting problems in measuring productivity? Economists differ in their answers, but almost all would agree that despite these measurement problems, the bottom-line conclusion from this analysis remains unchanged: Productivity differences among countries are very large.

The Contribution of Productivity to Income Differences among Countries

Having derived a measure of productivity for different countries, we can now ask how much variations in productivity contribute to variations in income. The answer to this question will also tell us what role variations in factor accumulation play in these income variations.

---

[1]Hall and Jones (1999), Klenow and Rodriguez-Clare (1997).

Economist Lant Pritchett begins his analysis of the problems of measuring physical capital with a joke:

> While on a foreign trip, Mr. A, a government official, visits the penthouse apartment of his friend Mr. B, a bureaucrat of a poor country. After admiring the fine residence and furnishings, A says: "Be honest B, I know that with your official salary you cannot possibly afford this. What gives?" Taking his friend to the window, B replies, "See that superhighway running through town? 10 percent." Some time later B has the occasion to visit the even poorer country of his friend A and finds himself in an even larger and more luxuriously appointed penthouse apartment. Says B, "I know your official salary must be even lower than mine, yet your house is much nicer. What gives?" Taking his friend to the window, A points out and says, "See that superhighway running out into the jungle?" After straining his eyes for a minute B replies, "But there is no highway out there." "Exactly," says A with a wink, "100 percent."

The joke, observes Pritchett, contains more than a nugget of truth: Much of the money that is allegedly spent on investment in new capital is diverted along the way into other uses. In one infamous project, the Ajaokuta steel mill in Nigeria, half of the total "investment" of $4 billion was siphoned off into the pockets of various officials. Even in cases in which money meant for investment is not stolen, it is often wasted, as in the example of a nuclear power plant built in the Philippines under the government of Ferdinand Marcos. Although the price tag was $2 billion, the plant never produced any electricity.

In many developing countries, the diversion of investment funds away from the actual building of new capital is particularly severe. The reasons are twofold. First, a large fraction of investment in these countries is done by governments, which tend to be less efficient than the private sector in converting investment spending into capital. Second, both governments and private-sector corporations in many developing countries are corrupt.

Pritchett's observations on the measurement of capital raise several important issues for economists studying growth. Most directly, the waste of investment spending may itself be an important reason poor countries are poor. We return to this issue in Chapter 12, in which we study the role of government more extensively.

With respect to the current chapter, the relevance of Pritchett's argument is that it implies that our measures of productivity may be wrong. As we have seen, measuring productivity requires a measure of the stock of physical capital. But if Pritchett is right, in many countries, the quantity of investment that economists *think* is taking place is larger than what is actually taking place. Therefore, the quantity of capital that economists think is present is much larger than what is actually there.

Because this kind of overstatement of the capital stock is likely to be a bigger problem in poor countries than in rich countries, the *actual* gap between capital stocks in rich and poor countries is larger than the gap in capital stocks *estimated* by economists. This discrepancy in turn implies that actual gaps in productivity between rich and poor countries are smaller than economists have estimated because the productivity gap is what is required to explain differences in output that are not explained by accumulation of factors such as capital.

How severe is the problem in the actual data? Pritchett estimates that over the period 1960–1987, the true growth rate of capital in the Middle East, North Africa, sub-Saharan Africa, and South Asia was less than half the growth rate one would believe from looking at official statistics. The actual level of the capital stock at the end of the period ranged between 57% and 75% of the officially measured capital stock.[*]

*Pritchett (2000).

As we saw previously, we can break down the difference in income between any two countries into a part that is a result of productivity and a part that is a result of factor accumulation. Stated mathematically,

ratio of output = ratio of productivity × ratio of factor accumulation.

In the numerical example in the last section, output in Country 1 is 24 times as large as output in Country 2, productivity in Country 1 is 2 times as large as productivity in Country 2, and factor accumulation in Country 1 is 12 times as large as in Country 2. In this theoretical example, factor accumulation clearly explains more of the gap in income between the two countries than productivity does.

What happens when we look at data from real countries? Which is more important in explaining income differences—factor accumulation or productivity? To answer this question, we can calculate the two terms on the right side of the previous equation for every country for which we have data. In each case, we will compare the country with the United States. The results are shown in Figures 7.3 and 7.4.

Figure 7.3 presents data on factor accumulation. All the countries for which there are data are divided into five groups, ranging from poorest to richest in terms of income per capita. For each group, we then calculate the average level of factors of production relative to the United States. In the richest group of countries (which includes the United States), the average level of factor accumulation is equal to 94% of the U.S. level; in the poorest group of countries, factor accumulation equals only 19% of the U.S. level.

▶ FIGURE 7.3

Role of Factors of Production in Determining Output per Worker, 2009

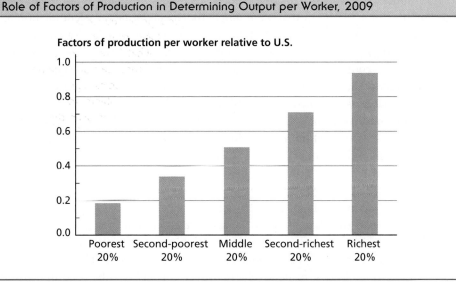

Factors of production per worker relative to U.S.

For sources, see Table 7.2.

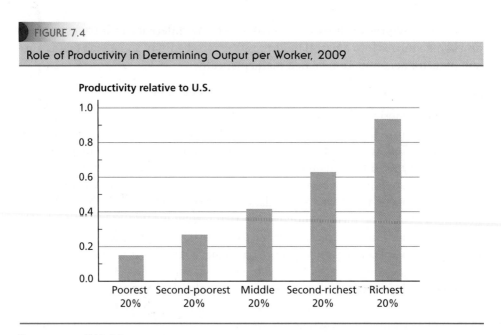

FIGURE 7.4

Role of Productivity in Determining Output per Worker, 2009

Productivity relative to U.S.

For sources, see Table 7.2.

Figure 7.4 shows the same analysis for productivity. For the same five groups of countries, the figure graphs the average level of productivity relative to the United States. In the richest group of countries, productivity averages 94% of the U.S. level; in the poorest group of countries, productivity averages 15% of the U.S. level.

To understand how the data in Figures 7.3 and 7.4 explain differences in output among countries, recall that we *multiply* the effects of factor accumulation and productivity to determine a country's output per worker. Consider, for example, the typical country in the middle-income group. According to Figure 7.3, factor accumulation in such a country equals 51% of the U.S. level. In other words, if such a country had productivity that equaled productivity in the United States, its income would be only 51% as large as U.S. income. According to Figure 7.4, the productivity of countries in this middle-income group is in fact only 41% of the U.S. level. The combined effect of factor accumulation and productivity is that countries in this group have output per worker that is only 21% (i.e., 0.51 × 0.41) of the U.S. level.

Looking at Figures 7.3 and 7.4 together, we can draw a number of interesting conclusions. What is most striking is how similar the two figures are. As we survey the set of countries from poor to rich, the levels of factor accumulation and productivity seem to rise at roughly the same rate. Among the richest one-fifth of countries, productivity and factor accumulation are of almost equal importance in explaining the gap in income relative to the United States: They are 94% and 93% of the United States, respectively. However, for all the other country groups, productivity is slightly more important than factor accumulation. For example, among the poorest countries, factors of production are on average 19% of the U.S. level, whereas their productivity is only 15% of the U.S. level. The mathematical box "The Relative Importance of Productivity and Factor Accumulation" performs a more formal analysis of these data to reach a similar conclusion. Specifically, 47% of the variation in output per worker among countries is a result of factor accumulation, and 53% is a result of productivity.

MATHEMATICAL EXTENSION

The Relative Importance of Productivity and Factor Accumulation

Define

R_i^y = the ratio of output per worker in Country i to output per worker in the United States

R_i^p = the ratio of productivity in Country i to productivity in the United States

R_i^f = the ratio of factor accumulation in Country i to factor accumulation in the United States

The relationship among these three variables, as derived in the text, is:

$$R_i^y = R_i^p \times R_i^f.$$

Taking logarithms of this equation, we get:

$$\ln(R_i^y) = \ln(R_i^p) + \ln(R_i^f).$$

If we look across a large sample of countries, we can use this equation to decompose the variance of $\ln(R_i^y)$ as follows:

$$\text{Var}(\ln(R_i^y)) = \text{Var}(\ln(R_i^p)) + \text{Var}(\ln(R_i^f)) + 2\,\text{Cov}(\ln(R_i^p), \ln(R_i^f)).$$

For the countries analyzed in Figures 7.3 and 7.4, the values of these terms are:

$\text{Var}(\ln(R_i^y)) = 1.64$

$\text{Var}(\ln(R_i^p)) = 0.49$

$\text{Var}(\ln(R_i^f)) = 0.38$

$\text{Cov}(\ln(R_i^p), \ln(R_i^f)) = 0.39$

In dividing the responsibility for variations in income between the two sources (factor accumulation and productivity), we follow the common practice of evenly splitting the covariance term. Thus:

$$\frac{\text{fraction of income variance}}{\text{due to productivity}} = \frac{\text{Var}(\ln(R_i^p)) + \text{Cov}(\ln(R_i^p), \ln(R_i^f))}{\text{Var}(\ln(R_i^y))},$$

(continued)

MATHEMATICAL EXTENSION (*CONTINUED*)

The Relative Importance of Productivity and Factor Accumulation

$$\text{fraction of income variance due to factor accumulation} = \frac{\text{Var}(\ln(R_i^f)) + \text{Cov}(\ln(R_i^p), \ln(R_i^f))}{\text{Var}(\ln(R_i^y))}.$$

Substituting the values for our data, we find that productivity is responsible for 53% of the variation in income per capita and that factor accumulation is responsible for 47%.

7.3 DIFFERENCES IN THE GROWTH RATE OF PRODUCTIVITY AMONG COUNTRIES

Using development accounting, we aimed to determine what explains differences in the level of income per capita among countries. We found that differences in both productivity and factor accumulation played a role, with factor accumulation being the more important of the two. We now study how countries' income grows over time, once again investigating the relative importance of productivity and factor accumulation. Specifically, we examine how much of a country's income growth is accounted for by growth in productivity and how much by growth in the quantity of factors of production, using a technique called *growth accounting*.

Having derived this result, we then ask two follow-up questions. First, how much income growth *on average* is accounted for by productivity growth, and how much by increases in factors of production? Second, when we look at variation in growth rates among countries (i.e., at fast-growing versus slow-growing countries), how much of this variation is explained by variation in productivity growth, and how much by variation in growth in the quantity of factors of production?

Measuring Countries' Productivity Growth

We once again start with the Cobb-Douglas production function, in per worker terms:

$$y = Ak^\alpha h^{1-\alpha}.$$

As in Section 7.2, we can interpret this equation as saying that:

$$\text{output} = \text{productivity} \times \text{factors of production},$$

where the term $k^{\alpha}h^{1-\alpha}$ is a composite of the two factors of production. We now transform this equation into an equation relating the growth rates of output, productivity, and factors of production:[2]

$$\text{growth rate of output} = \text{growth rate of productivity}$$
$$+ \text{ growth rate of factors of production.}$$

Recall that output and factors of production are measurable but that productivity is derived only by measuring other things. Rearranging the preceding equation gives:

$$\text{growth rate of productivity} = \text{growth rate of output}$$
$$- \text{ growth rate of factors of production.}$$

Using our notation of putting a hat ($\wedge$) on top of a variable to indicate its growth rate, the growth rate of productivity is $\hat{A}$, and the growth rate of output is $\hat{y}$. Using calculus, we can show that the growth rate of the composite factors of production is given by $\alpha\hat{k} + (1 - \alpha)\hat{h}$.[3] Thus, we can rewrite the preceding equation as:

$$\hat{A} = \hat{y} - \alpha\hat{k} - (1 - \alpha)\hat{h}.$$

This equation shows how, given data on a country's growth rates of output, physical capital, and human capital, we can measure its growth rate of productivity. This technique for deriving the growth rate of productivity is called **growth accounting.**

As with our analysis using development accounting, we begin with a theoretical example in which the numbers work out easily. The first two rows of Table 7.3

TABLE 7.3

Data for Calculating Productivity Growth in Erewhon

	Output per Worker, y	Physical Capital per Worker, k	Human Capital per Worker, h
Erewhon in 1975	1	20	5
Erewhon in 2010	4	40	10
Annual Growth Rate	4%	2%	2%

---

[2]To accomplish this transformation, we apply the rule that if $Z = X \times Y$, then $\hat{Z} = \hat{X} + \hat{Y}$; where a hat ($\wedge$) indicates a variable's growth rate.

[3]Mathematical Note: Define X as the composite factors of production:

$$X = k^{\alpha}h^{1-\alpha}.$$

Taking natural logarithms of this equation,

$$\ln(X) = \alpha \times \ln(k) + (1 - \alpha) \times \ln(h).$$

Differentiating with respect to time yields

$$\hat{X} = \alpha\hat{k} + (1 - \alpha)\hat{h}.$$

show data on the levels of output, physical capital, and human capital per worker in the country of Erewhon in 1975 and 2010. The first step in calculating productivity growth in Erewhon is to calculate the growth rates of each of these quantities over the 35-year period we are examining. The results of this calculation appear in the bottom row of the table. For example, the growth rate of output is calculated as:

$$\text{growth rate of output} = \left(\frac{\text{output in 2010}}{\text{output in 1975}}\right)^{1/35} - 1 = 4^{1/35} - 1 = 0.04 = 4\%.$$

Substituting the numbers for annual growth rates into our formula and using a value of 1/3 for α gives:

$$\hat{A} = 0.04 - \frac{1}{3} \times 0.02 - \frac{2}{3} \times 0.02 = 0.02.$$

In other words, productivity in Erewhon grew at a rate of 2% per year over this period.[4]

We now apply this technique to actual data. We examine data for the period 1975–2009. In the United States, output per worker grew at a rate of 1.34% per year, physical capital per worker grew at 2.20% per year, and human capital per worker grew at 0.11% per year. Putting these numbers together (and using a value of $\alpha = 1/3$), we get:

$$\hat{A} = 0.0134 - \frac{1}{3} \times 0.022 - \frac{2}{3} \times 0.0011 = 0.0054.$$

In other words, productivity grew at a rate of 0.54% per year over this period. Given that the growth rate of output per worker in the United States over this period was 1.34% per year, we can see that productivity growth explains 40% (= 0.54/1.34) of output growth in the United States. The other 60% of output growth is explained by the accumulation of factors of production.

The Contribution of Productivity to Growth Differences among Countries

In our discussion of Figures 7.3 and 7.4, we examined what fraction of the variation in income per capita among countries was a result of variation in factors of production and what fraction was a result of variation in productivity. We found that 47% of the variation resulted from factors of production and 53% resulted from productivity. We can interpret this finding by comparing the typical rich country with the typical poor country. The typical rich country has both higher productivity and higher factor accumulation than the typical poor country. The part of the income difference

---

[4]Another way to calculate productivity growth is first to calculate the value of productivity, A, in each period by using data on y, k, and h, and then to compute the growth rate of productivity from these derived values of A.

FIGURE 7.5

Role of Factors of Production in Determining Growth, 1975–2009

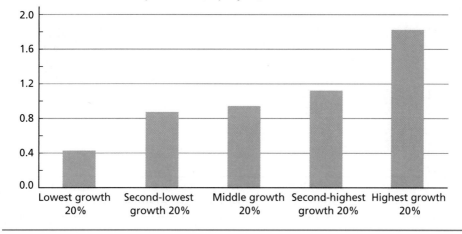

Growth rate of factors of production (% per year)

For sources, see Table 7.2.

between the two countries that is explained by the difference in productivity is a bit larger than the part explained by the difference in factors of production.

Now suppose that we examine growth rates of income, comparing the typical fast-growing country with the typical slow-growing country. How much of the faster income growth in one country is the result of faster productivity growth, and how much is the result of faster growth of factors of production? That is, what fraction of the variation in growth rates of income results from variation in the growth rate of productivity, and what fraction results from variation in the growth rate of factors of production?

To answer these questions we divide countries into five groups, from fastest-growing to slowest-growing. For each group, we calculate the average growth rate of factors of production and the average growth rate of productivity. These results are presented in Figures 7.5 and 7.6.

As shown in Figures 7.5 and 7.6, both productivity and factor accumulation contributed to differences in growth rates of output per worker among countries. As we move from the slowest- to the quickest-growing countries, we see that both productivity and factor accumulation grow faster. In the case of factor accumulation, average growth rates range from 0.43% per year in the slowest-growing group of countries to 1.83% per year in the fastest-growing group of countries. The gap between these groups is 1.40% per year. In the case of productivity growth, the range is broader. There is a gap of 2.75% per year between the average productivity growth rate of the fastest-growing group and that of the slowest-growing group.

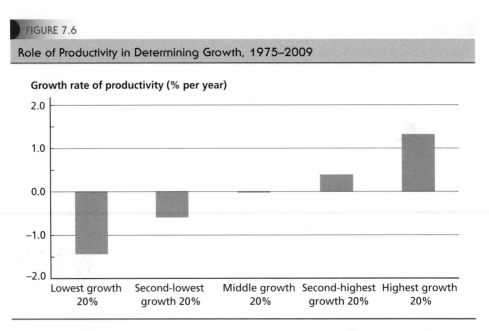

FIGURE 7.6

Role of Productivity in Determining Growth, 1975–2009

Growth rate of productivity (% per year)

For sources, see Table 7.2.

Also, both the slowest- and second-slowest-growing groups have *negative* rates of productivity growth.

Looking at Figures 7.5 and 7.6, it appears that productivity growth is a much more important source of differences in output growth rates than is growth of factors of production. To confirm this visual evidence, we can perform a mathematical calculation similar to the computation we used to analyze country differences in the level of output per worker. In this case, the result is that 68% of the variation in growth rates is the result of variation in productivity growth, whereas 32% of the variation in growth rates is the result of variation in factor accumulation.[5]

7.4 CONCLUSION

A country can produce more output either by increasing the factors of production at its disposal or by using its factors more effectively. This chapter has introduced two techniques for looking at productivity, or the differences among countries in the effectiveness with which they combine factors of production to produce output. Development accounting analyzes the sources of differences in the level of income per capita among countries. Growth accounting studies productivity growth over time.

---

[5]Mathematical Note: These percentages are derived using the methodology described in the mathematical box in Section 7.2. The data used are $\text{Var}(\hat{y}) = 2.42$, $\text{Var}(\hat{y}^p) = 1.26$, $\text{Var}(\hat{y}^f) = 0.41$, and $\text{Cov}(\hat{y}^p, \hat{y}^f) = 0.38$, where $\hat{y}^p$ is the growth rate of productivity and $\hat{y}^f$ is the growth rate of factors of production.

A TALE OF TWO CITIES

Hong Kong and Singapore have long fascinated economists studying economic growth. Both were among the fastest-growing countries in the world since World War II. Between 1960 and 1996, GDP per capita in Hong Kong grew at an annual pace of 6.1%, whereas in Singapore, growth was 7.0% per year. Given the similarity in their growth rates and the fact that they were both independent city-states (until Hong Kong's absorption by China in 1997), one might have expected that the two countries would have had similar sources of economic growth. Thus, it was a great surprise when a detailed study by economist Alwyn Young found that growth in the two countries was quite different.

Young used growth accounting techniques similar to those presented in this chapter to analyze growth in the two countries over the period 1966–1990. He found that although productivity growth played a large role in the growth of Hong Kong's income, Singapore's income growth was almost entirely driven by factor accumulation. In Hong Kong, productivity grew at a pace of 2.3% per year; in Singapore, the comparable figure was 0.2% per year.

Young's findings were seen as bad news for Singapore because growth resulting from factor accumulation cannot continue indefinitely. As we saw in Chapter 3, a country that raises its investment rate will experience transitional growth as the economy moves toward the new steady state, but such growth will eventually die out. To keep growth constant, the investment rate would have to rise continually. Indeed, in Singapore, investment as a fraction of GDP rose from 11% to 40% between 1966 and 1990. But of course, the investment rate cannot keep rising forever. Similarly, the level of education of the Singaporean work force rose at a rapid pace that is unlikely to be sustained into the future (between 1966 and 1990, the fraction of the labor force with a high school education rose from 15.8% to 66.3%).

In an influential article in *Foreign Affairs* magazine, economist Paul Krugman took Young's ideas to their logical conclusion: Singapore's factor-driven growth would soon have to slow down. Unless the country could boost productivity growth, Singapore was fated to follow in the path of the Soviet Union, which grew rapidly for several decades as a result of factor accumulation, only to stagnate eventually because of failed productivity.

In 1996, in response to the controversy set off by Krugman's article, Singapore began a drive to raise its productivity growth rate. The government launched campaigns to get companies to share productive ideas and put up posters telling workers that "doing a good job will make you feel proud." Even the 46,000 vendors selling food on Singapore's streets were targeted through programs that offered training in cooking and management, centralized kitchens, and the franchising of the most successful operators.[*]

[*]Young (1995), Krugman (1994), McDermott (1996).

The introduction to this chapter raised four questions for these techniques to address. Let's review the answers:

1. *How much does productivity differ among countries?* Quite a lot. According to our calculations, productivity in many poor countries is only a small fraction of productivity in rich countries. For example, productivity among the poorest one-fifth of countries is only 15% of the U.S. level. Put differently, equal quantities of physical and human capital would produce more than six times as much in the United States as in these poor countries. Even among richer countries, there are surprisingly large differences in productivity. For example, productivity in the Japan is 70% of the level of the United States.

2. *How much of the variation in income per capita among countries is explained by productivity differences?* We found that both productivity and factor accumulation were important in explaining differences in the level of income among countries, with productivity being the more important of the two. Specifically, 53% of the variation in income per capita among countries is explained by variation in productivity, and 47% is explained by variation in factors of production.

3. *How much does productivity* growth *differ among countries?* Once again, the answer was, quite a lot. In the fastest-growing one-fifth of countries, productivity growth averaged 1.33% per year over the period 1975–2009; in the slowest-growing one-fifth, productivity growth averaged –1.42% per year.

4. *How much of the variation in growth rates among countries is explained by variation in productivity growth, and how much by variation in factor accumulation?* Although productivity is slightly more important than factor accumulation in explaining variation in the level of income, productivity growth is far more important than factor growth in explaining variation in income growth rates. Overall, 68% of the variation in income growth among countries was explained by productivity growth and 32% by factor accumulation.

These findings raise two questions: What explains differences in productivity among countries, and why does productivity grow so quickly in some countries while holding constant or even falling in others? The exercises that we have conducted shed no light on these issues. Although we can measure the coefficient *A*, we do not know what it really is because we cannot observe *A* directly. Rather, we have observed the inputs and outputs of production and inferred the value of *A* from these. For this reason, the results of this exercise are often called "a measure of our ignorance."[6]

In the next four chapters, we probe this area of ignorance.

KEY TERMS

productivity   **179**   development accounting   **185**   growth accounting   **193**

---

[6]Abramovitz (1956).

QUESTIONS FOR REVIEW

1. Why is measuring productivity more difficult than measuring output, physical capital, labor, and human capital?

2. What is development accounting?

3. What is growth accounting?

4. What is the difference between development accounting and growth accounting?

5. How important are factor accumulation and productivity in explaining differences in the level of income among countries?

6. How important are factor accumulation and productivity in explaining differences in income growth among countries?

PROBLEMS

1. In Figure 7.1, panel (c) shows the case where Country 1 has higher output than Country 2 because it has more factors of production and higher productivity than Country 2. Draw similar diagrams showing the following two situations:

   a. Country 1 has both higher output per worker and higher productivity than Country 2, but it has a lower level of factors of production than Country 2.

   b. Country 1 has both higher output per worker and more factors of production than Country 2, but it has a lower level of productivity than Country 2.

2. If a country's physical and human capital both double over the course of 100 years, and output increases by a factor of eight, by what factor does productivity increase during this time?

3. Consider the following data on the fictional countries of Sylvania and Freedonia. The production function is $y = Ak^\alpha h^{1-\alpha}$, where $\alpha = 0.5$.

   a. Calculate the level of productivity, A, in each country.

   b. Calculate the countries' relative levels of output if all differences in output were the result of productivity.

   c. Calculate the countries' relative levels of output if all differences in output were the result of factor accumulation.

	Sylvania	Freedonia
Output per Worker, y	100	200
Physical Capital per Worker, k	100	100
Human Capital per Worker, h	25	64

4. Consider the following data, which apply to countries X and Z in the years 1975 and 2010. In both countries, the production function (in per-worker terms) is $y = Ak^\alpha h^{1-\alpha}$, where $\alpha = 1/3$.

Country	Year	Output per Worker, y	Physical Capital per Worker, k	Human Capital per Worker, h
X	1975	100	1	1
	2010	1,200	27	8
Z	1975	50	2	2
	2010	1,200	54	16

Which country had higher productivity growth between 1975 and 2010? Show how you got your answer. (You do not need to use a calculator to answer this question.)

5. The following table provides data on output per worker, physical capital per worker, and human capital per worker, all relative to the United States. For each of the three countries listed, calculate factor accumulation and productivity relative to the United States. In which country does factor accumulation play the largest role in explaining income relative to the United States? In which country does productivity play the largest role?

Country	Output per Worker, y	Physical Capital per Worker, k	Human Capital per Worker, h
Netherlands	0.87	0.81	0.94
Paraguay	0.097	0.094	0.80
Pakistan	0.092	0.067	0.65

6. The following table provides data on the annual growth rates of output, physical capital, and human capital per worker for three countries. For each country, calculate the growth rates of productivity and factor accumulation. In which country does factor accumulation account for the largest share of growth? In which country does productivity account for the largest share of growth?

Country	Growth Rate of Output per Worker, $\hat{y}$ (%)	Growth Rate of Physical Capital per Worker, $\hat{k}$ (%)	Growth Rate of Human Capital per Worker, $\hat{h}$ (%)
Argentina	0.66	0.31	0.52
Uruguay	1.82	1.83	0.51
Panama	1.73	0.90	0.84

7. The data on human capital we used throughout this chapter measured the number of years of schooling attained by members of each country's working-age population. However, countries differ in the number of days of school that make up a school year. Rich countries tend to have more days in their school years than do poor countries. Suppose that instead of data on school years, we used data on school days. How would these new data change our assessment of the role of productivity in explaining variations in output per worker among countries?

For additional exploration and practice using the Online Data Plotter and data sets, please visit www.pearsonhighered.com/weil.

THE ROLE OF TECHNOLOGY IN GROWTH

To see evidence of technology's role in economic growth, we just need to look around. Growth in living standards is so wrapped up with technological progress that often the two are indistinguishable. Modern inventions have changed the ways in which goods are produced, enabling workers to produce immensely more than they did a few generations ago. Technological progress also has allowed us to consume new goods and services ranging from air travel to zippers, that did not exist at the beginning of the 20th century.

While nature... shows a tendency to diminishing return, man... shows a tendency to increasing return...[Knowledge]is our most powerful engine of production; it enables us to subdue nature and...satisfy our wants.

—Alfred Marshall

Beyond these observations, we can also turn to more formal measures to show the importance of technological change in economic growth. As we saw in Chapter 7, the exercise of growth accounting shows that changes in productivity have contributed substantially to countries' economic growth. When productivity improves, the same quantities of factors of production can be combined to produce more output. A natural explanation for productivity improvements is improved technology—for example, the invention of a new production process.

The observation that technological change has been a powerful driver of growth raises two questions. First, what explains technological progress itself? Second, although technological change seems to be an obvious explanation for the productivity growth in the richest countries over the last two centuries, can technological gaps explain differences in the levels of productivity among countries today?

In this chapter, we take up several issues relating to technology. We begin by examining the nature of technological progress, paying particular attention to the incentives for technology creation that are faced by potential inventors. We then analyze how changes in the resources devoted to technology creation affect the rate of output growth and how technological progress spills across national boundaries. Finally, we consider the barriers that prevent the transfer of technology from rich to poor countries.

We revisit the determinants of technological progress in Chapter 9, where we also address the question of how quickly technology can be expected to improve in the future. In Chapter 10, we return to the question of how much technology differences can explain productivity differences between rich and poor countries.

8.1 THE NATURE OF TECHNOLOGICAL PROGRESS

As an example of technological progress, we can look at something as familiar as a piece of software. Consider what happens when you add new software to your computer. The capital (the computer) and labor (you, the user) involved in production have not changed at all. But suddenly, with the newly installed software, the output that you can produce with this capital and labor has increased.

In terms of our modeling of the production function, technological progress of this sort is captured as a change in value of the parameter A in the Cobb-Douglas production function, $y = Ak^{\alpha}h^{1-\alpha}$, where y is output per worker, A is productivity, k is physical capital per worker, and h is human capital per worker. In other words, an improvement in technology will mean that given quantities of physical and human capital can be combined to produce more output than was previously possible.

Because technology changes the way in which factors of production are combined to produce output, changes in technology can affect the process of economic growth. A crucial aspect of technological change is that it allows an economy to transcend the limitations imposed by diminishing returns. This is the theme of the quotation from Alfred Marshall at the beginning of this chapter. Recall from Chapter 6 that the amount of human capital per worker, h, cannot grow indefinitely. Similarly, Chapter 3 showed that diminishing returns prevent physical capital accumulation alone from leading to permanent growth of output. Thus, even if all of society's resources were devoted to producing factors of production, the economy would eventually reach a steady state in which growth ceased. However, the dismal arithmetic of diminishing returns is undone once we allow for improvements in technology. As long as the parameter A can get bigger, income per capita can continue to grow. (The mathematical appendix to this chapter lays out how technological progress can be incorporated into the Solow model of Chapter 3.)

Technology Creation

Creating new technologies requires investment. As in the case of capital creation, someone must use resources that could have been devoted to something else to create, refine, and put into practice a productive idea. The nature of this investment in technology has varied greatly across different places and times. Modern economies devote vast resources to research and development (R&D) in a systematic effort to create new products or processes. In the year 2009, the United States devoted 2.8% of its GDP to R&D. Table 8.1 shows data on the number of researchers (defined as

> TABLE 8.1

Researchers and Research Spending, 2009

Country	Number of Researchers	Researchers as a Percentage of the Labor Force	Research Spending ($ billions)	Research Spending as a Percentage of GDP
United States	1,412,639	0.89%	398.2	2.8%
Japan	655,530	1.00%	137.9	3.4%
Germany	311,519	0.74%	82.7	2.8%
France	229,130	0.80%	48	2.2%
South Korea	236,137	0.96%	43.9	3.3%
OECD Total	4,199,512	0.70%	965.6	2.4%

Source: OECD Main Science and Technology Indicators database.

professionals engaged in the conception or creation of new knowledge, products, processes, methods, and systems) working in the top five R&D countries, along with the percentage of the labor force engaged in research and the amount spent on research. The table also shows total figures for the Organisation for Economic Co-operation and Development (OECD) group of wealthy countries.

This deliberate channeling of such great resources to technology creation is a fairly recent phenomenon, however. Before the mid-19th century, technological advance was primarily the product of "tinkerers" rather than formally trained scientists. Even today, the formal R&D of big corporations is often overshadowed by the efforts of independent inventors working in their spare time out of a garage.

Most R&D is conducted by private firms seeking to maximize profits. However, the unique nature of technology has long led governments to play a role in research. For example, in 1714 the British government offered a prize of £20,000 for the creation of an accurate means of measuring longitude.[1] In the United States in 2009, 27.1% of R&D was sponsored by the government, although a good deal of the effort targeted military rather than productive applications. To give one prominent example, the Internet was created and nurtured under government auspices. The most important way in which government aids R&D, however, is by providing inventors with legal protection against the copying of their work, in the form of a patent. Patents are discussed at length in the next section.

Transfer of Technology

The observation that the accumulation of better technology has led to a higher level of output does not immediately convey the difference between technology and other inputs to production. After all, we have already seen that the accumulation of physical and human capital also has led to higher output. The difference

---

[1]Sobel (1995).

between technology and conventional factors of production (like physical and human capital) is that although conventional factors of production are *objects* (even human capital exists as neural pathways inside a person's brain), technologies are essentially *ideas* lacking a concrete physical existence.

One result of technology's nonphysical nature is that although conventional factors of production are **rival** in their use, technology is **nonrival.** If a piece of physical capital such as a hammer is being used by one person, it cannot be used by another. Similarly, a piece of human capital such as an engineer's technical training can be used in only one productive task at a time. Exactly the opposite is true of technology. One person's use of a piece of technology in no way prevents others from using it just as effectively. Thomas Jefferson noted this property of technology: "Its peculiar character, too, is that no one possesses the less, because every other possesses the whole of it. He who receives an idea from me, receives instruction himself without lessening mine; as he who lights a taper at mine, receives light without darkening me."[2]

The nonrival nature of technology means that, in studying it, we will have to focus much more on transfers among firms or countries than we would with the more traditional factors of production. In many cases, this transferability can be a great boon. If a country is poor because it lacks capital, then it can raise its income only by undertaking the costly investment of building new capital. Taking capital from a rich country and moving it to a poor country would make the poor country better off but the rich country worse off. By contrast, if a country is poor because it lacks technologies, then technologies can be transferred from elsewhere without making the country from which they were taken any worse off.

But there is a dark side to this magical quality of technology: The nonrivalry of ideas is often bound up with a low level of excludability. **Excludability** is the degree to which an owner of something (such as a good or an input into production) can prevent others from using it without permission. Physical capital has a high degree of excludability. Because physical capital is a piece of property, its owner can easily prevent other people from using it. And because its use is excludable, the owner of a piece of physical capital is able to earn a return by charging other people for its use. By contrast, ideas are often nonexcludable—their very nature makes it hard to prevent someone else from using them. Often, because of nonexcludability, the person who has created a new technology will not reap most of the benefits from its creation. This fact diminishes the incentives for creating technology.[3]

Determinants of R&D Spending

Most R&D spending is undertaken privately by firms. The concentration of technology creation in the private sector is even more apparent once we look beyond the formal R&D that is conducted in laboratories. Firms also spend a great deal of

---

[2]Jefferson (1967), p. 433.
[3]Romer (1990).

effort tinkering with production processes to raise quality or lower costs—a process known as *shop-floor R&D*. Thus, the pace of technological change will depend on the decisions of private firms, and if we wish to understand the determinants of R&D spending, we should look at the problem facing a firm that is deciding whether to do R&D and how much.

Profit Considerations. A firm will engage in R&D in the hope of inventing something: a new product or a new, more efficient way of producing some existing product. If the firm succeeds, it will be able to raise its profits. In the best case (from the firm's point of view), its invention will give it a monopoly on the sale of some product, allowing it to earn supernormal profits. Alternatively, a new invention may give the firm a means of producing a product being sold by other firms, but to produce it at a lower price. In either case, the extra profits that arise from this competitive advantage are the incentive that makes the firm do R&D in the first place. The larger the profits associated with having invented something, the more the firm is willing to spend in the effort to invent it. This observation suggests several of the considerations affecting the amount of R&D that firms conduct.

First, the amount the firm will want to spend on R&D will depend on how much of an advantage a new invention will confer. If other firms can easily copy the new technology and use it in their own production, then the firm that did the R&D will not have benefitted from its spending. For many inventions, the key to maintaining competitive advantage comes from having an invention that can be patented and thus protected from imitation.

Second, the firm will be influenced by the size of the market in which it can sell its product. The larger the available market, the greater the profits that the new invention will earn. Thus, by allowing inventors to sell their products in more countries, international economic integration increases the incentive to conduct R&D.

Third, the firm will take into account how long the advantage conferred by a new invention will last. Will competitors be able to come up with a product that does almost the same thing? Will someone else invent an even better product in a few years? If the invention can be patented, how long does the patent last? The longer the firm will have a competitive advantage as a result of its invention, the more money it will be willing to spend on R&D to achieve such an advantage.

Finally, the uncertainty surrounding the research process will influence a firm's R&D spending. If a firm invests $1 billion in building a new factory, it can be fairly confident that it will have a useful piece of capital in the end. By contrast, $1 billion spent on R&D might yield a new market-dominating product, or it might yield nothing at all. This observation suggests that firms that are better able to share the risks of R&D investments, or economies where such risks are better shared, will be more likely to undertake such risky investments. The recent expansion of venture capital funds (which direct investments to start-up companies) and the appetite of investors for "tech stocks" have greatly increased the flow of money into R&D.

Creative Destruction. This description of the incentives that a firm faces in deciding how much R&D to do makes clear a further point: Much of the time, the profits a firm earns as a result of creating a new technology come at the expense of *other* firms. Economist Joseph Schumpeter gave the name **creative destruction** to the process by which new inventions create profits for firms, these profits serve as the incentive to engage in research in the first place, and the new technologies so created (often, along with the firms that created them) are eventually supplanted by yet newer technologies.[4] Schumpeter's phrase nicely captures the double-edged nature of the process. Although we often celebrate the triumphs of new technologies, our enthusiasm ignores the dislocations suffered by firms and workers that the new technologies displace. History abounds with examples of people who have been adversely affected by technological progress and have fought back—the most famous example being the Luddites, who in the early 19th century smashed weaving machinery that was putting them out of work. More prosaically, firms with market-dominating technologies have often tried to stifle new generations of technologies. For example, in 2000, a U.S. district court found Microsoft guilty of having abused its monopoly in operating systems to stymie innovations in the computer industry.

Because technological change can be so destructive, establishing an economic system that encourages technological change can be a delicate business. Because economic systems do not always get the incentives right, the adoption of new technologies is often blocked.

8.2 PATENTS AND OTHER FORMS OF INTELLECTUAL PROPERTY PROTECTION

As we have seen, technology's unique quality—the ease of its transfer from one person or firm to another—has the downside of making it difficult for the creator of a new technology to reap its financial benefits. This nonexcludability reduces the incentive to create new technologies in the first place. It has long been recognized that allowing an inventor to enjoy more of the benefits that result from his or her labor increases the rate of invention of new technologies. The preamble to Venice's patent law of 1474 makes exactly this point: "[If] provisions were made for the works and devices discovered by men of great genius, so that others who may see them could not build them and take the inventor's honor away, more men would apply their genius… and build devices of great utility to our commonwealth."[5] The Constitution of the United States similarly authorizes Congress to enact laws "to promote the progress of science and useful arts, by securing for limited times to authors and inventors the exclusive right to their respective writings and discoveries."

---

[4]For a modern analysis of creative destruction, see Aghion and Howitt (1992, 2008).
[5]Mokyr (1990), p. 79.

A **patent** is a grant made by a government that confers on the creator of an invention the sole right to make, use, and sell that invention for a set period of time, generally 20 years. Patentable items include new products and processes, chemical compounds, ornamental designs, and even new breeds of plants. (Copyright, a related form of intellectual property protection, applies to writing, music, images, and software, among other things). To receive a patent, an inventor must produce something that is both novel (i.e., not something that was already known) and nonobvious. Further, one cannot patent laws of nature, physical phenomena, or abstract ideas. Inventors generally must file for a patent separately in every country where they want to protect their invention.

Although in theory the rules for what can be patented are straightforward, in practice it can be complicated to apply them. For a start, the issue of whether an invention is novel and nonobvious turns out to be in the eye of the beholder. In the 1860s, the U.S. Supreme Court ruled that attaching a rubber eraser to the back of a pencil was not a patentable idea because it was not novel. However, in 2003, the J. M. Smucker Company was successfully able to patent

> A crustless sandwich made from two slices of baked bread. The sandwich includes first and second matching crustless bread pieces. The bread pieces have the same general outer shape defined by an outer periphery with central portions surrounded by an outer peripheral area, the bread pieces being at least partially crimped together at the outer peripheral area. A central composite food layer is positioned between the central portions of the bread pieces and spaced inwardly of the crimped outer periphery area. The composite food layer includes a first and second layer of a first food spread and a second food spread that is substantially encapsulated between the first and second layer of the first food spread,

which to many people sounds like nothing more than a peanut butter and jelly sandwich with the crust cut off. Another recent controversial patent was Amazon's successful laying claim to the idea of "one click" purchasing. This is an example of a more general class of patentable ideas called business method patents that have become increasingly important as information technology has opened up new forms of commerce.

A second issue that arises for many patents filings is the verification of the underlying science. Until the end of the 19th century in the United Kingdom, patents could be registered without any official check on their feasibility. A significant fraction of patents in the steam engineering industry in the Britain during that period were granted for devices that could never work, including a large number of perpetual motion machines that were patented after 1860, when it was proved that such at thing was impossible.[6] In modern patent systems, scientifically trained examiners must approve each patent, but their resources can be overwhelmed by the flood of applications.

---

[6]Mcleod et al. (2003).

A third difficulty in applying the rules of a patent system is in deciding which inventor deserves the patent. There are two types of standards used. In a "first to file" system, the party (inventor or corporation) that brings its application to the patent office first receives the patent; in a "first to invent" system, the patent is granted to whoever can prove that they were the first to come up with the idea. The drawback of the first to invent system is that it can involve complex investigation and litigation to establish who actually came up with an idea first. Further, a patent in the first to invent system is never fully secure because it is always possible that a previous inventor will show up and take it away. This makes it difficult for inventors to sell their patents and makes firms less confident in investing in patented technologies. A first-to-file system creates certainty but introduces other problems. Established firms with large legal departments have a significant advantage in filing patents relative to small startups. Further, under a first-to-file system, firms may be forced to file patents before their inventions are fully developed, running the risk that they will give away the thrust of their research without receiving a patent. In 2011, the United States switched from using a first-to-invent system to using a first-to-file system, aligning its law with most other countries.

Problems with the Patent System

Although the monopoly rights that a patent grants serve as an incentive to inventors, and thus speed technological progress, there are downsides to patents as well. The first is simply the inefficiency associated with any monopoly (a point discussed further in Chapter 10). Once a firm has developed a particular technology, the firm will act as a monopolist, maximizing its revenue by charging a high price and, in doing so, limiting the benefits of the technology. Potential users of a technology, or those who cannot afford to pay the monopolist's price, often resent the profits earned under patent protection. This resentment is most pointed in the case of pharmaceuticals, which are often sold at an enormous markup over the marginal cost of production.

A second problem with patents is that in some cases, the balance between encouraging new R&D, on the one hand, and holding back progress of other firms doing similar work, on the other, can go awry. In the 1980s and early 1990s, U.S. patent law was changed to make patents both easier to procure and easier to enforce and also to allow for those whose patents were infringed on to obtain large legal settlements.[7] The number of patents granted annually rose from 62,000 in 1982 to 244,000 in 2010. The stock of patent examiners, whose job it is to decide on whether a patent should be granted, has not kept up with the flood of new applications, resulting in less careful scrutiny and thus the inappropriate granting of patents. At the same time, the backlog of unprocessed patent applications has

---

[7]Jaffe and Lerner (2004).

grown. By 2011, the average waiting time for a patent to be granted had reached three years. The result has been a flood of litigation. Between 1982 and 2010, the number of patent lawsuits commenced quadrupled.

The changed environment gave birth to a new type of firm known as a "patent troll." Patent trolls are companies that collect patents that they have no intention of using themselves, often buying them in bulk from firms that are going bankrupt. Patent trolls also often take out numerous patents related to technologies that have not yet been developed. Unlike firms that invent portfolios of useful technology that they can then license to others who want to use them, and thus publicize their patents and actively look for users, the goal of a patent troll is to wait until another firm independently develops and incorporates into its own products technology similar to a patented technology already in the troll's portfolio. Once the target company has become locked in to using the new technology, the patent troll sues for infringement and threatens to shut down the operations of the target company, allowing the patent troll to extort a hefty payment. Another strategy used by patent trolls is to patent technologies that are already in wide use, having been viewed by other firms as being too obvious to patent.

The most famous example of an attack by a patent troll was in the case of NTP, a firm founded in 1991 by inventor Thomas Campana and attorney Donald Stout. The firm made no attempt to produce anything or find buyers for its technologies. It simply sat on a portfolio of patents and waited for someone to wander into its technological trap. The firm that did so was Research in Motion (RIM), creator of the Blackberry wireless e-mail device. In 2002, a jury found that RIM had unknowingly infringed on several NTP patents. Legal battles continued for several years, reaching a head in early 2006, when a court came within days of shutting down RIM's entire e-mail network. The federal government even tried unsuccessfully to intervene in the case, arguing that a loss of Blackberries would pose a threat to national security. At this point RIM caved in and paid NTP $612 million to settle the case. In November 2006, NTP announced plans to file a similar lawsuit against Palm Inc, the maker of the Palm Pilot, causing shares in that company to fall in value by 6.5%. In a similar case, the Internet auction firm eBay was forced to pay millions of dollars in damages to a small firm that had previously patented the "buy it now" feature.

The existence of patent trolls holds back technological progress because potential inventors fear that much of the value of their new idea could be siphoned off by patent trolls. New products might contain thousands of conceivably patentable components, making it impossible for innovators to be certain that a new product is immune to an infringement suit. In 2005, in the software industry alone, there were 300 such lawsuits under way, with an estimated litigation cost of $500 million. The threat of patent trolls also forces companies to engage in "defensive patenting" of any technology that could conceivably be related to the products they want to produce, further wasting resources that could be devoted to researching productive technology.

Even without the threat of patent trolls, computer and telecommunications companies have been engaged in acquiring patents for the purposes of suing each other or for deterring other firms from suing them. In 2011, a portfolio of patents of the bankrupt firm Nortel was sold for $4.5 billion, with much of it going to Apple and Microsoft. The threat from these firms is part of what induced Google to acquire Motorola, which had a rich patent portfolio of its own, for $12.5 billion. In late 2011, Apple successfully sued HTC, a maker of smartphones running the Google Android operating system. The suit had the potential to block the import of several of HTC's most popular phones. Apple claimed that the phones violated a 1999 patent that Apple obtained for the system by which a smartphone scans text to find items like phone numbers and then offers to add them to an address book or call them with one tap.

Alternatives to Patents

Sometimes patents are not the best way for firms to protect their innovations because patenting an invention requires a detailed public description. Such a description may make it easy for competitors to come up with a close substitute—and once the patent has expired, others will be able to copy it exactly. For this reason, the formula for Coca-Cola was never patented and has remained secret for more than a century. A 1994 survey of the managers of R&D laboratories found that they considered secrecy to be twice as important as patents in protecting new production processes.[8]

Patents are also only useful if the legal sanctions against copying an invention can be enforced. In the case of a crop such as potatoes, a farmer who purchases seed potatoes once from a company can use seed potatoes from his or her first year's harvest to plant in a second year and can even provide seed potatoes to friends. Such behavior may technically be illegal, but as a practical matter, the seed company cannot do anything about it. Thus, a company that has invested heavily in the creation of a new breed of plant will find itself with only a limited opportunity to sell its seeds—and as a result will be reluctant to undertake such an investment in the first place. In an interesting twist, the Monsanto Corporation tried to deal with this problem by developing a "terminator gene" that allowed the first year's crop to grow normally but ensured that any resulting seeds were infertile.[9]

Although the patent system protects intellectual property and restricts access to reward innovators financially, money is not the only incentive that can produce innovation. In the last decades, an important force in the software industry has been the "open source" movement, in which programmers work together to create programs not protected by copyright. An example of open source software is the Linux operating system, which dominates among web servers. Some open source development

---

[8]Cohen, Nelson, and Walsh (2000).
[9]Pollan (1998).

work is by individuals who want to establish their reputation in the open-source world before selling their expertise privately. But for the vast majority of participants, writing open source software seems to be a form of creative expression. They get utility from participating in a cooperative venture and having their work appreciated by peers. Indeed, the participants in this movement often seem to be motivated not by profit but by honor, which is something that economists do not understand well.

8.3 MODELING THE RELATIONSHIP BETWEEN TECHNOLOGY CREATION AND GROWTH

In this section we examine two models of the relationship between technology and growth. We start with a model of a single country. We then move to a two-country model so that we can study the impact of technology transfer. To keep the models simple, we ignore the details of who in a country is creating new technologies or what incentives they face. Instead, we take the effort that each country puts into technology creation as a given and consider how growth is affected by different levels of technology creation.

One-Country Model

To focus on the issues that are introduced once we start thinking about technology creation, we use a simplified version of the production function that we examined in previous chapters.[10] Specifically, we ignore the roles of both physical and human capital, so the only input to production is labor. Let L_Y be the number of workers who are involved in producing output. Similarly, let L_A be the number of workers who are involved in creating new technologies. The total size of the labor force is L and because producing output and creating new technologies are the only activities that can occupy workers, we have the equation:

$$L = L_Y + L_A.$$

Define γ_A as the fraction of the labor force engaging in R&D. Stated mathematically:

$$\gamma_A = \frac{L_A}{L}.$$

(Recall that when we discussed capital accumulation, we used γ to stand for the fraction of output invested in new capital. Here we use it to mean something else, but it is intended to be analogous.) We can thus express the number of workers involved in producing output as:

$$L_Y = (1 - \gamma_A)L.$$

---

[10]The treatment in this section draws on Lucas (1988) and Mankiw (1995).

Because we assume that workers are the only input into producing output—that is, we ignore the role of physical and human capital—the production function is simple. Total output is equal to the number of workers involved in producing output multiplied by the level of productivity:

$$Y = AL_Y.$$

Combining the previous two equations, we can rewrite the production function as:

$$Y = A(1 - \gamma_A)L,$$

or in per-worker terms:

$$y = A(1 - \gamma_A). \tag{8.1}$$

This equation says that the level of output per worker is higher when the level of productivity A is higher and, for a given value of A, when a smaller fraction of the labor force is involved in doing R&D. At first it may seem paradoxical that having fewer people doing R&D would raise the amount of output produced. To resolve this apparent paradox, note that if fewer people are doing R&D today, more people are producing output today—but if fewer people are doing R&D today, the level of productivity, and thus output, will indeed be lower in the future.

We now turn to the process of productivity growth, that is, to the creation of new technologies. We assume that the rate of technological progress is a function of the number of workers who are devoting their time to R&D. Specifically, we model technological progress as being determined by the equation:

$$\hat{A} = \frac{L_A}{\mu},$$

where, as in previous chapters, a hat (^) over a variable indicates its rate of growth. Thus $\hat{A}$ is the growth rate of productivity. On the right side of this equation, L_A is the number of workers engaged in R&D, and μ is the "price" of a new invention, measured in units of labor. In other words, μ tells us how much labor is required to achieve a given rate of productivity growth. The larger μ is, the more labor must be devoted to R&D to achieve a given rate of technological growth.[11]

We can rewrite the equation for technological progress as:

$$\hat{A} = \frac{\gamma_A}{\mu} L. \tag{8.2}$$

To analyze the behavior of this model, we begin with the case in which the fraction of the population engaged in R&D, γ_A, is constant. Looking at the

---

[11]In Chapter 9 we will discuss this "technology production function" in some detail and will consider alternative forms for it.

production function in per-worker terms, Equation 8.1, we see that as long as γ_A is constant, the level of output per worker, y, is just proportional to the level of technology, A. Therefore, the two variables must grow at the same rate, that, is:

$$\hat{y} = \hat{A}.$$

Combining this equation with the equation for the growth rate of technology, Equation 8.2, we get:

$$\hat{y} = \hat{A} = \frac{\gamma_A}{\mu} L. \tag{8.3}$$

This equation says that increases in the fraction of the population involved in R&D, γ_A, will increase the growth rate of output. It also says that growth will be higher if the cost of new inventions is lower, that is, if μ is smaller.

Let's now consider what will happen if γ_A suddenly increases. From Equation 8.3, we know that this increase in γ_A will increase the growth rates of both output, y, and productivity, A. But there is a second effect of increasing γ_A: Moving workers into the R&D sector will mean involving fewer workers in producing output. From the production function (Equation 8.1), it is clear that output will thus fall. Figure 8.1 combines these two effects. Panel (a) of the figure illustrates how the value of A changes over time, and panel (b) shows how the value of y changes over time. (In both panels, the vertical axis is plotted as a ratio scale. As we saw in Chapter 1, a variable that grows at a constant rate will form a straight line when plotted on a ratio scale.)

As panel (a) shows, when γ_A rises, the growth rate of technology rises as well. The increasing steepness in the line representing A illustrates this rise. In panel (b), the line representing y also becomes steeper, indicating that the growth rate of output per worker has increased. But at the moment γ_A increases, there is a jump downward in y, representing the loss of output from workers shifting away from production and into R&D. Panel (b) makes clear that eventually output will regain and then pass the level it would have reached had there been no change in γ_A. Thus, a country that devotes more of its resources to R&D will suffer a reduction in output in the short run but be better off in the long run.

The conclusion that spending more on R&D lowers output in the short run but raises it in the long run has some similarity to our findings in Chapter 3 about investment in physical capital. According to the Solow model, raising investment will lower the level of consumption in the short run because output that was previously consumed is devoted to building new capital. But in the long run, higher investment will lead to higher output and thus an increase in consumption. There is a crucial difference, however, between the Solow model's findings with respect to physical capital investment and this chapter's findings with respect to R&D spending. In the model we consider in this chapter, an increase in R&D leads to a *permanent* increase in the growth rate of output. In the Solow model, an increase

FIGURE 8.1

Effect of Shifting Labor into R&D

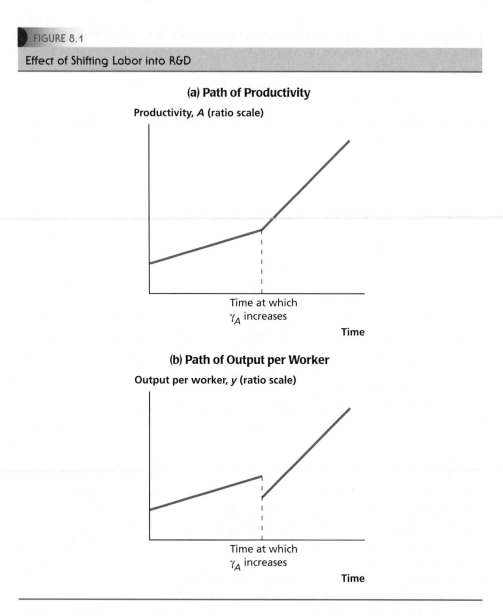

(a) Path of Productivity

Productivity, *A* (ratio scale)

Time at which
γ_A increases

Time

(b) Path of Output per Worker

Output per worker, *y* (ratio scale)

Time at which
γ_A increases

Time

in investment leads to a higher steady-state level of output, so the investment increase's effect on output growth is only transitory.

Finally, this one-country model allows us to examine how population size relates to technology growth. An implication of Equation 8.3 is that the bigger the labor force, *L*, the larger the growth rate of technology, $\hat{A}$ (holding μ and γ_A constant). The logic for this result is simple: If two countries devote the same fractions of their labor force to inventing new technologies, then the country with more people will have more workers doing R&D. It stands to reason that more people doing R&D should be able to come up with more inventions, so the more populous country should have faster technological progress.

This finding would suggest that, over time, countries with more people should have higher levels of technology, and thus should be richer, than countries with fewer people. Yet this prediction does not hold true in the data: There is no evidence that countries with more people either grow faster economically or are systematically richer than countries with few people.

The explanation for this "failure" of the model is that a country's level of technology depends on R&D done not only within that country's borders but also abroad. Technologies cross borders. This transfer of technology is the subject of the rest of this chapter. The idea that larger population means faster technological progress is a topic that we return to in Chapter 9, where we consider the future of technology. There we explore whether higher population means higher technological progress at the level of the planet as a whole, rather than at the level of an individual country.

Two-Country Model

From the discussion in Section 8.1 of firms' decisions about technology creation, it is clear that the transfer of technologies among firms is an important consideration. What about the transfer of technology among countries? (See box "International Technology Transfer.")

Our analysis of technology transfer stresses the interplay of two different means by which a country can acquire a new technology.[12] The first is **innovation**—the invention of a technology. The second is **imitation,** or copying a technology from elsewhere.

Consider two countries, labeled 1 and 2. We assume that the labor forces of the two countries are the same size: $L_1 = L_2 = L$. However, we allow the two countries to have different levels of technology, designated A_1 and A_2. As in the model of the last section, the labor force within each country is divided between output production and R&D. The levels of output per worker in the two countries are thus:

$$y_1 = A_1(1 - \gamma_{A,1}),$$

and

$$y_2 = A_2(1 - \gamma_{A,2}),$$

where $\gamma_{A,1}$ is the fraction of the labor force in Country 1 that is doing R&D, and $\gamma_{A,2}$ is the same thing in Country 2.

Countries acquire new technologies either by creating them from scratch (invention) or by copying from abroad (imitation). Of course, technologies can

---

[12]The model in this section draws on Barro and Sala-i-Martin (1997).

INTERNATIONAL TECHNOLOGY TRANSFER

In 1950 Eiji Toyoda, an engineer whose family's firm had built trucks for the Japanese army during World War II, visited the Ford Motor Company's River Rouge automobile plant in Michigan. At the time, River Rouge was among the most technologically advanced automobile factories in the world, and Toyoda spent two months carefully observing its operations. Why Ford was willing to let Toyoda study its plant in such detail is not recorded, but presumably the management felt there was no threat of competition from a small company in war-ravaged Japan. It was a decision that Ford would bitterly regret when Toyoda's firm, renamed Toyota, later rose to become a world automotive superpower.[*]

This transfer of technology across international borders was part of a long history. Europe, which would later be an exporter of advanced technologies, benefitted immeasurably in the Middle Ages from technologies that it imported from the rest of the world—for example, paper and gunpowder from China and the decimal numeral system (Arabic numerals)

from India. And when Europeans first reached the New World, one of the most important things they took back with them was the "technology" contained in the DNA of new food crops: potatoes, corn (maize), tomatoes, and chili peppers, among others.

Technological advantage has sometimes been viewed as a precious commodity to be guarded within national borders. In the 18th and 19th centuries, for example, Britain banned the emigration of skilled craftsmen and the export of some kinds of machines, in an effort to keep its technology from spreading. Such barriers were not fully effective, however. In 1789 Samuel Slater slipped out of England in disguise, having memorized cutting-edge technology in textile manufacture. He later built the first water-powered textile mill in the United States, in Pawtucket, Rhode Island, and became known as the father of the U.S. Industrial Revolution.[†]

Even as some governments have tried to prevent technologies from spreading abroad, others have done their best to import technologies from

be copied from abroad only if they have already been invented—a country cannot copy something that does not yet exist. Thus, the option of imitation is open only to the country that is the "technology follower." The "technology leader" will have to acquire new technologies through invention. We assume that if a given technology already exists in the leading country, it will be less expensive for the follower country to imitate the technology than to reinvent the technology on its own.

In our model, the variable A represents the level of technology. Thus, the technology leader will have a higher value of A than the technology follower. We assume that the fraction of the labor force engaged in R&D, γ_A, is higher in Country 1 than in Country 2: $\gamma_{A,1} > \gamma_{A,2}$. This assumption (along with the assumption that the countries have equal-size labor forces) guarantees that Country 1 will be the technology leader and Country 2 the technology follower in the model's steady state.

more advanced countries. In 1697 Czar Peter the Great adopted a false identity and took a job at a Dutch shipyard to learn advanced technologies to bring back to Russia. During the Industrial Revolution, Britain's European rivals, jealous of the country's technological superiority, attempted to copy British technologies by various means: encouraging the migration of skilled workers, setting up government research projects, and even sending out industrial spies. Following the restoration of the Meiji emperor in the 1860s, Japan embarked on an ambitious program to bring in the best of foreign technology from abroad. In one of the oddest stories of technology transfer, the Soviet Union found a valuable information source for its attempt to develop its own hydrogen bomb: analysis of the airborne fallout from the U.S. tests as it circulated the whole planet.

Today, nations rarely attempt to restrict the transfer of technology outside their borders for economic reasons (as opposed to national security reasons), to a large extent because firms that do R&D view their domestic competitors as just as much of a threat as their foreign rivals. Large multinational firms further reduce the relevance of national borders. If Ford develops a new technique at its factory in Detroit, the company might be willing to share the innovation with its foreign subsidiaries but will strive to keep it out of the hands of its domestic competitors just as strongly as it will try to prevent foreign companies from copying it.

A number of developing countries have embarked on ambitious strategies to encourage the transfer of technology. Among the most successful has been Taiwan, which encouraged foreign investment (through tariff protections and subsidies) with the condition that foreign firms help in the creation of local technological capability, for example, by buying product components locally.[‡]

[*]Womack, Jones, and Roos (1991).
[†]Clark (1987), Landes (1998), ch. 18.
[‡]Pack and Westphal (1986), Romer (1992).

In the case of the technology leader, the process of creating new technologies is the same one that we examined previously:

$$\hat{A}_1 = \frac{\gamma_{A,1}}{\mu_i} L_1.$$

The only difference is that we have now designated the cost of invention—which in the last section was simply called μ—as μ_i, where i stands for "invention."

We now turn to Country 2. Call μ_c the cost of acquiring a new technology via imitation (the c is for "copying"). Our key assumption is that the cost of copying goes down as the technology gap between the follower and the leading country widens. There are several ways to justify this assumption. One justification is that not all technologies are equally easy to imitate, and that the farther behind the leader a follower is, the more easy-to-imitate technologies there are available to copy. Alternatively, we could say that what affects the cost of imitation is the time since a new technology was invented—thus the farther the follower lags behind the leader, the older (and thus easier to copy) are the technologies that the follower wants to imitate.

To formulate this assumption mathematically, we say that μ_c is a function of the ratio of technology in Country 1 to technology in Country 2, where the function that describes the relationship is denoted as $c(\ )$:

$$\mu_c = c\left(\frac{A_1}{A_2}\right).$$

We make three assumptions about this "cost of copying" function. First, we assume that it is downward sloping—that the cost of copying falls as the technology gap between the two countries increases (i.e., as the ratio of technology in Country 1 to technology in Country 2 increases). Second, we assume that as the ratio of A_1/A_2 goes to infinity, the cost of copying falls to 0. In other words, if the gap in technology were infinitely large, then imitation would be costless. Finally, we assume that as the ratio of A_1/A_2 approaches 1, the cost of copying approaches the cost of invention. This means that if the follower country is very near the technology leader, it gets little benefit from copying technology rather than inventing its own. (The cost-of-copying function is not defined if A_1/A_2 is less than 1 because in this case, there would be nothing for Country 2 to copy.) Figure 8.2 shows what the cost-of-copying function might look like.

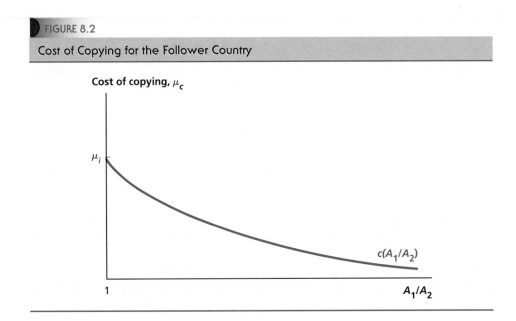

▶ FIGURE 8.2

Cost of Copying for the Follower Country

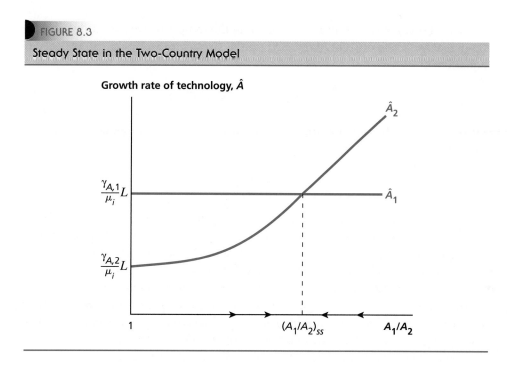

FIGURE 8.3

Steady State in the Two-Country Model

Given a value of μ_c, the rate of technology growth in Country 2 is given by an equation in the same form as the growth rate of technology in Country 1:

$$\hat{A}_2 = \frac{\gamma_{A,2}}{\mu_c} L_2.$$

We are now in a position to look at the steady state of the model. The key insight is that, in the steady state, the two countries will grow at the same rate. Figure 8.3 shows why this is the case: It graphs the growth rate of A in each country as a function of A_1/A_2, the ratio of technology in the leader country to technology in the follower country. If this ratio were 1—that is, if Country 2 had the same level of technology as Country 1—then we would know that technology would be growing more quickly in Country 1 than in Country 2. The reason is that, in this case, the two countries would have the same cost of creating new technologies, whereas Country 1 has a higher value of γ_A than does Country 2. By contrast, if this ratio were infinite, then the cost of acquiring new technologies in Country 2 would be 0, and Country 2 would be experiencing faster technological growth than Country 1. Thus, at some ratio of A_1/A_2 between 1 and infinity, the two countries will have the same growth rates of A, and the ratio of the levels of technology in the two countries will remain constant. This will be the steady state. Note also that this steady state is stable: If the ratio A_1/A_2 starts off above the steady state, then A_2 will grow faster than A_1, and the ratio will fall. If the ratio starts off below the steady state, the opposite will occur.

Given that the two countries will grow at the same rate, we can easily solve for their relative levels of technology. Setting the two growth rates equal, we get the equation:

$$\frac{\gamma_{A,1}}{\mu_i} L = \hat{A}_1 = \hat{A}_2 = \frac{\gamma_{A,2}}{\mu_c} L.$$

Of these terms, the only one that can adjust is μ_c, the cost of copying. Thus, we know that:

$$\mu_c = \frac{\gamma_{A,2}}{\gamma_{A,1}} \mu_i.$$

We can summarize these mathematical manipulations as follows. First, we know that in the steady state, the two countries must grow at the same rate. If Country 2 were growing faster than Country 1, then Country 2 would become the technology leader, an impossibility given that Country 2 spends less on R&D than Country 1. If Country 1 were growing faster than Country 2, the technological gap between them would grow infinitely large, and the cost of copying for Country 2 would be 0—in which case Country 2 would grow faster than Country 1. Given that the two countries grow at the same rate and that Country 2 devotes less effort to R&D than Country 1, Country 2 must have a lower cost of technology aquisition than Country 1, and we can determine the specific cost by comparing the levels of R&D effort in the two countries. For example, if Country 2 devotes half as much effort to R&D as Country 1 (i.e., $\gamma_{A,2}/\gamma_{A,1} = 1/2$), then the cost of technology copying in Country 2 must be half as large as the cost of invention in Country 1 (i.e., $\mu_c/\mu_i = 1/2$).

Once we know the value of μ_c in steady state, we can use the function that determines μ_c to figure out the steady-state value of A_1/A_2, that is, the relative level of technology in the two countries. (See end-of-chapter problem 7 for an example.)

An interesting question arises as we examine the steady state of this model: Is the technology-leading country necessarily better off than the follower? The answer is no. Although the technology leader is more productive, it also devotes a higher fraction of its labor force to R&D and thus has fewer workers producing output. Whether it is possible for the follower to have a higher level of income than the leader will depend on the costs of imitation relative to innovation. If imitation is inexpensive, then a follower country will have a level of productivity near that of the leader while devoting a much smaller share of its labor force to R&D. In this case, it will be possible for the follower to have higher income than the leader. By contrast, if imitation is expensive, then the follower country either will have to devote almost as much of its labor force to R&D as does the leader, in which case its level of technology will be close to the leader's, or else will have a level of technology that is far behind that of the leader, if it devotes only a small part of its labor force to R&D.

We can use this two-country model to think about the effects of changes in "policy," here interpreted as changes in the parameter γ_A. These effects differ from what would be seen in the one-country model.

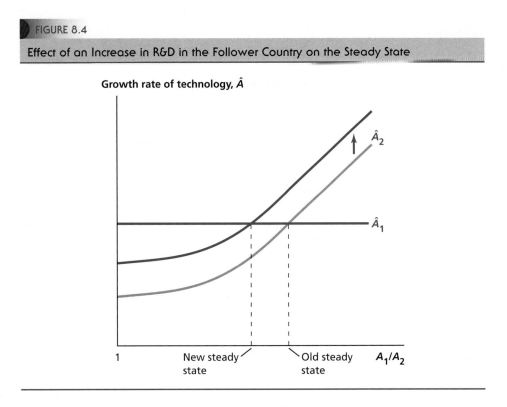

FIGURE 8.4

Effect of an Increase in R&D in the Follower Country on the Steady State

Growth rate of technology, $\hat{A}$

$\hat{A}_2$

$\hat{A}_1$

1   New steady state   Old steady state A_1/A_2

Consider the following scenario. The two countries are in steady state, with $\gamma_{A,1} > \gamma_{A,2}$. Suppose now that Country 2 raises its value of γ_A but that the new value is still below the value in Country 1. Figure 8.4 shows how this change affects the steady-state levels of technology in the two countries. The curve representing $\hat{A}_2$ shifts upward. This shift means that for any given value of A_1/A_2 (and thus for any given cost of copying), Country 2 is growing faster than it would have grown before the increase in $\gamma_{A,2}$. As the figure shows, the new steady state occurs at a lower value of A_1/A_2, that is, a smaller gap in technology between the two countries.

Figure 8.5 shows how the levels of A_2 and y_2 behave over time. (As in Figure 8.1, the vertical axis is plotted on a ratio scale, so that a variable growing at a constant rate appears as a straight line.) Panel (a) of the figure shows that the growth rate of technology in Country 2 temporarily rises after $\gamma_{A,2}$ increases (as seen by the increasing steepness of the line representing A_2). Over time, however, an A_2 moves closer to A_1, technological growth in Country 2 returns to its old level. The reason is that the steady-state growth rate of technology in Country 2 is determined by the growth rate of technology in Country 1, the technology leader.

Panel (b) of Figure 8.5 shows that the immediate effect of an increase in $\gamma_{A,2}$ is to reduce the level of output in Country 2, y_2, because a smaller fraction of the labor force is involved in producing output. But the increase in R&D effort leads to

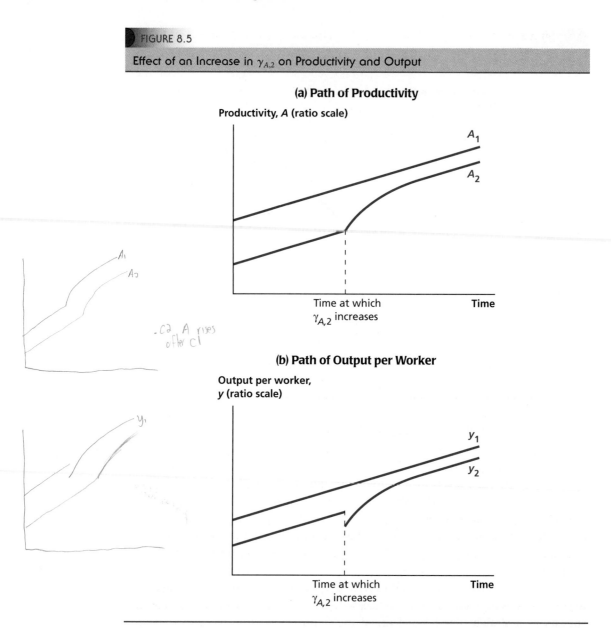

FIGURE 8.5

Effect of an Increase in $\gamma_{A,2}$ on Productivity and Output

(a) Path of Productivity

Productivity, A (ratio scale)

A_1

A_2

Time at which
$\gamma_{A,2}$ increases

Time

(b) Path of Output per Worker

Output per worker,
y (ratio scale)

y_1

y_2

Time at which
$\gamma_{A,2}$ increases

Time

faster growth in A_2 and thus in y_2. Growth in Country 2 is temporarily high while the level of technology in Country 2 is moving toward the level in Country 1, but once the new steady-state ratio of A_1/A_2 has been reached, growth in Country 2 returns to its rate before the change in $\gamma_{A,2}$.

This finding that an increase in R&D in the follower country causes a *temporary* increase in the growth rate of output is in stark contrast to the result of the one-country model, in which an increase in R&D produced a *permanent* increase in growth. As far as the follower country is concerned, this model of growth through technology creation shares one of the properties of the models of factor accumulation that we studied in Chapters 3, 4, and 6: A change in "policy" (such as the investment rate, γ, in the Solow model, or the level of R&D spending, $\gamma_{A,2}$, in this model) will lead to a *transitory* change in the growth rate of output. Eventually, the growth rate of output will return to its level preceding the change in policy, although the level of output will differ from what it would have been without the policy change.

The result that a change in R&D spending will lead to only a transitory change in the growth rate of output does not hold true for the leader country in this two-country model. Because the leader country does not have the option to imitate technology from abroad, it is effectively in the same situation described in the one-country model: A change in R&D will lead to a permanent change in its growth rate of output.

This stark difference between the predictions of the model for Country 1 (the leader) and Country 2 (the follower) raises the question of how we can apply such a model to the real world. Should we try to determine which country in the world is the technology leader? If we can identify this leader, can we confidently conclude that an increase in its R&D will raise the world growth rate of technology, but that an increase in any other country's R&D will improve only that country's relative position, without affecting the world growth rate? The answer to these questions is almost certainly no. The scenario of one country leading the world in every technology, with every other country playing catch-up, might have been nearly correct at some points in history—for example, for the United Kingdom in the early 19th century and for the United States soon after World War II. But in the world today, technological superiority is much more diffuse, with many countries crowding the "technological frontier" and different countries leading in different industries.

The lack of a single "technology leader" in the world today does not mean that the model fails to serve a useful purpose. Rather, it suggests that we should focus on the model's general lesson instead of the particular results. The general lesson of the model is that increased R&D spending within a given country will have two effects. First, it will change that country's relative position in the world technological hierarchy and thus bring a period of transitory growth in both technology and income within the country. Second, increased R&D spending in a given country will lead to faster growth in technology for the world as a whole.

8.4 BARRIERS TO INTERNATIONAL
· TECHNOLOGY TRANSFER

The model of international technology transfer that we just examined gives a fairly hopeful conclusion with regard to technologically backward countries. As long as technologically advanced countries continue to do R&D, cutting-edge technology will advance. This technological advance will eventually bring productivity improvements even to a country far from the cutting edge. Even if a technologically backward country does almost no R&D, it someday will be able to copy, and thus benefit from, the inventions of the most advanced countries.

This optimistic prediction does not always seem to work out in practice, however. In particular, although technologies move fairly freely among the most developed countries, many technological advances in the rich countries appear to have little impact on the poorest countries. In this section, we examine two reasons technological transfer from the developed to the developing world may not always flow so easily.

Appropriate Technology

In our two-country example of technology transfer, we assumed that the technologies that are useful in one country will be useful in another. Technology was summarized by the parameter A, and if two countries had different technologies (i.e., different values of A), then clearly the country with a higher value of A had the better technology. Further, because a follower country would be better off using the leading country's technology, the fact that the follower country does not immediately switch to the leading country's value of A implies that there is some barrier, such as patent protection or secrecy, hindering the transfer of technology.

With respect to the transfer of technology among relatively developed countries, this description is probably correct. But in the case of technology transfer between the developed and developing worlds, other issues intrude.[13] It is possible that technologies developed in the richest countries will not be "appropriate" to poorer countries. For example, rich countries tend to have more physical and human capital per worker than do poor countries. If technologies created in rich countries are specific to the mix of factors found there—that is, if the technologies work only with high levels of human and physical capital—then such technologies will not be useful in poor countries. For example, an advance in the technology for magnetic levitation trains—a highly capital-intensive form of transportation—will do little to raise productivity in a country that relies primarily on bicycles and battered buses to move people around. Similarly, rich countries tend to be in temperate climate zones, where advances in agriculture include the development of crops unsuited to the tropics. If a particular new technology is available to but not appropriate for a poor country, it is unlikely to be used there.

We can represent the idea of appropriate technology with our familiar diagram of a production function, graphed with physical capital per worker on the horizontal axis and output per worker on the vertical axis. (We do not include human capital in the analysis because doing so would require drawing the diagram in three dimensions.)

Let's first consider the situation in which technological change is "neutral" in the sense that it does not apply differently to different mixes of factors of

---

[13]Atkinson and Stiglitz (1969), Basu and Weil (1998), Acemoglu (2002).

FIGURE 8.6

Neutral Technological Change

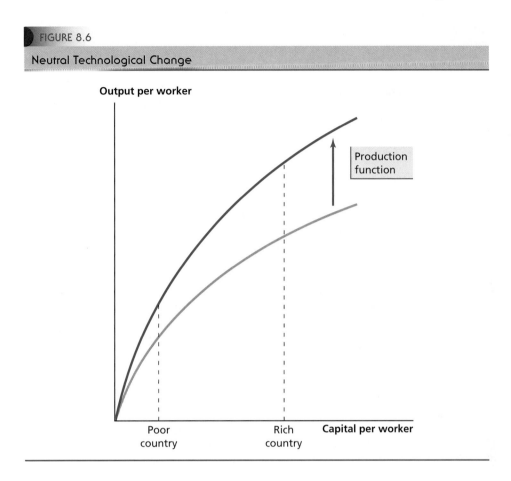

production. This would be the case if, for example, the production function was of the Cobb-Douglas form, $y = Ak^{\alpha}$, and technological change took the form of an increase in the parameter A. As shown in Figure 8.6, this technological advance would be represented by a proportional shift upward in the production function. This shift would be just as significant—that is, just as large a percentage of the country's income—for a poor country as for a rich country. Thus, if technological change took this neutral form, a poor country would benefit just as much as a rich country from a technological advance, even if the invention itself took place in the rich country.

The alternative case is a "capital-biased" technological change—that is, a technological change that is useful only to capital-rich countries. Figure 8.7 shows this alternative. For a country with high capital per worker, capital-biased technological change will lead to an increase in output per worker. But a country with low capital per worker will experience little or no increase in output.

Why might technological progress be biased toward high levels of capital per worker? The reason is that the countries that do most of the R&D have high

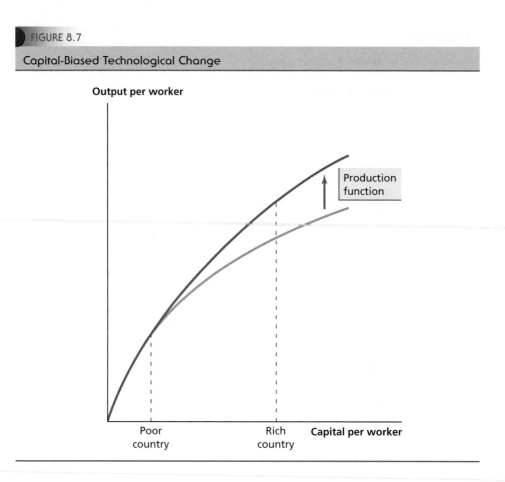

FIGURE 8.7

Capital-Biased Technological Change

levels of capital per worker, and firms in those countries do R&D to improve the productivity of the factor mix they are working with. In the year 2000, R&D spending per capita was $932 in the United States and $775 in Japan, but only $42 in South America and $6 in Africa. Africa, with 13.3% of world population, accounted for 0.6% of world R&D spending.[14]

   This analysis leaves open the question of why R&D labs in developed countries do not create technologies that developing countries can use. One reason is that developing countries typically enforce property rights to new technologies laxly. The inventor of a new technology that benefits producers in poor countries will find it almost impossible to get those producers to pay to use his or her invention and thus to earn a return on his or her investment. Such slack enforcement weakens the incentive to create technologies that are useful in poor countries.

---

[14]National Science Foundation (2006), Figure 4-33 and Appendix Table 4-57.

Tacit Knowledge

The model of appropriate technology assumes that any technology used in a rich country is available for use in a poor country, but that the poor country may choose not to use it. An alternative explanation for why technology is not transferred from rich to poor countries is that poor countries are *unable* to use technology developed in rich countries. In other words, there are barriers to the transfer of technologies among countries.

At first, there would seem to be a limit to the size of these barriers to technology transfer. For example, patents expire in 20 years, after which time a technology (which must be fully described in the patent application) is freely available to anyone who wants to use it. Similarly, firms that rely on secrecy rather than patents to protect their technologies generally relax their guard when it comes to technology they used 10, 20, or 30 years ago. These considerations suggest that technologies should take at most a few decades to flow from the richest to the poorest countries. This rapid speed of technology transfer would seem to impose a limit on exactly how technologically backward poor countries can really be.

But experience with the transfer of technologies from rich to poor countries has shown that there is much more to such transfer than simply carrying the blueprints for new production processes across national borders. In addition to the codified knowledge represented by a set of blueprints, there also exists **tacit knowledge** in the minds of engineers—thousands of small details about the workings of a technology, learned over years of experience and transferred from person to person, not in written form but through informal training. Often the users of a technology are unaware themselves of the extent of this tacit knowledge, so the transfer of blueprints alone, without tacit knowledge, can (and frequently does) lead to expensive failures.

Scientist and philosopher Michael Polanyi, who popularized the idea of tacit knowledge, described two countries' strikingly different experiences with a machine for producing light bulbs. Imported into Hungary in the 1950s, the device could not produce a single bulb that was not defective for a whole year. Meanwhile, an identical machine worked perfectly in Germany. Similarly, in the 1960s, a U.S. company, Cummins Engine, set up joint ventures in Japan and India to manufacture the same truck engine. The Japanese plant quickly reached the same levels of quality and productivity as Cummins's plants in the United States. In the Indian plant, by contrast, costs were more than three times as high as in the United States, and quality remained low. In these cases, the crucial difference lay neither in the quality of physical capital nor in the formal education of workers in different countries, but in the practical experience of key engineers and managers.[15]

---

[15]Polanyi (1962), Acemoglu and Zilibotti (2001).

EMBODIED TECHNOLOGICAL PROGRESS AND LEAPFROGGING

In Section 8.1 on technological progress, we used the example of a new generation of software. New software represents a new and better technology. The physical capital and human capital inputs (the computer and the worker) do not change, but with new software, they are more productive.

Not all examples of technological progress are as simple as software. New technology is often built into capital goods. This linking of technology to specific pieces of capital is called **embodied technological progress** (by contrast, software is an example of disembodied technological progress). If a technological change is embodied in capital, the technology is not upgraded until the capital good is replaced.

We can similarly think of technological progress as being embodied in the human capital that students acquire during their schooling. Education has both a general component (skills that are always applicable) and a specific component (e.g., skills for using current technology). As in the case of software, it is possible to upgrade the "wetware" inside a worker's head to deal with a new technology, but such skill upgrades require new investment in human capital. And as workers get older, improving the technology that they can work with gets more difficult and less worthwhile because the working life over which older workers can use their new skills is shorter. Thus, these workers are less likely to be able to use the most advanced technologies.

The fact that technology is embodied in physical and human capital means, in turn, that we cannot so easily separate factor accumulation from technological progress. A country with a high investment rate will have, on average, capital goods that are younger (more recently produced). As a result, these capital goods will embody more recently developed technologies, and the country with high investment will be technologically more advanced than one with low investment. Similarly, a country with an older population will have a harder time staying on the technological cutting edge, for a large fraction of its workers will have been educated farther in the past.

We can see this effect of embodied technology in the adoption of the basic oxygen furnace, one of the most important innovations in the steel industry, which was invented in the early 1950s. In the United States, where the steel

The existence of tacit knowledge complicates technology transfer. Recognizing the importance of tacit knowledge also helps explain other phenomena. First, tacit knowledge makes it much more difficult for technology to pass from developed to developing countries than within developed countries because much of the tacit knowledge is not specific to a given technology so much as to a given *type* of technology. Second, if tacit knowledge is important, the successful transfer of a single technology to a developing country may have a large externality effect because in the process, the stock of tacit knowledge will build up, allowing the easy transfer of further technologies. This externality effect might explain how countries such as South Korea and Taiwan were able, in the space of a few decades, to advance through a series of technological stages and quickly catch up to cutting-edge technologies.

industry expanded only slowly after World War II, the diffusion of this new technology was slow. In Japan, by contrast, the steel industry was growing much faster over this period, so steel plants adopted the new technology much more quickly. By 1968, 75% of Japanese steel was produced using the basic oxygen furnace, compared with only 40% of U.S. steel.[*]

The embodiment of technology in capital goods also gives rise to the possibility of technological **leapfrogging,** the process by which technologically backward countries or firms jump ahead of the leaders. One of the best examples of leapfrogging comes from software, which is where our present discussion began. Software is constantly being improved, but the typical computer user does not find it worthwhile to upgrade every time a new version of software becomes available. Instead, the user will stick with his or her current version of a program until it is antiquated enough that replacing it is worthwhile, at which point he or she will adopt the newest available version. Thus, there is a constant process of leapfrogging, by which the users with the most antiquated software jump ahead to install the most modern program.[†]

Leapfrogging can also occur at the level of countries. In countries where recently developed technology is incorporated into capital goods, firms may not find it worthwhile to scrap their existing capital to adopt the newest innovations. Countries that are farther behind, by contrast, will do so. Telephones provide a good example. In countries where telephones have been common for decades, an extensive infrastructure of telephone wires ("land lines") leads to every house and business. In the 1990s, the existence of these land lines reduced the demand for the new cellular phone technology. As a result, many countries with an initially poor infrastructure adopted cell phones faster than countries with an entrenched infrastructure. In 2001, Africa became the first world region in which cell phones outnumbered land lines. Between 2001 and 2010, the number of cell phone subscriptions increased by a factor of 14. Africa also leads the world in the use of cell phones for informal banking, money transfer, and small transactions.

[*]Ruttan (2001).
[†]Brezis, Krugman, and Tsiddon (1993).

8.5 CONCLUSION

In this chapter we have analyzed the role of technological progress in economic growth. Improvements in technology mean that the same inputs can produce a larger quantity of output. Thus, technological progress holds the key to continual economic growth.

As in the case of physical and human capital, the creation of new technology requires the investment of resources. For technology, this investment is referred to as R&D.

Two key characteristics of technology are that it is nonrival and that it is also frequently nonexcludable. Nonrivalry refers to the fact that one person's use of a piece of technology does not prevent others from using it. Nonexcludability refers to the fact that it is often difficult for the creator of a technology to prevent other people from using it. Both of these properties result from the fact that technologies are essentially ideas rather than objects. In this respect, technology differs fundamentally from factors of production such as physical capital and human capital.

The upside of technology's nonrivalry is that not everyone who uses a new technology has to go through the effort of creating it. If this same thing were true for human capital, then you could learn calculus by having one of your friends take the class. The downside of technology's nonexcludability is that this quality makes it difficult for the creator of a new technology to reap the benefits from his investment. The history of technology is rich with examples of inventors trying to restrict the spread of the knowledge that they created to earn a return on their investment.

We have also probed into why technologies might transfer more easily among rich countries than from rich to poor countries. We saw that certain technologies may fail to flow from rich to poor countries either because they are not appropriate for use, given the poor countries' available factors of production, or because poor countries lack the tacit knowledge required to make the technologies function. This issue of technology transfer from rich to poor countries is of crucial importance because the overwhelming majority of world R&D occurs in rich countries.

We return to the subject of how technology and growth are related several more times in the book. Much of the next chapter is devoted to the technology production function that determines how inputs of R&D translate into technological progress. There we also consider historical data on the speed of technological progress and see what the available data can tell us about the future of technological progress. In Chapter 10, we more closely examine the relationship between technology and productivity, asking to what extent differences in productivity among countries are explained by differences in technology. In Part IV we examine some "fundamental" determinants of growth and consider whether several specific factors (culture, geography, and government) have either facilitated or impeded technological transfer across national boundaries. And in Chapter 16, where we look into how constraints on natural resources might limit growth, we weigh the possibility that technological changes can provide a way out of the problem.

KEY TERMS

rival (inputs into production) **204**	creative destruction **206**	tacit knowledge **227**
nonrival (inputs into production) **204**	patent **207**	embodied technological progress **228**
excludability **204**	innovation **215** imitation **215**	leapfrogging **229**

QUESTIONS FOR REVIEW

1. How does technological progress differ from the accumulation of factors of production as a source of economic growth?

2. What does it mean to say that technology is nonrival? What does it mean to say that technology is often nonexcludable?

3. What factors influence a firm's decision to engage in R&D?

4. What is a patent? How do patents affect the incentives of firms to do R&D?

5. What are the short-run effects of an economy's devoting more resources to R&D? What are the long-run effects?

6. How does the effect of raising the fraction of resources devoted to R&D differ in a follower country compared with a leading country? Why are the effects different?

7. How does the existence of appropriate technology or tacit knowledge impede the transfer of technology from rich to poor countries?

PROBLEMS

1. For each of the following goods, indicate whether the good is rival or nonrival and whether it is excludable or nonexcludable.

    a. national defense

    b. a cookie

    c. access to a password-protected web site (assuming that the password cannot be stolen)

    d. fruit that grows on a tree in the middle of a public square

2. The monopoly pricing that results from patents is often criticized, especially in the case of life-saving prescription drugs. What are the advantages and disadvantages of patent laws in this situation? Is there any alternative you can think of? What are the advantages and disadvantages of this alternative?

3. Consider a country described by the one-country model in Section 8.3. Suppose that the country *temporarily* raises its level of γ_A. Draw graphs showing how the time paths of output per worker (y) and productivity (A) will compare under this scenario with what would have happened if there had been no change in γ_A.

4. Consider the one-country model of technology and growth that was presented in Section 8.3. Suppose that $L = 1$, $\mu = 5$, and

$\gamma_A = 0.5$. (These numbers are not meant to be realistic but rather are chosen to make the calculations easier. There has certainly never been a country where half of the labor force was engaged in R&D!) Calculate the growth rate of output per worker. Now suppose that γ_A is raised to 0.75. How many years will it take before output per worker returns to the level it would have reached if γ_A had remained constant? (Note: You can solve this problem by using a calculator or computer or by applying some of the tricks for working with growth rates discussed in Chapter 1.)

5. Consider the two-country model of Section 8.3. Suppose that $\gamma_{A,1} > \gamma_{A,2}$ and that the two countries are in steady state. Suppose now that Country 1 raises the fraction of the labor force that is doing R&D. Draw a picture showing how the rates of growth in Countries 1 and 2 will behave over time.

6. Consider the two-country model of Section 8.3. Suppose that $\gamma_{A,1} > \gamma_{A,2}$ and that the two countries are in steady state. Now suppose that Country 2 raises the fraction of the labor force that is doing R&D so much that $\gamma_{A,1} < \gamma_{A,2}$. Draw a picture showing how the rates of growth in Countries 1 and 2 will behave over time.

7. Consider the two-country model of Section 8.3. Suppose that the cost-of-copying function is:

$$\mu_c = \mu_i \left(\frac{A_1}{A_2} \right)^{-\beta},$$

where $0 < \beta < 1$. Assume that the two countries have labor forces of equal size.

a. Using this function, solve for the steady-state ratio of technology in the leading country to technology in the follower country (i.e., A_1/A_2) as a function of the values of γ_A in the two countries. Show how this depends on the value of β, and explain what is going on.

b. Assume that $\beta = 1/2$, $\mu_i = 10$, $\gamma_{A,1} = 0.2$, and $\gamma_{A,2} = 0.1$. Calculate the steady-state ratio of technology in Country 1 to technology in Country 2.

For additional exploration and practice using the Online Data Plotter and data sets, please visit www.pearsonhighered.com/weil.

INCORPORATING TECHNOLOGICAL PROGRESS INTO THE SOLOW MODEL

We start with the Solow model using a Cobb-Douglas production function. The production function is:

$$Y = AK^\alpha L^{1-\alpha},$$

where Y is output, K is physical capital, L is labor, and A is a measure of productivity. In Chapter 3, we assumed that A was constant. Now we consider what happens when A grows over time. We use a hat ($\wedge$) to designate growth rates, so the growth rate of A is $\hat{A}$.

Before we proceed, it is convenient to define a new measure of productivity, which will simply be a transformation of our old measure, A. We define a new variable e:

$$e = A^{1/(1-\alpha)}, \text{ or alternatively, } e^{1-\alpha} = A.$$

The production function is thus

$$Y = e^{1-\alpha}K^\alpha L^{1-\alpha} = K^\alpha(eL)^{1-\alpha}.$$

With the equation in this form, we can think of the technology variable, e, as measuring the number of *effective workers* per actual worker. That is, increasing e and increasing L have the same effect on the total amount of output. The product of these two variables, eL, is the total number of effective workers in the economy.

In Chapter 3 we transformed the production function by dividing both sides by L to put output and capital in per-worker terms. Now we divide both sides by eL to put output and capital in per-effective-worker terms. We define:

$$\text{output per effective worker} = y = Y/eL,$$

$$\text{capital per effective worker} = k = K/eL.$$

The production function thus becomes:

$$y = k^\alpha.$$

To derive the equation for the change in the capital stock over time, we start with the definition of capital per effective worker and differentiate with respect to time. (Recall that we use a dot over a variable to indicate a derivative with respect to time.)

$$\dot{k} = \frac{d\left(\frac{K}{eL}\right)}{dt} = \frac{\dot{K}eL - \dot{L}Ke - \dot{e}KL}{(eL)^2} = \frac{\dot{K}}{eL} - \frac{\dot{L}}{L}\left(\frac{K}{eL}\right)$$

$$-\frac{\dot{e}}{e}\left(\frac{K}{eL}\right) = \frac{\dot{K}}{eL} - (\hat{L} + \hat{e})k.$$

We substitute into this equation the differential equation describing the evolution of the aggregate capital stock:

$$\dot{K} = \gamma Y - \delta K,$$

where γ is the fraction of output that is invested and δ is the depreciation rate. This substitution, along with the assumption that the growth rate of the labor force, $\hat{L}$, is 0, yields:

$$\dot{k} = \gamma y - (\hat{e} + \delta)k = \gamma k^{\alpha} - (\hat{e} + \delta)k. \tag{8.A.1}$$

The intuition for this equation is that $\hat{e}$, the growth in the number of effective workers per actual worker, is playing the same role that population growth played in the version of the Solow model studied in Chapter 4. Specifically, when $\hat{e}$ is large, it dilutes the amount of capital per effective worker.

Steady State

We can analyze the steady state of the model exactly as we did in Chapters 3 and 4. In particular, we can draw a figure like Figure 3.4, showing how the steady-state level of capital per effective worker is determined. We can also algebraically solve for the steady state by setting the equation for the growth rate of capital per effective worker equal to 0 (that is, $\dot{k} = 0$).

$$0 = \gamma k_{ss}^{\alpha} - (\hat{e} + \delta)k_{ss}.$$

We can solve this equation for k_{ss}:

$$k_{ss} = \left(\frac{\gamma}{\hat{e} + \delta}\right)^{1/(1-\alpha)}.$$

The steady-state level of output per effective worker is given by the equation

$$y_{ss} = k_{ss}^{\alpha} = \left(\frac{\gamma}{\hat{e} + \delta}\right)^{\alpha/(1-\alpha)} \tag{8A.2}$$

Output per effective worker, y, is constant in the steady state. What about *total* output? To answer this question, we start with the definition of y,

$$y = Y/(eL),$$

and taking logs and differentiating with respect to time:

$$\hat{y} = \hat{Y} - \hat{e} - \hat{L}.$$

We have assumed that there is no growth in the labor force, so this equation can be rewritten as:

$$\hat{Y} = \hat{y} + \hat{e}.$$

Finally, in the steady state, $\hat{y} = 0$, so we have the equation:

$$\hat{Y} = \hat{e}.$$

In other words, total output grows at the growth rate of e. We can rewrite this equation in terms of our original measure of productivity, A, by starting with the definition of e, taking logs, and differentiating with respect to time, to get:

$$\hat{e} = \left(\frac{1}{1 - \alpha}\right)\hat{A}$$

and thus:

$$\hat{Y} = \left(\frac{1}{1 - \alpha}\right)\hat{A}.$$

The Effect of a Change in Technology Growth

Equation 8A.2, which shows the steady-state level of output per effective worker, says raising the growth rate of technology, $\hat{e}$, will *lower* the steady-state level of output per effective worker. At first this result seems counterintuitive in that we would expect an increase in technological progress to *raise* the level of output. The resolution to this mystery is that faster technological progress does raise the level of output per worker, even as it lowers the level of output per effective worker be-cause it raises the number of effective workers per worker—that is, e. We can see this effect by tracing through the chain of events that follows from an increase in the growth rate of technology, that is, in $\hat{e}$.

Previously we derived the equation:

$$\hat{Y} = \hat{y} + \hat{e},$$

which says that the growth rate of total output is the sum of the growth rate of output per effective worker and the growth rate of effective workers per actual worker. In the steady state, $\hat{y}$ is 0. Now consider an economy that is in steady state. Suppose that there is an increase in the growth rate of technology—that is, $\hat{e}$ rises. Two forces will be acting on the growth rate of total output. On the one hand, $\hat{e}$ has risen. On the other hand, because the steady-state level of output per effective worker has fallen, $\hat{y}$ will become negative (having been 0 in the steady state). Which of these effects will dominate?

To answer this question, we rewrite Equation 8A.1 by dividing both sides by k:

$$\hat{k} = \frac{\dot{k}}{k} = \gamma k^{\alpha-1} - (\hat{e} + \delta).$$

In the steady state, $\hat{k}$ is 0. Let the increase in $\hat{e}$ be denoted $\Delta \hat{e}$. Because the right side of the preceding equation is equal to 0 before the increase in e, we have that following the increase:

$$\hat{k} = -\Delta\hat{e}.$$

The relationship between the growth rates of y and k can be derived by starting with the production function in per-effective-worker terms, taking logs, and differentiating with respect to time:

$$\hat{y} = \alpha\hat{k}.$$

Combining the two preceding equations:

$$\hat{y} = -\alpha\Delta\hat{e}.$$

The growth rate of total output will thus be:

$$\hat{Y} = \hat{y} + \hat{e} + \Delta\hat{e} = \hat{e} + (1 - \alpha)\Delta\hat{e},$$

so the initial effect of a rise in the growth rate of technology by some amount $\Delta\hat{e}$ will be to raise the growth rate of total output by $(1 - \alpha)\Delta\hat{e}$. Over time, however, as the economy moves to a new steady state, y will fall and $\hat{y}$ will approach 0. In the new steady state, the growth rate of total output will have risen by the full amount $\Delta\hat{e}$.

Figure 8.8 puts all these results together. It shows the time paths of e, y, and Y for a country that starts in steady state and then experiences an increase in $\hat{e}$. (The graphs use a ratio scale on each vertical axis, so a variable growing at a constant rate will appear as a straight line.)

FIGURE 8.8

Effect of an Increase in Technological Progress

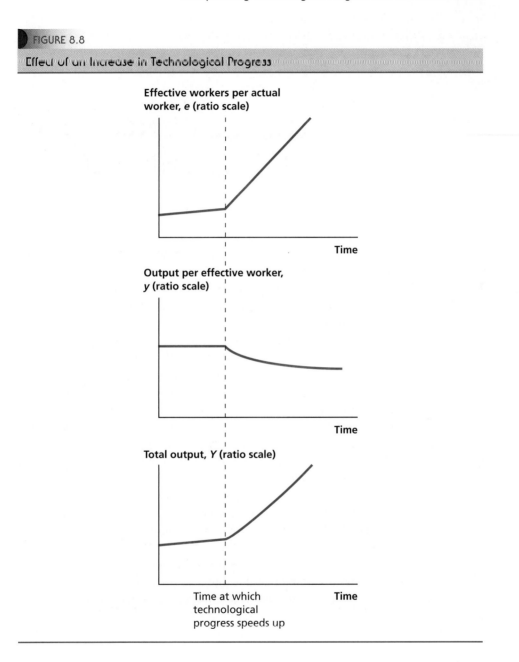

Effective workers per actual worker, *e* (ratio scale)

Time

Output per effective worker, *y* (ratio scale)

Time

Total output, *Y* (ratio scale)

Time at which technological progress speeds up

Time

THE CUTTING EDGE
OF TECHNOLOGY

I believe that
the motion picture is
destined to revolutionize
our educational system
and that in a few years it
will supplant largely, if not
entirely, the use of textbooks.

—Thomas Edison, 1922[1]

The phrase "cutting edge of technology" refers to new techniques that are just moving out of development and into production. Cutting-edge technologies hold great promise for higher productivity, although they are not guaranteed to work. Today, examples of cutting-edge technologies include quantum computing, gene therapy, and supercapacitors.

One characteristic of cutting-edge technologies is that they do not remain that way for long. With time, technologies that are at the cutting edge become commonplace or even obsolete. Conveniences that we take for granted—automobiles, refrigerators, electric lights, and even the flush toilet—were revolutionary inventions in their day. A whole host of technologies that were once cutting edge are now outmoded and no longer used: movable type, the steam piston engine, the telegraph, and the player piano, to name but a few.

Technological advance has allowed us to enjoy the high standard of living that we see in the developed world today. Of course, it is not technology alone that makes rich countries rich; if it were, then no countries would be poor today. But technology is essential—we could hardly imagine a country with a 21st-century standard of living using 19th-century technology.

It is common to take for granted not only the technological advances that have made our current standard of living possible, but also the process of technological change itself—that is, the fact that there is a cutting edge of technology and that it is always changing. Yet this process of rapid technological change is historically unusual. The era of rapid technological progress dates back only 250 years in the most advanced countries. Before this period, technological advance was slow and sporadic. Even within the current era of rapid advance, waves of progress have alternated with periods when the pace of technological change has slackened.

---

[1]Quoted in Cuban (1986).

In this chapter we look at the process of technological change. In contrast to Chapter 8, where our focus was on how technology differs among countries, this chapter examines technology in only the most advanced countries, those at the cutting edge. We consider both the speed with which technology advances and the factors determining that advance. We will see how growth accounting can provide information about changes in technological progress over time. With respect to the sources of technological progress, we will examine data on the inputs into new technologies (such as the number of researchers) and the growth rate of technology, to see what we can learn about the "technology production function" that relates the two.

The last part of the chapter considers the future course of technological progress. Although most of us assume that technological advance will continue at its current pace, some economists (who are generally a pessimistic bunch) are not so sure. We will explore whether inventions are getting harder and harder to come up with as the stock of possible new ideas is depleted. We will also ask whether the fact that some sectors of the economy are experiencing rapid technological progress while others remain technologically stagnant could lead to problems in the future.

9.1 THE PACE OF TECHNOLOGICAL CHANGE

To get a sense of the pace of technological progress, we can think about specific revolutionary inventions and when they were made. Granted, such an approach poses many problems. For example, how do we judge the importance of one invention versus another? Nonetheless, even a quick consideration of the list of momentous inventions in the box "Some Milestones of Technological Progress" shows a concentration of inventions in the last few centuries.

An alternative way to examine technological progress is to apply one of the techniques introduced in Chapter 7. There we used data on factor accumulation to conduct a growth accounting exercise, which shows how productivity has changed over time. We concluded that most productivity change is properly associated with technological progress. In the rest of this section, we apply growth accounting to three broad historical periods.

Technological Progress before the 18th Century

To set the stage for an examination of economic growth in the last several centuries, we begin by looking further back in the past. We focus on Europe, which not only is the area for which the best data are available but also had become the world's technology leader by 1700.

Conducting a growth accounting exercise for such an early period poses a number of problems. For one thing, the available data are quite sparse. There are

SOME MILESTONES OF TECHNOLOGICAL PROGRESS

- *Food production* (8500 B.C.)—The step from hunting and gathering to planting crops and raising livestock allowed for higher population densities and the rise of complex civilizations.

- *Wheel* (3400 B.C.)—Invented in the region of the Black Sea, the wheel spread through Europe and Asia within a few centuries. The wheel was also invented in Mexico before the arrival of Europeans, but it never found practical application there.

- *Writing*—Invented in Mesopotamia around 3000 B.C., writing was also independently developed in Central America before 600 B.C.

- *Padded horse collar*—Invented in China around 250 B.C. and independently in Europe in the ninth century, the padded collar allowed a horse to pull a heavy load without choking itself, thus producing a leap in the efficiency of animal power.

- *Mechanical clock* (around 1275)—This invention revolutionized the organization of economic activity by allowing people to coordinate their actions.

- *Movable type* (1453)—Johannes Gutenberg's invention made it practical to manufacture books on a printing press. In the 50 years that followed, more books were produced in Europe than during the preceding millennium, stimulating vast social as well as economic changes. Movable type was also invented in China some six centuries previously but did not take off there.

- *Steam engine* (1768)—This innovation was the first practical method for converting chemical energy into mechanical energy.

- *Textile manufacture* (second half of the 18th century)—A series of inventions mechanized the spinning and weaving of cotton textiles, which were the premier industry of the Industrial Revolution. The price of cotton cloth declined by 85% between 1780 and 1850.

- *Network electricity* (last quarter of 19th century)—This was not a single invention but a series, including the dynamo (1870), the light bulb (1879), the transformer (1885), and the alternating current electric motor (1889). Together, these devices revolutionized the transmission and use of energy.

- *Mass production of automobiles* (1908)—Henry Ford did not invent the car, but by standardizing design and streamlining production, he brought the price of automobiles within reach of the average family.

- *Transistor* (1947)—This tiny electronic switch laid the basis for modern computers and telecommunications.

- *ARPANET* (1969)—The predecessor to the Internet, this network was created by the U.S. Department of Defense. Originally it

no data at all on the accumulation of physical and human capital, whereas data about population and income per capita are only imprecise estimates. Thus, we must consider any results we obtain as rough approximations.

A second issue in doing this kind of growth accounting exercise on historical data relates to a consideration we discussed in Chapter 3: the important role that land played as an input in preindustrial economies. Ignoring the role of land, as we

connected 4 host computers. A decade later, there were 188 hosts. By 2011, there were over 849 million Internet hosts.

- *Polymerase chain reaction* (1985)—This technique, by which a DNA fragment is rapidly reproduced, is a key tool of genetic engineering.

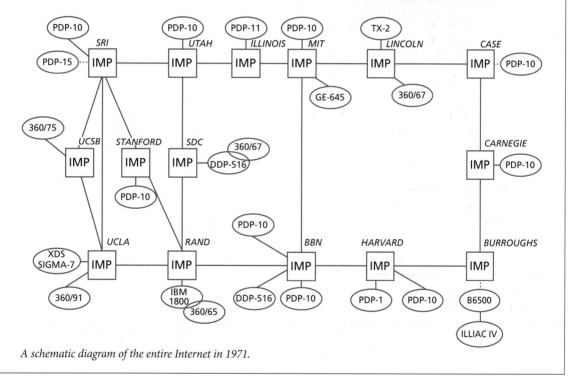

A schematic diagram of the entire Internet in 1971.

did in our growth accounting exercise in Chapter 7, would not be appropriate in studying a time period when most people worked as farmers and most wealth was held in the form of land.

Taking account of these problems, we consider a production function in which the only factors of production are labor (L) and land (X):

$$Y = AX^\beta L^{1-\beta}.$$

This is a Cobb-Douglas production function of the same sort that we examined in previous chapters. The exponent β will be equal to the fraction of national income that is paid to owners of land. As in previous chapters, Y measures output and A measures productivity.

Dividing both sides of this production function by L, we get an expression for output per worker (y):

$$y = A\left(\frac{X}{L}\right)^{\beta}. \tag{9.1}$$

Following the same procedure we used in Chapter 7, we can write this equation in terms of growth rates as:[2]

$$\hat{y} = \hat{A} + \beta\hat{X} - \beta\hat{L}, \tag{9.2}$$

where a hat (^) over a variable indicates its annual rate of growth. Because we are considering a geographical area of constant size, the quantity of land does not change ($\hat{X} = 0$). Rearranging the remaining terms in Equation 9.2, we get an expression for productivity growth:

$$\hat{A} = \hat{y} + \beta\hat{L}. \tag{9.3}$$

To calculate the growth rate of productivity, $\hat{A}$, we need data on the growth rates of income per capita and the size of the population.

The final piece of our calculation is a measure of the parameter β, the exponent on land in the production function. We use a value of $\beta = 1/3$, based on evidence that in preindustrial economies, the share of national income paid to land owners was around one-third.[3] Table 9.1 presents the results of this calculation for two time periods. During the first period, from A.D. 500 to 1500, income per capita in Europe did not grow at all; as we saw in Chapter 4, the Malthusian model

TABLE 9.1

Growth Accounting for Europe, A.D. 500–1700

Period	Annual Growth Rate of Income per Capita, $\hat{Y}$	Annual Growth Rate of Population, $\hat{L}$	Annual Growth Rate of Productivity, $\hat{A}$
500–1500	0.0%	0.1%	0.033%
1500–1700	0.1%	0.2%	0.166%

---

[2]Mathematical Note: Taking logarithms of Equation 9.1,

$$\ln(y) = \ln(A) + \beta\ln(X) - \beta\ln(L).$$

Differentiating with respect to time, we get Equation 9.2.

[3]Kremer (1993).

of population, which implies that income per capita should be roughly constant, fit Europe well in these centuries. Population grew during this period at a rate of 0.1% per year. The table shows that the calculated rate of productivity growth was 0.033% per year. This calculation implies that over the entire 1,000-year period, the value of *A* rose by a factor of 1.39. In other words, a given quantity of land and labor would have produced 39% more output in the year 1500 than it did in 500.

The second period examined, 1500–1700, saw a quickening of economic growth in Europe. Having been roughly constant for a millennium, income per capita grew at a rate of roughly 0.1% per year, and population growth rose to 0.2% per year. The growth rate of productivity, 0.166% per year, was five times as high as it had been during the preceding 1,000 years. But even during this latter period, the growth rate of productivity was extremely slow in comparison to what we see in the world today. For example, in Chapter 7, we saw that the average growth rate of productivity in the United States over the period 1975–2009 was 0.54% per year.

The Industrial Revolution

The most significant turning point in the history of technological progress was the **Industrial Revolution,** which is generally dated between 1760 and 1830 in Britain, spreading somewhat later to continental Europe and North America. The Industrial Revolution was a period of rapid technological innovation in a number of industries. Most significantly, businesses began to mechanize production in ways that would allow the transfer of tasks that had been performed by skilled artisans to machines that could work faster and tirelessly. The three most important areas of change were

- *Textiles*—Innovations in the manufacture of textiles, particularly cotton textiles, were the centerpiece of the Industrial Revolution. A wave of new inventions revolutionized the processes of spinning, weaving, and printing fabric. For example, the time required for a worker to spin one pound of cotton into thread fell from 500 hours to only 3. British production of cotton textiles rose by a factor of 125 between 1770 and 1841, and prices plummeted.[4] As a consequence, the use of underwear became common for the first time.

- *Energy*—Wind, water, animals, and human muscle had been the only sources of mechanical energy for millennia. The steam engine, in which burning fuel produced steam to drive a piston, represented a revolutionary break with the past. Using the steam engine tapped the vast chemical energy contained in coal deposits (already used as fuel for heating) as a source of mechanical energy. Between 1750 and 1850, British production of coal rose 10-fold.[5] Steam engines also revolutionized transportation, beginning with

[4]Harley (1993).
[5]Pollard (1980).

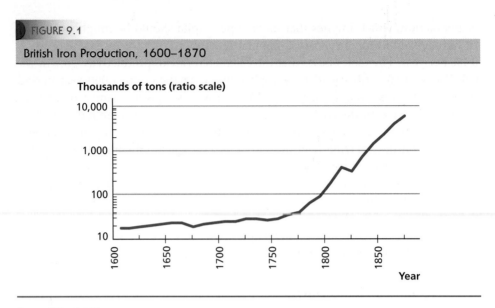

FIGURE 9.1

British Iron Production, 1600–1870

Thousands of tons (ratio scale)

Source: Riden (1977).

Robert Fulton's steamboat in 1807 and spreading later to railroads (the first steam railway opened in 1825).

- *Metallurgy*—The widespread replacement of wood with coal as a source of fuel in iron smelting, as well as several important technical innovations, dramatically drove down the cost of iron production. Figure 9.1 shows the resulting increase in output. Production of iron, which had been relatively constant for the previous two centuries, rose from 34,000 tons in 1760 to 680,000 tons in 1830 and 5,960,000 tons in 1870. By 1825 England, with 2% of the world's population, was producing half of the world's iron.[6] Iron was used in turn in the construction of buildings, bridges, and railways.

Along with these changes in production technology came shifts in the overall structure of the economy—shifts in where people worked and lived. Between 1760 and 1831, the fraction of the British labor force employed in agriculture, forestry, and fishing fell by half, from 48% to 25%, whereas the fraction of the labor force employed in industry and mining rose from 22% to 41%.[7] The fraction of the British population living in cities rose from one-sixth to one-half over the period 1700–1850. To move food, raw materials, and finished products around an increasingly integrated national economy, some 2,400 miles (4,000 kilometers) of canals were constructed in Britain between 1760 and 1835.

---

[6]Riden (1977), Bairoch (1988), p. 245.
[7]Stokey (2001).

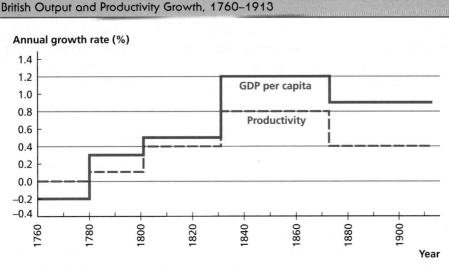

FIGURE 9.2

British Output and Productivity Growth, 1760–1913

Annual growth rate (%)

Source: Crafts (1996).

How did the Industrial Revolution affect Britain's economic growth? Figure 9.2 shows data on the growth rates of GDP per capita and productivity in Britain from 1760 to 1913.[8] One striking aspect of the figure is that despite the technological upheavals of the Industrial Revolution, the pace of economic growth was quite slow by modern standards. For example, in the years 1801–1831, during which Britain rose to be the world's dominant political and economic power, GDP per capita grew at only 0.5% per year and productivity at only 0.4% per year—rates we would consider fairly dismal today.

As is also evident in Figure 9.2, growth in productivity and output did not stop or even slow down with the end of the Industrial Revolution in 1830. In the later 19th century, mass production in factories replaced decentralized cottage industries. Economic historians identify a "Second Industrial Revolution," dated roughly 1860–1900, with innovations in industries such as chemicals, electricity, and steel.

Given these two observations—that growth during the Industrial Revolution was not particularly fast and that growth did not slow down when the Industrial Revolution ended—what was really so revolutionary about the period? There are two answers. First, the technologies introduced during the Industrial Revolution were indeed revolutionary, but their immediate impact on economic growth was

---

[8]Crafts (1996).

small because they were initially confined to a few industries. More significantly, the Industrial Revolution was a *beginning*. Rapid technological change, the replacement of old production processes with new ones, the continuous introduction of new goods—all of these processes that we take for granted today got their start during the Industrial Revolution. Although the actual growth rates achieved during this period do not look revolutionary in retrospect, the pattern of continual growth that began then was indeed revolutionary in contrast to what had come before.[9]

Technological Progress since the Industrial Revolution

Figure 9.3 shows the growth rates of GDP per capita and productivity in the United States for the years 1870–2007. During this period the United States overtook Britain to become the wealthiest and most technologically advanced country in the world (see Figure 1.5).[10]

One striking feature of Figure 9.3 is the period of high growth of total factor productivity lasting from 1890 to 1971. During this remarkable period—roughly the length of one human lifetime—daily life in the most developed countries was transformed more dramatically than ever before. Among the most important

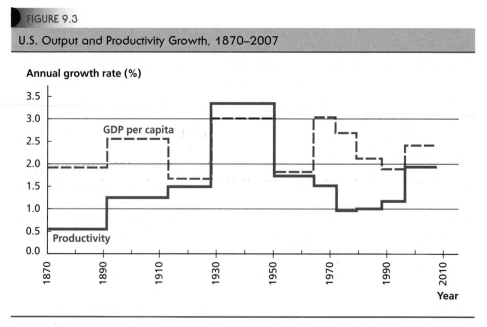

FIGURE 9.3

U.S. Output and Productivity Growth, 1870–2007

Sources: Gordon (1999, 2010).

---

[9]Mokyr (1990), Chapter 5.
[10]Gordon (1999, 2000).

changes were electric lights, refrigeration, air conditioning, the telephone, the automobile, air travel, radio, television, and indoor plumbing. Many of these technologies were invented previously in the 19th century, but they took several decades to spread to the economy as a whole—a process that is known as **diffusion.** For example, the electric light bulb was invented in 1879, but by 1899 only 3% of U.S. households had electric light. It took another three decades, until 1929, before 70% of households were using this technology.[11]

A second trend that emerges from Figure 9.3 is the dramatic reduction in the growth of productivity starting in the early 1970s. Having averaged 1.99% per year over the period 1890–1971, productivity growth fell to an annual rate of 1.06% between 1972 and 1995. This **productivity slowdown,** which took place not only in the United States but also throughout the developed world, was one of the most puzzling phenomena of the post–World War II era. Many observers feared that the rapid technological progress that had done so much to improve living standards had abruptly come to an end. Compounded over time, the change in productivity growth would have an enormous impact on the standard of living.

What caused the productivity slowdown? In explaining this phenomenon, it is important to remember a point from Chapter 2: Productivity is not the same as technology. In the long run, it is clear that productivity growth mostly comes from improvements in technology, but in any given time period, there can be changes in productivity that have more to do with the organization of the economy than with changes in technology—in other words, changes in what we have called *efficiency.* Thus, the slowdown in productivity growth in the 1970s and 1980s does not necessarily mean that the growth rate of *technology* fell. Indeed, there is good reason to think that the period of time of the productivity slowdown is one in which the efficiency of the U.S. economy fell. Large increases in the price of oil in 1973 and 1979 threw the economies of all of the industrial economies into chaos (and, indeed, the slowdown in productivity growth was largest in industries that were related to the production and use of energy, such as motor vehicles and electricity production).[12] Two massive recessions—one in 1974 and another in 1981–1983—left a significant fraction of the capital stock sitting idle. Both inflation and unemployment reached their post-World War II peaks during this period. One interpretation of these data on productivity is that negative changes in the efficiency of production undid the positive progress in technology.

A final striking aspect of Figure 9.3 is that, starting in the mid-1990s, there was another change in the trend. Productivity growth averaged 1.95% per year between 1995 and 2007, almost exactly the same as its average level between 1890 and 1971. Although this apparent change in trend is based on only a few years' worth of data, it has already excited a great deal of discussion. Some economists see in these data the beginning of a "Third Industrial Revolution," centered on

---

[11]David (1991a), Gordon (2000).
[12]Nordhaus (2004).

information technologies such as computing and telecommunications. Skeptics point out, however, that although technological progress in information industries has been breathtaking, these industries by themselves do not constitute a large fraction of the economy. Whether information technology will indeed transform other parts of the economy and have as large an effect on productivity as previous generations of technological progress remains to be seen.

9.2 THE TECHNOLOGY PRODUCTION FUNCTION

Thomas Edison, who invented the light bulb, phonograph (the first device for recording sound), and motion picture, once commented that "genius is one percent inspiration and ninety-nine percent perspiration." As true as this was for a great inventor like Edison, it is even more so for the men and women who are responsible for most research and development. In other words, technological progress does not occur spontaneously but rather as a result of deliberate effort.

In Chapter 2 we first encountered the idea of a production function that relates the inputs (factors of production) to the quantity of output produced in an economy. In this section our goal is to think about a similar concept: a **technology production function.**[13] This is a function in which the output is new technologies and the inputs are the things we use to create these new technologies. In a modern economy, the inputs to the technology production function are the labor and human capital of researchers, along with the capital (laboratories, computers, and so on) that they use.

A first step in thinking about such a technology production function is to measure the inputs and outputs themselves. We focus on the years since World War II because this is the only period for which good data are available. Over the period 1950–2007, the number of researchers engaged in research and development (R&D) in the G-5 countries (the United States, United Kingdom, France, Germany, and Japan) increased from 251,000 to 3.5 million—a factor of 14.[14] Regarding the output of the technology production function, the best evidence we have is the growth rate of productivity, shown in Figure 9.3. Here the evidence points to falling, or at best constant, productivity growth over the post–World War II period. Although productivity growth is not a perfect measure of technological change, the data do not give much evidence of a long-term rise in the rate of technological progress.

Using these data to compare inputs into and outputs of the technology production function, a startling fact emerges: *The input to technological progress has grown substantially over time, whereas the growth rate of technology has not.* In this section, we discuss the implications of this fact for the nature of the technology production function.

---

[13]This treatment follows Jones (1995).
[14]Jones (2002), OECD MSTI database.

GENERAL-PURPOSE TECHNOLOGIES

How does technological progress proceed? In an even flow or in waves? In recent years, economists studying technological change have focused on the latter view: that there are certain momentous technological innovations, called **general-purpose technologies,** that change the entire nature of the economy. These technologies, which include the steam engine, network electricity, and railroads, have two important characteristics. First, they change the mode of production in many different sectors of the economy, and second, they trigger a chain reaction of complementary inventions that take advantage of the new technological paradigm. Because of the trail of complementary inventions that follow in its wake, the period of growth resulting from a single general-purpose technology can go on for several decades.

The electric motor provides a good case study of the far-reaching changes brought about by a general-purpose technology. Although electric motors were first used in manufacturing in 1883, their diffusion was initially slow. At the beginning of the 20th century, steam engines provided 80% of the mechanical drive used in U.S. factories, with most of the remainder supplied by water wheels and turbines. By 1929, however, electric motors powered 79% of mechanical drive.

The first effect of electric power was a gain in energy efficiency, but this was only the beginning. More important, electricity would change the production process itself. In factories powered by steam, a large steam engine turned a shaft that ran the length of the factory; individual machines were powered by belts that brought power from the central shaft. With this setup, machines had to be laid out along the line of the power shaft, and as long as any machines were in use, the central steam engine had to operate. At first, electric motors in factories simply replaced the central steam engine with a similarly powerful electric motor. Over time,

however, engineers learned that using electric motors would let them radically change the layout of the factory. When smaller motors powered individual pieces of equipment, engineers could organize factories in whatever layout used capital, labor, and raw materials most efficiently, rather than designing around power shafts leading to a steam engine. Between 1899 and 1929, output per hour in manufacturing grew at a rate of 2.6% per year. The use of individual motors also saved more energy because it became unnecessary to run a large central motor when only a few pieces of machinery were in use.[*]

The most recent general-purpose technology is the semiconductor (i.e., the transistor and the integrated circuit), which forms the basis for modern computers. As with other general-purpose technologies, the initial diffusion of the semiconductor was slow. (The first products to incorporate transistors, in the early 1950s, were hearing aids.) Over time, however, semiconductor-based computers have penetrated almost every sector of the economy. But as computers spread through the economy in the 1980s, the growth rate of productivity remained dismally low. In 1987 economist Robert Solow commented despairingly that "you can see the computer age everywhere except in the productivity statistics." The failure of ever more powerful computers to produce faster productivity growth was referred to as the "computer paradox." Finally, in the second half of the 1990s, productivity growth sped up (as Figure 9.3 shows). In the view of many economists, this productivity speedup was the result of the computer's finally coming into its own as a productive instrument. Just as businesses had taken decades to learn how to apply electric motors to redesign their production processes, they had needed decades to learn how to exploit the capabilities of semiconductors.

[*]Devine (1983), Atkeson and Kehoe (2001).

Recall that in Chapter 8 we used a simple form of the technology production function, relating the rate of change of technology to the amount of labor devoted to research and development, L_A, and the "price" of a new invention, measured in units of labor, μ:

$$\hat{A} = \frac{L_A}{\mu}, \tag{9.4}$$

where a hat (^) over a variable indicates its rate of growth. Thus, $\hat{A}$ is the growth rate of technology.

Although Equation 9.4 looks simple, it incorporates two important assumptions about how new productive technologies are created. In this section we explore each of these assumptions and discuss what may be more reasonable alternatives. We then look at the implications of these alternatives for the future growth rate of technology.

The Relationship between Technology Level and the Speed of Technological Progress

"If I have seen farther than others," wrote mathematician Isaac Newton, "it is because I have stood on the shoulders of giants." Newton's point was that scientific knowledge is cumulative: Researchers today begin their investigations where those who came before them left off. The same incremental nature is true for the productive technologies that interest economists.

The cumulative nature of technological progress has both positive and negative effects on the ease of doing R&D. On the one hand, researchers today have a larger base of knowledge on which to build and a larger set of tools than did those who came before them. Thus, we would expect researchers today to be more productive than researchers in the past. On the other hand, researchers today might have more difficulty making discoveries or thinking of new technologies than their predecessors simply because the easiest discoveries have already been made. This negative effect of past discoveries on the ease of making discoveries today is called the **fishing out effect** (a body of water is said to be "fished out" when all the good fish have been caught). Further, because more is known today than in the past, it takes more effort for a researcher to learn everything required to work at the cutting edge.

Equation 9.4 makes a subtle but important assumption about this issue. Specifically, it assumes that the growth rate of technology depends *only* on the amount of resources devoted to R&D, not on the level of technology itself. In other words, the benefits of having better tools to work with exactly cancel out the negative effects of having already made the easier discoveries.

This assumption is probably not justified. The easiest way to see this is to consider the data discussed previously on the pace of technological progress and

SCIENCE AND TECHNOLOGY

Science represents our understanding about how the world works, that is, about physical and biological processes. Technology, by contrast, represents the knowledge of production techniques. What is the relationship between the two?

For most of human history, technological advance was largely unrelated to any scientific understanding of the rules by which the universe operated. Productive technologies were discovered by trial and error rather than through any understanding of why a certain procedure led to a given outcome. Indeed, if there was any connection between science and technology, it was that technological advance opened the way for greater scientific understanding.

There are at least two important ways in which advances in science have resulted from technological improvements. First, technology has posed many puzzles that scientists have then striven to solve. In one of the most famous cases, French scientist Sadi Carnot worked out the laws of thermodynamics in 1824 by trying to figure out why a high-pressure steam engine was more efficient than a low-pressure engine. Similarly, the mystery of why canned foods did not spoil was one of the puzzles that led Louis Pasteur into his studies of microbiology. More recently, two researchers at AT&T Corporation who were trying to understand technical problems with satellite communication stumbled onto the existence of background radiation, which confirmed one of the key predictions of the Big Bang theory of the universe (the researchers themselves did not know of the prediction).

Second, technological improvements have led to scientific advance by giving scientists tools to conduct better experiments and observations. Instruments such as the microscope (invented in 1590) and telescope (invented around 1600) literally opened up new worlds for scientific investigation. In a recent example of this phenomenon, the decoding of the human genome was vastly accelerated by the use of high-speed DNA-sequencing machines.

During the first half of the 19th century, scientists began to repay their debt to technology. The technologies of the Industrial Revolution (1760–1830), including advances in cotton spinning and steam power, had not depended on scientific discoveries. But the technologies of the Second Industrial Revolution (1860–1900), including innovations in steel, chemicals, and electricity, could not have been developed without new scientific understandings.

In the 20th century, this shift toward science-driven technological advance has continued. Technological breakthroughs like the semiconductor, laser, and nuclear power, for example, rested solidly on new scientific understandings of how the universe functions. This is not to say that science's debt to technology has been eliminated, however. Advances in physics depend crucially on new pieces of technology such as better particle accelerators. And there remain many examples of technological advance that do not result from new scientific understanding. For example, the key breakthrough in the invention of the ink-jet printer—which uses miniature heat sources to squirt tiny bubbles of ink onto paper—took place in 1977 when a researcher accidentally touched an ink-filled syringe with a hot soldering iron. Another example of technological advance that did not rely on science is the Windhexe, a device that uses compressed air traveling at supersonic speeds inside a closed chamber to instantly grind up and dry out liquid wastes such as poultry droppings. It was invented by a Kansas farmer with little education beyond high school, and as yet scientists still do not understand how it works.

the number of R&D researchers since World War II. The input of labor (as well as other resources) into R&D has risen dramatically, but the pace of technological progress has remained constant or even fallen. This finding seems to be evidence that the dominant effect is the negative one of having already made the easy discoveries. Were it not for the negative effect of past research on current R&D productivity, greater input into R&D would have resulted in faster technological progress.

Another way to see how much past technological progress has limited the productivity of present research is to look at the effort required to achieve some technological milestones. Many of the key breakthroughs of the 18th and 19th centuries resulted from the labors of lone scientists or inventors, often working in their spare time. By contrast, by the late 20th century, almost all advances were made by large and well-funded research teams.

Decreasing Returns to Scale in Technology Production

In Equation 9.4, the growth rate of technology is simply proportional to the number of people engaged in R&D. The equation says that if we doubled the number of researchers doing R&D (and doubled all other inputs into R&D as well), we would double the rate of technological progress. Is this a reasonable assumption? For many economic activities, the answer would be yes. That is, we often assume constant returns to scale, meaning an increase in all inputs will lead to a proportional increase in output.

For the technology production function, however, this assumption of constant returns to scale is not appropriate. Instead, this function is characterized by decreasing returns to scale. These decreasing returns to scale arise from the qualities of knowledge itself that we discussed in Chapter 8. Once a piece of knowledge has been created, it can be costlessly shared among any number of people. This quality of nonrivalry means that if several people (or groups of people) are all trying to create the same piece of knowledge, then the efforts of most of them will ultimately be wasted. After the first person has created the knowledge and shared it (or patented it), the efforts of all of the others who were trying to create that piece of knowledge will have been in vain.

The history of science and technology is replete with instances of this sort of duplication of effort. For example, 19th-century English naturalist Alfred Wallace worked for years on a theory of natural selection, only to be "scooped" by Charles Darwin. Similarly, the Bessemer process, which revolutionized the production of steel, was discovered simultaneously in 1856 by English engineer Henry Bessemer and U.S. inventor William Kelley. More recently, two competing research groups completed the sequencing of the human genome almost simultaneously. Parallel efforts to solve a particular technological problem often result in "patent races" in which the winner gets a patent and the loser(s) get nothing. For example, Alexander Graham Bell was able to reap a fortune from his invention of the telephone because he filed his patent application only two hours before a similar filing by a competing inventor, Elisha Gray. (At the time, U.S. patent law was based on a first-to-file system.)

When R&D is conducted on parallel tracks, the researchers often create parallel solutions to the same problem and develop parallel standards (e.g., the HD DVD and Blu-ray formats of high-definition optical disks). The more effort that is devoted to R&D, the more likely is this duplication of effort. Therefore, devoting more effort to R&D will not generate a proportional increase in the pace of technological progress.

Implications for the Future of Technological Progress

We can summarize the two modifications to our technology production function just described as follows. First, as the level of technology rises, finding new discoveries becomes ever harder. Second, as the effort devoted to R&D increases, the effectiveness of each new researcher falls. Both of these modifications imply that ever-increasing input into R&D will be required to maintain the current speed of technological progress. (The mathematical appendix to this chapter explores this issue more deeply.)

To get an idea of just how much more R&D effort will be required to maintain the current level of technological progress, we can look to historical data. We saw that from 1950 to 2007, the number of researchers in the G-5 countries grew from 251,000 to 3.5 million—a factor of 14 over 57 years. If this same ratio applies in the future, then maintaining the same rate of technological progress over the next 57 years will require a similar 14-fold increase in the number of researchers, from 3.5 million in 2007 to 49 million in 2064. Extending the analysis further, the effort will require 686 million researchers in 2121!

Is such an increase possible, or will technological progress inevitably slow down? To answer this question, we must look at three possible sources of growth in the amount of labor devoted to R&D:

- *The overall labor force could grow.*

  One of the factors that allowed the number of researchers to grow over the last half-century has been the expansion of the labor force, resulting from growth in the population and the increase in the labor force participation rate of women. For example, the labor force in the United States increased from 62 million to 153 million people between 1950 and 2011. Even if the fraction of the labor force engaged in R&D had remained constant, the number of researchers would have more than doubled.

  As we saw in Chapter 5, most of the world's richest countries, which are also those at the cutting edge of technology, are not expected to experience significant growth in population over the next several decades—and will probably never again experience the kind of rapid population growth that they did in the 19th and 20th centuries. Thus, population growth in these countries is unlikely to add much to the labor devoted to R&D. Similarly, growth in the labor force resulting from increased participation of women in the United States is bound to slow down because the labor force participation rate for women is almost as high as that for men (although this is not true in all of the technologically advanced countries).

- *The fraction of the labor force engaged in research could grow.*

In the United States, the fraction of the labor force that is engaged in R&D rose from 0.25% in 1950 to 0.92% in 2007, and similar increases occurred in other cutting-edge countries. Even more than the increase in the labor force, this increase in the fraction of the labor force doing research was responsible for the large rise in the number of researchers.

Will this expansion in the fraction of the labor force doing R&D continue into the future? In the very long run, the answer obviously has to be no; it is

WHERE IS THE CUTTING EDGE OF TECHNOLOGY?

In Chapter 8 we introduced the idea that some countries are at the cutting edge of technology ("technology leaders") whereas others trail behind ("technology followers"). In the world today, which countries are the technology leaders? Table 9.2 attempts to identify the cutting edge by looking at data on patents. Because patents are one means that inventors use to profit from their intellectual property, the number of patents, relative to a country's population, should be a good measure of inventive activity. Table 9.2 lists all of the countries that in 2010 had more than 30 patents granted in the United States for every million of their residents. (We omit the United States itself from the table because inventors are most likely to file for patents in their own countries, so we cannot compare data on patents granted to U.S. citizens with patents granted to foreign citizens.)

Patents are an imperfect measure of technological activity. Industries vary in how likely inventions are to be patented as opposed to being protected by other means. For example,

a survey of the managers of R&D labs found that the industry where patenting is considered most important in protecting intellectual property is pharmaceuticals, a result that explains why Switzerland, with its large pharmaceutical industry, has so many patents. By contrast, in the food and textiles industries, secrecy and lead time (i.e., being first to bring a product to market) are considered far more important than patents.* Countries that specialize in these industries may have a low rate of patenting even though they are technologically advanced. And even if a particular country is not at the forefront of technology, many localities in that country can be part of the technological cutting edge. The best example is the city of Bangalore in India, home to 120,000 information technology workers. Indeed, globalization has made it increasingly difficult to pinpoint a geographic area that corresponds to the cutting edge of technology.

*Cohen, Nelson, and Walsh (2000).

impossible for the fraction of the labor force doing R&D to rise above 100%. However, given the relatively small share of the labor force engaged in R&D today, the limit of 100% will not be binding for a long time. More realistically, however, if we accept that not *all* members of the labor force are capable of doing scientific research, the relevant limit may be much lower than 100%.

- *New members could be added to the set of countries doing cutting-edge research.*

From Table 9.2 it is clear that many countries at the cutting edge of research are newcomers. Japan, Taiwan, Israel, South Korea, and Singapore were not at the cutting edge of technology in the middle of the 20th century. Even fewer of the countries listed in that table would have been at the cutting edge

TABLE 9.2

U.S. Patents and Patents per Million Residents, 2010

Country	Patents	Patents per Million Residents
Taiwan	9,635	418.5
Japan	46,978	368.2
Israel	1,917	260.7
Finland	1,232	234.4
Switzerland	1,889	247.8
Sweden	1,594	175.7
South Korea	12,508	257.2
Germany	13,633	167.0
Canada	5,513	163.3
Hong Kong	716	101.0
Singapore	633	123.2
Luxembourg	44	88.4
Denmark	766	138.9
Netherlands	1,919	115.8
Iceland	25	80.9
Austria	905	110.2
Australia	2,079	96.6
Belgium	896	86.0
France	5,038	77.8
Norway	448	95.8
United Kingdom	5,038	80.8
Ireland	275	59.5
New Zealand	232	54.6
Italy	2,254	37.1

Source: U.S. Patent and Trademark Office, http://www.uspto.gov/web/offices/ac/ido/oeip/taf/cst_all.htm

of technology in 1900 or 1850. The addition of new members to the group of cutting-edge countries has expanded the labor pool from which researchers can be drawn. Even today, the countries at the cutting edge of technology account for only 14% of world population, so there is good reason to expect that this flow of newcomers will continue.

The upshot from this analysis is potentially hopeful, as long as we do not take too long run of a perspective. Even though continued technological progress requires devoting an increasing number of workers to R&D, no immediate constraint will prevent such an expansion. Given that only a small fraction of the labor force in the developed countries currently works in R&D, and that only a small fraction of the world lives in countries that are technological leaders, there is plenty of room to expand the number of researchers.

In the very long run, however, this analysis does become pessimistic. Assuming that the world's population eventually stabilizes, there will have to come a time when the amount of labor devoted to R&D will stop rising. At that point, the growth rate of technology will slow down.

9.3 DIFFERENTIAL TECHNOLOGICAL PROGRESS

In our analysis of technological progress, we have treated technology as a single measure that raises productivity in the economy as a whole. But simple observation shows that the pace of technological progress is radically different in various sectors of the economy. Some industries, such as communications, have changed beyond recognition over the past century. Other completely new industries have been created, among them television and air travel. By contrast, there are sectors in which production today looks much the same as it did a century ago. Barbers and teachers, for example, use many of the same tools as their great-grandparents did.

These differential changes in productive technology are reflected in changes in the relative prices of goods. Goods where there has been a lot of productivity growth have become cheap relative to goods where technological advance has been slow. For example, in 1927, one megawatt-hour of electricity cost slightly more than a fine men's suit ($55 versus $43). In 2010 the same amount of electricity cost only 12.4% as much as a similar suit ($98.80 and $795, respectively).[15]

What do these differential rates of technological progress imply for economic growth? One observation is obvious: Technological progress is more important when it occurs in a larger sector. For example, a huge productivity improvement in the toothbrush-producing industry will be less significant than a small productivity improvement in the automobile industry. More generally, we can say that

---

[15]Federal Reserve Bank of Dallas (1997), http://www.eia.gov/electricity/data.cfm#sales, http://www.hartschaffnermarx.com/mens-suits/.

the average rate of technological progress for the economy as a whole will be a weighted average of the rates of progress in the different sectors of the economy, with the weights of the different sectors proportional to the fraction of total output produced in that sector.

Differential Technological Progress: Two Theoretical Examples

The analysis presented previously only highlights a more important question: What happens to the fraction of the economy made up by a given sector when that sector experiences technological progress? Answering this question turns out to be quite complicated. But we can establish good intuition through two simple examples.

Example 1: Bread and Cheese. Imagine an economy in which only two goods are produced: bread and cheese. We will assume that these two goods are perfect complements, and thus consumed in a fixed ratio; one slice of bread is always eaten with one slice of cheese. Because no one will buy bread if there is no cheese to match, and vice versa, the production of bread will always equal the production of cheese.

Now suppose that there are different rates of technological progress in the two industries. Productivity in the bread industry rises at a rate of 2% per year, whereas productivity in the cheese industry does not rise at all. If the resources devoted to production of each good do not change, then bread production rises by 2% per year, whereas cheese production remains constant. Clearly this will not happen because it would result in the production of more bread than cheese. Instead, resources (capital and labor) are moved from bread production into cheese production. This movement of factors from the high-productivity industry (bread) to the low-productivity industry (cheese) slows productivity growth and partially offsets the technological progress taking place in the bread industry.

To see the long-run effect of this differential productivity growth, we can think about what this economy will look like far in the future, when technological progress in the bread industry has continued for a long time. At this point, bread production will be so technologically advanced that the economy will devote negligible resources to this industry. Rather, almost all of the economy's capital and labor will be devoted to producing cheese. Every year some of the capital and labor used to produce bread will be shifted over to the cheese industry, but the bread industry will use so few resources to begin with that these additions to the cheese industry will have only a minuscule effect on cheese production. The growth of output in the economy as a whole will therefore be almost zero—that is, almost the rate of productivity growth in the cheese industry.

Example 2: Butter and Margarine. Our second example also involves an economy in which only two goods are produced. But in this case, the two goods, butter and margarine, are perfect substitutes for each other, so consumers will want to consume only the cheaper of the two.

Suppose once again that there are different rates of technological progress. In the margarine industry, technology improves at a rate of 2% per year, whereas butter production technology does not improve at all. Further, suppose that in the year when we begin our analysis, butter is cheaper than margarine.

Initially, because butter is cheaper than margarine, consumers buy only butter. The economywide rate of technological progress is the same as the rate of progress in the butter industry—that is, zero. However, as margarine technology improves, the price of margarine falls relative to that of butter. At some point, margarine becomes cheaper than butter, and the economy switches from producing only butter to producing only margarine. At this point, the rate of growth of the economy as a whole increases because now the technological progress that is relevant is technological progress in the margarine industry.

The result in this example is exactly the opposite of what we saw in Example 1. In that case, technological progress eventually ground to a halt; in this case, the growth rate of technology for the economy as a whole speeds up over time.

Conclusions from the Examples. The key difference between these two examples is in what happens to the share of spending devoted to the sector with rapid technological progress. In Example 1 this share falls over time, so the economywide rate of technological progress falls as well. In Example 2 the share rises over time, so the economywide rate of technological progress rises as well. Although both examples are extreme, this general lesson carries over whenever we consider differential technological progress: If the fraction of income spent on the sectors with rapid technological growth rises over time, the overall growth rate of technology will also rise. If the share spent on these sectors falls, the overall rate of growth of technology will fall.

Which example is more applicable to the world today?

Technological Progress in the Real World: Goods versus Services

The most notable real-world case of this sort of differential technological progress is the production of goods versus services. Production methods for goods (i.e., manufacturing) have been one of the most technologically dynamic areas in the economy. By contrast, the production processes for many of the services we consume have changed little over the last century. As a result of this differential productivity growth, a change has occurred in the relative prices of goods and services. For example, in 1927 a pair of Levi's jeans cost roughly 13 times as much as a woman's haircut. By 2011, a pair of Levi's cost only 1.5 times as much as a woman's haircut. To give a more extreme example: In 2004 health insurance for a family of four was 2.5 times as expensive as a 37-in LCD television set. By 2011, health insurance was 35 times as expensive.[16]

To see whether this differential productivity growth will have a positive or negative impact on overall growth, we need to look beyond prices to the total amount of spending in these two areas. Here the news is bad: In the United States, the fraction of total consumption devoted to services rose from 40% in 1950 to 67% in 2010. Thus, economic activity is shifting into the sector with lower productivity growth. The economist William Baumol has called this shifting of expenditures into services, where productivity growth is slow, the **cost disease,** because relative costs rise in the sector with slow productivity growth. One notable sector with slow productivity growth and thus rising costs is education, as college students (and their parents) are all too well aware.

Does this analysis imply that growth will indeed grind to a halt? The future is not necessarily so bleak. Most important, although technological progress has in the past been faster in goods-producing industries than in service-producing industries, this fact will not necessarily hold true in the future. Plenty of entrepreneurs are trying to replace teachers with Internet technology, and if they succeed, a huge increase in productivity in this service industry will follow. Similarly, we find historical examples of technological change raising the productivity of a service industry. Music is a case in point. Before the late 19th century, a person who wanted to listen to music had to employ actual *musicians* to produce it for him. Thus, for most people, listening to music was limited to special venues such as concert halls. Few could afford the luxury of sitting at home and listening to music. Technological progress (starting with the player piano in 1896) changed all that, and today anyone can listen to music almost for free.

Technological Progress in the Real World: Information Technology

A second application of our analysis of differential technological progress is to the information technology industries, the most dynamic part of the economy today. Here rapid technological advance has been reflected in plummeting prices. Figure 9.5 shows how the price of computers has changed over 28 years. Between 1982 and 2010, the price index for computers (i.e., the amount that one would have to pay to buy a computer of constant processing power) fell at an average rate of 13.8% per year. Over the period as a whole, the price fell by a factor of 65.

Assuming that this technological progress continues, how will it affect the rate of technology growth in the economy as a whole? As we have seen, the answer

---

[16]Federal Reserve Bank of Dallas (1997), Goldman and McGlynn (2005), Young (2011), Schuman (2004), Hellmich (2010).

PREDICTING TECHNOLOGICAL PROGRESS

The big problem with forecasting progress in technology is simple to understand: The only way we can know now that something will be possible to do in the future is to know how it will be done—but if we know how it will be done, it has already been invented.

In 1965 Gordon Moore, one of the founders of Intel Corporation, made a prediction that has come to be known as **Moore's law,** which says that the power of microprocessors (the chips that are the "brains" of computers) would double every 18 months. Moore did not say how this change would come about, and the ways that it was accomplished were certainly unknown to him then. But the prophecy held roughly true. The Intel 4004 chip, released in 1971, contained 2,300 transistors; the Intel Xeon MP, released in 2008, had 1.9 billion (see Figure 9.4). The increase in capacity by a factor of 826,086 over the course of 37 years corresponds to a doubling every 22.6 months.

Moore's prediction is justifiably famous because it seemed outlandish at the time yet the increase in computer power he predicted has profoundly affected the global economy. Many predictions about technological progress now seem humorous, as the list here demonstrates.[*]

Too Optimistic

50 years hence…we shall escape the absurdity of growing a whole chicken in order to eat the breast or wing, by growing these parts separately under a suitable medium.

—Winston Churchill, British statesman, 1932

It is not too much to expect that our children will enjoy in their homes electricity too cheap to meter.

—Lewis L. Strauss, chairman of the U.S. Atomic Energy Commission, 1954

I do not hesitate to forecast that atomic batteries will be commonplace long before 1980.…It can be taken for granted that before 1980, ships, *aircraft, locomotives, and even automobiles will be atomically fueled.*

—David Sarnoff, television pioneer, 1955

Within 10 to 20 years' time we could have a robot that will completely eliminate all routine operations around the house and remove drudgery from human life.

—Professor M W Thring, "A Robot in the House," 1964

Some very likely technical innovations in the last third of the twentieth century:

- *some control of weather and/or climate*
- *direct electronic communication with the brain*
- *human hibernation for months or years at a time*
- *physically non-harmful methods of overindulging*
- *underwater cities*

—Herman Kahn and Anthony J. Weiner, *The Year 2000,* 1967

Too Pessimistic

If this thing were at all possible, then something similar would have been done a long time ago in antiquity by men like Archimedes or Moses. But if these wise men knew nothing of mirror pictures made permanent, then one can straightaway call the Frenchman Daguerre, who boasts of such an unheard of thing, the fool of fools.

—From a German publication in 1839, commenting on Louis Daguerre's announcement of the invention of photography

Well-informed people know it is impossible to transmit the voice over wires and that were it possible to do so, the thing would be of no practical value.

—Editorial in the *Boston Post,* 1865

When the Paris Exhibition closes electric light will close with it and no more be heard of.

—Erasmus Wilson, professor at Oxford University, 1878

Heavier-than-air flying machines are impossible.

—Lord Kelvin, president, Royal Society, 1895

There is not the slightest indication that [nuclear] energy will ever be obtainable.

—Albert Einstein, physicist, 1932

I think there is a world market for maybe five computers.

—Thomas Watson, chairman of IBM, 1943

Where a calculator on the ENIAC is equipped with 19,000 vacuum tubes and weighs 30 tons, computers in the future may have only 1,000 vacuum tubes and perhaps only weigh 1.5 tons.

—Popular Mechanics, March 1949

By 2005 or so, it will become clear that the Internet's impact on the economy has been no greater than the fax machine's.

—Paul Krugman, economist, 2000

*Sources: Wilson, Einstein, Kelvin, Churchill, Sarnoff, and Watson: Cerf and Navasky (1998); Thring: Kahn and Weiner (1967); Daguerre: Davidson (1988); Krugman: Krugman (2000).

FIGURE 9.4

Moore's Law as Seen in Intel Microprocessors

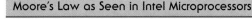

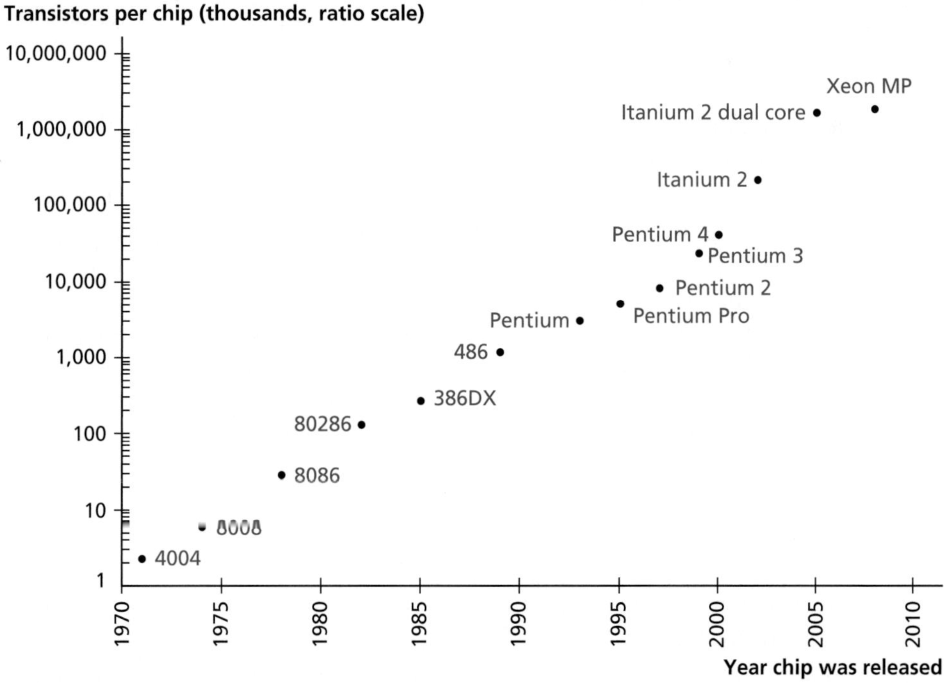

Transistors per chip (thousands, ratio scale)

Source: Intel Corporation.

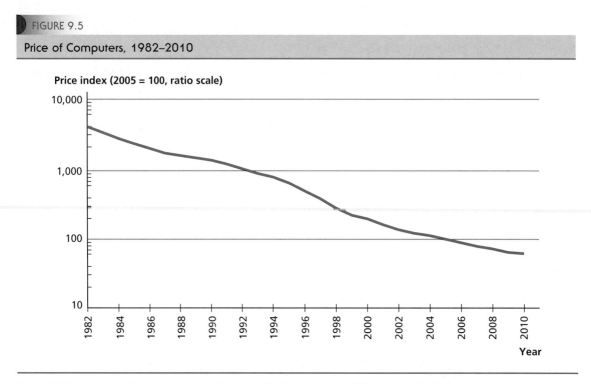

FIGURE 9.5

Price of Computers, 1982–2010

Source: U.S. Department of Commerce, National Income and Product Accounts, Table 1.5.4. Includes both computers and peripherals.

depends on how large a part of total output is composed of these information industries. People are getting more and better computers, cell phones, and so on, but the prices of these goods are falling, so it is not clear whether the total amount of spending on computers will rise, fall, or stay constant. Figure 9.6 shows that, at least so far, the answer has been "stay constant." The percentage of GDP invested in computers and peripherals in 2009 was essentially the same as the percentage invested in 1982. For people who bought several computers over this period (the author bought at least 15), this comes as no surprise: Despite the vast improvements in computer power and corresponding reductions in cost, the price of the computer that most people want has not changed all that much.

9.4 CONCLUSION

In the long run, technological progress is the major source of economic growth. In Chapter 8, where we first took up the subject of technological progress, we mainly focused on how technology differs among countries—specifically, why some countries are at the cutting edge of technology whereas others lag behind. In this chapter we have been concerned with the cutting edge itself: with the pace of technological progress and the process of technology creation.

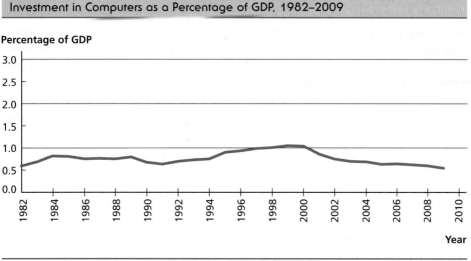

▶ FIGURE 9.6

Investment in Computers as a Percentage of GDP, 1982–2009

Percentage of GDP

Source: U.S. Department of Commerce, National Income and Product Accounts, Table 5.5.5. Includes both computers and peripherals.

Technological change dramatically accelerated with the Industrial Revolution (1760–1830) and has continued at a historically unprecedented pace ever since. Within this period of rapid growth, however, the pace of change has varied. Slack periods—most recently the productivity slowdown that afflicted most of the developed world from the mid-1970s through the mid-1990s—have alternated with waves of rapid growth associated with the arrival of new general-purpose technologies, the most recent being computers and information technology.

These 250 years of technological progress have altered the lives of residents of the world's richest countries almost beyond recognition. As economist Richard Easterlin puts it, "The transformation of living levels has been qualitative as well as quantitative. By comparison with the conveniences and comforts widely available in developed economies at the end of the 20th century, everyday life two centuries ago was most akin to what we would know today as 'camping out.'" Similarly, economic historian Joel Mokyr concluded that because of technological progress, daily life has changed more in the last 200 years than in the preceding 7,000 years.[17]

Will this rapid advance of technology continue? Our examination of the sources of technological progress provides some limited insight into this question. One of our most intriguing observations is that over the last six decades, the input into technological progress—that is, the number of people engaged in R&D—has

---

[17]Easterlin (2000), Mokyr (1990).

grown immensely, while at the same time the pace of technological progress has remained relatively constant. This observation suggests a negative effect of past R&D on current technological progress (i.e., a "fishing out" of good ideas) and decreasing returns to scale in the technology production function. Thus, maintaining the current pace of technological progress will require ever greater input into R&D. Luckily, there is little reason that the input into R&D cannot continue to grow at its current pace for the foreseeable future.

A second insight from our study of technological progress is that it is important in which sector such progress takes place. To raise standards of living, technological progress has to occur in sectors of the economy that represent a large fraction of total expenditure. Thus, a crucial question is whether those sectors where progress is fastest will absorb a rising or falling share of spending in the economy. A related question is whether technological progress will spill over from the goods-producing sectors, where it has historically been fastest, into the production of services, where technological progress has thus far been slow.

Beyond these general observations, the future of technology must by necessity remain a mystery. To know for sure that a certain technology can be invented in the future, one must have invented it already. The failures of past prognosticators should make any student of technology cautious.

KEY TERMS

Industrial Revolution **243**	technology production	fishing out effect **250**
diffusion **247**	function **248**	cost disease **259**
productivity slowdown **247**	general-purpose technologies **249**	Moore's law **260**

QUESTIONS FOR REVIEW

1. When did the Industrial Revolution take place? What were some of the most important industries affected? Why was it revolutionary?

2. What was the productivity slowdown? Was it necessarily caused by a slowdown in the growth rate of technology?

3. Why is the technology production function characterized by decreasing returns to scale?

4. How does the current level of technology affect the ability of current researchers to produce technological progress?

5. Given that technological progress proceeds at different speeds in different sectors of the economy, what implications do these differences have for the growth rate of aggregate output?

PROBLEMS

1. Over the period from 10,000 B.C. to A.D. 1, world population is estimated to have increased from 4 million to 170 million. Assuming that the level of income per worker was constant, the quantities of human and physical capital per worker did not change, and the exponent on land in the production function is one-third, calculate the total growth in productivity over this period. What was the *annual* growth rate of productivity, A?

2. The technology for cutting hair has changed little in the last 100 years, whereas the technology for growing wheat has improved dramatically. What do you think has happened to the relative prices of haircuts and wheat? What do you think has happened to the relative incomes of barbers and farmers? Explain how this is possible.

3. The *price elasticity of demand* for a good measures how much the quantity of the good demanded responds to a decline in the good's price. Specifically, the price elasticity of demand is the ratio of the percentage change in the quantity demanded to the percentage change in the price. How is a good's price elasticity of demand related to whether technological progress in producing that good will lead to a rise or decline in the share of the economy's total spending on that good?

4. Suppose that people consume only two goods, cheese and bread. They consume these two goods in a fixed ratio: One slice of bread is always eaten with one slice of cheese. Both cheese

and bread are produced using only labor as an input. Their production functions are:

$$Y_b = A_b L_b,$$

$$Y_c = A_c L_c,$$

where Y_b is the quantity of bread, Y_c is the quantity of cheese, L_b is the amount of labor devoted to producing bread, and L_c is the amount of labor devoted to producing cheese. The total quantity of labor in the economy, L, is constant, and $L_b + L_c = L$.

In the year 2000, $A_b = A_c = 1$. But technological progress takes place at different speeds in the two industries. Specifically, $\hat{A}_b = 2\%$, and $\hat{A}_c = 1\%$, where these growth rates of technology are exogenous.

a. What quantities of labor will be devoted to producing bread and cheese in 2000?

b. What will the growth rate of total output be in 2000? (Hint: Because the quantity of bread produced will always be the same as the quantity of cheese produced, the growth rate of total output equals the growth rate of the quantity of bread produced, which equals the growth rate of the quantity of cheese produced.)

c. Draw a graph showing the growth rate of output from the year 2000 onward. Show whether growth rises, falls, or stays constant, and explain why it does so. What will the growth rate of output be in the long run?

5. Do you expect the pace of technological progress to speed up, slow down, or remain constant over your lifetime? Explain your reasoning.

For additional exploration and practice using the Online Data Plotter and data sets, please visit www.pearsonhighered.com/weil.

AN IMPROVED VERSION OF THE TECHNOLOGY PRODUCTION FUNCTION

The technology production function first introduced in Chapter 8 was:

$$\hat{A} = \frac{L_A}{\mu},$$

where L_A is the labor force devoted to R&D, μ is the "price" of a new invention, measured in units of labor, and $\hat{A}$ is the growth rate of technology. Section 9.2 of this chapter discusses two potential problems with this formulation of the technology production function: first, a negative effect of the level of technology on the growth rate of technology (the fishing out effect), and second, decreasing returns to scale. We address each of these in turn.[18]

A simple way to model the fishing out effect is to raise the level of technology, A, by a negative coefficient and multiply it by the other terms on the right side of the equation:

$$\hat{A} = \frac{L_A}{\mu} A^{-\phi}, \quad 0 < \phi < 1.$$

This equation says that, holding constant L_A and μ, technological progress will be slower, the higher the current level of technology. The value of ϕ determines the strength of this effect. For example if $\phi = 1/2$, then quadrupling the level of technology would reduce by half the growth rate of technology produced by a given input of R&D. If $\phi = 1$, then quadrupling the level of technology would reduce by three-quarters the growth rate of technology produced by a given input of R&D.

We can incorporate decreasing returns to scale into our technology production function in a somewhat similar manner: We raise the input into R&D, L_A, to some power less than 1:

$$\hat{A} = \frac{L_A^{\lambda}}{\mu}, \quad 0 < \lambda < 1.$$

---

[18]This treatment draws heavily on Jones (1998).

This equation says that if the R&D effort (that is, L_A) is constant, then the growth rate of technology also should be constant. And if the R&D effort rises, then the growth rate of technology also should rise. However, because of duplication of effort, an increase in L_A will raise the growth rate of technology less than proportionally. For example, if $\lambda=1/2$, then raising L_A fourfold will only double the rate of technology growth.

Combining both of these effects produces the following technology production function:

$$\hat{A} = \left(\frac{1}{\mu} \right) L_A^\lambda A^{-\phi}.$$

Using this improved technology production function, we can calculate the relationship between the growth rates of R&D input on the one hand and technology on the other. If the growth rate of technology, $\hat{A}$, is constant, then it must also be the case that the product $L_A^\lambda A^{-\phi}$ is constant. Writing this as an equation:

$$x = L_A^\lambda A^{-\phi},$$

where x is a constant. Taking logarithms and differentiating with respect to time, we get:

$$0 = \lambda \hat{L}_A - \phi \hat{A}.$$

Finally, rearranging this equation yields:

$$\hat{A} = \frac{\lambda}{\phi} \hat{L}_A.$$

If we knew the values of λ and ϕ, we could use this equation to determine what rate of technological progress would be consistent with a given growth rate of the R&D labor force. Alternatively, we can use the equation, along with data on technological progress and growth of the R&D labor force, to learn about the parameters λ and ϕ themselves. For example, suppose that the growth rate of technology is 1% per year and that the growth rate of the number of researchers is 5% per year. This would imply that:

$$\frac{\lambda}{\phi} = \frac{\hat{A}}{\hat{L}_A} = \frac{0.01}{0.05} = 0.2.$$

Unfortunately, without additional data, we cannot learn the values of λ and ϕ separately. In the preceding example, it is possible that $\lambda = 0.2$ and $\phi = 1$, that $\lambda = 0.1$ and $\phi = 0.5$, and so on.

CHAPTER 10

EFFICIENCY

In my dream I came to a
room where men sat in a large
circle around a pot of soup. Each man
held a long spoon, which he could dip into
the pot. But the spoons were longer than the
men's arms, and so they could not bring the soup
to their mouths. The men were hungry, and cried
out in their misery. "This is hell," said my guide. Then
he took me to another room, similar to the first.
Once again men sat in a large circle around a pot
of soup, and once again each man's spoon was
so long that he could not bring it to his mouth.
But in this room the men were not hungry,
because they were feeding each other.
"This," said my guide, "is heaven."

—Variously attributed

In Chapter 7, in which we explored the subject of productivity, we found that productivity not only differs significantly among countries but also changes over time within a single country. A natural presumption is that much of the growth in productivity that occurs is the result of changes in technology. This premise seems especially reasonable for the most advanced, richest countries. Often we can even associate a particular technological advance—for example, the steam engine or network electricity—with a specific period of productivity growth. When we look at differences in productivity among countries, however, the picture gets complicated. Productivity is much lower in poor countries than in rich countries, but it is far from obvious that the reason is a gap in technology. The most significant piece of evidence against blaming the gap in productivity on technological backwardness is that many of the most advanced technologies are being used in poor countries. A good example is cellular telephones, which became widespread in developed countries only in the 1990s and have already spread to the poorest regions of Africa.

But if differences in productivity between rich and poor countries do not stem completely from differences in technology, then where else do they come from? In Chapter 2, we suggested a possible additional source of productivity differences, which we called *efficiency*. We defined efficiency as the effectiveness with which factors of production and technology are combined to produce output. Put differently, efficiency is an umbrella concept used to capture anything that accounts for differences in productivity *other* than differences in technology.

In this chapter, we explore the idea of efficiency in greater detail. We ask whether we can find any direct evidence of efficiency differences among countries. We also try to determine how much of the observed variation in productivity among countries is the result of differences in efficiency and how much is the result of differences in technology.

Part of our approach to studying efficiency will be mathematical and data driven. But we will also study efficiency in a more qualitative fashion, looking for "narrative" evidence of differences in efficiency among countries. One thing that will become clearer in this effort is that it is often easiest to study efficiency by looking at its absence. Just as doctors can best define what "healthy" means only with reference to sickness, it is easiest to understand what it means for an economy to be efficient by looking at examples of inefficiency.

10.1 DECOMPOSING PRODUCTIVITY INTO TECHNOLOGY AND EFFICIENCY

Productivity, as we have seen, is itself determined by two things: *technology*, which represents the knowledge about how factors of production can be combined to produce output, and *efficiency*, which measures how effectively given technology and factors of production are actually used. A natural way to think about this relationship in mathematical terms is that technology and efficiency are multiplied to determine productivity:

$$A = T \times E, \tag{10.1}$$

where A is a measure of productivity, T is a measure of technology, and E is a measure of efficiency.

We can motivate this formulation with the following example. Suppose that we are comparing the output of two farmers. The two farmers employ similar quantities of land, labor, and capital—in other words, there are no differences in the quantities of factors of production they use. There are two differences between the farmers, however. First, Farmer A uses a better variety of seed than Farmer B; indeed, each acre planted with the seed that Farmer A uses produces twice as much grain as each acre planted by Farmer B. The second difference is that the laborers who work for Farmer A insist that out of every two bushels of grain harvested, one bushel should be thrown away. Thus, in the end, the two farmers have the same level of output.

The difference in the seeds used by Farmer A and Farmer B captures the idea of technology. The difference stemming from Farmer A's workers throwing away part of the harvest illustrates the idea of efficiency. The technology of Farmer A is twice as good as that of Farmer B, but his production process is only half as efficient. As a result, the two farmers have the same level of productivity.

The difference in efficiency in this simple example may strike you as absurd. Although it is easy to believe that some farmers might have figured out how to do things that others have not yet done—in other words, that there is a differ-ence in technology—it is harder to believe that some farmers would do things in a manner that is so obviously inefficient. Yet as this chapter shows, examples of inefficiency are all too abundant once we examine real economies, although they are rarely as simple.

Analyzing Cross-Country Data

In Chapter 7, we saw how the technique of development accounting can be used to measure differences in productivity among countries. For example, Table 7.2 showed that in 2009, the level of productivity, A, in India was equal to 0.31, where A in the United States was normalized to 1. In other words, given quantities of capital and labor in India would produce only 31% as much output as the same quantities of capital and labor would produce in the United States. To what extent is this difference in productivity the result of a difference in technology, and to what extent is it the result of a difference in efficiency?

We can approach this question by thinking about how far India is behind the United States technologically. We found in Chapter 7 that the average growth rate of A in the United States over the period 1975–2009 was 0.54% per year. Suppose that all of this growth in A was because of improvement in technology—in other words, we assume that efficiency remained constant. Then, if we know how many years India is behind the United States technologically, we can compare the two countries' values of technology, T.

Suppose that India is G years behind the United States technologically. That is, the level of technology in India in 2009 was the same as the level of technology in the United States in the year 2009 – G. Mathematically:

$$T_{2009,\,\text{India}} = T_{2009-G,\,\text{US}}.$$

Let g be the growth rate of technology in the United States. The relationship be-tween technology in the United States in the years 2009 and 2009 – G is given by the equation:

$$T_{2009,\,\text{US}} = T_{2009-G,\,\text{US}} \times (1 + g)^G.$$

Substituting the first of these equations into the second yields:

$$T_{2009,\,\text{US}} = T_{2009,\,\text{India}} \times (1 + g)^G.$$

Finally, we can rearrange this equation as follows:

$$\frac{T_{2009,\,\text{India}}}{T_{2009,\,\text{US}}} = (1 + g)^{-G}. \tag{10.2}$$

Equation 10.2 gives the ratio of technology in India to technology in the United States as a function of the gap in technology measured in years, G, and the growth rate of technology in the United States, g. For example, suppose India is

10 years behind the United States technologically, and the annual growth rate of technology in the United States is 0.54% per year (as calculated in Chapter 7). The ratio of technology in the two countries is

$$\frac{T_{2009,\,\text{India}}}{T_{2009,\,\text{US}}} = 1.0054^{-10} = 0.95.$$

In other words, India has technology equal to 95% of the U.S. level.

To see how we can use Equation 10.2 to infer differences in efficiency between the two countries, we go back to Equation 10.1, which showed the relationship among productivity, efficiency, and technology. We can write this equation separately for India and the United States (where we leave out the subscript for years, as we are now considering only 2009):

$$A_{\text{India}} = T_{\text{India}} \times E_{\text{India}},$$
$$A_{\text{US}} = T_{\text{US}} \times E_{\text{US}}.$$

Dividing the first of these equations by the second:

$$\frac{A_{\text{India}}}{A_{\text{US}}} = \frac{T_{\text{India}}}{T_{\text{US}}} \times \frac{E_{\text{India}}}{E_{\text{US}}}. \qquad (\mathbf{10.3})$$

The term on the left side of this equation, which is the ratio of productivity in the two countries, is the value 0.31 that was calculated in Table 7.2. The first term on the right side, which is the ratio of technology in the two countries, can be calculated from Equation 10.2, given information on the growth rate of technology and the technology gap measured in years. Knowing these two ratios, we can calculate the final term on the right side of the equation, which is the ratio of efficiency in the two countries.

In Table 10.1, we use Equation 10.3 to calculate the ratio of efficiency in India to efficiency in the United States. Because we do not know the actual size of the technology gap (i.e., the number of years that India lags the United States), we consider a variety of possible values. These are listed in the left-most column. For each technology gap, the second column of the table shows the level of Indian technology relative to U.S. technology that would be implied by the size of the technology gap (using the value of U.S. technology growth, $g = 0.54$, per year, that we calculated in Chapter 7). For example, if India is 10 years behind the United States technologically, then Equation 10.2 says that T_{India} is equal to 95% of the U.S. level. Finally, the last column lists the value of efficiency in India relative to the United States. This value is calculated, following Equation 10.3, so that the product of technology in India relative to the United States and efficiency in India relative to the United States equals 31%. For example, if technology in India is equal to 95% of the U.S. level, then efficiency in India must equal 33% of the U.S. level because $0.95 \times 0.33 = 0.31$.

TABLE 10.1

Decomposition of Productivity Gap Between India and the United States

Years India Lags United States in Technology (G)	Level of Technology in India Relative to United States (T)	Level of Efficiency in India Relative to United States (E)
10	0.95	0.33
20	0.90	0.35
30	0.85	0.36
40	0.81	0.38
50	0.76	0.41
75	0.67	0.46
100	0.58	0.53
125	0.51	0.61

The message from this exercise is that, unless lags in technology are extremely large, most of the difference in productivity between India and the United States must be the result of a difference in efficiency. For example, given the speed with which many advanced technologies such as cell phones and computers have reached India, it is hard to believe that the average technology gap between India and the United States is 30 years. If the technology gap were indeed equal to 30 years, then technology in India would be at 85% of the U.S. level, whereas efficiency in India would be at 36% of the U.S. level—in other words, the difference in efficiency would be the dominant source of the difference in productivity between the two countries. As can be seen from Table 10.1, the "break-even point"—the technology lag at which technology and efficiency would be equally important in determining the productivity gap between India and the United States—would fall somewhere between 100 and 125 years. (The exact gap would have to be 109 years.)

Looking at other developing countries listed in Table 7.2 and performing a similar calculation makes this point even more strongly. Comparing Malawi and the United States, for example, technology and efficiency would play equally important roles only if the technology gap were equal to 227 years.[1]

---

[1]Mathematical Note: To calculate these break-even points, we set the ratio of technology in the two countries equal to the ratio of efficiency in the two countries and then combine Equations 10.2 and 10.3 to get

$$(1 + g)^{-G} = \left(\frac{A_{\text{India}}}{A_{\text{US}}} \right)^{1/2}.$$

Taking logarithms and rearranging,

$$G = - \frac{\ln(A_{\text{India}}/A_{\text{US}})}{2 \times \ln(1 + g)}.$$

10.2 DIFFERENCES IN EFFICIENCY: CASE STUDIES

Section 10.1 argues that differences in efficiency are an important determinant of differences in output among countries. But the argument is somewhat circumstantial. We have seen that there are large differences in productivity among countries and that these differences seem too large to be the result of differences in technology alone—and that therefore they must be the result of differences in efficiency.

Although this kind of argument can be useful, the case that efficiency is an important determinant of output would be greatly strengthened if we could observe efficiency more directly. This is the task to which we now turn. Unfortunately, we cannot measure efficiency systematically in a large sample of countries (or in a single country over time) in the same way that we can measure output and factor accumulation. Instead, we will examine a number of case studies, in which we can isolate efficiency. If we find that efficiency plays a strong role in these cases, we will have support for the argument that efficiency is important more generally.

Central Planning in the Soviet Union

The former Soviet Union provides one of the best examples of low output as a result of inefficiency. The Soviet economy was relatively good at accumulating factors of production: Its rate of investment in physical capital was higher than that of the United States, and its workforce was fairly well educated. In terms of technology, the USSR was in a more complicated position. In areas related to national defense, it was often at par with the rich Western countries, whereas in areas that were not viewed as national priorities, such as the production of consumer goods, it lagged behind. Nonetheless, given the tools at its disposal (and its proven ability to adapt technologies that were viewed as priorities), it is hard to believe that the USSR was too far behind the richest countries technologically.

Despite its technology, the USSR was a disaster in terms of producing output. In 1985, the year Mikhail Gorbachev took power, GDP per capita in the Soviet Union was less than one-third the U.S. level, and over the previous decade, per-capita income had grown at a rate of less than 1% per year.[2] Because this dismal performance could not have been the result of deficiencies in technology or factor accumulation, it must have been the result of low efficiency.

One cause of the Soviet economy's inefficiency was central planning, which began with Joseph Stalin's first "five-year plan" in 1928. Under central planning, government bureaucrats determined how labor, capital, and raw materials were allocated, what goods were produced, which firms supplied inputs to which other firms, and so on. In theory, such a centrally planned economy could produce output just as efficiently as, or even more efficiently than, a market economy. In practice, however,

---

[2]Maddison (2001), Appendix C.

central planners did a poor job of fulfilling the roles that prices play in coordinating activity in a market economy, such as channeling productive inputs to the firms that value them most, giving firms an incentive to produce goods that are in high demand, and equalizing the quantities of each good that are supplied and demanded. As a result, shortages were rampant. Waiting in line to purchase whatever consumer goods were available became an accepted part of life in the Soviet Union, and output was reduced because firms were frequently unable to obtain crucial inputs. Further, the need to meet production quotas often led firms to produce the wrong goods. In one infamous example, a nail factory was given a production target measuring the total weight of nails to produce. The factory's managers found that the easiest way to meet the target was to produce exceedingly large nails, which were of no use to consumers.

A second source of inefficiency in the Soviet economy was the lack of incentives for managers and workers. Because firms had no owners seeking to maximize profits, managers of firms had no incentive to minimize their production costs, much less to implement new technologies that would raise productivity. Because so many goods were in short supply, firms similarly had no incentive to maintain the quality of their output—consumers would snap up whatever the firms produced. Plant managers had little leeway to fire unproductive workers or to reward those who did a good job, so absenteeism and on-the-job drunkenness were rampant. The sorry state of affairs was captured in a popular joke: A visitor to a factory asks the manager, "How many people work here?" The manager replies, "About half."

The demise of the Soviet Union and the end of communism in the early 1990s replaced central planning with a new set of institutions, which so far have turned out to be little better. Free markets have been opened up, but much of the basic framework that supports a functioning market economy, such as the rule of law and clearly defined property rights, is still missing (we return to this topic in Chapter 12). Vast resources have been wasted in struggles to take possession of the resources that formerly belonged to the state. A study conducted in 1999 found that, on average, Russian productivity was only 19% of the U.S. level.[3] A follow up analysis found that eight years later, in 2007, productivity was 26% of the U.S. level.[4] Productivity this low is clearly the result of low efficiency rather than technological backwardness.

Textiles in 1910

In 1910 textile workers in New England earned 50% more than similar workers in England, twice as much as workers in France and Germany, 3 times as much as those in Italy and Spain, and more than 10 times as much as those in Japan, India, and China. In the early part of the 20th century, the U.S. government conducted a thorough study to determine the source of these large wage differentials.

---

[3]McKinsey Global Institute (1999).
[4]McKinsey Global Institute (2009).

Inspectors were sent to observe the cotton textile industry in all of the world's major manufacturing nations and to record data such as the type of machinery used, costs of raw materials, and quality of cloth produced. The results from this study offer a remarkable opportunity to examine a single industry (at the time, one of the most important in the world) in great detail.[5]

The most important finding of the government's research was that differences in technology, in the sense of some countries using more advanced productive methods than others, were almost completely irrelevant for explaining differences in wages. The reason was that the technology used in textile production in the countries studied was basically the same—indeed, most of the machines used in production were identical, having been manufactured in England and shipped throughout the world. Nor did differences in raw materials explain any of the differences in wages among countries.

What accounted for these large differences in wages then? The key factor seems to be the efficiency of the workers. In the textile industry, output was produced by combining capital, in the form of machines such as looms, with the labor of the workers who tended these machines. Figure 10.1 graphs data from

FIGURE 10.1

Wages and Machines in the Textile Industry, 1910

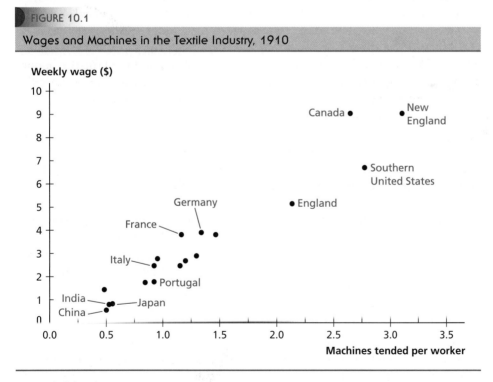

Source: Clark (1987).

[5]Clark (1987).

18 countries on the amount of machinery that each worker tended and the average weekly wage. The relationship is striking: In countries in which workers tended more machinery, wages were higher. Workers in high-wage countries tended up to six times as much machinery as workers in low-wage countries. Equally surprising, the fact that workers in the richest countries tended more machines did not mean that machinery in these countries was any less productive, as one might have expected if poor countries were substituting labor for capital. Rather, the opposite was true: Each loom in the more-developed countries, though tended by fewer workers, produced *more* output.

But if differences in the amount of machinery tended explain differences in wages, a new question arises: Why were workers in rich countries able to tend so much more machinery? Differences in factors such as workers' health and education do not seem to be the reason. Rather, differences in factory organization and in labor practices are evidently the main explanation. Workers in the poorer countries were capable of tending more machines, but something in the way the economy was organized prevented them from doing so. This "something" is exactly the concept of efficiency that we are examining in this chapter.

This huge variation in efficiency was just as puzzling to contemporary analysts of the textile industry as it is to economists examining the data today. A U.S. visitor to India in the 1920s, observing the number of machines tended by each worker, noted that "it was apparent that they could easily have taken care of more, but they won't.... They cannot be persuaded by any exhortation, ambition, or the opportunity to increase their earnings." In 1928 an attempt by managers to increase the number of machines per worker in Bombay sparked a major strike.

Differences in Productivity within an Industry

Recent studies by the consulting firm McKinsey have analyzed productivity in individual industries in the three largest industrial economies in the world: the United States, Japan, and Germany. The researchers collected detailed information on capital and labor inputs, as well as the organization of production, and for each industry, they calculated measures of productivity similar to those we examined in Chapter 7. Table 10.2 shows the results of these productivity calculations for four industries (automobiles, steel, food processing, and telecommunications), as well as an aggregate measure of productivity (which includes industries other than those listed here).[6]

As shown in the table, the studies found interesting differences in relative productivity among industries. Japan's steel and automobile industries were more productive than their U.S. and German counterparts, but food processing in Japan was less than half as productive as in the other countries. German productivity was

---

[6]Baily and Solow (2001).

TABLE 10.2

Productivity in Selected Industries in the Early 1990s

	United States	Japan	Germany
Automobiles	100	127	84
Steel	100	110	100
Food Processing	100	42	84
Telecommunications	100	51	42
Aggregate Productivity	100	67	89

close to that of the United States in three of the four industries examined but fell far behind in telecommunications. The differences in productivity at the industry level were much larger than those in aggregate productivity.

What was the source of these large differences in productivity? It seems unlikely that they were the result of differences in technology, because the three countries considered are clearly at the frontier of world technology, and ideas flow easily among them. Further, if technology differences were at the root of these differences in productivity, it would be hard to explain the pattern of productivity differences observed. As one commentator put it, "If we are going to attribute these productivity differences to differences in *technology*, it is hard to understand how Japanese businessmen can be so successful at learning and developing technologies for making automobile parts, and so inept at learning and developing technologies for freezing fish."[7] Another piece of evidence that something other than differences in technology explains these differences in productivity among countries is that some of these productivity differences hold true even within a single company. For example, Ford Europe failed to adopt Japanese just-in-time production techniques (by which a manufacturer holds small inventories of parts), even though these techniques were adopted by Ford USA. Finally, in some cases, productivity was low in a country even though the country clearly had better technology than its rivals. For example, productivity was low in the German beer-brewing industry, even though the most advanced brewing machinery was made in Germany and exported.

A better explanation for these productivity differences—and the one that the studies' authors seize on—is differences in the organization of production among the countries. Japanese automobile makers, for example, work closely with their parts suppliers to streamline procedures and improve productivity. In Germany and the United States, by contrast, the relationship between automakers and their suppliers is more antagonistic. Suppliers fear that if they improve their productivity, the firms to which they sell their parts will simply negotiate lower purchase prices,

---

[7]DeLong (1997).

and this reduces the incentive to become more efficient. Regarding the Japanese food-processing industry (which employs more workers than automobiles and steel combined), the authors of the study blame low productivity on "a Byzantine network of regulation and custom that surround agriculture and distribution."

Differences in productivity within a single industry are even visible *within* a single country. One such extensively studied industry is health care in the United States, which accounted for 18 percent of GDP in 2011. There are enormous differences among regions in the United States in the quantity of medical care that individuals receive, with little or no corresponding difference in the health outcomes that result from this spending. For example, the amount of medical care provided per person, adjusting for differences in the age of the population, is almost three times as high in Miami as it is in Honolulu.[8] Given that the same amount of output (health) is being produced with massively different amounts of inputs (health care spending), and with no variation in technology, this is clearly a case of varying efficiency.

The surgeon and journalist Atul Gawande performed a detailed examination of two Texas counties, with similar demographics, in which the rate of medical care use differed by a factor of two. Patients in McAllen country got more tests, hospital treatments, and surgery than those in El Paso county, but no better health outcomes. Gawande attributed the difference to varying norms among the doctors in the two regions regarding how much the incentive of extra revenue from doing additional procedures should be allowed to influence the practice of medicine.[9]

Subsurface Coal Mining in the United States, 1949–1994

In the previous two case studies, we compared the same industries in different countries. We saw evidence of large differences in productivity that did not seem attributable to differences in technology. We thus concluded that the large differences in productivity represented large differences in efficiency.

Still, with the previous case studies, we could worry that there were *hidden* differences in technology, and that these, rather than differences in efficiency, were the real explanation for the differences in productivity. In the case study that follows, we look at a single industry in a single country. Further, we focus on a case in which productivity *fell* dramatically. Because technology was unlikely to be moving backward over this period, we can safely conclude that the decline in productivity represented a decline in efficiency.

The industry we examine is subsurface coal mining in the United States.[10] Figure 10.2 plots coal output per hour worked over the period 1949–1994. For most of this period, output per worker-hour rose steadily, reflecting improvements in technology as well as the accumulation of capital. But between 1969 and 1978, a puzzling

---

[8]Gottleib et al. (2010).
[9]Gawande (2009)
[10]Parente and Prescott (2000).

FIGURE 10.2

U.S. Subsurface Coal Mining: Output, Price, and Output per Worker Hour, 1949 1994

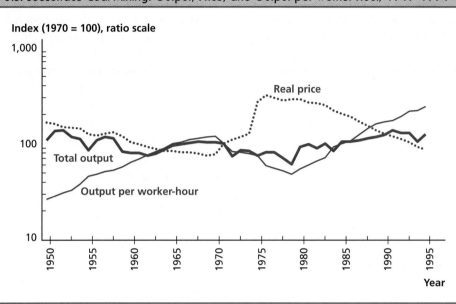

Source: Parente and Prescott (2000).

reversal of this trend occurred: Output per worker-hour fell by one-half. Over the same period, the total quantity of coal produced hardly changed at all. In other words, twice as much labor input was used to produce the same amount of coal.

The explanation for this drop in productivity is hinted at in the figure, which also shows the real price of coal over the same period of time. The price of coal shot up during the 1970s, mostly as a result of rising oil prices. Increased demand for coal made coal-mining companies highly profitable. The rise in profits in turn improved the bargaining position of the mine workers' union because it raised the cost that the union could impose on firms by going on strike. The union took advantage of its improved bargaining position to change work rules so as to raise the level of employment—and thus lowered productivity. This sort of behavior, in which employers are forced to hire more workers than are required for production, is called **featherbedding.**

The trend in coal productivity reversed itself again in the 1978–1994 period, when productivity rose by a factor of three. No burst of technological progress explains this jump in productivity. Rather, the driving factor was a decline in the price of coal, as oil prices fell and competition from nonunionized open-pit mines in the West increased. Subsurface coal mines faced the choice of improving productivity or closing down altogether, so the bargaining power of the coal miners' union weakened substantially.

10.3 TYPES OF INEFFICIENCY

The last section looked at several examples of inefficiency. Based on these (and the hundreds more that economists know about), we can confidently conclude that large inefficiencies indeed exist in most economies. Going further, it would be nice to have a complete theory of inefficiency, covering why it arises, where it is most severe, and so on. Although such a theory does not yet exist, we can try to generalize about inefficiency. For a start, we can try to categorize the different forms that inefficiency takes.

The next five subsections describe five different ways in which economies can be inefficient. In some cases, resources such as capital and labor are used for doing things that have no economic value, or they remain unused. Resources used in production may be channeled into the wrong parts of the economy or to firms that do not use them as well as possible. Finally, various forces may prevent the use of available technologies that yield a higher level of output for the available inputs of factors of production.

Unproductive Activities

One type of inefficiency occurs when resources are diverted from productive to **unproductive activities**—that is, uses without economic value. Obviously, for society as a whole, the fewer resources that are used for production, the less will be produced, and the less will be available for consumption. Thus, from society's point of view, unproductive activities waste resources. From the perspective of the individuals who engage in them, however, unproductive activities can be perfectly rational—people earn more for themselves by engaging in unproductive activities than they could by producing output. How can this be? The answer is that such an unproductive activity must necessarily involve some redistribution—that is, taking output away from others.

Certain unproductive activities, such as theft and smuggling, are illegal. In addition to wasting resources directly (in the case of burglary, using labor to break into houses rather than to produce output), such activities also require further nonproductive spending on the part of those who would rather not see their property taken away (e.g., hiring guards or installing alarm systems). In many countries, the costs of defenses against illegal appropriation are high. In 1992, for example, the standard fee paid by Russian retailers for "protection" (generally from the people charging the fees) was 20% of sales.[11] In some poor countries, unproductive activities also include kidnapping for ransom, banditry, and even civil war, where the object of conflict is the right to exploit natural resources. An example is the African country of Angola, which is richly endowed with oil, diamonds, and

---

[11] Åslund and Dmitriev (1999).

other minerals, and which experienced a 27-year civil war between 1974 and 2002. At the war's end, income per capita was lower than when the war began. But in the first seven years of peace, income per capita nearly doubled.

Unproductive activities that involve the use of laws or government institutions to bring private benefits are called **rent seeking.** (An **economic rent** is a payment to a factor of production that is in excess of what is required to elicit the supply of that factor.) Rent seeking usually arises in cases where government policy creates an artificial or contrived rent, such as through licenses or protected monopolies.

One of the most common instances of rent seeking occurs when developing countries use quotas to limit the imports of some goods. Because the domestic price of these goods is much higher than the world price, firms that obtain import licenses can make large profits. In pursuit of these licenses, the managers of import firms expend a good deal of effort—traveling repeatedly to the capital city to press their case, employing relatives of the officials who distribute import licenses, hiring the officials themselves into high-paying jobs when they leave government service, or engaging in outright bribery. One of the reasons that capital cities of many developing countries are so big (e.g., Mexico City, population 21 million, or Jakarta, Indonesia, population 19 million) is that firms locate there to maximize their chances of capturing rents generated by the government.[12] In addition to the direct costs expended on rent seeking, a second form of waste occurs when the best and brightest workers choose to enter government service to reap the rewards of bribery, rather than to work in the productive sector.

The extent to which people devote their efforts to producing output rather than trying to get a bigger slice of the pie depends, of course, on the relative rewards of these two activities. If rent seeking pays well, then talented people will pursue it. If talent is better compensated in productive activities, then that is where it will be applied. The relative rewards to these two activities depend in turn on the institutional structure of the economy. For example, if there is strong government control of the economy, then there will be large benefits to be reaped from influencing that control. One has only to look at the hallways of the U.S. Capitol building—nicknamed Gucci Gulch for the expensive shoes worn by the high-paid lobbyists who crowd them—to see how much talent and effort are wasted on rent seeking, even in a country with a relatively honest government.

Idle Resources

A second form of inefficiency results when labor or capital is simply not used at all. Such **idle resources** may take several forms. In the case of workers, the inefficiency includes both actual unemployment, where a worker has no job, and underemployment, where a worker has a job but spends only a fraction of his or her

---

[12]Ades and Glaeser (1995).

work time producing output. Capital can similarly be unemployed (a factory that sits unused) or underemployed (a factory running at less than full capacity).

Unemployment of workers and capital often results from macroeconomic instability. In 1939 President Franklin Roosevelt described the problem of the Great Depression as one of "idle men and idle capital." Indeed, the Great Depression was a period of great inefficiency in the U.S. economy: Between 1929 and 1933, GDP fell by 30%, without any declines in available technology or factors of production. In other words, the U.S. economy in 1933 was only 70% as efficient as in 1929. In developed countries, such business cycle downturns have been fairly mild and short-lived since World War II. But in many developing countries, chronic macroeconomic instability has remained a significant contributor to the inefficiency of the economy, and thus to a low level of output.

Underemployment frequently results from institutional arrangements that encourage the hiring of more workers than are needed. State-run enterprises are notorious for their overstaffing. Air Afrique, which until it was liquidated in 2002 was owned by a consortium of 11 African governments, is a prime example. In 2001 the airline had 4,200 employees but only 8 aircraft, a ratio of more than 500 employees per airplane. By contrast, the most efficient European airlines, such as Britain's EasyJet, had a ratio of 66 employees per airplane. Despite its huge staff, Air Afrique's service was appalling.[13] In a similar instance of overstaffing, many developing countries guarantee jobs for educated workers by hiring them into bloated and unproductive bureaucracies. But the problem of government-induced underemployment is not limited to developing countries. To give one example, during the middle of the 20th century, railroads in the United States and Canada switched from coal-fired steam locomotives to diesel engines. This change in technology eliminated the need for a "fireman" to shovel coal. However, government regulations and union contracts continued to require the presence of a fireman on diesel locomotives.

As in the case of unproductive activities, underemployment of workers entails a transfer of resources from one person to another rather than the production of more output. The employee who is paid for not working is receiving a subsidy from someone else in the economy—his employer, his fellow employees, the government, or the consumer of the goods that his firm is producing. Although he may be better off using his labor unproductively than he would be if he were using it productively, society as a whole is worse off.

Misallocation of Factors among Sectors

The two types of inefficiency just described—unproductive activities and idle resources—result when available resources are not used in productive activities. Another form of inefficiency occurs when resources are used in producing the wrong things. In such a case of **misallocation** the inefficiency will be less obvious

---

[13]"A New Air Afrique?" *The Economist*, August 25, 2001.

than in cases of resources not being used at all. Nonetheless, misallocation can have a large effect on efficiency.

With respect to economic growth, a significant form of this inefficiency is **misallocation among sectors**—that is, directing resources to the wrong sectors (distinct parts) of the economy. These sectors may simply be the different regions of a country. Alternatively, in most poor countries, we can distinguish between an urban sector, with advanced modes of production and organization, resembling a more industrialized economy, and a rural sector in which production technologies remain primitive.

Why would misallocation of factors among sectors ever take place? To see how misallocation can happen, we must step back and ask a more basic question: Why would we expect resources to be optimally allocated in the first place?

We consider this problem in a simple setting. Suppose there are two sectors in the economy, called Sector 1 and Sector 2. In each sector, there is a production function by which capital and labor are transformed into output. Total output of the economy is the sum of the output in the two sectors. We can now ask a simple question: If the quantities of capital in each sector are fixed, what is the optimal allocation of labor between the two sectors that will maximize the total output of the economy? The answer, which you may remember from previous economics courses, is that the value of output will be maximized when the marginal product of labor in the two sectors is the same.

Figure 10.3 illustrates the optimal allocation of labor. The quantities of labor in each of the two sectors are measured along the horizontal axis. One curve shows

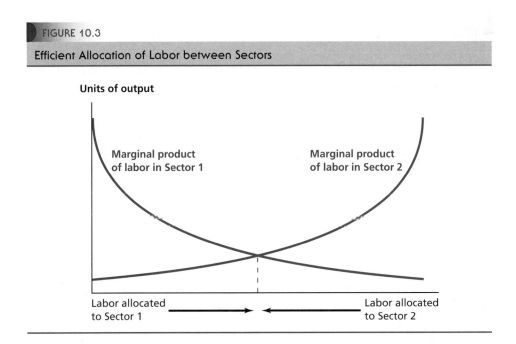

FIGURE 10.3

Efficient Allocation of Labor between Sectors

Units of output

Marginal product of labor in Sector 1

Marginal product of labor in Sector 2

Labor allocated to Sector 1

Labor allocated to Sector 2

the marginal product of labor in Sector 1 as a function of the quantity of labor in Sector 1, and the other curve shows the marginal product in Sector 2 as a function of labor in Sector 2. The curve describing Sector 2 is drawn with the horizontal axis reversed, so that a movement from left to right corresponds to a reduction in the quantity of labor used in Sector 2. The point where the two curves meet represents the optimal allocation of labor between the sectors.

Figure 10.4 illustrates a case in which the marginal products of labor in the two sectors are not equalized. In this case, labor is overallocated to Sector 1. The marginal product of labor in Sector 1 (MPL_1) is thus lower than the marginal product in Sector 2. Were one worker to move from Sector 1 to Sector 2, output in Sector 1 would fall by MPL_1, but output would rise in Sector 2 by MPL_2. The change in output would thus be $MPL_2 - MPL_1$. Moving from the inefficient allocation to the efficient allocation would raise output by an amount given by the shaded triangle in the figure.

In a well-functioning market economy, reaching the optimal allocation of labor between sectors occurs automatically, as a result of two forces. First, as we saw in Chapter 3, labor will be paid its marginal product as a wage. Second, if the marginal product (and thus the wage) for the same unit of labor is different in different sectors of the economy, then workers will have a strong incentive to move from the sector with low marginal product to the sector with high marginal product. This movement of labor will lower the wage in the sector that has high marginal product and will raise it in the sector with low marginal product. The movement of labor will continue until the two marginal products are equalized, and thus the

FIGURE 10.4

Overallocation of Labor to Sector 1

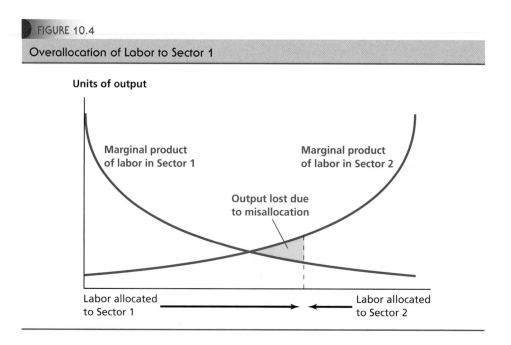

quantity of output is maximized. This mechanism, by which the choices of individual people who simply want to maximize their own wages will end up maximizing the amount of output that society produces, is exactly the "invisible hand" that Adam Smith celebrated in *The Wealth of Nations*.

Now we can address the previous question: Why might the optimum *not* be reached? The answer is that factors might not be allocated according to their marginal products. There are two possible reasons: Factors may not be able to move between sectors in response to the signal provided by differences in the payments they receive, or the payments received by factors may not reflect their marginal products. We consider these in turn.

Barriers to Mobility. If there are barriers to mobility between sectors, then a gap in wages may persist. The higher these barriers, the larger the gap between marginal products that can be sustained, and thus the larger the degree of inefficiency.

One type of barrier between sectors is geographic isolation. Because moving from one part of a country to another involves costs, both economic and psychological, interregional wage gaps may persist for a long time. However, as costs of communication and transportation fall, the availability of information about wage gaps will increase, as will the ease with which workers can move to the parts of a country where they are most valued, thus increasing efficiency.

Another type of barrier to mobility between sectors arises if a minimum wage is imposed in the high-wage sector. In this case, the process by which people move from the low-wage to the high-wage sector will be short-circuited. Firms in the high-wage sector will not be able to expand their payroll by hiring workers from the low-wage sector because this shift would involve lowering the marginal product of labor below the minimum wage.

Wages Not Equal to Marginal Product. If workers are not paid their marginal products, then a difference between sectors in the marginal product of labor will not automatically translate into a difference in wages, so workers will not have an incentive to move between sectors. A common example of this phenomenon is the overallocation of labor to family farms in developing countries. Family members who work together on a farm do not receive a formal "wage." Rather, the output of the farm is generally divided equally among the family members. In economic terms, the workers are receiving a payment of their *average* product rather than their marginal product. Because production on a farm, where the quantity of land is fixed, is characterized by declining marginal product of labor, the payment that is received by a worker will be higher than the marginal product of labor. By contrast, a worker who leaves the farm to work in the industrial sector will receive a wage equal to his or her marginal product there. Figure 10.5 shows that the resulting allocation of labor will mean that the marginal product in farming is lower than the marginal product in industry.

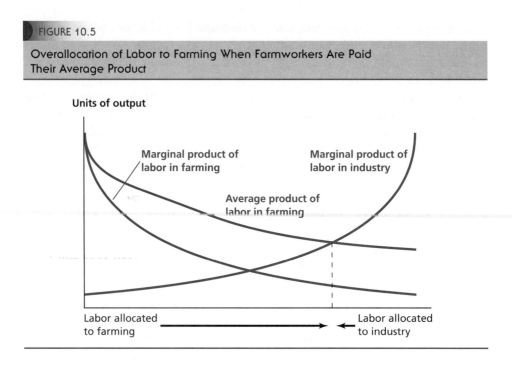

FIGURE 10.5

Overallocation of Labor to Farming When Farmworkers Are Paid
Their Average Product

Another reason that wages may not be equal to marginal products is if there is segmentation or discrimination in the labor market, such that potentially productive people are unable to work in certain sectors (and thus would receive zero wages if they did). To give an example, in the United States in 1960, 18% of white men worked in high-skilled occupations such as executives, managers, engineers, doctors, or lawyers. The corresponding figures for white women, black men, and black women were 3%, 3%, and 1%, respectively. Assuming that there are not inherent differences in ability among these groups, this stark sorting among occupations represents a misallocation of talent: People who would be productive in high-skilled occupations are working in some job for which they do not have a comparative advantage because of ethnic or gender discrimination. And indeed, as the legal and social environment changed in the United States, so did the allocation of labor. In 2007, 24% of white men worked in high-skilled occupations, whereas the fractions for white women, black men, and black women were 17%, 15%, and 13%, respectively. A recent study estimates that roughly 20% of the growth of average wages in the United States over the period 1960–2008 was the result of the reduction in barriers to efficient allocation of labor for women and African Americans. The lowering of these barriers also accounted for a substantial fraction of the income convergence between the South and the rest of the country.[14]

---

[14]Hsieh, Hurst, Jones, and Klenow (2011).

Efficiency Gains from Sectoral Reallocation. The preceding analysis shows how the misallocation of factors among sectors can be an important type of economic inefficiency. Correspondingly, the *reallocation* of factors between sectors—from sectors with a low marginal product to sectors with a high marginal product—can be a major source of growth. Indeed, if we see examples of growth through the reallocation of factors, this is good evidence of an initial misallocation and thus an initial inefficiency. (A chapter supplement, available on this book's Web site, analyzes how sectoral reallocation affects the growth rate of output.)

Sectoral reallocation out of agriculture and into manufacturing was a major component in the rapid growth of Taiwan and South Korea, two of the "Asian Tigers." In Taiwan, output per worker grew at a rate of 5.4% per year over the period 1966–1991; the shift out of agriculture accounted for 0.7 percentage points of that growth. Similarly, in South Korea, sectoral reallocation accounted for 0.6 percentage points of the annual growth rate of 5.6%. Between 1960 and 1990, the fraction of the South Korean labor force working in agriculture fell from 61% to 18%. In the United States, a similar transformation took place over a much longer time period. In 1880, 50% of the U.S. labor force worked in agriculture, and the average wage in agriculture was only 20% of the average wage in manufacturing. By 1980, the fraction of the population employed in agriculture had fallen to only 3%, and the wage in agriculture had risen to 69% of the industrial wage.[15]

Ease of geographic mobility may be one explanation for the particularly high efficiency of the U.S. economy. Americans are notoriously willing to relocate in search of economic advantage—and this willingness is aided by having a large country with a single language. By contrast, geographic mobility within Europe has traditionally been low, in part because Europeans have much deeper cultural roots in the places where they were born than do most Americans. For example, 3% of Americans moved between states each year during the 1980s and 1990s, but the rate at which Italians moved between regions during this period was only 1%.[16] In many countries, the lack of geographic mobility is abetted by policies that pay people to stay in economically depressed areas, rather than encouraging them to move to areas where there is more opportunity.

The most dramatic example of labor reallocation in the world today is China, where workers are moving both from agriculture to industry and from the impoverished interior of the country to more prosperous coastal regions. Between 1980 and 2008, the fraction of the labor force working in agriculture fell from 69% to 40%.[17] Average income in China's coastal provinces is now more than twice as high as in the interior of the country. The exact number of people who have migrated to the coast is not known (in part because much of the migration is illegal),

---

[15]Young (1995), Caselli and Coleman (2001), Gollin, Parente, and Rogerson (2001).
[16]Bertola (1999).
[17]World Development Indicators Database.

but it is thought to be well into the tens of millions. This ongoing reallocation of labor is part of the reason that China's economy is growing so quickly, but the shift is also putting enormous strains on the country's political and social structure.

Misallocation of Factors among Firms

Just as factors can be misallocated between sectors of the economy, there can also be **misallocation among firms.** Firms differ in their levels of productivity for any number of reasons. Some firms may have inferior technology; some may have poor organization; some may have bad management. In a well-functioning economy, resources will move from less productive to more productive firms, thereby raising the overall level of productivity in the economy. This shift happens naturally when firms compete with each other. A high-productivity firm can make a profit at prices that lead less productive firms to lose money. Less productive firms are thus driven out of business, and the capital and labor they used are absorbed by more productive firms.

Many things can get in the way of this reallocation of resources. If low- and high-productivity firms collude to maintain high prices rather than competing with each other, then low-productivity firms will be able to stay in business and thus not free up the factors they are using (although they will earn smaller profits than high-productivity firms). Similarly, many low-productivity firms manage to get government help staying in business, in the form of subsidies, favored contracts, trade protection (if the more productive firms are located abroad), or other means. For example, in India businesses that employ fewer than 10 workers are exempt from various regulations governing employment conditions, hours, and hiring and firing of workers. Not surprisingly, there are a lot of 9-worker firms in the country.

This sort of misallocation among firms becomes rampant in nonmarket economies (of which few are left in the world) and in firms that do not have to make a profit because they are owned by the government. In government-owned firms, workers' wages are not closely related to the amount of output they produce. Workers or other resources may be allocated among industries on the basis of managers' political power, for example, rather than on the basis of where they will be the most productive.

Monopoly power provides another reason that labor may be misallocated among firms. We saw in the discussion of misallocation among sectors that one condition required for a free-market economy to achieve an optimal allocation of labor is that workers are paid their marginal products. But a firm with a monopoly will restrict production to keep prices high, so it will not hire more workers even if the marginal product of labor is higher than the wage. As a result, the marginal product of labor will be higher in monopolized industries than in industries in which markets are competitive. Unlike government-owned firms, which tend to employ too much labor, monopolistic firms tend to employ too *little* labor from the point of view of economic efficiency.

A recent study gives a more detailed picture of what factor misallocation among firms can look like. If labor and capital are allocated efficiently among firms, their marginal products should be equal across all firms. Differences in marginal products between firms therefore indicate a misallocation of resources— for example, as a result of public subsidies or government restrictions. Economists Chang-Tai Hsieh and Peter Klenow examined manufacturing firms in India (1987–1994), China (1998–2005), and the United States (1977, 1987, and 1997). They found that differences in marginal products across plants were much larger in India and China than in the United States. For example, in the United States, the ratio of the average marginal product of capital and labor in the 75th percentile plant (i.e., the plant that was more productive than 75% of all plants) to the average marginal product of capital and labor in the 25th percentile plant was 1.3. For China, the corresponding ratio was 2.3, and in India it was 2.5. In other words, in the United States the high-productivity firms were 30% more productive than the low-productivity firms, whereas in both China and India, the high-productivity firms were more than twice as productive as the low-productivity firms. Hsieh and Klenow conclude that manufacturing productivity would increase by 25%–40% in China and 50%–60% in India if the degree of misallocation in those countries were the same as in the United States.[18]

Another indicator of the efficiency of allocation of factors among firms is the correlation between firm size and productivity level. Given a fixed degree of variation in productivity among firms, the economy as a whole will be more efficient to the extent that the larger firms are the more productive ones. In the United States the correlation is positive and large; in Western Europe it is smaller; and in Eastern Europe smaller still. In China, the correlation rose from being negative to being near zero over the years 1998–2005, a period when aggregate productivity in the country was growing rapidly.[19]

The box on the next page, "Finance and Growth," discusses the role of the financial system in allocating capital among different uses.

Technology Blocking

In Chapter 8 when we considered barriers to the transfer of technology among countries, we were generally concerned with barriers originating *outside* a country. Examples include patent protection and secrecy on the part of the inventor and a lack of the tacit knowledge required to implement a new technology in a potential recipient country. **Technology blocking** occurs when a technology could feasibly be used—that is, there are no barriers such as those just mentioned—but someone deliberately prevents its use. The technology in question can be either foreign or

---

[18]Hsieh and Klenow (2009).
[19]Haltiwanger (2011).

FINANCE AND GROWTH

One of the key determinants of how efficiently an economy functions is the performance of its financial system, which is composed of banks and other institutions (such as insurance companies and pension funds), markets for stocks and bonds, as well as the government agencies that monitor and regulate them. The financial system performs a number of functions that serve to raise the efficiency of production. Most importantly, it directs capital toward its most productive use by evaluating the potential returns from different investment projects, pooling the savings of many individuals to allow for large investments, monitoring the outcomes of investment projects to make sure that investors are properly compensated, and spreading the risk of any one project among a large number of individuals. The financial system also eases transactions, allowing for more specialization in production. In addition, by channeling investment funds from people who have money to people who have good investment projects (either good business projects or good opportunities for human capital investment) the financial system profoundly affects the degree of income inequality and intergenerational economic mobility—topics to which we return in Chapter 13.*

Economists use a variety of measures to assess the degree of financial development in a country. The size of the banking system is often measured by the value of bank deposits relative to gross domestic product (GDP). The degree of development of the stock market is measured at the "turnover ratio," that is, the value of shares traded in a given year divided by the total value of listed shares. Not surprisingly, there is a strong correlation between the degree of financial system development and the level of GDP per capita. Further, holding constant a country's level of income, those with better financial systems grow more quickly. Finally, we can use the development accounting framework discussed in Chapter 7 to examine how financial development is related to the different proximate determinants of GDP. The data show that the link is much tighter between financial development and productivity than it is between financial development and factor accumulation. This is consistent with the view that financial development raises economic efficiency.†

The strong correlation between income and financial development leaves open the question of whether differences in financial systems among countries are a cause of observed income differences, or whether differences in finance simply reflect other factors that determine income. This question has not yet been definitively answered, but a number of types of evidence point, at least tentatively, to causality running from finance to income.

The first type of evidence is based on timing. It appears that in many countries with good financial systems and rapid growth, the presence of the good financial system preceded growth. For countries in the bottom quartile of financial development in 1960, the average

domestic in origin. Because there is no physical or technical obstacle to the use of an intentionally blocked technology, we think of technology blocking as a form of inefficiency rather than as a type of technological backwardness. Some examples of technology blocking:

- Roman writers Petronius and Pliny the Elder record an apocryphal story of technology blocking. During the reign of the emperor Tiberius (A.D. 14–37), growth rate of GDP per capita between 1960 and 2000 was 1.2% per year. For countries in the top quartile, it was 3.2%.[‡] Similarly, episodes in which countries liberalized their financial markets are followed, on average, with an increase in the growth rate of output.

A second type of evidence comes from the history of banking deregulation in the United States. For much of the 20th century, state laws restricted the number of branches any one bank could open. As a result, the banking system was characterized by a large number of inefficient local monopolies. Starting in the early 1970s, states began loosening branching restrictions. States that liberalized their markets experienced faster economic growth than similar states that did not. Interestingly, the total quantity of bank lending did not rise in states that liberalized; rather, growth seems to have accelerated because what lending took place was being more efficiently allocated to borrowers with good investment projects.[§]

A third piece of evidence suggesting that causality runs from finance to growth is that in countries with well-developed financial systems, it is a particular set of industries—those that are dependent on the financial system—that do well. If it were the case that high income simply led to the development of a good financial system, then we would not expect to see this phenomenon.[**]

A final piece of evidence for the importance of finance in determining income comes from comparing the legal environment in which investment takes place. The commercial law that governs investment (creditors' rights, contract enforcement, and accounting standards) in most countries can be classified as deriving from one of four origin countries: England, France, Germany, or Scandinavia. Of the four, investors are most strongly protected under the English system, and least protected under the French. These differences in legal origin predict differences in the degree of financial development as well as economic growth among countries. Because it is hard to think of how the origin of a country's legal system should affect growth other than through financial development, this is strong evidence for causality running from finance to growth.[††]

How can countries improve the functioning of their financial systems? Existing evidence is that government-owned banks perform more poorly than those that are privately held, that countries that permit foreign banks to compete in their domestic banking systems have more efficient finance than those that do not, and that strong legal systems that protect the interests of small investors relative to corporate "insiders" lead to more efficient allocation of capital.

*Levine (2005).
[†]Beck, Levine, and Loayza (2000a).
[‡]King and Levine (1993).
[§]Jayaratne and Strahan (1996).
**Rajan and Zingales (1998).
[††]Beck, Levine, and Loayza (2000b).

a craftsman demonstrated a new type of unbreakable glass at the imperial court. The emperor, impressed with the beauty and practicality of the new glass, asked the craftsman whether he had shared his secret with anyone. When the craftsman said that he had not, the emperor had him executed and his workshop destroyed, out of fear that the new material would reduce the value of the imperial hoard of gold.

- Johannes Gutenberg's printing press using movable type, invented in 1453, threatened the livelihood of scribes, who for centuries had copied books by hand. Bibles produced on a printing press were sold for one-fifth the price traditionally charged by scribes, who said of printed Bibles that only the devil would be able to produce so many copies of a book in so little time. The scribes' guild in Paris succeeded in delaying the introduction of the printing press into their city for 20 years. Printing presses were also resisted by Islamic calligraphers and by the Brahmin caste in India.[20]

- The most famous episode of technology blocking—and the one that has become synonymous with resistance to technological change—involved the so-called **Luddites.** The Luddites were skilled artisans in the British textile industry whose livelihoods were being destroyed by mechanization. One example of that mechanization, the gig mill, introduced for finishing fine woolen cloth in 1793, allowed one man and two boys to accomplish in 12 hours what had formerly required one man working 88–100 hours. In 1811, large-scale rioting erupted among the Luddites, with workers destroying some 800 weaving and spinning machines and threatening mill owners who were considering adopting the new technology. In 1812 Parliament passed a law making machine breaking an act punishable by death. Britain dispatched 12,000 troops to quell the unrest, and 17 Luddites were hanged.

- In the first half of the 19th century, railroads were opposed for economic reasons by owners of canals, turnpikes (private roads), and stagecoaches, as well as by farmers who grew hay for horses. Moreover, people widely denounced them as unholy because they were not mentioned in the Bible, and one minister predicted that observers would be driven insane at the sight of locomotives moving with nothing to pull them. Railroad companies triumphed over these obstacles, of course, and then turned around and successfully suppressed a competing technology: steam-powered carriages, which were a potential predecessor to the internal combustion automobile. In the United Kingdom, railway interests (along with horse breeders) secured the passage of legislation providing that steam carriages remain below a maximum speed of four miles per hour in the country and two miles per hour in towns, and further that they have three drivers, one of whom must precede the vehicle, carrying a red flag in the day and a red lantern at night. The legislation was not repealed until 1896, thus dooming the steam carriage.[21]

- In the 1880s Thomas Edison tried to block the introduction of alternating current (AC) electric power, promoted by George Westinghouse, to maintain

---

[20]Mokyr (1990), Stern (1937), Brooks (2003), Chapter 8.
[21]Stern (1937).

the value of his own direct current (DC) distribution system. Edison filed patent lawsuits and tried to get state legislatures to adopt laws that would restrict AC power. To make the point that AC current was unsafe, he got New York State to adopt the electric chair, using AC current, as its official means of execution. Edison also encouraged the use of the term *Westinghoused* to describe being electrocuted. Despite these clever stratagems, Westinghouse's AC system won out in the end.[22]

- In 1869 the chemist Hippolyte Mege-Mouiries responded to Emperor Napoleon III's challenge to develop an inexpensive substitute for butter by inventing margarine. In North America, margarine makers immediately ran into stiff opposition from dairy farmers, who naturally wanted to maintain the demand for butter. A spate of anti-margarine laws was passed in the United States in the late 19th century. The federal government imposed a prohibitive tax on margarine that was colored yellow; seven states banned margarine entirely, and two required that it be colored pink. Regulation of margarine in the United States declined after World War II, in large part because of the shift by margarine manufacturers to soybean oil, which had its own politically powerful lobbying group to counter the weight of dairy farmers. The federal tax on margarine was repealed in 1950, and the last state restrictions (in Wisconsin, a dairy state) were repealed in 1967. Margarine consumption in the United States was only 15% of butter consumption in 1930, but by 1970 margarine was outselling butter two-to-one. Dairy farmers wielded even greater power in Canada, where margarine was entirely banned from 1886 to 1949. The province of Quebec, the last holdout in Canada, removed its ban on the sale of yellow margarine in 2008.[23]

- In a recent example of technology blocking, Microsoft attempted to suppress various new computer technologies, such as the Java programming language and the Netscape browser, that threatened the firm's Windows monopoly. According to the legal brief prepared by the U.S. Department of Justice, Microsoft tried to obstruct the distribution of innovative products—for example, by paying Internet service providers not to distribute the Netscape browser. The company also threatened to cut off access to Windows for partners such as PC manufacturers and applications software developers that adopted or distributed the new technologies. Finally, Microsoft used the technology blocking ploy of introducing its own versions of new technologies and making them incompatible with those of its rivals, a strategy that was branded "embrace, extend, extinguish."[24]

---

[22]David (1991b).
[23]Durpe (1999).
[24]Bresnahan (2002).

From these examples of technology blocking, we can draw several conclusions. First, the reason for most technology blocking is that a new technology, although beneficial for society as a whole, usually makes someone worse off. This outcome should not be a surprise. Economist Joseph Schumpeter coined the term *creative destruction* to describe the economic changes brought about by the introduction of a new technology. Those whose livelihoods stand to be destroyed by a new technology will do their best to block it. Although *Luddite* is often used as a term of derision, the Luddites themselves were not irrational in their opposition to new technology.

In addition, although opposition to new technologies often comes from workers, the phenomenon is far more widespread. Firms, even those in the high-tech sector, are prone to engage in technology blocking if it serves their best interests.

A third conclusion is that technology blocking does not always work; its success depends on the relative power of those who are hurt by a new technology and those who benefit from it. In the case of the Luddites, for example, the political power of the mill owners proved stronger than that of their workers. In the example of unbreakable glass, technology blocking triumphed because the person who stood to lose out from the new technology was the emperor. In the case of margarine, the rise of a countervailing force—soybean farmers who benefitted from allowing margarine to be sold freely—turned the tide against technology blocking.

Finally, although many of the forms of inefficiency we have examined in this chapter seem to be particularly serious problems in developing countries, rich countries may be even more prone to technology blocking than poor ones. The reason is that blocking a new technology often requires the assistance of a well-functioning government, which is more frequently found in rich countries than in developing countries.

10.4 CONCLUSION

Our analysis in this chapter has rested on the idea that we can separate country differences in productivity into differences in available technology and differences in the efficiency with which technology and factors of production are employed. Our most important conclusion is that differences in efficiency among countries are much larger than differences in technology. Thus, variation in efficiency explains most of the variation in productivity among countries.

The most important piece of evidence for the importance of efficiency is that, as we saw in Chapter 7, productivity differences among countries are quite large. These differences in productivity *could* be the result of differences in technology—but given the ease with which technology flows across borders, and the large technology gaps that would be required were technology differences to explain productivity differences, this explanation is doubtful. Rather, most of the variation in productivity among countries is probably the result of variation in efficiency.

We have considered both some explicit examples of inefficiency and a more general characterization of the different types of inefficiency. The inefficiencies discussed in the case studies in Section 10.2 in some instances fit neatly into the categories of inefficiency discussed in Section 10.3. For example, the failure of German brewers to use advanced brewing machinery that is made in Germany looks like a case of technology blocking, and featherbedding in the U.S. coal industry serves as a good example of idle resources. But in other cases the inefficiencies we considered in Section 10.2 do not fall into the categories presented in Section 10.3. In fact, the five types of inefficiency we examined in Section 10.3 are only a beginning when it comes to exploring the many different ways that an economy can fail to use available technology and factors of production effectively. Indeed, economists do not yet have a complete theory of economic inefficiency, even though they have been studying the subject at least since the time of Adam Smith.

One preliminary lesson that we can draw from our study of efficiency is that the level of efficiency in an economy depends crucially on its institutional structure. If individuals can profit from blocking the introduction of new technologies or from doing unproductive things, then they will do so. The difference between a society in which factors are channeled to their most productive use, new technologies are implemented, and resources are not wasted in rent seeking, on the one hand, and a society in which this happy state of affairs does not hold true, on the other, does not lie in the self-interest or energy of its citizens. Rather, the source of the difference is the institutional structure that rewards, or fails to reward, activities such as rent seeking and technology blocking.

In the next part of the book, much of our concern will be with factors that affect the efficiency of economies. Many of the examples of inefficiency in this chapter are related to aspects of government policy. In Chapter 12, we will look more directly at what governments do and why. One of the questions we will address in Chapter 13 is the degree to which an unequal distribution of income can lead to the creation of institutions that impede efficiency. And in Chapter 14 we will look at differences in culture—such as the attitudes of workers and employers—as a potential source of country differences in efficiency.

Before examining these influences on efficiency, however, in Chapter 11 we expand our framework to take account of an economy that is open to trade with the rest of the world. We will see that efficiency in an even more important issue for an open than a closed economy. We can think of the possibility to trade with other countries as a kind of technology: Through trade, a country can convert things it is good at producing into things it is not as good at producing. The failure to use the "technology" of international trade is perhaps the best example of the phenomenon of technology blocking.

KEY TERMS

featherbedding   279
unproductive
  activities   280
rent seeking   281
economic rent   281

idle resources   281
misallocation   282
misallocation among
  sectors   283

misallocation among
  firms   288
technology blocking   289
Luddites   292

QUESTIONS FOR REVIEW

1. What is efficiency? How are efficiency, technology, and productivity related?

2. How does knowing the technological "gap" between two countries allow us to infer differences in their levels of efficiency?

3. How does the evidence from the textile industry support the view that differences in efficiency among countries can be quite large?

4. List and briefly define the five types of inefficiency discussed in the text.

5. What are the conditions under which free movement of workers between sectors will achieve an efficient allocation of labor?

PROBLEMS

1. There are two countries, X and Z. Productivity in Country X is twice as high as productivity in Country Z. Technology in Country X is four times as high as technology in Country Z. How does efficiency in the two countries compare?

2. Perform a calculation similar to that in Table 10.1, using the following data: The level of productivity in Country X, relative to the United States, is 0.5. The growth rate of technology is 1% per year. Country X lags behind the United States in terms of technology by 20 years. What is the level of efficiency in Country X relative to the United States?

3. Looking at the calculation in Section 10.1, suppose that efficiency in India were equal to that in the United States. Based on the data on the countries' relative productivity and the growth rate of productivity in the United States of 0.54% per year, how large (in years) would the technology gap between the two countries be?

4. Give two examples of real-world inefficiencies (that are not given in the text), and for each one, explain which of the five categories of inefficiency it most closely corresponds to.

5. Which of the five types of inefficiency described in the chapter do you think is most economically significant in the country that you know best? Explain why and give examples.

6. In the two-sector model of an economy (described under the heading "Misallocation of Factors Among Sectors" in Section 10.3), use a diagram like Figure 10.3 to show how a minimum wage in the urban sector would lead to an inefficient allocation of labor.

7. Consider a country in which there are two
$|dy/dx$ sectors, called Sector 1 and Sector 2. The
production functions in the two sectors are:

$$Y_1 = L_1^{1/2}$$
$$Y_2 = L_2^{1/2}$$

where L_1 is the number of workers employed
in Sector 1 and L_2 is the number of workers
employed in Sector 2. The total number
of workers in the economy is L. The only
difference between the sectors is that in
Sector 1 workers are paid their *marginal*
products, whereas in Sector 2 they are paid
their *average* products. Workers move freely
between sectors so that the wages are equal.
Calculate how many workers will work in
each sector.

For additional exploration and practice using the Online Data Plotter and data sets, please visit
www.pearsonhighered.com/weil.

11

GROWTH IN THE OPEN ECONOMY

Economically, what is the difference between restricting the importation of iron to benefit iron-producers and restricting sanitary improvements to benefit undertakers?

—*Henry George*, Protection or Free Trade, *1886*

Countries interact in myriad ways. The most obvious interaction is trade: Countries do not consume only the goods and services produced within their own borders. An American can buy French wine and an Indian can consume U.S. wheat. In addition to these international flows of goods, there are flows of factors of production. For example, when savers in Japan invest in machinery to produce output in Indonesia, physical capital flows between those countries. Similarly, as people flow across borders through immigration, labor and human capital are moving from country to country. To this list we could add flows of technology; flows of ideas (e.g., democracy and communism); military conflict or foreign domination; and flows of international aid.

Thus far in our investigation of economic growth, we have mostly ignored economic interactions among countries. When we studied the accumulation of physical and human capital, population growth, and the efficiency of production, we assumed an economy that was closed off from the rest of the world. The one exception to our closed-economy approach has been in thinking about technology, where we explicitly studied the flow of ideas across borders.

In this chapter, we look directly at the effects of economic openness. Specifically, we investigate three questions relating to openness. First, how does being open to the world economy affect a country's economic growth? Second, what are the particular channels through which openness affects growth? Finally, why are some people opposed to openness? We begin by considering how to measure the openness of an economy, as well as how and why openness has increased in recent years.

11.1 AUTARKY VERSUS OPENNESS

We read all the time about *globalization*, the process that is eliminating the economic relevance of national borders. But what does it mean for an economy to be "open" to the world market?

As a starting point, we can consider the opposite of openness: an economy that has no interaction whatsoever with other countries. The perfectly closed economy has implicitly been the subject of most of our modeling so far in this book—not because it is an accurate description, but because it is the easiest place to begin. In a world of closed economies, the amount of output produced in each country is a function of the stocks of factors of production (physical capital, human capital, and labor) that each country has accumulated, as well as of the country's level of productivity.

Economists use the word **autarky** to refer to the situation in which a country does not interact economically at all with the rest of the world. In recent history, a few countries—among them North Korea, Albania, and Burma—have come close to achieving such a state. But even in these cases, there was some trade with outside countries and interactions other than trade, such as the flow of ideas and the threat of military conflict.

Once we allow for an economy to interact with other countries, we must be precise about the form of the interaction. Economists distinguish between two primary forms of economic integration among countries. The first is **trade**—the exchange of goods and services. The second is the **flow of factors of production** across borders. Although trade and factor flows are often loosely tossed together into the category of "openness," they differ in important ways. A country can be quite open to trade, for example, without allowing foreigners to own capital. Thus, in our analysis of the international aspects of economic growth, we must carefully distinguish between these two forms of openness.

In looking at trade and factor flows, we need to measure how open an economy is. One approach is to measure the quantities of goods or factors that flow among countries. If there is a large flow of goods into and out of a country, for example, then we can say confidently that it is open to trade. However, even if countries are open, goods or factors do not necessarily flow among those countries. Along with openness, there must also be a reason for economic interaction. If two countries produce the same goods or have the same factors of production, there might be no incentive for trade, even if trade is perfectly possible. In this case, we can use a different method of testing for openness. If two economies are open to trade with each other, then the **law of one price,** which says that the same good will sell for the same price in both markets, must hold true. If the prices are not the same and trade is possible, then entrepreneurs will be able to buy goods or factors in one country and sell them in another, making an instant profit. Thus, if countries are open to trade in goods, then the same good will sell for the same price in both countries. Similarly, if countries are open to movements of factors of production, then the same factor should earn the same income in both markets. Turning this notion around, we can measure the degree of integration between two economies by measuring the differences in prices.

We would never expect the law of one price to hold perfectly. It always costs something to transport goods and factors from place to place. But we can use the degree of similarity of prices as a measure of integration. The closer are the prices of the same goods in two countries, the more integrated are their markets for goods (in the sense of being able to trade). Likewise, the closer are prices of the same factors of production, the more integrated are the countries' markets for factors of production.

Using these two gauges of openness, we can measure where a country fits between the two extremes of perfect autarky and perfect openness. If we do so, we will find large differences among countries in their degree of openness, as well as large changes in openness over time.

Measuring Output in an Open Economy

Allowing for trade in goods among countries does not require a fundamental alteration in the conceptual framework we have been using to analyze national income. Once we allow for the international movement of factors of production, however, the picture becomes more complicated. To understand the reason for this complication, consider what happens when an American invests his or her capital in a foreign country—say, Italy. Recall from Chapter 3 that capital used for production earns a return that is paid to the owner of the capital. We have seen that capital income is part of national income. But in the instance of our U.S. investor, should that capital income be counted as part of income in Italy, where the production is taking place, or in the United States, where the capital is owned?

The answer is that there are two different ways of defining income. **Gross domestic product (GDP)** is the sum of all income earned by the factors of production *located in a given country*. **Gross national product (GNP)** is the sum of all income earned by the factors of production *owned by the residents of a given country*. In our example, the income of a piece of capital in Italy that is owned by a U.S. resident would count as part of U.S. GNP and Italian GDP. It would not count as part of either U.S. GDP or Italian GNP. Similarly, the wages of an Egyptian worker who takes a temporary job in Saudi Arabia will count as part of Egyptian GNP and Saudi GDP, but not as part of Egyptian GDP or Saudi GNP.

Whether GNP or GDP is a better measure depends on what we want to know. Most of the available data measure GDP because measuring the amount of output produced in a country is much easier than figuring out who owns what factors of production. But it is important to recognize that some of the international flows of factors we are considering can lead to a large discrepancy between GDP and GNP.

Globalization: The Facts

Although current observers tend to view the last several decades as a period of unprecedented integration of national economies, economic historians have pointed out that the current wave of globalization is really the second such wave to sweep the world. The first period of globalization began in the middle of the 19th century and peaked just before World War I. The period 1914–1950, featuring two world wars and the Great Depression, saw a retreat from global integration. Much of the increase in integration that has taken place since World War II has simply been a return to the level of integration that existed before World War I. This pattern of two waves of globalization is visible in Figure 11.1, which shows the ratio of world trade (specifically, the total value of world exports) to world GDP over the period 1870–2010. A striking feature of the figure is that in 1950, trade as a fraction of GDP was at almost the same level as 80 years previously.[1]

With respect to international flows of physical capital (the most mobile factor of production), we again see two waves of globalization. The golden age of international capital flows was the two decades before World War I. The British were the "bankers to the world" during this period: Of the total sum invested across national boundaries, half came from Britain. In 1911 Britain invested more than half of its savings abroad, and this foreign investment constituted 8.7 percent of Britain's GDP. Europeans financed a large fraction of the investment

▶ FIGURE 11.1

Growth of World Trade, 1870–2010

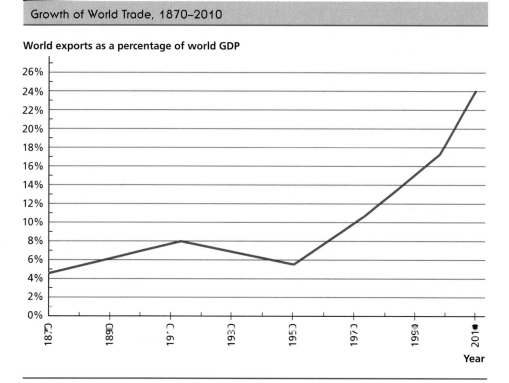

World exports as a percentage of world GDP

Source: Maddison (2001), World Bank (2007a).

[1]Maddison (2001).

that took place in much of the New World. Between 1870 and 1910, for example, foreigners financed 37% of investment in Canada. In 1913 foreigners owned almost half of the physical capital in Argentina and one-fifth of the physical capital in Australia.

International capital flows dried up after World War I and did not return to their previous levels until recent decades. In 2010, the world's biggest capital exporters were China ($305 billion), Japan ($196 billion), and Germany ($188 billion). The largest importer of capital was the United States ($471 billion).

Starting in the 1990s, there was a boom in investment in "emerging markets" in the developing world. Annual net private capital flows into developing countries averaged $92 billion over the period 1997–2000, and rose to $659 billion in 2010. However, these inflows of private capital have largely been matched by the accumulation of foreign reserves by developing country governments, so there has actually been a net flow of capital *out* of the developing world over the last decade.[2]

In one important respect—the movement of people among countries—the current wave of globalization has yet to reach the degree of integration seen in the surge that peaked in 1914. Between 1870 and 1925, roughly 100 million people changed countries, equal to about one-tenth of the world's population in 1870. About 50 million were emigrants from Europe (primarily eastern and southern) to the Americas and Australia. The rest primarily emigrated from China and India, bound for other parts of Asia, the Americas, and Africa. The end of colonialism, the rise of nationalism, and political changes in the receiving countries greatly reduced the importance of immigration after World War II. Of the countries that received large flows of immigration in the late 19th century, only the United States has maintained immigration near the rate it experienced then. In 1910, 14.7% of the U.S. population was foreign born; in 2010 the foreign-born percentage was 12.4%.[3]

Globalization: The Causes

Two major forces have driven globalization. Technological advances have eased the movement of goods and information, and changes in economic policies have lowered barriers to trade. We address these causes in turn.

Transport Costs. One of the driving forces in both waves of globalization has been a fall in the price of transportation. Before 1800, modes of transport had changed only gradually. Sailing ships, canal boats, and animal-drawn carts were slow and expensive means of transporting goods. As a result, international trade was profitable only when there was a large difference in the price of a good in the

---

[2]http://www.un.org/esa/analysis/wess/wesp2011files/2011chap3.pdf.
[3]DeLong (2001), *Current Population Survey.*

importing and exporting countries and when the goods to be transported had a high ratio of value to weight, as in the case of gold and spices.

In the 19th century, two key technologies—the railroad and the steamship— vastly reduced the cost of transportation and propelled economic integration. Railways integrated markets within individual countries and brought interior areas within reach of the world market. In 1850 the United States had 9,021 miles of railway; by 1910 it had 249,902 miles. In 1780 the 177-mile (283-kilometer) trip from Paris to Calais on the English Channel took three days by coach. By 1905 the trip by railroad took only three hours and 24 minutes.[4]

Regular steamship transport across the Atlantic Ocean began in 1838, al- though initially the cost was prohibitive for anything but high-value items. A series of technological improvements over the course of the 19th century drove the price of ocean transport down at a pace of 0.88% per year in the first half of the century and 1.5% per year in the second half. As shipping got cheaper, it also got faster. The fastest ocean liner in 1842 had a top speed of 10 knots; by 1912 the top speed was 18 knots. The opening of the Suez Canal in 1869 greatly reduced travel times between Europe and Asia—for example, cutting by 41% the trip between London and Bombay. The total carrying capacity of world shipping increased by a factor of 29 between 1820 and 1913.[5]

To see how the decline in transport costs led to greater economic integra- tion, we can look at the prices of the same good in different markets. Recall the law of one price: If there were no transport costs or other barriers to trade, a good would have to sell for the same price in different markets. In 1870 wheat was 58% more expensive in London than in Chicago, and rice was 93% more expensive in London than in Rangoon. By 1913 the gaps had fallen to 16% and 26%, respec- tively. These reductions in price differentials provide evidence of increased eco- nomic integration.[6]

In the 20th century, the cost of transport continued to decline. The average cost of shipping one ton of freight fell from $95 to $29 between 1920 and 1990 (in 1990 dollars).[7] The introduction of containerized freight in 1953 led to a 20-fold increase in the speed with which ships could be loaded. The growth of air freight, which barely existed at all before World War II, has allowed new commodities to enter trade. For example, annual exports of cut flowers from Kenya to Europe grew from nothing in the early 1960s to $446 million in 2008.

Finally, not only has the cost of transporting any particular item fallen, but the composition of countries' output has shifted toward goods that are easier to trans- port. Alan Greenspan, then chairman of the Federal Reserve Board, pointed out in 1996 that over the previous 50 years, the value of real output produced in the

---

[4]Braudel (1984), Dauzet (1948).
[5]Harley (1988), Maddison (2001), Table 2–25a.
[6]O' Rourke and Williamson (2002).
[7]International Monetary Fund (1997).

United States had risen threefold, whereas the weight of that output had increased only slightly. This change in the value/weight ratio of GDP has resulted both from a shift to lighter materials (transistors replaced vacuum tubes; fiber-optic cable and satellites replaced copper wire) and from a movement in the composition of output away from physical goods toward "weightless" goods such as entertainment, communications, and specialized knowledge.

Transmission of Information. A second force propelling economic integration is the faster flow of information. Access to current information aids both trade and capital investment. In the early 19th century, the time required for information to flow from London to New York via sailing ship was as long as three weeks. For that reason, the Battle of New Orleans, fought between the British and Americans in 1815, took place some two weeks after an armistice had been signed. By the 1860s, steamships could convey information across the Atlantic in just 10 days. With the inauguration of the transatlantic telegraph cable in 1866, the time required to transmit a message fell to two hours, and by 1914 it was less than one minute. The first U.S.-British telephone service (transmitted by radio) was introduced in 1927.

Information transmission has also gotten cheaper. During the last 70 years of the 20th century, the price of communication fell by 8% per year. For example, a three-minute telephone call between London and New York cost $300 in 1930, $50 in 1960, and about $1 in 1996 (all of these figures are in 1996 dollars).[8] Today, such a phone call can be made for free over the Internet. This steep reduction in communication costs has simplified the coordination of economic activity over long distances, allowing for freer flows of goods and factors of production.

Reductions in the cost of transmitting information have allowed the development of new types of trade. Traditionally, trade was confined to goods—that is, things that could be put on a boat and taken from place to place. By contrast, trade in services has been more difficult. For example, even though haircuts (a service) are far cheaper in India than in the United States, there is no way for an entrepreneur to take advantage of this price differential. But increasingly, many information-based services have become subject to trade. For example, the Internet service provider America Online imports customer-support services by hiring workers in the Philippines to answer 80% of its e-mail concerning technical problems and billing.

Trade Policy. The cost of transporting goods is only one of the barriers to trade and to the movement of factors of production. Restrictions on international trade are among the oldest forms of government economic policy (see box "Tariffs, Quotas, and Other Trade Restrictions"). Indeed, as transport costs have fallen, the legal barriers to trade that governments impose have become much more significant.

---

[8]"One World?" *The Economist,* October 18, 1997; Quah (1998).

TARIFFS, QUOTAS, AND OTHER TRADE RESTRICTIONS

The two most important forms of trade restriction are **tariffs** (taxes on the import of a good) and **quotas** (restrictions on the total amount of a good that can be imported). International agreements to reduce trade restrictions usually focus on the reduction of tariff rates and the elimination of quotas altogether. But tariffs and quotas are only the beginning when it comes to trade restriction.

Here are some other forms:

- *Voluntary export restraints (VERs)*—These are arrangements in which one country agrees to put a limit on exports bound for another country. For example, in 1981, facing a threat of U.S. tariffs, Japan agreed to limit automobile exports to the United States to 1.68 million vehicles per year. The policy, which was terminated in 1994, is estimated to have raised the price of Japanese cars in the United States by $1,200 on average. Reduced competition from Japan also raised the price of U.S.-made cars.[*] Because VERs are usually instituted in response to the threat of more severe actions on the part of the importing nation, the word *voluntary* should not be taken seriously.

- *Anti-dumping duties*—Dumping occurs when a firm charges a lower price in a market to which it is exporting than it does in its home market. Under the rules of the World Trade Organization (WTO), a country that is having products dumped in its markets is allowed to impose import duties (taxes) to offset the price differential. However, these anti-dumping duties are frequently abused. Sympathetic government officials are prone to find evidence of dumping in just about any case where a well-connected industry is suffering from foreign competition. The U.S. imposition of anti-dumping duties on imported steel in 2002, for example, owed more to the fact that the steel industry is concentrated in states that would be important in the 2004 presidential election than to any behavior on the part of foreign steel producers. In a more bizarre case, the United States imposed anti-dumping duties on golf carts manufactured in Poland between 1976 and 1980, even though no golf carts were sold in Poland. The share of worldwide anti-dumping actions that target exports from China rose from 13% in 1995 to 35% in 2008.[†]

- *Excessive standards*—Governments impose standards on all sorts of goods that are sold in their countries, ranging from regulations designed to protect public health (e.g., pure-food standards) to requirements that enable different pieces of equipment to work together. Often, however, standards are used to keep foreign products out of the domestic market. For example, Israel, with a population of only 6 million, requires the use of an electrical plug that is unique in the world, to give an advantage to local manufacturers of electrical equipment.

- *Bureaucratic creativity*—In 1982, during a trade dispute with Japan, France instituted a policy that all videocassette recorders (VCRs) imported into the country would have to enter through a single port, where only one customs officer was put in charge of processing the paperwork. The resulting bottleneck drove down the volume of Japanese VCR imports by 90%.[‡]

These sorts of obstacles to trade are collectively referred to as **nontariff barriers.** A study conducted in the late 1990s calculated that nontariff barriers were on average roughly equal in size to tariff barriers, although the ratio of the two varied by country. In Japan, for example, non tariff barriers were twice as important as tariffs.[§]

[*]Berry, Levinsohn, and Pakes (1999).
[†] http://www.antidumpingpublishing.com/
[‡] www.japanlaw.com/lawletter/nov82/vu.htm.
[§]Anderson and Neary (1999)

One force propelling the current wave of globalization has been a series of reductions in trade restrictions negotiated under the General Agreement on Tariffs and Trade (GATT) and its successor, the WTO. Average tariff rates in the industrial countries fell from 40% at the end of World War II to 6% by 2000. In the year 2010, average tariff rates were 2.8% among the wealthy countries of the Organisation for Economic Co-operation and Development (OECD), 8.2% among middle-income countries, and 11.0% among poor countries. Among industrial countries, some of the highest tariffs are in agriculture. In Japan, the tariff on wheat is 250%, and the tariff on rice is sufficient to maintain the domestic price at four times the world market price.[9]

11.2 THE EFFECT OF OPENNESS ON ECONOMIC GROWTH

Whether openness to foreign trade is good for a country's economy is one of the oldest questions in economics. As a starting point toward answering this question, we need to measure how countries differ in their degree of openness. Because a country has many means of restricting trade and factor movements, measuring a country's degree of openness requires some judgment.

The data used here are from two studies that examined a number of aspects of openness, such as the level of tariffs, manipulation of the exchange rate, and government monopolies on exports.[10] For every year between 1965 and 2000, each country is assigned a value of 1 if it was open and 0 if it was not. Figure 11.2 shows the relationship between openness and the level of GDP per capita in 2000. Countries are grouped into four categories: those that were never open during the period 1965–2000, those that were open some years but fewer than half, those that were open more than half of the time but not always, and those that were always open. As Figure 11.2 clearly shows, the more open to the world economy countries are, the more likely they are to be rich. Countries that were always open were, on average, 4.5 times as rich as countries that were never open. Countries that were open more than half the time were 1.5 times as rich as countries that were open less than half the time.

Although the result in Figure 11.2 is striking, it does not prove that being open to the world economy makes a country rich. Perhaps openness is a luxury that only rich countries can afford. Or similarly, maybe some third characteristic of countries tends to make them both rich and open. To determine whether being open to the world economy will *cause* a country to be rich, we take three approaches. First, we look at how growth rates (rather than levels) of income compare in open and closed countries. Second, we examine how growth rates change when countries

---

[9]World Bank (2011b), Dollar and Collier (2001), Department for Environment, Food, and Rural Affairs (UK), http://archive.defra.gov.uk/foodfarm/food/pdf/ag-price-annex%204.pdf
[10]Sachs and Warner (1995), Wacziarg and Welch (2008).

FIGURE 11.2

Relationship between Economic Openness and GDP per Capita

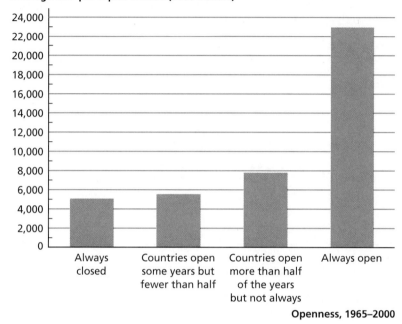

Sources: Sachs and Warner (1995), Wacziarg and Welch (2008).

become more open or less open. Finally, we consider the impact of geographic factors that affect a country's openness but, unlike trade policies, are not themselves affected by other characteristics of the country.

Growth in Open versus Closed Economies

Our first approach is to see how growth rates compare in open and closed countries. Figures 11.3 and 11.4 are both scatter plots in which each data point represents a single country. In both figures, the horizontal axis measures GDP per capita in 1965 (using a ratio scale), and the vertical axis measures countries' average growth rates over the period 1965–2000. The two figures use different samples of countries. Figure 11.3 examines countries that were closed, according to the measure discussed previously for some or all of the years with available data. Figure 11.4 looks at countries that were open for the entire period.

The results in these figures are striking in two respects. First, the average growth rate of income in the closed group, 1.5% per year, was significantly lower than in the open group, 3.1% per year. Second, among the economies that were

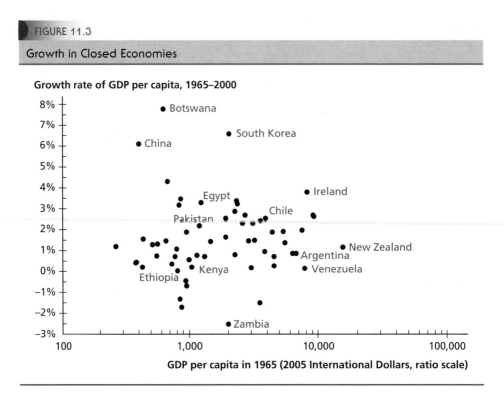

▶ FIGURE 11.3

Growth in Closed Economies

Sources: Sachs and Warner (1995), Wacziarg and Welch (2008), Heston et al. (2011).

closed some or all of the time, there is no observable relationship between the initial level of a country's GDP and its subsequent rate of growth. Among the countries open to trade, by contrast, we find strong evidence of convergence: Poorer countries that are open tend to grow faster than richer countries. Putting the results in the two figures together, we can see that poor countries that are open to trade grow faster than rich countries, and poor countries that are closed to trade grow more slowly than rich countries.

How Changes in Openness Affect Growth

Our second approach to exploring the effect of openness on growth is to consider how *changes* in a country's degree of openness affect growth rates. If within a particular country, a change in trade policy (a trade liberalization or the imposition of new trade restrictions) is followed by a change in the growth rate of output, this pattern can supply us with evidence about the way trade affects income.

One of the most sweeping examples of trade liberalization comes from 19th-century Japan. In the 12 years after Japan ended its self-imposed economic isolation in 1858, the value of Japanese trade with the rest of the world rose by a

FIGURE 11.4

Growth in Open Economies

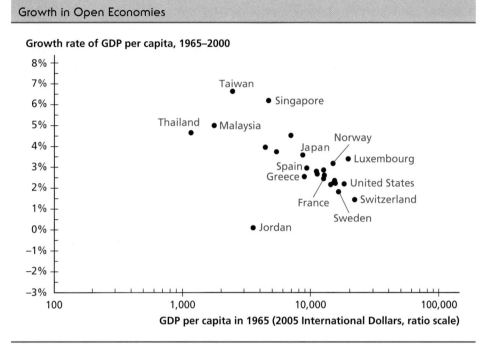

Sources: Sachs and Warner (1995), Wacziarg and Welch (2008), Heston et al. (2011).

factor of 70. The opening to trade is estimated to have raised Japanese real income by 65% over two decades, and put the country on a path of growth that would eventually cause it to catch up to European levels of income (see Figure 1.5). This same effect of trade liberalization has occurred in the 20th century as well. In South Korea, following a sweeping liberalization of trade in 1964–1965, income grew rapidly, doubling in the next 11 years. Similarly, Uganda and Vietnam experienced rapid growth in the 1990s, following their integration into the world economy.

In all these examples, increased openness led to higher growth. Conversely, when we look at cases in which openness *decreased*, we see evidence that lower growth followed. For example, the trade embargo instituted by President Thomas Jefferson in 1807–1809 spawned widespread unemployment and bankruptcy in the United States. Similarly, the wave of tariff increases throughout the world in 1930, including the U.S. Smoot-Hawley tariff, contributed to the severity of the Great Depression of the 1930s.[11]

---

[11]Huber (1971), Irwin (2002), Dollar and Collier (2001).

The Effect of Geographical Barriers to Trade

Our third approach to probing into whether openness is good for growth is to look beyond economic policy and examine another factor that influences whether a country is open to trade or capital flows: geography. Nineteenth-century economist Henry George, as a way to make a case for free trade, used the observation that natural barriers to trade can play the same role as those imposed by governments:

> If to prevent trade were to stimulate industry and promote prosperity, then the localities where he was most isolated would show the first advances of man. The natural protection to home industry afforded by rugged mountain-chains, by burning deserts, or by seas too wide and tempestuous for the frail bark of the early mariner, would have given us the first glimmerings of civilization and shown its most rapid growth. But, in fact, it is where trade could be best carried on that we find wealth first accumulating and civilization beginning. It is on accessible harbors, by navigable rivers and much traveled highways that we find cities arising and the arts and sciences developing.[12]

A study by economists Jeffrey Frankel and David Romer used George's observation to inquire into how openness to trade affects income per capita in a large number of countries. The authors proceeded in two stages. First, they examined the role that geographic factors play in determining trade. They found that the volume of trade between any two countries was partially determined by how far apart the two countries were, whether one of the countries was landlocked, and how large the countries were. Using data on geographic characteristics, the researchers could thus calculate how much trade they would expect each country to have. For example, on the basis of geography alone, they would expect Lesotho, a landlocked country in southern Africa far from major markets, to have only 40% of the trade volume of Belgium, an equal-sized country on the coast of Europe. In the second stage of their analysis, they asked how this geographically determined trade volume affected a country's income. Because geography—unlike trade policy—cannot itself be the result of differences in income or of some other factor, any relationship between geographically determined trade and income per capita must be the result of trade's affecting income. They found that raising the ratio of trade to GDP by one percentage point would raise income by an amount between 0.5% and 2.0%.[13]

The approach of using geographic barriers between countries to measure the difficulty of trading has the advantage that such barriers are clearly exogenous— that is, they are not determined by other country characteristics, such as income. However, the geographical measure has a corresponding difficulty, which is that distances between countries never change. Two recent studies by the economist

---

[12]George (1886).
[13]Frankel and Romer (1999).

James Feyrer get around this difficulty by looking at natural experiments in which trade costs between country pairs changed, even if their distance did not. The first natural experiment was the closing of the Suez Canal, as a result of fighting between Egypt and Israel, over the years 1967–1975. A significant fraction of world trade flowed through the canal before the closing, and the new routes that ships had to take significantly increased the shipping distances between some pairs of countries. For example, the sailing distance between Mumbai and London rose from 6,200 nautical miles to 10,800 nautical miles after the canal was closed. At the same time, many other country-pair distances were unaffected by the canal's closing. Feyrer finds that there was a significant reduction in trade volumes for countries that saw their effective trade distances increased.

The second natural experiment Feyrer examines is the change in effective distance among country pairs that has taken place as more of the value of trade has shifted from sea to air. The cost per ton of air freight fell by a factor of 10 between 1955 and 2004. The fraction of the value of U.S. exports that traveled by air rose from essentially zero in 1960 to over half by 2004 (excluding Mexico and Canada). A similar shift took place in much of the world. A key difference between air freight and traditional sea freight is that the former follows straight lines (literally, great circle routes on a globe), whereas the latter follows routes that depend on where oceans are. As a result of the rise of air freight, the effective distance between country pairs that were much closer in straight-line terms than in terms of sea routes (e.g., Japan and Germany) fell by much more than the effective distance between country pairs that were equally distant in terms of air and sea travel (e.g., Brazil and Spain). In this case, Feyrer finds an increase in trade volumes among country pairs where the effective distance fell as a result of air freight. In both of his studies, Feyrer finds that changes in a country's trade induced by changes in the effective distance to its trading partners resulted in corresponding changes in income; when trade rose, income rose, and when trade fell, income fell.[14]

The three types of evidence we have examined—comparisons of growth rates of open versus closed countries, studies of episodes of trade liberalization or restriction, and examination of the effects of geographic factors that limit openness—all point to the same conclusion: that being open to the world economy is good for a country's economic growth. This finding raises two questions. First, what specifically is it about openness that is good for growth? Second, if openness works so well as a policy, why do more countries *not* adopt it?

11.3 OPENNESS AND FACTOR ACCUMULATION

The analysis of data in the last section leads to the conclusion that openness makes an economy richer. But it does not indicate *how* openness affects growth; in other words, what are the particular channels by which being open to the outside

---

[14]Feyrer (2009a, 2009b).

world affects a country's level of income per capita? On the basis of the analysis in Chapter 7, a natural place to begin answering this question is to consider whether openness affects growth through the channel of factor accumulation or through the channel of productivity. In other words, are more open countries richer because they have more physical and human capital for each worker to work with, or are they richer because they use their factors of production more effectively?

We start by examining factor accumulation. Specifically, we consider how growth is affected by the flow of physical capital among countries. We focus on physical capital because it is the most mobile factor of production.

Physical capital flows across national borders through several channels. The largest is **foreign direct investment,** by which a foreign firm buys or builds a facility in another country. The second largest channel is **portfolio investment,** in which investors from a foreign country purchase stocks or bonds. The remaining sources of capital flows are government grants and lending from banks and multinational donor agencies such as the World Bank. Of the $659 billion in private capital that flowed into developing countries in 2010, $248 billion was foreign direct investment.[15]

Growth with Capital Mobility

A natural way to examine the effect of capital mobility on economic growth is to use the Solow model. When we first encountered this model, we examined an economy that was closed to capital flows, so that the level of investment was by necessity equal to the level of saving. Now we look at the same model in the case of an economy that is fully open to capital flows from the rest of the world, so that investment can be financed by foreign savings and, similarly, domestic savings can be used to finance foreign investment.

Because the economy is open to capital flows, we can use the law of one price to conclude that prices of any mobile factor of production must be the same in the country we are considering and in the rest of the world. Recall from Chapter 3 that the way we measure the "price" of capital is by its rental rate (i.e., the cost of renting one unit of capital for one unit of time). We therefore will assume that in an economy open to capital flows, the rental rate for capital will be the same as in the rest of the world. For analytic simplicity, we also make a second assumption: that the economy we are examining is small relative to the rest of the world. Thus, what happens in this economy has no effect on the prices of factors in the rest of the world. A final simplifying assumption is that we ignore the effect of human capital in our analysis.

As in our previous analysis, our starting point is the production function in per worker terms:

$$y = Ak^{\alpha},$$

---

[15]http://www.un.org/esa/analysis/wess/wesp2011files/2011chap3.pdf.

where y is output per worker, k is capital per worker, A is a constant that measures the level of productivity, and α is a coefficient between 0 and 1. In Chapter 3, we calculated the marginal product of capital, MPK, :

$$\text{MPK} = \alpha A k^{\alpha-1}.$$

This equation says that the marginal product of capital depends negatively on the amount of capital per worker, k. If a country has a relatively high level of capital per worker, it will have a lower marginal product of capital. In Chapter 3, we saw that, as a consequence of firms' maximizing their profits, the marginal product of capital is equal to the rental rate of capital. Defining r as the rental rate of capital gives us the equation:

$$r = \text{MPK} = \alpha A k^{\alpha-1}.$$

Our assumption of perfect openness to factor flows implies that the law of one price holds true: Factor prices in the country we are examining must be the same as factor prices in the rest of the world. We assume that there is some "world" rental rate of capital, denoted r_w. The assumption of perfect openness to capital flows implies that:

$$r = r_w.$$

Combining the preceding two equations, we get:

$$r_w = \alpha A k^{\alpha-1}.$$

Rearranging this equation to solve for the level of capital per worker, k, we get:

$$k = \left(\frac{\alpha A}{r_w}\right)^{1/(1-\alpha)}. \tag{11.1}$$

This analysis produces an important conclusion: With perfect capital mobility, the capital/labor ratio depends on the world rental rate of capital. This result is important because in our previous analysis of growth and capital accumulation in Chapters 3 and 4, we examined a situation in which the capital/labor ratio in a given country depends on domestic factors like the saving rate and the growth rate of the population.

To see the implication of capital mobility for the level of GDP per worker, we substitute the level of capital per worker from Equation 11.1 into the production function:

$$y = A k^\alpha = A\left(\left(\frac{\alpha A}{r_w}\right)^{1/(1-\alpha)}\right)^\alpha = A^{1/(1-\alpha)}\left(\frac{\alpha}{r_w}\right)^{\alpha/(1-\alpha)}. \tag{11.2}$$

The significance of this equation has to do with what is *not* in it. Recall from Chapter 3 that in the Solow model for a closed economy, the level of GDP per worker depends on the saving rate. A country that saves more will be richer in the steady state (see Equation 3.3, noting that for a closed economy the investment rate, γ, is equal to the saving rate). But the saving rate does not appear anywhere in Equation 11.2. Thus, Equation 11.2 says that GDP per worker will not be any higher in a country with a high saving rate than in a country with a low saving rate.

Does this mean that, if the economy is open to factor flows, a country with a high saving rate will not be richer than a country with a low saving rate? No! However, to see why a high-saving country will be better off than a low-saving country, we must look beyond GDP to GNP. Consider what would happen if a country raised its saving rate. In the closed-economy model of Chapter 3, this increase in saving would raise the level of domestic investment and thus raise the capital stock. But if the saving rate increased in an open economy, the increase in the capital stock would lower the marginal product of capital. At this point, owners of capital would find that they could earn higher returns abroad and would transfer their capital out of the country. This movement of capital abroad would continue until the marginal product of capital again equaled the world level; in this way, the capital stock would return to its former level. All of the rise in saving would result in increased ownership of capital in other countries.

Recall that GNP is the income of all factors of production that are *owned* by the residents of a given country. Thus, although changes in the saving rate will not affect GDP, they will have an impact on GNP because they will affect the quantity of capital owned abroad. A country that saves more will own more capital in total and consequently will earn more capital income, with the result that GNP will rise.

One important implication of this free-capital-flow model is that for a country with a low saving rate, openness to capital flows should raise the GDP. Capital that is not supplied domestically can be supplied from abroad. The same would hold true for any country that has a low level of capital—for example, a country in which a war or natural disaster destroyed part of the capital stock. If the economy is open to capital flows, then investment flowing into the country from abroad can produce growth in GDP per worker that is much more rapid than the country could produce with its own savings.

A final implication of the model is that for a country with a *high* saving rate, openness to capital flows will lower the level of GDP per worker, as capital will flow abroad to countries where its marginal product is higher. At first, this implication might seem to indicate that for a country with high saving, openness to capital flows is a bad thing. But this conclusion is incorrect. It can be shown algebraically that openness to capital flows will raise the level of GNP per worker in both high- and low-saving countries.

Assessing the Free-Capital-Flow Model

Having examined a model of growth in a world with perfect capital flows, we now assess whether this model is appropriate for understanding the real world. In the first part of this chapter, we examined data on the size of capital flows.

Now we ask whether these flows are large enough to justify the assumption of perfect capital mobility.

In the model we just developed, investment in a given country has no relationship to that country's level of saving. But investment does depend on the value of the productivity coefficient A. As Equation 11.1 shows, a country with a high value of A will have a large capital stock, which implies a high level of investment. Saving, by contrast, might depend on factors such as how present- or future-oriented people in a country are. Having a high saving rate does not necessarily make a country a good place to invest. Given these observations, we would not expect to see any particular relationship between saving and investment rates in the free-capital-flow model; in statistical terms, these rates should be uncorrelated. In contrast, in the closed-economy model of Chapter 3, saving and investment within a country were equal—so looking across countries, saving and investment would be perfectly correlated. That is, saving might not be the same in every country because countries differ in the saving propensities of their populations or in their investment climates; but the amount of saving in any country would always equal the amount of investment in that country.

This difference in the implications that the closed- and open-economy models have for the correlation between saving and investment suggests a test of which model is more appropriate for the real world. Across a sample of countries, the more highly correlated are saving and investment rates, the less appropriate it is to think of capital flowing freely across international borders. Figure 11.5 shows the results of just such a test from a famous study by economists Martin Feldstein

FIGURE 11.5

Saving and Investment Rates of Industrialized Countries, 1960–1974

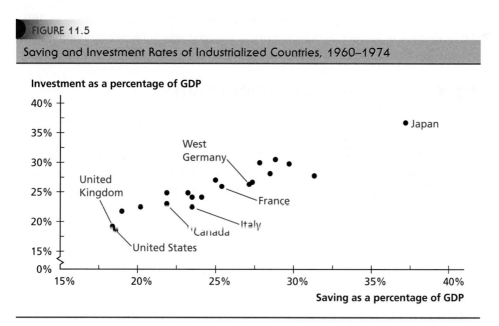

Sources: Feldstein and Horioka (1980).

and Charles Horioka, which examined data from a set of industrialized countries between 1960 and 1974. The message from this figure is clear: Saving and investment are highly correlated, so the presumption of free capital movement is inappropriate.[16]

Using the data in Figure 11.5, we can calculate a numerical indicator of the degree of capital market openness, called the **savings retention coefficient.** This coefficient, which equals the slope of a line drawn to fit the data points in the figure, measures what fraction of every dollar of additional saving ends up as additional domestic investment. In an economy closed to capital flows, the savings retention coefficient would be 1, meaning that an additional dollar of saving would lead to an additional dollar of investment. In a perfectly open economy of the type analyzed in the previous subsection, the savings retention coefficient would be 0. In the Feldstein and Horioka data, the coefficient is 0.89, indicating that the economies studied were almost perfectly closed to capital flows. A similar analysis looking at data for the period 1990–1997 found that the savings retention coefficient had fallen to 0.60, indicating that capital markets became more open. Interestingly, the savings retention coefficient in the several decades before World War I was approximately the same as it was in the 1990s, showing again that the current growth of world capital flows represents a return to the pre–World War I level of globalization.[17]

These results suggest that although the world has moved in the direction of capital market openness in recent years, economies remain closer to being closed to capital flows than they are to being perfectly open. There is also evidence that poorer countries—those most able to benefit from large foreign investment—are generally *less* open to capital flows than are rich countries. For example, in 2010, the total stock of foreign direct investment in India was $168 per capita; the comparable figure in Australia was $23,633 per capita.[18]

11.4 OPENNESS AND PRODUCTIVITY

In Section 11.2, we saw that being open to the world economy tended to raise the level of income per capita in a country. In the previous section, we found that openness to capital flows is *theoretically* a channel through which openness makes countries richer. However, our examination of the data showed that capital flows were simply not large enough to justify this theoretical possibility. Thus, the primary channel through which openness raises income per capita must be elsewhere: Specifically, openness must improve productivity.

As we saw in Chapter 10, productivity itself has two components: technology and efficiency. In this section, we consider those components in turn.

---

[16]Feldstein and Horioka (1980).
[17]Obstfeld and Rogoff (2000), Taylor (2002).
[18]http://unctadstat.unctad.org

Trade as a Form of Technology

The most important effect of trade on productivity is so obvious that it is easy to overlook: Trade makes a country more productive by allowing it to produce the things it is good at producing and then to sell them to other countries in return for things it is not as good at producing. From this perspective, trade is like a form of technology. Although trade does not literally convert one good into another in the way that a piece of technology such as a loom converts yarn into cloth, the effect is essentially the same (see box "The Rise and Fall of Consolidated Alchemy").

Potential gains from trade arise whenever a country has a comparative advantage in producing some good relative to another country. There can be many sources of such comparative advantage. A country may have natural endowments that make it easy to produce particular products (tropical fruit in Guatemala, salted codfish in Iceland). Or a country may specialize in some products because they are well suited to the factors of production it has in abundance (e.g., the polishing of small diamonds, which is labor intensive, is concentrated in India). Finally, a country may be particularly good at producing certain items simply because it has already specialized in them so that it has developed expertise (movies in the United States, fashion in France).

For a specific example of how gains from trade allow income to grow, we can go back to the case of Japan's economic opening in 1858. Table 11.1 shows the prices of two goods, tea and sugar, before and after Japan's opening of trade. Before the opening, one pound of tea in Japan cost roughly the same amount as one pound of sugar, indicating that the resources required to produce these two goods were equally valuable. Once Japan began to trade, however, the price of tea rose, and that of sugar fell. After the opening of trade, Japan could "produce" two and a half pounds of sugar by growing one pound of tea and exporting it. This method of obtaining sugar was far more productive than the alternative of growing and processing sugar domestically. Japan had a comparative advantage in the production of tea and within two decades was exporting 24 million pounds of it annually.

Although Japan's transition from almost complete autarky to free trade represents an extreme version of trade liberalization, the same possibilities of welfare gains arise whenever barriers to trade (either physical or legal) are lowered. For example, one study estimated that tariff reduction agreements under the Uruguay

TABLE 11.1

Prices in Japan before and after Opening to Trade

	Price before Opening (U.S. cents per pound)	Price after Opening (U.S. cents per pound)
Tea	19.7	28.2
Sugar	22.7	11.2

Source: Huber (1971).

THE RISE AND FALL OF CONSOLIDATED ALCHEMY

In the year 2015, a mysterious scientist and entrepreneur named Merle Lin announced to the world that he had finally solved the ancient problem of the transmutation of matter.* Using his secret process, Lin claimed, he could transform one type of object into another. Unlike the medieval alchemists who strove to turn iron into gold, however, Lin claimed that his process worked on more mundane materials. Wheat, for example, could be transformed into televisions, and tractors could be transformed into tomatoes.

Fearing that others would copy his new technology, Lin was obsessive about secrecy. In interviews with journalists, he hinted only that the process involved nanotechnology, artificial intelligence, and quantum tunneling. The few scraps of information that he did give out, however, were enough to whet the appetite of investors, who poured $5 billion into the initial public offering of his company, called Consolidated Alchemy. Lin used the money to build a facility on an isolated peninsula, protected from prying eyes by the latest in high-tech security equipment and staffed with workers sworn to secrecy.

Within six months, Consolidated Alchemy was up and running. Trucks pulled into Lin's factory to drop off tons of raw materials and drove away laden with the outputs of the transmutation process. Not only the United States, but foreign countries as well, sent their goods to Lin's factory to be transformed by his secret process.

As with many new technologies, Lin's transmutation process faced opposition. Firms producing goods that competed with Consolidated Alchemy complained of destructive competition and asked the government to limit the new company's output during a 10-year transition period. The farmworkers' union ran newspaper advertisements warning of potential long-term health consequences from eating tomatoes produced through transmutation. But this grumbling carried little weight with the legions of consumers who were eager to take advantage of the low prices offered by Consolidated Alchemy. And for every producer who felt the squeeze of competition from Consolidated Alchemy, there was another who profited from supplying Lin's company with raw materials. The employees of Consolidated Alchemy, who benefitted handsomely from stock options, also were happy. Despite inducements, both legal and illegal, from potential competitors, not one employee would even hint at the nature of the transmutation process.

Round of trade negotiations (begun in 1986 and completed in 1984) raised world purchasing power by $73 billion per year, equivalent to 0.2% of world GDP. The same study estimated that a further 33% reduction in all barriers to trade in agriculture, manufactured goods, and services that remained after the completion of the Uruguay Round would raise world purchasing power by $574 billion, or 1.7% of world GDP.[19] Another study estimated the cost to poor countries of rich-country protectionism to be $100 billion per year—a figure that is twice as large as foreign aid from rich to poor countries.[20]

---

[19] Brown, Deardorff, and Stern (2002). The implied value of world GDP used in this study is not comparable to other measures we have seen in this book.

[20] Dollar and Collier (2001), Chapter 2.

In the media, Merle Lin was compared to James Watt and Thomas Edison as one of the great heroes of technological advance. In Congress, the senator from the state where Consolidated Alchemy's factory was located said that those who opposed the new technology were no better than the Luddites. For any politicians who might have forgotten the virtues of free competition, Lin's political action committee, Americans for Unencumbered Transmutation, stood ready to supply a monetary reminder.

Then, as quickly as it had ascended to corporate stardom, Consolidated Alchemy came crashing to the ground. An investigation by *The New York Times*, using satellite photographs and a detailed examination of the records of the company's foreign subsidiaries, revealed that Merle Lin's secret transmutation process was a hoax. There was no advanced new technology. Consolidated Alchemy was nothing but a giant import-export business. The so-called raw materials that Lin bought from Americans and claimed to be transmuting were actually sold to foreigners, in return for the goods that Lin was claiming to have produced himself. And Lin had kept both sides in the dark about his operation! While Americans thought their wheat was being transmuted into televisions, the Chinese were told that their televisions were being transmuted into wheat.

The reaction among politicians was fierce. Congress set up an investigative committee. A team of 100 lawyers from the Justice Department combed through all of Consolidated Alchemy's corporate filings and, finding several instances of misplaced commas in a minor quarterly report, shut the company down.

The closing of Consolidated Alchemy threw thousands of workers out of high-paying jobs and also meant the end of the inexpensive products that the company had been supplying. But politicians universally agreed that this was a small price to pay for the protection of the American way of life. Politicians in foreign countries, who had similarly been misled about Lin's company, were equally vociferous in denouncing Lin's treachery. Throughout the world, politicians celebrated the fact that their countries had been saved from the dangers of trade.

*This story is adapted from James C. Ingram, "A Fable of Trade and Technology," in *International Economic Problems* (Wiley, 1966).

Openness and Technological Progress

The example of Consolidated Alchemy makes the point that trade is a form of technology. But openness can also affect technology in the more conventional sense. That is, even ignoring the benefits of trade, a country that is more open will have better technologies for producing output using its factors of production.

There are two ways in which economic openness contributes to a higher level of technology. First, countries that are open to trade are more able to import existing technologies from abroad. This technology transfer takes place through many channels, all of which are facilitated by openness. In the case of foreign direct investment, a firm building a factory in another country will transfer technology along with capital. Another channel is a technologically backward country's purchase of key inputs or of capital goods that embody a new technology from abroad. Finally, interactions among countries allow for the transfer of "softer" technologies such as innovative organizational techniques.

As a measure of the importance of technology transfer in raising a country's level of technology, one study investigated what fraction of technological progress in each of the OECD countries could be attributed to ideas that originated abroad, compared with ideas produced domestically. The study found that ideas produced abroad were the dominant source of technological progress in all but one country. In Japan, for example, only 27% of technological progress resulted from domestically produced ideas, and in Canada only 3% of technological progress resulted from domestically produced ideas. The United States is the only country in which the majority of technological progress (82%) derives from domestically produced ideas.[21]

In addition to facilitating technology transfer, a second way in which openness contributes to a higher level of technology is by expanding the incentives for the creation of new technologies. The primary motivator for firms or entrepreneurs to invest in research and development is the prospect of the profits they will earn by deploying a successful invention. Naturally, the larger the market in which a new invention will be used or a new product sold, the higher the profits accruing to the inventor. This lure of higher profits will give a greater incentive to R&D spending in an economy that is able to export its products. As Matthew Bolton, the partner of James Watt, who invented the steam engine, explained, "It is not worth my while to manufacture [your engine] for three countries only; but I find it very worth my while to make it for all the world."[22]

Openness and Efficiency

In Chapter 10 we saw that much of the variation among countries in productivity is not the result of technology but rather of the efficiency with which countries use the available technology and factors of production. There is good reason to believe that the openness of an economy makes an important contribution to the level of efficiency in production.

As we saw in Chapter 10, the presence of monopolies is one source of inefficiency—specifically, monopoly leads to the misallocation of factors of production. An important effect of trade is that it weakens the monopoly power of domestic firms, thus raising efficiency. A similar effect of trade is to allow the firms in a country to take advantage of economies of scale by giving them access to a larger market for their output.

In addition to these effects on efficiency, there is good evidence that foreign competition has a bracing effect on domestic firms. Over and over again, we see

---

[21]Eaton and Kortum (1996).
[22]Quoted in Mokyr (1990), p. 245.

examples of firms being exposed to competition from abroad and then raising their efficiency in production. The response of the U.S. automobile industry to Japanese competition is a classic example. In the two decades after World War II, automobile sales in the United States were dominated by four domestic firms. The picture changed in the 1970s, however. Rising gasoline prices pushed buyers toward cars that were smaller and more fuel efficient than Detroit's models, and U.S. consumers discovered the high quality of Japanese imports. Imports accounted for only 6% of the U.S. market in 1965 but 27% by 1980 (of which 75% was from Japan). Stung by foreign competition, the U.S. automobile industry sped up technical change, adopted new production methods, and greatly improved the quality and consumer appeal of its products. As can be seen in Figure 11.6, which shows data on the quality of U.S. and Japanese automobiles from 1980 to 2000, the U.S. industry was largely able to close the quality gap.

In the case of the U.S. automobile industry, no specific change in government trade policy drove up foreign competition. However, when a government reduces the trade protection it provides to domestic firms, efficiency does frequently rise. For example, after the completion in 1989 of a free-trade agreement between Canada and the United States, productivity among Canadian manufacturers that had formerly been protected by high tariffs rose three times

FIGURE 11.6

Quality of U.S.- and Japanese-made Automobiles

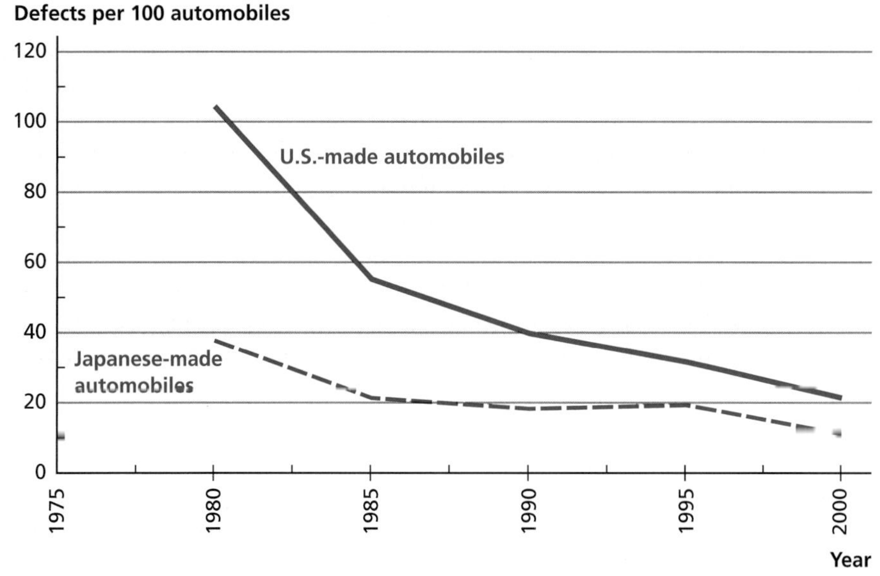

Sources: "Are Today's Cars More Reliable?" *Consumer Reports* 66(4) (April 2001), p. 12.

as fast as productivity among previously unprotected manufacturers. We find a similar case in the tool industry in India, which before 1991 was protected by a 100% tariff. When the Indian government slashed the tariff, Taiwanese firms quickly grabbed one-third of the Indian market. But in the next decade, Indian firms raised their productivity, won back most of their domestic market, and even began to export their products. The best Indian firms now almost match Taiwan's productivity, with wages that are only one-sixth the Taiwanese level, so they are competitive.[23]

This effect of openness to trade on the efficiency of production was stressed by the authors of the study on interindustry productivity comparisons that we considered in Chapter 10. The study concludes,

> Conventional explanations—differences in manufacturing technology, for example, or in economies of scale or in the cost of raw materials or in worker education—cannot systematically account for these variations in productivity. Instead, what does explain them is the degree to which the industry in question is open to the pressures of global competition. The rule-of-thumb is simple: Exposure to global competition, though painful, breeds high productivity; protection, whatever its motives and whatever its form, breeds stagnation.[24]

11.5 OPPOSITION TO OPENNESS

We have seen that being open to the world economy tends to make a country richer, and that the major channel through which this takes place is the effect of openness in raising productivity. These findings raise a natural question: If openness is so good, why do people so frequently oppose it?

Much of the explanation for the opposition to openness, and to free trade in particular, can be found in the observation made previously in the chapter that trade is like a form of technology that transforms things that a country is good at producing into things that it is not. As we saw in Chapter 10, many new technologies are good for a country on average, but are not good for every person and every industry in a country. Those who are hurt by a new technology will do their best to block its introduction. This same logic of technology blocking applies to trade. Workers and firms in the industries for which a country has a comparative *dis*advantage are natural supporters of trade protection. Similarly, domestic firms that will lose their monopoly positions with the opening of trade oppose openness. In both cases, what is good for a country on average is bad for a particular group.

The history of trade policy makes clear that the strongest supporters of trade restriction, although they often claim to be acting in the national interest, have

---

[23]Trefler (2001), Dollar and Collier (2001).
[24]Lewis et al. (1993).

generally been acting in their own self-interest. For example, the British Corn Laws of the 19th century, which placed tariffs on the import of grain, were supported by large land owners and opposed by manufacturers and industrial workers.

Some industries can maintain trade restrictions because of the way the costs and benefits of trade policy are distributed. Trade liberalization offers large benefits to an overall economy, but with only a small gain to each consumer. The costs of more open trade, by contrast, often fall on a small group of firms or workers. As a result, those who are hurt by trade liberalization tend to feel more strongly about it than those who benefit. In the United States, for example, restrictions on imports keep the domestic price of sugar at twice the world level. The costs of this program to consumers—roughly seven dollars per person per year—are barely perceptible. The benefits to producers, though smaller in total than the costs, are concentrated among a few farmers and processors, who have successfully lobbied politicians to maintain the program. Similarly, in 1990, the U.S. tariff on luggage was estimated to be protecting 226 U.S. jobs, at an annual cost to consumers of $211 million, or $934,000 for each job protected. In the late 1990s the cost of trade protection in the European Union was estimated to be 220,000 euros per year for each job saved.[25]

Beyond the self-interest of firms or workers in a particular industry, opposition to openness can also arise on the part of owners of factors of production that will become relatively less scarce if tariff protection is removed. For example, suppose that a country with relatively scarce capital opens up its market to international capital flows. Capital from abroad will enter the country, lowering the domestic rental rate for capital and raising the wage. The average level of income per capita will rise in such a case, but the income of capitalists (who rely on capital income rather than labor income) will fall.

Another example of how trade affects the returns to different factors of production is the case of human capital. As we saw in Chapter 6, the labor force in the United States has a high average level of schooling in comparison to the rest of the world. Put differently, highly educated workers are relatively abundant in the United States, and workers with a low level of education are relatively scarce. This scarcity of low-education workers in turn implies that, without trade, low-education workers would earn relatively good wages. As the United States has opened to trade, however, the scarcity of low-education workers in the country has been offset by the worldwide abundance of low-education workers and scarcity of high-education workers. Having a comparative advantage in goods and services produced by high-skill workers, the United States has exported these and imported goods embodying low-skill foreign labor. In this way, trade has contributed to the increase in the *skill differential* (the gap in wages between low- and high-education workers) in the United States.

---

[25]Hufbaur and Eliott (1994), Messerlin (2001).

ANTI-GLOBALIZATION

Our analysis of opposition to openness has been about opposition based on self-interest. That is, we have focused on cases in which workers or firms in a specific industry, or owners of particular factors of production, oppose free trade out of self-interest, even if such trade benefits their country as a whole.

In recent years, another sort of opposition to openness has emerged among people who see globalization as harmful to developing countries. Nongovernmental organizations (NGOs) and student activists have been at the forefront of this movement. Some of the concerns of the anti-globalization movement are quite legitimate, but others do not hold up to economic scrutiny. Among the issues are the following.

Exploitation of Workers

Critics of globalization often point to low wages, poor working conditions, and the employment of children in foreign-owned factories (or locally owned factories that produce goods for export) in developing countries. Commonly branded as sweatshops, these factories produce goods for export to the developed world, and if it were not for globalization, they would not exist.

Of all of the arguments against globalization, the charge of worker exploitation is the weakest. The willingness of workers to take jobs in factories—even sweatshops—to produce exports shows that such jobs are preferable to workers' available alternatives. Put differently, if it were not for globalization, the same workers would have jobs with even lower wages or worse working conditions. Not only do exporting firms provide better jobs than are available in the local economy, but they also raise overall wages in the economy by increasing the demand for labor.

Moreover, only 5% of children who are employed in developing countries work in the export sector, and their jobs are also apparently preferable to the alternatives. In 1995, a researcher from the British charity Oxfam reported on the effects in Bangladesh of a campaign by human rights groups to stop U.S. retailers from buying goods made by child labor. Some 30,000 to 50,000 children in Bangladesh lost their jobs in the textile industry. The majority of these children were forced to find work in more dangerous occupations, such as welding, or even prostitution.*

Inability of Poor Countries to Compete

A second criticism of globalization is that openness (as enforced by the rules of the WTO) forces small farmers and firms in developing countries to compete with large multinational companies on a "level playing field" where they are hopelessly outmatched. This argument confuses *competition*, in which one party wins and one loses, with *exchange*, which is the essence of trade. When countries compete, as in sports or war, the weaker country loses out. When countries exchange, a country that is weak (in the sense of having lower productivity or fewer factors of production) stands to gain just as much as a country that is strong.

Still, when a country, either poor or rich, opens up to the world economy, some sectors of the economy will indeed be unable to compete with imports. Other sectors will find themselves able not only to compete with imports but also to export their output. The movement of factors of production from sectors where the economy has a comparative disadvantage to the sectors where it has a comparative advantage is the essence of gains from trade. The proper policy response to the dislocations that occur in both rich and poor countries when trade is opened up is *adjustment assistance*—helping workers relocate to sectors with comparative advantage and cushioning the temporary reduction in income while they do so—not trade restriction.

Environmental Exploitation

Globalization can lead to environmental degradation through several channels. First, rich countries can export their pollution, either literally by shipping their waste abroad or, more commonly, by allowing their high-pollution industries to migrate abroad and then importing the products of these industries. The movement of polluting industries from rich to poor countries is not necessarily bad for poor countries—they may value the increase in income as worth the cost in environmental terms. However, if poor-country governments do not adequately regulate polluting industries or do not take into account the interests of the people who will be harmed by pollution (as is frequently the case), then trade in pollution-producing industries can be harmful.

A second way in which globalization can harm the environment is by opening up rich-country markets to poor-country exports that are produced in an environmentally harmful way. For example, the farming of shrimp for export to the developed world has destroyed coastal wetlands and mangrove forests in several tropical countries. However, this aspect of the harm from globalization can be exaggerated. Much of the economic activity that is displaced by globalization also is environmentally harmful. The destruction of the Amazonian rain forest, for example, is primarily being conducted by small farmers, driven by low rural incomes and population pressure. Similarly, 77% of logging in Asia and 89% of logging in Africa is done for the production of fuel for local use.[†] By opening up new livelihoods and new sources of products, globalization can also reduce some environmental harms.

Loss of National Sovereignty

Openness to the world economy imposes constraints on how governments behave. In so-called footloose industries (industries that can easily relocate production from one place to another), firms will shop around for the most profitable country in which to operate. Countries' attempts to attract or retain these firms will create a "race to the bottom" in which national governments compete to offer the fewest restrictions on environmental pollution, the weakest laws governing workers' rights, and so on.

A second loss of sovereignty associated with openness, particularly openness with regard to capital flows, is in a government's ability to levy taxes. More than workers, owners of capital can easily move their factor of production out of a country if they do not like the taxes they have to pay, so governments are constrained to keep capital taxes low. The burden of financing government expenditure thus shifts to taxes on labor or consumption goods. Because wealthy people tend to be the ones who own capital and earn capital income, the reduction in capital taxation induced by globalization exacerbates income inequality.

The Hidden Price of Foreign Capital

Although most economists accept the case for free international trade in goods, the virtues of openness with regard to flows of capital are more controversial. For a developing country, foreign investment can greatly speed growth by allowing rapid expansion of the capital stock (the United States owes much of its industrial progress in the 19th century to huge inflows of foreign capital). Also, flows of capital, particularly foreign direct investment, often carry with them the transfer of rich-country technology. But capital inflows create several problems.

First, a country that imports capital from abroad becomes subject to the whims of international investors. Waves of speculation and herd behavior—the forces that create volatility in stock markets—can lead to wild swings of capital flows and exchange rates, a situation

(*continued*)

ANTI-GLOBALIZATION (CONTINUED)

producing macroeconomic instability. The problem is particularly acute when the capital imports consist of short-term investments that can be withdrawn quickly. This was the case during the Latin American financial crisis of 1994–1995 and the Asian financial crisis of 1997. By the time of the 2008 financial crisis, many developing countries had built up large capital reserves to protect themselves from these market swings, which proved to be an effective defense.

A second problem with capital mobility is that it allows governments in developing countries to go irresponsibly into debt. Although government debt (e.g., to fund the construction of infrastructure) can be a useful development tool, rulers in poor countries all too often use borrowed money to maintain their hold on power or to enjoy a lavish lifestyle. When these rulers leave office, their former subjects are left with a crushing burden—in many developing countries, debt-service payments consume more than 25% of export earnings. In the last several years, a broad coalition of people ranging from Pope John Paul II to rock star Bono has agitated for rich countries to forgive the debt of the world's poorest countries. In 2005, the G-8 countries agreed to scrap the debt owed by 18 of the world's poorest nations, totaling roughly $40 billion.

Hypocrisy on the Part of Rich Countries

Finally, many critics of globalization point out that rich-country governments that press developing countries to open their markets are themselves often engaged in protectionism. The most flagrant example of this protectionism is the Common Agricultural Policy of the European Union, a system of import restrictions, price supports, and export subsidies.

Rich-country protectionism clearly harms developing countries by shutting down potentially profitable export markets. But protectionism also hurts rich countries themselves. For example, the Common Agricultural Policy uses up almost half of the European Union's budget (to protect an industry that employs 5% of the labor force), raises the price of food to consumers, and leads to environmental damage through overly intensive cultivation.

Although the charge of hypocrisy is justified, the anti-globalist conclusion that developing countries should engage in similar protectionism is not. Quite the contrary, rich-country protectionism lowers the average level of welfare in these countries while producing benefits only for small, well-connected groups. Both rich and poor countries would benefit from a reduction in poor-country protectionism, just as both would benefit from a reduction in rich-country protectionism.

---

*Irwin (2002), p. 217, "Ethical Shopping: Human Rights," *The Economist*, June 3, 1995, pp. 58–59.
†Irwin (2002), pp. 48, 51.

11.6 CONCLUSION

Globalization is not a new phenomenon. Countries have been linked economically through trade, capital flows, migration, and technology transfer for centuries. But the last 200 years, and particularly the period since World War II, have seen accelerated economic integration, fueled by reductions in the cost of transporting goods and information, as well as by coordinated reductions in the barriers that governments put in the way of trade. The ability to interact with other countries profoundly alters the process of economic growth. Foreign countries represent a potential supply of factors of production that may be scarce in a given country, as well as an outlet for factors that are plentiful. They are also a source of technology transfers, and they afford an opportunity for a country to specialize in the areas of production that it does best.

The most important finding of this chapter is that being open to the world economy is good for a country's economic growth. Three types of evidence point to this conclusion. First, openness leads to economic convergence: Poor countries that are open grow faster on average than do rich countries, whereas poor countries that are closed grow more slowly than rich countries. Second, countries that open up their markets to the world economy experience a speedup of growth, whereas countries that close their markets experience a slowdown of growth. Finally, countries that are less able to participate in world commerce because of their geographic position suffer from lower income as a result of their isolation.

Having established that openness benefits a country, we then examined the various channels by which openness might raise income. Although it is theoretically possible that the most important method by which openness promotes growth is via capital flows among countries, the empirical evidence does not support this theory. Rather, we have seen that the most important effect of openness is on productivity. Openness benefits a country by facilitating technology transfer, by exposing firms to additional competitive pressure, which improves efficiency, and by increasing the incentives for technological innovation. More important, however, we can think of international trade itself as a form of technology. Through trade, a country can transform things it is good at producing—because of natural endowments, the accumulation of factors, or simple specialization—into things it is not as good at producing.

One theme of this chapter is that, although openness benefits a country's residents on average, it rarely benefits *all* of them. This is another way in which openness is similar to technological progress. In the case of technological progress, there will usually be firms or workers who are made worse off by any particular new invention. In the case of openness, workers and firms in industries that are not competitive on the world market naturally oppose trade. So do people who own factors of production that are scarce in the country relative to the world as a whole. Most of those who are against free trade are just as rational in their opposition as were the Luddites in opposing the introduction of new weaving machinery.

KEY TERMS

autarky **299**

trade **299**

flow of factors
  of production **299**

law of one price **299**

gross domestic product
  (GDP) **300**

gross national product
  (GNP) **300**

tariff **305**

quota **305**

nontariff
  barriers **305**

foreign direct
  investment **312**

portfolio
  investment **312**

savings retention
  coefficient **316**

QUESTIONS FOR REVIEW

1. How can the law of one price be used to assess the degree of economic integration of two countries?

2. What factors have led to the increase in globalization over the last 200 years?

3. If an economy is perfectly open to capital flows from the rest of the world, how is the level of GDP related to the saving rate?

4. What determines the types of goods that a country imports and exports?

5. How does domestic production change when a country becomes open to international trade?

6. What possible sources of comparative advantage would lead a country to export a particular good?

7. Why is openness to trade similar to a form of technology?

PROBLEMS

1. A U.S. citizen takes a temporary job in France. How are the wages counted in U.S. GNP and GDP?

2. Give an intuitive explanation as to why higher saving rates are not associated with higher levels of GDP in an economy with perfect capital mobility, but they are in a closed economy. Does this mean that if you save a lot, you are better off in a closed economy? Why or why not?

3. Consider the model of an economy open to capital flows that was presented in Section 11.3. How will an increase in the growth rate of population, holding constant the saving rate, affect GDP per capita? How will it affect GNP per capita? How do these results contrast with the Solow model as presented in Chapter 3?

4. Consider the case of an economy that is perfectly open to the world capital market, as examined in Section 11.3. Suppose that the world rental price of capital, r_w, doubles. By what factor will the level of GDP per worker change? Assume that the value of α, capital's share in the production function, is 0.5.

5. People in a particular country that is closed to trade consume only cheese and bread. They always consume one slice of cheese with one slice of bread. It takes one labor-hour to produce a slice of cheese and two labor-hours

to produce a slice of bread. The country has a total of 60 labor-hours per day. How many slices of cheese and bread will be produced per day? Now suppose that the economy is opened to trade. On the world market, the price of one slice of bread equals the price of one slice of cheese. How does production in the country change? What is the new consumption of bread and cheese?

6. Suppose that the world consists of 10 countries. The countries are identical in terms of their levels of technology and efficiency, their quantities of factors of production, the preferences of their consumers, and so on. There are two industries in the world: pizzerias and automobile factories. Correspondingly, there are only two consumption goods: pizzas and cars. The big difference between pizzerias and auto factories is in their scale: Auto factories have to be large, whereas pizzerias can be small.

   The world starts off in autarky. In each country, the market is big enough to support only one auto factory, although there are many pizzerias. Now suppose that the world opens to trade. Both pizzas and autos can be traded (we ignore the fact that in real life problems of congealing cheese prevent trade in pizzas). Trade does not affect the production technology in any country.

What do you expect to happen to the relative prices of pizza and cars (i.e., the number of pizzas required to buy one car) as a result of the opening of trade? Will there be reallocation of factors of production into one or the other sector? How and why will the opening of trade affect efficiency?

7. A recent study has concluded that the tariff on the import of widgets has raised real wages in the domestic widget industry. Based on this finding, it has been suggested that tariffs be raised in all industries. Comment on the wisdom of this proposal.

For additional exploration and practice using the Online Data Plotter and data sets, please visit www.pearsonhighered.com/weil.

GOVERNMENT

One of the best ways to see how government can affect economic growth is by looking at pairs of countries that are similar in every respect except their governments. The Cold War resulted in two such pairs of countries: North and South Korea and East and West Germany.

At the end of the Korean War in 1953, North and South Korea were similar in many respects. Both had been devastated by decades of war, and they had similar endowments of natural resources, similar levels of education, and similar income per capita. The two Koreas also shared a common culture and 1,300 years of history as a united country. But the governments in the two countries—and in particular their economic policies—were quite different. Communist North Korea, under the one-man rule of Kim Il Sung (succeed by his son Kim Jong-il in 1994 and his grandson Kim Jong-un in 2011), followed a path of central planning and economic isolation from the rest of the world; South Korea had a relatively free market and strong orientation toward international trade. Although democracy had grown only gradually in South Korea (there were successful military coups in 1961 and 1980), by the end of the 20th century, the country was a genuine democracy.

The economic performance of the two Koreas could not have been more different. South Korea was one of the world's fastest-growing countries in the decades after 1960. North Korean economic growth was dismal. Today, the country suffers from massive food shortages, and years of underinvestment and mismanagement have left its industrial capital stock almost beyond repair. In 2009, income per capita in South Korea exceeded income per capita in North Korea by a factor of 16.

The story of East and West Germany was in many ways similar. The two Germanys had the same culture and history, similar natural resources, and were similarly devastated in World War II. Following the war, East Germany became a member of the Warsaw Pact military alliance and the Soviet-led Council for Mutual Economic Cooperation (COMECON). West Germany, firmly aligned with the North Atlantic Treaty Organization (NATO) and a founding member of the European Economic Community (predecessor to today's European

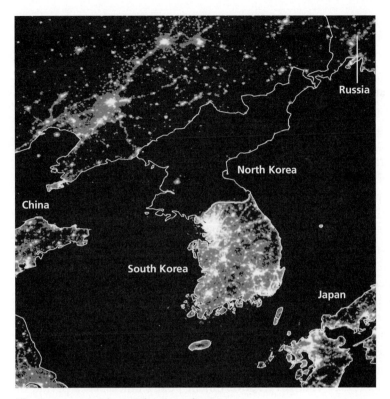

The Korean peninsula at night as seen from space.

Union), pursued a market-oriented economic policy. Unlike Korea, Germany had already been one of the richest countries in the world before World War II, and West Germany rapidly regained this status. East Germany was one of the most economically successful states of the communist bloc but badly trailed its neighbor. If the symbols of the West German economy were the powerful cars of Mercedes-Benz and BMW, their East German counterpart was the Trabant, a cramped, noisy, pollution-spewing, plastic and fiberglass automobile with a top speed of 60 miles (97 kilometers) per hour, whose design was hardly modified after 1957 and for which would-be buyers had to spend years on a waiting list. The contrast between the economically successful West and the depressed East is what led to the dissolution of the East German state in 1990.

We can also see the importance of government policies by looking at how growth changes within a single country when government policy changes. The recent history of China provides illustrations of policies' positive and negative effects on growth.

In 1958, Chairman Mao Zedong instituted the Great Leap Forward, a set of policies designed to bring China to the level of the most advanced countries in only a few years. Agricultural production was reorganized into vast communes, each made up of some 5,000 households. Industry was restructured as well, with commune-based "backyard blast furnaces" replacing traditional industrial establishments. But the policies of the Great Leap Forward failed horribly. The political operatives who managed the communes were incompetent, and the peasants in the communes had little incentive to work efficiently. The backyard blast furnaces produced iron of such poor quality that it was useless. In response to local officials' falsely glowing reports about increases in food production, government planners reduced the area of land to be sown with grain and diverted up to 100 million farm laborers to industrial projects and the construction of public works such as dams and roads. The grain harvest fell roughly 25% between 1958 and 1960, but local officials, eager to please their superiors in Beijing, reported that it had almost doubled. Because of these fabrications, the country continued to export grain even as shortages developed. In the ensuing famine, an estimated 30 million people died.[1]

Government policy in China again dramatically affected the economy starting in 1978, when senior leader Deng Xiaoping initiated a series of liberalizations. Land that had been held collectively in communes was leased back to peasant households, which could sell their surplus production. The Chinese government relaxed the grip of central planning by easing restrictions on non state-owned enterprises and by creating special economic zones that encouraged foreign investment. The share of output produced by state-owned enterprises fell from 78% in 1978 to 30% in 2009. Over the same period, international trade as a share of GDP rose fourfold.[2] These changes in government policy unleashed a period of rapid economic growth. Income per capita, which had grown only sluggishly in the previous two decades, increased by a factor of 13 over the period 1978–2009. Applying as it did to one-sixth of the world's population, this episode of economic growth was arguably the most spectacular in human history.

These examples demonstrate the power of government to affect how an economy develops. In this chapter we look more closely at the interaction of government and growth.

Government activity can be linked to all of the determinants of economic growth that we have examined so far. The simplest way in which the government affects economic growth is through the channels of factor accumulation that we discussed in Part II. Government affects the accumulation of physical capital directly through investments in government capital (e.g., infrastructure such as roads) and indirectly through its budget (because budget deficits absorb savings that would otherwise be invested in physical capital). We have also seen the hand of government in the accumulation of human capital because in most countries, government pays for a large fraction of education. And government also influences population growth, through pro- or anti-natalist policies.

---

[1]Ashton et al. (1984), Chen and Galenson (1969).
[2]Desvaux, Wang, and Xu (2004), OECD (2009), World Development Indicators database.

Beyond factor accumulation, government policy can significantly affect the speed of technological progress, both through direct government funding of research, and through government administration of the patent system, which allows researchers to reap rewards and thus provides an incentive for inventive activity. However, the area in which government plays its most important role is efficiency. Through taxation, regulation, administration of laws, and a host of other tools, governments create the environment in which firms and workers go about their activities. By setting the "rules of the game" for the economy, government can profoundly affect economic development.

Economists who examine government policy face a choice of two different perspectives. Sometimes they want to ask "What *should* government do?" about a specific issue. They use the tools of economic analysis to determine what policies will best promote a specific goal—for example, rapid economic growth. Such analysis, aimed at advising government on how it should act, is called the **normative** approach to government policy. At other times, economists want to ask "*Why* does government do what it does?*" The answer to this question explains behavior rather than recommending behavior. The people who make government policy are assumed to be acting in their own self-interest, just as we view firms or workers as behaving in their own self-interest. This attempt to describe rather than prescribe government actions is called the **positive** approach to government policy.

In this chapter we pursue both normative and positive analyses of government behavior. We begin with the normative issue of how government should act. We will find a broad scope of disagreement among economists on this issue. In addition to examining the general arguments for and against government intervention in the economy, we will analyze data on specific government policies and see how they affect growth. We will then turn to a positive analysis of why governments sometimes do things that are bad for growth. Finally, we will consider why poor countries seem to have governments that are particularly unfavorable to economic growth.

12.1 DEFINING GOVERNMENT'S PROPER ROLE IN THE ECONOMY

The question of government's proper role in encouraging growth is one of the oldest in economics. It was a primary concern of Adam Smith in *The Wealth of Nations*. The proposed answers have ranged from a vision of minimal government interference (*laissez-faire*) to complete government ownership of the means of production.

The Case for Government Intervention in the Economy

The starting point for most analyses of government intervention in the economy is **market failure,** the idea that in some circumstances unfettered markets will not produce an efficient outcome. Although market failure can take many forms, we focus here on four types: public goods, externalities, monopoly, and coordination failure.

The simplest form of market failure occurs when there are particular goods, called **public goods,** that the private market cannot supply—most commonly because there is no practical way to charge those who benefit from the use of such goods. The classic example of a public good is national defense. Other public goods that are relevant for determining economic growth include the rule of law (which we consider in Section 12.2), infrastructure such as airports and highways, the standardization of weights and measures, and a stable currency.

A second reason for government intervention in the economy is **externalities**: the incidental results of some economic activity that affect people who do not control the activity and are not intentionally served by it. In Chapter 8, we already saw an example of government policy motivated by externalities: The creation of a new technology often involves large externality benefits to people other than the inventor. Because the inventor does not take these *positive externalities* into account—and instead compares only his or her private benefit from making an invention to his or her cost in creating it—the amount of invention is naturally lower than the socially optimal amount. Such positive externalities are the reason that governments play a role in supporting research and development (R&D) through both direct spending and patent protections that raise the fraction of an invention's social benefits received by the inventor. A second example of a policy that is motivated by externalities is education. When a person chooses how much education to pursue, he or she weighs the private costs of an education against the benefits that he or she will receive. But it is often argued that education provides benefits to society beyond those that the individual receives: An educated person helps improve the quality of life of those around him or her. Because people ignore these external benefits, the quantity of education that individuals will decide on for themselves will be lower than the socially optimal amount, so the government has a role to play in encouraging education. Similarly, in the case of *negative externalities*, such as pollution, a private firm will tend to produce more than the socially optimal quantities. Government regulation is required to limit this externality.

A third form of market failure that can motivate government economic policy is the existence of **monopolies,** single firms that are the sole suppliers of a particular commodity. An industry such as electricity transmission is often viewed as a *natural monopoly* because it would be impractical for several companies to string electric wire to every house. In such a case, there is a role for government regulation to prevent the monopolist from charging an inefficiently high price.

The private market can also potentially fail in cases requiring the coordination of activities by many firms or many people. Some potential **coordination failures**—and the need for a government to correct them—are obvious. It is useful for everyone to drive on the same side of the road, and even the most diehard free marketer would have little objection to letting the government announce which side it should be. But coordination failure may also be more subtle. Consider a case in which firms are reluctant to invest in one industry—say, a bicycle factory—because they fear there will be no raw materials for them to purchase, whereas firms are reluctant to invest in a second industry—say, steel production—because they fear there will be no market for their output. It is often argued that in such cases, government planning can break the logjam and further the process of economic development.

Despite its prominence in this discussion, market failure is not the only reason that governments become involved in the economy. Another motivation for government to take a hand in economic matters concerns not the total quantity of output but rather the way that output is distributed among the citizens of a country. Governments may view **income redistribution**—the transfer of income from rich to poor, from working-age adults to the elderly, or from the general population to members of some favored group—as one of their proper roles.

The Case Against Government Intervention in the Economy

Few economists would argue that there should be *no* government intervention in the economy. Rather, it is a question of degree. For many economists, the reasons for government intervention are not sufficient to justify the degree of intervention that we observe. As a result, they argue, government intervention, at the margin, reduces economic welfare.

The case against government intervention starts with the observation that, although proper government policy can theoretically fix any market failure, in practice it often fails to achieve its goals. When government tries to take the place of private firms, the resulting enterprises tend to operate inefficiently because they lack the incentives (specifically, profit) that motivate private firms. Similarly, in cases in which industries are regulated as natural monopolies, often such regulation effectively preserves the absence of competition. In general, the success of any government intervention depends crucially on the ability and the honesty of the officials entrusted to carry it out. When these qualities are lacking, the resulting **government failure** can be worse than any market failure that government policy was designed to correct. Recognizing the difficulty that governments have when they try to intervene in the economy suggests that, whenever possible, the role of government should be defined as narrowly as possible.

Critics also argue that many fewer market failures exist than the proponents of activist government policy believe. In the case of public goods, the debate centers on the question of whether some of the goods that governments supply could have been supplied privately if government had not taken over their provision. In much of the world, functions previously performed by the government are being **privatized,** that is, handed over to the private sector. In various countries, privatized activities have included the building of roads and telephone networks and the operation of jails. A parallel trend has been the **deregulation** of industries (removing them from government supervision). In the United States, for example, the deregulation of telephones, airlines, and trucking led to steep declines in the prices paid by consumers.

The issue of income redistribution presents some of the most difficult questions regarding the proper role of government. For other issues, the costs and benefits of intervention can be measured in the same terms—for example, the inefficiency of monopoly versus the inefficiency of government regulation. In the case of income redistribution, however, the benefits of such a policy (a greater degree of equality) are of a different nature than the costs of the policy (a lower degree of efficiency). This so-called **equity-efficiency trade-off** will be at the heart of our examination of income inequality in Chapter 13. However, critics of big government point out that much of the income that governments redistribute does not flow from rich to poor. Rather, it is redistributed among people in the same income groups, who are at different stages of their life cycles, as when taxes are taken from working-age adults and transfers are paid to the elderly. Critics argue that these redistributions have a large effect on the efficiency with which the economy operates (for reasons that we will consider) but do little or nothing to improve equity.

Swings of the Pendulum

Although there has never been a consensus about government's proper role in the economy, either among economists or among those who govern, the 20th century saw two broad swings of the pendulum in the intellectual analysis and the practice of government intervention. Beginning around World War I, the idea that the government could play a decisive, active role in furthering economic development gained ground throughout the world. The most extreme example is the Soviet Union, where a series of five-year plans, including government owner-ship of factories and forced collectivization of agriculture, sparked impressive economic growth during the 1920s and 1930s. The economic collapse of the Great Depression, which seemed to be evidence of coordination failure on a massive scale, inspired forceful government intervention in the workings of the economy. The fascist states of Germany and Italy imposed strong controls over the market, with the apparent result that these countries were able to shake off the effects of the Depression more rapidly than their neighbors. Even in the United States, where politicians had long been hostile to government interference in the economy, President Franklin Roosevelt's New Deal program to promote economic recovery represented an unprecedented degree of government meddling in the economy, including price controls, purchases of surplus agricultural output, and direct job creation through public works. The Great Depression also inspired the theories of John Maynard Keynes, which provided an intellectual foundation for activist mon-etary and fiscal policies designed to maintain full employment.

Following World War II, governments in Western Europe developed elabo-rate welfare states providing nationalized health care, public housing, and gen-erous unemployment insurance and old-age pensions. In the developing world, the newly independent governments that emerged with the end of colonialism pursued a model of state-led industrialization and economic planning.

The last two decades of the 20th century witnessed a shift away from government control of the economy. This was most pronounced among the communist and former communist countries, most of which moved decisively toward a market system. In the industrialized world, there was a wave of deregulation and privatization of some functions of government, along with reduction in the generosity of welfare-state benefits. In the developing world, in response to the problems of economic planning that are discussed below, there was a turning away from state-led industrialization, toward a more market-based approach with an emphasis on free trade.

Following the financial crisis of 2007–2008, and the subsequent global recession, there may be yet another change of direction. It is hard not to notice that the countries that suffered the largest economic shocks were those with the freest markets. By contrast, China, with its heavy-handed government control, (as well as lack of democracy) suffered hardly at all. Whether the "Chinese model" of economic growth is something that can be exported to other countries remains to be seen.

12.2 HOW GOVERNMENT AFFECTS GROWTH

Having traced some of the theoretical arguments about what role government should play in the economy, we now look at how governments have affected growth in practice. We focus on three particular aspects of government action: the maintenance of the rule of law, the overall size of government, and the practice of planning.

Rule of Law

One of the most important public goods that governments provide is the rule of law. Consider for a moment the myriad ways in which a developed economy relies on laws to function. Firms that sign contracts with each other—for delivery of merchandise, for repayment of a loan, and so on—rely on the existence of courts that will enforce those contracts. Inventors rely on the enforcement of patent laws. Even more fundamentally, owners of private property depend on courts and police to enforce their ownership. As we saw in Chapter 10, a well-functioning financial system, which is reliant on the rule of law, contributes to economic efficiency through its role in optimally allocating capital.

The rule of law cannot be taken for granted in most of the world. In many countries, judicial systems are weak, and legal cases are as likely to be settled on the basis of who has better political connections as on legitimate legal claims. Douglass North, who won the Nobel Prize in economics in 1993, concluded, "The inability of societies to develop effective, low-cost enforcement of contracts is the most important source of both historical stagnation and contemporary underdevelopment in the Third World."[3]

---

[3]North (1990), p. 54.

The former Soviet Union provides one of the best examples of the importance of the rule of law. With the fall of communism, the legal structure surrounding basic economic activity became highly uncertain. The line between legitimate business and organized crime blurred because assets formerly owned by the government in trust for the citizenry as a whole rapidly found their way into the hands of a well-connected few. (The Russian slang term *biznesman* carries the connotation of someone who engages in semilegal, slimy transactions.) In this legally unstable environment, income per capita in the Russian Federation fell by 12% in the decade following the 1991 breakup of the Soviet Union.

In an environment in which the rule of law is weak, we would expect that factors of production would not be accumulated and that economic activity would be plagued by inefficiency. For both these reasons, output would decline. The available data are consistent with these predictions. The data we use measure rule of law as a composite of the enforceability of contracts, the effectiveness and predictability of the judiciary, and the incidence of crime. Sources for this information include surveys of businesspeople and citizens, as well as compilations of opinions of experts at nongovernmental organizations (NGOs), think tanks, and risk-rating agencies. The data are scaled to have a mean of 0 and range from –1.91 (Zimbabwe) to 1.94 (Switzerland). Figure 12.1 shows the relationship between the rule of law and the composite measure of

> **FIGURE 12.1**
>
> **Rule of Law and Factor Accumulation, 2009**

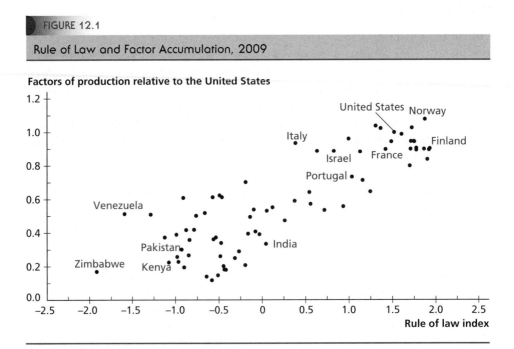

Source: Kaufmann, Kray, and Mastruzzi (2010). Data are scaled to have a standard deviation of 1.

FIGURE 12.2

Rule of Law and Productivity

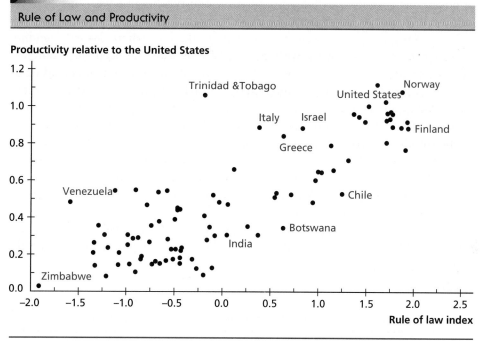

Source: Kaufmann, Kray, and Mastruzzi (2010). Data are scaled to have a standard deviation of 1.

accumulation of physical and human capital that we constructed in Chapter 7; Figure 12.2 shows the relationship between the rule of law and the productivity measure that we derived in Chapter 7. In both cases, there is a strong positive correlation, and the figures show that the channels of factor accumulation and productivity are of roughly equal importance in explaining the effect of the rule of law on income per capita. The exceptions to the general trend in these data are also interesting. For example, India has both low factor accumulation and low productivity, considering its level of the rule of law, whereas Italy has higher factor accumulation and higher productivity than would be expected, given its level of the rule of law.

Taxation, Efficiency, and the Size of Government

One of the most important ways in which government affects the state of the economy is by its sheer size. Big government—that is, government that spends a lot of money—requires big government revenue. With the exception of a few countries including Saudi Arabia, where a natural resource (oil) is the primary source of revenue, governments raise funds by taxing citizens and businesses. These taxes in turn affect the efficiency of economic activity.

In 1883 the German social scientist Adolph Wagner theorized that the size of government would inevitably increase as countries became wealthier because a more developed economy requires more complex regulation and because many public goods provided by the government are of the type where desired spending rises more than proportionally with income. **Wagner's law** has been borne out over the last century, as revealed in Figure 12.3, which shows government spending as a percentage of GDP in five of the richest countries in the world. In the United States, for example, government spending as a share of GDP grew from 3.9% in 1870 to 43% in 2009. Among the industrialized countries of the Organisation for Economic Co-operation and Development (OECD), the average share of government spending in GDP was 47% in 2009. (Of course, figures for 2009 were inflated by higher government spending and lower output that were lingering effects of the great recession of the late 2000's.) In Sweden, government spending peaked at two-thirds of GDP in 1996 but has declined since.

Examining the size of government in poorer countries reveals a second striking fact: Although these countries tend to have smaller governments than do

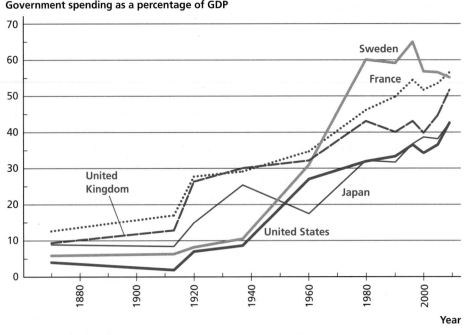

FIGURE 12.3

Growth of Government Spending, 1870–2009

Source: "The Future of the State," *The Economist*, September 20, 1997, *OECD*.

the richest countries, their governments are much larger than were rich-country governments at a comparable stage of economic development. For example, among the countries in the World Bank's Middle East and North Africa grouping, government employment over the period 1996–2000 averaged 25% of total employment. Average GDP per capita in that group of countries in 1997 was $4,580. The United States had reached the same level of GDP per capita in the first decade of the 20th century, but by 1929 (the earliest year for which data are available), total government employment in the United States was only 6.5% of total employment.

The increase in government spending has been funded by an equally large increase in the taxes that governments collect. Taxes are relevant for economic growth because they directly affect the efficiency with which output is produced. The relationship between efficiency and taxation can be illustrated using a simple diagram of supply and demand such as Figure 12.4. Consider the market for some good, in which there is an upward-sloping supply curve and a downward-sloping demand curve. The good in question could be anything that is taxed: For example, it could be labor if we are thinking of an income tax, or it could be gasoline or some other commonly taxed commodity. In the absence of taxes, the equilibrium price and quantity of the good would be determined by the intersection of the supply

FIGURE 12.4

Effect of a Tax

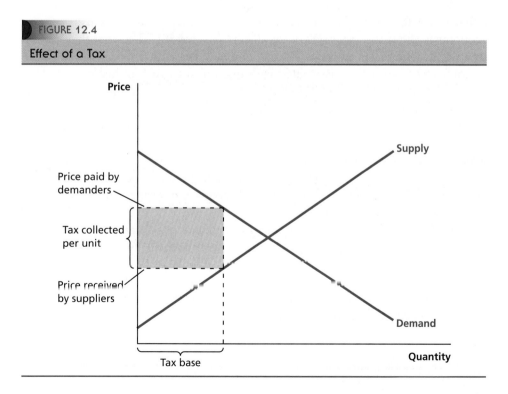

and demand curves. The effect of a tax is to place a wedge between the price that a supplier receives and the price that a demander pays. As the figure shows, the imposition of the tax will also lower the quantity of the good that is purchased; this quantity is called the **tax base.** The total revenue collected by the tax is equal to the tax base multiplied by the per-unit tax. This total revenue is represented by the shaded rectangle in Figure 12.4.

The larger is the gap between the price received by suppliers and the price paid by demanders—that is, the larger is the tax imposed in a given market— the smaller will be the number of transactions that will take place. In other words, raising the tax rate will lower the tax base. This is the source of the inefficiency associated with taxes: When taxes are high, some of the potential transactions between buyers and sellers will not take place, and these transactions would have made both groups better off. No tax will be collected on these forgone transactions, but by discouraging transactions, the tax made the potential buyers and sellers worse off.[4] The size of this inefficiency grows with the size of the tax. Because higher taxes shrink the tax base, increases in revenue collected when tax rates rise are not proportional to increases in tax rates. Indeed, once tax rates are high enough, further increases in the tax rate will not raise any revenue at all, because they will be more than offset by reductions in the tax base.

The analysis of Figure 12.4 raises a question about the real world: How inefficient are the taxes that are actually levied? There is no consensus among economists about the exact size of tax distortions, but it is clear that they can be significant. One recent estimate for the United States is that the marginal dollar of government revenue is associated with one dollar's worth of lost output. This means that the "cost" of one more dollar of government spending is actually two dollars: one dollar of taxation and one dollar of lost output.[5]

The fact that taxes cause inefficiency in the economy does not mean that there should be no taxes. As we have seen, government provides public goods without which the economy could not function at all. These public goods are paid for by taxation. Thus, even if the government were solely concerned with maximizing GDP per capita, the optimal choice of public goods and taxation involves a trade-off between the costs and benefits.

However, not all of the money that governments collect as tax revenue goes toward supplying public goods. Increasingly one of the major functions of government is to make transfers of income to people. The largest transfers are old-age pensions; other transfers include unemployment benefits and welfare payments to the poor. In the United States, such transfers now amount to 16% of GDP in 2010, and their share has more than doubled since the 1960s.

---

[4]Readers who have studied microeconomics will recognize the inefficiency discussed here as "deadweight loss."
[5]Feldstein (1997).

Planning and Other Industrial Policies

Economic planning occurs when the government takes responsibility for some or all of the decision making in an economy. The heyday of economic planning came in the decades after World War II, when governments in newly independent countries in the developing world experimented with various policies to improve their backward conditions. The motivations for government intervention in the economy, which we explored in Section 12.1, were viewed by many economists as being especially salient in the developing world. Several policy tools were common during this period:

- *State enterprises*—These were corporations owned by the government but functioning somewhat like private companies. Policy-makers thought it was particularly important that the government control the "commanding heights" of the economy—areas such as transportation and heavy industry. In many countries, state enterprises produced more than half of manufactured output.

- *Government-owned banks*—In no industry has government control been viewed as being more important than in banking. By directing the flow of investment, government-owned banks in theory have enormous leverage to overcome market failures—for example, steering funds to industries with large externalities or solving coordination problems. Control of banking also allows the government to accomplish social objectives such as distributing resources to underprivileged population groups or regions. Worldwide, national governments owned on average 42% of countries' 10 largest banks in 1995, a figure which had fallen from 59% in 1970. Government ownership of banks is much higher in developing than developed countries. As of 2006, government-owned banks accounted for 98% of bank assets in China, 75% in India, and 65% in Egypt. Among developed countries, the two with the highest share of assets in government-owned banks were Israel (46%) and Germany (42%).[6]

- *Marketing boards*—Many countries compelled farmers to sell their crops to a state marketing enterprise. Government planners thought that by pooling the output of all the farmers, the marketing board could get better prices on the international market.

- *Trade restrictions*—Governments imposed tariffs and quotas on imports, justifying these actions with the so-called infant industry argument: that local firms needed temporary protection from the vicissitudes of world markets to develop into first-class competitors.

---

[6]La Porta, Lopez De Silanes, and Shleifer (2002), Barth, Caprio, and Levine (2006).

THE OTHER PATH

Imagine that you are an entrepreneur in Lima, Peru. You'd like to start a small business: nothing fancy, just a sewing shop. You rent a small factory, buy a few sewing machines, and hire workers. Are you all set to become a respectable member of the Lima business community?

Not quite. If you want to operate your business legally, you first must jump a few bureaucratic hurdles. Be prepared to deal with seven separate government agencies, many of them more than once. You will have to get 11 different permits, licenses, certificates, and so on. Expect to be solicited by bureaucrats for bribes 10 times to speed up the process. Even if you try to avoid paying up, you will have to comply with at least two of these extortions, or the whole process will grind to a halt. To fulfill every regulation will take 289 days from start to finish, or about 10 months. Between the fees you will pay and the potential wages you will forgo going from one office to the next, the cost of your odyssey will be $1,231, or 32 times the Peruvian monthly minimum wage. These were the findings of the Liberty and Democracy Institute, a Peruvian research center, when it tried to open such a factory to demonstrate the difficulty of starting up a legal business in Peru.

Discouraged in your entrepreneurial endeavor, what will you do? Most likely, you will try to start your business informally, outside the established legal framework. You might rent a small room off an alley and put no sign out front to advertise your business. You will probably employ fewer than 10 people. You may parcel out piecework for laborers to do at home. Through these ploys, you will hope to avoid the prying eyes of government inspectors and tax authorities. And you will not be alone in your efforts. The Liberty and Democracy Institute estimates that 42.6% of all housing in Lima has been built informally. Likewise, 95% of the vehicles used in public transit in Lima are informal. In Peru as a whole, 61.2% of all hours worked are devoted to informal activities, and the informal sector accounts for 38.9% of Peru's GDP.[*]

The situation in Peru is not unusual. Worldwide, the underground economy is estimated to be worth $9 trillion per year. In rich countries, it is roughly 15% of GDP, whereas in the developing world, it averages roughly one-third of GDP. Some of the activity in the underground economy is criminal (e.g., drug dealing), but much of it is legal activity that is simply carried out "off the books" and out of sight of government officials.[†]

Although conducting business informally may be the best option available to many entrepreneurs, it leads to several sorts of inefficiencies. Informal firms cannot sign legally enforceable contracts or receive financing from banks. Informal firms must remain small to avoid detection—so they cannot take advantage of economies of scale.

[*]De Soto (1989). All of the figures cited are for 1984.
[†]"The Shadow Economy: Black Hole," *The Economist*, August 28, 1999.

In almost all cases, the policies failed. State enterprises, for example, were woefully inefficient. The managers of these enterprises, facing neither competition from other firms nor pressure from shareholders to produce profits, had little incentive to strive for efficiency in production. The hiring policies of the enterprises were often dictated by the desire to provide jobs for the well connected. The increase in efficiency that results when firms are no longer owned by the government is the key motivation for privatization. A study of 170 firms that

PLANNING IS NOT ALWAYS A FAILURE

Economists with a free-market orientation do not like economic planning, so they are intellectually satisfied when they see it fail. Unfortunately for these economists, there are several cases in which planning has functioned spectacularly well.

The most successful economic planning post–World War II has occurred among the East Asian "Tigers," most notably South Korea and Taiwan. In both countries, government engaged in heavy-handed industrial policies that seemed to have promoted some of the fastest growth of output ever observed.

The actual policies used in South Korea and Taiwan were not very different from those discussed on p. 212. The Korean government created public enterprises in steel and petro-chemicals, for example, to launch new industries in areas where private enterprises were reluctant to undertake new ventures. South Korea also directed investment into industries that government bureaucrats thought appropriate. The Taiwanese government allowed foreign firms to sell products in Taiwan only if they promised to transfer technologies to Taiwanese firms. Both countries liberally used tariffs to protect infant industries.

The ways that Korea and Taiwan differed from most of the rest of the world seem to have been in the execution of these policies, rather than in the policies themselves. The public enterprises that the Korean government created operated as autonomous, profit-seeking entities and in many cases were quickly moved into the private sector. And unlike many other countries, Korea and Taiwan were efficient in weaning their infant industries from protection. In Korea, the government insisted that to maintain protection of their domestic market, protected industries export a growing share of their output. This requirement forced protected industries to bring their level of productivity up to the world level within a short period of time. In Taiwan, the government similarly eliminated tariff protection from industries that failed to meet targets for productivity growth. In one notable incident, a Taiwanese bureaucrat not only threatened to remove tariff protection for the domestic light bulb industry if the quality did not improve, but also ordered the public destruction of 20,000 low-quality bulbs.*

Why did planning succeed in these cases when it failed in so many others? One lesson of these successes is that, not surprisingly, planning works best when administered by an efficient, honest bureaucracy. Those who are skeptical about the value of planning can also take comfort in the fact that Korea and Taiwan had many advantages in addition to their industrial policies—high rates of saving and human capital accumulation, and relatively egalitarian income distributions, for example—so it is not clear exactly how much planning contributed to their successes.[†]

*Romer (1992).
[†]Westphal (1990).

---

were privatized in Mexico in the 1980s and 1990s found that the cost per unit of output fell by an average of 23% following privatization. Firms that were privatized also went from making losses on average to being profitable. Most strikingly, the average number of employees at firms that were privatized fell by half, whereas the volume of output produced rose—evidence of a good deal of wasted employment.[7]

---

[7]La Porta and Lopez–De Silanes (1999).

The lending policies of government-owned banks have rarely matched the theory which justified this policy. Rather than being directed to sectors with large externality benefits, loans have often been used to swing key electoral constituencies or to reward political supporters. A study in Pakistan examined loans made by government banks between 1996 and 2002, a period during which such banks accounted for 64% of lending. The authors found that politically well-connected firms were able to borrow 45% more money from government banks and defaulted on their loans 50% more frequently than similar firms without such connections.[8] Additionally, government-owned banks often provide an easy way for corrupt politicians to extract money from the government: The bank makes a loan to the politician, who then defaults on it, keeping the money for himself.

Marketing boards, which were initially supposed to raise farmers' income, ended up doing just the opposite as government officials could not resist the temptation of the revenues that passed through their hands. In Ghana, for example, the share of revenue farmers received from sales by the cocoa marketing board fell from 77% in 1948 to 20% in 1979. In Zimbabwe in 2007, police were manning roadblocks throughout the country and conducting raids on farms to enforce the law that all grain be sold to the country's Grain Marketing Board (GMB). Not only did the GMB pay lower prices than the black market, but GMB payments were often delayed by several months, during which time rampant inflation eroded their value. There were also widespread accusations that officials of the GMB were diverting official purchases of grain into the black market for their personal profit.

Trade restrictions also were usually counterproductive. In theory, infant industry protection should have been offered only to industries where a country had a chance of someday being a competitive producer. In practice, governments protected any industry with enough political clout—and often all industries indiscriminately. Further, most of the "infant" industries that were protected never managed to grow up. Facing no pressure from foreign competition, they remained inefficient.

A final problem with industrial policies was that in an economic environment dominated by state controls, private entrepreneurs found that the easiest way to make profits was by securing the favor of government bureaucrats who decide on the allocation of investment and imports.[9] Rent seeking is an unproductive activity that reduces the efficiency of production.

Civil Conflict

The preceding discussion, and indeed most of this chapter, focuses on the effects of government policies that are intended to affect the economy. But in some cases, the economic effects of government arise not from a particular policy, but from struggles to control who will govern or from a complete absence of government.

---

[8]Khwaja and Mian (2005).
[9]Krueger (1990).

In 2011, 1.5 billion people lived in areas affected by state fragility, conflict, or large-scale, organized criminal violence, and these afflictions had resulted in there being some 42 million displaced persons. A major form of violence is civil wars, which have killed three times as many people as wars between countries in the period since World War II. Some 73% percent of the "bottom billion" poorest people in the world live in societies that are experiencing a civil war or have recently finished one.[10]

Conflicts such as civil wars reduce economic growth through numerous channels. Wars are inevitably accompanied by looting, flight of refugees, destruction of capital, restriction of commerce, weakening of social capital (a concept discussed in Chapter 14), and a cutback of government's role in supplying public goods (not to mention humanitarian costs that go far beyond economic damage). There is a massive reduction in investment, especially foreign investment, as well as trade. Each year of major violence raises a country's poverty rate by 1% on average. Evidence of the economic effects of violence is also visible when conflicts end. For example, over the 17 years of Mozambique's civil war (1977–1994), output fell at an annual rate of 1.3% per year. In the 15 peaceful years that followed, output grew at an average annual rate of 4.9%.

Although violence lowers a country's income, poverty similarly increases the risk of violence through several channels. For a start, people in dire economic straits are easy recruits for revolution or banditry simply because their opportunity cost is so low. This point was nicely stated by the Sudanese rebel leader John Garang (who held a PhD in economics): "Under these circumstances, the marginal cost of rebellion in the South became very small, zero or negative; that is, in the South it pays to rebel." Another way that low income raises the probability of civil conflict is simply that poor countries have bad roads and weak militaries and are therefore less able to put down insurgencies, especially in peripheral parts of the country. A study of conflict in Africa found that a reduction in economic growth of five percentage points raised the probability of civil conflict the next year by 50%.[11]

The economist Paul Collier has argued that repeated cycles of violence and economic failure, which feed upon each other, can function as a trap (in the sense of an economy having multiple steady states) as discussed in Chapter 3 of this book. A country caught in a **conflict trap** may not differ in any fundamental way from a country that is peaceful and prosperous. Circumstances or luck may have been all that made the difference. For example, a particularly good or bad leader or a temporary economic setback or boom may put a country on the path toward the conflict trap or move it decisively away from one.

Poverty is not the only determinant of violent conflict, of course. As discussed in Chapter 15, another powerful driver of conflict in developing countries is the presence of valuable natural resources, the rents from which make control of the

---

[10]World Bank (2011), Collier (2007).
[11]Miguel, Satyanath, and Sergenti (2004).

government particularly lucrative. Countries that score poorly on the rule of law and corruption indices discussed previously are also more likely to fall into civil war. By contrast, the grievances that are often central in the rhetoric of civil wars, such as oppression of an ethnic minority, appear to have little statistical power to predict the outbreak of war.

Luckily, the last two decades have seen a significant downward trend in fighting: 39 violent conflicts began during the decade of the 2000s, down from 81 that began in the 1990s. The number of ongoing civil wars peaked at 52 in 1992 and had fallen to 35 by 2008. And worldwide annual battle deaths in civil wars fell from 164,000 in the 1980s to 92,000 in the 1990s to 42,000 in the 2000s.[12] This downward trend is particularly encouraging because one of the most powerful predictors of whether a country will experience violence is whether it is has done so in the recent past. Wars inevitably leave in their wake resentments and economic damage, not to mention stocks of weapons and well-trained fighters. Over time, wounds heal, weapons rust, soldiers age, the fabric of society is repaired, and thus the probability of a relapse into conflict decreases.

12.3 WHY GOVERNMENTS DO THINGS THAT ARE BAD FOR GROWTH

As discussed in the introduction to this chapter, economic analyses of government behavior proceed from two perspectives: the normative (asking what governments should do) and the positive (asking why governments do the things they actually do). The analysis in the previous section has been primarily normative: We considered what actions governments can take to affect the growth rate of output. We also saw that governments often do not act in a fashion that maximizes growth.

In this section, we take a positive approach to government behavior. Specifically, we ask why governments do things that are bad for growth and why they fail to do things that are good for growth.

Some Other Goal

One reason that governments do things that are harmful for growth is that they are pursuing some other goal. Spending taxpayer money on national defense, the arts, or foreign aid, for example, may lower economic growth (because of the distortionary effect of taxation) but can still be viewed as being in the national interest.

Another possible goal of government that can result in lower economic growth is the reduction of pollution. Over the last several decades, governments throughout the world have introduced regulations limiting the discharge of pollution into the air and water by factories, automobiles, and so on. These regulations have forced the

---

[12]World Bank (2011).

installation of hundreds of billions of dollars' worth of new equipment such as catalytic converters on automobiles. Because anti-pollution regulations raise the amount of input used without raising the quantity of output produced, they reduce economic efficiency. However, governments view this reduction in efficiency as a price worth paying for a cleaner environment. Indeed, as we will see in Chapter 16, another way to view this issue is that reducing pollution only appears to be inefficient because we do not measure output properly. If we explicitly take into account the costs of pollution, then a government policy that reduces the production of goods but also reduces the amount of pollution produced may no longer seem inefficient.

Finally, the most important example of a policy goal that may impede economic growth is one that we already have touched on, and a subject to which we will return in the next chapter: income equality. Governments that redistribute income from rich to poor face an equity-efficiency trade-off. Reducing inequality (raising equity) lowers economic efficiency and thus reduces economic growth. This is a price that many governments are willing to pay.

Corruption and Kleptocracy

A second reason that governments do things that are bad for growth is that those who staff the government are acting in their own self-interest rather than in the interest of the country they are governing. Government corruption takes many forms, from a tax inspector who accepts a bribe to overlook income on which he is supposed to collect taxes, to a mayor who trades city contracts for cash payments, all the way up to a president who grants a lucrative monopoly to his son. When corruption reaches to the highest levels of government, it is labeled **kleptocracy,** meaning "rule by thieves."

Although corruption has existed as long as there have been governments, economists have only recently focused on it as an important factor in economic development. As evidence of this change in focus, during the 1980s, the word *corruption* was mentioned in the title or abstract of 3.2 out of every 10,000 published economics articles. By 2009, the rate was 72 out of every 10,000 articles. Further, before 1990, some economists argued that a certain amount of corruption could be beneficial. In their view, many government policies are themselves detrimental to economic growth, and corruption on the part of the officials who are supposed to carry out these policies could have a positive effect. Indeed, it was also argued that kleptocracy could be conducive to economic growth because even a ruler who has no interest in the country's economy other than what can be stolen from it will still want the country to be as prosperous as possible, so that there is more to steal. Such a ruler might even have a strong interest in suppressing any corruption at the lower levels of the bureaucracy to make sure that there is more left over to take. Finally, the stronger is the country's economy, the more likely are the citizens to be content with a kleptocrat's rule, and thus the more likely the ruler will be to remain in power and enjoy the spoils.

In the last decade, economists studying economic development have increasingly come to view corruption as one of the most important impediments to development. In a report in 2002, the World Bank identified corruption as "the single greatest obstacle to economic and social development" because it weakens the institutional foundation on which economic growth depends. In 2004, the World Bank estimated that $1 trillion in bribes are paid every year.

Some of the links between corruption and economic growth are straightforward. First, corruption directly wastes taxpayers' money. A corrupt government spends more than is necessary because, for example, contracts are awarded to the firm that pays the largest bribe rather than to the firm that puts in the lowest bid. Further, some taxes are diverted directly into the pockets of government officials. In 2001, for example, some $900 million, one-tenth of the country's GDP, simply disappeared from Angola's treasury.[13] Because raising tax revenue lowers the efficiency of production, this waste of tax revenue reduces growth.

The waste of government revenue is only the beginning of the inefficiency brought about by corruption. A second effect of corruption is that governments undertake policies solely to generate more opportunities for bribery. For example, a government may impose import quotas so that officials can trade import licenses for bribes, or a government may build an unnecessary road so that it can award contracts to well-connected companies. Corruption also undermines the rule of law, which as we saw previously is one of the most important public goods that government provides. Corrupt government officials have a strong interest in making sure there is not a strong judicial system to stand in their way. And firms that cannot be certain their contracts will be enforced (because judges respond to bribes rather than facts and law) will be reluctant to undertake investments.

Getting data on the extent of corruption is quite difficult. Not surprisingly, governments themselves do not collect any information on the topic. The data in Figure 12.5 were assembled using the same sources as those on rule of law in Figures 12.1 and 12.2: surveys of citizens as well as international experts. In the figure, control of corruption is measured so that the mean level is 0 with a range from –1.73 in Somalia to 2.42 in Denmark (data are for the year 2009). There is obviously a close relationship between corruption and the level of income per capita. No wealthy country has a high level of corruption, and most poor countries are ranked as being fairly corrupt. Of course, these data do not prove that corruption is what causes countries to be poor. In Section 12.4 we further interpret the data.

Self-Preservation

A final reason that governments do things that are bad for growth is that this tactic is often the best way to keep themselves in power. Many of the changes in social structure that inevitably accompany economic growth pose a threat to those in power. New

---

[13]Angola: Measuring Corruption," *The Economist*, October 26, 2002.

FIGURE 12.5

Government Corruption versus GDP per Capita, 2009

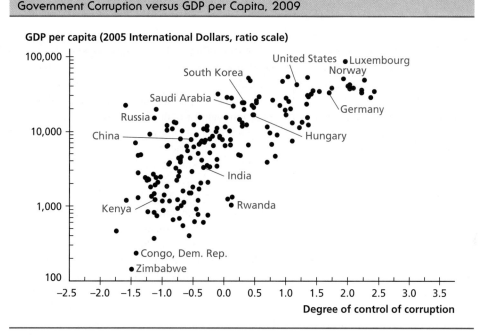

Source: Kaufmann, Kray, and Mastruzzi (2010).

technologies can redistribute economic power away from the groups that support the current ruler; rising education may introduce destabilizing new ideas; the movement of population from farms to cities creates a potential revolutionary class; and trade with the outside world can carry with it dangerous foreign ideas.

The fact that economic growth can be destabilizing does not mean that governments will always oppose it. A lack of economic growth can also threaten a government's survival—because a failure to grow may breed popular discontent and because a country that does not grow may be menaced by more advanced neighbors. During the Meiji period (1868–1912), the Japanese government made this second idea explicit in advancing the slogan "Rich Country, Strong Army." Thus, a government faces a trade-off in choosing policies that affect growth, and the policies it chooses will depend on the circumstances. A government with a weak grip on power will be inclined to preserve the status quo, at the cost of forgoing growth; a government that is secure in power will be willing to tolerate the social dislocations that accompany rapid growth. Similarly, a government that faces threats from abroad will be inclined to take the risks associated with growth that would be avoided by a government that feels no foreign pressure.

The history of Russia illustrates this trade-off between the threats posed by growth and failure to grow. In the early 19th century, Russia was noticeably

GOVERNMENT REGULATION: HELPING HAND OR GRABBING HAND?

Why does government do the things it does? Is it to benefit the public good—or to benefit those who do the governing? In practice, it is not always easy to distinguish which of these motivations is more important.

One study examined a specific government activity—regulating the creation of new firms—to determine which of these objectives is more significant.* The authors collected data from 75 countries on the legal requirements for opening a new firm. They counted the actual number of bureaucratic steps involved, measured how long the process took, and tallied the fees involved. The difficulty of creating a new firm varies considerably among countries. For example, an entrepreneur wanting to establish a new firm in Bolivia has to follow 20 procedures, wait 82 business days, and pay $2,696 in fees; in Canada, the same entrepreneur would have to follow two procedures, wait 2 days, and pay just $280.

Using these data, the authors set out to test two different theories of why there are such large differences among countries in the difficulty of creating firms. According to the first theory, which they call the "helping hand" view, governments regulate the entry of new firms to protect consumers from low-quality producers and also to limit negative externalities such as pollution. According to the second theory, which the authors call the "grabbing hand" view, regulation is imposed by governments to benefit either government bureaucrats themselves or those in the private sector who supply them with political or financial support.

The data strongly favored the grabbing hand view. Countries with more regulations did not have less pollution, higher-quality consumer products, or better health than countries with fewer regulations. This finding indicates that regulation of the entry of new firms is not serving to protect consumers, as is posited in the helping hand view. Further, there is strong evidence that the number of regulations is negatively related to the degree to which government represents the interests of citizens. In other words, more democratic countries tend to have fewer regulations, again indicating that the purpose of regulation is not to make citizens better off. Similarly, governments that are judged as being more corrupt also have more regulations, a relationship suggesting that government officials create these regulations to increase the number of opportunities to collect bribes.

*Djankov et al. (2002).

backward in comparison to its rapidly industrializing European neighbors and the United States. For example, in 1850, Russia had a total of 301 miles (501 kilometers) of railroad track, compared with 5,987 miles (9,979 kilometers) in the United Kingdom and 8,711 miles (14,518 kilometers) in the United States. But industrialization posed two threats to the Russian monarchy. First, the Russian rulers feared that industrial workers concentrated in cities would be susceptible to the contagion of revolutions such as those that swept Europe in 1848. Second, industrialization would undermine the land-based wealth of the elites who supported czarist rule.

Defeat in the Crimean War (1854–1856) drove home the degree of Russia's industrial backwardness. British and French rifles had three times the range of those used by Russian soldiers. Following the war, the czar embarked on a program of industrialization and railway building out of fear that foreigners would conquer more Russian territory. But the czar's previous apprehensions of industrialization's destabilizing effects proved correct, and after revolutions in 1905 and 1917, the monarchy was swept from power.[14]

The trade-off between economic growth and political security that concerned the czars in the 19th century was the same dilemma faced by Mikhail Gorbachev, the leader of the Soviet Union, at the end of the 20th century. The policies of *perestroika* (restructuring) and *glasnost* (political openness) that Gorbachev instituted in 1986 aimed to shake up the moribund Soviet economy, which was falling increasingly behind its competitors in the West. Once again, however, the price of economic modernization proved high: Within five years, Gorbachev was out of power, and the Soviet Union had dissolved.

As we have seen, some economists argued that a kleptocratic ruler—one who is using her position to amass wealth—would have an incentive to maximize economic growth so there would be more to steal. However, in practice, most kleptocrats are far more concerned with simply staying in power than with expanding the size of the economic "pie" from which they can take a piece. Many of the institutional arrangements necessary for economic growth (widespread literacy, rule of law) will appear threatening to a kleptocrat, and economic growth itself can create new elites who will compete for power with an established hierarchy. This perspective was summarized by President Mobutu Sese Seko of Zaire (now the Democratic Republic of the Congo), a notorious kleptocrat of the post–World War II era who amassed wealth estimated at between $5 billion and $10 billion while his country remained mired in poverty. In response to a request from the president of neighboring Rwanda for help in fighting an armed insurgency, Mobutu replied, "I told you not to build any roads.... Building roads never did any good. I have been in power in Zaire for thirty years, and I have never built one road. Now they are driving down them to get you."[15] Zaire had only one-tenth as much paved roadway in 1991 as at the time of its independence from Belgium in 1960. Despite his avoidance of investment in infrastructure, Mobutu was overthrown in 1997.

12.4 WHY POOR COUNTRIES HAVE BAD GOVERNMENTS

Our findings about why governments do things that are bad for growth apply to governments in both rich and poor countries. However, examination of data suggests that although no government is perfect, poor countries tend to have particularly bad governments. When we examined the rule of law and corruption, for example, we found that poorer countries tended to score much worse on these measures.

---

[14]Acemoglu and Robinson (2002), Landes (1998).
[15]Robinson (2001).

The fact that poor countries have bad governments raises an obvious question: Are these countries poor *because* of their bad governments, or is bad government a symptom, rather than a cause, of poverty?

The simple answer to this question is "some of each." Few economists would disagree that being richer tends to make a country have better government or that having a better government tends to make a country richer. But there is active debate about which of these channels of causation—from government to income, or from income to government—is more important in explaining the correlation between income and quality of government that we see in the data. In the remainder of this section, we examine the arguments on both sides.

Causation Running from Income to Government Quality

The argument that income primarily affects government quality, rather than the other way around, rests on two observations. The first is that bad government is not always an impediment to economic growth; second is that the quality of government often improves in response to growing income.

The history of currently developed countries provides evidence that bad government does not necessarily prevent growth. Many of the contemporary practices that international agencies such as the World Bank denounce were at one time not considered even improper. For example, until 1871 the main method by which officers in the British army were appointed or promoted was by purchasing their position. Officers were expected to recoup the price of their investment by, among other schemes, diverting some of the money allocated for buying provisions for the men under their command.[16]

The history of New York City provides a good example of growth proceeding despite bad government. Between 1825, when the opening of the Erie Canal connected New York City to the Great Lakes, and 1900, the city's population grew by a factor of 17, reaching 3.7 million. In 1900, New York trailed only London as the most important city in the world economy. It was also, by most accounts, a cesspool of corruption. One of the most infamous incidents of the era ironically surrounded the construction of a courthouse. Completed in 1880, the New York County Courthouse cost $15 million ($335 million in 2010 dollars)—twice what the United States had recently paid to purchase the territory of Alaska from Russia. Of those costs, more than three-quarters was stolen by a ring headed by the notorious William Marcy "Boss" Tweed. So powerful was Tweed's grasp that a special committee created to investigate allegations of corruption at the time not only reported no cause for concern, but also spent half its budget having its report printed by a Tweed-owned company. Boss Tweed eventually ran afoul of the law when his detailed accounting books were leaked to *The New York Times*. In an effort to free

---

[16]Bruce (1980).

New York City government as depicted by the cartoonist Thomas Nast in 1871.

himself from prison, shortly before his death, Tweed wrote out a confession, complete with documentary evidence, that implicated half of the city government.[17] Muckraking journalist Lincoln Steffens, in his book *The Shame of the Cities* (1904), detailed the extent of municipal corruption and concluded that "the spirit of graft and of lawlessness is the American spirit."

The example of New York City's rapid growth in the face of widespread corruption is hardly unique. The period since World War II has also seen plenty of cases in which bad government did not hold back economic growth. Between 1950 and 1990, for example, growth in Japan was not noticeably slowed by "crony capitalism," a business culture based on connections, often between government officials and the firms they were supposed to regulate; nor was growth in Indonesia notably slowed by the corruption of President Suharto, whose family accumulated a fortune of $15 billion. In both of these cases, bad government was the focus of scrutiny only after growth had slowed down for other reasons. Today the most interesting case in this dimension is China, which is growing with astonishing rapidity but ranks only 117th out of the 186 countries in the control of corruption measure used in Figure 12.5.

Just as there is good evidence that bad government does not necessarily impede growth, there are many channels through which rising national income improves the quality of government. The simplest channel is that richer countries

---

[17]Kolbert (2002).

DEMOCRACY AND ECONOMIC GROWTH

One of the most interesting questions economists have explored regarding government is the relationship between economic growth and democracy. Figure 12.6 shows the relationship between income per capita and a measure of political rights (specifically the competitiveness of the electoral system and the accountability of elected leaders) as compiled by the organization Freedom House.* The data are on a 7-point scale, with 1 being least democratic and 7 being the most democratic. The figure shows that political rights are greater in richer countries. But as with the other measures of government that we have been studying, these data do not tell us the source of the relationship. Does being a democracy make a country rich, or is democracy somehow a consequence of a country's wealth?

Unlike some other measures of "good government," including rule of law and absence of corruption, democracy may not always be good for economic growth. Economists point to both positive and negative influences of democracy on growth. On the one hand, by imposing limits on the power of rulers, democracies can avoid the worst excesses of kleptocracy. There is also evidence that more democratic countries are less likely to have corrupt government officials.[†] On the other hand, democracies can be prone to political instability; also, democratic politicians, to retain their office, are often tempted to implement policies that produce short-run gains rather than long-run growth. Some economists also claim that democratic governments emphasize policies that redistribute income to the detriment of economic growth.

An interesting case study of the effects of democracy on economic growth comes from comparing the economic performances of India and China, the world's two most populous countries. India has been a functioning democracy since it gained independence from Britain in 1947. China has been nondemocratic since the communist victory in 1949. In 1980, India was the richer of the two countries, with income per capita of $1,018 compared with China's $714 (both in 2005 dollars). The two countries had also suffered similar problems of slow growth. In the last two decades of the 20th century, both countries began liberalizing their slow-growing, state-controlled economies and opening up to the world market.

Of the two countries, China has undeniably been more successful at liberalizing and growing. Average growth over the period 1975–2009 was 7.9% per year, compared with 3.7% per year in India. Part of this difference in growth rates seems directly attributable to the degree of democracy. Whether it is licensing new investment projects, modernizing regulations, or building infrastructure, the Indian government is often hampered by the constraints of a democracy such as bickering between different levels of government (e.g., state versus national), changes of direction when new politicians come into office, and the ability of small constituencies to hold up projects until their own interests are satisfied. By contrast, the Chinese government is able to execute decisions with remarkable speed and efficiency. Nowhere is the difference between the two countries more apparent than in the construction of public works. Expressway mileage in China increased from less than 1,000 km in 1993 to 74,000 km, roughly equal to that of the United States, in 2011. In that same year, India had 600 km of expressways. (Of course nondemocratic governments can also execute bad policies with speed and efficiency. A policy disaster like China's Great Leap Forward would not have occurred in a democracy like India.)

Foreign investors clearly prefer the kind of stability associated with nondemocratic government to the uncertainty of a democracy. In 2010, foreign direct investment inflows as a share of GDP were twice as high in China as in India.

The economist Robert Barro, studying data from a large cross-section of countries, concluded that some democracy was good for economic growth but that beyond a moderate level, additional democracy was bad for growth. According to his calculations, the optimal level of democracy is roughly in the middle of the 7-point scale used in Figure 12.6.§ Examples of countries with this level of democracy are Pakistan, Honduras, and Kenya. If Barro's analysis is correct, then the fact that the richest countries in the world are also the most democratic must reflect causation running from income to democracy. Democracy, beyond a moderate level, is a luxury good that wealthy countries choose to consume even though it reduces their income.

*Freedom House (2011).
†Treisman (2000).
§Barro (1997).

FIGURE 12.6

Democracy and GDP per Capita

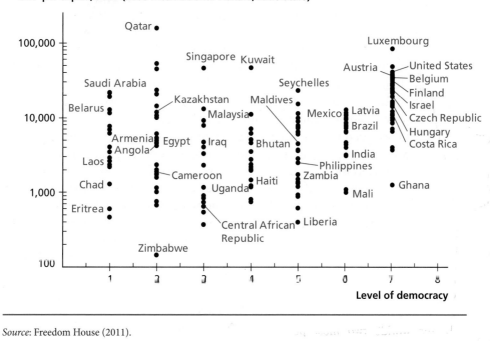

GDP per capita, 2009 (2005 International Dollars, ratio scale)

Source: Freedom House (2011).

can afford to pay their civil servants reasonable wages, thus shutting off one of the prime motivations for corruption. A second channel through which prosperity improves the quality of government is that when there is a larger (or growing) pie to split up, there is typically less of the destructive competition between interest groups that is often expressed in the form of governmental gridlock. Finally, the sense of public spiritedness that can lead to honest government may be a "luxury good" affordable only to people in relatively wealthy countries. As the box "Democracy and Economic Growth" shows, the same is true of democracy.

Causation Running from Government Quality to Income

Economists who believe that bad government is primarily a cause rather than a symptom of economic underdevelopment principally base their views on the abundant evidence of government's ability to affect the economy. We have seen numerous examples of policies that have encouraged or impeded economic growth, such as those of North and South Korea. Given that government policies are so important in affecting growth, and that these policies differ so much among countries, it is natural to conclude that variation in government policy explains a significant fraction of variation in income among countries.

A second component of the argument that causality runs primarily from government quality to income is that there is an obvious explanation for why some countries have bad governments that has nothing to do with their income. That explanation is the legacy of colonialism. Most of the poorly governed countries in the world are former European colonies. For example, of the 30 most corrupt countries as measured in the data described previously, 22 are former European colonies (of the remainder, 5 are parts of the former Soviet Union).

Colonialism led to bad governments through two channels. First, in many former colonies, colonial powers installed government systems that were explicitly designed to maximize the revenue that could be collected from the populace rather than to encourage economic or social development. For example, in Latin America in the 17th and 18th centuries, the colonial powers (Spain and Portugal) created a system of state monopolies and trade restrictions designed to extract resources from the population. Colonial governments in Africa, most of which was colonized in the second half of the 19th century, were even more brutally efficient in their drive to mine the wealth of their colonies. At the beginning of the 20th century, for example, France was extracting 50% of the GDP of its colony Dahomey (now Benin). The European exploitation of Africa reached its zenith in the Belgian colony of the Congo, where the colonial masters relied on forced labor and extortion in their pursuit of rubber to provide bicycle tires for Europeans. Over the period 1880–1920, between 5 million and 10 million Congolese natives died as a result of colonial brutality.[18]

---

[18]Hochschild (1998).

When European colonizers departed (or were ejected), these extractive forms of government were left in place—and frequently the European colonizers were simply replaced by a local strongman or ruling native elite. Of course, Europeans did not leave behind bad governments in all of their ex-colonies. The United States, Canada, and Australia are all former colonies. The difference is that in countries where large numbers of Europeans settled, they tended to establish governmental systems that mirrored those of Europe itself. But in the colonies where large numbers of Europeans did not settle—because of inhospitable climate and debilitating disease—institutions were created that later led to bad governments.

The second reason that former colonies often have bad governments is that colonial rule created states with ethnic mixes that made good government difficult. European colonizers often drew the boundaries between colonies (which would later become the borders between states) without regard to the ethnic composition of the population. Further, colonial powers often played one ethnic group off against another as part of a "divide and rule" strategy that allowed a small group of Europeans to maintain control. The period since independence in most former colonies has been characterized by destructive struggles for power, as well as by the use of government machinery to channel money to favored ethnic groups.

Economists examining data from a large sample of countries have argued that this colonial legacy is the most important determinant of how the quality of government varies among countries. If they are correct, then the correlation of government and income must be the result of causality running from government to income and not the other way around.

12.5 CONCLUSION

The issue of which government policies can maximize growth is one of the oldest questions in economics. Government intervention in the economy is justified by the existence of market failures—cases in which the unfettered operation of the market fails to produce the best possible outcome. Market failures include externalities like pollution and the inability of private firms to provide public goods such as roads. But the problem of government failure—the inefficiencies that arise through incompetence, malfeasance, or just plain politics—reduces the usefulness of government intervention. The debate over how best to balance these two competing risks is not likely to be resolved anytime soon.

In this chapter we reviewed some of the tools that governments use to influence the economy. These tools include the provision of the rule of law, regulation of how firms behave, planning (direction of resources to certain targeted industries), trade policies such as tariffs and quotas, and outright ownership of the means of production. Governments also affect the level of economic efficiency by their sheer size (i.e., by the amount that they tax and spend). How these tools are used has varied among countries and over time. In some cases, we have enough evidence to tell us what policies are good. For example, rule of law is unambiguously good for economic growth, and complete government direction of the economy does not work. In many other cases, however, there is more uncertainty about what policy is best. Government planning and the protection of infant industries with tariffs have often but not always failed. Similarly, there is no consensus about the optimal size of government or the optimal degree of income redistribution.

In addition to asking what government *should* do, economists also ask *why* governments do the things they do. Governments often institute policies that are bad for economic growth or fail to enact measures that would be good for growth. In some cases, the explanation for this behavior is that the government is trying to accomplish some other legitimate policy goal that conflicts with growth—for example, redistributing income from rich to poor or reducing pollution. Often, however, the motives for growth reducing actions are less noble. The abuse of public office for private gain—either by the head of government or by lower-level officials—reduces growth by eroding the rule of law, among other things. Similarly, the desire to stay in power may conflict with actions that would promote economic growth.

On average, governments in poor countries behave in a manner more detrimental to growth than regimes in rich countries. Specifically, poor-country governments do a worse job of maintaining the rule of law and are more likely to be corrupt than are rich-country governments. Poor-country governments also tax and spend more than did rich-country governments when they were at a similar stage of development. Pinpointing the direction of causality—whether bad government leads to low growth or vice versa—is one of the most challenging and intriguing questions that economic researchers are addressing today.

KEY TERMS

normative **333**	coordination	equity-efficiency trade-off **336**
positive **333**	failure **334**	Wagner's law **340**
market failure **333**	income redistribution **335**	tax base **342**
public goods **334**	government failure **335**	conflict trap **347**
externality **334**	privatized **335**	kleptocracy **349**
monopoly **334**	deregulation **335**	

QUESTIONS FOR REVIEW

1. What is the difference between positive and normative analyses of government economic policy?

2. What market failures are often cited as justification for government intervention in the economy? In each case, explain how economic policy can address the market failure.

3. What is the equity-efficiency trade-off?

4. What is a conflict trap and why is it relevant for economic development?

5. What are some of the reasons why governments do things that are bad for economic growth?

6. What are some explanations for the positive correlation between GDP per capita and the quality of government?

PROBLEMS

1. For each of the following government actions, explain where it fits into the discussion of the rationales for government policy listed in Section 12.1. What market failure, if any, does the policy address? Does the policy stimulate economic growth? Is the policy an example of government failure? Whose interests are served by the policy?

   a. In 238 B.C., the Chinese emperor Qin Shi Huang Di enacted a law standardizing the length of axles on carts so that the wheels of carts could more easily follow in the ruts of those that had gone before.

   b. Most countries have central banks (such as the Federal Reserve System in the United States) that are responsible for controlling the quantity of money and regulating the price level.

   c. In 1996, the Indonesian government announced the creation of a "national car" called the Timor. The car was to be produced by a company under the control of Tommy Suharto, the president's son, whose only experience in the automobile industry was as a race-car driver. Although the car was actually manufactured in South Korea, it was exempt from duties and luxury taxes paid by other imported automobiles. Tommy Suharto's company promised that within three years, 60% of the content of the car would be domestically produced. (His father's government fell in 1998, and Tommy Suharto was subsequently convicted of ordering the murder of a judge.)

   d. Many governments subsidize vaccinations against infectious diseases or require that children be vaccinated before attending school.

   e. In many countries, it is illegal to operate a private mail service in competition with the government post office.

   f. Many governments impose a minimum wage.

   g. The World Bank concluded in 1994 that the failure of African governments to spend $12 billion on the maintenance of roadways over the previous decade had necessitated the expenditure of $45 billion on roadway reconstruction.

   h. Many governments pay some or all of the costs of college education for their citizens.

2. Use a diagram like Figure 6.4 (page 157) to analyze the theories of causation running between income per capita and the quality of government that are discussed in Section 12.4 of this chapter.

3. Coffee is primarily made from two different beans, Arabica and Robusta. The beans grow in different countries. Suppose that in the year 2008, a major scientific study finds that drinking coffee made from Arabica beans contributes to heart disease, whereas drinking coffee made from Robusta promotes better health. As a result, the price of Arabica beans falls and the price of Robusta beans rises. An economist reads about these goings-on and says "Great. This will help me understand the connection between income and quality of government." Explain the thinking, what data would be looked at to carry out this investigation, and how the results would be interpreted. Also explain why looking at this data would be superior to simply examining the correlation between income and the quality of government.

4. The supply and demand curves in a particular market are given by the following equations:

$$Demand: Q = 100 - P$$

$$Supply: Q = P,$$

   where P is the price of the good and Q is the quantity supplied or demanded.

   a. Solve for the market-clearing price in the absence of a tax.

   b. Suppose that the government taxes the good at a rate of τ. Specifically, if P is the price that demanders pay for the good, then the government collects τP as tax, and the supplier receives $(1-\tau)P$. Calculate the equilibrium values of P and Q.

c. Solve for the tax rate that will maximize the government's revenue.

5. A country is ruled by a wise, unselfish, absolute dictator. The government collects a tax on wages and spends the money on a public good. There is no corruption, nor are there any political considerations regarding how much of the public good the government produces. How would the amount of the public good supplied by this dictator compare in the case where labor is supplied inelastically versus the case where the labor supply curve is upward sloping? Explain your answer.

6. Consider an extension of the Solow model from $\int_{dy/dx}$ Chapter 3 to encompass a second type of capital, called government capital, which consists of publicly funded infrastructure such as roads and ports. Let x denote the quantity of government capital per worker, k the quantity of physical capital per worker, and y the quantity of output per worker. The economy's production function (in per-worker terms) is:

$$y = Ak^{1/3}x^{1/3}.$$

We assume that the government collects a fraction τ of national income in taxes and spends all of this revenue producing government capital. We also assume that a constant fraction y of after-tax income is invested in producing physical capital. Both government capital and physical capital depreciate at rate δ. The equations describing how government capital and physical capital change over time are thus:

$$\Delta x = \tau Ak^{1/3}x^{1/3} - \delta k.$$

$$\Delta k = \gamma(1 - \tau)Ak^{1/3}x^{1/3} - \delta k.$$

a. Solve for the steady-state level of output per worker.

b. What value of τ will maximize output per worker in the steady state?

For additional exploration and practice using the Online Data Plotter and data sets, please visit www.pearsonhighered.com/weil.

INCOME INEQUALITY

Our study of economic growth has so far been concerned with what determines the average level of income per capita in a country. But beyond the average level of income, economists are also interested in how that income is divided among the country's residents—that is, in the **distribution of income.**

One reason to pay attention to the distribution of income is its relationship to poverty. For any given average level of income, if income is distributed more unequally, more people will live in poverty. An example makes this point clear. In the year 2005, average income per capita in India ($2,557) was 21% larger than average income per capita in Pakistan ($2,112). But the fraction of the population living on an income of less than $1.25 per day was 41.6% in India, compared with only 22.5% in Pakistan.[1] The reason for the difference was the distribution of income. Pakistan has a more equal distribution of income than does India.

Beyond its link to poverty, the distribution of income is also intimately tied to the process of economic growth. We will see in this chapter that there are a number of channels through which income inequality affects economic growth. Although the empirical evidence is inconclusive, it is possible that a high level of inequality is good for growth at some stages of development and bad for growth at others. Economic growth, in turn, feeds back to affect the degree of income inequality.

Another reason to study income inequality is that, as we saw in Chapter 12, reducing inequality is frequently one of the most important goals of government economic policy. Some policies may achieve the twin goals of reducing income inequality and raising economic growth. A good example of such a policy is the public provision of education. In other cases, however, the goals of maximizing economic growth and reducing income inequality are in conflict. In this chapter we discuss one such case in detail—the redistribution of income through taxation.

Finally, income inequality within a country is, for residents of a country itself, often a more salient issue than differences in income among countries. A poor

> An imbalance between rich and poor is the oldest and most fatal ailment of all republics.
>
> —Plutarch

---

[1] *World Development Indicators* database, Heston, Summers, and Aten (2011).

person in the United States is probably more aware of where he or she stands in relation to rich people in the United States than he or she is of her status relative to people in countries that are much poorer than the United States. To the extent that people derive their happiness not from the absolute level of their consumption but from how their consumption compares with that of the people around them, income inequality within a country may be more important than differences in income among countries. This is a topic to which we will return in Chapter 17.

In this chapter we begin by discussing how income inequality is measured and how movements in inequality have historically been related to economic growth. We then look at the determination of inequality itself: what factors influence it and what mechanisms cause the degree of inequality to change over time. We next examine—both theoretically and empirically—how income inequality affects economic growth. Finally, we consider economic mobility, a concept that is closely related to income inequality.

13.1 INCOME INEQUALITY: THE FACTS

Thus far, most of our measurements have been concerned with *country averages*—we have looked at countries' average levels of income per capita, average levels of fertility per woman, average quantities of capital per worker, and so on. In studying income inequality, we will focus on how the residents of a country differ from the country's average, and thus also how they differ from each other.

We can look at income distribution in two complementary ways. One approach is to divide the population into several equal-sized groups and to measure how much income each group earns. The other way is to divide income into equal-sized intervals and to ask how much of the population falls into each interval.

Table 13.1 presents an example of the first way of looking at the distribution of income. The data are on household income in the United States in the year 2009.[2]

TABLE 13.1

Household Income in the United States by Quintiles, 2009

Quintile	Average Household Income	Share of Total Household Income (%)
1st (Lowest)	$11,552	3.4
2nd	$29,257	8.6
3rd	$49,534	14.6
4th	$78,694	23.2
5th (Highest)	$170,844	50.3

Source: DeNavas-Walt, Proctor, and Smith (2010).

---

[2]DeNavas-Walt, Proctor, and Smith (2010). The specific measure used is pretax money income, including government cash transfers and excluding capital gains.

Households are divided into five income *quintiles*, each made up of 20% of the population. The first quintile is the one-fifth of households with the lowest income. The second quintile is the next-lowest one-fifth of households in terms of their income rank, and so on. The second column of the table shows the average level of household income within each quintile, and the last column shows each quintile's share of total household income.

A second way to view income distribution is to divide the population into different categories of income and to look at the fraction of the population in each. Figure 13.1 applies this analysis to the same data on the United States as in Table 13.1. Income categories are plotted along the horizontal axis, and the height of each bar shows the percentage of households in each category. For example, the category with the most households (which is called the **mode** of the distribution) is between $20,000 and $24,999. This category includes 6.0% of households.

Two useful statistics for summarizing a distribution are the **mean** (the simple average) and the **median** (the value that has exactly as many observations below it as above). For the United States in 2009, mean household income was $67,976, and median household income was $49,777. The fact that the mean was higher than the median is not unusual—for all income data that have ever been observed, this fact holds true. The reason is that income distributions are always **skewed**—that is, they have a long right tail, rather than being symmetric around their means. (Figure 13.1 does not show the full extent of the long right tail because such an illustration would require a page several yards wide! For that reason, the figure does not include the 3.8% of households with income of $200,000 or higher.) In a skewed income distribution, a few households with very high income raise the mean level of income without having much effect on median income.

Using the Gini Coefficient to Measure Income Inequality

Tabulations of data such as those presented in Table 13.1 and Figure 13.1 effectively show inequality within a country at a single point in time. However, if we want to compare income inequality among countries or examine inequality trends in one country over time, it is useful to have a single number that summarizes the degree of income inequality in a country. The measure most frequently used is called the **Gini coefficient**.

To construct the Gini coefficient for income inequality, we begin with data on the incomes of all the households (or a representative sample of households) in a given country. We can arrange these households from lowest to highest income, and from this arrangement of the data, we can calculate a series of figures. We first ask what fraction of the total income in the country is earned by the poorest 1% of households. Then we find the fraction of total income earned by the poorest 2% of households, and so on. We can do calculations for each fraction of households

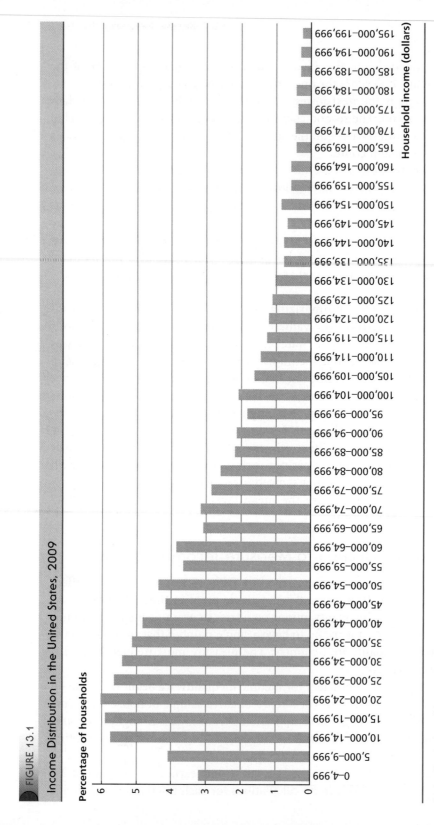

FIGURE 13.1

Income Distribution in the United States, 2009

Percentage of households

Household income (dollars)

Source: DeNavas-Walt, Proctor, and Smith (2010).

through 100% (where, of course, the fraction of income earned by the poorest 100% of households is 100%). Graphing these data produces a **Lorenz curve.**

Figure 13.2 shows the Lorenz curve for the data on U.S. household income that we analyzed in Table 13.1 and Figure 13.1. The points on the curve corresponding to the poorest 20%, 40%, 60%, and 80% have been labeled. These points can be derived directly from Table 13.1. For example, the first line of Table 13.1 shows that the poorest 20% of households earn 3.4% of total household income. Adding the first and second lines of the table shows that the poorest 40% of households in the United States earn 12.0% of total household income.

The Lorenz curve has a bowed shape because of income inequality. If income were distributed perfectly equally, then the poorest 20% of households would receive 20% of total household income, the poorest 40% would receive 40% of total household income, and so on. In this case, the Lorenz curve would be a straight line with a slope of 1; this is the "line of perfect equality" in Figure 13.2.

> **FIGURE 13.2**

The Lorenz Curve for the United States, 2009

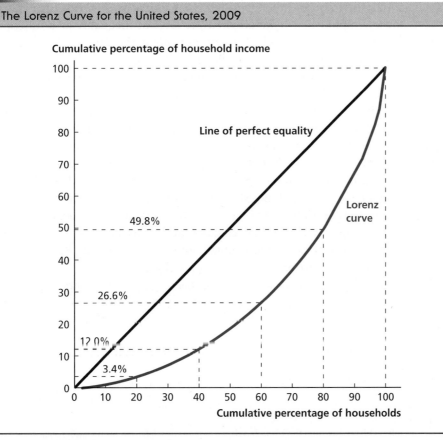

Source: De Navas-Walt, Proctor, and Smith (2010).

The more bowed out is the Lorenz curve, the more unequally income is distributed. We can use this property of the Lorenz curve to construct an index that summarizes inequality in a single number. This index is the Gini coefficient. The Gini coefficient is constructed by measuring the area between the Lorenz curve and the line of perfect equality and dividing this area by the total area under the line of perfect equality. The more bowed out is the Lorenz curve, and thus the more unequal is the distribution of income, the higher will be the value of the Gini coefficient. If income is distributed perfectly equally, then the value of the Gini coefficient will be 0. If income is distributed as unequally as possible—that is, if a single household receives all household income in the country—then the Gini coefficient will be 1. The Gini coefficient for the household income data from the United States graphed in Figure 13.2 is 0.468. Later in this chapter, we will see that Gini coefficients can also be used to measure inequality of other economic characteristics, such as holdings of financial wealth.

The Kuznets Hypothesis

In 1955, economist Simon Kuznets hypothesized that as a country developed, inequality would first rise and then later fall (we will discuss his reasoning later). Kuznets's theory implies that if we graphed the level of inequality as a function of the level of gross domestic product (GDP) per capita, the data would trace out an inverted-U shape.[3] This relationship, illustrated in Figure 13.3, has come to be known as the **Kuznets curve.** In the years since Kuznets wrote, more data have been collected, and his hypothesis has served as a touchstone for research in this area as economists attempt to prove, disprove, or explain the Kuznets curve.

One can look for evidence of a Kuznets curve either by examining the level of inequality in a single country over time or by looking at a single point in time in a cross-section of countries with different levels of income. Figure 13.4 takes the first approach, showing the Gini coefficient in England and Wales from 1823 to 1915. This was a period of rapid industrialization during which income per capita increased by a factor of roughly three. The data show a large rise in inequality during the first half of the period and an even larger decline in the second half, so that by 1915, income was distributed more equally than it had been in 1823. Thus, in these historical data, the Kuznets curve is clearly visible.

Figure 13.5 takes the cross-sectional approach, graphing income per capita on the horizontal axis and the Gini coefficient on the vertical axis.[4] The figure shows many interesting patterns. Many of the most unequal countries are in Latin America. The countries with the lowest levels of inequality are relatively rich countries with well-developed welfare states, such as Sweden and Norway, or else

---

[3] Kuznets (1955).

[4] Data on the Gini coefficient are from the *World Development Indicators* database, for the most recent year available after 2000.

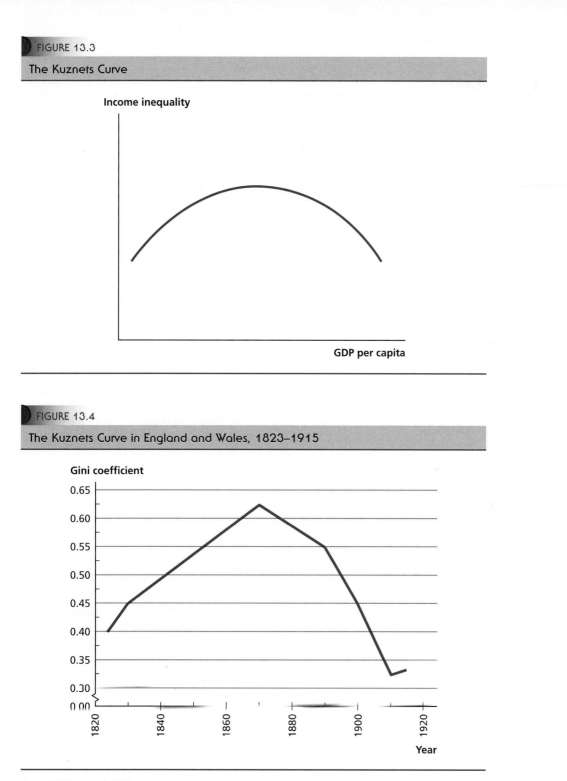

FIGURE 13.3

The Kuznets Curve

FIGURE 13.4

The Kuznets Curve in England and Wales, 1823–1915

Source: Williamson (1985).

369

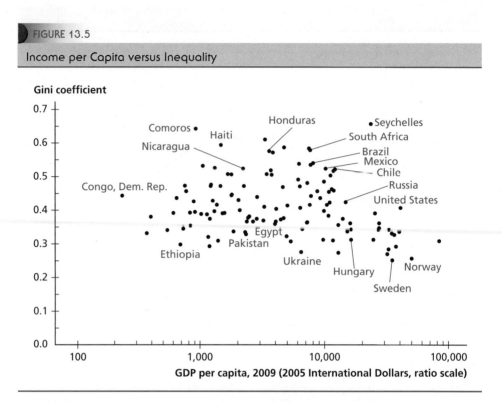

FIGURE 13.5

Income per Capita versus Inequality

Source: World Development Indicators database, Heston et al. (2011).

countries with a recent communist past, such as Hungary and Ukraine. The United States stands out as having an unusually high level of inequality for a rich country.

The data in Figure 13.5 do not provide strong evidence of the inverted-U-shaped relationship between development and income inequality that Kuznets hypothesized. However, using more advanced statistical techniques, a number of researchers believe there is still good evidence for the Kuznets curve. The problem, they argue, is that many other factors, in addition to the level of development, affect a country's level of inequality. Once the analysis accounts for these factors, the Kuznets curve "comes out of hiding," to use the phrase of one researcher. According to a study by the economist Robert Barro, the peak of the Kuznets curve comes at a per-capita income level of $4,815 (in 2000 dollars), corresponding roughly to the income level of Romania in the figure. Barro's estimates imply that a quadrupling of income per capita from the value that is at the peak of the Kuznets curve (as would happen if Romania grew to have the level of income per capita of the United Kingdom) would lead to a reduction of 0.05 in the Gini coefficient.[5]

---

[5]Barro (2000), Table 6, column 2, Higgins and Williamson (1999).

IS GROWTH GOOD FOR THE POOR?

One reason economists care about income inequality is that it is related to poverty: Holding constant the average level of income per capita in a country, a higher degree of income inequality will mean that poor people are worse off. This observation implies that if there *is* a Kuznets curve—that is, if for poor countries, an increase in income per capita also means an increase in inequality—then it is theoretically possible that economic growth can be bad for the poorest people in a country. Specifically, growth's effect of raising the average level of income may be counteracted by a widening of inequality as the poorest people fall farther below the average.

Whether this theoretical possibility corresponds to reality—that is, whether growth may be bad for the poor—is an empirical question. One path to the answer is to look directly at the incomes of the poor. Figure 13.6 shows data on the average income of the poorest quintile (that is, the poorest 20%) of the population, as well as the average level of GDP per capita for the population as a whole, assembled by economists David Dollar and Aart Kraay.* The data come from various years over the period 1956–1999 and cover 137 countries, with an average of three observations for each country.

The data in Figure 13.6 show how average GDP and the degree of inequality work together to determine the income of the poor. For example, Mexico in 1989 and South Korea in 1988 had almost the same level of GDP per capita ($8,883 and $8,948, respectively), but because South Korea's income distribution was so much more equal than Mexico's, the average income of the poorest quintile in South Korea was twice as high as that in Mexico ($3,812 and $1,923, respectively). Similarly, in 1975, Taiwan (another country with a relatively equal distribution of

income) had almost the same level of income of the bottom quintile ($1,925) as did Mexico in 1989, but a much lower level of GDP per capita ($4,854). Points along the upper edge of the mass of data points are countries with relatively egalitarian income distributions—that is, a high level of income of the bottom quintile relative to the income overall. Points along the lower edge of the mass of data points represent countries with an unequal income distribution.

Although the influence of inequality on the income of the poor is apparent in Figure 13.6, the overall impression that the figure gives is that the most important determinant of the incomes of the poor is a country's average level of GDP. Poor people in a rich, unequal country are far better off than poor people in a poor, egalitarian country.

Using these data, Dollar and Kraay examined whether specific policies had different effects on the income of the poor versus overall income. Their key finding was that policies that affect growth for good or ill generally do *not* significantly affect the distribution of income. For example, rule of law and openness to trade raise overall income in a country and have positive but minor effects on the share of income going to the lowest quintile. Similarly, a high rate of inflation and a high level of government consumption are bad for overall income and reduce (but only slightly) the share of income going to the poor.

Another approach to the question of how growth affects the incomes of the poor is to look at individual episodes of economic growth. A recent study examined 88 episodes in which the average level of income per capita in a country grew over the course of a decade. In each case, the authors looked at data on the distribution of income at the beginning and ending points

(*continued*)

IS GROWTH GOOD FOR THE POOR? (CONTINUED)

of the episode. They found that in 77 cases, the income of the poorest fifth of the population also grew. In all but one of the other cases, either growth of average income was very low, or the decline in the income of the poor was temporary and was reversed in subsequent decades. In only one case (Colombia between 1970 and 1980) was there rapid growth of average income (2% per year) while the lowest quintile experienced a reduction in income.[†]

Summarizing the results of these studies, growth is almost always good for the poor, and so are the policies that lead to growth.

[*]Dollar and Kraay (2002).
[†]Deininger and Squire (1996).

FIGURE 13.6

Income per Capita versus Income of the Bottom Quintile

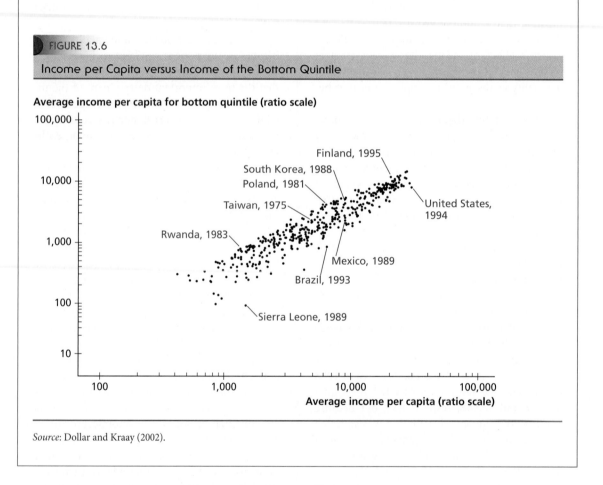

Source: Dollar and Kraay (2002).

13.2 SOURCES OF INCOME INEQUALITY

The previous section looked at the measurement of income inequality and also examined data on how inequality has historically been related to economic growth. We now want to probe more deeply into the sources of income inequality: What are the economic mechanisms that lead it to vary among countries and to change over time? Before answering these questions, however, we need to address a more fundamental issue: Why is there income inequality at all?

The reason income inequality exists is that people in an economy differ from each other in many ways that are relevant to their incomes. Differences occur in human capital (both education and health), in where people live (city versus countryside or different geographical regions of a country), in their ownership of physical capital, in the particular skills they have, and even in their luck. These differences are translated into differences in income by the economic environment. A man may be rich because he has a skill that is in high demand, because his parents gave him money when he was born, or because he just happened to be in the right place when a good job became available. He might be poor because he lives in a part of the country that is economically depressed, because he suffers from a physical ailment that limits his earning, or because he had no access to an education.

In considering the reasons that inequality differs among countries, then, we should think both about the distribution of different economic characteristics among a population and about how different characteristics translate into different levels of income. A country may have a high degree of inequality either because there is great disparity in these characteristics (e.g., some people have a high level of education and some have none at all) or because there is a large effect of differences in some characteristic on the amount of income that a person earns (e.g., people with nine years of education earn much higher wages than people with eight years). Similarly, inequality in a given country could change over time because of a change in the way characteristics are distributed or rewarded.

We can be more concrete about this analysis by limiting ourselves to a single characteristic. Suppose that the only characteristic that determines income is the number of years of education. For simplicity, we assume that the maximum possible number of years of education is four. Panel (a) of Figure 13.7 gives an example of what the distribution of education might look like. The figure shows the fraction of the population in each of the possible educational categories: 15% of the population have zero years of education, 20% have one year of education, and so on.

To get from this distribution of education to a distribution of income, we need to know how education translates into income. A useful concept, introduced in Chapter 6, is that of the *return to education*: the percentage rise in earnings that results from an additional year of education. For the purposes of our example, we use a return to education of 10% per year. Thus, if a worker with no education earns an income of 100, a worker with one year of education will earn 110, a worker with two years of education will earn 121, and so on. This return to education is shown

> FIGURE 13.7

Determination of Income Inequality

(a) Distribution of Education

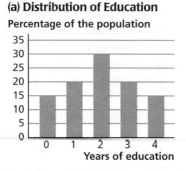

(b) Relationship between Education and Income

(c) Distribution of Income

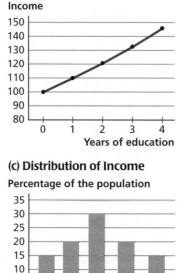

in panel (b) of Figure 13.7, where income is graphed against the number of years of education.

Putting together data on the distribution of education and the return to education, we can derive the distribution of income—that is, the fraction of the population that earns each level of income. For example, the 15% of the population with zero years of education will earn 100, the 20% of the population with one year of education will earn 110, and so on. Panel (c) of Figure 13.7 graphs this distribution.

Using this analysis, we can examine what determines differences in the distribution of income among countries and what causes the distribution of income to change over time within a given country. Differences among countries or changes over time must have their source in either the return to education or the distribution of education.

Figure 13.8 looks at the effect of changing the return to education. The right and left sides of the figure consider two different countries. As shown in panel (a), the two countries have the same distributions of education. But panel (b) shows that the two countries differ in their returns to education—on the left, the return to education is 10%, whereas on the right, it is 5%. Thus, the line representing the relationship between education and income has a steeper slope on the left than on the right. Panel (c) shows that this lower return to education on the right leads to a more tightly compressed distribution of income—that is, a lower level of income inequality. Changing the return to education from 10% to 5% lowers the Gini coefficient from 0.068 to 0.035. (Both of these Gini coefficients are lower than one would observe in real data—but in real data, there is far more variation in the sources of inequality than in this theoretical example.)

Figure 13.9 does a similar analysis of the effect of changing the distribution of education. In this case, the two countries have the same return to education, as shown in panel (b). But as panel (a) indicates, the two countries differ in their distributions of education: The country on the right has a narrower distribution of education—that is, more people in the middle educational groups and fewer people in the lowest and highest educational groups. As panel (c) shows, this narrower distribution of education on the right translates into a narrower distribution of income as well—the Gini coefficient is 0.068 for the data on the left and 0.049 for the data on the right.

In Figures 13.8 and 13.9, we changed only one determinant of inequality at a time. More realistically, however, we would expect that both might change simultaneously, either reinforcing each other or working in opposite directions. For example, in a given country, the distribution of education might become more equal while the return to education rises. In such a case, the total effect on inequality would depend on which force was stronger. Further, once we move beyond this simple model, we must remember that *many* characteristics affect income. Fully accounting for the determination of inequality—why it differs among countries or why it changes over time—would require knowing the distribution of each of these characteristics, as well as the rate of return that it earns in the labor market. Such a full accounting is impossible in practice because many of the characteristics that affect an individual's income are not observable by economists. For example, economists can gather data on people's education and health but not on their persistence, energy, or ambition, even though these latter factors clearly influence income. Despite these difficulties, the framework is useful for understanding the determinants of inequality.

This framework can be used to understand Kuznets's hypothesis that income inequality would first grow and then fall as countries developed. Kuznets reasoned that economic growth—represented by the arrival of new technologies and changes

FIGURE 13.8

How the Return to Education Affects the Distribution of Income

(a) Distribution of Education

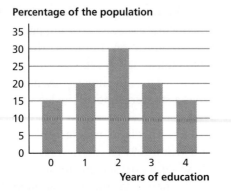

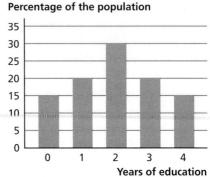

(b) Relationship between Education and Income

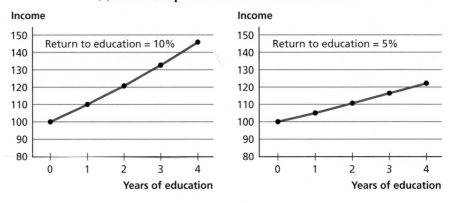

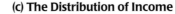

(c) The Distribution of Income

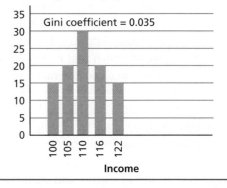

FIGURE 13.9

How the Distribution of Education Affects the Distribution of Income

(a) Distribution of Education

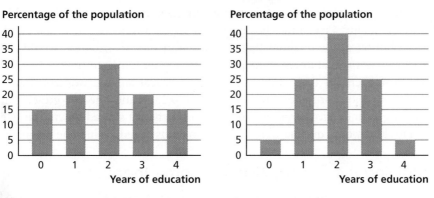

(b) Relationship between Education and Income

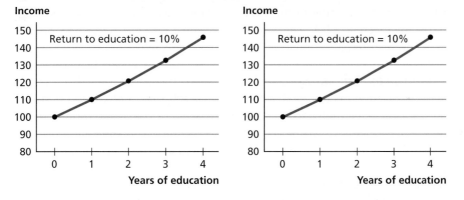

(c) Distribution of Income

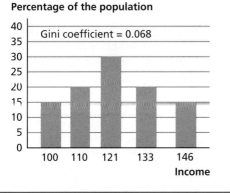

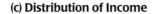

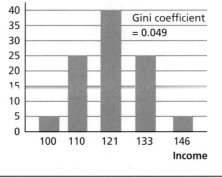

in the structure of the economy—would initially raise the rate of return to skills, such as education and entrepreneurial ability, because skilled workers are better than unskilled workers at adapting to new modes of production. Similarly, new technologies will raise the rate of return to physical capital because technologies are often embodied in new capital goods. Because skills and capital are found at the high end of the income distribution, this increase in the rate of return to them would raise income inequality. Over time, however, new forces would begin to operate. First, the distribution of the qualities that determine income distribution would change over time in a way that lowered inequality. The higher return to skills would induce unskilled workers (or their children) to get an education, and workers would migrate out of regions or sectors that were falling behind and into fast-growing areas. Second, as technological progress and structural change slowed down, the rates of return to skills would decline, a trend that also tends to reduce income inequality.

Explaining the Recent Rise in Income Inequality

Figure 13.10 graphs the Gini coefficient in the United States from 1947 to 2009.[6] As the graph shows, inequality declined slightly in the quarter-century that followed World War II, but starting in the 1970s, income inequality has increased sharply. This rise in inequality has been observed in most other advanced economies as well. Economists have examined several possible explanations.

Technological Advances. In Chapter 9 we discussed the idea that technological progress occurs in discrete waves, each one centered on a so-called general-purpose technology. The most recent general-purpose technology is the semiconductor, which laid the basis for the revolution in information technology. Many economists believe that the coming of age of this technology was the source of the speedup in economic growth in the United States that took place in the second half of the 1990s.

As with other increases in technological progress, information technology increased the rate of return to certain characteristics of workers—most importantly, education. Computers complemented the skills that educated workers already possessed, making such workers more productive, while doing less to raise the productivity of uneducated workers. In 2003, among workers with a high school degree or less education, 35.7% used a computer at work and 21.8% used the Internet. Among workers with a bachelor's degree or more education, the corresponding percentages were 83.8 and 72.9.[7] The new technology also created a fluid situation in which there was a high return to flexibility (to work with a new technology) or entrepreneurial spirit.

---

[6]Weinberg (1996), Jones and Weinberg (2000), DeNavas-Walt, Proctor, and Smith (2010). Data for 1992 and earlier years are adjusted to reflect a change in data collection methodology in 1993.
[7]US Bureau of Labor Statistics, http://www.bls.gov/news.release/ciuaw.nr0.htm. Autor, Katz, and Krueger (1998).

FIGURE 13.10

Income Inequality in the United States: 1947–2009

Sources: Weinberg (1996), Jones and Weinberg (2000), DeNavas-Walt, Proctor, and Smith (2010).

If this explanation for increased inequality is correct, we should expect that at some point the inequality-inducing effects of the current technological revolution will dissipate, and the level of inequality will return to where it stood before the new technology arrived.[8]

Increases in International Trade. As we saw in Chapter 11, trade changes the effective scarcity of different inputs into production. The opening up of trade lowers the rate of return to qualities that are scarce in a given country but plentiful in the world as a whole. Similarly, trade raises the rate of return to qualities that are plentiful in a given country but scarce in the world as a whole. The effect of trade on inequality in a given country depends on how the skills whose returns are affected are distributed in the population. For example, education is more plentiful in a developed country than in the rest of the world, so opening trade will tend to raise the return to education, thus raising inequality. A second effect of trade is to change the payoff from living in different regions of a country. For example, as China opened up to international trade over the last two decades, the economic advantages of coastal provinces

---

[8]Galor and Tsiddon (1997), Caselli (1999).

have increased relative to those in the interior. Because the coastal provinces were already richer, international trade has increased the degree of income inequality.

"Superstar" Dynamic. Observers of the labor market have pointed to the rise of a "superstar" dynamic in many occupations, by which people with the highest levels of some qualities earn much more than people with only slightly lower qualifications. The most obvious example of the superstar phenomenon is in sports, where the best athletes earn enormous premiums over those who are almost as good. A similar dynamic—perhaps driven by the rise of communication technologies that enable a single individual to interact with a broader range of others—has been observed in occupations such as entertainment, law, corporate management, and finance. The superstar system represents a rise in the return to certain qualities and thus increases income inequality.[9]

13.3 EFFECT OF INCOME INEQUALITY ON ECONOMIC GROWTH

Having examined how inequality is measured and what factors affect the level of inequality, we now examine how inequality affects growth. We begin with a theoretical examination of four different channels through which inequality has been hypothesized to affect economic growth, both for good and ill. These four channels are the accumulation of physical capital, the accumulation of human capital, government redistribution policy, and sociopolitical instability. We then consider what light the data shed on the question of inequality's overall effect on growth, as well as on the different theoretical channels that have been suggested.

Effect on the Accumulation of Physical Capital

One channel through which income inequality can have a beneficial effect on economic growth is saving rates. We saw in Chapter 3 that saving, which leads to the accumulation of physical capital, can significantly affect economic growth. A country with a higher saving rate will have a higher steady-state level of income per capita, and a country that raises its saving rate will experience a period of transitional growth as it moves toward a new steady state.

Inequality is related to the saving rate for the simple reason that saving rates tend to rise with income. That is, the higher a person's income is, the higher his or her saving rate is likely to be. The total amount of saving in a country is the sum of saving by people in all different income groups. The more unequal is income—that is, the higher the fraction of total income earned by richer people—the higher will be total saving.

This principle can be demonstrated using data from the United States. Table 13.2 shows the median saving rates of households in different income quintiles. Quintiles

---

[9]Rosen (1981).

TABLE 13.2

Saving Rates by Income Quintile, 2003

Income Quintile	Median Saving Rate (%)
1 (Lowest)	9.0
2	13.5
3	17.2
4	19.2
5 (Highest)	24.4

Source: Dynan, Skinner, and Zeldes (2004), Table 3. Data are for households with heads aged 30–59.

with higher income consistently have higher saving rates. The saving rate for the highest quintile is almost three times the saving rate for the lowest quintile. Using the numbers in Table 13.2, we can gauge the quantitative effect of inequality on saving rates. For example, suppose that we took one dollar of income away from a household in the richest quintile and gave it to a household in the poorest quintile. Such a redistribution of income would reduce the degree of inequality in the country. But because the average saving of the poor out of their income (9.0 cents per dollar) is smaller than the average saving of the rich out of their income (24.4 cents per dollar), the effect of redistributing income would be to reduce total savings by 15.4 cents (that is, 24.4–9.0) for every dollar transferred.

The view that more inequality would lead to a higher level of capital accumulation has been shared by observers from all parts of the political spectrum, ranging from Karl Marx to Ronald Reagan (economics makes for strange bedfellows). John Maynard Keynes, writing of the late 19th and early 20th centuries, argued that income inequality, which put money in the hands of those least likely to spend it on consumption, was an essential, though distasteful, prerequisite for economic growth:

> It was precisely the inequality of the distribution of wealth which made possible those vast accumulations of fixed wealth and of capital improvements which distinguished that age from all others. The immense accumulations of fixed capital which, to the great benefit of mankind, were built up during the half century before the war, could never have come about in a society where wealth was divided equitably.[10]

Effect on the Accumulation of Human Capital

Although a more unequal distribution of income is beneficial for accumulating physical capital, the situation is the opposite in the case of human capital: A more unequal distribution of income leads to lower human capital accumulation. The

---

[10]Keynes (1920).

source of the difference between these two cases goes back to one of the funda-mental differences in the two factors of production. Human capital is "installed" in a specific person; it works only when its owner works, and it cannot be transferred from one person to another. By contrast, a piece of physical capital can be used by different people at different times and can easily be sold by one person to another. As a result, it is fairly easy for one person to own physical capital that is used in production by a different person. For example, a rich woman may own a factory that uses the labor of hundreds of other people. But it is almost impossible for a person to own the human capital that is installed in someone else. Thus, unlike the case for physical capital, the opportunities that any one person has to invest in human capital are limited to the human capital that he can install in himself.

The effect of inequality in the presence of this limitation on human capital investment can be easily seen in a simple example.[11] Consider two people, one rich and one poor. Each person has two types of investment that can be made: in human capital or in physical capital. We assume that at low levels of investment, the marginal product of human capital is very high. But as the quantity of human capital that is invested in any one person increases, its marginal product goes down. By contrast, the marginal product of physical capital that any one investor faces does not depend on the amount that person invests in physical capital because any single person's investment is minuscule in relation to the national level of capital.

The relationship between the quantities that an individual invests in human and physical capital and the marginal products earned by these investments is shown in Figure 13.11. The horizontal axis measures the quantity invested in each form of capital. Because the marginal product of human capital declines with the quantity that an individual invests, the line representing the marginal product of human capital is downward sloping. The line representing the marginal product of physical capital is horizontal. The level of investment at which the two curves cross is labeled I^*. If a person invests less than I^* in human capital, the marginal product of human capital will be higher than the marginal product of physical capital. If a person invests more than I^* in human capital, then the marginal product of human capital will be less than for physical capital.

As Figure 13.11 makes clear, if a person has only a little money, he or she will invest in human capital rather than in physical capital because it is always better to invest in the form of capital with the highest marginal product. But people with a lot of money to invest will invest their marginal dollars in physical capital. More specifically, if a person has less than I^* available to invest, he or she will invest it all in human capital. If he or she has more than I^* to invest, then he or she will invest I^* in human capital and the rest of his or her money in physical capital.

Before going on, we can check whether this story is consistent with the data. One of the implications of this story is that human capital will be distributed much

---

[11]Galor and Zeira (1993).

FIGURE 13.11

Marginal Products of Physical and Human Capital

Quantity invested by one person

more equally than physical capital. The reason is that many poorer people will do all of their investment in the form of human capital and therefore will own no physical capital, whereas many wealthy people will hold almost all of their wealth in the form of physical capital. This prediction is indeed borne out by the data. Recall the definition of the Gini coefficient, which measures the degree of income inequality in a country, with 0 corresponding to perfect equality and 1 to the highest possible degree of inequality. Gini coefficients can also be used to measure the degree of inequality in the ownership of specific assets such as physical capital and human capital. In the United States, the Gini coefficient is 0.78 for physical capital and 0.14 for years of education.[12] Thus, ownership of physical capital is indeed more unequal than that of human capital.

How does inequality affect the accumulation of human capital? Let's consider two people, one with more than I^* available to invest, and the other with less than I^*. The person with less than I^* will invest all of the wealth in human capital; the person with more than I^* will invest I^* in human capital and the rest of the wealth in physical capital. Notice that the marginal product of the last dollar invested by the poor person is higher than the marginal product of the last dollar invested by

---

[12]Thomas, Wang, and Fan (2000), Diaz-Giménez, Quadrini, and Ríos-Rull (1997). Data for education apply to 1990, and those for wealth apply to 1992.

the rich person. If income is redistributed from the rich person to the poor person, two things will happen. First, human capital accumulation will rise because the poor person will invest extra money in human capital, whereas the rich person will reduce investment in physical capital. Second, total output will go up because the marginal product of human capital being invested in by the poor person is higher than the marginal product of physical capital that the rich person invests in.

The different effects of inequality on physical and human capital accumulation—beneficial in the case of physical capital and harmful in the case of human capital—suggest that inequality may have different effects on the pace of economic growth at different stages of growth. As Keynes's quotation suggests, the driving force of 19th-century economic growth was the accumulation of physical capital. For example, many of the new technologies of this period were oriented toward the more effective use of physical capital—that is, building better machines. Thus, in this period, inequality may have contributed to economic growth. However, as discussed in Chapter 6, economic growth in the last several decades, at least among the most developed countries, has been driven by the accumulation of human capital rather than physical capital. In this circumstance, inequality is detrimental to growth.[13]

For developing countries, openness to international capital flows (as discussed in Chapter 11) also will influence how inequality affects factor accumulation. If a country is open to flows of physical capital, then the beneficial effects of inequality on the saving rate will no longer be relevant because investment does not have to be financed out of domestic savings. On the other hand, the negative effects of inequality on human capital investment will remain. Thus, the level of inequality that maximizes factor accumulation will be lower in a country open to capital flows than in one that is closed to capital flows.

Income Inequality, Income Redistribution, and Efficiency

The preceding two channels through which income inequality may affect growth involve mechanisms by which a country's level of income inequality can affect the accumulation of factors of production, specifically physical and human capital. As we have seen in previous chapters, differences in the accumulation of factors of production are not the only source of differences in income among countries. Rather, differences in the productivity with which these factors of production are used play an equally important role in explaining income differences among countries. We now turn to the question of how inequality may affect a country's productivity. Recall from Chapter 10 our division of productivity into two parts: one representing the available technology for combining factors of production, and the other representing the efficiency with which available technology and factors were used. In this section and the next, we examine how income inequality can reduce the efficiency of an economy.

---

[13]Galor and Moav (2004).

The first way in which inequality can affect the efficiency of production is through the channel of income redistribution, the process by which governments take money away from those with high income and give it to those with low income. When incomes are unequal, governments face pressure to redistribute income. Governments accomplish this goal through taxation. But as we saw in the last chapter,, taxation leads to inefficiency. So by raising the likelihood that the government will want to use taxes to redistribute income, inequality can indirectly lower the level of efficiency, and thus output.

To examine this relationship between inequality and efficiency in detail, we consider a simple model of the process of income redistribution.[14] To keep our model tractable, we assume that the income redistribution is the *only* thing the government does—that is, we ignore other government functions such as the provision of public goods. We assume that redistribution takes the following form. First, the government taxes all workers at the same *rate*. That is, all workers pay the same fraction of their income as taxes, so workers with high incomes pay more taxes than those with low income. Second, the government takes the revenue that it collects from this tax and pays it back to workers in equal *amounts*. This sort of payment is known as a **lump-sum transfer.** In real life, governments not only redistribute money but also provide services. However, because many of these services, including education and health care, would otherwise be paid for by households themselves, their provision by the government has an effect similar to distributing cash payments.

Taxes and transfers are important because they affect workers' incomes. A worker's **pretax income** is the income that he or she earns before any taxes are collected. A worker's **disposable income** is his or her pretax income minus the taxes paid and plus the transfer that he or she receives from the government. The difference between a worker's pretax income and disposable income will depend on where in the income distribution he or she falls. Because we are assuming that the government uses all of its revenues to make lump-sum transfers, the size of the lump-sum transfer each worker receives will equal the mean amount of taxes collected per worker, which in turn will equal the tax rate times the mean of pretax income. Thus, a worker who had pretax income exactly equal to the mean pretax income would receive a lump-sum transfer exactly equal to what was paid in taxes. A worker who had pretax income below the mean would receive a lump-sum transfer larger than what he or she paid in taxes, and a worker who had pretax income above the mean would receive a transfer smaller than what he or she paid in taxes.

Because taxes serve to redistribute income from high income to low income workers, the distribution of disposable income will be more equal than the distribution of pretax income. Further, we can use the tax rate (i.e., the fraction of pretax income collected by the government) as a measure of the degree of redistribution. If

---

[14]The approach here is based on Alesina and Rodrik (1994) and Persson and Tabellini (1994).

the government collects only a small percentage of pretax income and redistributes it, then disposable income will be almost as unequally distributed as pretax income. If the government collects a large fraction of pretax income and redistributes it, then disposable income will be distributed much more equally than pretax income.

Now let's consider the relationship between taxes and productivity. When taxes are high, taxpayers have an incentive to avoid paying them, either legally or illegally. But avoidance entails nonproductive activities, ranging from a firm's keeping two sets of books (an illegal means of evading taxes) to a person's staying home rather than working (a legal means of tax avoidance). As a result, taxes will lower efficiency and so will lower pretax income for all workers. Further, as shown in Chapter 12, the effect of taxes on productivity grows larger as the tax rate rises. When taxes are low, the decrease in efficiency that results from an increase in taxes is relatively small; when taxes are high, the marginal loss of efficiency from a further increase in taxes is large.

We can now examine how much redistribution different workers would prefer. Consider first a worker with pretax income above the mean level in the country. This worker will be made worse off by redistribution for two reasons. First, he or she will receive less back in the form of a lump-sum transfer than he or she paid in taxes. Second, the reduction in economic efficiency resulting from redistributive taxation will also lower the worker's pretax income. Thus, a worker with pretax income above the mean will favor a tax rate of zero.

In the case of a worker with pretax income exactly equal to the mean, only one of the two effects previously described is operative. This worker receives a lump-sum transfer exactly equal to his or her tax payment, so in this sense he or she is not hurt by redistribution. But the negative effect of redistributive taxes on efficiency, and thus on pretax income, nonetheless makes him or her worse off. Therefore, this worker also will be against redistribution.

For a worker who earns *less* than the mean pretax income, the two effects of a tax work in opposite directions. The lump-sum payment he or she will receive from the government will be larger than taxes, so his or her disposable income rises. However, the inefficiency resulting from high taxes lowers his or her pretax income, making him or her worse off. Thus, a worker with income below the mean faces a trade-off between the benefits that he or she gets from redistribution and the costs of inefficiency as a result of taxation. The level of taxation (and thus redistribution) that maximizes such a worker's disposable income will depend on how far below the mean his or her level of pretax income is. The farther below the mean the pretax income, the more important to him or her is redistribution, the less harmful is reduced pretax income, and the higher the level of taxation he or she will prefer. A worker who had zero pretax income—that is, one whose disposable income consisted solely of the lump-sum transfer he or she received—would prefer a tax rate that maximized total government revenue and thus the size of the per-person transfer.

To summarize this discussion graphically, Figure 13.12 illustrates the relationship between a worker's desired tax rate and his or her level of pretax income. All

FIGURE 13.12

Relationship between Income Inequality and the Desired Tax Rate

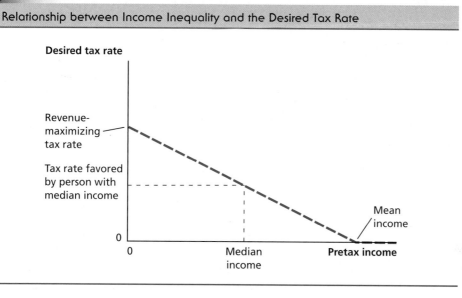

workers with pretax income greater than or equal to the mean will want a tax rate of zero. Workers with pretax income below the mean will want a positive tax rate. This desired tax rate will be higher for workers with lower pretax income.

Using our analysis of desired rates of taxation (and thus redistribution), we can address the question of how actual rates of taxation are determined. The answer is that the determination of tax rates is a political process. To analyze this process, we can think about a simplified version of politics. Suppose that each person has one vote and that the only issue over which there is voting is whether to raise or lower the tax rate. In this situation, the tax rate is easy to calculate: It will be the rate that is optimal for the voter with the *median* level of pretax income. The logic is simple. We have already established that people with higher pretax incomes will favor lower tax rates and that everyone at or above the mean level of pretax income will favor a tax rate of zero. If the tax rate is higher than the level favored by the voter with median pretax income, then he or she would be in favor of lowering the tax rate, as would everyone with pretax income higher than his or hers. By definition, half the population has pretax income above the median level. If all these people, as well as the person with median income, favor lowering the tax rate, then a majority will support lowering taxes. Similarly, if the tax rate is lower than the level favored by the person with median pretax income, then a majority will favor raising the tax rate. Thus, the tax rate chosen will be the one preferred by the person with the median level of pretax income, who is often referred to as the **median voter.**

Figure 13.12 shows the median level of pretax income and the tax rate favored by the worker with that level of pretax income. Notice that the median level of

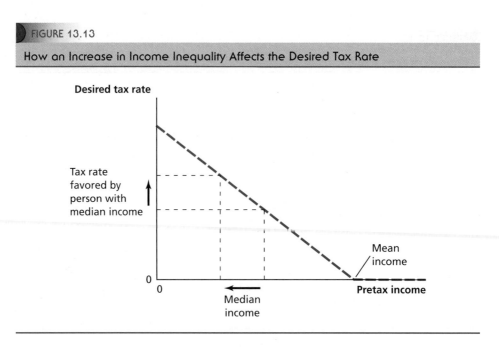

FIGURE 13.13

How an Increase in Income Inequality Affects the Desired Tax Rate

pretax income is below the mean level of pretax income, in accordance with the fact mentioned in Section 13.1 that median income is *always* (at least in all of the countries for which we have data) below the mean. Thus, the tax rate selected by the median voter will be above zero.

Finally, we can analyze the effect of income distribution on the level of taxes, and thus the effect on efficiency. Consider what happens when the distribution of pretax income changes, holding constant the mean of income. Suppose, for example, that income becomes more unequal. The wider the distribution of income is, the farther will the median level of pretax income be below the mean. Put another way: If two countries have the same average pretax income, then the median level of pretax income will be lower in the country with a more unequal distribution of income. As Figure 13.13 shows, when median pretax income falls, the rate of taxation favored by the median voter rises. Higher inequality leads to more redistribution and more taxation—and, for the reasons discussed in Chapter 12, a lower level of efficiency. Through this channel, inequality lowers the average level of income.

Sociopolitical Unrest in Response to Income Inequality

The model of redistribution through taxation just presented took a simplistic view of the political process: More inequality results in more demand for redistribution, so more redistribution takes place. A more realistic view of the political process would acknowledge that decisions are not necessarily made by simple majority voting, either in formal democracies (where, despite the rule of "one person, one vote," wealthier classes exert political power beyond their numbers) or in non-democratic countries. Given this observation, we might revise our conclusion to say that countries with a more unequal distribution of income might have more *pressure* for redistribution but not necessarily more actual redistribution.

The pressure for redistribution is expressed in several ways, all of them slowing growth. One expression is through political instability because different groups compete for power. Unstable political situations discourage investment, as occurs when, for example, people who build factories worry that their property might be confiscated following some potential future revolution or other change in government.

A second expression of the pressure for redistribution is crime. Property crime is often the attempt by poor people to redistribute resources through channels other than the political system. Other forms of social unrest that can be motivated by severe inequality, such as rioting, also lead to the destruction of property, even if they do not result in a redistribution of income. Crime not only wastes the time and the energy of criminals themselves, it also wastes the resources of those who have to spend money preventing it. In *The Wealth of Nations* (1776), Adam Smith wrote of societies with a high degree of inequality that "civil government, so far as it is instituted for the security of property, is in reality, instituted for the defence of the rich against the poor, or of those who have some property against those who have none at all." By this logic, greater inequality requires a larger government—and, thus, reduced economic efficiency—simply to secure the property rights of the rich.

The history of Latin America in the 20th century provides endless examples of the growth-decreasing effects of political instability rooted in economic inequality. Most recently in Venezuela, conflict between leftist president Hugo Chavez and a coalition led by business leaders produced a general strike that shut down large parts of the country's economy in late 2002 and early 2003.

Empirical Evidence

In this section we've surveyed one channel whereby inequality may increase growth and three channels by which it may slow growth. A natural question is: Which of these effects dominate? Does inequality raise or lower growth?

Unfortunately, available statistical data are unable to answer this question. Although some economists claim to find evidence that inequality is on average bad for growth, others claim the data point in the opposite direction. One of the obstacles to getting a clear answer is that inequality itself is difficult to measure. Thus, we cannot say that inequality has *no* effect on growth, only that the data are not yet sufficient to tell us what the possible effect is.[15]

One reason it is hard to tease out the effect of income inequality on economic growth is that the effect may depend on a country's stage of growth, as well as

---

[15]Barro (2000), Forbes (2000).

other factors such as whether a country is open to capital flows from abroad. In a country where growth is driven by physical capital accumulation, income inequality will be more conducive to growth than in a country where growth is driven by human capital accumulation. Similarly, in a country open to flows of physical capital from abroad, income inequality will be less conducive to growth than in a country that is closed to capital flows.

Economists have been more successful in examining the individual channels, just explored, by which inequality might affect growth. Their efforts do not measure inequality's overall effect on growth but do provide evidence on which of the channels are likely to be important. Among their findings:

- In countries where income inequality is higher, the accumulation of human capital through education is lower. This finding matches the theoretical prediction discussed in this section. A related finding is that in countries where income inequality is higher, the total fertility rate is higher. This is another channel through which income inequality is bad for growth (as we saw in Chapter 4, high fertility slows growth).

- To test the theory that income inequality leads to sociopolitical unrest, economists have constructed an index of sociopolitical instability. The index records perceptions of how likely it is that the government will be overthrown by unconstitutional or violent means, such as terrorism, and also captures the occurrence of riots and violent demonstrations. The smaller the value of this index, the less the degree of instability in the country. Figure 13.14 graphs this index of sociopolitical instability on the vertical axis, against the Gini coefficient, measured along the horizontal axis. The figure shows that, in contrast to the theoretical channel discussed in this section, there is no statistical tendency for countries with less equal income distributions to have higher degrees of instability.

- In contradiction to the discussion of taxation and redistribution presented in this section, there is no evidence that higher income inequality leads to a higher level of redistributive taxation. Indeed, countries with higher inequality tend to have *lower* taxes than countries where income inequality is low.[16] One explanation is that where income inequality is high, political power is firmly controlled by the wealthy, who are able to block redistribution.

As an alternative to these statistical analyses, some economists have looked at the historical evidence on economic growth to learn about the effects of inequality. The clearest case of the importance of inequality in affecting economic growth is the contrast between the history of Latin America and that of the United States and Canada.

---

[16]Perotti (1996).

> FIGURE 13.14

Relationship between Income Inequality and Sociopolitical Instability

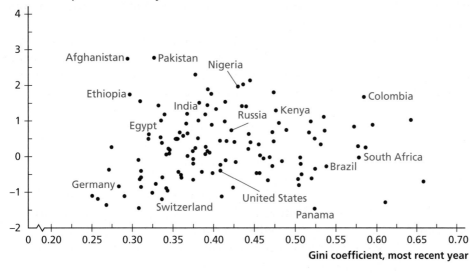

Sources: Kaufmann, Kraay, and Mastruzzi (2010), Heston et al. (2011).

The inequality gap between the two regions can be traced back to their colonization by Europeans starting in the 16th century. Many Latin American colonies quickly specialized in the cultivation of sugar, coffee, and other exportable crops. Production for export led to the organization of agriculture into large plantations and resulted in an extremely unequal distribution of income—a phenomenon exacerbated by the use of slaves. In other parts of Latin America, notably Peru and Mexico, rich mineral resources and Europeans' ability to exploit dense native populations led to the formation of large estates.

By contrast, the colonies that would eventually become the United States and Canada were neither able to grow highly prized commodities like sugar nor were endowed with valuable minerals or dense native populations that could be effectively harnessed. As a result, the northern colonies were economically far more marginal than their neighbors to the south. For evidence of just how economically marginal they were, consider that following the Seven Years' War (1756–1763), the victorious British actively debated which of two territories they should take from the defeated French as reparations: the Caribbean island of Guadeloupe or Canada.

The majority of labor in the colonies that would become the United States and Canada was supplied by voluntary European immigrants and their descendants, as opposed to slaves and American Indians. The relatively homogeneous population of these regions, and the absence of plantation-style agricultural production for export, led to an economy based on small family farms, resulting in a relatively equal distribution of income. The U.S. South, growing export crops such as rice, tobacco, and cotton and using slave labor, was closer to the Latin American model. But even in the South, the use of slaves and the level of income inequality were more modest than in the sugar-growing regions.

The patterns of relative inequality in North and South America persisted long after the end of the economic bases for their initial differences in inequality (i.e., slavery, the primacy of coffee and sugar as export crops, and so on). Indeed, they endure today: Many of the most unequal countries in the world are in Latin America. An underlying factor in this persistence is the extent to which inequality was built into the political institutions in Latin America. The region lagged far behind the United States and Canada in the fraction of the population that was eligible to vote, as well as in democratic innovations such as the secret ballot. The institutional structure in Latin America placed power in the hands of a small elite that was able to extract resources from the majority of the population. In the United States and Canada, political institutions restricted the power of government, protected private property, and assured the rule of law.

One of the most important effects of inequality was on investment in human capital. The United States and Canada were leaders in the public provision of education. In contrast, the elites that governed the highly unequal countries of Latin America had little interest in supporting schooling. They would gain little economically from it, and they feared that a more educated population might want a larger share of political power. By 1870, both Canada and the United States had reached 80% literacy, a level that the rest of the Americas would not reach for 75 years.

The failures to invest in human capital and to construct institutions of the type conducive to economic growth, along with the instability that resulted from conflict over income distribution, were among the major contributors to Latin America's failure to keep up with the United States and Canada. Across the span of centuries, it is easy to see the negative effect of income inequality on growth. Unfortunately, it is also clear from this history just how persistent inequality can be.[17]

13.4 BEYOND INCOME DISTRIBUTION: ECONOMIC MOBILITY

Analysis of a distribution of income (e.g., as depicted in Figure 13.1) reveals how the residents of a country compare at a single point in time. But these are not the only important data pertinent to inequality. A second key aspect of inequality is **economic mobility**: the movement of people from one part of the income distribution to another.

---

[17]Engerman and Sokoloff (2002).

To see the importance of economic mobility, let us consider two countries that have the same distributions of income but different levels of mobility. In one country, people are constantly shifting from one part of the income distribution to another, whereas in the second country, people always remain at the same position in the income distribution. Clearly, the first country—with higher mobility—has greater equality in an important sense, even though an economist looking only at the Gini coefficients in the two countries would not observe this.

Economic mobility can be measured on many different time horizons. For example, we might be interested in year-to-year or decade-to-decade movements of individuals through the income distribution. Economists frequently examine **intergenerational mobility** (i.e., the change in the economic status of families from one generation to the next). Intergenerational mobility is often described as "equality of opportunity." A high degree of intergenerational mobility means that the children of poor parents have the same prospects—that is, the same probability of being rich or poor—as do the children of wealthy parents. Where intergenerational mobility is low, children are likely to be in the same part of the income distribution as their parents.

One way to study mobility is to look at a **transition matrix,** a table showing the probabilities that individuals will move from one income group to another. Table 13.3 is an example of a transition matrix using data on families in the United States. The rows of the matrix consider different income groups of the parents. The top row represents the parents in the lowest quintile of the income distribution, the second row represents parents in the second quintile, and so on. Within each row, the columns are the probability that children of these families were found in specific quintiles when they were adults. For example, there is 6% probability that a person whose parents were in the lowest income quintile will be in the highest income quintile.

The entries along the diagonal of the transition matrix indicate the probability that a child will end up in the same income quintile as his or her parents. These

TABLE 13.3

Intergenerational Income Mobility in the United States

	Children's Income Quintile				
Parents' Income Quintile	1st (bottom)	2nd	3rd	4th	5th (top)
1st (bottom)	0.42	0.23	0.19	0.11	0.06
2nd	0.25	0.23	0.24	0.18	0.10
3rd	0.17	0.24	0.23	0.17	0.19
4th	0.08	0.15	0.19	0.32	0.26
5th (top)	0.09	0.15	0.14	0.23	0.39

Source: Isaacs (2011a).

entries tend to be large. But these data also indicate a fair degree of mobility: For example a person whose parents were in the middle income quintile has a 17% chance of ending up in the bottom quintile and a 19% change of ending up in the top quintile.

Measuring mobility is much more difficult than measuring inequality, because it requires being able to track families over a long period of time. For that reason, we know much less about how mobility compares among countries than we do about comparisons of inequality. One study that put together consistent estimates for nine countries found the lowest mobility in the United States and United Kingdom, mid-range mobility in France, Germany, and Sweden, and the highest mobility in Canada, Finland, Norway, and Denmark.[18]

Unfortunately, detailed data on mobility are not available for enough countries to allow for a statistical analysis of how mobility is related to a country's level of income per capita or its rate of economic growth. However, economists have several theories about how mobility affects a country's rate of growth and how economic mobility itself is determined.

As with income inequality, there are several possible channels through which mobility might affect economic growth. First, a society with a high degree of mobility is likely to be more able to use the talents of all of its citizens. The talents that can contribute to economic growth may arise in people born into any part of the income distribution. A society in which anyone can grow up to be the president or a scientist or a corporate CEO will have more gifted presidents, scientists, and corporate CEOs than a society in which access to these careers is limited to members of a small class.

A second channel through which mobility affects economic growth is the political sphere. Recall our finding that a higher degree of income inequality leads to greater pressure for income redistribution, so that in more unequal societies, there is either more redistribution (with the accompanying inefficiency of higher taxes) or more social conflict over redistribution (with accompanying instability, which also is bad for growth). The degree of economic mobility can moderate the desire for income redistribution. A person in the bottom of the income distribution who knows that his or her children have a good chance of moving up in the world will have much less interest in income redistribution than a poor person who knows that his or her children will also remain in the bottom of the income distribution. In this way, income mobility contributes to a reduction in class strife. Indeed, one theory for why the United States has had much less class-oriented politics than the developed countries in Western Europe is that Americans *perceive* class mobility to be higher than do Europeans, even if this does not match reality.[19] In a survey of 27 countries regarding perceptions of mobility and inequality, the United States ranked highest in fraction of the

---

[18]Corak (2006).
[19]Benabou and Ok (2001).

population that agreed with the statement "People get rewarded for their intelligence and skills" and just below the highest in the percentage who agreed with the statement "people get rewarded for their effort." These statements indicate that Americans believe that family background is not an important determinant of an individual's success in life. The United States also ranked last in the fraction of the population that agreed with the statement "it is the responsibility of the government to reduce the differences in income."[20]

As to the determinants of mobility, the most important influence is probably access to education. Education opens a path to upward movement in the income distribution for the children of the poor. In countries with generous public education systems, such transitions are more likely. Similarly, public health policies and broad access to medical care will make it less likely that the children of the poor will be stunted physically or mentally by ill health, raising the degree of economic mobility.

A second determinant of economic mobility is the nature of a country's institutions and government. As we saw in examining the influences of technology and trade, growing countries can undergo wrenching changes. New technologies can economically harm whole regions or whole sectors of the economy. Powerful interest groups attempt to block these changes, and they often succeed. If new technologies or openness to trade are blocked, specific groups benefit, but economic growth often suffers. This same ability of interest groups to block technology and trade also limits economic mobility. By definition, economic mobility means that people at the top of the income distribution are being replaced by others who were formerly lower down in the distribution. Thus, the most powerful people in society often oppose policies that raise the degree of mobility. The larger is the degree to which the rich control economic policy, the less likely are mobility-enhancing policies to be implemented.

A third determinant of economic mobility is the nature of marriages in a country. When people marry those of their own economic and social class—a phenomenon known as **assortative mating**—economic mobility tends to be impeded. To the extent that people marry for other than economic reasons—that is, for love—there will naturally be more mixing of classes. In a marriage involving two classes, a certain amount of intergenerational mobility is guaranteed because a child of that marriage cannot be in the same class as both parents were. Recent research shows that the degree of assortative mating varies significantly among countries. The researchers measured husbands' and wives' social class by looking at their education levels—not a perfect measure but the best one available. They found that the correlation between the education of husbands and wives is twice as great in Colombia and Ecuador (the countries where assortative mating is most

---

[20]Isaacs (2011b)

prevalent) as in Australia and Israel (the countries where it is least prevalent.) One determinant of the propensity to marry across class lines is the level of inequality in a country. Evidently, it is easier for a rich person to "marry down"—that is, to marry someone from a lower-income group—in a country where the income gap between the groups is not too large.[21]

Finally, racial or ethnic discrimination will also lower economic mobility. The children of those in discriminated-against groups will be similarly discriminated against.

13.5 CONCLUSION

In the Preface to *Democracy in America* (1835), French aristocrat Alexis de Tocqueville wrote that "among the novel objects that attracted my attention during my stay in the United States, nothing struck me more forcibly than the general equality of condition among the people.... The more I advanced in the study of American society, the more I perceived that this equality of condition is the fundamental fact from which all others seem to be derived and the central point at which all my observations constantly terminated." The benefits that Tocqueville perceived as arising from equality included improvements in morality and marital fidelity, a belief on the part of the whole population in the possibilities of self-improvement, and the encouragement of democracy.

In our analysis in this chapter, we have taken a much narrower view of the effects of income inequality than what Tocqueville would have found appropriate. We have asked what economic factors influence the level of inequality and have examined how inequality affects the determination of the average level of income per capita. This is not to say that the effects of equality that Tocqueville saw are unimportant—only that economics currently lacks the tools to comprehend them.

We have also avoided addressing other important aspects of income distribution: whether equality of income is a good thing in and of itself, and what price is worth paying to achieve it. For example, suppose that we concluded that reducing the level of inequality in a country by a specific amount—say, a reduction in the Gini coefficient from 0.54 (the level in Brazil) to 0.25 (the level in Sweden)—could be achieved only at a given cost—say, a reduction in the average level of GDP per capita by 20%. Would such a trade-off be worth making? This is the sort of question that politicians and policy makers wrestle with all the time. Yet economists have found it difficult to develop tools to answer this question.

---

[21]Fernandez, Guner, and Knowles (2005).

KEY TERMS

distribution of
  income   363
mode   365
mean   365
median   365
skewed distribution   365

Gini coefficient   365
Lorenz curve   367
Kuznets curve   368
lump-sum transfer   385
pretax income   385
disposable income   385

median voter   387
economic mobility   392
intergenerational
  mobility   393
transition matrix   393
assortative mating   395

QUESTIONS FOR REVIEW

1. How are poverty and inequality related?

2. How is the Gini coefficient constructed? What values of the Gini coefficient correspond to perfect equality and perfect inequality?

3. How do the distribution of characteristics and the return to characteristics interact to determine the level of income inequality in a country?

4. What are some possible explanations for the rise in income inequality in the United States over the last three decades?

5. How does income inequality affect the accumulation of physical and human capital?

6. How does income inequality affect the efficiency of production?

7. What does the history of the Americas tell us about the sources of inequality and inequality's effect on economic growth?

8. What is economic mobility? How is it related to income inequality?

PROBLEMS

1. In a certain country, the population consists of five blue people and five green people. Each green person has an income of $1 per year. Each blue person has an income of $3 per year.

    a. Draw the Lorenz curve for this country.

    b. On your diagram from part a, indicate clearly what area you would divide by what other area to calculate the Gini coefficient.

    c. [Difficult] Calculate the Gini coefficient. [Hint: The area of a triangle is equal to one-half base times height.]

2. Many companies are working to perfect "distance learning" technology, by which a single professor can teach students at dozens or even hundreds of colleges and universities.

Using the framework of Section 13.2, explain how such a technological change would affect the distribution of income among professors.

3. How would the availability of student loans to finance education influence the relationship between inequality and the accumulation of factors of production? In particular, how would student loans affect the level of inequality that maximizes factor accumulation?

4. What is the relationship between a poor person's perception of economic mobility and his or her desire to see a high level of redistributive taxation? How would the degree of redistributive taxation compare in two countries that had the same distribution of income but different levels of economic mobility?

5. The table below shows the probability that a mother in a given part of the income distribution (given by the row) will have a daughter in a given part of the income distribution (given by the column). So, for example, the daughter of a woman with income in the bottom third of the income distribution will herself have a 60% chance of being in the bottom third, a 25% chance of being in the middle third, and a 15% chance of being in the top third.

What is the probability that the *granddaughter* (along the maternal line) of a woman in the middle third of the income distribution will herself be in the middle third of the income distribution? Show how you got your answer.

| | Income Group of Daughter | | |
Income Group of Mother	Bottom Third	Middle Third	Top Third
Bottom third	0.6	0.25	0.15
Middle third	0.25	0.5	0.25
Top third	0.15	0.25	0.6

For additional exploration and practice using the Online Data Plotter and data sets, please visit www.pearsonhighered.com/weil.

CULTURE

From our day-to-day experience, most of us would agree that a person's attitudes are an important determinant of economic success. People who work hard and plan for the future are more likely to succeed than those who are lazy or take a passive attitude. This is not to say that attitudes are the *only* determinant of economic success. A lazy person may be born rich or be so talented that he or she can succeed without working hard. But attitudes certainly have a large effect.

If we learn anything from the history of economic development, it is that culture makes all the difference.

—David Landes, The Wealth and Poverty of Nations

If differences in attitude can be important for individual success, a natural question is whether they can also be important for the success of a country as a whole. Is it possible that differences among countries in **culture**—the values, attitudes, and beliefs prevalent in a society—are partially responsible for differences in economic outcomes?

The idea that culture is a determinant of national wealth is an old one. Sociologist Max Weber (1864–1920) argued that the rise of a "Protestant ethic," which celebrated hard work and the acquisition of wealth, led to an explosion of economic growth in northern Europe starting in the 16th century. More recently, scholars have debated whether the rapid growth of such countries as Taiwan, Singapore, and South Korea can be explained by their adherence to "Asian values," a term coined by *The Economist* magazine in 1980.

Despite these examples, however, economists have generally been reluctant to apply themselves to culture, a topic that is more familiar to anthropologists, sociologists, and historians. Culture makes economists uncomfortable because it is difficult to quantify, depriving economists of the mathematical tools with which they are most familiar. For many of the more "economic" characteristics we have examined in other chapters (physical capital, human capital, and so on), we have widely accepted measurements and sources of data. In contrast, there is no single set of data that summarizes cultural differences among countries—for some aspects of culture, there are no formal data at all. Further, discussions of culture run the risk of offending because they may seem to imply that some cultures are good and others are bad (a point we return to in the conclusion to this chapter). Despite these difficulties, we shall see in this chapter that there is enough evidence that culture *does* affect economic growth and that it cannot be ignored.

We begin our excursion into culture by examining its different aspects and their economic effects. We then turn to the question of what determines culture. We examine both noneconomic factors that affect culture and also how culture is altered by economic growth. The fact that growth affects culture is especially important. It raises the possibility that the association between particular cultural attributes and the level of income per capita may involve income affecting culture, rather than vice versa. We also address the question of whether some cultural attributes are good for growth in some circumstances and bad for growth in others.

14.1 THE EFFECT OF CULTURE ON ECONOMIC GROWTH

To demonstrate that culture is important for economic growth, we have to show first that culture has potentially important aspects that vary among countries and second, that these aspects of culture significantly affect economic outcomes. Neither of these tasks is easy because culture is so hard to measure. Not only does culture have many different dimensions, but even when we restrict ourselves to a single aspect of culture, we often lack any objective (much less quantitative) measure and have to rely on the observers' subjective assessments. Similarly, in some cases there is direct evidence of culture's economic effects, whereas in other cases such effects can only be inferred. Compounding these challenges, because measures are necessarily so subjective, the way an observer assesses a culture may be affected by what he or she knows of the economic success of the country being examined.

This section of the chapter comprises six subsections. The first four look at individual aspects of culture: openness to new ideas, belief in the value of hard work, saving for the future, and the degree to which people trust one another. The last two subsections consider broader characterizations of culture, one called *social capital* and the other called *social capability*.

Openness to New Ideas

Scholars who have examined the historical process of economic growth have often stressed the importance of a society's openness to importing new ideas from abroad. We saw in our discussion of technology that many of the technologies used in any particular country were invented in other countries, so a country that more readily adopted technologies from abroad would be more technologically advanced. History is full of institutions—as diverse as the Roman Catholic Church in Europe before the Protestant Reformation and the former Soviet Union—that felt threatened by new ideas and did their best to suppress them. Indeed, cultures that are genuinely open to new ideas are a historical rarity.

Scholars often view countries' differences in willingness to adopt foreign technology as part of the explanation for a great mystery in the history of economic growth: the divergence between Europe and China. In their dealings with the wider world, Europeans showed a great willingness to copy the best that other countries had to offer. Inventions from the rest of the world, such as paper and gunpowder from China itself, were eagerly adopted by Europeans and played a crucial role in Europe's economic ascent. China, by contrast, took a disdainful attitude toward the rest of the world. Contacts with foreigners were treated as opportunities to display the superiority of Chinese culture. The European outlook is exemplified by German mathematician Gottfried Leibniz's instructions to a European traveler going to China "not to worry so much about getting things European to the Chinese, but rather about getting remarkable Chinese inventions to us." Contrast this view with the haughty letter that the Chinese emperor Qian Long sent to King George III, turning down the British request to open a trade mission in China (1793): "Our dynasty's majestic virtue has penetrated unto every country under Heaven, and Kings of all nations have offered their costly tribute by land and sea. As your Ambassador can see for himself, we possess all things. I set no value on objects strange or ingenious, and have no use for your country's manufactures."[1] Partially as a result of this difference in openness to new ideas, the technological gap between China and Europe became a yawning chasm in the centuries between 1500 and 1900.

Scholars also theorize that the ability to accept ideas from abroad influenced development in Japan and in the Islamic world. Japan, the most economically successful country with cultural roots outside of Europe, enthusiastically borrowed technologies and ideas from Europe. Finding itself at a technological disadvantage to the most advanced countries in the middle of the 19th century, Japan undertook a period of technological emulation that is still without equal in world history. Japan sent delegations of observers to Europe and America, and they brought back not only productive technologies but also institutions, legal codes, and military organization. One explanation for Japan's ability to follow such a course is that the Japanese had traditionally been cultural borrowers from China, so they could simply transfer the target of their emulation.

In the case of the Islamic world, we see the opposite: a tendency to reject outside ideas, which has arguably been the greatest impediment to economic growth. One symbol of this resistance to foreign ideas was the rejection of the printing press, which Muslims viewed as an instrument of sacrilege. The first printing press in the Ottoman Empire was not established until 1728, some 275 years after Gutenberg's invention. This rejection of foreign ideas has continued into the present day. There are more than 280 million Arabic speakers in the

---

[1]Mokyr (1990), p. 188, Backhouse and Bland (1914), pp. 322–331.

world, but only about 330 foreign books are translated into Arabic each year. Five times as many books are translated into Greek, a language spoken by only 13 million people.[2]

Hard Work

Throughout human history, in every culture, almost all adults have had to work to survive. But cultures have differed in their view of that work: as a necessary evil or as an activity with an intrinsic value. We would expect that in cultures where work was viewed as good in and of itself, people would work harder and produce more output.

In Europe, disdain for work has its roots in classical Greek culture. The Greeks viewed work as best left to slaves, so that it did not get in the way of the important pursuits of philosophy, art, and politics. In a similar vein, the Bible portrays work as a curse that God imposed on humans as punishment for their sins. The turning point for European attitudes toward work was the Protestant Reformation of the 16th century, particularly the writings of John Calvin, who stressed that "all men were created to busy themselves with labor" and that material success was a sign of God's favor. These attitudes toward work were subsequently secularized and popularized as part of Western culture by, among others, U.S. patriot Benjamin Franklin ("No man e'er was glorious who was not laborious"). In a 1985 survey that asked whether work or leisure was more important, 46% of Americans chose work and only 33% chose leisure. The fraction of Protestants who said that work was more important than leisure was 10% higher than the corresponding figure for Roman Catholics.[3] Sociologist Max Weber argued that this devotion to hard work partly explained the early development of the Protestant regions of Europe.

We do not have data on attitudes toward work in the period that Weber wrote about, but we can use data from the world today to check his theory. To look for evidence that attitudes toward work affect economic growth, we examine data from the World Values Survey, which interviewed large samples of people in a number of countries between 2000 and 2011.[4] One question asked people to rate the importance of work versus leisure on a five-point scale, with 1 indicating "It's leisure that makes life worth living, not work" and 5 indicating "Work is what makes life worth living, not leisure." Figure 14.1 shows the average value in each country on the horizontal axis and the level of income per capita on the vertical axis.

Figure 14.1 certainly provides no support for the theory that attitudes toward hard work are a determinant of economic success. Quite the contrary, people in

---

[2]United Nations Development Program (2002b).
[3]Lipset (1990), Hill (1992).
[4]www.worldvaluessurvey.org, waves III, IV, and V.

> FIGURE 14.1

Value of Work versus GDP per Capita

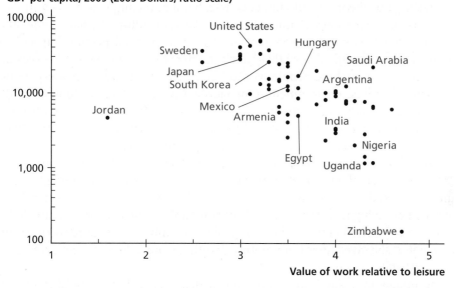

GDP per capita, 2009 (2005 Dollars, ratio scale)

Source: World Values Survey.
*Scored on a 5-point scale where 1 indicates higher value on leisure, and 5 indicates higher value on work.

poor countries are more likely to think that work is important than people in rich countries. Further, the data do not bear out certain common cultural stereotypes. For example, Mexicans, usually viewed as easygoing, believe in hard work more than the Japanese, who are stereotyped as industrious.

The data are hard to interpret because people in rich countries can afford more leisure and thus may have come to believe more in its importance. What we would really like to know is how Mexicans and Japanese would feel about work versus leisure if the countries had the same level of income per capita.

Saving for the Future

We saw in Chapter 3 that a country's economic growth is strongly affected by its saving rate. We also saw that there are large differences in saving rates among countries. If cultural differences among countries affected their saving rates, then these differences could in turn affect the level of economic growth.

In the post–World War II period, the most dramatic examines of high saving rates have all been in East Asia: Japan, South Korea, Taiwan, Singapore, and most recently China. All of these countries have cultures that were strongly influenced by China, suggesting the idea that there is a common "Confucian" element that may explain their common behavior. According to this view, the virtues of diligence and thrift, celebrated by Confucius some 2,500 years ago, have become deeply embedded in East Asian culture.

Testing this theory is difficult, of course, because the high-saving countries of East Asia also share many characteristics unrelated to culture. Perhaps some other aspect of the economic environment in these countries led people to have high saving rates. To test the theory that culture matters for saving, then, it is necessary to examine a case where people with different cultural backgrounds experience the same economic environment. One clever way to do so is to look at people who have all immigrated to the same country. Presumably such immigrants retain some of the culture of their countries of origin, but no matter where they are from, they face the same economic environment in their new home.

Two studies of the saving of immigrants—one in Canada and one in the United States—took exactly this approach. The authors calculated saving rates of immigrants and asked whether immigrants from high-saving countries tended to have higher saving rates than immigrants from low-saving countries. Both studies found no correlation between the saving rate of an immigrant's source country and the amount she saved after immigrating. In other words, there was no evidence of a cultural effect on saving.

Although this result is interesting, the evidence against the cultural view is not as strong as it might appear. First, the studies examined only saving; other aspects of culture may be important. Second and more significantly, immigrants are not a randomly selected group by any means. They are unlikely to be a perfect reflection of the culture they left behind. Indeed, by the fact that they moved (almost always in pursuit of economic opportunity) and others from their country did not, we know that they have different attitudes toward making sacrifices for a better future. Finally, in looking at immigrants, we are not seeing culture in its purest form. The original culture of the source country will have been mixed with the culture of the new home, so it is harder to detect cultural effects on economic behavior.[5] (See box "What Parking Tickets Say about Culture" for a more successful application of this same approach.)

Trust

Economic interactions often involve reliance on a person to keep his word. An employee trusts that at the end of the week that the boss will give him or her a paycheck. A merchant trusts that a customer's promise to pay will be fulfilled. Investors in a firm trust that they will receive their share of the profits. Without trust, economic activity would be reduced to a crude level, and huge resources would have

---

[5]Carroll, Rhee, and Rhee (1994, 1999).

WHAT PARKING TICKETS SAY ABOUT CULTURE

We saw in Chapter 12 that there are large differences among countries in the degree of political corruption and that corruption is strongly negatively correlated with the level of gross domestic product (GDP) per capita. It is easy to think of channels by which corruption impedes economic development. But what causes differences among countries in the degree of corruption? This finding suggests that corruption may be a *cause* of low income.

One theory is that differences in corruption among countries reflect differences in the economic calculus facing public officials, that is, the costs and benefits of corrupt behavior. In poor countries, where official salaries are low and legal enforcement is weak, corruption is optimal. A second theory is that differences in corruption reflect differences among countries in social norms, which are an aspect of culture.

The natural way to test the hypothesis that there is a cultural dimension to corruption is to look at how corruption behaves when the economic environment changes, or how individuals behave when they move from one economic environment to another. This is what economists Ray Fisman and Edward Miguel do, by studying diplomats from around the world gathered at the United Nations in New York City.* The behavior Fisman and Miguel examine is not corruption in the classic sense, but it is something close: abuse of power. Before November 2002, diplomats serving at the United Nations, along with their families, benefited from diplomatic immunity that allowed them to avoid paying parking fines. Between 1997 and 2002, diplomats accumulated 150,000 unpaid parking tickets, resulting in outstanding fines of more than $18 million. The most common violation (43% of cases) was for parking in a "No Standing—Loading Zone."

Fisman and Miguel measured the average number of parking tickets per diplomat over the five years before November 2002. The range is enormous, from zero (for diplomats from Norway, Japan, the Netherlands, and the United Kingdom, among others) to 58.6 for Nigeria, 69.4 for Pakistan, and 246.2 for Kuwait. There is also a strong correlation between the number of violations per diplomat and the index of corruption (as discussed in Chapter 12) in their home country. Overall, the data predict that going from a corrupt country such as Nigeria to an honest one like Norway is associated with an 80% drop in parking violations per diplomat. The fact that diplomats from noncorrupt countries will behave in a law-abiding manner, even when the law does not apply to them, is a testament to the strong role that culture plays in determining behavior.

On the other hand, culture is clearly not everything. In November 2002 New York City police began stripping diplomatic parking plates from vehicles that accumulated more than three unpaid parking violations. Violations fell by 98% within two months. This demonstrates that even though corrupt behavior has a cultural component, good legal enforcement can overcome the cultural effect.

*Fisman and Miguel (2007).

to be devoted to making sure that people came through on their promises. Society would lose the advantages gained by creating complex organizations—for example, allowing people to specialize in specific tasks or exploiting gains from trade. Obviously, a society in which one could not rely on others to hold to their commitments would be poorer.

John Stuart Mill wrote in 1848, "The advantage to mankind of being able to trust one another, penetrates into every crevice and cranny of human life: the economical is perhaps the smallest part of it, yet even this is incalculable." He added, "There are countries in Europe... where the most serious impediment to conducting business concerns on a large scale, is the rarity of persons who are supposed fit to be trusted with the receipt and expenditure of large sums of money."[6] In a similar vein, the economist Kenneth Arrow wrote, "Virtually every commercial transaction has within itself an element of trust, certainly any transaction conducted over a period of time. It can be plausibly argued that much of the economic backwardness in the world can be explained by the lack of mutual confidence."[7]

Although it is obvious that a society in which everybody deals honestly will be better off than one in which people do not, it is less obvious what incentives cause individuals to be honest. One force that makes people honest is the power of the state. If the person with whom I write a contract fails to fulfill his obligations, I can take him to court. But the roots of trust go much deeper than the power of the state. There are numerous instances of economic interaction in which neither party is in a position to call a police officer or a lawyer, but in which people nonetheless carry through on their promises. The amounts of money may be too small to justify bringing to bear the power of the state, for example, or the terms of the contract may be so informal as to make suing for noncompliance impossible. In the extreme, it may even be impossible for one of the parties to a transaction to observe whether the other one has complied with the terms of the agreement. For example, a rural vegetable stand may be left unattended, with instructions that customers add up their own bills and deposit money in a box. It is here that we often suspect the workings of culture as a countervailing force that can explain why people act honestly, even when it is not in what appears to be their best interest.

If societies differ in their degree of trustworthiness, we would expect this variation to be reflected in economic outcomes.[8] But how do we measure trust? Researchers have relied on a number of strategies. One approach has been simply to ask people. Surveys in 92 countries asked respondents, "Generally speaking, would you say that most people can be trusted, or that you can't be too careful in dealing with people?" The mean response, averaging across all of the countries, was that 25.1% of respondents thought that most people could be trusted. But there was a good deal of variation in the answer. In Norway 74.2% of respondents thought that most people could be trusted, whereas in Turkey only 4.9% of people thought so.

These perceptions of trustworthiness presumably reflect the experiences of the people who answered the survey and thus should tell us something about the

[6]Mill (1909), Book 1, Chapter 7.
[7]Arrow (1972).
[8]Knack and Zak (2001).

PITFALLS OF CULTURAL EXPLANATIONS FOR ECONOMIC GROWTH

The Japanese are a happy race, and being content with little, are not likely to achieve much.
— a Western observer in 1881

To see your men [Japanese] at work made me feel that you are a very satisfied easy going race, who reckon time is no object. When I spoke to some managers they informed me that it was impossible to change the habits of national heritage.
— a Western observer in 1915*

These two quotations from Western observers show how silly cultural interpretations of economic growth can look in retrospect. By the end of the 20th century, the shoe was on the other foot: Not only were cultural traits being invoked to explain Japanese economic success, but the cultural characteristics attributed to the Japanese were the exact opposite of those that had seemed obvious a century previous. A poll conducted in 1992 found that 94% of Americans characterized the Japanese as "hardworking," whereas only 15% of Japanese thought the same way about Americans.[†]

What happened?

Perhaps the culture of Japan changed dramatically over this period; still, such an explanation is not very attractive—especially because late-20th-century advocates of the superiority of Japanese culture believed that some ancient quality of the culture was important. It is also possible that Japanese culture did not change, but the circumstances in which the Japanese found themselves did. The cultural attributes that were useful in the context of a late-20th-century economy might somehow have been less useful a century previous. The final possibility is that culture simply mattered less to the productivity of Japanese workers than the observers thought.

The sources of difficulty in interpreting culture as a determinant of economic growth are not hard to find. Because researchers cannot objectively measure many aspects of culture, they must rely on subjective measures. But there is a natural tendency for observation of a country's economic situation to affect the observer's assessment of its culture. Countries that are prospering economically naturally appear to have cultures that are good for growth, whereas those that are trailing economically seem to have cultures that are bad for growth.

This problem of **observer bias**—in which the assessment of some attribute variable is clouded by the observer's knowledge of how that variable is related to other things—is not unique to the problem of assessing culture's effect on economic growth. Indeed, it is a general problem in science. It is the reason, for example, that new medicines are tested using a double-blind methodology, in which doctors who assess whether a patient's condition has improved (as well as the patient himself or herself) do not know whether the patient received the real medicine or a placebo.

*Both quotations appear in Landes (1998), p. 350.
[†]Reported in *Time* magazine, February 10, 1992.

countries in which they live. But answers to a survey may not be a perfect measure; for example, people in some countries may be more prone to giving optimistic answers that do not reflect either their experience or their behavior. A second measure comes from a more direct experiment. In each of 15 different countries, a number of wallets containing $50 in cash and the name and address of their owner were intentionally "lost" in public places. Researchers then kept track of the fractions of wallets that were returned with their contents intact. The correlation coefficient of

FIGURE 14.2

Relationship between Trust and Investment

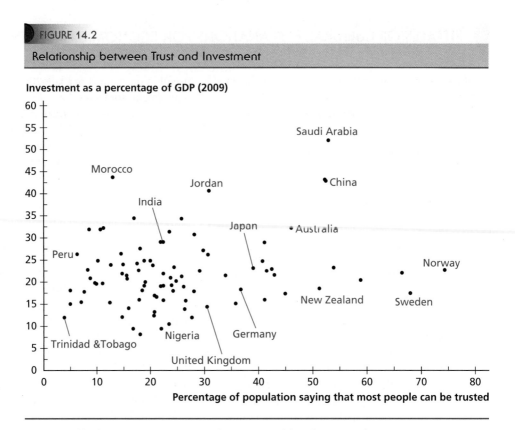

Investment as a percentage of GDP (2009)

Sources: World Values Survey, Waves III, IV, and V; Heston et al. (2011).

this measure with the survey responses about trustworthiness was 0.67, indicating that people's assessments of their environments were fairly accurate.[9]

To examine the economic importance of differences in trustworthiness, we analyze how trust is related to investment. Investment is the economic interaction that is most reliant on trust because it involves a long time lag between when a person relinquishes money and when he or she expects to get it back. Figure 14.2 shows that across countries, there is indeed a positive relationship between the measure of trust and the fraction of output that is invested.

Social Capital

The previous section showed the importance of trust for economic growth. But what determines the level of trust in a country? Economists and sociologists have identified one of the determinants of trust as **social capital.** Social capital refers to

---

[9]Knack and Keefer (1997), Felten (2001).

the value of the social networks that people have and of the inclination of people in those networks to do things for each other. In a society where people have large circles of acquaintance, and where people who know one another are inclined to be helpful, social capital is high. In a society where people are isolated socially, or where there is no norm of helping out those one knows, social capital is low. Social capital is the glue that holds society together.

Social capital arises when people interact in any number of settings, ranging from membership in an organization to dinner with a group of friends. In some cases, the creation of social capital is deliberate, as when a business owner joins a club so he or she can make useful contacts. In other cases, social capital is produced as a by-product of other activities, such as attendance at religious services.

Social capital makes people more trustworthy because a person is less likely to cheat someone who is a member of his or her social network. The larger your network—your own friends and acquaintances or the people you can reach through them—the more people you can trust. An illustration of the benefits from trust that social capital can produce is given by sociologist James Coleman in this description of the wholesale diamond market in New York:

> In the process of negotiating a sale, a merchant will hand over to another merchant a bag of stones for the latter to examine in private at his leisure, with no formal insurance that the latter will not substitute one or more inferior stones or a paste replica. The merchandise may be worth thousands or hundreds of thousands of dollars. Such free exchange of stones for inspection is important to the functioning of this market. In its absence, the market would operate in a much more cumbersome, much less efficient fashion.

The reason that the market can function so efficiently is that all the participants are Hasidic Jews linked to each other through a dense network of family, community, and religious ties. A diamond dealer who cheated his fellow merchants would suffer a painful severing of those ties.[10]

Beyond its role in facilitating trust, social capital has many additional economic benefits. Information—about jobs, investments, or potential customers—flows easily within social networks, so a well-networked society will more efficiently match people to economic opportunities. People within a social network also can provide mutual aid. Neighbors keep an eye on one another's homes, thus reducing crime; similarly, a community can come together to help a family suffering from an unexpected setback, providing a form of insurance. Social capital also facilitates collective action because people who already have a relationship with each other can trust one another to do their part in some joint enterprise. For example, where there is good social capital, parents will be more able to work together to achieve the common goal of improving the quality of schooling. (See box "Importance of Social Capital at the Village Level.")

---

[10]Coleman (1988).

IMPORTANCE OF SOCIAL CAPITAL AT THE VILLAGE LEVEL

Although we have been primarily interested in the ability of culture to explain differences in economic status among countries, useful evidence about the role of culture can also be found by focusing on a much more local level. One study looked for evidence of the effect of social capital on economic growth by studying 84 villages in Tanzania, one of the poorest countries in the world.* The authors constructed an index of social capital based on information about people's membership in voluntary groups, the most prevalent being churches, mosques, the village burial society, women's groups, and the political party. The more people were members of such groups, and also the more "inclusive" rather than "exclusive" these voluntary groups, the higher the village's index of social capital.

The theory that the study's authors sought to test was that the existence of this social capital would facilitate trust and cooperation, so villages with higher social capital would also have higher levels of income. Specifically, they hypothesized that in villages with higher social capital, people would be more likely to work together to solve common problems, to share information about economic opportunities and new technologies, and to provide informal insurance to one another.

The study found evidence to support the theory. Higher social capital was correlated with more parental involvement in the schools, higher school quality, and greater participation in projects to repair village roads. Households in villages with higher social capital were also more likely to adopt improved agricultural practices such as use of fertilizer or agrochemicals.

Finally, the study found that households in villages with high social capital had higher income. The authors calculated that for a typical village, in which the average household had membership in 1.5 voluntary groups, raising the average household's membership by an additional one-half group would raise the level of income per capita by 20%.

*Narayan and Pritchett (1999).

One of the most important effects of social capital is improving the functioning of government. People who care about their fellow community members are more likely to vote. Similarly, politicians in an environment in which social capital is high are less inclined to abuse their constituents for personal gain. In a study that examined different regions in Italy, the degree of social capital was measured by counting how many people participated in groups such as soccer clubs and choral societies. The authors concluded that in regions in which social capital was higher, government functioned more efficiently.[11]

Based on such evidence, there is good reason to suspect that social capital is a source of country differences not only in trust but also in quality of government. Unfortunately, this theory is difficult to test because we have no systematic data on differing levels of social capital among countries.

Political scientist Robert Putnam has recently argued that social capital in the United States has declined in the last half century. In 2000, Americans were half as

---

[11]Putnam, Leonardi, and Nanetti (1993).

likely to belong to a church-, mosque-, or synagogue-affiliated social group or to belong to a union as they had been 40 years previously. Americans also were members of fewer clubs and donated a smaller fraction of their income to charity. Even bowling, the country's most popular competitive sport, has changed. In the mid-1960s, 8% of American men and 5% of American women belonged to bowling teams that competed in organized leagues. By 2000, membership for both men and women had fallen to 2%. Bowling itself has remained popular, but Americans now more commonly bowl with a few friends rather than in a larger group. One manifestation of this trend in social capital in the United States is that the number of lawyers per capita, having held constant between 1900 and 1970, doubled between 1970 and 2000. Presumably, the increased need for lawyers reflects a decline in people's ability to trust each other or to solve disputes through informal means.[12]

Putnam suggests several possible reasons for the decline in social capital in the United States, including the physical sprawl of U.S. cities and the fading memory of shared sacrifice during World War II. One prime suspect is the rise of television, which came to dominate American's leisure time during the period in which social capital was declining. But, as with many of the correlations discussed in this book, there is a severe problem in inferring causality in this case. Perhaps social capital declined for some other reason, and television time simply expanded to fill the void. Or perhaps the two are unrelated and just happened to occur simultaneously. To solve this inference problem, the economist Ben Olken studied villages in rural Java in Indonesia. Because of Java's mountainous terrain, there is great variability among villages in the number of radio and television stations that people could tune into. This variation in reception serves as a natural experiment to test the causal effects of media. Olken finds that in villages with better reception, people indeed spend more time listening to radio and watching television (10 additional minutes per day per channel received), and conversely are members of fewer village social groups. He also finds that reception of more television channels is associated with a decline in people's self-reported willingness to trust others. Thus, television does seem to have a negative causal effect on social capital.[13]

Social Capability

The last dimension of culture that we examine is **social capability,** a term used by economist Moses Abramovitz to refer to the social and cultural qualities that allow a country to take advantage of economic opportunities.[14] In Abramovitz's description of the growth process, countries that are economically underdeveloped but that have sufficient social capability can take advantage of the opportunities that

---

[12]Putnam (2000, 2001).
[13]Olken (2009).
[14]Abramovitz (1986).

arise from interaction with the developed world, through technology transfer, trade, and flows of capital. Such countries will rapidly catch up to leading countries' living standards. Poor countries that lack social capability will be condemned to economic stagnation. Social capability includes the following elements:

- The experience of the population with the organization and management of large-scale enterprises.

- The ability of residents of a country to take advantage of market economics, such as through specialization and trade.

- An outlook compatible with empirical science—that is, a belief in cause and effect, in contrast to superstition or magic.

- A social view that focuses on life on earth, rather than seeing life as relatively unimportant in contrast to spiritual existence.

Although there is good reason to believe that qualities under the heading of social capability should have a large effect on the process of economic development, social capability is difficult to measure. Any researcher who measured social capability and then tried to evaluate whether it was correlated with economic growth would risk biasing the assessment of social capability according to the sort of economic growth observed—the problem of observer bias discussed in the box "Pitfalls of Cultural Explanations for Economic Growth" (page 407).

There is a way around the problem of observer bias, however: We can use a measure of social capability that was constructed *before* the period of economic growth we are studying. Such an index is not subject to the criticism that it might be influenced by a knowledge of how countries actually fared.[15]

The index that we use for this analysis was constructed in 1961 by economists Irma Adelman and Cynthia Taft Morris. It covers 74 countries that were considered "developing" at that time. The index is based on quantitative data and on field experts' assessments of qualities related to culture, such as "modernization of outlook" and "character of basic social organization," which are usually left out of formal economic analyses.

As Figure 14.3 shows, there is a strong positive relationship between Adelman and Morris's index of social development and the level of income per capita in 1960. However, this strong correlation is not a proof of the importance of social capability, for two reasons. First, Adelman, Morris, and the experts on whom they relied observed the level of income per capita in 1961. Thus, their assessments of culture could well have been biased toward labeling the cultures of richer countries as more socially capable. Second, it is possible that the cultural elements the researchers defined as important were the result of countries' being richer rather than unchanging aspects of culture.

---

[15]Temple and Johnson (1998).

FIGURE 14.3

Social Capability versus GDP per Capita in 1960

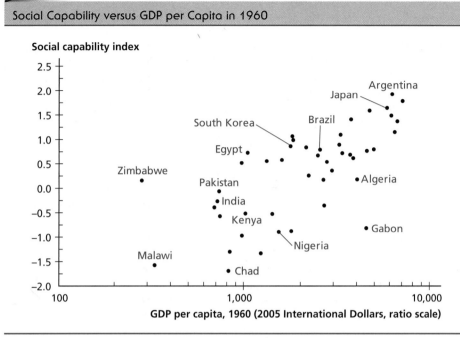

Sources: Temple and Johnson (1998); Heston, Summers, and Aten (2011).

We can solve both of these problems if we examine the performance of countries following the construction of the Adelman-Morris index. Specifically, we can take advantage of an idea introduced previously in this book: that if two countries have the same level of income but different underlying characteristics, then the country with a higher steady-state level of income will grow more quickly.

From Figure 14.3 we can see that some countries have surprisingly high indices of social capability, given their level of output, and some countries have surprisingly low indices. For example, Pakistan's index is high relative to other countries with the same level of income, and Chad's index is lower than that for countries with the same level of income (indeed, in 1960 Chad had higher income per capita than Pakistan but a lower value of the social capability index).

We can use this observation to construct a test of the importance of social capability. Suppose that social capability were the only determinant of a country's steady-state level of income per capita. In that case, if we saw two countries that had the same level of income but different levels of social capability, we would know that the country with a higher level of social capability would experience higher growth in the future. (This is exactly the logic of "convergence" we considered in Chapter 3 when we were examining investment rates.) Of course, social

CHANGES IN APPROPRIATE CULTURE

Our focus in this section has been on whether some cultural attributes are good for growth and others are bad for growth. Another possibility is that some cultural attributes are good for growth at some stages of development and bad for growth (or neither good nor bad) at others. This possibility should not be surprising because it is similarly the case with other factors that affect economic growth. We know that the types of personal attributes that earn a large return in the labor market, presumably reflecting workers' productivity, change with the stage of development. For example, before mechanization, physical strength was an important determinant of a person's worth, but over time has become much less important. Similarly, the mental capacities that are rewarded change. For example, the ability to add numbers quickly or to spell is less important in a computerized workplace than in previous times. So we should not be surprised if cultural values that are conducive to growth at some stages of development, or in some environments, will be hindrances at other times.

An example of a cultural attribute that may either help or harm economic growth, depending on a country's stage of development, is the degree of sharing among people. At a low level of economic development—for example, within a small band of hunter-gatherers—sharing is essential for survival. But for a more developed economy, there can be such a thing as too much sharing. If society expects that all of a person's belongings will be shared with the extended family, village, or tribe, then the incentive to invest in capital—either physical or human—is greatly diminished.

Japan provides a vivid example of changing views about what constitutes a good cultural attribute. During the 1980s, when Japanese manufacturers were rising to world dominance, commentators gave much of the credit for this success to the mind-set of the Japanese worker. Japanese conformity and "groupism," according to this view, allowed factories to operate at levels of efficiency unachievable elsewhere. One commentator observed: "Japanese capitalism has been more successful than its American counterpart in building large organizations that command intense, sometimes passionate loyalty from their members. Arguably, this has provided Japanese companies a culture-based source of competitive advantage."*

A decade later, however, Japanese culture was being viewed as an impediment to economic success. A government-appointed panel concluded that conformity and adherence to rules had "leached Japan's vitality." The key to economic success, said the panel, was to downplay the traditional Japanese preference for group consensus and instead to promote tolerance, self-reliance, and the empowerment of individuals.[†]

Thus, in the space of a decade, a dramatic shift occurred in the perception of how well Japanese culture was suited to the current economic environment. Whether this change in the perceived appropriateness of Japanese culture represents a real change in the economic environment—or whether it instead reflects a shift in thinking by practitioners of economic prognostication—is not at all clear. The reassessment of culture came after a decade of disastrous performance on the part of the Japanese economy, which in turn may have had nothing to do with cultural factors. Indeed, the episode is a good reminder of the problem of observer bias: Perceptions of culture can be affected by economic performance.

*Berger (1994).
[†]Struck (2000).

capability is unlikely to be the *only* determinant of a country's steady state, but even if there are other determinants, the logic just described should still apply on average. Specifically, for a given level of income, the mean growth rate of countries with high social capability should be larger than the mean growth rate of countries with low social capability.

To implement this test thus requires two steps. First, we determine how each country's level of social capability compares with our expectations, given the country's level of income. Graphically, we can draw the line that best fits the data points in Figure 14.3, and then, for each country, we can measure the gap between the country's actual level of social capability and the level predicted by the fitted line. As a second step, we take these gaps between the actual and predicted level of social capability for each country (which economists call "residuals") and compare them with subsequent economic growth. If our theory is correct, countries with larger residuals—that is, countries that had higher levels of social capability relative to their levels of income—should have experienced higher growth.

This exercise yields the results shown in Figure 14.4: a strong, positive relationship between the "residual" part of social capability and subsequent economic growth. Countries that had high levels of social capability relative to their income, including South Korea, Japan, and Thailand, grew quickly. Countries

FIGURE 14.4

Social Capability and Economic Growth

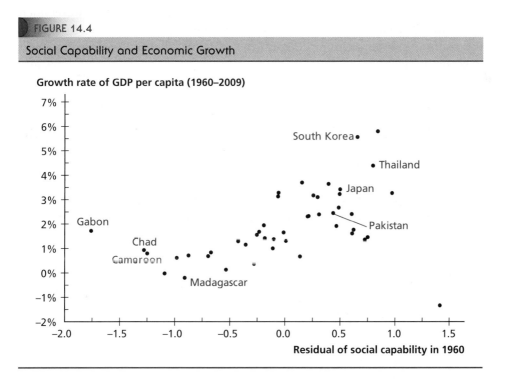

Growth rate of GDP per capita (1960–2009)

Residual of social capability in 1960

where social capability was low relative to income, including Cameroon, Madagascar, and Chad, grew slowly.[16]

14.2 WHAT DETERMINES CULTURE?

A theory of culture's effect on economic growth has two parts. The first component—an explanation of how culture affects economic outcomes—has been our concern in Section 14.1. The second component is an examination of culture itself, the subject to which we now turn.

As much of the foregoing discussion made clear, one of the prime determinants of culture is religion. The forces that shape what religion a country's people follow are themselves complex. One important determinant is the historical record of conquest and settlement. For example, Latin America is primarily Catholic today because it was colonized by Spain and Portugal. Similarly, Islamic conquests over several centuries largely determined the countries where Islam is practiced today. But religion is also shaped by inspiration and faith of vast numbers of ordinary people and of pivotal individuals such as Confucius (551–479 B.C.); Gautama Buddha (563–483 B.C.), the founder of Buddhism; the Roman emperor Constantine (A.D. 288–337) who converted the Roman Empire to Christianity; the prophet Muhammad (A.D. 570–632), who founded and spread Islam; and Martin Luther (1483–1546), an early leader of the Protestant Reformation. Tracing the interplay between the historical events and the distribution of religions among countries today—much less explaining why prophets and preachers arose when and where they did—would take us far beyond the scope of this book. Instead, in this section, we examine some determinants of culture that are more easily subject to economic analysis.

Climate and Natural Resources

In the next chapter, we will explore several different channels through which climate and natural resources may explain differences in income among countries. Here we consider whether these factors affect growth through an influence on culture.

The most plausible linkage between climate and culture centers on the need for a person to behave in a forward-looking manner. In a temperate climate such

---

[16]Mathematical Note: Students with a background in econometrics will recognize that this two-step procedure is equivalent to regressing growth on social capability and initial GDP. The results from running this regression (with standard errors in parentheses) are:

$$\text{growth} = 0.057 + 0.0100 \text{ social capability} - 0.0054 \ln(\text{GDP per capita in 1960})$$
$$(0.0028) \qquad\qquad (0.0032)$$

$$R^2 = 0.48$$

as that of Europe, crops mature seasonally, and one must provide for shelter and heat for the winter. A temperate climate instills values such as saving and planning ahead. These values might shape a culture in a way that is conducive to modern economic growth.

The explanation for a link between natural resources and culture is similar to that for climate: If a country has resources that allow people to survive without working hard, then there will be less of a cultural imperative to work. In 1576 the French political philosopher Jean Bodin wrote, "Men of a fat and fertile soil, are most commonly effeminate and cowards; whereas contrariwise a barren country makes men temperate by necessity, and by consequence careful, vigilant, and industrious."[17] A related effect of natural resources on culture is that the presence of resources may allow countries to avoid modernization and thus may slow development. A salient example is the effect of oil on the culture of many of the Persian Gulf states.

If climate and resources do affect culture, an important question is whether these effects are long lasting. That is, when people's environment changes, do the cultural attributes that arose in response to that environment also change? For example, it is true that people living in Sweden before industrialization had to be more forward-looking than those living in Tahiti because in Sweden the failure to plan for the severe winter could lead to death by starvation or freezing, whereas in Tahiti the climate is gentle and food crops grow year-round. But the conditions that made planning necessary in Sweden are no longer present. The average Swede can buy food at a grocery store rather than having to stockpile it. If cultural traits induced by climate are persistent, then modern Swedes might still be forward-looking, even though such behavior is no longer necessary. But if these cultural traits are *not* persistent, then we would expect that the current residents of tropical countries (which tend to be poor) will have values more favorable to hard work and saving than the residents of rich countries that are located in temperate zones because in rich countries life is relatively easy.

Cultural Homogeneity and Social Capital

And the Lord said, "Behold, they are one people, and they have all one language; and this is only the beginning of what they will do; and nothing that they propose to do will now be impossible for them. Come, let us go down, and there confuse their language, that they may not understand one another's speech."

—*Genesis 11*[18]

---

[17]Bodin (1967).
[18]Revised Standard Version of the Bible, copyright 1952 [2nd edition, 1971] by the Division of Christian Education of the National Council of the Churches of Christ in the United States of America. Used by permission. All rights reserved.

Researchers examining culture's role in economic growth often point to the degree of homogeneity within a country as an important influence on growth. The idea is not that some cultures are good for growth and some bad, but rather that it is beneficial for everyone in a single country to share the same culture. The story of the Tower of Babel, from which the preceding quotation comes, makes this same point about language, something that is similar to culture. If people in a country speak a variety of different languages, then communication will be difficult, and the gains obtained from economic cooperation will be reduced.

Even when people speak the same language, there may also be a role for cultural or ethnic homogeneity in allowing an economy to function more efficiently. Social capital—the strength of social networks that we considered previously—is likely to be higher in a country where people belong to the same ethnic group. Similarly, trust is higher where there is ethnic homogeneity because people are more likely to deal dishonestly with members of other ethnic groups than with members of their own. Evidence of this trust within ethnic groups is that international mercantile networks have often been organized along ethnic lines—for example, Chinese merchants in Southeast Asia and Indians in East Africa. Moreover, one study found that in Cote d'Ivoire, the extent of environmental degradation of the land was lower in ethnically homogeneous than ethnically heterogeneous villages, suggesting that people have an easier time cooperating for the common good with others of the same ethnicity.[19]

To test whether ethnic homogeneity is important at the country level, researchers have constructed an **index of ethnic fractionalization,** which is the probability that two randomly selected people in a country will not belong to the same ethnic group. A country in which everyone is a member of the same ethnic group will have an index of 0 because there would be no chance that two randomly selected people would belong to different ethnic groups. A country with two equal-sized ethnic groups would have an index of 0.5, and a country with 10 equal-sized groups would have an index of 0.9. A country with an index of 1 would be completely fractionalized—every person would be a member of a different ethnic group, so the probability that any two individuals were from different ethnic groups would be 100%.[20]

Figure 14.5 shows data on ethnic fractionalization and its relationship to the level of gross domestic product (GDP) per capita. The values for the fractionalization index cover a wide range, from nearly complete ethnic homogeneity, with fractionalization near 0, to a high fractionalization of 0.93 (in Uganda). The figure also shows that there is a negative relationship between the degree of fractionalization

---

[19]Ahuja (1998).

[20]Mathematical Note: The index of ethnic fractionalization is defined as:

$$1 - \sum_{i=1}^{I} n_i^2,$$

where I is the number of ethnic groups in the country and n_i is the fraction of the population belonging to group i.

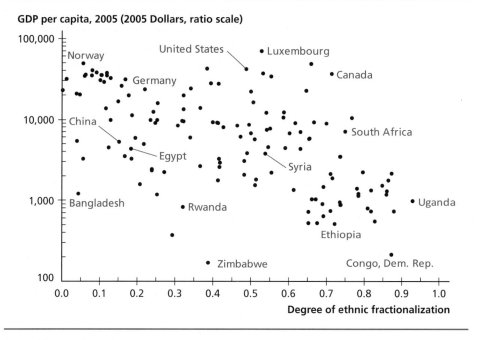

FIGURE 14.5

Ethnic Fractionalization versus GDP per Capita

Source: Alesina et al. (2003).

and the level of a country's income. The mass of data points in the upper left (high income, low ethnic fractionalization) includes such European countries as the United Kingdom, France, Italy, Sweden, and Portugal, all of which have ethnic fractionalization between 0.05 and 0.12. Even lower fractionalization is measured in Japan (0.012) and South Korea (0.002). By contrast, the 15 most fractionalized countries in the world are all poor and in Africa. There are a number of interesting exceptions to the general relationship between ethnic fractionalization and income per capita, however. The United States, Canada, Belgium, and Switzerland all have relatively high degrees of fractionalization despite being rich, whereas Bangladesh, Haiti, and Egypt are all poor despite being ethnically homogeneous.

The negative correlation between ethnic fractionalization and income per capita suggests that fractionalization may slow a country's growth. Other available evidence supports this theory. Countries with a high degree of ethnic fractionalization tend to have worse governments, as measured by high corruption or the inability to provide public goods such as roads and telephone networks. As with many correlations like this, however, it is also possible that ethnic fractionalization does not cause countries to be poor but some third factor causes both fractionalization and poverty. A natural candidate for this third factor is countries' colonial histories. As we saw in Chapter 12, one reason for Africa's high ethnic fractionalization is that European colonial powers drew the boundaries between their colonies (which later became the borders between countries) with little regard to the distribution of ethnic groups. Another legacy of colonization was bad government. Thus, it is possible that ethnic fractionalization and bad government are related only because they are both the result of colonization, not because ethnic fractionalization causes bad government.

Researchers who have studied ethnic fractionalization have also looked at two other measures of heterogeneity within countries: *linguistic fractionalization* (people speaking many different languages) and *religious fractionalization* (people belonging to many different faiths). Linguistic fractionalization is similar to ethnic fractionalization: Both tend to be high in the same countries, and poorer countries tend to have higher levels of linguistic fractionalization than rich countries. Religious fractionalization, however, is positively (although weakly) correlated with income: Richer countries tend to be more religiously fractionalized than poorer countries. One possible explanation is that religious fractionalization is a sign of tolerance on the part of government, and that governments that are more tolerant of minority rights tend to also be more democratic, honest, and efficient—qualities that promote economic growth.

Population Density and Social Capability

Previously in this chapter, we saw that undeveloped countries with a high level of *social capability*—the social and cultural qualities that allow a country to take advantage of economic opportunities such as technology transfer, trade, and factor flows—are in a position to catch up rapidly with leading countries. But what determines social capability? Researchers have identified **population density**—the number of people living on each square mile of land—as one potential source. Countries that are poor but densely populated tend to have many of the aspects of social capability we examined. Higher population density facilitates the division of labor by raising the number of consumers in each producer's immediate neighborhood. By contrast, in sparsely populated areas, self-sufficiency is the rule, and people have little experience with economic transactions beyond their own family or village. Similarly, densely populated areas are likely to have more extensive government and more historical experience with government than sparsely populated areas. Experience with centralized government gives residents in densely populated areas experience with formal organizations, laws, written contracts, and other institutions that are helpful for taking advantage of economic opportunities from abroad. Countries with the longest histories of centralized governments (i.e., kingdoms, empires, or states that comprise more than a few thousand households) are mostly found in Europe, Asia, and the Middle East. By contrast, many African and South American countries have short histories of centralized government.[21]

---

[21]Bockstette, Chanda, and Putterman (2002).

If higher population density raises social capability, then countries with high population density will be able to grow rapidly in the proper economic circumstances. For example, if a country had a dense population but was poor due to the lack of arable land, then the opening-up of international trade would allow the country to bypass the constraint on its resources and to grow quickly.

Figure 14.6 explores the relationship between population density and growth over the period 1960–2005. As we saw in Chapter 11, this was a time of rising globalization, during which many developing countries were indeed able to take advantage of economic opportunities from abroad. The figure shows a striking correlation between countries' levels of population density and their growth rates of income per capita. (The positive relationship between density and growth remains statistically significant even if we exclude the high-density, rapidly growing city-states of Hong Kong and Singapore.) Among the fast-growing countries were many in East Asia, among them China and South Korea. These countries had dense populations and, as we would expect, long traditions of commercial culture, economic specialization, and centralized government rule. Many of the slow-growing, sparsely populated countries in Africa and South America were

FIGURE 14.6

Population Density versus Economic Growth

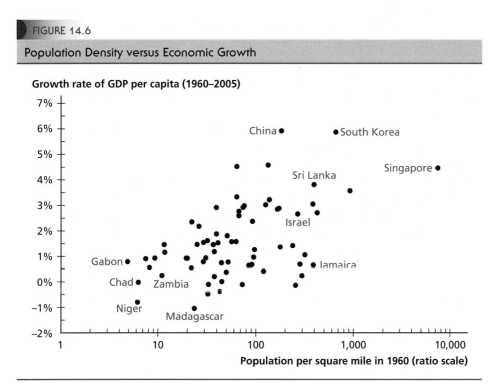

Source: Burkett, Humblet, and Putterman (1999).

characterized by subsistence agriculture, a low level of economic specialization, and a short history of centralized government.[22]

Identifying population density as an important contributor to social capability raises the further question of how density itself is determined. One of the important factors is geography, the focus of our next chapter. Geographic characteristics such as soil quality, amount of rainfall, and length of the growing season determine how large a population can be supported on a given quantity of land. Thus, the steppes of Mongolia—arid, windswept, and far above sea level—inevitably are able to support much lower population density than the delta of the Yangtze River, with its rich soils and a moderate climate. Other factors that influence population density include a country's level of technology (which raises the amount that can be produced with a given input of land), openness to trade (which allows for the import of food), and quality of government.

14.3 CULTURAL CHANGE

Now that we have examined how cultural factors affect economic growth and looked at some of the determinants of culture, we turn to the subject of cultural change. Specifically, we explore how the economically relevant aspects of culture vary over time, as a result of deliberate action (e.g., on the part of the government), economic growth itself, or as a consequence of other events.

The histories of Japan and the Islamic world demonstrate the importance of cultural change. As we saw in Section 14.1, one of the keys to Japan's rapid economic growth in the 19th and 20th centuries was its willingness to accept ideas from abroad, whereas an aversion to accepting ideas from abroad has been one of the factors that held back growth in the Islamic world over the last several centuries. These attitudes toward accepting ideas from abroad are cultural attributes—but they are not *unchanging* cultural attributes. Indeed, in both cases, recent attitudes toward accepting ideas from abroad sharply contrast with previous ones. In the case of Japan, the period of cultural borrowing from abroad followed a period of 230 years in which Japan had intentionally sealed itself off from the West to *prevent* the inflow of new ideas. In the case of the Islamic world, resistance to ideas from abroad dates from the 13th and 14th centuries. For five centuries before this period, the Islamic world was remarkably open to ideas from abroad. Arab scholars preserved and advanced classical science, mathematics, and philosophy during Europe's Dark Ages, adopted the decimal number system (called "Arabic numerals" in English) from India, and invented the idea of experiments. Similarly, the Islamic world adopted papermaking technology from China centuries before Europe did. The reasons for the Islamic

---

[22]Burkett, Humblet, and Putterman (1999), Chanda and Putterman (1999).

DETERMINANTS OF COOPERATION: AN EXPERIMENTAL APPROACH

The ability of people in a society to cooperate for the common good is an important determinant of economic success. Many researchers have speculated that this ability to cooperate is influenced by culture, but determining whether this is so is complicated by the fact that we do not usually observe people's *propensity* to cooperate, only whether they actually do cooperate. Perhaps differences in cooperation are determined by the different environments in which people find themselves rather than by differences in culture. To find the true extent to which culture determines the propensity to cooperate, we would like to observe how much people from different cultures cooperate when placed in the same environment.

Economists have recently conducted experiments to probe into cultural differences in behavior, holding fixed the economic environment. In one study, researchers examined 15 small, economically less-developed societies including foragers, slash-and-burn horticulturalists, nomadic herders, and small-scale settled farming communities. Members of these communities were enrolled in an experiment in which they played a so-called ultimatum game. In this game, people were paired off randomly and anonymously. One member of a pair, called the proposer, was given a sum of money (or in the case of societies that did not use money, tobacco, or other goods) and allowed to propose a division between himself and the other member of the pair, called the responder. The responder could then either accept the proposed division, in which case the two players received the proposed amounts, or reject the division, in which case neither player received anything.

The researchers found significant differences among the societies studied in how experimental subjects behaved and concluded that these social differences were much more important than an individual's age, sex, or economic status in determining behavior. Specifically, proposers were more likely to make offers near to equal division in societies in which economic production involved a greater degree of cooperation (e.g., communal whale hunting compared with individual foraging) and in which people relied on market exchange rather than self-sufficiency. These results seem to indicate that experience with one form of reciprocity induces people to act cooperatively in other spheres of interaction.

Another interesting finding in the study challenges the common presumption that people in developed economies have lost their sense of community. When the ultimatum game was played in industrialized countries, the average proposed division was closer to equal than in most of the undeveloped economies that were studied. In industrialized societies, the modal offer—that is, the offer made most frequently—was always equal division. In many of the less developed societies studied, the modal offer was that the proposer keep 75% or more of the pot.*

*Henrich et al. (2001).

world's change in attitude toward ideas from the outside world are not well understood. Some scholars have pointed to the trauma of military defeat as the source of Islamic insularity. In 1258 the city of Baghdad, one of the Arab world's commercial and cultural centers, was sacked by the Mongols, who slaughtered 800,000 of the city's residents.

Economic Growth and Cultural Change

The first part of this chapter makes the case that there is a systematic relationship between aspects of a country's culture and its level of income per capita. This statistical relationship is not proof, however, that differences in culture *cause* differences in economic outcomes. A second possibility is that countries differ in their levels of income for reasons that have nothing to do with culture, and that these differences in income in turn determine differences in culture.

There is good reason to think that economic growth changes a country's cultural values. The most important aspect of this change is the substitution of market relations for other modes of production and exchange. Urbanization, exposure to foreign ideas, and increased education also have significant impacts on the worldview of residents of a growing country.

Using Figure 14.7, we can take a simplified approach to considering the implications of culture and economic growth's being jointly determined. We assume that there is some one-dimensional measure of culture, which we call modernization, that both is determined by the level of income per capita and in turn plays a role in determining income. We measure the level of income per capita, Y, on the horizontal axis and the degree of modernization of culture, M, on the vertical axis. The curve $Y(M)$ shows how modernization affects income, and the curve $M(Y)$

▶ FIGURE 14.7

Simultaneous Determination of Income and Modernization

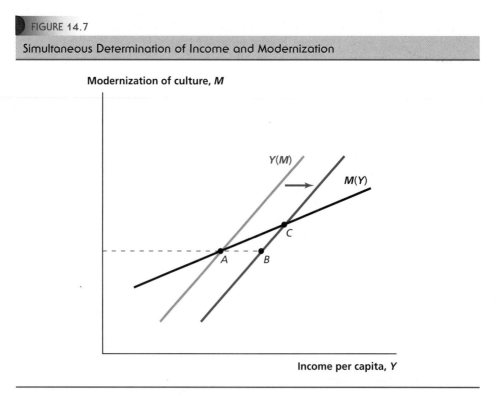

shows the effect of income on modernization. Both curves are upward sloping: More modern culture raises the level of income, and higher income leads to a more modern culture. The point A represents an initial equilibrium.

Now consider what happens when some exogenous change affects the $Y(M)$ curve—that is, some change in the economic environment raises the level of income for any given level of culture. Examples of such an exogenous change are the development of a new productive technology and the opening of a country to international trade. Because culture takes time to change, the initial effect of this exogenous change will be to shift the economy from point A to point B. Over time, however, the level of culture will begin to adjust to the new level of income, and there will be a further period of growth toward point C. Depending on the slopes of the two curves in the picture, this second period of growth, in which modernization and growth of income reinforce each other, could account for much more income growth than the initial, exogenous change in the economic environment. Thus, the mechanism of cultural change will produce a multiplier that magnifies other factors affecting income.

Government Policy and Cultural Change

One of the forces that can change culture is the government. In some cases, government policies are explicitly targeted at changing culture, either as a means of achieving some noneconomic end (e.g., fostering national unity) or to create a culture more conducive to economic growth. In other cases, cultural changes resulting from government policies are an accidental by-product of a policy designed to do something else.

An example of a policy aimed at a noneconomic end is linguistic unification. We saw previously in the chapter that poor countries tend to be more linguistically fragmented than rich countries. This fragmentation partially reflects the arbitrary borders drawn by the European powers between their colonies, which later became sovereign states. But it also reflects a long history of deliberate policies of linguistic unification in the richer countries. For example, France is linguistically unified today only because of policies implemented in the 19th century to suppress numerous regional languages such as Breton and Provencal.[23] Many developing-country governments today take a similarly strong hand in promoting such national languages as Swahili in Tanzania and Bahasa in Indonesia. These attempts to achieve linguistic unity are generally aimed at political rather than economic goals—specifically, to forge a national identity and prevent separatist movements. Nevertheless, linguistic unification also has important economic effects in fostering greater market integration.

---

[23]Jardin (1983).

A Soviet propaganda poster.

An example of a policy with both economic and non-economic goals is the campaign of Mustafa Kemal Atatürk (1881–1938), the founder of the Turkish state, to modernize and secularize his nation's culture. Starting in the 1920s, Atatürk worked to bring Turkey culturally closer to Europe by moving the written language from an Arabic to a Latin alphabet, replacing the Islamic calendar with a Western one, and promoting political rights and education for women. He introduced European dress and even outlawed, on penalty of death, the traditional Turkish hat, the fez. These changes have had a lasting influence on Turkish culture and in turn on economics and politics. Turkey is a functioning democracy in a region dominated by hereditary rulers and military strongmen, and the country scores much better than its Arab neighbors on measures such as the rule of law and the control of corruption.

The Japanese government's pro-saving campaign, which we encountered in Chapter 3, as well as many of the family-planning campaigns described in Chapter 4, exemplify policies explicitly targeted at changing a cultural attribute to achieve an economic end. Another example is the Soviet Union's decades-long attempt—largely unsuccessful—to inspire a greater work ethic in the country's labor force. Propaganda deployed in the campaign—including posters, films, and poems—celebrated the accomplishments of workers who exceeded their production quotas. Typical of the effort is the novel *Time, Forward!* (1932) in which the plot's dramatic tension revolves around the attempt to build a huge steel plant in record time.

Conservative critics of the social welfare states that have developed in the world's richest countries often stress the unintentional effects of government policy on culture. In the view of these observers, government policies aimed at helping people in need have the negative side effect of undermining the cultural values that helped make these countries rich in the first place. Consider the example of a typical welfare-state policy: early retirement benefits for disabled workers. In an economy where there is a strong work ethic, the majority of people taking advantage of such a program are workers who must leave the labor force because of a genuine disability; only a small minority of beneficiaries are abusing the system by retiring early when they are capable of working. Over time, however, the existence of some successful shirkers will erode the ethical stricture against receiving benefits that one does not deserve. More and more of the program beneficiaries will be undeserving, and the cost of the program relative to the genuine benefit will rise. Swedish economist Assar Lindbeck calls this change in values resulting from an overprotective state "learned helplessness." He argues that because of this change in culture, the long-run costs of a given social policy—that is, the costs taking account of how a policy affects culture—are much larger than the short-run costs incurred during the period when culture has not yet been affected.[24]

Media and Cultural Change

A final influence driving cultural change is media, especially television. In 2010, 72% of households in developing countries had a television set, up from almost zero a few decades ago.[25] As discussed previously in this chapter, one way television affects culture is by reducing people's interactions with each other and thus weakening social capital. But television also has a direct effect on culture by influencing people's world views and aspirations, something that advertisers have long known.

One study examined the effect of television on cultural attitudes in Brazil, a country where the most popular form of television entertainment is a type of serialized drama known as a *telenovela*. Telenovelas strive for realism in many dimensions, including the use of colloquial language and incorporating contemporary events, seasons, and holidays into their stories. In one dimension, however, the people who inhabit telenovelas are not typical Brazilians: they have much lower fertility. 72% of female main characters in telenovelas have no children at all, and 21% have only one child. The study compared fertility in different communities, depending on when the television transmission of the telenovelas started in their area. The authors find that in communities that were reached by television soap operas, fertility fell by more than in areas not reached, presumably because the telenovelas changed perceptions about ideal family size. The authors conclude that the influence of telenovelas was a significant contributor to the rapid reduction in Brazil's total fertility rate, from 5.8 children per woman in 1970 to 2.9 in 1991. During that same period, the fraction of households owning a television set rose from 8% to 81%.[26]

A similar study examined cultural attitudes in rural India during a period in which satellite/cable television (a single satellite receiver hooked up by cable to numerous village households) was growing rapidly in the country. Satellite television portrayed an urban lifestyle featuring smaller families, later marriage, more education, and empowered women, which was alien to deeply traditional villages. The arrival of satellite television led to an increase of roughly 40% in the fraction of household who said they watched television in the previous week. The authors compared survey responses about attitudes in villages before and after the arrival of satellite television, using as comparison groups villages that had satellite television

---

[24]Lindbeck (1995).
[25]ITU (2010).
[26]La Ferrara, Chong, and Duryea (2008).

for the entire study period as well as those that did not receive it at all during the study period. They found that the arrival of satellite television led to a decline in the extent to which survey respondents said that domestic violence against women was acceptable, a decrease in reported preference for sons, and an increase in female autonomy (e.g., not needing to ask permission from their husbands to visit the market). All of these changes moved attitudes in the rural setting closer to those of survey respondents in urban areas. The authors also found evidence that increased exposure to satellite television lowered fertility and raised school enrollment.[27]

14.4 CONCLUSION

Culture—people's values, attitudes, and beliefs—is not usually discussed in economics courses. But an increasing number of economists argue that culture matters for economic growth. Culture influences many of the economically relevant decisions people make, including how hard they work, how much they save, how much education they give their children, and how well they cooperate with their peers. If countries differ in how their cultures influence these decisions, such cultural differences should affect economic outcomes.

The first part of the chapter examined six different aspects of culture. We looked at how they varied among countries and considered evidence that this cultural variation affected economic growth. The reasons for examining so many different aspects of culture were that culture is by its nature multidimensional, and we lack an ideal measure of culture. By its nature, culture is hard to quantify, and drawing the link from some aspect of culture to observed economic outcomes is much harder than is the case for a more conventional determinant of output such as physical capital or human capital. Despite these obstacles, there is enough evidence to conclude, at least tentatively, that cultural differences do play some role in explaining differences in income per capita among countries. Aspects of culture that may affect income include openness to new ideas (which affects the ability to assimilate technology from abroad), inclination to work hard and to save for the future (which leads to the accumulation of physical capital and human capital), and level of social capital (which influences how much people trust one another and thus indirectly has an impact on both the accumulation of physical capital and the overall efficiency of production).

The conclusion that culture matters for economic growth is only the beginning for research in this area. Ideally, we would like to measure *how much* culture matters, in the same way that we can measure how much the accumulation of human capital or physical capital matters in determining a country's level of output. Answering this question will have to await better measures of culture than those that are currently available.

---

[27]Jensen and Oster (2009).

We also looked at the determinants of culture. We found evidence that factors such as climate, population density, and the ethnic makeup of a country play a role in shaping culture. We saw that cultures change over time, in response to economic growth itself, government policies, and exposure to media. Finding some factors that influence culture, however, hardly means that we fully understand why culture varies among countries. Much of what determines culture, such as religion and the accidents of history, is far outside the sphere of economists' understanding.

A final key point is that a cultural attribute that leads to economic growth is not necessarily good in any moral sense, nor is a cultural change that raises growth necessarily desirable. Indeed, the idea that the cultural attributes necessary for economic growth are actually bad was championed by none other than the great economist John Maynard Keynes. In his view, many of the cultural attributes that promoted economic growth—the love of money, the glorification of hard work, and the focus on how to improve things in the future rather than living in the moment—were downright distasteful. Keynes cautioned that once the economy has grown rich enough that human wants have been satisfied, the necessity of admiring such values will be removed:

> When the accumulation of wealth is no longer of high social importance, there will be great changes in the code of morals. We shall be able to rid ourselves of many of the pseudo-moral principles which have hag-ridden us for two hundred years, by which we have exalted some of the most distasteful of human qualities into the position of the highest virtues.... All kinds of social customs and economic practices, affecting the distribution of wealth and of economic rewards and penalties, which we now maintain at all costs, however distasteful and unjust they may be in themselves, because they are tremendously useful in promoting the accumulation of capital, we shall then be free, at last, to discard.[28]

But Keynes stressed that until the goal of economic growth has been achieved, it is not proper to discard the culture that fosters it: "For at least another hundred years we must pretend to ourselves and to everyone that fair is foul and foul is fair; for foul is useful and fair is not. Avarice and usury and precaution must be our gods for a little longer still. For only they can lead us out of the tunnel of economic necessity into daylight."

KEY TERMS

culture　**399**　　　　social capability　**411**　　　　population density　**420**
observer bias　**407**　　index of ethnic
social capital　**408**　　　fractionalization　**418**

---

[28]Keynes (1930).

QUESTIONS FOR REVIEW

1. What are some aspects of culture that are relevant for economic behavior?

2. What evidence suggests that economically relevant aspects of culture differ among countries?

3. Why is the problem of observer bias particularly severe when we study the effects of culture on economic growth? What are some potential solutions to the problem?

4. What is social capital, and why is it related to trust?

5. How is social capital related to ethnic fractionalization?

6. What are some ways in which government policy affects a country's culture?

PROBLEMS

1. For each of the following attributes, give an example from a distinct culture that you know well. The culture could be that of a country, region, ethnic group, organization (such as a school or corporation), or a similar group. Be as specific as possible in describing the specific cultural attribute and how it functions.

   a. A cultural attribute that is useful in achieving some goal.

   b. A cultural attribute that holds back the group from accomplishing something desirable.

   c. A cultural attribute that has been intentionally instilled in the members of the group in question.

2. Based on the data in Figure 14.3, but not on what you know of their subsequent history, which country would you expect to have a higher growth rate over the period since 1960, Algeria or Zimbabwe? Explain why.

3. In a certain country, there are three ethnic groups: 50% of the population belongs to Group A, 25% of the population belongs to Group B, and 25% of the population belongs to Group C. What is the country's index of ethnic fractionalization?

4. Consider Figure 14.7, which shows the relationship between cultural modernization and income per capita. In which case will the "modernization multiplier" be larger: when the $M(Y)$ curve is flat, or when it is steep, although less steep than the $Y(M)$ curve? What is the economic interpretation of the slope of the $M(Y)$ curve?

5. Use Figure 14.7 to show how an exogenous increase in "modernization," which might result from exposure to foreign culture, will affect economic growth. Assuming that modernization responds only slowly to income, show how the initial effect of the exogenous increase differs from its long-run effect.

6. Imagine that you are playing the "ultimatum game" described in the box "Determinants of Cooperation" (page 423). The other player (whom you cannot observe) is of your same economic and social group. The sum of money to be divided in the game is $1,000.

   a. If you were the responder, what minimum payout would you accept? Explain why.

   b. If you were the proposer, what division would you propose? Explain your reasoning.

   c. How would your responses to parts a and b have differed if the sum of money to be divided was $10 instead of $1,000? Why?

7. Do the following informal survey of six of your friends or family members. First explain to them the rules of the ultimatum game described

in the box "Determinants of Cooperation." Then tell them to imagine they are the proposer, that the responder is someone from their own economic and social group, and that the sum of money to be divided is $1,000. Ask them what division they would propose and why. Report the results of your survey, and then draw conclusions about what explains differences among your respondents regarding their proposed divisions.

For additional exploration and practice using the Online Data Plotter and data sets, please visit www.pearsonhighered.com/weil.

GEOGRAPHY, CLIMATE, AND NATURAL RESOURCES

Geography is destiny.

—Napoleon Bonaparte

In examining the fundamental determinants of income differences among countries, we have repeatedly grappled with the issue of whether the variables we were measuring were really so fundamental. How can we be sure that the nature of a country's government determines its level of income, for example, when there is also a compelling case that income affects government? The same holds true for income inequality and for culture.

In this chapter we look at a set of potential determinants of income—geography, climate, and natural resources—that are clearly immune to this problem. As we shall see, however, our difficulties are not completely behind us. To give a preview, Figure 15.1 shows a scatter plot comparing income per capita and a nation's latitude—that is, its distance from the equator. There is clearly a strong relationship in the data: The farther a country is from the equator, the richer it is, on average. Further, there is certainly no danger of "reverse causation," that is, no risk that the relationship in the data occurs because becoming rich causes a country to move farther from the equator. But what *does* the relationship between income and latitude tell us? What economic machinery underlies this relationship?

In this chapter we examine data on how geography, climate, and natural resources differ among countries. We will see that there are good theoretical reasons why each of these characteristics should affect income. In the case of two of these characteristics—geography and climate—we will also find good empirical evidence that the effect is significant. We will also see how these characteristics have been incorporated into theories of why the Eurasian landmass developed before the rest of the world and into two different explanations for why Europe developed before China.

One conclusion from this chapter is that the natural resources available in a given country today are not a great constraint on growth because countries can import resources from abroad. But this finding leaves open the question of whether the availability of resources at the *world* level may not constrain worldwide growth. We return to this topic in Chapter 16.

FIGURE 15.1

Relationship between Latitude and Income per Capita

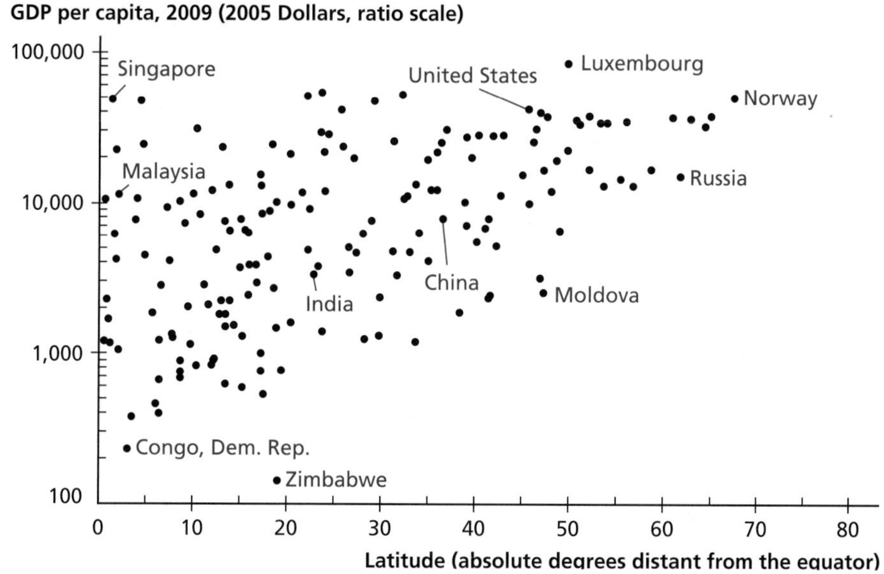

GDP per capita, 2009 (2005 Dollars, ratio scale)

Sources: Heston, Summers, and Aten (2011), Gallup, Mellinger, and Sachs (2001).

15.1 GEOGRAPHY

The population of the world passed the 7 billion mark on about October 31, 2011. This population inhabited planet earth's surface area of 58 million square miles (150 million square kilometers) of land. These numbers imply an average population density of 121 people per square mile (47 people per square kilometer). But as the map of world population density inside this book's back cover shows, the population of the planet is not spread out evenly. Mountains, deserts, and polar regions have extremely low population densities. In total, 90% of the world's population lives on only 10% of the land. Population densities of countries range from 5.2 people per square mile in Mongolia and 7.8 people per square mile in Australia up to 3,271 people per square mile in Bangladesh. The United States has 88.1 people per square mile.

That some parts of the world have low population densities is no surprise. It is difficult to live at all—let alone to produce output—in some of the earth's inhospitable regions. Most people live in places where conditions are favorable for production and for living: where temperatures are moderate, the ground is level, soil is fertile, and there is neither too much nor too little precipitation.

In this section we consider how the standard of living (as opposed to the density of population) is related to geographic characteristics. We examine effects of geography on economic growth through the channels of international trade, cross-border influences of neighboring countries, and geographic influences on government. We also look at the role that geographic factors played in economic growth in the millennia before the continents were linked by transoceanic travel. Then, in Section 15.2, we explore the effects on economic growth caused by one of geography's most important aspects: climate.

Location, Trade, and Growth

In Chapter 11 we considered how international trade affects economic growth. We saw that openness to international trade raises income per capita primarily through its effect on productivity: Openness facilitates technology transfer, leads to a more efficient organization of the economy, and raises income by allowing a country to specialize in the goods it is best at producing.

Recall that one of the determinants of openness to trade is geography. Unlike other determinants of trade, such as tariffs and quotas, a country's geography is unchangeable. If geography determines trade, and if trade helps a country grow rich, then some countries (or regions of countries) have a fundamental advantage over others.

The most important geographic determinant of a country's ability to participate in international trade is its proximity to the ocean. In *The Wealth of Nations* (1776), Adam Smith wrote:

> As by means of water carriage a more extensive market is opened to every sort of industry than what land carriage alone can afford it, so it is upon the sea-coast, and along the banks of navigable rivers that industry of every kind begins to sub-divide and improve itself, and it is frequently not till a long time after that those improvements extend themselves to the inland part of the country.

As in Smith's day, today ocean transport is the cheapest way to ship goods. And geographic evidence bears out the importance of ocean transport in determining where people live and what standard of living they enjoy. Only 17.4% of the world's landmass is located within 60 miles (100 kilometers) of an ocean or a river that is navigable as far as the sea. However, 49.9% of the world's population lives on this land, and 67.6% of the world's gross domestic product (GDP) is produced on it. GDP per capita in areas that are within 60 miles of the sea is, on average, twice as high as GDP per capita in areas farther inland.[1]

Proximity to the sea can also go far toward explaining large differences in economic success among regions of the world. Figure 15.2 shows a strong positive relationship between the fraction of a region's population that lives within 60 miles

---

[1]Mellinger, Sachs, and Gallup (2000).

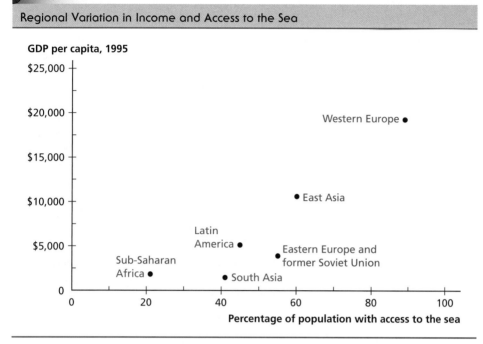

FIGURE 15.2

Regional Variation in Income and Access to the Sea

GDP per capita, 1995

Source: Gallup, Sachs, and Mellinger (1999).

of an ocean or a navigable river and the region's average level of GDP per capita. Particularly striking in the figure is the low fraction of the population in sub-Saharan Africa, only 21%, that has access to the sea. This is caused by several factors, including a dearth of natural ports and an absence of navigable rivers (e.g., the enormous Congo River system is blocked by waterfalls only 83 miles inland). In addition, sub-Saharan Africa has a low ratio of coastline to land area (Western Europe has one-eighth the land area of Africa, but its coastline is 50% longer). Furthermore, Africa's population is concentrated in the interior highlands, where the tropical heat is somewhat reduced.

Besides access to waterways, another determinant of a country's openness to trade is its location with respect to major centers of economic activity. On average, each 600 miles (1,000 kilometers) of distance from one of the most developed regions of the world (the United States, Western Europe, or Japan) raises transport costs by one percentage point. Similarly, increasing the distance between two countries by 1% lowers the volume of trade between them (relative to GDP) by 0.85%.

Together, access to the sea and distance from major centers of economic activity help account for differences in the cost of transporting goods. The average cost of transporting imports, expressed as a ratio to the total value of imports, is 3.6% for the United States, 4.9% for Western Europe, 9.8% for East Asia, 10.6% for Latin

GUNS, GERMS, AND GEOGRAPHY

Some 500 years ago, there began one of the most pivotal events in human history. Over three centuries, starting with Christopher Columbus's voyage to the Americas in 1492 and ending with James Cook's discovery of Australia in 1770, human populations that had been geographically isolated from each other for millennia came into violent contact. The impetus for this collision of civilizations was the spread of Europeans—explorers, traders, colonists, and conquerors—throughout the world.

The most dramatic impact of this clash of civilizations occurred in the Americas and in Australia, where much of the native culture, language, and population were wiped out and replaced with European imports. Most of Asia, by contrast, either was never colonized by Europeans at all or, if colonized, managed to maintain its precolonial civilization, population, and language. Sub-Saharan Africa's fate lay between these two extremes: European control was more complete than in Asia, but it never resulted in the wholesale displacement of the native population, as it had in the Americas.

Many of the proximate causes of Europe's domination are fairly obvious: Europeans of the 16th century had better weaponry and more sophisticated social organizations than did the American, Australian, and African natives with whom they came into contact. The considerably smaller technological gap between Europeans and Asians explains why Europeans failed to dominate Asia as they did other regions. But

what was the source of this discrepancy? Why had the Americas, Australia, and sub-Saharan Africa not developed to the same level as the civilizations of Europe and Asia by the time that they all came into close contact?

In *Guns, Germs, and Steel: The Fates of Human Societies*, biologist Jared Diamond argues that it was geography that determined this outcome.* According to Diamond, Eurasia, the landmass composed of the continents of Europe and Asia, had several key advantages over the rest of the world that allowed it eventually to dominate.

Eurasia's most important advantage was its good fortune in having numerous species of plants and animals that could be domesticated. The large mammals that formed the basis for premodern agricultural economies—cows, horses, pigs, sheep, and goats—were all native to Eurasia. By contrast, in the Americas, the only mammals that could be domesticated were llamas and alpacas, both of which were localized in their habitats and of limited economic usefulness. Similarly, of the 56 large-seeded grass species that could potentially be domesticated as food grains, 39 were native to Eurasia, 11 to the Americas, 4 to sub-Saharan Africa, and only 2 to Australia.

This advantage in the range of species that could be domesticated stemmed partially from plain luck. It also resulted from a second advantage that Eurasia had: its size. Including North Africa, to which it was both culturally and economically linked, the Eurasian landmass is 50%

America, and 19.5% for sub-Saharan Africa. These differences in transport costs correlate well with differences in trade volume and income per capita.[2]

Access to trade explains differences in income not only among countries but also among the regions of a single country. The case of China provides an interesting

---

[2]Bloom and Sachs (1998), Gallup, Sachs, and Mellinger (1999), Frankel and Romer (1999).

larger than the Americas, two-and-a-half times as large as sub-Saharan Africa, and eight times as large as Australia. A larger area is likely to contain more useful plant and animal species. If the employment of these species then spreads throughout the landmass, residents of a larger area ultimately have the benefit of a higher number of useful species.

Another advantage of Eurasia was in its geographic orientation along an east-west axis. This orientation allowed for the spread of agricultural techniques and of useful plant and animal species throughout a zone of relatively similar climates. Thus, the chicken, domesticated in China, could spread to Europe, whereas grains first domesticated in the Fertile Crescent of southwest Asia spread as far east as Japan. By contrast, the north-south orientation of the Americas meant that climactically similar zones, which could potentially have shared agricultural technologies, were separated by areas in which these technologies would not be useful and thus would not spread. Similarly, although the climates of southern Africa and the Mediterranean basin were similar enough that European crops would have grown in southern Africa, the two regions were separated by a whole continent in which European crops would not flourish. Consequently, these crops did not reach southern Africa until they arrived by sea.

The availability of food crops and domestic animals in Europe and Asia allowed for more efficient food production, denser populations, and the rise of advanced civilizations. Surplus food could support a large class of rulers, priests, and warriors. This context fostered the rise of new technologies, including writing, metallurgy, and the oceangoing ships that took European colonizers around the world. The east-west orientation of the Eurasian landmass allowed important inventions such as the wheel (invented around 3000 B.C. in the Black Sea region) to spread throughout the continent. And the vastness of the Eurasian landmass permitted a large population to share these new technologies. As a result, Eurasia was more economically advanced—and more densely populated—than any other part of the earth.

Finally, domestic animals and dense populations gave Europeans one more crucial benefit. People's close association with large animals allowed many animal diseases, such as measles and smallpox, to transfer to humans. And dense populations caused Europe to sustain a number of endemic diseases that, in a sparser population, would have died out. Over time, Europeans developed partial immunity to these diseases, although they still harbored the agents of infection. Thus, when Europeans came into contact with unexposed American Indians, the results were devastating. Diseases killed far more Americans than any deliberate action of the Europeans, and the massive depopulation left the Americas (and later Australia as well) open to domination and colonization.

*Diamond (1997).

example. Before 1978, government policy closed the Chinese economy to most foreign trade. In the 25 years following the liberalization of trade policy, the ratio of trade to GDP quadrupled. The fastest growth in trade occurred in China's coastal regions, which also experienced much faster income growth than did the country's interior provinces. Thus, once the artificial barrier of government trade policy was removed, geographic differences in the ease of trading with the rest of the world led to an increase in income inequality among different regions in China.

Geographic Concentration and Spillovers

A look at the world map inside the front cover of this book suggests that wealthy countries tend to be near one another. Europe is the best example. Among non-European countries that are wealthy, there is also a good deal of clustering, such as Canada and the United States, Japan and South Korea, and Australia and New Zealand.

One possible explanation for this clustering is that it reflects countries' influence on their neighbors. Economists use the term **spillovers** to describe these cross-border effects. We already saw that countries that are near each other are more likely to trade with each other. Wealthy countries also tend to spread jobs to their poor neighbors to take advantage of low wages; one prominent example is the **maquiladora** assembly plants in Mexico that import components from the United States and ship their output back over the border. A wealthy neighbor also provides a positive example, a source for ideas to copy, and opportunities for training. In contrast, a politically unstable neighbor is likely to be a source of refugees or military aggression. Because poor countries are more prone to suffer from such instability, having rich neighbors is an aid to a country's growth.

A second possible explanation for this clustering is that nearby countries share common characteristics that are important for growth. For example, countries that are close to each other share the same climate. Similarly, neighboring countries may have common characteristics that are difficult for economists to measure. In Chapter 14, for example, we weighed the possibility that the fast-growing East Asian countries share a Confucian culture.

Depending on the exact source of the relationship between a country's income and that of its neighbors, the fact that wealthy countries are geographically clustered may represent an additional obstacle for the development of many poor countries. Specifically, if the clustering of economic growth is indeed the result of spillover effects, then this is good news for a few developing countries that are near richer countries (e.g., Mexico, Morocco, and China), but it is bad news for most of the developing world, particularly for sub-Saharan Africa. If, however, the clustering of economic growth simply reflects common factors among neighboring countries, then the clustering itself does not represent additional bad news. According to this second interpretation, countries that put in place the building blocks of growth—good government, accumulation of physical capital and human capital, and so on—will grow rich even if their neighbors remain poor.

Geography's Effect on Government

Another way in which geography has been theorized to affect economic growth is through its effects on the size of states as well as the conduct of government.[3] The background to this theory is the observation of differences in the historical

---

[3]Jones (1987).

formation of states in Europe in comparison to most of the rest of the world—and, in particular, in comparison to China—in the period before the Industrial Revolution. Europe was exceptional for its lack of a unified government. The division of Europe into a large group of independent countries has been a feature of the continent's history since the dissolution of the Roman Empire. In 1600, there were 500 more or less independent political units in Europe, and even in 1900, after centuries of consolidation, there were 25 independent European states.

In contrast to Europe, China has had a history of remarkable centralization, beginning with the first unified Chinese state in 221 B.C. The last extended period of partition ended in the 13th century. Even as China was conquered by foreigners including the Mongols (13th century A.D.) and the Manchus (1644), the country continued to be governed as a single unit. Beyond China, empires were also the general rule in most of the preindustrial world.

Was Europe's lack of unification good for economic growth? A priori, we might expect exactly the opposite. A large, unified country will have a large market and thus the potential for gains from specialization. Productive ideas should also spread more easily in a unified country. Disunity raises the prospect of war between neighboring states, which wastes resources—and indeed, preindustrial Europe experienced a great deal of fighting among neighboring states.

Despite these theoretical advantages of unification, historical experience points to a number of ways in which the lack of centralization in Europe proved advantageous for economic growth. First, external competition served as a check on governments' power. Although a given ruler might be tempted to enact policies that would stifle economic innovation to maintain the status quo, there was always the danger that neighboring countries would allow innovation and thus gain an advantage. Government's size was limited by the ability of capital owners to move their wealth—and of workers to move themselves—from one jurisdiction to another if they found taxes or other restrictions too burdensome. These constraints forced Europe's monarchs to be less prone to wasteful extravagance than their Chinese peers. Second, when governments did try to suppress destabilizing economic innovation (or the destabilizing ideas that went along with it), the innovators often could move to a neighboring country. In China, by contrast, there was usually no outside competition for the government to worry about, nor was there any place for suppressed innovators to go.

The danger of the unified government in China was most forcefully demonstrated in the 15th century, when the imperial court turned violently against oceanic exploration. The huge Chinese fleets, which had sailed as far as the east coast of Africa, fell into disrepair. By 1500, building a ship with more than two masts had become a crime punishable by death. The advantage of European fragmentation was demonstrated in a similar area: When Genoese navigator Christopher Columbus was unable to get financing for his voyage of exploration from the Portuguese, he turned to their neighbors, and competitors, the Spanish. Europeans were no less disposed to suppress useful ideas than were Chinese—witness the trial of Galileo in 1633, in which the great astronomer was forced to recant his belief that the earth rotates around the sun (his writings were not removed from the Catholic Church's index of banned books until 1835). But even though Galileo's work was suppressed in Catholic areas, his ideas continued to advance in Protestant regions.

In sum, the historical record seems to show that the virtues of competition—which we examined in Chapters 10 and 11 with respect to firms— apply to countries. The question then becomes: What was the source of Europe's exceptionalism? In other words, why did Europe remain politically fragmented while large empires were the norm in the rest of the world?

One prominent theory attributes Europe's fragmented political structure to geography. Figure 15.3 shows that Europe's most fertile lands—areas including the

FIGURE 15.3

Core Areas in Preindustrial Europe

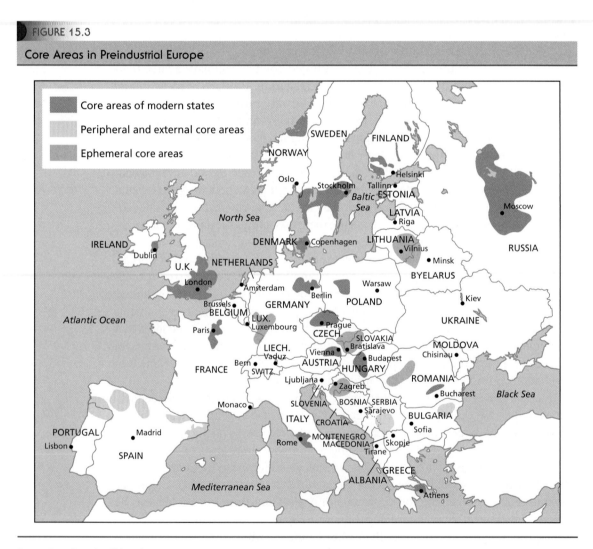

Source: Pounds and Ball (1964).

London basin, the Ile de France, and the plain of the Po River, which would become the cores of modern states—are widely dispersed among large areas of reduced fertility.[4] As historian Eric Jones writes, "On the modern map the intervening spaces have been cleared, drained, cultivated and filled up with people, but until the end of preindustrial times Europe was a succession of population islands in a sea of forest and heath."[5] Europe is also cut apart by numerous natural barriers, including mountain chains such as the Alps and the Pyrenees, as well as bodies of water such as the English Channel. Although the different parts of the continent can communicate and trade with one another, they are sufficiently separated that they are difficult to govern as a single unit. By contrast, as shown in Figure 15.4, China has only four such core

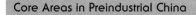

FIGURE 15.4

Core Areas in Preindustrial China

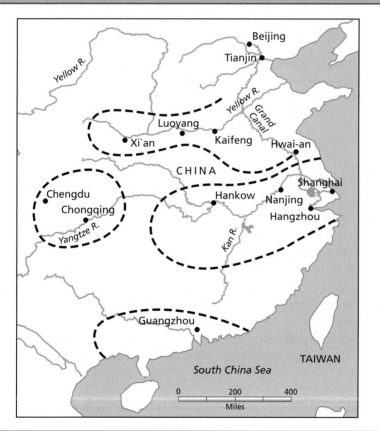

Source: Stover (1974).

---

[4]Pounds and Ball (1964).
[5]Jones (1987), p. 106.

regions, of which two, centered along the Yellow and Yangtze rivers, are dominant.[6] Further, the main core areas of China were connected by the Grand Canal in the fourth century B.C. Thus, geography made it likely that China would be governed as a single unit, a circumstance that held back economic growth.

Like many other explanations for the different historical experiences of Europe and China, however, this theory has to be treated with some caution. An interesting counterexample comes from the history of the Indian subcontinent, which has a geography much like Europe's with scattered areas of fertile land separated by desert, hills, and jungle. India was not politically unified between the Gupta empire in the fifth century A.D. and the Mughals in the 16th century A.D. Yet political fragmentation in India did not have the same growth-inducing effects that it did in Europe. This example is a useful reminder that geography is not necessarily destiny—geography may be part of the explanation of why Europe developed before the rest of the Eurasian continent, but not all of it.

15.2 CLIMATE

One of the most important aspects of a country's geography is its climate—that is, the seasonal patterns of temperature, precipitation, winds, and cloud cover. We begin our analysis of climate by looking at data on how income and population differ among the world's climate zones. We then investigate some of the potential causes of this variation.

Previously in this chapter, we noted the strong relationship between a country's distance from the equator (i.e., its latitude) and its income per capita. Because latitude is linked to climate, this finding suggests a role for climate in determining income per capita. But climate does not depend on latitude alone; factors such as prevailing weather systems, distance from the ocean, and altitude also matter. Thus, for example, the nations of Western Europe, because they are warmed by the Gulf Stream, are not as cold as other countries at similar latitudes. Altitude explains why the highlands of Kenya are relatively moderate in their climate despite their proximity to the equator. For an accurate assessment of climate's role in determining income per capita, we need to look at detailed data on how climate varies.

Geographers divide the earth's climate into 12 zones, which are detailed in Table 15.1. The left-most column of the table gives the climate designation according to the Koppen-Geiger system of climate classification (the exact meaning of these designations is not important for our purposes).[7] The second column describes the climate zone, and the third column lists some representative cities in each zone. The fourth and fifth columns show the percentage of the world's

---

[6]Chi (1963).
[7]For a full discussion, see Strahler and Strahler (1992).

TABLE 15.1

World Climate Zones

Climate Zone	Description	Representative Cities	Percentage of World Landmass	Percentage of World Population	GDP per Capita Relative to World Average
Af	Tropical Rain Forest	Jakarta, Indonesia; Manaus, Brazil	4.0	4.4	0.64
Am	Tropical Rain Forest with Seasonal Monsoon	Manila, Philippines; Cochin, India; Belém, Brazil	0.8	2.4	0.41
Aw	Tropical Savannah	Dhaka, Bangladesh; Kinshasa, Congo; Havana, Cuba	10.8	17.5	0.38
Cw	Subtropical: Mild Humid with Dry Winter	Hanoi, Vietnam; Kanpur, India; Lilongwe, Malawi	4.3	16.0	0.44
Cf	Mild Humid Climate with No Dry Season	New York, USA; Paris, France; Shanghai, China; Sydney, Australia	7.7	19.5	2.24
Cs	Mediterranean Climate: Mild, Humid with Dry Summer	San Francisco, USA; Rome, Italy; Santiago, Chile	2.2	4.3	2.10
Df	Snowy-Forest Climate with No Dry Season	Chicago, USA; Moscow, Russia	23.0	5.8	1.90
Dw	Snowy-Forest Climate with Dry Winter	Seoul, South Korea; Vladivostok, Russia	6.2	5.3	0.64
BS	Semi-arid Steppe	San Diego, USA; Odessa, Ukraine	12.3	11.8	0.55
BW	Desert: Annual Precipitation Less than 15 in. (38 cm)	Cairo, Egypt; Karachi, Pakistan	17.3	6.2	0.58
H	Highlands	Mexico City, Mexico	7.3	6.8	0.78
E	Ice Climates: Average Temperature in Warmest Month Less Than 50° F (10° C)	Nuuk, Greenland	4.0	<0.1	—

Source: Data on landmass, population, and GDP per capita are from Mellinger, Sachs, and Gallup (1999).

landmass in each zone and the percentage of the world's population living in each zone. Finally, the sixth column of the table presents average GDP per capita in each zone relative to the world average.

The first three climate zones in Table 15.1 (Af, Am, and Aw) are classified as tropical. These are areas in which average temperatures during the coldest month of the year do not fall below 64° F (18° C). As the table shows, these tropical regions, which together contain 24.3% of the world's population, are poor. As a group, their income per capita is only 43% of the world average. The fourth climate zone, designated Cw, is subtropical and shares many of the characteristics of the tropical group, including its relative poverty.

The second group of four climate zones (Cf, Cs, Df, and Dw) is referred to as the temperate region. As can be seen in Table 15.1, these are generally the wealthiest parts of the world, the exception being the relatively small Dw zone, which falls exclusively in northeastern Asia. Taken together, the temperate region contains 34.9% of the world's population and has income per capita that is 1.94 times the world average. In western Europe, 96% of the population lives in temperate zones. In North America, the percentage is 88%. By contrast, only 12% of Latin Americans and 4% of sub-Saharan Africans live in such zones, and South Asia has no temperate climate zone whatsoever.

In this section, we investigate the links between climate and economic growth. Climate has direct effects on productivity, most importantly in agriculture. Climate also influences the human input into production because the prevalence of disease is linked to climate and because people's ability to work is affected by temperature. Finally, climate affects the economy by making a location more or less pleasant as a place to live.

Climate and Agricultural Productivity

In 2009, agriculture accounted for 35% of world employment. Historically, the figure was much higher, and in many developing countries this is still the case. For example, the share of employment in agriculture is 59% in sub-Saharan Africa and 54% in South Asia.[8] Thus, differences in agricultural productivity among countries profoundly affect income per capita.

Measures of agricultural output per worker differ greatly between tropical and temperate regions. Figure 15.5 shows the relationship between a country's latitude and the production per worker in agriculture. The range of the data is enormous, with workers in wealthy, temperate countries producing as much as 300 times the agricultural output of workers in poor, tropical countries.

The finding that agricultural output per worker is low in the tropics does not necessarily mean that the tropics are a bad place for agriculture. That is, this fact alone does not indicate whether low agricultural output in tropical countries is the result of inherent differences in the agricultural environment, such as can be traced to climate, or whether there is some other cause. Other factors that might explain the gap in agricultural output between tropical and temperate countries include differences in the use of inputs to production such as agricultural machinery and fertilizers, the human capital of farmers, and the amount of land available per farmer. Similarly, differences in agricultural productivity might result from differences in the institutional environment, such as the quality of government, between tropical and nontropical countries. Only after we account for all of these other potential sources of difference can we judge whether climate can explain the low output of tropical agriculture.

---

[8]International Labour Organization (2011).

FIGURE 15.5

Latitude versus Agricultural GDP per Agricultural Worker

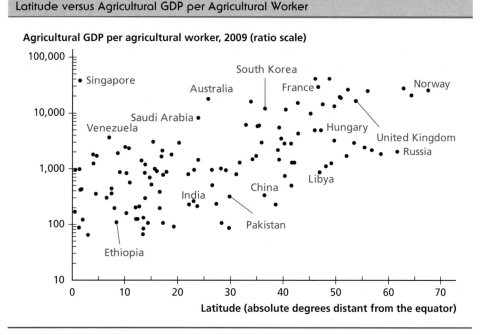

Agricultural GDP per agricultural worker, 2009 (ratio scale)

Source: United Nations Food and Agriculture Organization (2010).

Studies of the agricultural production function, employing techniques similar to those we used in Chapter 7 to analyze the production function for the economy as a whole, show that even when we account for differences in farm machinery, fertilizer inputs, and the human capital of workers, agricultural productivity in tropical countries is lower than in the temperate zone. One estimate is that using the same capital, labor, and fertilizer inputs, land in wet tropical climates produced 27% less and land in the dry tropics produced 31% less output than land in the wet temperate zone. Land in the dry temperate zone produced 15% less than land in the wet temperate zone.[9]

At first, the finding that tropical climates are inhospitable to agriculture may be surprising because we tend to associate tropical climates with lush vegetation. Tropical areas also have longer growing seasons than do temperate regions. On closer inspection, however, tropical climates suffer from several disadvantages in producing useful crops. Although the tropics do receive heavy rainfall, the pattern in which rain falls is not good for farming. In much of the tropics, rain falls seasonally, so torrential monsoons alternate with long dry seasons. Even where this

---

[9]Gallup (1998), Table 2.

seasonal pattern does not occur, tropical rain tends to fall in deluges that can erode the soil. For example, on the island of Java, home to the majority of Indonesia's population, a quarter of annual rain comes in storms of 2.4 inches (60 millimeters) per hour. Similarly, the seasonal pattern of sunlight in the temperate zones—long days in the summer and short days in the winter, as opposed to the relative constancy of sunlight in the tropics—is optimal for growing staple grains such as wheat and corn (maize).

Even more significant as a factor affecting agricultural productivity in the tropics is the absence of frost. Frost, which occurs when the ground-level temperature falls below freezing, has been called "the great executioner of nature" for its effect in killing exposed organisms. Tropical areas are characterized by a wealth of insect life, which competes vigorously with humans in consuming food crops. A second benefit of frost is that by killing some of the microorganisms in the soil, frost slows the decay of organic materials. In tropical regions, the rapid breakdown of organic matter into its component minerals causes farmed land to lose its fertility rapidly unless farmers apply fertilizer. Finally, frost helps to control the types of animal diseases that place a heavy burden on tropical agriculture.[10]

Climate and Disease

In Chapter 6 we looked into how the health of a country's residents affects income per capita. Healthy people can work harder and longer than unhealthy people; they can also think more clearly. Similarly, students who are healthier do a better job of accumulating human capital in the form of education. We saw a strong correlation between health, as measured by life expectancy, and income per capita.

Much of the correlation between health and income per capita results because people in richer countries can afford better inputs into health. But differences in health may also result from factors other than income—the "health environment" of a country that we identified in Chapter 6. In our analysis of the simultaneous determination of income and health, we found that if countries differ in their health environment, these differences will affect both income and actual health. Countries with a poor health environment will in equilibrium be both poorer and less healthy than countries with a good health environment. Further, differences in the health environment among countries will be subject to a multiplier effect: Countries with better health environments will have healthier workers who produce more output, allowing for better nutrition and medical care, which will further improve health.

There is good evidence that the tropics constitute a bad health environment. Tropical regions are rife with diseases that are harmful to humans, including malaria, yellow fever, sleeping sickness, and schistosomiasis (also called bilharzia), to

---

[10]Masters and McMillan (2001), Sachs (2000).

name but a few. The concentration of diseases in the tropics results from two factors. First, regions where the temperature never reaches freezing support a much wider selection of parasites and disease-carrying insects than do temperate zones. Second, because protohumans evolved in tropical regions of Africa and spent millions of years there, local parasites had ample time to evolve to take advantage of them. Starting in the 15th century, Europeans inadvertently spread these African parasites to other tropical areas. In contrast to the tropics, the temperate zones have been home to humans for only a few tens of thousands of years, so fewer disease parasites in these regions have evolved to attack humans.[11]

Of all tropical diseases, malaria has the largest effect on economic growth. In 2010, there were an estimated 216 million cases of malaria, resulting in 655,000 deaths; 80% of cases and 90% of deaths occurred in Africa.[12] A typical bout of the disease entails four to six days of nearly total incapacitation, followed by four to eight days of fatigue. Long-term effects on children include brain damage and learning disabilities and on adults include anemia, which lowers the energy level.

Malaria is caused by a one-celled parasite called a plasmodium and is transmitted among humans by the bites of mosquitoes of the *Anopheles* genus. Female mosquitoes that bite an infected person carry away some of the parasite along with the blood they ingest; when the mosquitoes bite another person, the parasite is transmitted into that person's bloodstream. The malaria parasite has no host other than mosquitoes and humans, and a person who is infected with the parasite will become noninfectious within about two months of having received the parasite. Therefore, malaria can be maintained only in climates where mosquitoes are active almost year-round.

Today malaria is confined almost exclusively to the tropics in what is a significant retreat from its earlier geographic extent. Before 1945, areas at a high risk for malarial infection included Greece, Spain, Italy, and large parts of the U.S. South. For example, in 1935 there were 135,000 cases of malaria and 4,000 deaths from the disease in the United States. In Europe some geographical areas, such as the Pontine Marshes in central Italy and the Plain of Marathon in Greece, were considered uninhabitable because of the pervasiveness of malaria.

As with other tropical diseases, malaria's restriction to the tropics could conceivably be the result of the poverty of tropical nations rather than to any characteristic of malaria itself. That is, tropical countries might be poor for some reason unrelated to malaria (e.g., the effect of climate on agricultural productivity that we considered in the previous section), and such countries might suffer from malaria because they are too poor to undertake proper preventive measures. To assess this issue, researchers have constructed an index of "malaria ecology" for various countries. The malaria ecology index measures the susceptibility of a

---

[11]McNeill (1976).
[12]World Health Organization (2011).

country's climate to mosquito breeding (which depends on adequate rainfall and warm temperatures), as well as the prevalence of mosquito species that feed only on humans (because human malaria is transmitted by a single mosquito biting two people, transmission is much more likely when mosquitoes limit their meals to humans).

As Figure 15.6 shows, the malaria ecology index is closely related to the actual incidence of malaria, measured as the fraction of the population that was exposed to risk of malaria in 1994. Among countries with low values for the malaria ecology index, little or none of the population was at risk for the disease. In most of the countries with a high value for the index, 100% of the population was at risk. For intermediate values of the malaria ecology index, we find interesting variation among countries. For example, Spain and India have roughly the same malaria ecology index—that is, their climates are equally hospitable to malaria mosquitoes—but 66% of India's population was at risk for the disease whereas none of Spain's population was. Other countries are notable as outliers. For instance, Pakistan had surprisingly high exposure to malaria given its climate, and Brazil had very low malaria given its climate.

FIGURE 15.6

Malaria Ecology versus Incidence of Malaria

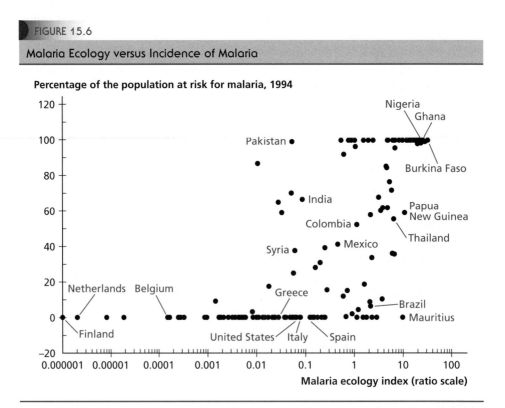

Percentage of the population at risk for malaria, 1994

Sources: Kiszewski et al. (2004).

Overall, Figure 15.6 shows that malaria ecology is the dominant factor in explaining the actual incidence of malaria. This finding is profoundly bad news for the development prospects of tropical countries. For countries such as Pakistan and India, with moderate levels of malaria ecology, there are hopeful examples in which countries that have a similar climate have eliminated the disease. But for countries with a very high malaria ecology index, there are almost no examples of the successful eradication of the disease. The only country with an extremely favorable malaria ecology that has wiped out the disease, Mauritius, is a special case. The environment of Mauritius is so favorable to malaria that in 1867 an epidemic of the disease killed 10% of the country's population. However, Mauritius has the advantage of being a small island of only 788 square miles (2,040 square kilometers). Being small made it relatively easy for the country to eradicate malaria by draining swamps and spraying DDT. Once malaria was eliminated, Mauritius did not face the common problem of the reintroduction of the disease from neighboring areas because it was cut off by the ocean.[13]

Climate and Human Effort

A final aspect of climate's effect on economic growth is associated with the effort that people put into their work. French philosopher Montesquieu observed in 1748 that "people are more vigorous in cold climates."[14] Montesquieu's own explanation for this phenomenon—involving nervous juices, bodily fibers, humors (fluids thought to affect health and temperament), and other aspects of 18th-century medical theory—has been discredited, as has been his belief that a warm climate makes a person more sensitive to both pleasure and pain. But there is a more straightforward explanation for the relationship between temperature and vigor, based on human physiology. Simply put, people in warm climates cannot work hard because they will overheat. Three-quarters of the energy released by a working muscle takes the form of heat, which must be dissipated in order for the body to go on functioning. In a warm climate—especially a warm, humid climate, where the evaporation of sweat cannot keep the body cool—people must work slowly if they are to survive.

The relationship between climate and effort can be modified by technology. Humans, after all, are tropical creatures. In their natural state, humans are far more vulnerable to exposure during winters in the temperate zone than to overheating in the tropics. This vulnerability to cold is the reason that humankind spent most of its history in the tropics. Technological progress in the form of clothing, shelter, and fire allowed humans to leave Africa and populate the rest of the planet. So successfully did preindustrial technology keep people warm that human habitation

---

[13]World Health Organization (2003), Gallup and Sachs (2001).
[14]Montesquieu (1914), Book XIV.

spread as far north as the Arctic Circle. But technological development in the area of temperature control has been asymmetric: We have been able to warm ourselves for thousands of years, but only in the last century, following the invention of the air conditioner in 1902, did we learn to cool ourselves. Even now, cooling technology is much more cumbersome and much less portable than heating technology in the form of clothing.

Because of its high cost, air-conditioning has had most of its impact so far in developed countries rather than poor countries in the tropics. In the United States, for example, air-conditioning has contributed to the rise of the "Sun Belt" in the decades since 1950, when air-conditioning started to come into widespread use. The fraction of the U.S. population living in the South, having declined in the first half of the 20th century, rose from 31% in 1950 to 37% in 2010. Cities such as Houston, Atlanta, Phoenix, and Las Vegas owe much of their rapid growth to the fact that air-conditioning made them livable year-round. Many pundits have argued that the air conditioner also deserves some of the credit for the growth of big government in the United States after World War II. Before the invention of air-conditioning, Washington, D.C. was so miserable in the summer that the federal government almost closed down for several months each year.

In most tropical countries, with a few exceptions like Singapore, air-conditioning has thus far had little impact on worker productivity. Ironically, as tropical countries grow wealthier, the last occupation that will benefit from air-conditioning is the occupation that is most prevalent in the tropics: agriculture. It is much easier to air-condition a factory or an office than it is to keep a farmer cool out in the fields.

15.3 NATURAL RESOURCES

One seemingly obvious geographic determinant of income is the presence or absence of natural resources. Output is not produced by capital, labor, human capital, and technology alone: Also needed are natural resources such as farmland, forests, and minerals, which are combined with capital and labor to produce output. It seems obvious that countries with more natural resources per capita should be richer than those without resources. Yet the relationship between resource endowments and income has proved to be more complex than one would initially think.

The Relationship between Natural Resources and Growth

Until the 19th century, the most important natural resource for determining economic growth was fertile land. Although European colonists were first drawn to the New World in pursuit of gold and silver, the availability of abundant land is what drove most of the economic growth of the Americas. The importance of land as a natural resource is not surprising because, as we saw in Chapter 3, land was more significant than capital as a factor of production (and earned a higher fraction of national income) before industrialization. The newly settled, land-abundant countries were among the richest in the world in the 19th century. In 1870 Australia, the United States, and Canada had higher real wages than any country in Europe, and Argentina's real wages were higher than those of any European country other than Great Britain. Not surprisingly, these land-rich countries were magnets for immigration: In the hundred years following 1820, some 60 million Europeans set sail for the New World.[15] Along with this flow of labor came an inflow of European capital. As we saw in Chapter 11, financial markets were globalized in the 19th century, and a good deal of the investment that took place in the Americas was financed in Europe. Thus, growth of many countries in the Western Hemisphere was very much "resource driven." Observers of the time took it for granted that a country's bounty of natural resources was a primary determinant of its economic success.

And yet, for all the countries that grew rich from natural resources, in many others, abundant natural resources did not result in economic growth. The sugar-producing islands of the West Indies, which at the time of the American Revolution were the richest parts of the British Empire in America, remained economically stagnant after 1800. Similarly, Mexico and Peru were the most important Spanish New World colonies because of their rich endowments of gold and silver, but they failed to move beyond resource extraction into sustained growth. During the 19th century, there were booms in the production of cotton (Egypt), copper (Chile), sugar (Cuba), coffee (Brazil, Colombia, and Costa Rica), guano (Peru), and nitrate (Chile), all of which failed to lay the foundation for long-term growth.

In the post–World War II period, the relationship between economic growth and natural resource endowments has also been uneven. Many countries—most notably, the oil-exporting countries of the Persian Gulf—have grown rich from natural resources. But there are also prominent examples of countries that have grown rich despite being exceedingly poor in resources. Conversely, many countries have remained poor despite a generous endowment of resources.

To assess more systematically the role of natural resources in determining countries' income, we use World Bank data that measure each country's natural capital. **Natural capital** is the value of a country's agricultural lands, pasture lands, forests, and subsoil resources, including metals, minerals, coal, oil, and natural gas.[16] Unlike physical and human capital, natural capital is not created by

---

[15]O' Rourke and Williamson (1999).
[16]World Bank (2006).

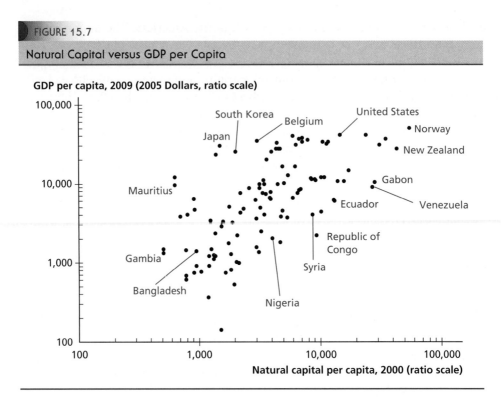

FIGURE 15.7

Natural Capital versus GDP per Capita

Sources: World Bank (2006), Heston, Summers, and Aten (2011).

deliberate investment. Rather, a country's natural capital represents the resources that exist irrespective of human activity.

As shown in Figure 15.7, natural capital and GDP per capita are positively related: Countries with more natural resources tend to have higher income. (Several wealthy, oil-rich countries such as Saudi Arabia, Kuwait, and Qatar are omitted from the figure because of lack of data.) However, there are many exceptions to the rule that resources make a country richer. Japan, South Korea, and Belgium are among the world's most resource-poor nations but are also among those with the highest income per capita. Similarly, Syria, Venezuela, Ecuador, and the Republic of Congo all have low income relative to their levels of natural resources. Thus the figure suggests that natural resources are helpful to economic growth but are neither necessary nor sufficient to achieve growth.

Analyses similar to Figure 15.7 but looking at the growth of income rather than the level of income have come to a conclusion that is even less favorable to natural resources. For example, one study examined the role of natural resources by calculating the share of total national wealth (defined as natural plus physical plus human capital) that consisted of natural capital. The author found that countries where natural capital made up a large fraction of national wealth grew significantly more slowly over the period 1965–1998 than did countries where natural capital made up a small share of national wealth. Similarly, another study found that countries that relied on natural resource exports grew more slowly between 1970 and 1990 than those that did not rely on such exports.[17]

These studies present a puzzle. Surely, a bounty of natural resources should, other things being equal, make a country better off. Yet the effect of natural resources on income is weak at best. In the next section, we explore potential solutions to this puzzle.

Explanations for the Resource Curse

As we have seen, an abundance of natural resources is often a spur to economic growth. At the same time, many countries' experience with natural resources has been surprisingly disappointing. This negative experience has led some observers to conclude that in the long run, the presence of natural resources can actually impede economic growth—in effect, that there is a "resource curse."

Where could such a resource curse come from? In Chapter 14, we identified one possible channel: that countries rich in natural resources do not develop the cultural attributes necessary for economic success. In addition to this culture-based explanation, three other prominent theories attempt to come to grips with this phenomenon, one focusing on the level of saving, one on the process of industrialization, and one on politics.

Overconsumption. One explanation for the resource curse begins with the observation that booms in income resulting from natural resources tend to be temporary. The discovery of a new resource or a sudden increase in the price of a resource will lead to a spurt in a country's export earnings. Eventually, however, either the resource runs out, or its price in the world market decreases as importing countries find a substitute or as new sources of supply come on line.

Windfalls of income associated with resource booms seem to lead countries to raise their consumption to levels that cannot be sustained once the boom ends. As a result, countries in which booms have ended experience low rates of saving (and thus investment) in an effort to maintain their consumption. Because economic growth requires investment, the final result is a lower level of income after a temporary resource boom than if the boom had never taken place.

In some cases, the situation is even worse. During a resource boom in developing countries, their governments sometimes assume that revenue from the

---

[17]Gylfason (2001), Sachs and Warner (2001).

resource not only will remain high but will *keep on rising*. In anticipation of higher future revenues, such governments borrow money on the world market, often to fund ill-conceived public investment projects. When the resource boom ends, these countries are left with unsupportable overhangs of foreign debt.

What is bad for growth is not the presence of natural resources per se, but rather the interaction of natural resource abundance with some other factor. In the case of a temporary resource boom, a country whose people or government was sufficiently forward-looking could take a large fraction of the resource windfall and invest it productively for the future. Thus, the country could end up richer in the long run.[18]

Dynamics of Industrialization. A second explanation for the resource curse is that natural resources distort the structure of an economy in a way that produces short-run benefits but long-run costs. A country with natural resources to export will import other products, generally manufactured goods, for its own consumption. The shift to importing manufactured goods will cause the country's own manufacturing sector to contract. In the short run, this contraction represents an efficient adjustment. However, manufacturing industries are those with the most rapid technological progress. A country that imports its manufactures will miss out on this progress and may be worse off in the long run than a country that lacks a natural resource to begin with. The process by which the presence of a natural resource is ultimately detrimental to the domestic manufacturing sector is called the **Dutch disease** because it was first analyzed when the development of large natural gas fields off the coast of Holland in the early 1960s led to a contraction of that country's manufacturing sector.

One of the most prominent historical examples of the Dutch disease is the experience of Spain after Europe's discovery of the New World. Spain became fantastically rich from the inflow of gold and silver from the Americas. This inflow had the same effect on the Spanish economy as if the resources had actually been located in Spain itself. Spain traded its gold and silver to the rest of Europe in exchange for manufactured goods. But when the flow of gold and silver ran out, other countries had gained experience and knowledge in production, and Spain was left an economic backwater.

One implication of this theory is that the effect of resources on a country's economic growth will depend crucially on the degree to which the exploitation of a natural resource stimulates or impedes production in other sectors of the economy. Resource extraction can stimulate production in other sectors through **backward linkages,** in which locally produced goods are used as inputs by the resource extraction industry, and **forward linkages,** in which the natural resource is processed or used to produce other goods. When backward and forward linkages

---

[18]Rodriguez and Sachs (1999).

are present, the exploitation of a natural resource can drive the development of the economy as a whole. Backward linkages may provide enough demand to allow for the creation of industries for which the country otherwise would have been too small. Similarly, countries may start up the ladder of industrial development by processing their own natural resources. Finally, industrial development resulting from backward or forward linkages can stimulate growth in other economic sectors. For example, a railway line built to take iron ore from a mine in a country's interior to a port on the coast can also link farmers in the country's interior to world markets.

Whether exploiting a given natural resource will result in backward and forward linkages that promote economic growth depends on the nature of the resource, transport costs, and the state of the economy in which the resource is found. In the case of a land-rich country such as the United States in the 19th century, the export of grain, a resource-intensive product, involved a rich set of forward and backward linkages. The economy required agricultural machinery to harvest crops, railroads to move them to ports, and a banking system to finance the whole operation. Through these linkages, resources contributed to the industrialization of the United States itself.

Ironically, one consequence of the reduction in transport costs over the last 200 years is that much of the processing of natural resources now occurs in a place other than where the resources are located. In the late 19th century, the United States, Britain, and Germany all experienced rapid growth in their steel industries owing to the availability of domestic iron and coal deposits. By contrast, after World War II, Japan and South Korea became major steel producers using imported raw materials. For resource-producing countries, the reduction in transportation costs means that the production of natural resources is often unaccompanied by significant forward or backward linkages. Some resource exports in the developing world today take the form of **enclaves**—small pockets of economic development that have almost no contact with the rest of the country's economy. The most extreme version of such an enclave is offshore oil production, in which capital and workers are imported and oil is pumped and exported without any contact with the local economy.

Politics. The theories of why resources may not lead to development we've considered so far—overconsumption, the Dutch disease, and lack of linkages—all suggest that government actions can play a role in turning the resource curse into a blessing. Government policy, for example, can help to ensure that the windfall income from a commodity boom is used for investment or put aside for a rainy day rather than being used for consumption. Similarly, because many resource extraction industries are owned by a government itself, government policy can be used to establish forward and backward linkages between resource extraction and other sectors of the economy. In addition, governments can collect taxes on resource exports and use this revenue to provide a public good such as infrastructure or to invest in education. Thus, we might expect that, with proper government policy, the presence of natural resources could be a significant boon to growth.

The fact that natural resources frequently do not support growth suggests, then, that governments are not undertaking effective policies. But many observers go one step further, arguing that the presence of natural resources actually makes governments undertake *worse* policies than they otherwise would. That is, natural resources may have a toxic effect on the political system.

The negative effects of natural resources on government policy come through two channels. First, natural resources often lead to an overexpansion of the government sector of the economy. This ballooning of government occurs both because resources provide a ready source of government revenue and because large government is often a means by which the revenue from natural resources is distributed, legally or otherwise, to powerful groups within a country. Second, by increasing the revenue that the government can distribute to favored groups, the presence of natural resources raises the stakes in the struggle for control of the government, thus encouraging people to put more effort into maintaining or seizing power.

The following description of Venezuela during the oil boom of the 1970s captures the typical ways in which natural resource revenue is redistributed to favored groups:

> In this climate, massive government contracts were awarded outside of regular procurement procedures; large sums of money passed through state agencies without controls; millions of dollars worth of loans were granted without regulation. Previously existing forms of illegality were exacerbated: for example, the juggling of bank accounts, the awarding of contracts without a public bidding process, the private purchase of properties with public monies, the diversion of budgetary funds for purposes other than their allocation, the awarding of commissions on loans and contracts, [and] the issuance of large loans without sufficient security.

From 1970 to 1978, the size of the public sector of Venezuela's economy (government and government-owned firms) doubled, and the country's foreign debt rose by a factor of nine.[19]

The struggle for the control of government that results from these opportunities to grab a share of natural resource revenue takes a variety of forms, from political corruption to civil war to foreign invasion. The 10-year war that displaced a third of Sierra Leone's population in the 1990s, fought over and funded by lucrative diamond exports, is one of the worst cases of this sort of struggle. In countries in which resources are distributed unevenly along ethnic lines, the situation is even more terrible. For example, in Sudan a 20-year civil war pitting the politically dominant Muslim north of the country against the non-Muslim, oil-rich south

---

[19]Karl (1997), p. 146, Table 8, and Table A.9.

killed 1.9 million civilians. (A peace treaty was signed in January 2005, and the new country of South Sudan was established in 2011.)

The toxic effects of natural resources on the political system are most severe in the case of resources associated with large economic rents. Recall from Chapter 10 that an economic rent is a payment to a factor of production that is in excess of what is required to elicit the supply of that factor. Where there are large economic rents, the benefits of rent seeking are larger, and so, correspondingly, are the resources wasted on such activities. Resources produce large rents if they are easily extracted relative to their price. For example, in Saudi Arabia the cost of producing oil, inclusive of capital expenditures, is in the neighborhood of $4-6 per barrel.[20] In early 2012, that oil was selling for more than $100 per barrel. Similarly, resources produce rents if extraction is done by foreigners; for example, when oil is produced by platforms off the coast of Angola, the foreign companies that pump the oil simply send royalty payments to the Angolan government, without requiring anyone in Angola to do anything. By contrast, resources such as fertile farmland produce smaller (or no) rents because getting value out of farmland requires capital and labor.

Of course, the presence of rent-producing natural resources does not *necessarily* lead to political problems. In Norway, for example, large oil exports have fattened the government's coffers, but the country has remained free of the rent seeking, corruption, and mismanagement that have plagued most oil exporters. In addition, Norway has managed to put much of its extra income aside as a reserve to be used when oil revenues fall. The southern African country of Botswana provides another example in which government has apparently been immune to the toxic effects of natural resources. Despite a heavy reliance on diamond production (which accounts for 33% of the country's GDP), Botswana has maintained a stable, democratic, efficient, and honest government. In the 43 years following independence in 1966, GDP per capita grew at an annual rate of 6.0%. Why has Botswana been able to profit from natural resources whereas so many other African countries have failed? Among the explanations that have been put forward are Botswana's high degree of ethnic homogeneity, the survival of precolonial tribal institutions that constrained political elites and allowed for the expression of dissent, and the exceptional talent and lack of greed of Botswana's first postindependence leader, Seretse Khama.[21] The examples of Norway and Botswana imply an important interaction between the presence of natural resources and other factors—for example, culture and human capital—that also influence the quality of government. Perhaps once a country is rich enough or has a long enough tradition of honest government, it is relatively immune to the toxic effects of natural resources on the political system.

---

[20]Reuters (2009).
[21]Acemoglu, Johnson, and Robinson (2003), Beaulier (2003).

In an effort to moderate the most toxic effects of resources on development, the Extractive Industries Transparency Initiative (EITI) was created in 2002. The initiative brings together corporations in the oil, gas, and mining industries with governments of resource producing countries. Corporations agree to report all payments (taxes, royalties, bonuses) made to governments in resource producing countries and to submit to external auditing of their accounts, whereas governments agree to disclose all revenues received from corporations. An independent group in each country is then appointed to reconcile the two sets of reports. As of 2011, 60 of the world's largest oil, gas, and mining companies, and 35 governments, mostly in Africa, had signed on to the initiative. The hope is that transparency will prevent the worst abuses associated with resource extraction. Corporations will not be able to disguise bribe payments as other items in their account books. Similarly when citizens know exactly how much revenue was turned over to their governments, they will be in a position to demand that the money be used well. Whether the EITI is successful remains to be seen, however. Pessimists argue that with prices for the extractive products rising once again, the incentives faced by corporations to cut corners to secure supplies will simply be too great to resist. Further, the entry into the market of large Chinese buyers, which may not be constrained by scruples that western governments impose on their corporations, may undo some of the benefits of the EITI.

15.4 CONCLUSION

Is geography (along with climate and natural resources) destiny? Because a country's geography, climate, and natural resources are not determined by human activity, these characteristics are particularly attractive as fundamental explanations for differences in economic outcomes among countries. It is intellectually more satisfying to say that "Country X developed before Country Y because of differences in these fixed characteristics" than it is to cite accidents of history. In this chapter we have seen strong evidence that geographic and climatic characteristics are related to countries' economic outcomes. In the case of natural resources, the evidence is much weaker.

Still, some obstacles stand in the way of concluding that geography and climate are destiny. To see the difficulties, we can return to the chapter's opening example of latitude and income per capita. Countries near the equator have more disease-prone and enervating climates, are generally farther from the centers of economic activity, and have lower agricultural productivity than countries at higher latitudes. These characteristics might be underlying channels that explain the strong correlation between income per capita and distance from the equator. Many of these explanations would lead to the depressing conclusion that countries near the equator will never catch up to the developed world. But even with these potential explanations for the link between latitude and income, we still cannot be fully confident that proximity to the equator necessarily explains why these countries are poor. For every one of the channels we considered as a way in which geography can affect income, we can find exceptions. For example, even though most economic activity is conducted near seacoasts and in temperate climates, the fastest-growing city in the United States is Las Vegas, which is located in a desert, far inland. Similarly, the prevalence of disease in tropical areas has not *always* been a barrier to economic achievement. For example, although the French attempt to build a canal across Panama in the 1880s was defeated by yellow fever and malaria, at the cost of some 20,000 lives, in a subsequent effort by Americans, these diseases were eradicated before construction took place. Indeed, even the relative unhealthiness of the tropics is not an exogenous factor for certain. One reason that the tropics are so unhealthy for humans is that less money has been spent on studying tropical diseases than on studying diseases of temperate climates. This imbalance in spending is easily explained by the fact that rich countries—whose citizens buy new medicines and whose governments sponsor research—are located in temperate climates. Similarly, one reason that tropical agriculture is relatively unproductive is that agricultural research and development (R&D) is concentrated in temperate zones, so the technologies developed in these regions are not appropriate for the tropics.

Given these doubts, there is always the possibility that our explanations for the poverty of tropical countries are after-the-fact rationalizations. Perhaps if Sweden were poor rather than rich, economists would blame its poverty on the difficulties produced by cold weather and snow or the depressing effects of long winters.

An even more difficult question is what the existing relationship between latitude and income per capita tells us about income growth in the future. The example of the air conditioner altering the pace of economic activity in the U.S. South suggests that technological progress can significantly change the relationship between geographic factors and economic growth. It is also possible that the climate-income correlation we observe reflects the circumstances of history rather than any deleterious effects of climate on health or productivity today. We saw in Chapter 12 that climate was an important determinant of the kind of government Europeans established in their colonies. In climates in which disease took a heavy toll on European settlers, colonial powers tended to create "extractive" institutions. Conversely, in climates in which the mortality of Europeans was lower, permanent settlers brought with them European forms of government. The institutions created by colonial powers tended to carry over into the postcolonial period, endowing tropical former colonies with bad governments, which in turn stifled economic growth. If this mechanism is the primary explanation for the relationship between climate and income in the world today, then tropical countries that manage to improve their governing institutions will not experience any negative effect of climate on economic growth.[22]

One of this chapter's most important lessons is that a country's natural resources have only a limited effect on economic growth. Countries that lack many of the raw materials necessary to produce output in a modern economy can

---

[22] Acemoglu, Johnson, and Robinson (2001).

RESOURCES AND EARLY INDUSTRIAL DEVELOPMENT: THE CASE OF COAL

Much of the evidence in this chapter points to the conclusion that the presence of natural resources is not essential for economic growth in the world today. Simply put, countries can make up for any resources they lack by importing them from abroad. A different issue is whether the presence or absence of natural resources helps to explain the history of economic growth. In this area, many scholars argue that natural resources help to shed light on one of the most puzzling phenomena in economic history: the emergence of the Industrial Revolution in Europe rather than China, despite the latter's longer history of economic integration and, for many centuries, its more advanced level of technology.

The particular natural resource underlying this theory is coal. In Chapter 9 we saw the central role that coal played in the Industrial Revolution in Europe. Coal was the fuel that allowed for a vast increase in iron production starting in the 18th century. Even more significantly, coal-fired steam engines powered factories and drove the railways and ships that produced such a spectacular increase in trade in the 19th century.

China has vast coal deposits and today is the world's largest coal producer. But from the perspective of early industrialization, China had two pieces of bad luck involving coal. The first disadvantage was the location of the coal. China's deposits are primarily in the northwest of the country, particularly in the province of Shanxi, far from centers of population and economic activity, and are inaccessible to any easy water transport. Engineering and railroad technology were not advanced enough to exploit Chinese coal deposits until long after the beginning of industrialization. By contrast, Europe's largest coal deposits reside in Britain, the country that led the Industrial Revolution. British coal is located near centers of economic activity that predated the Industrial Revolution and is easily accessible to canals and ocean transport.

The second piece of bad luck for China derives from differences in the geology of the Chinese and British coal mines. Because British coal mines are susceptible to flooding, constant effort has to be applied to pump water out of them. This coincidence of a great need for mechanical energy for pumping at the same location as a cheap source of fuel ensured a ready demand for coal-fired steam engines. Indeed, early steam engines were so woefully inefficient in their use of energy and so bulky that they had no practical use *other* than pumping out coal mines. Only after several decades, as experience with steam power produced a series of technological improvements raising energy efficiency and reducing engine size, did the steam engine move beyond coal mines to become the dominant source of power for the Industrial Revolution.

In contrast to the British mines, Chinese coal mines are dry, and the greatest danger is not flooding but spontaneous combustion. To prevent spontaneous combustion, the Chinese developed sophisticated ventilation technology. Unlike the steam engine, however, this technology did not have uses in other parts of the economy.*

*Pomeranz (2000).

nonetheless grow rapidly, and countries that are well endowed with resources often grow slowly. The explanation for this surprising finding is simply that many natural resources are easy to transport across country borders.

The observation that the resources available to a given country do not determine its growth tells us nothing about whether the resources available to the world as a whole will affect global growth. Unlike individual countries, the world as a whole cannot import natural resources, at least for the foreseeable future. We return to the issue of natural resources at the world level in Chapter 16.

KEY TERMS

spillovers   438
maquiladora   438
natural capital   451

Dutch disease   454
backward linkages   454
forward linkages   454

enclaves   455

QUESTIONS FOR REVIEW

1. Why are geography, climate, and natural resources particularly interesting to study as possible determinants of economic growth? How do these characteristics differ from other factors affecting economic growth, such as quality of government, income inequality, and culture?

2. What evidence do we have that proximity to ocean transport is an important contributor to economic growth?

3. How did the availability of useful plant and animal species affect economic development in different regions before the 16th century? Why were Europe and Asia advantaged in this regard?

4. How were differences in geography reflected in the political histories of Europe and China? How did these political differences in turn affect economic growth?

5. Through what channels might a country's climate affect the country's level of income per capita?

6. What characteristics of tropical climates are particularly hostile to economic growth?

7. What is natural capital? In what ways is it similar to physical capital and human capital? In what ways is it different?

8. What is the resource curse? What are some potential explanations for it?

PROBLEMS

1. What does the Malthusian model presented in Chapter 4 predict will be the effects of climate-based differences in agricultural productivity on population density and on the standard of living in different geographic regions? Does this prediction match what we see in the data?

2. What does Jared Diamond's theory regarding the role of geography in explaining preindustrial economic growth say about the different fates of Europe and China?

3. How does globalization change each of the following relationships? In each case, cite specific examples.

   a. The relationship between a country's natural resources and its level of income per capita

   b. The relationship between a country's geographic characteristics and its level of income per capita

   c. The relationship between a country's climate and its level of income per capita

4. How have past changes in technology changed each of the following relationships? In each case, cite specific examples.

    a. The relationship between a country's natural resources and its level of income per capita

    b. The relationship between a country's geographic characteristics and its level of income per capita

    c. The relationship between a country's climate and its level of income per capita

5. Give an example of a possible (or at least conceivable) technological advance that would alter the relationship between countries' natural resource endowments and their levels of income per capita. Do the same for a possible techno-logical advance that would alter the relationship between countries' geographic characteristics and their levels of income per capita, and for a possible technological advance that would alter the relationship between countries' climates and their income per capita.

6. Study the history and geography of each of the following countries. Then write a short descrip-tion of how geography, climate, and natural resources have influenced each country's eco-nomic development and current economic status. Discuss whether the different theories presented in this chapter are borne out in these particular cases.

    a. Bolivia

    b. Panama

    c. Singapore

For additional exploration and practice using the Online Data Plotter and data sets, please visit http://www.pearsonhighered.com/weil.

16

RESOURCES AND THE ENVIRONMENT AT THE GLOBAL LEVEL

We first examined the interaction of natural resources and economic growth in Chapter 15. There we saw that a country's endowment of natural resources has surprisingly little impact on its level of economic development. The explanation is that countries can trade with each other, so they can import the resources they need. When we look at the relationship between resources and economic growth from a worldwide perspective, trade is irrelevant, at least for the foreseeable future. Unlike a single country, the world cannot make up for a shortage of natural resources by importing. Thus, although a lack of natural resources may not put one country at a disadvantage relative to others, natural resource shortages could be a problem for the world as a whole.

> Anyone who believes exponential growth can go on forever on a finite planet is either a madman or an economist.
>
> —Kenneth Boulding

In this chapter, we inquire into how natural resources interact with economic growth at the global level. We will see that this issue is far more contentious than other aspects of growth we have explored in this book. There is an immense intellectual gap between scholars who see the constraints imposed by natural resources as a crucial check on growth and those who argue that natural resources do not pose much of a problem. Further, the two sides in the debate often appear to be speaking different languages, and communication between them often takes the form of insults.

We begin by laying out a basic framework for measuring natural resources and incorporating resource inputs into the analysis of production. We then explore how to account for natural resource depletion in analyzing economic growth and whether mankind's current use of natural resources is sustainable in the long run. Finally, we examine how economic growth affects the environment. We will see that many of the concepts we applied in thinking about natural resources also carry over to the study of environmental degradation if we envisage a pristine environment as a resource that is depleted when pollution is created.

In our analysis of the interaction of resources and economic growth, we stress three related concepts: substitution, prices, and property rights. Substitution occurs when firms or consumers switch from using scarce resources to abundant resources. Resource prices signal a resource's scarcity to resource users (who will attempt to find substitutes) and to resource producers (who will attempt to produce more). Finally, when property rights over resources are well established, owners of resources have an incentive to preserve them, so looming resource shortages are reflected in higher prices. When this mechanism linking property rights, prices, and substitution functions properly, it automatically limits the impact of natural resource scarcities on the economy. In cases in which this mechanism breaks down, natural resource shortages pose their most severe threat to economic growth.

The roles of resource prices and property rights are particularly relevant when we examine how economic growth affects the environment. The key difference between a clean environment and other natural resources is that most of the time, no one owns a clean environment, so no market price is attached to creating pollution. For this reason, environmental degradation—particularly for the aspects of the environment that are least subject to property rights, such as the atmosphere—is more likely to be a problem associated with economic growth than is a shortage of natural resources.

16.1 NATURAL RESOURCE CONCEPTS

We begin by examining the different forms of natural resources, their measurement, and their use in economic activity.

Nonrenewable Resources

A **nonrenewable resource** is one that exists in a fixed quantity on the earth. When a nonrenewable resource is consumed, it is gone forever. A common measure of the availability of a nonrenewable resource is the level of **current reserves**, or the known quantity of the resource that can profitably be extracted at current prices using existing technology. Changes in the quantity of current reserves are brought about through four processes. The first two of these are the obvious ones: discoveries of new stocks of the resource raise reserves and depletion of existing stocks lowers reserves. The third way in which reserves can change is when the price of the resource changes: for example, if the price rises, then known deposits that were previously not worth extracting can become economically viable, increasing reserves. Finally, changes in technology can also make it worthwhile to extract a resource from a known deposit, even if the resource's price has not changed. In recent years, an important example of this effect has been the development of hydraulic fracturing ("fracking"), a technique that allows for the recovery of natural gas and oil from deep shale formations.

To look in more detail at data for a nonrenewable resource, we examine the most important one in the world today: oil. In 2011, oil accounted for 33% world

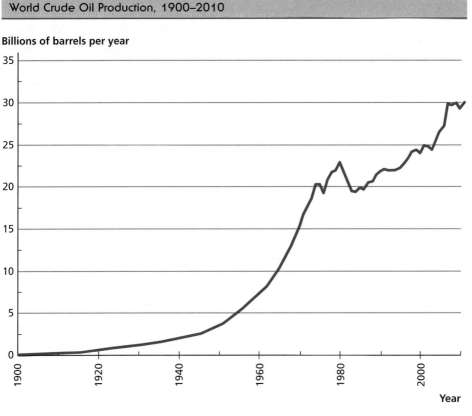

Sources: Jenkins (1977), p. 85 and Table 2, U.S. Department of Energy, Energy Information Administration (2007), Chapter 11, BP (2011)

energy production, followed by coal (28%), natural gas (22%), renewables (11%), and nuclear (5%).[1]

Figure 16.1 shows world production of crude oil since 1900. Oil production has quadrupled since 1960. The rich countries of the Organisation for Economic Co-operation and Development (OECD) account for 52% of world oil consumption, with the United States alone consuming 22%. By the end of 2010, the world had consumed 1,164 billion barrels of oil since the first well was drilled.

Table 16.1 presents data on oil reserves, production, and additions to reserves from 1945 to 2010. The table shows a pattern that is quite common in analyses of nonrenewable resources: even though production during the period examined was quite high compared with the quantity of reserves, the quantity of reserves continued

---

[1]U.S. EIA International Energy Outlook 2011: http://www.eia.gov/forecasts/ieo/world.cfm.

> **TABLE 16.1**

World Crude Oil Production and Reserves (Billions of Barrels)

	1945–1960	1961–1970	1971–1980	1981–1990	1991–2000	2001–2010
Reserves at Beginning of Period	51	292	612	649	1,001	1,108
– Production	77	119	205	217	253	253
+ Additions to Reserves	318	439	242	569	360	380
= Reserves at End of Period	292	612	649	1,001	1,108	1,236

Sources: Adelman (1995), Table 2.2; BP (2011)

to grow over time. In other words, more oil was discovered than was used. From 1945 to 2010, 1,123 billion barrels of oil were pumped, but 2,308 billion barrels of oil were added to reserves, primarily through discovery but also through changes in technology that made feasible the pumping of oil that had already been discovered.

Because oil is nonrenewable, this pattern of consumption rising but discovery rising even faster cannot continue indefinitely. The question is: When will it end? Answering this question requires estimating the amount of undiscovered oil in the world, by necessity a somewhat speculative exercise. An assessment by the U.S. Geological Survey in 2000 estimated the amount of ultimately recoverable oil (i.e., the amount that existed on the planet before humans withdrew any) at 3.0 trillion barrels.[2] Using this figure, we could say that out of the 3.0 trillion barrels of oil that existed before humankind started using oil, 1,164 billion barrels, or 39%, have already been used, 1,236 billion barrels (41%) have been discovered but not used, and 600 billion barrels (20%) remain to be discovered.

These estimates imply that 1,836 billion barrels of ultimately recoverable oil remained on earth at the end of 2010. Thus at the current rate of use of 30 billion barrels per year, all the oil will be gone in 61 years. If oil usage rises over time, as it has in the past, oil will run out sooner. For example, world oil usage grew at an annual rate of 1.6% per year between 1983 and 2010. If usage continues to rise at this same rate in the future, all the oil will be gone in 43 years.[3] Even before oil

---

[2]U.S. Geological Survey (2000).

[3]Mathematical Note: We calculate the time until the resource runs out as follows. Let $U(t)$ be the annual usage, $S(0)$ the total stock of the resource remaining at time 0, g the annual rate of growth of usage, and T the date on which the resource will run out. The relationship among these variables is given by the equation

$$S(0) = \int_0^T U(0)e^{gt}dt.$$

Integrating this equation and rearranging gives

$$T = \frac{\ln\left(1 + g\dfrac{S(0)}{U(0)}\right)}{g}.$$

runs out entirely, production will start to decline. The term **peak oil** is used to refer to the date when world production reaches its maximum. Estimated dates for when peak oil will be reached vary widely, but years in the range 2020–2030 are often mentioned.

Given the importance of oil in the world economy, does this looming stockout of oil mean that we are headed for economic disaster? Much of this chapter will be devoted to discussing exactly such questions.

Renewable Resources

A **renewable resource** is one that is replenished by natural processes and thus can be used repeatedly. Some renewable resources are not affected by the quantity that humans use. The simplest example is sunlight. The amount of sunlight available every year is roughly the same, and the amount that humans use in any given year does not affect the amount that will be available in future years. For other renewable resources, the situation is more complex. With respect to plants and animals, for example, the amount of the resource that is available at any time depends on past consumption. Although these resources can regenerate themselves, the speed with which they do so depends on usage. If too much of such resources is used at any one time, they may not be able to renew themselves in the future. Thus, it is possible to overuse renewable resources.

To illustrate this process, we can construct a simple mathematical framework. We define S_t as the resource stock at the beginning of period t, H_t as the quantity of the resource harvested in period t, and G_t as the quantity that grows in period t. The change in the stock from period to period is the difference between the amount of the resource that grows and the amount that is harvested. That is:

$$\Delta S_t = S_{t+1} - S_t = G_t - H_t.$$

The growth of the resource is a function of two variables: the existing stock of the resource, S, and the **carrying capacity** of the environment, which is the largest quantity of the resource that would exist in nature if humans never harvested the resource. If the stock of the resource is equal to the carrying capacity of the environment, then growth will be zero because there is no room for additional growth of the resource. Thus, when we are considering levels of the resource stock that are close to the carrying capacity of the environment, lower resource stocks will lead to higher growth. But if the resource stock is *too* low, then a second factor sets in—the rate at which the stock can grow depends on the quantity of the stock. In the case of fish or animals, for example, if so few members of a species remain in an environment that breeding pairs cannot find each other, then no regeneration of the stock will occur.

Figure 16.2 summarizes this discussion with a hump-shaped curve that shows the growth of a renewable resource as a function of its stock. The exact shape of this curve depends on the resource being considered. For species that

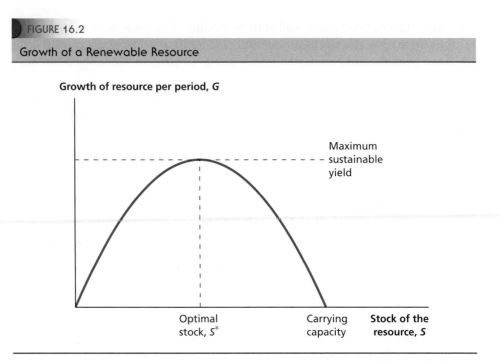

▶ FIGURE 16.2

Growth of a Renewable Resource

can reproduce rapidly to fill up an environmental niche, the peak of the curve (the maximum amount of growth) will occur when the stock is small relative to the carrying capacity. For species that naturally reproduce slowly, the maximum growth will be at a higher level of the stock relative to the carrying capacity—in other words, the peak of the curve will shift to the right.

The peak of the curve in Figure 16.2 is called the **maximum sustainable yield,** which is the largest quantity of the resource that can be harvested per period of time without diminishing the quantity of the resource available for future use. Corresponding to the maximum sustainable yield is an optimal stock of the resource, S^*.

For a resource that has not been used at all, the stock will be equal to the carrying capacity. If the resource is then harvested at the maximum sustainable yield, the stock will decline temporarily before stabilizing at the optimal stock, S^*. However, if the harvest of the resource is greater than the maximum sustainable yield for too long a period of time, the stock will fall below S^* and eventually reach 0. Further, once the stock of a resource has moved below S^*, the stock cannot be restored simply by reducing the harvest to equal the maximum sustainable yield. Rather, a period of harvesting *below* the maximum sustainable yield is required to restore the stock of the resource to the optimal level.

Unfortunately, a pattern of harvests above the maximum sustainable yield leading to stock below S^* describes the condition of many renewable resources in the world today. One of the most common examples of resources that experience overharvesting is fish. For example, Georges Bank, off the coast of New England, was once among the most productive fisheries in the world. The estimated maximum sustainable yield of groundfish (cod, haddock, and flounder) in this area is 217 million pounds (99 million kilograms) per year. By the mid-1960s, however, the annual catch had risen to 1.5 billion pounds (682 million kilograms). As stocks of fish declined, fishers used ever better technology in an effort to maintain their catch, but this effort was increasingly futile. By 1993 the annual catch had plummeted to 66 million pounds (30 million kilograms), and even at this level, it appeared that the population was not regenerating itself. This pattern of overfishing has been replayed throughout the world. Most recently, there has been a sharp drop in the stock of Atlantic tuna fish, which is commonly used in sushi.

Another important renewable resource that is vulnerable to overuse is underground aquifers containing fresh water that can be pumped to the surface. Aquifers from which a moderate amount of water is pumped will be naturally recharged as rainwater percolates through the soil above them. However, pumping too much water at once can render the aquifer unusable. For example, excessive pumping from an aquifer near a coastline can allow seawater to replace the fresh water. The aquifer that supplies almost all of the water used in the Gaza Strip under Palestinian Authority control is currently being pumped out at a rate that will lead to its total collapse within two or three decades.[4]

Property Rights over Resources

Another aspect of resources that will become important in our analysis is the degree to which their use is governed by property rights. Resources can be classified according to the degree of control that individuals, corporations, or governments can exert over their use. At one end of the spectrum are land and minerals, which are generally covered by well-established property rights. At the other end of the spectrum are fish in the sea, which are subject to little or no ownership.

The degree to which a resource is covered by property rights affects how it is used. Specifically, resources not covered by property rights are susceptible to inefficiently high rates of use. In the case of nonrenewable resources, overrapid depletion results. For a renewable resource, the consequence is extraction beyond the maximum sustainable yield. In both cases, the absence of property rights takes away a producer's incentive to limit present production to increase future stocks. For example, a fisherman who reduced his catch so as to maintain the stock of fish for the future would most likely see others harvest these fish. Similarly, if more than one person has the right to exploit a nonrenewable resource, each will have an incentive to use it quickly, before someone else does.

---

[4]United Nations Environmental Program (2002).

The tendency to overexploit resources to which there are no property rights is called the **tragedy of the commons.** The term refers to the practice in preindustrial England of reserving some of a village's land as a "commons" on which all residents were free to graze their livestock. In 1833 economist William Forster Lloyd noted a stark contrast between commons land and privately owned land. "Why," he asked, "are the cattle on a common so puny and stunted? Why is the common itself so bare-worn, and cropped so differently from the adjoining inclosures?" His answer was that while property owners raising livestock on their own lands faced an incentive to limit grazing so as to preserve the fertility of the land for the future, no such incentive was present for those using the commons. As a result, commons land was frequently overgrazed and rendered unproductive.[5]

One solution to the tragedy of the commons is to establish property rights. In the case of common grazing land, for example, creating property rights would mean dividing the commons into a number of private pastures. Assigning private property rights is not always practical, however. For example, in the case of an underground aquifer that runs beneath several people's property, it is impossible to assign a fixed fraction of the aquifer to each property owner. An alternative to private property rights is control of the resource by government or some other authority that can take into account the negative externality that results from the use of the resource. (Recall from Chapter 6 that an externality is an incidental effect of some economic activity for which no compensation is provided.) For example, in the case of a common pasture, the government or some other authority can limit the number of livestock that each herder is allowed to graze. Such an arrangement makes all herders better off.

Proper management of a commons requires an authority that has not only the wisdom and honesty to decide how much of the resource should be used, but also the wherewithal to enforce such decisions. Often, when resources are overexploited, one of these prerequisites is lacking. Forests are among the most overexploited resources in many developing countries. Governments formally own and manage most of this land but are often powerless to stop illegal logging. It is estimated that up to 70% of logging in Indonesia is illegal. Even when government can control access to a resource, political expediency (such as the desire to win an upcoming election or to please a powerful interest group) often favors overuse.

Finally, the most severe cases of the tragedy of the commons occur when resources do not fall under the control of any single government. In the world today, the two most important resources in this category are the ocean and the atmosphere. In recent years, countries have extended economic exclusion zones far beyond their coastlines in an effort to claim property rights over ocean fish—indeed, in 1975, Britain and Iceland came to the brink of war over Iceland's declaration of a 200-mile (320-kilometer) exclusion zone for cod fishing. Despite such efforts,

---

[5]Lloyd (1833), Hardin (1968).

many fish that swim in international waters are being overexploited. The total quantity of wild fish harvested worldwide rose from 20 million tons in 1950 to 96 million tons in 2009. According to the Food and Agriculture Organization, 53% of world fish stocks are currently being exploited at the maximum sustainable yield, and 28% are being exploited beyond that level.[6] In the case of the atmosphere, the problem is not the depletion of a resource but rather pollution. As we will see later in this chapter, however, the economic analysis is the same. Because no one "owns" an unpolluted atmosphere, there is a tragedy of the commons in which producers abuse their ability to dump pollutants into the atmosphere.

Resources and Production

Our interest in natural resources stems from the fact that resources are used in the production of output. Without land to grow food, raw materials from which to make goods, and energy to power machines, economic activity would cease altogether.

Table 16.2 looks at the use of a particularly important resource, energy, by countries grouped according to income. (The data are for the year 2008). The table shows, not surprisingly, that energy consumption rises with income per capita. When we compare the richest with the poorest group of countries, per capita energy use differs by a factor of 14. Using Table 16.2, we can do a simple calculation: Suppose that everyone in the world used the same per-capita quantity of energy as people in the high-income group of countries. How much would world energy consumption rise? The answer is that it would rise by a factor of 2.9. If everyone in the world used as much energy per capita as citizens of the United States (7,481 kilograms of oil equivalent per capita), world energy consumption would rise by a factor of 4.2!

TABLE 16.2

Energy Use by Different Country Groups

Country Group	Population (Millions)	GDP per Capita ($)	Commercial Energy Use per Capita (Kg of Oil Equivalent)	Energy Intensity (Kg of Oil Equivalent per $ GDP)
Low Income	764	1,061	364	0.309
Lower Middle Income	2,392	2,988	671	0.224
Upper Middle Income	2,419	8,063	1,825	0.227
High Income	1,113	33,691	5,112	0.151

Source: World Bank (2011).

---

[6]United Nations Food and Agriculture Organization (2010).

A useful idea for thinking about the role of resources in production is the **resource intensity** of production, that is, the amount of a resource required to produce a unit of output. Applying this idea, the last column of Table 16.2 calculates the energy intensity of production—in other words, the amount of energy used per dollar of GDP produced. Energy intensity falls with income, but the difference between the poorest and the richest groups of countries is only a factor of two. This relative equality of resource intensity is not necessarily true for all resources. For example, intensity of land use per dollar of GDP is much lower in rich than in poor countries because a lower fraction of rich-country GDP is composed of food products. Nor is resource intensity for any given resource constant over time. Intensity of use will rise or fall with changes in technology, changes in the composition of output (e.g., goods versus services), changes in the price of the resource itself, and changes in the price of resources that are close substitutes for a given resource. For example, energy intensity in the United States fell by 1.9% per year between 1973 and 2000, in response to the rise in energy prices that began with the Arab oil embargo.

Using the concept of resource intensity, we can examine how economic growth, population growth, and the growth of resource use are related. Define y as GDP per capita, L as the size of the population, I as resource intensity, and R as resource consumption. The definition of resource intensity is:

$$I = \frac{R}{yL}.$$

We can rearrange this equation to be:

$$R = IyL.$$

Now we can rewrite this equation in terms of growth rates (using a ^ to denote a growth rate):[7]

$$\hat{R} = \hat{I} + \hat{y} + \hat{L}.$$

This equation says, for example, that if output per capita is growing at 1% per year, population is growing at 1% per year, and resource intensity is constant, then total resource use will grow at 2% per year.

The equation can also be turned around and used to illustrate how resource limitations affect economic growth. For example, assume that the quantity of a resource available for use is constant, as in the case of a renewable resource that is already being exploited at the maximum sustainable yield. This assumption implies that $\hat{R} = 0$. The previous equation can then be rewritten as:

$$\hat{y} = -\hat{I} - \hat{L}.$$

---

[7]Mathematical Note: Specifically, we take logarithms of both sides of the equation and then differentiate with respect to time.

In this form, the equation says that for output per capita to have a positive growth rate, resource intensity must be falling faster than population is growing.

16.2 INCORPORATING NATURAL RESOURCES INTO THE ANALYSIS OF ECONOMIC GROWTH

The finite nature of nonrenewable resources implies that an economy faces a trade-off between the present and the future: The more of a resource that is used today, the less will be left for tomorrow. Of course, this trade-off between the present and the future is not unique to natural resources. We saw in previous chapters that investments in physical capital, human capital, and technological progress all have the potential to raise the standard of living in the future, at the cost of lower consumption today. But even if this sort of trade-off is not unique to natural resources, it is certainly most salient in this area. If we do not invest in physical capital or human capital now, later generations can always get around to doing so themselves. But if we consume all of the oil on the planet, future generations may be unable to rectify the situation.

Discussion of the relationship between natural resources and economic growth is often organized around the concept of **sustainable development.** This term was defined by the 1987 United Nations Commission on Environment and Development (also called the Brundtland Commission, after its chair) as "development that meets the needs of the present without compromising the ability of future generations to meet their own needs."

From an economic viewpoint, there are many problems with implementing this definition. First, economists do not like to talk about "needs"—especially in the case of rich countries, in which average levels of consumption are a huge multiple of human needs in any biological sense. A second problem with the approach taken by the Brundtland Commission is that by focusing only on whether income in the future will be higher than income today, the definition leaves much out. For example, suppose that the current path of economic growth is sustainable in the sense that future generations will be *slightly* better off than the current generation. Also, suppose some change in policy would make the current generation only a little worse off but would make those who followed us much better off. Both policies are sustainable, so the sustainability criterion will not help us to choose between them.

A final problem with the definition of sustainable development is that it is much easier to apply it in an ex post sense (i.e., looking backward in time) than in an ex ante sense (looking forward). If shortages of natural resources cause declines in the standard of living, then future observers will correctly conclude that the economic growth we are now experiencing was unsustainable (see box "Resource Disasters"). By contrast, if world income per capita grows steadily over the next 200 years, then it will clearly be true that today's economic development was sustainable. Because we can not see into the future, it is hard to know which of these scenarios will happen.

RESOURCE DISASTERS

The observations that resources are important for production and are in limited supply have often inspired forecasts that resource constraints will inevitably put a damper on economic growth. The intellectual grandfather of this school of thought is none other than Thomas Malthus, who wrote that "the power of population is so superior to the power in the earth to produce subsistence for man, that premature death must in some shape or other visit the human race."[*]

Malthus's prophecy was fairly general; he did not give a date and time for the predicted apocalypse. Many of his successors have been more specific about the nature of the coming resource cataclysm. In 1865 economist Stanley Jevons predicted that Britain would soon run out of coal, with disastrous results. In his assessment of future development in the 1930s, English author H. G. Wells pointed to the fixed supply of phosphorus (necessary for agriculture) as the factor limiting future growth.[†]

Pessimism about future resources peaked in the 1970s, during what was, not coincidentally, a period of rising resource prices. One expression of this pessimism was an exhaustive study called *The Limits to Growth*.[‡] The authors created a computerized "world model" that incorporated feedback loops between economic growth, birth and death rates, stocks of renewable and nonrenewable resources, and pollution. They employed data from the period 1900–1970 to establish a baseline of past behavior and then used their model to forecast what would happen over the period 1970–2100. Figure 16.3 shows the forecast time paths of world population, food per capita, industrial output per capita, nonrenewable resources, and pollution. According to their model, food and industrial output per capita both peak around the year 2000, after which they fall as a

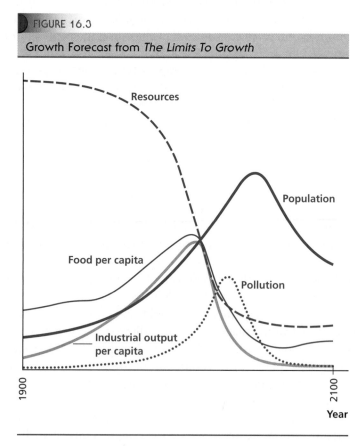

FIGURE 16.3

Growth Forecast from *The Limits To Growth*

Source: Meadows et al. (1972), Figure 35.

result of shortages of nonrenewable resources. Population continues to rise for several decades after the peak of income because of demographic momentum, but sometime in the middle of the 21st century, the death rate is driven upward by lack of food and health services.

So far, these doomsday scenarios have been utterly wrong. Agricultural productivity has risen faster than population, allowing the world to avoid the mass starvation that Malthus forecast. Jevons underestimated the quantity of available coal, the ability of engineers to mine the coal he knew about, and the role that oil would play in the 20th century. Food production, output per capita, and stocks of nonrenewable resources thus far show no evidence of the "overshoot and collapse" predictions of *The Limits to Growth*.

Unfortunately, the past miscalculations of prophets of doom are no guarantee that current forecasters will be wrong. And although there has been no planetwide resource cataclysm, more localized disasters have occurred.

Archaeologists have only recently pieced together the story of one such catastrophe, which took place on Easter Island in the middle of the Pacific Ocean. The island was settled by about 40 Polynesian migrants around A.D. 400. At the time of its settlement, Easter Island was covered with a forest of palm trees. The settlers found life in their new home easy. They cut down trees to build boats, caught fish in the rich waters off the island, hunted birds that lived in the forest, and farmed the fertile soil. With food so abundant, the population naturally grew. At its peak, from A.D. 1100 to 1400, the island supported a population of 10,000. During this period, the island's society was wealthy enough to maintain a special class of artisans, who carved the giant statues that to this day ring the island.

But the rise in population was more than the island's resources could sustain. Trees were cut down faster than they could regenerate, and the size of the forest declined. The birds that the settlers had hunted disappeared, and eventually no good trees were left for making fishing boats. Without the forest cover, the soil started to erode. There is archaeological evidence that the residents started fighting among themselves at this point and stopped building statues.

The Europeans who arrived at the island in 1722 found a population of only 3,000 and a level of civilization far below what had been required to build the giant statues. Further, the island was devoid of trees, and no one could figure out how, without wooden rollers, the giant statues could have been moved to their locations. (The fact that the island had ever supported a forest was not known until archaeologists examined evidence from pollen in recent decades.) The islanders believed that the statues had walked there by themselves.

Easter Island is far from being the only example of how shortages of natural resources can lead to the decline of a civilization. The Sumerian society that flourished in what is now southern Iraq in the third millennium B.C. was the world's first literate culture, with farms productive enough to support a large state bureaucracy and army. But Sumerian irrigation practices caused the soil to become waterlogged, and eventually salt built up on the ground's surface. Crop yields fell 65% between 2400 B.C. and 1700 B.C., and today the region is largely desolate and treeless.[§]

---

[*]Malthus (1798), Chapter 7.
[†]Jevons (1865), Wells (1931).
[‡]Meadows et al. (1972).
[§]Brander and Taylor (1998), Ponting (1991).

Despite the problems associated with implementing the specific definition of sustainable development as formulated by the Brundtland Commission, there is clearly a need for *some* way of assessing whether the path of resource use followed by an economy (or the world as a whole) will lead to a major disaster. We now explore one such approach.

Revising National Accounts

Throughout our study of growth, we have used data on gross domestic product (GDP). The measurement of GDP is part of a broader analytic framework called national income accounting, which was created by economist Simon Kuznets in the 1930s. In recent years, some scholars have tried to extend the system of national income accounting to take into account issues such as resource depletion and environmental degradation.

One approach starts with the idea of natural capital—the value of a country's agricultural lands, pasture lands, forests, and subsoil resources—that we introduced in Chapter 15. Natural capital is conceptually similar to measures of physical and human capital, with the important difference that most of the "investment" in natural capital is negative. That is, a country's natural capital generally declines over time as nonrenewable natural resources are used up. Natural capital can also rise, as occurs when a degraded renewable resource is restored—but such increases are rare. A decline in the stock of natural capital indicates that a country has destroyed an asset that would be valuable in the future.

We can incorporate natural capital into the framework of national income accounting by constructing a measure called green GDP. **Green GDP** is equal to conventionally measured GDP (the value of all the goods and services produced in a country in a given year) minus the value of natural capital that has been depleted or destroyed in that year.

This kind of adjustment is easiest to make in the case of nonrenewable resources. Measuring the quantity of a resource that is depleted in a given year is relatively easy. The harder question is what value to assign to this depletion. We observe the price of the resource in the market, but some of this price represents the effort that went into extracting the resource. Thus, the real value that we will want to use in our calculation is the **in-ground price** of the resource: what the resource sells for minus what it costs to extract. Table 16.3 shows a calculation of the costs of depletion (the adjustment that one would apply to calculate green GDP) for the 14 most important minerals. (Data are for 1994.)

The most important result from Table 16.3 comes from adding up the value of the exhausted resources for these 14 minerals. That total is $341 billion. By contrast, world GDP in 1994 was $25.2 trillion. Thus, the cost of depletion of these 14 minerals was only 1.4% of world GDP. Although not insignificant, this cost is smaller than what many believe to be the costs of resource depletion.

> **TABLE 16.3**
>
> **Calculation of the Value of Depletion for the 14 Most Important Minerals**

Mineral	World Consumption (Thousands)	Price per Unit ($)	Production Cost per Unit ($)	In-Ground Price per Unit (Price– Production Cost) ($)	Value of Exhausted Resource (Consumption: In-ground Price) ($ Million)
Crude Oil	3,012,984	113	56.6	56.4	169,932
Natural Gas	95,925	2,133	958.3	1,174.7	112,683
Hard Coal	3,967,054	40	32.6	7.4	29,356
Brown Coal (Lignite)	1,119,937	11	9.4	1.6	1,792
Bauxite (Aluminum)	132,315	33.8	14.5	19.3	2,554
Copper	9,539	2,330	1,385.2	944.8	9,012
Iron Ore	604,679	40	23.9	16.1	9,735
Lead	2,718	679	658.1	20.9	56.8
Nickel	783	6,278	5,239.9	1,038.1	812.8
Phosphate	136,482	38	31.7	6.3	859.8
Tin	166	5,428	4,209	1,219	202.4
Zinc	6,964	1,033	894.4	138.6	965.2
Gold	1.74	12,346,000	10,822,700	1,523,300	2,652
Silver	10	169,872	129,763.5	40,108.5	401.0
Total					341,015

Source: Weitzman (1999). Quantities are all metric tons, except for natural gas, which is measured in trillions of joules. Prices correspond to the unit of quantity used. Data are for 1994.

Applying this accounting to individual countries can produce more dramatic results. For example, in 2009, Saudi Arabia's measured GDP was $373 billion, and the country produced 3.6 billion barrels of oil. The average price of oil during the year was $56.35 per barrel, and Saudi production costs were roughly $5.00 per barrel, implying an in-ground price for Saudi oil of $51.35 per barrel.[8] Multiplying the in-ground price by the quantity of oil produced implies a downward adjustment of $185 billion (50% of GDP) to account for resource depletion.

Extending this methodology to renewable resources is difficult because the value of natural capital composed of renewable resources is not reduced one for one by the amount of the renewable resource used. If the renewable resource is being managed properly and harvested at less than the maximum sustainable yield, then the value of natural capital will not fall at all. If the resource is being overused

---

[8]Reuters (2009).

to the point where it cannot regenerate itself, then the decline in the value of natural capital will be much larger than the value of the resource harvested.

A third area to which we would like to extend the methodology of green GDP accounting is to analyze the effects of environmental degradation (the topic of Section 16.3). Here the problem is that no "price" is associated with pollution in the same way that nonrenewable resources have a price.

For the methodology of adjusting national income to account for resource depletion, it is crucially important to use the correct prices. That is, the resource price must reflect the cost of the resource being depleted. In calculating green GDP, the most frequently used price is the market price of the resource in question. If this price does not reflect the true scarcity of the resource, then the amount by which GDP is reduced to account for the depletion of the resource also will be wrong. We now consider whether resource prices accurately reflect the costs associated with scarcity.

Resource Prices

The prices that were previously used in calculating green GDP were the actual market prices of resources. For this calculation to make sense as a way to evaluate the cost of depleting resources today for the welfare of future generations, today's prices must accurately reflect the resources' value to future generations. If this condition does not hold—if, for example, people in the future end up putting a high price on resources that we consider cheap today—then our calculation will have understated the cost of resource depletion.

Not only are resource prices important for calculating green GDP, but they also play a crucial role in substitution and technological progress, two processes through which an economy minimizes its use of scarce resources, as we will see. A high price for a resource gives users an incentive to find substitutes. Similarly, a high price signals to potential inventors that finding a technological fix could be profitable.

For all these reasons, then, it is important that today's resource prices correctly reflect the value that people in the future will place on the same resources. The question then becomes: Are today's resource prices correct? Specifically, do prices reflect future resource scarcities?

There is a theoretical reason to think resource prices should indeed—at least in some cases—reflect the future value of resources. The key insight is that a relationship should exist between the scarcity of a resource in the future and its price today. The source of the relationship is the behavior of those who supply the resource. Suppose, for example, that a given resource has a low price today but is expected to be in short supply, and thus expensive in the near future. Owners of the resource will want to hold back their supply today, so they can take advantage of higher prices later on. The lower supply on the market will drive up the price today, and the addition of the resource stocks not used today will lower the price in the future. Exactly the opposite will happen if prices are high today but are expected to be low in the future. Owners of the resource will have an incentive to extract it as quickly as possible, so they can take advantage of the currently high price. Extra supply will drive down the price today, and lower available resources will raise the price in the future. As these examples show, the behavior of suppliers links current prices to expected future prices. Furthermore, because suppliers prefer, all things being equal, to have their money today rather than in the future, the in-ground price of resources should grow over time at the rate of interest.[9]

This mechanism by which the current price of resources reflects their future scarcity can break down for many reasons. If people who own the resource are not forward-looking, for example, then they will not take into account high future prices and will extract too much of the resource today. In this case, resource prices will rise faster than the interest rate. A similar scenario can occur when property rights over resources are poorly defined, so that those with access to the resource know that if they do not extract it today, the resource will not be available to extract tomorrow. Conversely, if resource extraction is limited by some artificial means, such as a cartel of producers, then prices could be high even though there is no long-run scarcity of a resource. In this case, prices might fall over time if the cartel's power weakens.

Thus, it is an empirical question whether the mechanism linking current resource prices to future scarcity holds roughly true. That is, on average, do the in-ground prices of natural resources rise over time at the rate predicted?

In practice, it is usually impossible to look at the in-ground prices of resources, so we focus on the prices of resources themselves. A further issue is that the mechanism linking current prices and future scarcity should hold only *in expectation*. The *actual* prices that we observe for a resource do not necessarily equal the prices that were expected (as future prices) at some time in the past. Things do not always turn out as expected. In the case of some resources, a new, unexpected source of demand may arise. In other cases, there may be an unexpected discovery of a new source of the resource or of some way to substitute something else for the resource. Instances of both phenomena abound. For example, the invention of the Hall-Heroult process in 1886 reduced the costs of aluminum refining by 95% and thus raised the value of bauxite (aluminum ore). Similarly, the development of fiber optic technology greatly decreased the demand for copper in telephone wires. Thus, the actual path of resource prices will combine people's expectations with the effects of unexpected events.

Despite these problems, we can certainly learn something by looking at the long-term history of natural resource prices. If prices are slowly rising over time, then perhaps the mechanism linking future scarcity to current production is mostly functioning. If prices are rising rapidly, this would be good evidence that

---

[9]Hotelling (1931).

decisions over how much resource to extract are *not* taking future scarcity into account.

To apply these principles to historic prices, Figure 16.4 shows data on the prices of natural resources over the period 1850–2010. The data are for a basket of commodities that has been altered over time to reflect changing demand in the most developed countries. The index excludes energy and precious metals. The figure shows a marked declining trend over the span of 160 years, interrupted by fluctuations associated with wars and economic booms and busts. There is also a notable recent surge in commodity prices that was only slightly dented by the worldwide economic crisis of 2008. Despite the recent surge, commodity prices fell by more than 50% over the entire period. Figure 16.5 shows similar data for the price of crude oil in the period 1861–2010. Here the most significant price movements during the last century are associated with the first assertion of power by Organization of the Petroleum Exporting Countries (OPEC) and the Arab oil embargo (1973), the Iranian Revolution (1979), the First Gulf War (1990–1991), and, once again, the takeoff in commodity prices that started around 2005. Until recently, at least, oil prices seem to have been more sensitive to political factors and

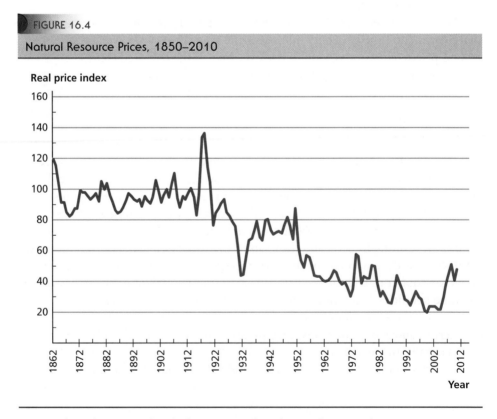

FIGURE 16.4

Natural Resource Prices, 1850–2010

Source: Cashin and McDermott (2002), *The Economist* industrial commodity price index

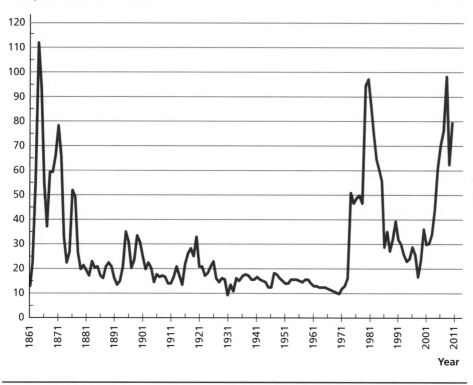

FIGURE 16.5

Real Price of Oil, 1861–2010

Price per barrel (2010 dollars)

Source: BP (2011).

to the success or failure of the producers' cartel in holding back supply than to any running down of the available stock of the resource.

From Figures 16.4 and 16.5 we can only conclude that the mechanism linking current resource use to future resource prices has not worked in practice in the way suggested by theory. But rather than showing that people were short-sighted and used resources too quickly—behavior that would imply rapidly rising resource prices over time—the evidence points to the conclusion that anyone who held back on producing natural resources in order to wait for higher prices in the future was making a mistake. (See box "The Bet.")

With respect to green GDP, the evidence of falling commodity prices suggests that the current prices of natural resources *overstate* the value of these resources to future generations. Thus, when we calculated the amount by which to adjust GDP for the exhaustion of nonrenewable resources, we overstated that adjustment.

THE BET

Scholars usually confine their disagreements to written and spoken words. But in 1980, Paul Ehrlich, a biologist, and Julian Simon, an economist, put their money where their mouths were. Ehrlich, the author of the best-selling book *The Population Bomb* (1968), was a well-known pessimist. He had predicted that the world was heading into a period of catastrophic resource shortages and famine. Simon, on the other hand, was a defender of the theory that human ingenuity is sufficient to compensate for any shortage of natural resources. In a book called *The Ultimate Resource* (1981), Simon summarized his view that people were the only input into production that the world could ever run short of.

Ehrlich's predictions of coming shortages implied that natural resource prices would rise over time. So Simon offered Ehrlich a bet on the prices of resources over the next decade. Ehrlich chose five minerals (tungsten, nickel, copper, chrome, and tin) and calculated what quantity of each could be purchased with $200 in 1980. The two scholars agreed that in 1990, they would calculate the price of the same quantities of the minerals. If the total price was higher than $1,000 (adjusted for inflation), Simon would pay Ehrlich the difference; if it was lower, Ehrlich would pay Simon.

Despite an increase in the world population by 921 million people (21%) during the 1980s, Simon won the bet. The basket of minerals that had cost $1,000 in 1980 was worth only $642 (in 1980 dollars) in 1990. The problem was not with the particular minerals that Ehrlich picked. Indeed, of 37 minerals, 35 declined in price during the 1980s. Simon offered to repeat the bet, but Ehrlich refused the challenge. In fact, the same basket of minerals that was worth $1,000 in 1980 fell further in price, to $415 in 2000, before significantly recovering to $773 in 2009 (both prices in 1980 dollars).* By 2011, the basket was back to being worth almost exactly $1,000 in 1980 dollars.†

*Mineral prices from US Geological Survey, http://minerals.usgs.gov/ds/2005/140/#talc. Deflated using the Consumer Price Index.
†"The Revenge of Malthus: A Famous Bet Recalculated," *The Economist* August 6, 2011.

The finding that natural resource prices have fallen over time, even for nonrenewable resources that are in fixed supply, puzzles many observers. In the next section, we survey the mechanisms that underlie this decline and allow growth to continue despite a fixed quantity of natural resources.

Why Resource Limitations Do Not Prevent Economic Growth

The decline in natural resource prices over time seems to provide evidence that the world is not running out of natural resources. Similarly, the exercise of adjusting national income and product accounts to factor in the cost of depletion of nonrenewable resources suggests that this cost is relatively small. These findings mystify many noneconomists. How can economic growth continue unimpeded when it uses up resources that are in finite supply?

As a starting point for thinking about this kind of issue, we can go back to the data on resource use that were presented in Section 16.1. For nonrenewable resources, we can take oil as an example. From Table 16.1, we saw that the total quantity of oil remaining on the planet is enough to cover roughly 61 years' worth of consumption at the current rate of use. For other nonrenewable resources, the ratio of the ultimately recoverable quantity of the resource to current use is higher, but the same result holds: Eventually, if use continues as its current rate, the resource will run out. Indeed, a moment's thought makes it obvious that *no* rate of depletion of a nonrenewable resource is sustainable indefinitely. In the case of renewable resources, it is possible to sustain use indefinitely, but only at a limited level. If GDP is growing and resource use is already at the maximum sustainable yield, then resource intensity (the quantity of resource used per unit of output) must fall over time.

These considerations would seem to suggest that our current level of resource consumption may indeed not be sustainable. The question is: Does that mean that our level of *income* is not sustainable?

The answer to this question is a definitive no, for two reasons. First, even though the resources that we use now exist in fixed supply, there are frequently possibilities for substituting different resources. Second, although resource depletion is a drag on growth, other factors, most notably technological progress, may be sufficient to overcome this drag and allow income to keep rising. We address these issues in turn. The mathematical appendix to this chapter further explores the relationship between technological progress and the sustainability of economic growth.

Substitution. Substitution is one of the most basic notions in economics. When firms choose the inputs they will use in production, they face a number of choices that will accomplish the same goal. Firms choose among these different possible inputs based on their prices. If a particular input becomes more expensive, the firm can substitute, using less of this input and more of some others. Similarly, consumers substitute among the different goods that can accomplish the same purpose (e.g., potatoes, bread, and rice) based on their prices.

For natural resources, numerous kinds of substitution are relevant. An example of this substitution is using labor and capital, in the form of irrigation and intensive cultivation, to make a given piece of land more productive. Similarly, a machine that uses raw materials more precisely so that it wastes less of them is an example of capital substituting for natural resources. In other cases, one natural resource can be substituted for another, as when coal gas and kerosene replaced whale oil as primary sources of illumination in the mid-19th century. In addition to substitution in production, there can also be substitution into less resource-intensive forms of consumption. For example, many of us value printed books, which require natural resources to produce. However, closer examination shows that what we value is not so much the books themselves, but the information within. If that information were equally accessible through another channel such as an electronic book, then we could indeed substitute this new medium for the natural resources used in producing printed books.

The ability of firms and consumers to substitute for a particular good will be reflected in the **price elasticity of demand**, which is the percentage change in the quantity of a good demanded divided by the percentage change in the good's price. A good for which close substitutes are easily available will have a high (in absolute value) price elasticity of demand—that is, when its price goes up, the quantity demanded will fall a lot. A good for which there are no close substitutes will have a price elasticity of demand that is closer to zero.

Knowing the price elasticity of demand for a particular natural resource tells us how reductions in the supply of that resource will affect its price. For resources with a large price elasticity of demand, reductions in supply will have little effect on prices because a small price increase will prompt firms or consumers to switch to substitutes. By contrast, if a natural resource has a small price elasticity of demand, then a reduction in supply will have a large effect on price.

A numerical example can make this point more concretely. Suppose we are looking at two natural resources. Resource A has a price elasticity of demand of –2, and resource B has a price elasticity of demand of $-1/2$. Suppose that the available quantities of both resources fall by 10%. How much will the prices of the two resources change? In the case of resource A, a 1% price increase will lead to a 2% decline in demand, so a 10% decline in quantity demanded will follow a 5% increase in price. In the case of resource B, each 1% increase in price will produce only a $1/2$% decline in the quantity demanded, so a reduction in quantity of 10% will require a 20% price increase.

This relationship between price elasticities of demand and resource prices is particularly important when combined with another observation: *Price elasticities of demand are almost always smaller (in absolute value terms) in the short run than in the long run.* Put another way, it takes resource users time to economize on their use of a given resource. Therefore, when a price changes, the short-run change in quantity demanded will usually be smaller than the long-run change in quantity demanded.

The reason for this difference between short-run and long-run price elasticities of demand is that resource intensity is embodied in capital goods, which are long-lived. Once a piece of capital equipment has been installed, it is difficult to change the mix of natural resources it uses in production. Rather, new equipment must be created for substituting inputs or incorporating resource-saving technologies. Thus, when the price of a resource rises, many owners of equipment may regret that they did not purchase more efficient equipment initially, but they will continue to use their old capital. Purchasers of new equipment, by contrast, will respond to the new, higher price of the resource by buying efficient equipment that substitutes other inputs for the scarce resource or that embodies resource-saving technologies. Over time, as old equipment wears out and new equipment replaces it, resource intensity will fall.

As an example of the importance of the time horizon in allowing for substitution, a study of gasoline demand in Canada found that the price elasticity of demand in the first year after a price increase was –0.31. This reduction in the quantity demanded reflected primarily the effect of people reducing the number of miles driven. At a five-year horizon, the price elasticity of demand was –0.70, and at a 10-year horizon, it was –1.01. At longer horizons, the primary way people reduced gasoline consumption was by switching to more fuel-efficient cars.[10]

This analysis makes clear that the key to economizing on the use of a resource is price. It also explains why potential resource shortages usually look worse than actual shortages. Looking at the quantity of a given resource used in production today, we conclude that if that resource were not present, output would have to fall. But as a resource begins to run short, increases in its price will induce substitution away from it. To a large extent, the bitter disagreements between those who believe that resource limitations pose a limiting factor to economic growth (mostly environmentalists) and those who think differently (mostly mainstream economists) come down to questions about the degree of substitution.

Technological Progress. In Chapters 8 and 9 we examined the role of technological progress in long-term growth. When we consider the interaction of resource constraints with technological progress, the most interesting question centers on the extent to which technology permits the substitution of resources that are not in short supply for resources that are scarce. Our discussion of substitution took as given that the possibilities for substituting for a resource are already known. But in practice, the technologies for substitution are not known. We do not really see these possibilities until there is demand for them.

History is full of examples of new technologies that have eased resource constraints that were impeding economic growth. We have seen several examples of this sort of technological progress in the chapter already, and the box "Resource-Saving Technologies" presents some additional cases. However, there are also cases where no magic technology arrived—for example, those in the earlier box "Resource Disasters." Finally, it is always possible that the resource shortages facing the world in the future will be less amenable to technological fixes than those in the past. Resource optimists take heart from the history of resource-saving technologies and argue that new inventions will come along to take care of any shortages that may arise. Resource pessimists argue that proceeding under the assumption that "something will turn up" is irresponsible at best and suicidal at worst.

If economists can contribute anything to this debate, it is the observation that for technological progress to work its magic, potential inventors must receive a signal that a new technology is needed—and that signal is the prices of resources that are (or will be) in short supply. The incentive to do research on solar energy or more efficient automobile engines is much higher when oil is selling for $100 rather than $15 per barrel. Resource prices that do not reflect future scarcities—for

---

[10]Eltony (1993).

RESOURCE-SAVING TECHNOLOGIES

In Chapter 9 we saw that technological advances are by nature hard to predict; the only way to know that something is technologically feasible is to do it. This fact is equally true for technologies that conserve or substitute for natural resources. History is replete with examples of inventions that have allowed economies to bypass seemingly insurmountable natural resource constraints. But in other cases, promises of resource-conserving technologies have not been fulfilled. This box considers two successes, one failure, and one case that is still undecided.

Nitrogen

The greatest resource constraint facing humanity at the beginning of the 20th century was a shortage of nitrogen, a vital input into plant growth. Although it is the most plentiful element in the earth's atmosphere, nitrogen must be "fixed," that is, converted to a biologically accessible form, before it can be used by plants. Before the 20th century, only certain bacteria and fungi, such as those that live symbiotically in the roots of leguminous plants, were capable of fixing nitrogen. In 1909 a young German chemist, Fritz Haber, solved the problem of nitrogen fixation by converting atmospheric nitrogen into ammonia to create the first synthetic chemical fertilizer. Scientists estimate that, without Haber's process, there would be enough food for only two-thirds of the earth's current population.

Rubber

In 1941, 99.6% of the rubber consumed in the United States was natural, produced from sap that dripped from trees. The primary source for natural rubber was plantations in Southeast Asia. Following the Japanese attack on Pearl Harbor in 1941, this source was cut off. Responding to the shortage of this crucial wartime material, the U.S. government organized a crash scientific program to develop synthetic rubber. In terms of its use of scientific and industrial resources, the synthetic rubber program was second only to the Manhattan Project, which developed the atomic bomb. By 1945, U.S. rubber consumption exceeded its prewar level, and 85% of the rubber consumed was synthetic.*

Nuclear Fusion

One of the most promising technologies of the post–World War II period has been nuclear fusion, the reaction that powers the sun and also

example, because of a commons problem in which the resource is not owned by any one individual—short-circuit the mechanism by which high prices produce resource-saving inventions.

The incentive provided by prices is also important for thinking about technologies that reduce pollution, which is the subject of Section 16.3. When firms face little incentive to reduce their emissions of pollution, potential inventors have little incentive to devise technologies that reduce pollution.

16.3 GROWTH AND THE ENVIRONMENT

This section examines the relationship between economic growth and environmental pollution. Our conceptual framework will be similar to the one we used in studying natural resources more generally. The key idea is that a clean the hydrogen bomb. Fuel for the reaction can be extracted from water and so is in practically limitless supply. Further, fusion reactors will not contribute to global warming or produce long-lived nuclear waste of the type that is generated by existing fission reactors. Unfortunately, decades of research, at a cost of billions of dollars, have yet to produce a controlled fusion reaction that yields more energy than it consumes. As *The Economist* magazine wryly commented in 2002, fusion reactors "are reckoned to be 50 years from commercialisation—and have been for most of the 50 years since people first started trying to build them."[†]

Solar Energy

Sunlight is plentiful, clean, and cheap. Photovoltaic cells, which make electricity directly from sunlight, have existed for more than a century, but for most of that time, they have been so expensive that their use was limited to special applications. The first practical use in power generation was in the 1950s, when photovoltaic cells costing $200,000 per watt of electricity produced were used to power satellites. Between 1975 and 2009, the price of photovoltaic cells fell from $50 to $1.27 per watt of electricity. Even at the current price, however, photovoltaic cells are economically viable for generating electricity only in places not connected to the regular electricity grid or where there is a significant government subsidy for their use. In 2010, photovoltaics accounted for 0.1% of world electricity production.[‡]

The future price of photovoltaic cells will depend on technological progress and the economies of scale that can be achieved as the market broadens. One estimate, based primarily on extrapolating past trends, is that the price of electricity produced from photovoltaics will fall below the price of electricity from burning coal around the year 2030.[§] If this comes to pass, it will have a profound impact on the world economy, displacing fossil fuels that cause global warming and providing a particular boost to the many poor countries where sunshine is abundant.

[*]Mowry and Rosenberg (1998).
[†]"Here we go again," March 9, 2002.
[‡]http://www.eia.gov/cneaf/solar.renewables/page/solarreport/solarpv.html, BP(2011)
[§]Chakravorty, Roumasse, and Tse (1997).

environment is a resource just like other resources. As we pollute, we "use up" the clean environment.

We can directly import many of the same concepts we used in addressing resources into the study of environmental issues. For example, we can view pollution as having both renewable and nonrenewable components. The absence of sewage in a lake is a renewable resource. If we add only a little sewage, then after a while, the lake will have naturally restored its purity. Just as with other renewable resources, we can calculate the capacity of an environment to accept pollution; this is the analog of sustainable yield for a renewable resource. If we add less than this amount, the quantity of pollution will be stable over time; if we add more, pollution will build up, and we may destroy the environment's ability to renew itself. Some pollutants, however, are not naturally cleansed by the environment, and so their accumulation is more analogous to the consumption of a nonrenewable resource.

The key difference between the environment and most other natural resources involves property rights. No one owns a clean environment—or, put differently, access to the resource of emitting pollution is available for free. Thus, the tragedy of the commons, discussed in Section 16.1 in the context of resource use, is particularly acute in the case of environmental pollution.

With respect to the environment, the roles played by price, substitution, and technological progress will be similar to those they play for more conventional resources. If emitting pollution has no cost, producers will have no incentive to limit their emissions. But when polluting has a price, producers will find ways to substitute away from emitting pollution. A high price on emitting pollution will also give firms an incentive to research and develop ways to limit emissions.

Another important characteristic of pollution is that the people who suffer from environmental degradation are seldom the same as the people who benefited from the activity that created the pollution. Pollution is a classic negative externality. Indeed, success in controlling pollution generally is inversely proportional to the distance between those who suffer from pollution's effects and those who produce the pollution. When pollution affects those nearby—for example, when a factory discharges waste into a local lake—political mechanisms are frequently sufficient to overcome the externality problem. This is especially true in countries in which governments are representative and effective. When the people who suffer pollution's effects are far away—for example, when power plants in the U.S. Midwest create acid rain that destroys forests in New England—the political obstacles to controlling the negative externality are greater. In the case of problems with the largest geographic scale, such as global warming, the difficulties are most severe.

The Environmental Kuznets Curve

In Chapter 13 we first encountered the Kuznets curve: a curve looking like an upside-down U, relating income inequality and the level of economic development. According to the Kuznets curve, countries experience first rising and later falling inequality over the course of development.

This same sort of analysis has been applied to the relationship between pollution and economic growth. The **environmental Kuznets curve** is an inverted-U relationship between the level of economic development and the level of environmental pollution. The logic behind the environmental Kuznets curve is fairly straightforward. At low levels of economic development, countries simply do not engage in enough production to cause significant pollution. As income per capita grows, environmental damage initially grows with it. At a high income level, however, a second factor comes to the fore: People are rich enough to care about pollution and take steps to reduce it. In microeconomic terms, a clean environment is a luxury good for which people are willing to spend more as they become wealthier.

Figure 16.6 shows an example of an environmental Kuznets curve. The horizontal axis measures income per capita, and the vertical axis measures the level of

> FIGURE 16.6

An Environmental Kuznets Curve

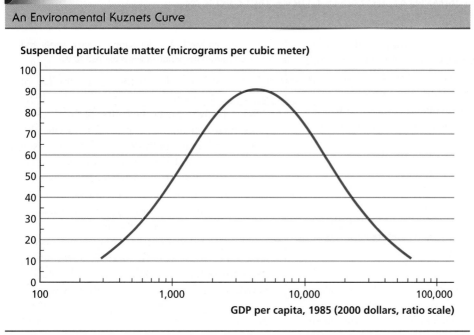

Suspended particulate matter (micrograms per cubic meter)

GDP per capita, 1985 (2000 dollars, ratio scale)

Source: Shafik (1994).

suspended particulate matter, a form of air pollution. The curve is fitted to data from 48 cities in 31 countries in 1986. The figure shows that particulate matter concentration rises with income up to a level of $4,717 (2000 dollars), roughly equivalent to El Salvador's GDP per capita in 2000. Above this level, higher income is associated with lower pollution, so that, for example, a country with five times El Salvador's level of GDP per capita would have half its level of suspended particulate matter. (See box "The Environmental Kuznets Curve in London.")

The logic of the environmental Kuznets curve has implications for rich and poor countries. First, the curve implies that as countries get richer, they are willing to pay more to get rid of pollution. Second, the reason that very poor countries have low pollution is not that they place a high value on a clean environment. Rather, they have no opportunity to trade off higher pollution for more income. Put another way, the costs of pollution, measured in dollars, are lower in a poor country than in a rich country.

This difference in the value that rich and poor countries place on pollution suggests a possibility for gains from trade. The potential was most famously outlined in a 1991 memorandum signed by the World Bank's chief economist at the time, Lawrence Summers.[11] The memorandum raised the question of whether the

---

[11]"Let Them Eat Pollution," *The Economist*, February 8, 1992.

THE ENVIRONMENTAL KUZNETS CURVE IN LONDON

In considering the environmental Kuznets curve, we have focused on differences among countries at a single point in time (called a *cross-sectional analysis*). However, just as with the Kuznets curve for inequality, we can look at the environmental Kuznets curve in a single place over time.

The city of London provides an example of this environmental Kuznets curve in action. Historically, the most significant source of pollution in London was the burning of coal, which became the city's primary fuel in the 17th century, following the extensive deforestation of the surrounding countryside. As early as 1661, an observer wrote:

> …inhabitants breathe nothing but an impure and thick Mist accompanied with a fuliginous and filthy vapour, which renders them obnoxious to a thousand inconveniences, corrupting the Lungs, and disordring the entire habits of their Bodies; so that Catharrs, Phthisicks, Coughs and Consumptions rage more in this one City than in the whole Earth besides…It is this horrid Smoake which obscures our Churches, and makes our Palaces look old, which fouls our Clothes, and corrupts the waters, so as the very Rain, and refreshing Dews which fall in the several Seasons, precipitate this impure vapor, which,

with its black and tenacious quality, spots and contaminates whatsoever is expos'd to it.*

Figure 16.7 shows the concentration of smoke in London over the period 1585–1940. After a steady rise over the course of three centuries, smoke concentrations peaked in the late 19th century and then rapidly declined. The sources of the decline included limits on industrial smoke emissions; the regulation of smokestack heights; the replacement of domestic open-coal fires with more efficient central heating; and the substitution of gas, oil, and electricity for coal.

The improvement in air quality accelerated after World War II. In 1952, 3,800 deaths were attributed to a "killer smog," during the height of which smoke concentrations soared to 4,500 micrograms per cubic meter. By the 1980s, during episodes of similar weather conditions (subfreezing temperatures, calm winds, and a low-level inversion), smoke concentrations rarely exceeded 500 micrograms per cubic meter. Between 1950 and 1985, the average amount of sunshine visible in London during the winter increased from 1.00 to 1.75 hours per day.†

*Evelyn (1661).
†Elsom (1995).

World Bank should actually be encouraging the migration of dirty industries from rich to poor countries. Among the points it made were:

- People in rich countries put a higher dollar value on reducing pollution than do people in poor countries. This is the case both because people in rich countries earn higher wages and thus have more money to spend on everything and because the health costs associated with pollution are more relevant in rich countries, where mortality from more easily preventable causes is so much lower. Thus, if a unit of pollution could be moved from a rich to a poor country, along with sufficient payment (less than the value that the rich country put on the pollution but more than the value that the poor country put on it), both countries would be better off.

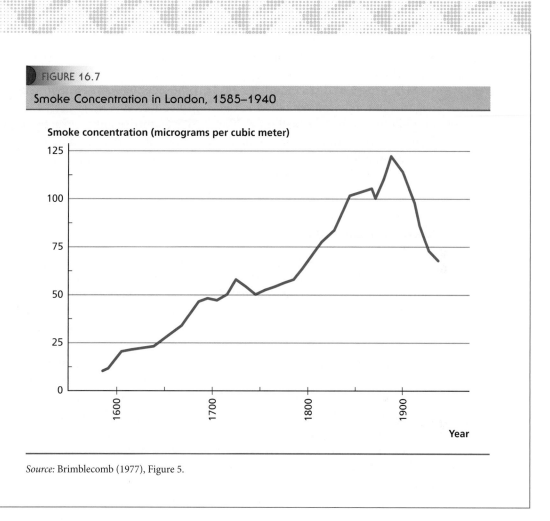

FIGURE 16.7

Smoke Concentration in London, 1585–1940

Smoke concentration (micrograms per cubic meter)

Source: Brimblecomb (1977), Figure 5.

- The negative effects of additional units of pollution rise with the quantity of pollution that is already present in an environment. For example, the health damage caused by increasing suspended particulate matter by 10 micrograms per cubic meter is larger in a country where there is already a particulate concentration of 80 grams per cubic meter than in a country where there is no pre-existing air pollution. Thus, moving polluting industries from high- to low-pollution countries will lower the overall damage done by pollution.

Although Summers's memorandum was widely condemned (and was meant to be a stimulus to discussion rather than a serious policy proposal), it is nonetheless true that there *has* been a migration of polluting industries from developed to developing countries. Indeed, this migration has often been the means by which developed countries have been able to enjoy cleaner environments. Examples of polluting industries that have largely relocated out of developed countries in response to environmental regulation are leather tanning and the recycling of lead-acid batteries.

The export of dirty industries has become a contentious issue in recent trade negotiations. Environmentalists in developed countries want the same limitations on pollution to be imposed on rich and poor countries alike—exactly to prevent dirty industries from simply changing countries rather than finding other ways to reduce pollution. But many representatives of developing countries object to this sort of regulation. Their countries would rather have both the jobs and the pollution of these industries than neither.

Global Warming

In analyzing the environmental Kuznets curve, we noted that as countries got richer, they had more ability to produce pollution but were also willing to pay more to improve their environment. However, previously in this section, we also saw that the sacrifices a country (or a person) will make for a cleaner environment also depend on the amount of the benefit it will receive. The more "global" is a pollution problem, the less any one country will benefit from reducing its emissions. The most extreme version of this phenomenon is the case of global warming.

Global warming refers to a rise in the temperature of the atmosphere near earth. The phenomenon can clearly be seen in Figure 16.8, which shows global average surface temperature over the period 1880–2010. Other indicators confirm this climactic warming: Global mean sea level increased by 6.7 inches (17 centimeters) during the 20th century.[12] There has been a widespread retreat of nonpolar glaciers, a thinning of polar ice, and a lengthening of the growing season in the Northern Hemisphere by one to four days.

The cause of current global warming is the accumulation in the atmosphere of so-called greenhouse gases, which absorb thermal radiation coming from the earth that would otherwise dissipate into space. The most significant greenhouse gas is carbon dioxide (CO_2). The atmospheric concentration of CO_2 increased by approximately 38% between the beginning of the Industrial Revolution and 2010 and is now rising at 0.5% per year. Roughly 80% of the rise in CO_2 has resulted from the burning of fossil fuels, with the other 20% as a result of deforestation and other changes in land use.[13]

The relationship between GDP per capita and CO_2 emission, shown in Figure 16.9, is quite strong. In this figure GDP per capita and the emission of CO_2 per capita are both plotted on a ratio scale. The reason is that the

[12]Intergovernmental Panel on Climate Change (2007).
[13]Intergovernmental Panel on Climate Change (2007), Lomborg (2001).

FIGURE 16.8

Average Global Temperatures

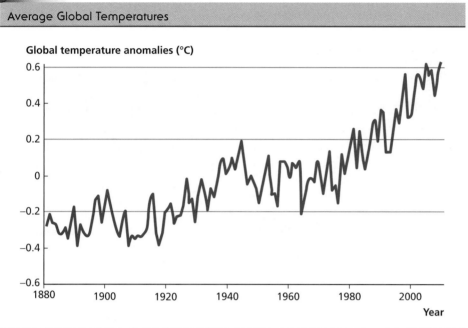

Source: www.giss.nasa.gov

differences among countries in CO_2 emission per capita, like those in income per capita, are so large that a ratio scale is necessary to make the data for poor countries visible. For example, U.S. emissions in 2007 were 19.3 tons per capita, whereas in Bangladesh emissions were only 0.3 tons per capita. In 2008, China was the world's largest CO_2 emitter, accounting for 21.9% of the world total. The United States was second highest, at 17.7% of the world total.[14]

Figure 16.9 makes clear that there is no environmental Kuznets curve when it comes to CO_2. This finding is consistent with the observation that, unlike the effects of other forms of pollution, the harm done by a given country's emission of CO_2 is concentrated on people who live far away. The absence of an environmental Kuznets curve implies that, without a significant change in policy, economic growth in poor countries will greatly exacerbate CO_2 emissions.

Prediction of Future Warming. Global warming is of concern because of the potentially large effects on economic activity, health, and habitability that could result if the warming trend continues or accelerates. Unfortunately, predicting the exact magnitude of future warming is notoriously difficult. Future

---

[14]Carbon Dioxide Information Analysis Center, U.S. Department of Energy, http://cdiac.ornl.gov/.

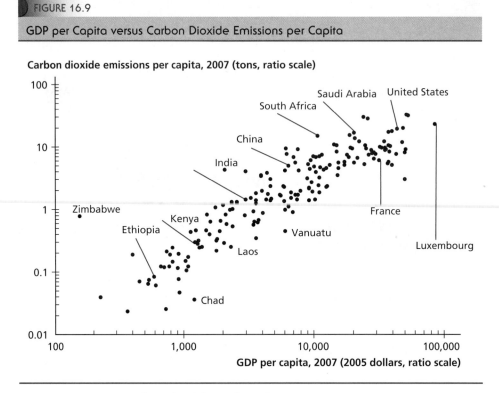

FIGURE 16.9

GDP per Capita versus Carbon Dioxide Emissions per Capita

Sources: Heston, Summers, and Aten (2011), http://cdiac.ornl.gov/.

increases in CO_2 concentration will depend on demographic and economic growth, technological unknowns such as the rate of progress in nuclear fusion and solar energy, and scientific uncertainties such as how the planet's absorption of atmospheric CO_2 will change as the concentration of the gas rises. One scenario examined by the Intergovernmental Panel on Climate Change (IPCC), which shared the 2007 Nobel Peace Prize for its work, entails a peaking of world population in the mid-21st century and 3% annual growth of world GDP, with the economy remaining largely dependent on fossil fuels. Under this scenario, CO_2 concentration rises 56% above its year 2000 level by 2050, and 166% above its year 2000 levels by 2100.

Calculating how a given rise in atmospheric CO_2 will translate into increased temperature involves another layer of scientific uncertainty. For the scenario just described, the IPCC estimates that mean temperature would rise 3.2° F (1.8° C) above its year 2000 level by 2050, and by a further 2.9° F (1.6° C) between 2050 and 2100. However, there is a great deal of uncertainty (roughly ± 1° C at the horizon of one century) associated with this forecast. The IPCC similarly forecasts that under this scenario, the rise in sea level over the course of the 21st century would be between 8.3 and 18.9 inches (21 and 48 centimeters).[15] Average precipitation is forecast to rise, and there will be an increase in the variability of weather, and particularly a rise in extreme climatic events such as floods, droughts, heat waves, and cyclones.

Estimating the economic effect of a given amount of global warming is equally difficult. Warming will close down some forms of economic activity while opening up others. For example, warming will put a larger fraction of U.S. land in the Mediterranean and subtropical climate zones, making growing conditions less hospitable to grains such as corn and wheat but raising the production of fruit, vegetables, and cotton. One study, using a survey of experts, estimated the costs of a 5.4° F (3° C) rise in temperatures by 2090. The average estimate of the most likely effect was that world output would be reduced by 3.6%. However, a good deal of uncertainty was attached to this estimate. The experts projected a 10% chance that the reduction in output would be less than 0.7%, and also a 4.8% percent chance that there would be a catastrophic reduction in world output of more than 25%.

Global warming will affect countries with differing degrees of severity. Countries that rely on agriculture and those with extensive coastlines will be most negatively affected. The vulnerability of the United States to global warming is roughly half the world average. The most severe effects of warming will be felt in the tropics, both because this part of the world is hottest already and because poor countries, which tend to be located in the tropics, have fewer resources with which to deal with changes in weather patterns, including a higher frequency of floods and droughts. In addition, an expansion will occur in the habitat hospitable to the mosquitoes that transmit tropical diseases such as malaria and dengue fever. A rise in the global sea level of 3.3 feet (1 meter)—which is more than most of the IPCC scenarios suggest will take place over the next century—would leave 17% of Bangladesh underwater and displace 10 million of the country's residents.[16]

Must Prevention of Global Warming End Economic Growth? The most significant attempt to control global warming has been the Kyoto Protocol, an agreement signed in 1997 and ratified by most countries in the world, with the notable exception of the United States. The Kyoto Protocol called for developed countries to reduce their greenhouse emissions by an average of 7% below their 1990 levels by the year 2012. Developing countries were not subject to any limitations. Attempts to extend the Kyoto Protocol beyond 2012, and to include targets for emissions for poor as well as rich countries, have thus far not been successful. However, a commonly discussed target is that developed countries reduce their total CO_2 emissions by 50% between by 2050.

Does reducing CO_2 emission require a cessation of growth? The answer is no, for the same reasons that reducing the use of any scarce resource does not

---

[15]Intergovernmental Panel on Climate Change (2007).
[16]Rijsberman and van Velzen (1996), Nordhaus (1994), Chapter 4 and Table 7.2.

require slower growth. We can examine this question in terms of the concept of resource intensity. In this case, the resource of interest is emission of CO_2. Consider a country that aims to halve emissions over the period 2010–2050. This would require reducing emissions at an annual rate of 1.7% per year. At the same time, suppose that growth of output per capita during this period is 2% per year and population growth is 1% per year. Recall from Section 16.1 that the equation relating the growth rates of resource use, resource intensity, output per capita, and population is:

$$\hat{R} = \hat{I} + \hat{y} + \hat{L},$$

where R is resource use, I is resource intensity, y is income per capita, L is population, and a hat over a variable indicates its growth rate. Rearranging this equation, we get:

$$\hat{I} = \hat{R} - \hat{y} - \hat{L}.$$

Using the values from the preceding scenario:

$$\hat{I} = -0.017 - 0.02 - 0.01 = -0.047.$$

In other words, the CO_2 intensity of output would have to fall by 4.7% per year to reach the target. This rate of decline of resource intensity is large by historical standards but hardly unprecedented.

The examples of other natural resources suggest that the key to achieving a rapid and sustained decline in the CO_2 intensity of output is price—specifically, the price of emitting CO_2. Emitting CO_2 is currently free. Raising the price of emissions would encourage firms and consumers to find substitutes and would spur progress on low-emissions technologies. A fairly simple policy, a **carbon tax** (i.e., a tax on the emission of CO_2), would accomplish all these goals. According to one evaluation of a range of different models, a carbon tax that brought the United States into compliance with the Kyoto Protocol would make GDP per capita in 2010 between 0.45% and 1.96% lower than it otherwise would have been.[17]

16.4 CONCLUSION

Natural resources are necessary to produce output. For centuries, economists and other scholars have considered the question of whether available resources are sufficient to sustain economic growth in the future. Despite numerous dire predictions, shortages of natural resources have had little effect—at least so far—in reducing economic growth. For example, contrary to Malthus's prediction of mass starvation, technological progress and the ingenuity of farmers have kept food production well ahead of population growth.

---

[17]Intergovernmental Panel on Climate Change (2001b), Table 8.4.

The explanation for why most doomsday scenarios have not come to pass can be summed up in one word: prices. High prices for a natural resource give producers an incentive to find new sources of supply and encourage consumers to find substitutes, while inducing inventors to look for ways of getting around resource bottlenecks. The anticipation of future scarcities gives resource owners an incentive to hold back supply today, automatically conserving scarce resources for future use and further spurring the search for substitutes.

But prices do not always circumvent resource shortages. The most common cause of failure is an absence of property rights. Where there is no ownership of a natural resource, no one has the incentive to husband it for the future. Indeed, such cases give producers an extra motivation to use the resource now, before someone else does. When this happens, a resource may be in abundant supply—with a commensurately low price and lack of incentive to find substitutes—until it runs out altogether. The most severe cases of overexploited resources in the world today—for example, fish in international waters—can be traced to ill-defined property rights.

The prime example of a resource for which there is no property right, causing a failure of the price mechanism, is a clean environment. No one "owns" a clean environment, so the price of emitting pollution is zero. The normal mechanism that would give polluters an incentive to substitute into nonpolluting forms of production is absent.

In the absence of property rights to a clean environment, another mechanism through which pollution can be controlled is government regulation. Government is better at controlling pollution when the harm that the pollution causes is localized. The most difficult forms of pollution to control are those that affect the planet as a whole, such as the accumulation of CO_2 that causes global warming.

If the history of other natural resource problems is a good guide, reducing the emissions of CO_2 need not cause a large reduction in economic growth. Rather, if producers of pollution face the right incentives—that is, if there is a price attached to CO_2 emission commensurate with the environmental cost—then the processes of substitution and technological progress will allow growth to continue.

KEY TERMS

nonrenewable
  resources   **464**
current reserves   **464**
peak oil   **467**
renewable
  resources   **467**
carrying capacity   **467**

maximum sustainable
  yield   **468**
tragedy of the
  commons   **470**
resource intensity   **472**
sustainable
  development   **473**

green GDP   **474**
in-ground price   **474**
price elasticity of
  demand   **484**
environmental Kuznets
  curve   **488**
carbon tax   **496**

QUESTIONS FOR REVIEW

1. What is the tragedy of the commons? For what types of natural resources is it relevant?

2. What is sustainable development? What are some problems with the Brundtland Commission's definition of the term?

3. How does the calculation of green GDP take into account the depletion of natural capital?

4. What is the theoretical relationship between current and future prices for a natural resource? What can cause this mechanism to break down?

5. Why is the long-run price elasticity of demand for a resource generally higher than the short-run price elasticity of demand?

6. Why does the environmental Kuznets curve have an upside-down U shape?

PROBLEMS

1. The following table presents data on population, GDP per capita, and total energy consumption in a country in 1965 and 2000. At what annual rate did the energy intensity of output grow over this period?

Year	Population	GDP per Capita	Energy Consumption
1965	1,000	1,0000	200
2000	2,000	2,0000	400

2. The quantity of fish in a lake grows according to the equation:

$$G_t = \frac{S_t \times (100 - S_t)}{100},$$

where S_t is the stock of fish at the beginning of period t and G_t is the amount of fish that grow during period t, both measured in tons.

  a. Suppose that in a certain year, the stock of fish in the lake is equal to 20 tons. Furthermore, both the stock of fish and the size of the harvest have been constant for a long period of time. How big is the annual harvest of fish, H_t?

  b. Calculate the optimal stock of fish in the lake and the maximum sustainable yield. You can do this either by trial and error or by using calculus.

3. Using Table 16.2, answer the following question: How would total energy use in the world compare to current energy use if everyone in the world used the same energy per capita as is currently used by residents of upper-middle-income countries?

4. Assume that the world has a 1,000-year supply of some resource at the current rate of use. Suppose that the rate of use grows at 2% per year. How long will the supply last?

5. Suppose that the price of gasoline has been $1 per gallon for a long period of time. Now consider two possible scenarios:

| Long-Term Increase | The price rises to $2 per gallon, and everyone expects it to remain at this level for a long time. |
| Short-Term Increase | The price rises to $2 per gallon, and everyone expects that after five years, it will drop back to $1 per gallon. |

How would the quantity of gasoline consumed in the first year after the price increase differ in these two scenarios? How would the quantity consumed in the fourth year after the change in price differ? Explain the source of the difference.

6. It has just been announced that large deposits of oil have been discovered in Chile. It will take five years for production to begin, but after that time Chile will become the world's largest oil producer by a large margin.

   a. How and why does this announcement affect the world supply curve for oil in the period before Chile's production comes online?

   b. How and why does this announcement affect the world demand curve for oil in the period before Chile's production comes online?

   c. Based on your answers to parts a and b, what can you say about what will happen to the world price and quantity of oil consumed in the period before Chile's production comes online?

7. The World Bank estimates that in 1992, between 300 million and 700 million women and children suffered from severe indoor air pollution produced by cooking fires, with effects on health that were often equivalent to smoking several packs of cigarettes per day. Discuss how the analysis of indoor air pollution differs from other types of pollution discussed in this chapter.

8. Governments often impose taxes on the emission of specific pollutants, such as the carbon tax discussed in Section 16.3. What is the relationship between the short-run effect and the long-run effect of such a tax on the quantity of pollution emitted? What is the relationship between the revenue collected by such a tax in the short run versus in the long run? Explain.

For additional exploration and practice using the Online Data Plotter and data sets, please visit http://www.pearsonhighered.com/weil.

TECHNOLOGICAL IMPROVEMENT VERSUS RESOURCE DEPLETION

Despite common intuition, there is nothing inconsistent about forecasting economic growth in the presence of depleting natural resources. Here we look at a simple example, concentrating on the case of a nonrenewable resource. Call $X(t)$ the quantity of the resource that exists at time t and $E(t)$ the quantity of the resource that is extracted and used at time t. The relationship between E and X (using a dot over a variable to denote its derivative with respect to time) is:

$$\dot{X}(t) = -E(t).$$

For simplicity, we consider this resource to be the *only* input into production; that is, we ignore physical capital, human capital, and labor. (Including these factors in our analysis would not change the general conclusion but would complicate the algebra.) The production function is:

$$Y(t) = A(t)E(t),$$

where Y is output and A is a measure of the state of technology.

If the state of technology, A, does not change over time, then eventually output will fall to 0 in this economy, as no more of the resource can be extracted. However, counteracting the depletion of the resource, we allow the level of technology to grow over time at some exogenous rate, g:

$$\hat{A}(t) = \frac{\dot{A}(t)}{A(t)} = g.$$

Using this setup, we can address the issue of sustainability. Specifically, we ask, "What is the trade-off between producing output today and leaving behind resources so that output can be produced tomorrow?" We formalize this problem by allowing for a choice of the rate at which the natural resource supply is used up. Specifically, let ϵ be the rate of extraction (the fraction of the resource extracted per period of time), which we assume to be constant:

$$E(t) = \epsilon X(t).$$

Given that the extraction rate is constant, it is easy to see that the quantity of the resource remaining will decline exponentially over time. If $X(0)$ is the quantity that existed at time 0, then we have:

$$X(t) = X(0) e^{-\epsilon t}.$$

We can now examine how both the growth rate of output and the level of output at time 0 are related to the extraction rate, ϵ. The level of output at time 0 is:

$$Y(0) = A(0)(\epsilon X(0)).$$

Thus, a lower extraction rate ϵ will lead to a lower level of initial output. To find the growth rate of output, we take logarithms of the production function and differentiate with respect to time, noting that the growth rate of extraction will be the same as the growth rate of the resource stock. This gives:

$$\hat{Y} = \hat{A} + \hat{E} = g - \epsilon.$$

This equation shows that a higher extraction rate leads to a lower growth rate of output. Indeed, if the extraction rate is too high, then the growth rate of output will be negative. There will also be a particular level of extraction that is consistent with zero growth of output. We can solve for the extraction rate that yields a constant level of output, ϵ^*, by setting the growth rate of output equal to 0 in the previous equation:

$$\epsilon^* = g.$$

Figure 16.10 shows some examples of possible paths of output that can result from choosing different extraction rates. If the extraction rate chosen is above ϵ^*, then

FIGURE 16.10

Relationship between Resource Use and Growth

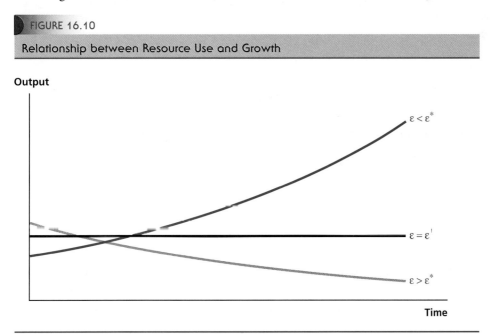

Output

$\varepsilon < \varepsilon^*$

$\varepsilon = \varepsilon^!$

$\varepsilon > \varepsilon^*$

Time

initial output will exceed the sustainable level but decline over time. If the extraction rate chosen is below ϵ^*, initial output will be below the sustainable level but will eventually rise above it.

PROBLEM

A.1. Suppose that output in a country is produced using only a nonrenewable resource. The rate of extraction of the resource is 1% per year. After 36 years, total output in the economy has doubled. What was the rate of technological progress? After how many years will the stock of the resource be reduced to one-eighth of its initial level?

For additional exploration and practice using the Online Data Plotter and data sets, please visit www.pearsonhighered.com/weil.

WHAT WE HAVE LEARNED AND WHERE WE ARE HEADED

17.1 WHAT WE HAVE LEARNED

The astounding variation in income per capita among countries is one of the most striking facts about the world today. Gross domestic product (GDP) per capita in the world's richest countries exceeds GDP per capita in the world's poorest countries by a factor of 40. The one-fifth of the world's population that lives in the richest countries receives 60% of world income. Meanwhile, 1.1 billion people survive on incomes of less than $1 per day. People in rich countries enjoy longer lives, better health, more leisure, and more amenities than do their poor-country counterparts.

These massive differences in country incomes are largely a product of economic growth during the last two centuries. Before 1800, differences in income per capita among countries were relatively small, and there had been no significant growth in the standard of living over hundreds of years. Today the poorest countries have living standards that are close to those in 1800, whereas rich countries' living standards have risen sharply. Thus, the increase in world inequality has come about because some countries have experienced economic growth whereas others have not. Although most of the richest countries in the world today are those whose economies started growing earliest, some countries that started later, notably Japan, have experienced bursts of rapid growth as they caught up with the leaders. These periods of swift growth have become more dramatic over time.

Our goal has been to understand these differences in income and growth among countries. Let's review how we approached the question and what we have learned.

Factor Accumulation

The most straightforward explanation for differences in income among countries is differences in their accumulation of factors of production. Workers in wealthy countries use more machines, computers, and infrastructure—that is, physical capital—than do workers in poor countries. Workers in rich countries also have more and better education—human capital—than do workers in poor countries. Finally, workers in rich countries are healthier than are workers in poor countries. These differences in the physical and human capital available to workers are clearly an important cause of income differences between rich and poor countries.

There is a chicken-and-egg aspect to these differences in capital between rich and poor countries. One reason that poor countries have low levels of physical and human capital is that they are poor. Households in a poor country may be just as desirous of investing in physical capital and providing human capital for their children as are households in a rich country, but a poor country simply lacks the means to make the same investments as a rich country. Because it is easier for a country to accumulate capital once it already has some capital, capital accumulation restricts the rate of growth in poor countries. Even if a poor country does everything else right—that is, it removes all of the other impediments to growth that we have considered—many decades will elapse before the accumulation of capital brings its income up to the level of its rich peers.

Theoretically, it would be possible for low capital accumulation to explain poor countries' poverty fully. However, our quantitative analysis showed that low capital accumulation was not by itself the answer. The former Soviet Union, which did a good job of accumulating physical and human capital but failed economically, clearly exemplifies how factor accumulation alone cannot explain economic growth.

Productivity

To the extent that differences in income among countries are not the result of accumulation of factors of production, they must be the result of productivity (i.e., the effectiveness with which factors of production are converted into output). Productivity differences among countries are large. Using development accounting, we saw that given quantities of labor, physical capital, and human capital would produce more than six times as much output in the richest one-fifth of countries as in the poorest one-fifth. Similarly, productivity growth is a major source of growth in output (explaining 40% of growth in output per worker in the United States between 1975 and 2009). Variations in productivity growth among countries are the most important explanation for variations among countries in the growth rate of output per capita.

These findings motivated us to examine productivity closely. What accounts for the differences in the quantity of output that can be produced with fixed quantities of factors of production? To analyze productivity, we divided it into two parts: technology and efficiency. Technology is knowledge about how to produce output. Technology can be discussed in terms of research and development, the dissemination of information, and scientific advance. The other component of productivity, efficiency, is related to the organization of the economy, the incentives that people and firms face, a country's institutions, and so on.

Technology. Technological progress is the primary factor explaining productivity growth over long stretches of time. The vast multiplication in the wealthiest countries' living standards over the last several centuries was the result of the invention of new goods and new ways of producing old goods.

Like the construction of physical and human capital, technological progress requires the use of resources, specifically research and development spending. But technology has unusual characteristics that make it unique as an engine of growth. Technology is nonrival, meaning that many people can use a single piece of technology at once. Thus, rich-country technology can be transferred to poor countries without being any less available to rich countries. But because technology is often nonexcludable (it is hard for the inventor of a technology to prevent others from using it), there is often insufficient incentive for the creation of new technologies. Historically, societies have rarely gotten the balance right—rewarding inventors enough to encourage research and development while preventing entrenched interests from blocking new technologies.

Technology explains much less of the productivity differences among countries today than it explains of the growth in productivity over time. The reason is that technologies cross borders relatively easily. The productivity gaps among countries are so large that, if such gaps were only the result of technology, poor countries would have to be using the same technology as rich countries used a century or more ago. Although some technological gaps certainly exist—caused by patent protection and secrecy on the part of those who have recently developed new technologies, and by the inappropriateness of certain new technologies to the factor mix found in poor countries—these gaps are not nearly as large as this logic would require.

Efficiency. We saw direct evidence of significant gaps in the efficiency of production among countries. Even using identical technologies, countries differ starkly in the amounts of output they can produce with a given quantity of capital and labor. In many developing countries, woefully overstaffed government-owned firms are an important form of inefficiency. It is also common for developing countries to devote excessive capital and labor to sectors of the economy that produce output of low value. In rich and poor countries alike, vast resources are wasted in struggles to take possession of existing output, rather than being used in producing additional output.

Efficiency is shaped by the institutions in an economy, which determine the opportunities and incentives that individuals and firms face. People in countries with low economic efficiency are no less hardworking and no more selfish than people in more efficient countries. A country's institutions shape how its citizens' efforts are directed—to productive activities, accumulation of factors of production, and invention of new technologies, on the one hand, or to technology blocking, rent seeking, and other unproductive activities, on the other. Perhaps the most difficult problem facing economic policy-makers—those in developing countries and those in the developed world who want to further poor countries' growth—is how to build institutions that are conducive to growth.

A particularly salient aspect of the efficiency of a country's economy is the degree to which it can take advantage of the benefits of specialization and gains from trade by interacting with other countries. Openness to the world economy also affects a country's technology and accumulation of factors of production, but these effects are secondary to the improved efficiency that results from international trade.

Fundamentals

Factor accumulation, technology, and efficiency are *proximate* determinants of a country's level of income per capita. That is, they directly affect income. Furthermore, by definition, these three measures are the *only* proximate determinants of income. Any difference in income per capita between two countries must be the result of some combination of differences in these three determinants; similarly, any growth in income per capita in a country must be the result of growth in one or more of these determinants.

But analyzing the proximate determinants of a country's wealth or poverty did not tell us everything that we wanted to know. To say that a country is poor because it has low factor accumulation, technology, or efficiency does not fully answer the question of *why* the country is poor. It is vital to understand the fundamental or deeper determinants that underlie these proximate determinants. In the last part of the book, we examined some of these fundamental determinants.

One particularly strong influence on all three proximate determinants of income is government behavior. Governments affect factor accumulation (e.g., by providing education), and they influence technological progress (e.g., by supporting research and development). But the most important effect of government is on the efficiency of the economy. By setting the rules of the game for firms and workers, government has a crucial impact on how much effort is devoted to productive versus unproductive activities and on how production in the economy is organized. The data clearly show that poor countries have governments that are bad for growth in several dimensions—they are more corrupt, more wasteful in their expenditures, and more likely to restrict trade and the formation of new businesses. Less clear is the extent to which bad government is a cause or a symptom of these countries' poverty.

Regarding other possible fundamental determinants of a country's economic development—income inequality, culture, and geographic factors—we found mixed evidence. Income inequality has both positive and negative effects on the accumulation of factors of production. More inequality is good for accumulating physical capital but bad for accumulating human capital. The more significant effects of income inequality run through its relationship with government: Unequal countries have more political instability and pressure for income redistribution, although not necessarily more actual redistribution. The other striking finding about income inequality is its persistence; in the most unequal countries in the world, the roots of current income inequality go back for centuries.

Our examination of culture showed several intriguing correlations between culture and economic outcomes. But as in the case of government, there is as yet no good way of sorting out how much of the causality runs from culture to economic growth and how much runs in the other direction.

In the case of geography, climate, and natural resources, this problem of causality is absent. We know that geography affects growth and not the other way around. The strong correlation between the level of GDP per capita and geographic factors such as distance from the equator provides clear evidence that geography has been one of the shaping forces of the current world income distribution. But the exact channel through which geography operates (through its historical effect on institutions, its effect on agricultural productivity, or its effect on the disease environment) is less clear. It is also uncertain to what extent the geographic forces that shaped income growth in the past will continue to operate in the future.

Fundamental determinants, working through the channels of factor accumulation, technological development, and the efficiency of production, are the ultimate forces shaping a country's economic destiny. But it would be presumptuous to say that fundamentals—or at least the set of fundamentals we have considered in this book—are destiny. In explaining why some countries are rich and some poor, we should allow for historical accidents such as the ascent of an especially unscrupulous leader at a key time in a country's history. In addition, there may be fundamental forces that economists have not yet even thought about. Finally, we may see changes in the way that fundamentals affect the economy. Characteristics of a country that were detrimental to growth in the past may be rendered irrelevant, or even helpful, by technological progress or other changes in the structure of the world economy.

17.2 WHAT THE FUTURE HOLDS

Understanding economic growth is hard enough—predicting growth is so difficult that we will not attempt it. Instead, in this section, we highlight some crucial issues to track over the next several decades.

WILL GROWTH MAKE US HAPPY?

In 1930 John Maynard Keynes wrote a remarkable essay, "Economic Possibilities for Our Grandchildren." Keynes reviewed the history of economic growth and considered what would happen if compound growth continued at its current pace for another century. Such growth, he calculated, would raise the standard of living by a factor of between 4 and 8. Keynes concluded that with growth of this magnitude, humanity would be within sight of solving what he called the *economic problem* of scarcity. With another century of growth, Keynes forecast, the central problem facing an individual would shift from how to acquire enough goods and services to how to meaningfully enjoy his abundant free time, "how to use his freedom from pressing economic cares, how to occupy the leisure, which science and compound interest will have won for him, to live wisely and agreeably and well."[*]

Despite the Great Depression, World War II, and other events that followed Keynes's writing, the fact is that compound growth *did* continue at roughly the rate Keynes had forecast. Income per capita in the United Kingdom has already quadrupled since Keynes wrote. But with four-fifths of the time period he considered having already elapsed, it is clear that the second part of Keynes's prediction was terribly wrong. The boom in leisure that he forecast has failed to come about. Rather than worrying about how to spend their abundant free time, people in many of the wealthiest countries are working as hard as their predecessors did 80 years ago, apparently because they feel that doing so is necessary to attain the standard of living they desire. For example, economist Juliet Schorr reports in her book *The Overworked American: The Unexpected Decline of Leisure* (1992) that the trend in the United States is toward people's putting in longer hours, taking work home from the office, and increasingly feeling squeezed in their ability to spend time on leisure pursuits or with their families. Nor does people's failure to move beyond the economic problem of want apply only to the poor. For example, in the last several U.S. presidential campaigns (including 2012), one of the few issues that all candidates could agree on was that the middle class was struggling economically. Even in the world's richest countries, the economic problem of scarcity seems no closer to having been solved than during Keynes's time.

Consideration of these facts raises the question, is it is possible that growth will not make people happier, or at least not as much happier as they expect? As a starting point in answering this question, we can look at the relationship between income and happiness within a single country. Figure 17.1 shows the relationship between self-reported happiness and income in the United States from surveys conducted in 1994–1996. The data points are the average level of income and the average level of happiness for each decile of the income distribution. Happiness is self-reported by households, on a scale where 1 is "not too happy," 2 is "pretty happy," and 3 is "very happy." Income is not the only determinant of happiness, but clearly happiness rises with income—doubling income raises happiness by approximately 0.09 points. This finding that income is correlated with happiness within a country is quite robust: it has been replicated dozens of times in a large number of countries.

One might think that the finding that rich people within a county are happier than poor people would automatically imply that people in rich countries are on average happier than people in poor countries, and similarly that average happiness in a country rises as the average level of income per capita rises. This is not necessarily the case, however. In fact it is easy to think of scenarios under which it would not be true.

Consider what happens, for example, if people's economic satisfaction depends not only on how much they consume but also on how their consumption relates to some benchmark that they use for comparison. That benchmark might be the consumption of other people around them, for example, other people in the country where they live. Someone who consumes, say, $20,000 per year will be happier if she lives in a country where average consumption is $10,000 than she would be if she lived in a country where average consumption is $30,000. A particularly simple form of this phenomenon is if people care not about their absolute level of consumption, but rather about their *rank* in the hierarchy of consumption. (Caring about one's relative standing seems to be an inherent human trait. Julius Caesar said, "I would rather be first in a small village in Gaul than second in command in Rome.")

If people compare their consumption to the average consumption around them, then growth will not make people any happier on average because it will raise people's benchmark just as much as it raises their consumption. A similar phenomenon can occur if what people compare their consumption to is what they are used to—that is, to their own past consumption. In this case, continual growth is required just to maintain a constant ratio of current consumption to the benchmark level. This interpretation would explain why Keynes' forecast did not come true: Keynes did not grasp that people would not be satisfied with income four times as large as his own because he was putting himself in their places—that is, imagining that people 100 years in the future would apply the same benchmarks as he was using. He failed to realize that

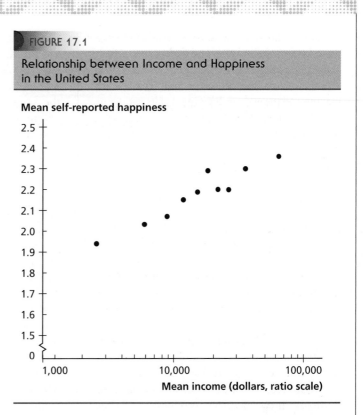

FIGURE 17.1

Relationship between Income and Happiness in the United States

Source: Frey and Sturtzer (2002). Data are for deciles of the income distribution.

after 100 years of growing consumption, people would have changed their benchmarks. They would have gotten used to a higher standard of consumption, so they would not feel as well off as he imagined they would.

Both of these cases are examples of what economists call "comparison utility."[‡] A more colorful name for the same thing is the "hedonic treadmill," which nicely captures the idea of running forward but never getting anywhere.

Given that growth making people happy is no longer logically necessary, the question then becomes empirical: in practice, does growth actually make people happier? The first economist to systematically consider this question was Richard

(Conitnued)

WILL GROWTH MAKE US HAPPY? (*CONTINUED*)

Easterlin, who wrote a series of studies on the topic beginning in 1974. His conclusion, which came to be known as the Easterlin Paradox, was that there is no link between a country's level of income and the average happiness of its residents.

Easterlin and his followers looked at data from surveys of average happiness in various countries. From their studies, two findings emerged. First, in cross-sectional analyses, it seemed that average happiness rose with income per capita up to some income level—generally around $15,000 per capita—but that after that the relationship was flat. Second, within countries over time, there did not seem to be any statistically significant relationship between the growth rate of income and the increase over time in happiness. In one of the more striking findings along this line, self-reported life satisfaction in Japan did not change over the period 1958–1991, even though real GDP per capita increased by a factor of 6.[†] Easterlin attributed these findings to exactly the sort of comparison utility just discussed.

More recent work has cast doubt on these findings, however. The economists Betsey Stevenson and Justin Wolfers performed an extensive reanalysis of data on happiness, using information over a longer time period and for more countries than previous work.[‡] They also made corrections for a number of problems that naturally came up in assessing something as slippery as happiness. Among other data problems, Stevenson and Wolfers found a number of changes in the wording of questions over time. For example, in Japan, happiness was measured on a five-point scale. In the early surveys, the top level of happiness was defined as "Although I am not innumerably satisfied, I am generally satisfied with life now." Later on, the top happiness category was changed to "completely satisfied," which was much more demanding.

Stevenson and Wolfers find that, at least for countries looked at in cross-section, the Easterlin paradox completely disappears: not only does average happiness rise with income, but the slope of the "well being-income gradient" (the amount of extra happiness associated with a 1% increase in income) is also roughly the same whether looking at the individuals within a country or comparing average happiness and average income among countries.

Looking at growth of happiness in a single country over time, things are more complicated. Stevenson and Wolfers claim to find evidence that a country's average happiness grows when its average income grows (with the same well-being income gradient observed in the other cases). But Easterlin, in a rebuttal to their work, claims that this relationship between happiness and income only holds true over business cycles, (booms and recessions), not in the long run.[§] In any case, however, the lack of statistically significant evidence that growth in a country raises happiness is not the same thing as a finding that growth does not raise happiness.

Whether the failure of the Easterlin Paradox would be good or bad news depends on one's perspective. For people in wealthy countries, it seems like good news. Under Easterlin's view, future growth in rich countries would not raise happiness, because people would constantly raise the standard to which they were comparing themselves. If Easterlin is wrong, however, there is no reason that another century of good growth cannot make everyone even happier.

On the other hand, the Easterlin hypothesis being right would have a significant upside when it comes to thinking about inequality in the world. The reason is that to the extent that the Easterlin hypothesis is correct, inequality in happiness is far lower than inequality in income. This would be good news for anyone who feels weighed down by the unfairness of some people being so much better off than others.

[*]Keynes (1930).
[†]Frey and Stutzer (2002).
[§]Easterlin et al. (2010).
[‡]Stevenson and Wolfers (2008).

What Will Happen to the World Income Distribution?

After rising for 150 years, the level of world income inequality flattened out in the last few decades of the 20th century. This relative constancy of income inequality is in turn the result of two forces working in opposite directions. On the one hand, the super rapid growth of some poor countries has narrowed income inequality in the world. In this respect, no country has been more important than China, with one-fifth of the world's population. China's GDP per capita was 3.5% of the U.S. level in 1980; by 2009 it was 19% of the U.S. level. On the other hand, the persistent failure of some poor countries to grow at all serves to increase the world's income inequality. Over the period 1975–2009, GDP per capita actually fell in 26 countries that accounted for 5.5% of the world's population.

More people exited poverty over the period 1980–2010 than ever before in human history. If the "contagion of growth" that affected China and some other poor countries continues to spread, then the next several decades could see a similarly massive reduction in world poverty and a narrowing of the world income distribution.

Will Technological Progress Continue Apace?

For countries that are currently rich, the most important determinant of future economic growth will be technological progress. Whether technological progress speeds up, slows down, or remains constant will have more impact on living standards 50 years hence than just about anything else. However, the determinants of technological progress are poorly understood. During the productivity slowdown of the 1970s and 1980s, the pace of technological progress seemed to be flagging. But the period since 1995 has seen particularly rapid technological change, as firms have learned how to apply the general-purpose technology of computers to restructuring their businesses and raising productivity.

By its very nature, technological progress is hard to forecast. (Moore's law, which has accurately predicted progress in the production of computer chips since 1965, is famous exactly because so many other predictions of future technology have been so woefully misguided.) In the last half-century, technological progress in the most advanced countries has been sustained by ever-growing inputs of labor and capital into research and development. It seems likely, although not certain, that such rising R&D input can be sustained, at least for the next 50 years. But even if R&D does continue to rise, there is no guarantee that the pool of available new inventions is bottomless. Whether the current wave of rapid technological progress will soon peter out or will continue for several more decades, and whether a new general-purpose technology will soon arise to spur on economic growth—these are questions that only time will answer.

What Is the Future of World Demographics?

The 20th century saw spectacular demographic changes: a quadrupling of world population, steep increases in longevity, and equally sharp declines in fertility. During the 21st century, the world will enter new demographic territory. The two great unknowns hanging over demographic developments are the progress of the AIDS epidemic and the path of fertility.

AIDS has already reversed the decades-long trend of rising life expectancy in a number of African countries. If the epidemic remains unchecked, it may have similar effects in other parts of the developing world.

In many of the world's richest countries, below-replacement fertility over the last few decades virtually guarantees unprecedented population aging and shrinkage in total population size. If fertility remains far below the replacement level for a few decades more, the resulting demographic change will have seismic effects on these countries' economies, societies, and place in the world. Some developing countries have had such a rapid fertility decline that they, too, may soon have below-replacement fertility, whereas in other parts of the developing world, fertility may remain far above replacement for half a century or more. Even if high-population-growth countries such as Pakistan and Nigeria do reach replacement fertility relatively quickly, demographic momentum will ensure that populations more than double over the next 50 years.

Will Global Economic Integration Continue?

Globalization has driven economic growth by facilitating the transfer of technology and factors of production and especially by allowing countries to specialize in producing the things they are good at. Although gains from trade raise the average standard of living in a country that participates in the world economy, there are undeniably groups within every country that lose out as a result of globalization. The dislocations that it causes have provoked serious opposition to globalization in both rich and poor countries. Governments have in the past used their power to reduce international economic interactions, and there is some chance that they will do so again.

If governments do not use their power to halt globalization, then we can expect to see yet further economic integration over the next several decades. Falling costs of transporting goods and the advent of nearly free transmission of information will lead to entirely new forms of economic interaction. Most significantly, there may be expanded trade in services. For example, students in rich countries may find themselves being taught by teachers half a world away.

Ongoing globalization will be good for rich countries, but it holds even more promise for the poor. For countries that are ill favored by geography—those lacking natural resources and those with low agricultural productivity because of their tropical climate—globalization holds the promise of eliminating barriers to growth. Access to the world market will also allow firms and workers to bypass the inefficient institutions that have held back growth in so many countries.

Will Shortages of Natural Resources Constrain Economic Growth?

For well more than a century, economists and other scholars have worried about the potential of natural resource shortages to limit economic growth. So far, their concerns have proved unwarranted. Although there have been shortages of specific resources, economies have shown great flexibility in substituting abundant resources for scarce resources. Technological progress has also circumvented many resource bottlenecks.

Although growth has not been constrained by resource shortages in the past, shortages theoretically could constrain growth in the future. The future of resource-saving technologies, like the future of technology more generally, is difficult to forecast.

The mechanism by which shortages of a natural resource raise its price, encouraging innovation and substitution, is short-circuited in the case of resources that are not privately owned. The most significant such resource in the world today is the atmosphere. World emissions of carbon dioxide from the burning of fossil fuel are likely to rise significantly as poor countries move toward the lifestyle of the developed world. The resulting global warming has the potential to alter the earth's climate radically, with unpredictable results.

17.3 A FINAL THOUGHT

Economic growth is an important topic because it has such a significant impact on the welfare of so many people. It is also an interesting topic because it is an ongoing story. The passage of time brings new data, new events, and new policy experiments. Finally, it is a field of active research, in which new ideas are constantly being proposed, debated, and tested. Readers who take from this book a desire to learn more about the questions we have raised—whether in further academic work or in casual observation of the world—will find their curiosity amply rewarded.

REFERENCES

Abramovitz, Moses. 1956. "Resource and Output Trends in the United States Since 1870." *American Economic Review* 46 (May): 5–23.

———. 1986. "Catching Up, Forging Ahead, and Falling Behind." *Journal of Economic History* 46 (June): 385–406.

Acemoglu, Daron. 2002. "Directed Technical Change." *Review of Economic Studies* 69 (October): 781–810.

———. 2010. "Theory, General Equilibrium, and Political Economy in Development Economics." *Journal of Economic Perspectives* 24 (Summer): 3.

Acemoglu, Daron, and David H. Autor. Forthcoming. "Skills, Tasks and Technologies: Implications for Employment and Earnings," in Orley Ashenfelter and David E. Card (eds.), *Handbook of Labor Economics Volume 4*. Amsterdam: Elsevier.

Acemoglu, Daron, and Simon Johnson. 2007. "Disease and Development: The Effect of Life Expectancy on Economic Growth." *Journal of Political Economy* 115(6): 925–985.

Acemoglu, Daron, Simon Johnson, and James A. Robinson. 2001. "The Colonial Origins of Comparative Development: An Empirical Investigation." *American Economic Review* 91(5): 1369–1401.

———. 2003. "An African Success Story: Botswana," in Dani Rodrik (ed.), *Search of Prosperity: Analytic Narratives of Economic Growth*. Princeton, NJ: Princeton University Press.

Acemoglu, Daron, and James A. Robinson. 2002. "Economic Backwardness in Political Perspective." *Mimeo* (May).

Acemoglu, Daron, and Fabrizio Zilibotti. 2001. "Productivity Differences." *Quarterly Journal of Economics* 116 (May): 563–606.

Adelman, Morris A. 1995. *The Genie out of the Bottle: World Oil Since 1970*. Cambridge: MIT Press.

Ades, Alberto F., and Edward L. Glaeser. 1995. "Trade and Circuses: Explaining Urban Giants." *Quarterly Journal of Economics* 110 (February): 195–227.

Aghion, Philippe, and Peter Howitt. 1992. "A Model of Growth Through Creative Destruction." *Econometrica* 60:2, 323–351.

———. 2008. *The Economics of Growth*. Cambridge: MIT Press.

Ahuja, Vinod. 1998. "Land Degradation, Agricultural Productivity, and Common Property: Evidence from Côte d'Ivoire." *Environment and Development Economics* 3 (February): 7–34.

Alesina, Alberto, Arnaud Devleeschauwer, William Easterly, Sergio Kurlat, and Romain Wacziarg. 2003. "Fractionalization." *Journal of Economic Growth* 8 (June): 155–194.

Alesina, Alberto, and Dani Rodrik. 1994. "Distributive Politics and Economic Growth." *Quarterly Journal of Economics* 109 (May): 465–490.

Anderson, James E., and J. Peter Neary. 1999. "The Mercantilist Index of Trade Policy." NBER Working Paper 6870 (January).

Arrow, Kenneth J. 1972. "Gifts and Exchanges." *Philosophy and Public Affairs* 1(4): 343–362.

Ashton, Basil, Kenneth Hill, Alan Piazza, and Robin Zeitz. 1984. "Famine in China, 1958–61." *Population and Development Review* 10 (December): 613–645.

Åslund, Anders, and Mikhail Dmitriev. 1999. "Economic Reform Versus Rent Seeking." In Anders Åslund, and Martha Brill Olcott (eds.), *Russia After Communism*, Washington, DC: Carnegie Endowment for International Peace.

Atkeson, Andrew, and Patrick J. Kehoe. 2001. "The Transition to a New Economy After the Second Industrial Revolution." Working paper, Federal Reserve Bank of Minneapolis.

Atkinson, Anthony B., and Joseph E. Stiglitz. 1969. "A New View of Technological Change." *Economic Journal* 79 (September): 573–578.

Autor, David H., Lawrence F. Katz, and Melissa S. Kearney. 2008. "Trends in U.S. Wage Inequality: Revising the Revisionists." *Review of Economics and Statistics* 90(2): 300–323.

Autor, David H., Lawrence F. Katz, and Alan B. Krueger. 1998. "Computing Inequality: Have Computers Changed the Labor Market?" *Quarterly Journal of Economics* 113 (November): 1169–1214.

Babbage, Charles. 1851. *The Exposition of 1851.* London: John Murray.

Backhouse, E., and J. O. P. Bland. 1914. *Annals and Memoirs of the Court of Peking.* Boston: Houghton Mifflin.

Baily, Martin Neil, and Robert Solow. 2001. "International Productivity Comparisons Built from the Firm Level," *Journal of Economic Perspectives* 15 (Summer): 151–172.

Bairoch, Paul. 1988. *Cities and Economic Development: From the Dawn of History to the Present.* Translated by Christopher Braider. Chicago: University of Chicago Press.

———. 1993. *Economics and World History: Myths and Paradoxes.* Chicago: University of Chicago Press.

Banerjee, Abhijit V., and Esther Duflo. 2011. *Poor Economics: A Radical Rethinking of the Way to Fight Global Poverty.* New York: Public Affairs.

Barro, Robert. 1997. *Determinants of Economic Growth: A Cross-Country Empirical Study.* Cambridge: MIT Press.

———. 2000. "Inequality and Growth in a Panel of Countries." *Journal of Economic Growth* 5 (March): 5–32.

Barro, Robert, and Jong-Wha Lee. 2011. "Education Attainment Dataset." http://www.barrolee.com/

Barro, Robert, and Xavier Sala-i-Martin. 1997. "Technological Diffusion, Convergence, and Growth." *Journal of Economic Growth* 2(1): 1–26.

Barth, James, Gerald Caprio, Jr., and Ross Levine. 2006. *Rethinking Bank Regulation: Till Angels Govern.* Cambridge: Cambridge University Press.

Basu, Susanto, and David N. Weil. 1998. "Appropriate Technology and Growth." *Quarterly Journal of Economics* 113 (November): 1025–1054.

Baumol, William J., and Alan S. Blinder. 1997. *Economics: Principles and Policy*, 7th ed. New York: Dryden Press.

Beaulier, Scott A. 2003. "Explaining Botswana's Success: The Critical Role of Post-Colonial Policy." Working paper, George Mason University.

Beck, Thorsten, Ross Levine, and Norman Loayza. 2000a. "Finance and the Sources of Growth." *Journal of Financial Economics* 58(1–2): 261–300.

———. 2000b. "Financial Intermediation and Growth: Causality and Causes." *Journal of Monetary Economics* 46(1): 31–77.

Benabou, Roland, and Efe Ok. 2001. "Social Mobility and the Demand for Redistribution: The POUM Hypothesis." *Quarterly Journal of Economics* 116 (May): 447–487.

Berg, Alan, and Susan Brems. 1989. *A Case for Promoting Breastfeeding in Projects to Limit Fertility.* World Bank Technical Paper 102.

Berger, Peter. 1994. "Gross National Product and the Gods." *McKinsey Quarterly* 1: 97–110.

Berhanu, Betemariam, and Dennis P. Hogan. 1997. "Women's Status and Contraceptive Innovation in Urban Ethiopia." Population Studies Training Center Working Paper 97 03, Brown University.

Bernanke, Ben S., and Refet S. Gürkaynak. 2001. "Is Growth Exogenous? Taking Mankiw, Romer, and Weil Seriously," in Ben S. Bernacke and Kenneth Rogoff (eds.), *NBER Macroeconomics Annual 16.* Cambridge: MIT Press.

Bernard, Andrew, and Meghan Busse. 2004. "Who Wins the Olympic Games: Economic Resources and Medal Totals." *Review of Economics and Statistics* 86(1), 413–417.

Berry, Steven, James Levinsohn, and Ariel Pakes. 1999. "Voluntary Export Restraints on Automobiles: Evaluating a Trade Policy." *American Economic Review* 89(3): 400–430.

Bertola, Giuseppe. 1999. "Labor Markets in the European Union." *Mimeo*, European University Institute (September).

Bloom, David E., and Jeffrey D. Sachs. 1998. "Geography, Demography, and Economic Growth in Africa." *Brookings Papers on Economic Activity* 2: 207–273.

Bloom, David, and Jeffrey Williamson. 1998. "Demographic Transitions and Economic Miracles in Emerging Asia." *World Bank Economic Review* 12(3): 419–455.

Bockstette, Valerie, Areendam Chanda, and Louis Putterman. 2002. "States and Markets: The Advantage of an Early Start." *Journal of Economic Growth* 7 (December): 347–369.

Bodin, Jean. 1967. *Six Books of a Commonwealth*. Translated and edited by M. J. Tooley. New York: Barnes and Noble.

Bongaarts, John. 1994. "Population Policy Options in the Developing World." *Science* 263 (February): 771–776.

———. "Fertility and Reproductive Preferences in Post-Transitional Societies." *Population and Development Review* 27 supplement: 260–281.

Bourguignon, François. 2011. "A Turning Point in Global Inequality…and Beyond." *Mimeo*.

Bourguignon, François, and Christian Morrison. 2002. "Inequality Among World Citizens: 1820–1992." *American Economic Review* 92 (September): 727–744.

BP Statistical Review of World Energy. 2011.

Brander, James A., and M. Scott Taylor. 1998. "The Simple Economics of Easter Island: A Ricardo-Malthus Model of Renewable Resource Use." *American Economic Review* 88 (March): 119–138.

Braudel, Fernand. 1984. *The Perspective of the World, Civilization and Capitalism 15th–18th Century*. Vol. 3. Translated by Sian Reynolds. New York: Harper and Row.

Bresnahan, Timothy F. 2002. "The Microsoft Case: Competition, Innovation, and Monopoly." Manuscript.

Brezis, Elise, Paul Krugman, and Daniel Tsiddon. 1993. "Leapfrogging in International Competition: A Theory of Cycles in National Technological Leadership." *American Economic Review* 83 (December): 1211–1219.

Brimblecomb, Peter. 1977. "London Air Pollution, 1500–1900." *Atmospheric Environment* 11: 1157–1162.

Brooks, Daniel J. 2003. *The Culture of World Civilizations*. Manuscript, Aquinas College.

Brown, Drusilla K., Alan V. Deardorff, and Robert M. Stern. 2002. *Computational Analysis of Multilateral Trade Liberalization in the Uruguay Round and Doha Development Round*. Discussion Paper 489, Research Seminar in International Economics, University of Michigan (December 8).

Bruce, Anthony. 1980. "The Purchase System in the British Army 1660–1871." *Studies in History*, Series No. 20, Royal Historical Society.

Burkett, John, Catherine Humblet, and Louis Putterman. 1999. "Pre-Industrial and Post-War Economic Development: Is There a Link?" *Economic Development and Cultural Change* 47(3): 471–495.

Cain, Mead. 1977. "The Economic Activities of Children in a Village in Bangladesh." *Population and Development Review* 3 (September): 201–227.

Carroll, Christopher, Jody Overland, and David N. Weil. 1997. "Comparison Utility in a Growth Model." *Journal of Economic Growth* 2 (December): 339–367.

———. 2000. "Saving and Growth with Habit Formation." *American Economic Review* 90 (June): 341–355.

Carroll, Christopher, Byung-Kun Rhee, and Changyong Rhee. 1994. "Are There Cultural

Effects on Saving? Some Cross-Sectional Evidence." *Quarterly Journal of Economics* 109 (August): 685–699.

———. 1999. "Does Cultural Origin Affect Saving Behavior? Evidence from Immigrants." *Economic Development and Cultural Change* 48 (October): 33–50.

Caselli, Francesco. 1999. "Technological Revolutions." *American Economic Review* 89 (March): 78–102.

Caselli, Francesco, and Wilbur J. Coleman II. 2001. "The U.S. Structural Transformation and Regional Convergence: A Reinterpretation." *Journal of Political Economy* 109 (June): 584–616.

Cashin, P., and C. J. McDermott. 2002. "The Long-Run Behavior of Commodity Prices: Small Trends and Big Variability." *IMF Staff Papers* 49: 175–199.

Cerf, Christopher, and Victor Navasky. 1998. *The Experts Speak: The Definitive Compendium of Authoritative Misinformation.* New York: Villard.

Chakravorty, Ujjayant, James Roumasse, and Kinping Tse. 1997. "Endogenous Substitution Among Energy Resources and Global Warming." *Journal of Political Economy* 105 (December): 1201–1234.

Chanda, Areendam, and Louis Putterman. 1999. "The Capacity for Growth: Society's Capital." Working paper, Brown University.

Chen, Nai-Ruenn, and Walter Galenson. 1969. *The Chinese Economy Under Communism.* Chicago: Aldine Publishing Co.

Chi, Ch'ao-Ting. 1963. *Key Economic Areas in Chinese History: As Revealed in the Development of Public Works for Water-Control.* New York: Paragon Book Reprint Corp.

China Statistics Press. 2006. *China Statistical Yearbook.*

Clark, Gregory. 1987. "Why Isn't the Whole World Developed? Lessons from the Cotton Mills." *Journal of Economic History* 47 (March): 141–173.

Coale, Ansely J., and Melvin Zelnik. 1963. *New Estimates of Fertility and Population in the United States.* Princeton, NJ: Princeton University Press.

Cohen, Daniel, and Marcello Soto. 2007. "Growth and Human Capital: Good Data, Good Results." *Journal of Economic Growth* 12(1): 51–76.

Cohen, Joel. 1995. *How Many People Can the Earth Support?* New York: W. W. Norton.

Cohen, Wesley M., Richard R. Nelson, and John P. Walsh. 2000. "Protecting Their Intellectual Assets: Appropriability Conditions and Why U.S. Manufacturing Firms Patent (or Not)." NBER Working Paper 7552 (February).

Coleman, James S. 1988. "Social Capital in the Creation of Human Capital." *American Journal of Sociology* 94 (S): S95–S120.

Collier, Paul. 2007. *The Bottom Billion: Why the Poorest Countries Are Failing and What Can be Done About It.* Oxford University Press.

Corak, Miles. 2006. "Do Poor Children Become Poor Adults? Lessons from a Cross Country Comparison of Generational Earnings Mobility." IZA Discussion Paper No. 1993. Bonn: Institute for the Study of Labor.

Costa, Dora. 2000. "American Living Standards 1888–1994: Evidence from Consumer Expenditures." NBER Working Paper 7650 (April).

Cox, Michael W., and Richard Alm. 1999. *Myths of Rich and Poor: Why We're Better Off Than We Think.* New York: Basic Books.

Crafts, Nicholas F. R. 1996. "The First Industrial Revolution: A Guided Tour for Growth Economists." *American Economic Review* 86 (May): 197–201.

Cuban, Larry. 1986. *Teachers and Machines: The Classroom Uses of Technology Since 1920.* New York: Teachers College Press.

Cutler, David, Winnie Fung, Michael Kremer, and Monica Singhal. 2007. "Mosquitoes: The Long-term Effects of Malaria Eradication in India." Mimeo.

Dauzet, Pierre. 1948. *Le Siècle des Chemins de Fer en France (1821–1938).* Fontenay-aux-Roses, Siene: Imprimeries Bellenand.

David, Paul A. 1991a. "Computer and Dynamo: The Modern Productivity Paradox in a

Not-Too-Distant Mirror," in *Technology and Productivity: The Challenge for Economic Policy.* Paris: OECD, 315–345.

———. 1991b. "The Hero and the Herd in Technological History: Reflections on Thomas Edison and the Battle of the Systems," in Patric Higonnet, David S. Landes, and Henry Rosovsky (eds.), *Favorites of Fortune: Technology, Growth, and Economic Development Since the Industrial Revolution.* Cambridge: Harvard University Press.

Davidson, Marshall B. 1988. *Treasures of the New York Public Library.* New York: Harry N. Abrams.

De Soto, Hernando. 1989. *The Other Path: The Invisible Revolution in the Third World.* New York: Harper & Row.

Deane, Phyllis, and Cole, W. A. 1969. *British Economic Growth 1688–1959.* Cambridge: Cambridge University Press.

Deininger, Klaus, and Lyn Squire. 1996. "A New Data Set and Measure of Income Inequality." *World Bank Economic Review* 10 (September): 565–591.

DeLong, J. Bradford. 1997. "Cross-Country Variations in National Economic Growth Rates: The Role of 'Technology,'" in Jeffrey Fuhrer and Jane Sneddon Little (eds.), *Technology and Growth.* Boston: Federal Reserve Bank of Boston.

———. 2001. *Slouching Toward Utopia: An Economic History of the Twentieth Century.* Manuscript.

DeNavas-Walt, Carmen, Bernadette D. Proctor, and Jessica Smith. 2010. *Income, Poverty, and Health Insurance Coverage in the United States: 2009.* Current Population Reports, P60-238, U.S. Census Bureau. Washington, DC: U.S. Government Printing Office.

Desvaux, Georges, Michael Wang, and David Xu. 2004. "Spurring Performance in China's State-owned Enterprises," *McKinsey Quarterly,* Special Edition, 96–105.

Devine, Warren D., Jr. 1983. "From Shafts to Wires: Historical Perspective on Electrification." *Journal of Economic History* 43 (June): 347–372.

Diamond, Jared. 1997. *Guns, Germs, and Steel: The Fates of Human Societies.* New York: W. W. Norton and Co.

Díaz-Giménez, Javier, Vincenzo Quadrini, and José-Víctor Ríos-Rull. 1997. "Dimensions of Inequality: Facts on the U.S. Distributions of Earnings, Income, and Wealth." *Federal Reserve Bank of Minneapolis Quarterly Review* 21 (Spring): 3–21.

Djankov, Simeon, Rafael La Porta, Florencio Lopez-De-Silanes, and Andrei Shleifer. 2002. "The Regulation of Entry." *Quarterly Journal of Economics* 117 (February): 1–37.

Dollar, David, and Paul Collier. 2001. *Globalization, Growth, and Poverty: Building an Inclusive World Economy.* Washington, DC: World Bank.

Dollar, David, and Aart Kraay. 2002. "Growth Is Good for the Poor." *Journal of Economic Growth* 7 (September): 195–225.

Drucker, Peter F. 1997. "The Future That Has Already Happened." *Harvard Business Review* 75 (September–October): 20–24.

Durpe, Ruth. 1999. "'If It's Yellow, It Must Be Butter': Margarine Regulation in North America Since 1886." *Journal of Economic History* 59 (June): 353–371.

Dynan, Karen E., Jonathan Skinner, and Stephen P. Zeldes. 2004. "Do the Rich Save More?" *Journal of Political Economy* 112(2): 397–444.

Easterlin, Richard A. 2000. "The Worldwide Standard of Living Since 1800." *Journal of Economic Perspectives* 14 (Winter): 7–26.

Easterlin, Richard, et al. 2010. "The Happiness–Income Paradox Revisited" *Papers of the National Academy of Science,* December 13.

Easterly, William. 1995. "Explaining Miracles: Growth Regressions Meet the Gang of Four," in Tako Ito and Anne O. Krueger (eds.), *Growth Theories in Light of the East Asian Experience.* Chicago: University of Chicago Press.

Easterly, William, and Stanley Fischer. 1995. "The Soviet Economic Decline." *World Bank Economic Review* 9 (September): 341–372.

Eaton, Jonathan, and Samuel Kortum. 1996. "Trade in Ideas: Patenting and Productivity in the OECD." *Journal of International Economics* 40 (May): 251–278.

Ehrlich, Paul R. 1968. *The Population Bomb.* New York: Ballantine Books.

Elsom, Derek M. 1995. "Atmospheric Pollution Trends in the United Kingdom," in Julian L. Simon (ed.), *The State of Humanity.* Cambridge: Blackwell.

Eltony, M. 1993. "Transport Gasoline Demand in Canada." *Journal of Transport Economics and Policy* 27 (May): 193–208.

Engerman, Stanley L., and Kenneth L. Sokoloff. 2002. "Factor Endowments, Inequality, and Paths of Development Among New World Economics." NBER Working Paper 9259 (October).

Ettling, John. 1981. *The Germ of Laziness: Rockefeller Philanthropy and Public Health in the New South.* Cambridge: Harvard University Press.

Evelyn, John. 1661. *Fumifugium: or The Inconveniencie of the Aer And Smoak of London Dissipated. Together With some Remedies humbly Proposed.* London: Printed by W. Godbid for Gabriel Bedel, and Thomas Collins.

Federal Reserve Bank of Dallas. 1997. *Time Well Spent: The Declining Real Cost of Living in America.* Annual report.

Feldstein, Martin. 1997. "How Big Should Government Be?" *National Tax Journal* 2 (June): 197–213.

Feldstein, Martin, and Charles Horioka. 1980. "Domestic Saving and International Capital Flows." *Economic Journal* 90 (June): 314–329.

Felten, Eric. 2001. "Finders Keepers?" *Reader's Digest* April, 103–107.

Fernandez, Raquel, Nezih Guner, and John Knowles. 2005. "Love and Money: A Theoretical and Empirical Analysis of Household Sorting and Inequality," *Quarterly Journal of Economics* 120(1): 273–344.

Fernandez-Armesto, Felipe. 1995. *Millennium.* New York: Bantam.

Fisman, Raymond, and Edward Miguel. 2007. "Corruption, Norms and Legal Enforcement: Evidence from Diplomatic Parking Tickets." *Journal of Political Economy* 115(6): 1020–1048.

Fogel, Robert W. 1964. *Railroads and American Economic Growth: Essays in Econometric History.* Baltimore: Johns Hopkins University Press.

———. 1997. "New Findings on Secular Trends in Nutrition and Mortality: Some Implications for Population Theory," in Mark R. Rosenweig and Oded Stark (eds.), *Handbook of Population and Family Economics*, Vol. 1A. Amsterdam: North Holland.

Forbes, Kristin. 2000. "A Reassessment of the Relationship Between Inequality and Growth." *American Economic Review* 90(4): 869–887.

Fox, Matthew, et al. 2004. "The Impact of HIV/ AIDS on Labour Productivity in Kenya." *Tropical Medicine and International Health* 9(3): 318–324.

Frankel, Jeffrey, and David Romer. 1999. "Does Trade Cause Growth?" *American Economic Review* 89 (June): 379–399.

Freedom House. 2011. *Freedom in the World, 2011.*

Frey, Bruno S., and Alois Stutzer. 2002. "What Can Economists Learn from Happiness Research?" *Journal of Economic Literature* 40 (June): 402–435.

Fuchs, Rachel. 1984. *Abandoned Children, Foundlings, and Child Welfare in Nineteenth-Century France.* Albany: State University of New York Press.

Fylkesnes, Knut, et al. 1997. "The HIV Epidemic in Zambia: Socio-demographic Prevalence Patterns and Indications of Trends among Childbearing Women." *AIDS* 11(3): 339–345.

Gallup, John L. 1998. "Agricultural Productivity and Geography." Harvard Institute of International Development.

Gallup, John L., and Jeffrey D. Sachs. 2001. "The Economic Burden of Malaria." *American Journal of Tropical Medicine and Hygiene* 64(1–2 S): 85–96.

Gallup, John L., Jeffrey D. Sachs, and Andrew D. Mellinger. 1999. "Geography and Economic Development." *International Regional Science Review* 22(2): 179–232.

———. 2001. "Geography Datasets." Center for International Development, Harvard University, http://www.cid.harvard.edu/ciddata/geography-data.htm

Galor, Oded, and Omer Moav. 2006. "Das Human Kapital." *Review of Economic Studies* 73(1): 85–117.

———. 2004. "From Physical Capital to Human Capital: Inequality and the Process of Development." *Review of Economic Studies* 71(4), 1001–1026.

Galor, Oded, and Daniel Tsiddon. 1997. "Technological Progress, Mobility, and Economic Growth." *American Economic Review* 87(3): 363–382.

Galor, Oded, and David N. Weil. 1996. "The Gender Gap, Fertility, and Growth." *American Economic Review* 86 (June): 374–387.

———. 2000. "Population, Technology, and Growth: From Malthusian Stagnation to the Demographic Transition and Beyond." *American Economic Review* 90 (September): 806–828.

Galor, Oded, and Joseph Zeira. 1993. "Income Distribution and Macroeconomics." *Review of Economic Studies* 60(1): 35–52.

Garang, John. 1987. *John Garang Speaks*. London: Kegan Paul International.

Garon, Sheldon. 1998. "Fashioning a Culture of Diligence and Thrift: Savings and Frugality Campaigns in Japan, 1900–31," in S. Minichiello (ed.), *Japan's Competing Modernities: Issues in Culture and Democracy, 1900–1930*. Honolulu: University of Hawaii Press.

George, Henry. 1886. *Protection or Free Trade; An Examination of the Tariff Question, with Especial Regard to the Interests of Labor*. New York: H. George and Co.

Goldman, Dana, and Elizabeth McGlynn. 2005. "US Health Care: Facts about Cost, Access, and Quality." Rand Corporation, http://www.rand.org/pubs/corporate_pubs/2005/RAND_CP484.1.pdf

Gollin, Douglas. 2002. "Getting Income Shares Right." *Journal of Political Economy* 110 (April): 458–474.

Gollin, Douglas, Stephen L. Parente, and Richard Rogerson. 2001. "Structural Transformation and Cross-Country Income Differences." *Mimeo* (December).

Gordon, Robert. 1999. "U.S. Economic Growth Since 1870: One Big Wave?" *American Economic Review Papers and Proceedings* 89 (May): 123–128.

———. 2000. "Does the 'New Economy' Measure Up to the Great Inventions of the Past?" *Journal of Economic Perspectives* 14 (Autumn): 49–74.

———. 2010. "Revisiting U.S Productivity over the Past Century with a View of the Future." NBER Working Paper 15834 (March).

Gylfason, Thorvaldur. 2001. "Natural Resources, Education, and Economic Development." *European Economic Review* 45 (May): 847–859.

Hall, Robert, and Charles Jones. 1999. "Why Do Some Countries Produce So Much More Output per Worker than Others?" *Quarterly Journal of Economics* 114 (February): 83–116.

Haltiwanger, John. 2011. "Firm Dynamics and Productivity Growth." *EIB Papers* 16: 1.

Hamermesh, Daniel, and Jeff Biddle.1994. "Beauty and the Labor Market." *American Economic Review* 84 (December): 1174–1194.

Hardin, Garret. 1968. "The Tragedy of the Commons." *Science* 162 (December): 1243–1248.

Harley, C. Knick. 1988. "Ocean Freight Rates and Productivity 1740–1913: The Primacy of Mechanical Invention Reaffirmed." *Journal of Economic History* 48 (December): 854–876.

———. 1993. "Reassessing the Industrial Revolution: A Macro View," in Joel Mokry (ed.), *The British Industrial Revolution: An Economic Perspective*. Boulder: Westview Press.

Hellmich, Nanci. 2010. "Bad Hair Day Can Hit Women's Self-Esteem, Wallet" *USA Today*, April 12. http://www.usatoday.com/news/health/2010-04-12-bad-hair_N.htm

Henderson, Vernon, Adam Storeygard, and David N. Weil. 2012. "Measuring Economic Growth from Outer Space." *American Economic Review*, 102(2), 994–1028.

Henrich, Joseph, Robert Boyd, Samuel Bowles, Colin Camerer, Ernst Fehr, Herbert Gintis, and Richard McElreath. 2001. "In Search of Homo Economicus: Behavioral Experiments in 15 Small–Scale Societies." *American Economic Review* 91 (May): 73–78.

Heston, Alan, Robert Summers, and Bettina Aten. 2011. *Penn World Table Version 7.0*, Center for International Comparisons of Production, Income and Prices at the University of Pennsylvania, May.

Higgins, Matthew, and Jeffrey Williamson. 1999. "Explaining Inequality the World Round: Cohort Sizes, Kuznets Curves, and Openness." NBER Working Paper 7224 (July).

Hill, Roger Brian. 1992. "The Work Ethic as Determined by Occupation, Education, Age, Gender, Work Experience, and Empowerment." Ph.D. diss., University of Tennessee, Knoxville.

Hochschild, Adam. 1998. *King Leopold's Ghost: A Story of Greed, Terror, and Heroism in Colonial Africa*. Boston: Houghton Mifflin.

Hotelling, Harold. 1931. "The Economics of Exhaustible Resources." *Journal of Political Economy* 39 (April): 137–175.

Hsieh, Chang-Tai, Erik Hurst, Charles I. Jones, and Peter J. Klenow. 2011. "The Allocation of Talent and U.S. Economic Growth." Working Paper.

Hseih, Chang-Tai, and Peter Klenow. 2007. "Misallocation and Manufacturing TFP in China and India." *Quarterly Journal of Economics* 124 (November): 1403–1448.

Huber, Richard J. 1971. "Effect on Prices of Japan's Entry into World Commerce After 1858." *Journal of Political Economy* 79 (May): 614–628.

Hufbauer, Gary Clyde, and Kimberly Ann Eliott. 1994. *Measuring the Costs of Protection in the United States*. Washington, DC: Institute for International Economics.

Inglehart, Ronald, and Hans-Dieter Klingermann. 2000. "Genes, Culture, Democracy and Happiness," in Ed Diener and E. M. Suh (eds.), *Subjective Well-Being Across Cultures*. Cambridge: MIT Press.

Ingram, James C. 1966. *International Economic Problems*. New York: Wiley.

Intergovernmental Panel on Climate Change. 2007. *The IPCC Fourth Assessment Report*.

International Energy Agency. 2002. *World Energy Outlook 2002*.

International Labour Organization. 2011. *Global Trends in Employment*. Geneva.

International Monetary Fund. 1997. *World Economic Outlook*.

Irwin, Douglas A. 2002. *Free Trade Under Fire*. Princeton, NJ: Princeton University Press.

Isaacs, Julia B. 2011a. "Economic Mobility of Families Across Generations," in Julia B. Isaacs, Isabel V. Sawhill, and Ron Haskins (eds.), *Getting Ahead or Losing Ground: Economic Mobility In America*. Washington, The Brookings Institution.

———. 2011b. "International Comparisons of Economic Mobility," in Julia B. Isaacs, Isabel V. Sawhill, and Ron Haskins (eds.), *Getting Ahead or Losing Ground: Economic Mobility In America*, Washington, The Brookings Institution.

ITU. "The World in 2010: ICT Facts and Figures," 2010.

Jaffe, Adam B., and Josh Lerner. 2004. *Innovation and Its Discontents: How Our Broken Patent System Is Endangering Innovation and Progress, and What to Do About It*. Princeton, NJ: Princeton University Press.

James, Estelle. 1998. "New Models for Old Age Security: Experiments, Evidence and Unanswered Questions." *World Bank Research Observer* 13 (August): 271–301.

Jardin, A. 1983. *Restoration and Reaction, 1815–1848.* Paris: Maison des Sciences de l'Homme; Cambridge: Cambridge University Press.

Jayaratne, Jith, and Philip E. Strahan. 1996. "The Finance-Growth Nexus: Evidence from Bank Branch Deregulation." *Quarterly Journal of Economics* 111(3): 639–670.

Jefferson, Thomas. 1967. *The Jefferson Cyclopedia.* Vol. 1. Edited by John P. Foley. New York: Russell and Russell.

Jenkins, Gilbert. 1977. *Oil Economists' Handbook.* New York: Applied Science Publishers.

Jensen, Robert, and Emily Oster. 2009. "The Power of TV: Cable Television and Women's Status in India." *Quarterly Journal of Economics* 124(3): 1057–1094.

Jevons, W. Stanley. 1865. *The Coal Question: An Inquiry Concerning the Progress of the Nation, and the Probable Exhaustion of our Coal-Mines.* London: Macmillan.

Jones, Arthur F., and Daniel H. Weinberg. 2000. "The Changing Shape of the Nation's Income Distribution 1947–1998," Current Population Report P60-204, U.S. Census Bureau (June).

Jones, Charles. 1995. "R&D-Based Models of Economic Growth." *Journal of Political Economy* 103 (August): 759–784.

———. 1998. *Introduction to Economic Growth.* New York: Norton.

———. 2002. "Sources of U.S. Economic Growth in a World of Ideas." *American Economic Review* 92 (March): 220–239.

Jones, Eric L. 1987. *The European Miracle: Environments, Economies and Geopolitics in the History of Europe and Asia,* 2nd ed. Cambridge: Cambridge University Press.

Joshi, Shareen, and T. Paul Schultz. 2007. "Family Planning as an Investment in Development: Evaluation of a Program's Consequences in Matlab, Bangladesh." Yale Economic Growth Center Discussion Paper No. 951.

Kahn, Herman, and Anthony Weiner. 1967. *The Year 2000: A Framework for Speculation on the Next Thirty-Three Years.* New York: Macmillan.

Kalemli-Ozcan, Sebnem. 2002. "Does Mortality Decline Promote Economic Growth?" *Journal of Economic Growth* 7 (December): 411–439.

Kaneko, Ryuichi, et al. 2008. "Population Projections for Japan: 2006–2055, Outline of Results, Methods, and Assumptions." *The Japanese Journal of Population* 6(1): 76–114.

Karl, Terry Lynn. 1997. *The Paradox of Plenty: Oil Booms and Petro-States.* Berkeley: University of California Press.

Kaufmann, Daniel, Aart Kraay, and Massimo Mastruzzi. 2010. "Governance Matters IX: Governance Indicators for 1996–2009," World Bank Policy Research Paper 5430.

Kelly, Morgan. 1997. "The Dynamics of Smithian Growth." *Quarterly Journal of Economics* 112 (August): 939–964.

Kendrick, John W. 1976. *The Formation and Stocks of Total Capital.* New York: Columbia University Press.

Kertzer, David I. 1993. *Sacrificed for Honor: Italian Infant Abandonment and the Politics of Reproductive Control.* Boston: Beacon Press.

Keyfitz, Nathan. 1989. "The Growing Human Population." *Scientific American* 261 (September): 119–126.

Keyfitz, Nathan, and Wilhelm Flieger. 1968. *World Population: An Analysis of Vital Data.* Chicago: University of Chicago Press.

———. 1990. *World Population Growth and Aging: Demographic Trends in the Late 20th Century.* Chicago: University of Chicago Press.

Keynes, John Maynard. 1920. *The Economic Consequences of the Peace.* London: Macmillan.

———. 1930. "Economic Possibilities for Our Grandchildren." Repr. in *The Collected Writings of John Maynard Keynes,* vol. 9, *Essays in Persuasion.* London: Macmillan, 1972.

Khwaja, Asim Ijaz, and Atif Mian. 2005. "Do Lenders Favor Politically Connected Firms? Rent Provision in an Emerging Financial Market." *Quarterly Journal of Economics* 120: 4.

King, Robert, and Ross Levine. 1993. "Finance and Growth: Schumpeter Might Be Right." *Quarterly Journal of Economics* 108(3): 717–737.

———. 1994. "Capital Fundamentalism, Economic Development and Economic Growth." *Carnegie-Rochester Series on Public Policy* 40 (June): 259–292.

Kiszewski, Anthony, Andrew Mellinger, Andrew Spielman, Pia Malaney, Sonia Ehrlich Sachs, and Jeffrey D. Sachs. 2004. "A Global Index Representing the Stability of Malaria Transmission." *American Journal of Tropical Medicine and Hygiene* 70(5): 486–498.

Klenow, Peter, and Andres Rodriguez-Clare. 1997. "The Neoclassical Revival in Growth Economics: Has It Gone Too Far?" *NBER Macro Annual*, pp. 73–103.

Knack, Stephen, and Philip Keefer. 1997. "Does Social Capital Have an Economic Payoff? A Cross-Country Investigation." *Quarterly Journal of Economics* 112 (November): 1251–1288.

Knack, Stephen, and Paul J. Zak. 2001. "Trust and Growth." *Economic Journal* 111 (April): 295–321.

Kolbert, Elizabeth. 2002. "Fellowship of the Ring: Boss Tweed's Monument Just Can't Stay Out of Trouble." *New Yorker*, May 6, 86–91.

Kremer, Michael. 1993. "Population Growth and Technological Change: One Million B.C. to 1900." *Quarterly Journal of Economics* 108 (August): 681–716.

Kremer, Michael, and Edward Miguel. 2004. "Worms: Identifying Impacts on Education and Health in the Presence of Treatment Externalities." *Econometrica* 72(1): 159–217.

Krueger, Anne O. 1990. "Government Failures in Development." *Journal of Economic Perspectives* 4 (Summer): 9–23.

Krugman, Paul. 1994. "The Myth of Asia's Miracle." *Foreign Affairs* 73 (November/December): 62–78.

———. 2000. "Why Most Economists' Predictions Are Wrong." *Red Herring*, May 18.

Kuznets, Simon. 1955. "Economic Growth and Income Inequality." *American Economic Review* 45 (March): 1–28.

La Ferrara, Eliana, Alberto Chong, and Suzanne Duryea. 2008. "Soap Operas and Fertility: Evidence from Brazil." Working Paper.

La Porta, Rafael, and Florencio Lopez-De-Silanes. 1999. "The Benefits of Privatization: Evidence from Mexico." *Quarterly Journal of Economics* 114 (November): 1193–1242.

La Porta, Rafael, Florencio Lopez-i-Silanes, and Andrei Shleifer. 2002. "Government Ownership of Banks," *Journal of Finance*, 57: 1.

Landes, David S. 1998. *The Wealth and Poverty of Nations: Why Some Are So Rich and Some So Poor.* New York: W. W. Norton.

Larsen, Ulla, and James W. Vaupel. 1993. "Hutterite Fecundability by Age and Parity: Strategies for Frailty Modeling of Event Histories." *Demography* 30 (February): 81–102.

Lee, Ronald D. 1990. "Long-Run Global Population Forecasts: A Critical Appraisal," *Population and Development Review*, 16, Supplement: Resources, Environment, and Population: Present Knowledge, Future Options, 44–71.

Levine, Ross. 2005. "Finance and Growth: Theory and Evidence," in Philippe Aghion and Steven Durlauf (eds.), *Handbook of Economic Growth.* Amsterdam: Elsevier Science.

Lewis, W. Arthur. 1954. "Economic Development with Unlimited Supplies of Labor." *Manchester School* 22(2): 139–191.

Lewis, William W., Hans Gersbach, Tom Jansen, and Koji Sakate. 1993. "The Secret to Competitiveness—Competition." *McKinsey Quarterly* 4: 29–43.

Lindbeck, Assar. 1995. "Hazardous Welfare-State Dynamics." *American Economic Review* 85 (May): 9–15.

Lipset, Seymour Martin. 1990. "The Work Ethic—Then and Now." *Public Interest* 98 (Winter): 61–69.

Livi-Bacci, Massimo. 1997. *A Concise History of World Population*, 2nd ed. Translated by Carl Ipsen. Malden, MA: Blackwell Publishers.

Lloyd, William F. 1833. *Two Lectures on the Checks to Population.* Oxford: Oxford University Press.

Lomborg, Bjørn. 2001. *The Skeptical Environmentalist: Measuring the Real State of the World.* Cambridge: Cambridge University Press.

Lucas, Adrienne. 2007. "The Impact of Disease Eradication on Fertility and Education." Wellesley College. *Mimeo.*

Lucas, Robert E. 1989. "On the Mechanics of Economic Development." *Journal of Monetary Economics* 22 (May): 3–42.

———. 1993. "Making a Miracle." *Econometrica* 61 (March): 251–272.

Maddison, Angus. 1995. *Monitoring the World Economy 1820–1992.* Paris: Development Center of the Organization for Economic Cooperation and Development.

———. 2001. *The World Economy: A Millennial Perspective.* Paris: Development Center of the Organization for Economic Cooperation and Development.

———. 2008 *Historical Statistics of the World Economy 1-2006,* http://www.ggdc.net/maddison/Maddison.htm

Malthus, Thomas R. 1798. *An Essay on the Principle of Population, as It Affects the Future Improvement of Society with Remarks on the Speculations of Mr. Godwin, M. Condorcet, and Other Writers.* London: Printed for J. Johnson in St. Paul's Church-Yard.

———. 1826. *An Essay on the Principle of Population,* 6th ed. London: J. Murray.

John A. Maluccio, et al. 2009. "The Impact of Improving Nutrition During Early Childhood on Education Among Guatemalan Adults." *The Economic Journal* 119 (April): 734–763.

Mankiw, N. Gregory. 1995. "The Growth of Nations." *Brookings Papers on Economic Activity* 1 (Spring): 275–310.

Mankiw, N. Gregory, David Romer, and David N. Weil. 1992. "A Contribution to the Empirics of Economic Growth." *Quarterly Journal of Economics* 107 (May): 407–437.

Mankiw, N. Gregory, and David N. Weil. 1989. "The Baby Boom, the Baby Bust, and the Housing Market." *Regional Science and Urban Economics* 19 (May): 235–258.

Masters, William A., and Margaret S. McMillan. 2001. "Climate and Scale in Economic Growth." *Journal of Economic Growth* 6 (September): 167–186.

McArthur, John W., and Jeffrey D. Sachs. 2001. "Institutions and Geography: Comment on Acemoglu, Johnson and Robinson." NBER Working Paper W8114 (February).

McDermott, Darren. 1996. "Singapore Swing: Krugman Was Right." *Wall Street Journal,* October 23.

McKinsey Global Institute. 1999. "Unlocking Economic Growth in Russia." Moscow: McKinsey Global Institute (October).

———.2009. "Lean Russia: Sustaining Economic Growth Through Improved Productivity." Moscow: McKinsey Global Institute (April).

McLaren, Angus. 1990. *A History of Contraception: From Antiquity to the Present Day.* Oxford: Basil Blackwell.

Mcleod, Christine, et al. 2003. "Evaluating Inventive Activity: The Cost of Nineteenth-Century UK Patents and the Fallibility of Renewal Data." *The Economic History Review,* New Series, 56(3): 537–562.

McNeill, William H. 1976. *Plagues and Peoples.* New York: Doubleday.

Meadows, Donella H., Dennis L. Meadows, Jørgen Randers, and William W. Behrens III. 1972. *The Limits to Growth: A Report for the Club of Rome's Project on the Predicament of Mankind.* New York: Universe Books.

Mellinger, Andrew, Jeffrey Sachs, and John Gallup. 2000. "Climate, Coastal Proximity, and Development," in Gordon L. Clark, Maryann P. Feldman, and Meric S. Gertler (eds.), *Oxford Handbook of Economic Geography.* Oxford University Press.

Miguel, Edward, Shanker Satyanath, and Ernest Sergenti. 2004. "Economic Shocks and Civil Conflict: An Instrumental Variables Approach." *Journal of Political Economy* 112(4): 725–753.

Mill, John Stuart. 1909. *Principles of Political Economy.* Edited by William James Ashley. London: Longmans, Green and Co. Library of Economics and Liberty, http://www.econlib.org/library/Mill/mlP7.html.

Mokyr, Joel. 1990. *The Lever of Riches: Technological Creativity and Economic Progress.* New York: Oxford University Press.

Montesquieu, Charles de Secondat, Baron de. 1914. *The Spirit of Laws.* Translated by Thomas Nugent. London: G. Bell and Sons.

Mowry, David C., and Nathan Rosenberg. 1998. *Paths of Innovation: Technological Change in 20th-Century America.* Cambridge: Cambridge University Press.

Narayan, Deepa, and Lant Pritchett. 1999. "Cents and Sociability: Household Income and Social Capital in Rural Tanzania." *Economic Development and Cultural Change* 47 (July): 871–897.

National Science Foundation. 2006. *Science and Engineering Indicators.* http://www.nsf.gov/statistics/seind06/

Nordhaus, William. 1994. *Managing the Global Commons: The Economics of Climate Change.* Cambridge: MIT Press.

———. 2004. "Retrospective on the 1970s Productivity Slowdown." National Bureau of Economics Working Paper 10950.

North, Douglass. 1990. *Institutions, Institutional Change, and Economic Development.* Cambridge: Cambridge University Press.

Obstfeld, Maurice, and Kenneth Rogoff. 2000. "Six Major Puzzles in International Macroeconomics: Is There a Common Cause?" In Ben Bernacke and Kenneth Rogoff (eds.), *NBER Macroeconomics Annual 2000.* Cambridge: MIT Press.

Olken, Benjamin A. 2009. "Do Television and Radio Destroy Social Capital? Evidence from Indonesian Villages." *American Economic Journal: Applied Economics* 1(4): 1–33.

Organization for Economic Cooperation and Development. 2002. *China in the World Economy: Domestic Policy Challenges.* Paris: OECD.

———. 2009. "State Owned Enterprises in China: Reviewing the Evidence." OECD Working Group on Privatisation and Corporate Governance of State Owned Assets, http://www.oecd.org/dataoecd/14/30/42095493.pdf

O'Rourke, Kevin H., and Jeffrey G. Williamson. 1999. *Globalization and History: The Evolution of the 19th Century Atlantic Economy.* Cambridge: MIT Press.

———. 2005. "From Malthus to Ohlin: Trade, Growth, and Distribution Since 1500." *Journal of Economic Growth* 10 (March): 5–34.

Pack, Howard, and Lawrence Westphal. 1986. "Industrial Strategy and Technological Change: Theory vs. Reality." *Journal of Development Economics* 22 (June): 87–126.

Parente, Stephen, and Edward Prescott. 2000. *Barriers to Riches.* Cambridge: MIT Press.

Perotti, Roberto. 1996. "Growth, Income Distribution, and Democracy: What the Data Say." *Journal of Economic Growth* 1 (June): 149–187.

Persson, Torsten, and Guido Tabellini. 1994. "Is Inequality Harmful for Growth? Theory and Evidence." *American Economic Review* 84 (June): 600–621.

PISA. 2009. "OECD Program for International Student Assessment." www.pisa.oecd.org.

Polanyi, Michael. 1962. *Personal Knowledge: Towards a Post-Critical Philosophy.* New York: Harper Torchbooks.

Pollan, Michael. 1998. "Playing God in the Garden." *New York Times Magazine,* October 25.

Pollard, Sidney. 1980. "A New Estimate of British Coal Production, 1750–1850." *Economic History Review* 33 (May): 212–235.

Pomeranz, Kenneth. 2000. *The Great Divergence: China, Europe, and the Making of the Modern World Economy.* Princeton, NJ: Princeton University Press.

Ponting, Clive. 1991. *A Green History of the World: The Environment and the Collapse of Great Civilizations.* New York: Penguin.

Population Reference Bureau. 1999. "Breastfeeding Patterns in the Developing World." Wall chart: Population Reference Bureau (July).

Pounds, Norman J. G., and Sue Simmons Ball. 1964. "Core-Areas and the Development of the European States System." *Annals of the Association of American Geographers* 54(1): 24–40.

Pritchett, Lant. 1994. "Desired Fertility and the Impact of Population Policies." *Population and Development Review* 20 (March): 1–55.

———. 2000. "The Tyranny of Concepts: CUDIE (Cumulated Depreciated Investment Effort) Is Not Capital." *Journal of Economic Growth* 5 (December): 361–384.

———. 2001. "Where Has All the Education Gone?" *World Bank Economic Review* 15(3): 367–391.

Putnam, Robert D. 2000. *Bowling Alone: The Collapse and Revival of American Community.* New York: Simon & Schuster.

Putnam, Robert. 2001. "Social Capital: Measurement and Consequences," *Canadian Journal of Policy Research* 2(1): 45–51.

Putnam, Robert D., Robert Leonardi, and Raffaella Y. Nanetti. 1993. *Making Democracy Work: Civic Traditions in Modern Italy.* Princeton, NJ: Princeton University Press.

Quah, Danny T. 1998. "A Weightless Economy." *UNESCO Courier* (December).

Rajan, Raghuram, and Luigi Zingales. 1998. "Financial Dependence and Growth." *American Economic Review* 88(3): 559–586.

Reuters. 2009 "FACTBOX-Oil production cost estimates by country," July 28. http://www.reuters.com/article/2009/07/28/oil-cost-factbox-idUSLS12407420090728

Revell, Jack. 1967. *The Wealth of the Nation: National Balance Sheet for the United Kingdom 1957-61.* Cambridge: Cambridge University Press.

Riddle, John M. 1992. *Contraception and Abortion from the Ancient World to the Renaissance.* Cambridge: Harvard University Press.

Riden, Philip. 1977. "The Output of the British Iron Industry Before 1870." *Economic History Review* 30 (August): 442–459.

Rijsberman, Frank R., and Andre van Velzen. 1996. "Vulnerability and Adaptation Assessments of Climate Change and Sea Level Rise in the Coastal Zone: Perspectives from the Netherlands and Bangladesh," in Joel B. Smith, et al. (eds.), *Adapting to Climate Change: An International Perspective.* New York: Springer.

Robinson, James A. 2001. "When Is the State Predatory?" *Mimeo.*

Rodriguez, Francisco, and Jeffrey D. Sachs. 1999. "Why Do Resource-Abundant Economies Grow More Slowly?" *Journal of Economic Growth* 4 (September): 277–303.

Romer, Paul. 1990. "Endogenous Technological Change." *Journal of Political Economy* 98(5, pt. 2) (October): S71–S102.

———. 1992. "Two Strategies for Economic Development: Using Ideas and Producing Ideas." *Proceedings of the World Bank Annual Conference on Development Economics, Supplement to the World Bank Economic Review,* 63–91.

Rosen, Sherwin. 1981. "The Economics of Superstars." *American Economic Review* 71 (December): 845–858.

Rosen, Stacey, and Shahla Shapouri. 2001. "Effects of Income Distribution on Food Security." U.S. Department of Agriculture Information Bulletin 765–2 (April).

Rostow, W. W. 1998. *The Great Population Spike and After: Reflections on Population and the Economy in the 21st Century.* New York: Oxford University Press.

Ruttan, Vernon W. 2001. *Technology, Growth, and Development: An Induced Innovation Perspective.* New York: Oxford University Press.

Sachs, Jeffrey D. 2000. "Tropical Underdevelopment." Working paper, Harvard University.

Sachs, Jeffrey D., and Andrew Warner. 1995. "Economic Reform and the Process of Global

Integration." *Brookings Papers on Economic Activity* 195 (1): 1–118.

———. 2001. "The Curse of Natural Resources." *European Economic Review* 45 (May): 827–838.

Sadik, Nafis, ed. 1991. *Population Policies and Programs: Lessons Learned from Two Decades of Experience.* United Nations Population Fund. Distributed by NYU Press.

Schorr, Juliet. 1992. *The Overworked American: The Unexpected Decline of Leisure.* New York: Basic Books.

Schultz, T. Paul. 1997. "The Demand for Children in Low Income Countries," in Mark Rosenzweig and Oded Stark (eds.), *The Handbook of Population and Family Economics.* Amsterdam: Elsevier.

Schuman, Michael. 2004. "Flat Chance." *Time Magazine*, Monday, Nov. 22.

Shafik, Nemat. 1994. "Economic Development and Environmental Quality: An Econometric Analysis." *Oxford Economic Papers* 46 (October): 757–773.

Shastry, Gauri Kartini, and David N. Weil. 2003. "How Much of Cross-Country Income Variation Is Explained by Health?" *Journal of the European Economic Association* 1 (April–May): 387–396.

Simon, Julian L. 1981. *The Ultimate Resource.* Princeton, NJ: Princeton University Press.

Sobel, Dava. 1995. *Longitude: The True Story of a Lone Genius Who Solved the Greatest Scientific Problem of His Time.* New York: Walker.

Sohn, Byungdoo. 2000. "Health, Nutrition, and Economic Growth." Ph.D. diss., Brown University.

Stern, Bernhard. 1937. "Resistance to the Adoption of Technological Innovations." In *Technological Trends and National Policy,* edited by National Resources Committee. Washington, DC: U.S. Government Printing Office.

Stevenson, Betsey, and Justin Wolfers. 2008. "Economic Growth and Subjective Well Being: Reassessing the Easterlin Paradox," *Brookings Papers on Economic Activity*, Spring.

Stokey, Nancy. 2001. "A Quantitative Model of the British Industrial Revolution, 1780–1850." *Carnegie-Rochester Conference Series on Public Policy* 55: 55–109.

Stover, Leon E. 1974. *The Cultural Ecology of Chinese Civilization: Peasants and Elites in the Last of the Agrarian States.* New York: Pica Press.

Strahler, Alan, and Arthur Strahler. 1992. *Modern Physical Geography.* New York: Wiley.

Strauss, John, and Duncan Thomas. 1998. "Health, Nutrition, and Economic Development." *Journal of Economic Literature* 36 (June): 766–817.

Struck, Douglas. 2000. "In Japan, a Nation of Conformists Is Urged to Break Out of the Mold." *Washington Post* News Service, January 21.

Taylor, Alan M. 2002. "A Century of Current Account Dynamics." *Journal of International Money and Finance* 21(6): 725–748.

Temple, Jonathan, and Paul A. Johnson. 1998. "Social Capability and Economic Growth." *Quarterly Journal of Economics* 113 (August): 965–990.

Thomas, Vinod, Yan Wang, and Xibo Fan. 2000. "Measuring Education Inequality: Gini Coefficients for Education." World Bank Working Paper 2525 (December).

Tobler, W., V. Deichmann, and J. Gottsegen, 1995. The global demography project. Technical Report TR-95-6. National Center for Geographic Information Analysis. Univ. Santa Barbara, CA.

Tocqueville, Alexis de. 1839. *Democracy in America*, 3rd American ed. Translated by Henry Reeve New York: G. Adlard.

Trefler, Daniel. 2004. "The Long and Short of the Canada U.S. Free Trade Agreement." *American Economics Review* 94 870–895.

Treisman, Daniel. 2000. "The Causes of Corruption: A Cross-National Study." *Journal of Public Economics* 76 (June): 399–457.

UNAIDS. 2010. Global Report on the AIDS Epidemic. New York: United Nations.

UNESCO. 1999. *UNESCO Yearbook.* Paris: UNESCO.

———. 2000. *World Education Forum, EFA 2000 Assessment.* Paris: UNESCO.

United Nations. 2011. "World Contraceptive Use 2011." Chart. Department of Social and Economic Affairs, UN Population Division.

United Nations Development Program. 2000. *Human Development Report: 2000.* New York: Oxford University Press.

———. 2002a. *Human Development Report: 2002.* New York: Oxford University Press.

———. 2002b. Arab Human Development Report.

———. 2003. *Human Development Report 2003.* New York: Oxford University Press.

———. 2007. UNDP database. http://hdr.undp.org/en/statistics/data/.

———. 2010. *Human Development Report 2010.*

United Nations Environmental Program. 2002. "Desk Study on the Environment in the Occupied Palestinian Territories."

United Nations Food and Agriculture Organization. 2002. *The State of the World's Fisheries: 2000.* New York: United Nations.

———. 2010. *Statistical Yearbook.*

United Nations Population Division. 1998a. *World Population Projections to 2150.* New York: United Nations.

———. 1998b. *World Population Prospects: The 1998 Revision.* New York: United Nations.

———. 2000. *World Population Prospects: The 2000 Revision.* New York: United Nations.

———. 2002. *World Population Prospects: The 2002 Revision Population Database.*

———. 2010. *World Population Prospects: The 2010 Revision.* http://esa.un.org/unpd/wpp/index

U.S. Department of Energy, Energy Information Administration, *International Petroleum Monthly,* July 2007.

U.S. Geological Survey. 2000. *World Petroleum Assessment.* http://pubs.usgs.gov/dds/dds-060/.

U.S. Patent and Trademark Office. 2006. *Patents by Country, State, and Year—All Patent Types.* http://www.uspto.gov/web/offices/ac/ido/oeip/taf/cst_all.htm

Wacziarg, Romain, and Karen Horn Welch. 2003. "Trade Liberalization and Growth: New Evidence." NBER Working Paper #10152.

Wade, Alice H. 1989. *Social Security Area Population Projections 1989.* Actuarial Study no. 105, U.S. Department of Health and Human Services, Social Security Administration.

Wehrwein, Peter. 1999/2000. "The Economic Impact of AIDS in Africa." *Harvard AIDS Review* (Fall/Winter).

Weinberg, Daniel H. 1996. "A Brief Look at Postwar U.S. Income Inequality." Current Population Report P60–191, U.S. Census Bureau, June.

Weir, Shandra, and John Knight. 2000. "Education Externalities in Rural Ethiopia: Evidence from Average and Stochastic Frontier Production Functions." Centre for the Study of African Economies, Oxford University (March).

Weitzman, Martin. 1999. "Pricing the Limits to Growth from Minerals Depletion." *Quarterly Journal of Economics* 114 (May): 691–706.

Wells, H. G. 1931. *The Work, Wealth, and Happiness of Mankind.* Garden City, NY: Doubleday, Doran & Co.

Westphal, Larry E. 1990. "Industrial Policy in an Export-Propelled Economy: Lessons from South Korea's Experience." *Journal of Economic Perspectives* 4 (Summer): 41–59.

Williamson, Jeffrey. 1985. *Did British Capitalism Breed Inequality?* Boston: Allen & Unwin.

Womack, James P., Daniel T. Jones, and Daniel Roos. 1991. *The Machine That Changed the World.* New York: Harper Collins.

World Bank. 1997. "Expanding the Measure of Wealth: Indicators of Environmentally Sustainable Development." Environmentally Sustainable Development Studies and Monographs Series, no. 17 (June).

———. 2002a. *Globalization, Growth, and Poverty: Building an Inclusive World Economy.* New York: Oxford University Press.

———. 2002b. *Global Development Finance 2002: Financing the Poorest Countries.* Washington, DC: World Bank.

———. 2003a. *World Development Report 2003.* Washington, DC: World Bank.

———. 2006. Where is the Wealth of Nations: Measuring Capital for the 21st Century. Washington, DC: World Bank.

———. 2011a. *World Development Indicators.* Online database.

———. 2011b. *World Development Report, 2011.* Washington, DC: World Bank.

World Health Organization. 2003. *Malaria Fact Sheet.* http://www.who.int/inf-fs/en/fact094.html

———. 2011. *World Malaria Report.* http://www.who.int/malaria/world_malaria_report_2011/en/

Worldwatch Institute. 1998. "A Matter of Scale." *World Watch* 11 (May/June): 39.

Yashiro, Naohiro. 1998. "The Economic Factors for the Declining Birthrate." *Review of Population and Social Policy* 7: 129–144.

Young, Alwyn. 1995. "The Tyranny of Numbers: Confronting the Statistical Realities of the East Asian Growth Experience." *Quarterly Journal of Economics* 110 (August): 641–680.

———. 2005. "The Gift of the Dying: The Tragedy of AIDS and the Welfare of Future African Generations." *Quarterly Journal of Economics* 120(1): 243–266.

———. 2007. "In Sorrow to Bring Forth Children: Fertility Amidst the Plague of HIV." *Journal of Economic Growth* 12(4): 283–327.

Young, Jeffrey. 2011. "Health-Benefit Costs Increase the Most in Six Years, Surpassing $15,000." Bloomberg News Service, September 27. http://www.bloomberg.com/news/2011-09-27/health-benefit-costs-rise-most-in-six-years-surpassing-15-000-per-family.html

GLOSSARY

age-specific fertility rate   The average number of children that a woman of a given age will bear in a given year. (p. 118)

assortative mating   The phenomenon of people marrying within their own economic and social class. (p. 395)

autarky   The situation in which a country does not interact economically with the rest of the world. (p. 299)

backward linkages   The situation in which production in an industry (such as resource extraction) stimulates the growth of other industries in a country by demanding their outputs. (p. 454)

capital   Tools that workers have at their disposal to produce goods and services. (pp. 30, 48)

capital dilution   The negative effect of population growth on capital per worker. (p. 93)

capital's share of national income   The fraction of national income that is paid out as rent on capital. If the production function is of the Cobb-Douglas form and factors of production are paid their marginal products, then the parameter α is equal to capital's share of national income. (p. 56)

carbon tax   A tax on the emission of carbon dioxide. (p. 496)

carrying capacity   The largest stock of a renewable resource that would exist in an environment if there were no harvesting of the resource by humans. (p. 467)

Cobb-Douglas production function   A specific functional form of the production function defined as $F(K, L) = AK^{\alpha}L^{(1-\alpha)}$ where K is the quantity of capital, L is the quantity of labor, A is a measure of productivity, and α is a parameter that has a value between 0 and 1. (p. 52)

college premium   The ratio of the wages of workers with a college education to those with a high-school degree. (p. 164)

composition effect   The effect by which a redistribution of world population from rich to poor countries lowers the average growth rate of world income per capita. (p. 146)

conflict trap   A situation in which civil violence and economic failure feed back upon each other to hold country at a low steady state level of income. (p. 347)

constant returns to scale   A characteristic of a production function such that when we multiply the quantities of each input by some factor, the quantity of output will increase by that same factor. (p. 51)

convergence toward the steady state   The process by which GDP per worker in a country will grow or shrink from some initial position toward its steady-state level. (p. 67)

coordination failure   A form of market failure in which the absence of a planner to coordinate actions among firms leads to a reduction in output. (p. 334)

correlation   The degree to which two variables tend to move together. (p. 40)

correlation coefficient   A number between −1 and 1 that measures the degree of correlation between two variables. (p. 40)

cost disease   The shifting of expenditures into services, which has the effect of lowering overall productivity growth in an economy. (p. 259)

creative destruction   The process by which new inventions create profits for some firms while driving others out of business. (p. 206)

cross-sectional data   Observations of different units at a single point in time. (p. 44)

culture   The values, attitudes, and beliefs prevalent in a society. (p. 399)

current reserves   The known quantity of a resource that can profitably be extracted at current prices using existing technology. (p. 464)

demographic momentum The phenomenon whereby a country where fertility has been high will continue to experience population growth even after fertility reaches the replacement level. (p. 132)

demographic transition The process by which a country's mortality and fertility rates decline as it develops. (p. 97)

depreciation The wearing-out of capital. (p. 51)

deregulation The removal of government supervision from an industry. (p. 335)

development accounting A technique used to decompose gaps in the level of income among countries into a part resulting from variation in productivity and a part resulting from variation in factor accumulation. (p. 185)

difference (in a variable) The change in the value of a variable from one time period to the next, symbolized by Δ (uppercase Greek letter delta). (p. 59)

diffusion The process in which a newly invented technology is spread throughout the economy. (p. 247)

diminishing marginal product A property of the production function implying that if we keep adding units of a single input (holding the quantities of any other inputs fixed), the quantity of new output that each new unit of input produces will be smaller than that added by the previous unit of the input. (p. 52)

disposable income A worker's pretax income minus the taxes paid plus the transfer payments received from the government. (p. 385)

distribution of income The manner in which a country's total income is divided among its residents. (p. 363)

Dutch disease The process by which the presence of a natural resource, by stimulating the import of manufactured goods, can harm a country's domestic manufacturing sector. (p. 454)

Easterlin Paradox The theory that there is no link between a country's level of income and the average happiness of its residents. (p. 510).

economic mobility The movement of people from one part of the income distribution to another. (p. 392)

economic model A simplified representation of reality that can be used to analyze how economic variables are determined, how a change in one variable will affect others, and so on. (p. 37)

economic rent A payment to a factor of production that is in excess of what is required to elicit the supply of that factor. (p. 281)

efficiency A measure of how well the available technology and inputs into production are actually used in producing output. (p. 31)

embodied technological process The situation in which new technologies cannot be implemented until they are incorporated into new pieces of capital. (p. 228)

enclaves Small pockets of economic development that have almost no contact with the rest of a country's economy. (p. 455)

endogenous variables Variables that are determined within an economic model. (p. 70)

environmental Kuznets curve An inverted-U-shaped relationship between a country's level of economic development and its level of environmental pollution. (p. 488)

equity-efficiency trade-off The trade-off between the benefits of income redistribution (a greater degree of equality) and the costs of the policy (a lower degree of efficiency). (p. 336)

excludability The degree to which an owner of something (such as a good or an input into production) can prevent others from using it without permission. (p. 204)

exogenous variables Variables that are taken as given when an economic model is analyzed. (p. 70)

externality An incidental effect of some economic activity for which no compensation is provided. (pp. 334, 175)

factors of production Inputs into production such as physical capital, human capital, labor, and land. (p. 34)

featherbedding A practice in which employers are forced to hire more workers than are required for efficient production. (p. 279)

fertility transition The decline in the birthrate that accompanies economic development. (p. 97)

fishing out effect The negative effect of past discoveries on the ease of making discoveries today. (p. 250)

flow of factors of production The movement of a factor of production such as capital from one country to another. (p. 299)

foreign direct investment Investment that takes the form of a firm's buying or building a facility in another country. (p. 312)

forward linkages The situation in which production in an industry (such as resource extraction) stimulates the growth of other industries in a country by supplying inputs into production. (p. 454)

fundamentals Underlying characteristics of a country that influence output via their effects on productivity or the accumulation of factors of production. (p. 32)

general-purpose technologies Momentous technological innovations that change the mode of production in many sectors in the economy and trigger a chain reaction of complimentary inventions. (p. 249)

Gini coefficient A measure of the degree of income inequality in an economy. (p. 365)

government failure Ill-conceived or improperly implemented government economic policies, particularly those designed to correct market failures. (p. 335)

green GDP Conventionally measured GDP minus the value of domestic natural capital that has been depleted or destroyed in a given year. (p. 474)

gross domestic product The value of all final goods and services produced in a country in a year. (pp. 300, 3)

gross national product The value of all income earned by the factors of production owned by the residents of a country. (p. 300)

growth accounting A technique used to measure the growth rate of productivity in an economy by subtracting growth due to factor accumulation from total growth of output. (p. 193)

growth rate The change in a variable from one year to the next, divided by the value of the variable in the initial year. (p. 59)

human capital Qualities such as education and health that allow workers to produce more output and that are themselves the result of past investment. (p. 150)

idle resources A form of inefficiency in which available factors of production are not used in producing output. (p. 281)

imitation The copying of a technology, as from another country. (p. 215)

income redistribution The transfer of income from rich to poor, from working-age adults to the elderly, or from the general population to members of some favored group. (p. 335)

index of ethnic fractionalization The probability that two randomly selected people in a country will not belong to the same ethnic group. (p. 418)

Industrial Revolution A period of rapid technological innovation in a number of industries, generally dated between 1760 and 1830 in Britain, and somewhat later in continental Europe and North America. (p. 243)

in-ground price The market price of a resource minus the cost of extraction. (p. 474)

innovation The invention of a new technology. (p. 215)

intergenerational mobility The change in the economic status of families from one generation to the next. (p. 393)

investment Goods and services devoted to the production of new capital rather than consumption. (pp. 30, 49)

kleptocracy The situation in which government is used to enrich a country's rulers. Also known as "rule by thieves." (p. 349)

Kuznets curve An inverted-U-shaped relationship between a county's level of income and its degree of income inequality. (p. 368)

law of one price The claim that if two economies are open to trade with each other then the same good will sell for the same price in both of them. (p. 299)

leapfrogging   The process by which technologically backward countries or firms jump ahead of the leaders. (p. 229)

life expectancy at birth   The average number of years that a newborn baby can be expected to live. (p. 98)

linear scale   The commonly used scale on a graph whereby equal spaces on an axis correspond to equal increments in the variable being graphed. (p. 10)

Lorenz curve   A graph showing what fraction of the total income in a country is earned by the poorest 1% of households, 2% of households, and so on through 100% of households. (p. 367)

Luddites   Workers in the British textile industry who destroyed machines that were threatening their livelihoods in the early 19th century. (p. 292)

lump-sum transfer   A government transfer payment in which each person receives an equal amount. (p. 385)

maquiladora   An assembly plant on the Mexican side of the border with the United States that imports components from the United States and ships its output back over the border. (p. 438)

marginal product   The extra output produced when one more unit of a particular input is used in production. (p. 52)

market failure   The idea that in some circumstances unfettered markets will not produce an efficient outcome. (p. 333)

maximum sustainable yield   The largest quantity of a renewable resource that can be extracted per period of time without diminishing the quantity of resource available for future use. (p. 468)

mean   The simple average. (p. 365)

median   The value in a set of observations that has exactly as many observations below it as above. (p. 365)

median voter   The voter with the median value of whatever characteristic (e.g., pretax income) determines the preferred choice of a particular economic policy (e.g., the tax rate). (p. 387)

misallocation   A form of inefficiency arising when resources are not efficiently allocated among different productive uses. (p. 283)

misallocation among firms   A form of inefficiency arising when resources are not directed to the most productive firms. (p. 288)

misallocation among sectors   A form of inefficiency arising when resources are inefficiently allocated among sectors. (p. 283)

mode   The value occurring most frequently in a series of observations. (p. 365)

monopoly   A single firm that is the sole supplier of a particular commodity. (p. 334)

Moore's law   The prediction made in 1965 that the power of microprocessors would double every 18 months. (p. 260)

mortality transition   The increase in life expectancy that accompanies economic development. (p. 97)

multiple steady states   A phenomenon in which a country's initial position determines which of several steady states it will move toward. (p. 74)

natural capital   The value of a country's agricultural lands, pasture lands, forests, and subsoil resources, including metals, minerals, coal, oil, and natural gas. (p. 451)

net rate of reproduction   The number of daughters to which each girl who is born can be expected to give birth, assuming that she goes through her life with the mortality and fertility of the current population. (p. 102)

nonrenewable resources   Resources that exist in a fixed quantity on earth. (p. 464)

nonrival (inputs into production)   An input into production, such as technology, that can be used by an unlimited number of producers simultaneously without reducing the degree to which each producer benefits from it. (p. 204)

nontariff barriers   Government-imposed limitations on international trade other than tariffs and quotas. (p. 305)

normative   An approach to government policy aimed at advising government on how it should act. (p. 333)

observer bias   The phenomenon by which the assessment of some attribute variable is clouded by the observer's knowledge of how that variable is related to other things. (p. 407)

omitted variable   A variable that is not included in a statistical analysis but that influences the observed correlation between two variables that are under study. (p. 41)

outlier   An observation that is inconsistent with the overall statistical relationship between two variables. (p. 38)

patent   A grant made by a government that confers on the creator of an invention the sole right to make, use, and sell that invention for a set period of time (usually 20 years). (p. 207)

peak oil   The date on which world oil production will reach its maximum (p. 467)

population density   The number of people living on each square mile or square kilometer of land. (p. 420)

portfolio investment   A form of international capital flow in which investors purchase stocks or bonds issued in a foreign country. (p. 312)

positive   An approach to the analysis of government policy aimed at describing rather than prescribing government actions. (p. 333)

pretax income   The income that a worker earns before any taxes have been collected and any transfers have been made. (p. 385)

price elasticity of demand   The percentage change in the quantity of a good demanded divided by the percentage change in the good's price. (p. 484)

privatization   The transfer of functions previously performed by the government to the private sector. (p. 335)

production function   A mathematical description of how the inputs a firm or country uses are transformed into output. (p. 34)

productivity   The effectiveness with which factors of production are converted into output. (pp. 31, 179)

productivity slowdown   The reduction in the growth of productivity in most developed countries that took place between the early 1970s and the early 1990s. (p. 247)

proximate cause   An event that is immediately responsible for causing some observed result. (p. 33)

public goods   Goods such as national defense and the rule of law that the private market cannot supply, often because they are nonexcludable. (p. 334)

purchasing power parity   A set of artificial exchange rates used to convert amounts from other countries and time periods into a common currency. (p. 4)

quota   A restriction on the total amount of a good that can be imported. (p. 305)

ratio scale   A scale used for graphing data whereby equal spaces on the vertical or horizontal axis correspond to equal proportional differences in the variable being graphed. Also called a logarithmic scale. (p. 10)

renewable resources   Natural resources that are replenished by natural processes and thus can be used repeatedly. (p. 467)

rent seeking   Unproductive activities that involve the use of laws or government institutions to bring private benefits. (p. 281)

replacement fertility   The level of fertility that is consistent with a constant population size in the long run. (p. 125)

resource intensity   The amount of a natural resource required to produce one unit of output. (p. 472)

return to education   The percentage increase in wages that a worker would receive if he or she had one more year of schooling. (p. 162)

reverse causation   A situation in which one might think that X causes Y when in fact the opposite is true. (p. 40)

rival (input into production)   An input into production that can only be used by a limited number of people at one time. (p. 204)

rule of 72   A formula for estimating the amount of time it takes something growing at a given rate to double. If g is the growth rate in percent per year, then doubling time $\approx 72/g$. (p. 10)

savings retention coefficient   The fraction of every additional dollar of saving in a country that ends up as additional domestic investment. It is an indicator of the degree of capital market openness. (p. 316)

scatter plot A graph in which one variable is measured along each axis and each observation is represented by a single point. (p. 38)

skewed distribution A distribution that is not symmetric around the mean, but rather has a long right or left tail. (p. 365)

social capability The social and cultural qualities that allow a poor country to take advantage of economic opportunities that arise from interaction with the developed world. (p. 411)

social capital The value of the social networks that people have and of the inclination of people in those networks to do things for each other. (p. 408)

spillovers Influences on economic growth that cross a country's borders to affect its neighbors. (p. 438)

steady state A condition of the economy in which output per worker and capital per worker do not change over time. (p. 60)

survivorship function A function showing the probability that a person will be alive at different ages. (p. 117)

sustainable development Term coined by the United Nations Commission on Environment and Development as "development that meets the needs of the present without compromising the ability of future generations to meet their own needs." (p. 472)

tacit knowledge Knowledge about production processes gained through experience and transferred from person to person through informal training. (p. 227)

tariff A tax on the import of a good. (p. 305)

tax base The quantity of a good or service that is subject to taxation. (p. 342)

technology The available knowledge about how inputs can be combined to produce output. (p. 31)

technology blocking A form of inefficiency arising when a technology could feasibly be used but someone deliberately prevents its use. (p. 289)

technology production function A production function in which the output is new technologies and the inputs are the labor and human capital of researchers along with the physical capital used in research and development. (p. 248)

tempo effect The temporary reduction in the total fertility rate resulting from a rise in the average age of childbirth. (p. 129)

total fertility rate The number of children that a woman would have if she lived through all of her childbearing years and experienced the current age-specific fertility rates at each age. (p. 100)

trade The exchange of goods and services across national borders. (p. 299)

tragedy of the commons The overuse of resources that occurs when there are no property rights. (p. 470)

transition matrix A table showing the probabilities of moving from each of many groups to each other group. (p. 393)

ultimate cause Something that affects an observed result through a chain of intermediate events. (p. 33)

unproductive activities A form of inefficiency in which resources are devoted to activities without economic value. (p. 280)

variable A characteristic of the observation that we are examining. (p. 38)

Wagner's law The claim that the size of government tends to increase as countries become wealthier. (p. 340)

INDEX

Abandonment, of children, 105
Abortion, 105, 119
Abramovitz, Moses, 198n, 411, 411n
Abuja conference, 160
AC. *See* Alternating current
Accounting. *See* Development
  accounting; Growth accounting
Acemoglu, Daron, 43n, 157n,
  161n, 164n, 165n, 224n, 227n,
  353n, 457n
Acid rain, 488
Adelman, Irma, 412–413
Ades, Alberto F., 281n
Adjustment assistance, 324
Africa. *See also* Sub-Saharan Africa;
  specific countries
  AIDS in, 125, 126–127, 511–512
  cell phones in, 229, 268
  ethnic fractionalization in, 420
  GDP in, 127
  GDP per capita in, 16
  malaria in, 160
  population forecasting for, 131
  standard of living in, 3
Age-specific fertility rate, 118
  in Nigeria, 119
  population forecasting and, 123
  in U.S., 119
Age-specific survivorship function,
  population forecasting and, 123
Aghion, Philippe, 206n
Aging, of population, 138–143
Agricultural productivity
  climate and, 444–446
  latitude and, 445
  population and, 475
Agriculture
  global warming and, 495
  income inequality and, 391
  in Industrial Revolution, 244
  sectoral reallocation from, 287
Ahuja, Vinod, 418n
AIDS, in Africa, 125, 126–127, 511–512
Air Afrique, 282

Air-conditioning, 450
Air pollution, in London, 490–491
Albania, autarky in, 299
Alesina, Alberto, 385n, 419n
Alm, Richard, 2n
Alternating current (AC),
  292–293
Aluminum, 479
America Online, customer service
  for, 304
Anderson, James E., 305n
Angola, 350
  natural resources of, 280–281
Animals
  domestication of, 436–437
  as renewable resource, 467–469
Anti-dumping duties, 305
Anti-globalization, 324–326
Appropriate technology, 224–226
Aquifers, 469
  property rights and, 470
Arbitrage, 26
Argentina
  old-age pension fund in, 72
  standard of living in, 2
ARPANET, invention of, 240–241
Arrow, Kenneth, 406, 406n
Ashton, Basil, 332n
Asia. *See also specific countries*
  values of, 399
Asian Tigers, 287
Åslund, Anders, 280n
Assortative mating, 395–396
Atatürk, Mustafa Kemal, 426
Aten, Bettina, 4n, 7n, 12n, 15n, 16n,
  62, 65, 131, 153, 154, 170, 186,
  363n, 413, 433, 452, 494
Atkeson, Andrew, 249n
Atkinson, Anthony B., 224n
AT&T Corporation, 251
Australia
  automobiles in, 1
  discovery of, 436
  patents in, 255

Austria, patents in, 255
Autarky, *versus* economic openness,
  298–306
Automobiles
  in Australia, 1
  in Bangladesh, 1
  from Canada, 321–322
  in Germany, 331
  from Japan, 321
  productivity in, 276–278
  tariffs on, 321–322
  from U.S., 321
Autor, David H., 164, 165, 378n
Aztecs, 19

Babbage, Charles, 48n
Baby boom, 128
  working age fraction and, 141
Baby bust, 128
Backhouse, E., 401n
Backward linkages, 454–455
Baily, Martin Neil, 276n
Bairoch, Paul, 18, 18n, 244n
Ball, Sue Simmons, 440n, 441n
Banerjee, Abhijit V., 43n
Bangladesh
  anti-globalization and, 324
  automobiles in, 1
  birth control in, 107
  children in, 112
  population aging in, 142
  population density in, 433
  working age fraction in, 142
Banking, 290
  deregulation of, 291
  government and, 343, 346
Barriers
  to international technology
    transfer, 223
  to mobility, 285
  nontariff, 305
  to trade, 305
Barro, Robert, 159, 166, 170, 186,
  215n, 357, 370n

Barth, James, 343n
Basu, Susanto, 224n
Baumol, William, 2n, 259
Bauxite, 479
Beaulier, Scott A., 457n
Beck, Thorsten, 291n, 457n
Belgium
 natural resources of, 452
 patents in, 255
Bell, Alexander Graham, 252–253
Benabau, Roland, 394n
Benin. *See* Dahomey
Berg, Alan, 106n
Berger, Peter, 414n
Berhanu, Betemariam, 108n
Bernanke, Ben S., 54n, 55
Bernard, Andrew, 145n
Berry, Steven, 305n
Bertola, Giuseppe, 287n
Bessemer, Henry, 252
Between-country income inequality,
 18–19
Bias
 capital-biased technological
 change, 225–226
 observer, 407
Big Bang theory, 251
Bilharzia, 446
Birth control, 105–109
 in Bangladesh, 107
 government toward, 106
 technology for, 106
Blackberry, 209
Black market, 20
Bland, J.O.P., 401
Bleakley, 161n
Blinder, Alan S., 2n
Bloom, David E., 143n, 436n
BMW, 331
Bockstette, Valerie, 420n
Bodin, Jean, 417n
Bolton, Matthew, 320
Bongaarts, John, 106n, 129n
Bono, 326
Botswana
 AIDS in, 126
 GDP per worker in, 65
 natural resources in, 457
Bourguignon, François, 19
Brander, James A., 475n

Braudel, Fernand, 303n
Brazil
 development accounting for, 186
 life expectancy in, 2
 malaria in, 161
 television in, 427
Breast-feeding
 fertility and, 106
 in Indonesia, 106
Brems, Susan, 106n
Bresnahan, Timothy F., 293n
Brezis, Elise, 229n
Bribery, 281
Brimblecomb, Peter, 491
Britain. *See also* England
 coal in, 460
 Corn Laws of, 323
 development accounting for, 186
 food in, 152
 GDP per capita in, 9–12
 height in, 2, 151
 investment by, 301–302
 patents in, 207, 255
 railroads in, 292
 R&D in, 248
Brooks, Daniel J., 292n
Bruce, Anthony, 354n
Brundtland Commission, 473
Buddha, 416
Burkett, John, 292n, 421, 422n
Burma, autarky in, 299
Business cycles, *versus* economic
 growth, 13
Busse, Meghan, 145, 145n
Butter, 293

Cain, Mead, 112n
Calvin, John, 402
Campaign to Encourage Diligence
 and Thrift, in Singapore, 72
Campana, Thomas, 209
Canada
 automobiles from, 321–322
 development accounting for, 186
 GDP of, 6
 growth rate in, 14
 income inequality in, 390–392
 patents in, 255
 saving in, 404
 textiles and, 275

Capital, 30. *See also* Human
 capital; Marginal product of
 capital; Natural capital; Social
 capital
 accumulation of, 57
 anti-globalization and, 325–326
 depreciation of, 51, 57
 developing countries and, 384
 export of, 301–302
 GDP and, 163
 income and, 48–76
 income inequality and, 380–381
 in India, 48
 investment and, 49–50
 land and, 58
 measurement of, 188
 in Mexico, 48
 misallocation among firms
 and, 289
 mobility of, 311–314, 325–326
 national income and, 54
 nature of, 49–51
 output and, 93–94
 in poor countries, 75, 504
 production and, 51–56
 production function and, 51–54
 return from, 50, 54–56
 rise and fall of, 58, 75
 rivalry with, 50
 saving and, 73
 Solow and, 56–68
 in Soviet Union, 75
 steady state and, 80
 in U.S., 48
 in wealthy countries, 504
Capital-biased technological change,
 225–226
Capital dilution, population and,
 93–95
Capital/labor ratio, 313
Capital per worker
 depreciation and, 94
 GDP and, 48–49
 growth rate and, 80
 investment and, 94
 in Japan, 186
 population and, 93–95
 Solow model and, 56–63, 94
 steady state for, 63, 95, 234–235
Capital's share of income, 56

Capital stock
    population and, 94
    steady state and, 66–67, 80
Caprio, Gerald, Jr., 343n
Carbon dioxide (CO_2), 492–496
Carbon tax, 496
Carnot, Sadi, 251
Carroll, Christopher, 404n
Carrying capacity, 467–469
Cars. See Automobiles
Caselli, Francesco, 287n, 379n, 387n
Cashin, P., 480
Catholic Church
    foundlings and, 105
    Galileo and, 440
    in Latin America, 416
Causation, 40–41. See also
        Proximate cause
Cell phones
    in Africa, 229, 268
    in India, 272
    in poor countries, 268
Central African Republic,
        GDP per worker in, 65
Central Council for Savings
        Promotion, in Singapore, 72
Cerf, Christopher, 261
Cervical cap, 106
Chad, population of, 82
Chakravorty, Ujjayant, 487n
Chanda, Areendam, 420n, 422n
Chavez, Hugo, 389
Chen, Nai-Ruenn, 332n
Chi, Ch'ao-Ting, 442n
Children. See also Fertility
    anti-globalization and, 324
    in Bangladesh, 112
    contaminated water and, 1
    in developed countries, 112
    in developing countries, 112
    economic growth and, 111
    with malaria, 161
    price of, 111
    quality-quantity trade-off with,
        112–113
Chile, old-age pension fund in, 72
China. See also Hong Kong; Taiwan
    coal in, 460
    corruption in, 355
    before 1820, 19–22
    fertility in, 130

GDP per capita in, 16, 511
GDP per worker in, 65
government in, 331–332, 439–442
Great Leap Forward in, 331–332
income in, 2
India and, 356–357
labor reallocation in, 287–288
marginal product in, 289
misallocation among firms in, 289
one-child policy of, 108
openness to new ideas in, 401
population of, 88
preindustrial, 441
saving in, 404
technology in, 88
textiles and, 275
trade and, 436–437
Cholera, 100
Chong, Alberto, 427n
Churchill, Winston, 260
Civil conflict, government and,
    346–348
Clark, Gregory, 217n, 275
Climate. See also Latitude
    agricultural productivity and,
        444–446
    culture and, 416–417
    disease and, 446–449
    geography and, 442–450
    hard work and, 449–450
    output per worker and, 444
    technology and, 449–450
    zones of, 442–444
Clinton, Bill, 37
CO_2. See Carbon dioxide
Coal, Industrial Revolution
    and, 460
Coale, Ansely J., 101
Cobb-Douglas production function,
    52–54, 79–81
    education and, 169–170
    factor payments and, 55–56
    human capital and, 168
    for measuring productivity
        growth, 192–193
    for neutral technology, 225
    productivity and, 95
    steady state and, 63
    for technology, 202
Coca-Cola, 210
Cohen, Joel, 135n

Cohen, Wesley M., 210n, 254n
Cole, W.A., 58n
Coleman, James, 409n
Coleman, Wilbur J., 287n
College premium, in U.S., 164–165
Collier, Paul, 306n, 309n, 318n,
        322n, 347n
Colombia
    malaria in, 161
    old-age pension fund in, 72
Colonialism, 302
    ethnic fractionalization and,
        419–420
    government and, 358–359
    land and, 450–451
Columbus, Christopher, 436, 439
COMECON. See Council for Mutual
        Economic Cooperation
Commons land, 470
Composition effect, 145–146
Computers
    in India, 272
    investment in, 263
    price index for, 262
    productivity and, 249
Condoms, 106
Conflict trap, 347
Confucius, 404
Consolidated Alchemy, 318–319
Constantine (Emperor), 416
Constant returns to scale, 51–52
    for technology, 252–253
Consumer price index (CPI), 25
Consumption
    investment and, 50
    of oil, 465
    population and, 82
    Solow model and, 213
Contaminated water, children and, 1
Contraception. See Birth control
Contracts, 337
    corruption and, 350
Convergence toward the steady state,
        67–68
    saving and, 74
    speed of, 79–81
Cook, James, 436
Cooperation, culture and, 423
Coordination failures, 334–335
Copper, fiberoptic technology and, 479
Copyright, 207

Corak, Miles, 394n
Corn Laws, of Britain, 323
Correlations, 38–41
Correlation coefficient, 39–40, 40n
Corruption
  GDP per capita and, 351
  in government, 349–350
  in poor countries, 353–359
Costa, Dora, 2n
Cost disease, 259
Cost of copying function, 218
Cotton spinning, invention of, 251
Council for Mutual Economic
  Cooperation (COMECON), 330
Country averages, of income per
  capita, 364
Cox, Michael W., 2n
CPI. *See* Consumer price index
Crafts, Nicholas F.R., 245n
Creative destruction, 294
  R&D and, 206
Crichton, Michael, 13
Crime, income redistribution and, 389
Crony capitalism, 355
Crops. *See* Agriculture
Cross-sectional data, 44
  environmental Kuznets curve
  and, 490
Cuban, Larry, 238n
Cultural change, 422–428
  economic growth and, 424–425
  government and, 425–427
  media and, 427–428
Cultural homogeneity, social capital
  and, 417–420
Culture, 399–429
  climate and, 416–417
  cooperation and, 423
  determinants of, 416–422
  economic growth and, 400–416
  hard work and, 402–403
  natural resources and, 416–417
  openness to new ideas and, 400–402
  parking tickets and, 405
  saving and, 403–404
  sharing and, 414
  social capability and, 411–416
  social capital and, 408–411
  trust and, 404–408
Cummins Engine, 227
Currency, exchange rates for, 25–26

Current reserves, 464
Customer service, for America
  Online, 304
Cutler, David, 161n
Cutting edge of technology,
  238–264

Dahomey, 358
Darwin, Charles, 252
Dauzet, Pierre, 303n
David, Paul A., 247n, 293n
Davidson, Louis, 261
DC. *See* Direct current
DDT, 158, 161, 449
Deadweight loss, 342n
Deane, Phyllis, 58n
Deardorff, Alan V., 318n
Deininger, Klaus, 371n
DeLong, J. Bradford, 277n, 302n
Democracy
  economic growth and, 356–357
  GDP per capita and, 357
Democracy in America
  (Tocqueville), 396
Democratic Republic of
  the Congo, 353
Demographics
  in future, 512
  for India, 104–105
  for Nigeria, 104–105
Demographic change, economic
  consequences of, 136–146
Demographic momentum
  in poor countries, 147
  women and, 132–133
Demographic transition, population
  and, 97
DeNavas-Walt, Carmen, 364, 364n,
  366, 378n, 379n
Deng Xiaoping, 332
Denmark, patents in, 255
Depreciation
  of capital, 51, 57
  capital per worker and, 94
  of human capital, 150
  investment and, 57, 60
  Solow model and, 57, 95
  steady state and, 60
Deregulation, 335
Derivative with respect to time, 59
Desired fertility, 107

  in developing countries, 109
  TFR and, 109
De Soto, Hernando, 344n
Desvaux, Georges, 332n
Developed countries. *See also*
  Wealthy countries; *specific
  countries*
  children in, 112
  education level changes in, 159, 166
  human capital in, 168
  investment by, 315
  population age in, 139
  saving rate by, 315
Developing countries. *See also* Poor
  countries; *specific countries*
  capital and, 384
  children in, 112
  civil conflict in, 347–348
  desired fertility in, 109
  education in, 175–176
  education level changes in, 159, 166
  family-planning programs in, 108
  fertility in, 101, 104, 130
  forests in, 470
  human capital in, 167
  international technology transfer
  in, 217
  investment in, 75
  life expectancy in, 99
  mortality in, 104
  mortality transition in, 100
  population age in, 139
  rent seeking in, 281
  TFR in, 109, 130
Development accounting, productivity
  and, 185–186
Devine, Warren D., 249n
Diamond, Jared, 436n
Díaz-Giménez, Javier, 383n
Difference, 59
Differential technological progress,
  256–262
Diffusion, 247
Diminishing marginal product, 52
  MPK and, 79
Direct current (DC), 293
Disease. *See also specific diseases*
  climate and, 446–449
  income per capita and, 156–157
  mortality transition and, 100
Disposable income, 385

Distribution of income. *See also* Income
    inequality; Income redistribution
  economic growth and, 363
  economic mobility and, 392–396
  in future, 511
  Kuznets curve and, 368–370
  poverty and, 363
  in U.S., 364–365, 366
Divide and rule, 359
Djankov, Simeon, 352n
Dmitriev, Mikhail, 280n
DNA-sequencing machines,
    invention of, 251
Doctors, 154
Dollar, David, 309n, 318n, 322n,
    371, 372
Domestication, of animals, 436–437
Down and Out in Paris and London
    (Orwell), 71
Drinking water
  mortality transition and, 100
  population with, 1
Drucker, Peter F., 127n
Duflo, Esther, 43n
Dumping, 305
Durpe, Ruth, 293n
Duryea, Suzanne, 427n
Dutch disease, 454
Dynan, Karen E., 381n

Easter Island, 475
Easterlin, Richard, 263n, 510n
  on happiness, 510
Easterlin Paradox, 510
Easterly, William, 14n, 75n
Eastern Europe, GDP per capita in, 16
East Germany, West Germany and,
    330–331
EasyJet, 282
Eaton, Jonathan, 320n
eBay, 209
Economic growth
  versus business cycles, 13
  capital mobility and, 311–314
  children and, 111
  cultural change and, 424–425
  culture and, 400–416
  democracy and, 356–357
  differences among countries,
    194–196
  distribution of income and, 363

  in economic openness, 298–327
  environment and, 486–497
  factors of production and, 195
  finance and, 290–291
  food and, 152
  geography and, 434–437, 507
  government and, 337–348
  happiness and, 508–510
  in Hong Kong, 197
  income and, 67
  income inequality and, 380–392
  investment and, 67
  leisure and, 508
  measurement of changes in, 59
  natural resources and, 450–453,
    473–486
  from outer space, 20–21
  population and, 82–114, 146–147
  population density and, 421–422
  poverty and, 371–372
  productivity and, 194–196
  proximate cause of, 33
  railroads and, 44
  rule of law and, 337–338
  in Singapore, 197
  social capability and, 415
  technology and, 201–230
  ultimate cause of, 33
Economic mobility, distribution of
    income and, 392–396
Economic models, 37
Economic openness
  versus autarky, 298–306
  economic growth in, 298–327
  efficiency and, 320–322
  factor accumulation and, 311–316
  GDP per capita and, 306–307, 309
  increase in, 307–308
  measurement in, 300
  opposition to, 322–323
  productivity and, 316–322
  saving rate and, 314
  technology and, 319–320
Economic planning, by government,
    343–346
"Economic Possibilities for Our
    Grandchildren" (Keynes), 508
Economic rent, 281
Ecuador, natural resources of, 452
Edison, Thomas, 238, 292–293
Education

  changes in level of, 159–161
  economic mobility and, 395
  externalities and, 175–176
  GDP and, 160
  GDP per capita and, 170
  human capital and, 158–176, 390
  income and, 161–163, 373–378
  income inequality and,
    373–378, 390
  as investment, 158
  opportunity cost in, 160
  as positive externality, 334
  productivity in, 259
  quality of, 174–175
  quantitative analysis of, 169–176
  return to, 162, 373
Effective workers, 233
Efficiency, 31, 33, 268–295. *See also*
    Inefficiency
  case studies on, 273–279
  cross-country data on, 270–272
  economic openness and, 320–322
  government and, 505–506
  hard work and, 505
  of health care, 278
  income inequality and, 384–388
  in India, 270–272
  output and, 505
  productivity and, 268, 269–272,
    504–505
  from sectoral reallocation,
    287–288
  in Soviet Union, 273–274
  of subsurface coal mining,
    278–279
  technology and, 269–272
  in textiles, 274–276
  in U.S., 270–272
Egypt
  GDP per worker in, 65
  life expectancy in, 2
Ehrlich, Paul, 134, 135n, 482
Einstein, Albert, 261
EITI. *See* Extractive Industries
    Transparency Initiative
Electricity
  as general-purpose technology, 249
  network, 240
  in Sub-Saharan Africa, 1
Electric light, 247
Eliott, Kimberly Ann, 323n

Elsom, Derek M., 490n
Eltony, M., 485n
Embodied technological progress, 228
Emerging markets, 302
Enclaves, 455
Endogenous variables, with saving
    rates, 70–71
Energy. *See also specific types*
    income and, 471
    in Industrial Revolution, 243–244
Engerman, Stanley, 392n
England
    in Industrial Revolution, 244–245
    iron in, 244
    textiles and, 275
    TFR in, 102
Environment
    economic growth and, 486–497
    globalization and, 463–497
    Kuznets curve for, 488–492
    natural resources and, 463–497
    pollution and, 487–488
    property rights and, 488
Environmental exploitation, anti-
    globalization and, 325
Equity-efficiency trade-off, 336
Essay on the Principle of Population
    (Malthus), 85
Ethiopia
    education in, 175
    family-planning programs
        in, 108
    GDP per capita in, 8
Ethnic fractionalization, 418–420
Europe. *See also specific regions and
    countries*
    government in, 439–442
    growth accounting for, 242
    preindustrial, 440
Evelyn, John, 490n
Exchange rates, for currency,
    25–26
Excludability, 204
Exogenous variables
    with culture, 425
    with health, 156–158
    with income, 158
    with saving rates, 70–71
Experimental data, 38
Export, of capital, 301–302
Externalities

education and, 175–176
government and, 334
human capital and, 175–176
Extractive Industries Transparency
    Initiative (EITI), 458

Factor accumulation
    economic openness and, 311–316
    government and, 333, 506
    income inequality and, 384, 506
    output per worker and, 195
    in poor countries, 194, 503–504
    productivity and, 191–192
    relative importance of, 191–192
    rule of law and, 338
    in wealthy countries, 194, 503–504
Factor payments, 54–56
Factor shares, 54–56
Factors of production, 34
    economic growth and, 195
    flow of, 299
    land as, 58
    before 19th century, 58
    output and, 180
    output per worker and, 189
    in poor countries, 191
    rule of law and, 338
    technology and, 202
Factors of production per worker,
    34–35
Failures
    coordination, 334–335
    government, 335
    market, 333
Family-planning programs, 108
Fan, Xibo, 383n
Featherbedding, 279
Federal Reserve Bank of Dallas, 2n,
    256n, 259n
Feldstein, Martin, 315–316, 342n
Felten, Eric, 408n
Fernandez, Raquel, 396n
Fernandez-Armesto, Felipe, 19n
Fertility. *See also* Age-specific fer-
    tility rate; Desired fertility;
    Replacement fertility; Total
    fertility rate
    breast-feeding and, 106
    in China, 130
    in developing countries, 101,
        104, 130

forecasting of, 125–132
    of French Canadians, 85
    in Great Depression, 101
    of Hutterites, 85
    income and, 110–111
    marriage and, 106
    mortality and, 102–105, 110
    motives for reduction in, 109–113
    in poor countries, 130–132
    reduction of, 105–109
    in sub-Saharan Africa, 130
    in Sweden, 103
    in wealthy countries, 83, 126–130
Fertility transition, population and,
    97, 100–101
Feyrer, James, 311n
Fiberoptic technology, copper
    and, 479
Final goods, 25
Finance, economic growth and,
    290–291
Finland, patents in, 255
First to file
    for patents, 208
    for telephone patent, 253
First to invent, for patents, 208
Fischer, Stanley, 75n
Fishing
    in Britain, 470
    in Iceland, 470
    in Industrial Revolution, 244
    maximum sustainable yield for,
        469, 471
    property rights and, 470–471
Fishing out effect, 250
Fisman, Ray, 405, 405n
Flieger, Wilhelm, 103
Flow of factors of production, 299
Fogel, Robert, 44–45, 100, 100n, 152
Food
    in Britain, 152
    economic growth and, 152
    GDP and, 152–153
    health and, 153
    height and, 151
    in Industrial Revolution, 244
    mortality transition and, 100
    in poor countries, 152–153
    population and, 1, 90
    productivity in, 276–278
    secrecy in, 254

Food (*Continued*)
  steady state and, 61
  technology and, 240
  in U.S., 2
  in wealthy countries, 152–153
Footloose industries, 325
Forbes, Kristin, 389n
Forcible sterilization, in India, 108
Ford, Henry, 240
Ford Motor Company, 216
Forecasting
  of fertility, 125–132
  of mortality, 124–125
  of population, 122–136
Foreign direct investment, 312
Forests
  in developing countries, 470
  on Easter Island, 475
  in Indonesia, 470
  in Industrial Revolution, 244
  overexploitation in, 470
Forward linkages, 454–455
Foundlings, Catholic Church and, 105
Fox, Matthew, 127n
Fracking, 464
France
  national language for, 425
  patents in, 255
  R&D in, 203, 248
  textiles and, 275
  TFR in, 102
Frankel, Jeffrey, 310n, 436n
Franklin, Benjamin, 402
Free-capital-flow model, 314–316
Freedom House, 357n
Freeman, Richard, 164
French Canadians, fertility of, 85
Frey, Bruno S., 509, 510n
Frost, 446
Fuchs, Rachel, 112n
Fulton, Robert, 244
Fundamentals, 32, 506–507
  RCTs and, 43
  saving and, 70
Future. *See also* Forecasting
  demographics in, 512
  distribution of income in, 511
  globalization in, 512–513
  global warming and, 493–495
  natural resources and, 478–482, 512
  population and, 121–147

poverty and, 71
replacement fertility in, 512
of technology, 253–256, 511
Fylkesnes, Knut, 127n

Galenson, Walter, 332n
Galileo, 439–440
Gallup, John L., 161n, 433, 434n, 435, 436n, 443, 445n, 449n
Galor, Oded, 92n, 111n, 168n, 379n, 382n, 384n
Garang, John, 347
Garon, Sheldon, 72, 72n
GATT. *See* General Agreement on Tariffs and Trade
Gawande, Atul, 278n
GDP. *See* Gross domestic product
GDP per capita
  in Britain, 9–12
  in China, 511
  CO_2 and, 492
  corruption and, 351
  by country group, 16
  democracy and, 357
  economic openness and, 306–307, 309
  education and, 170
  energy use and, 471
  ethnic fractionalization and, 418–419
  versus GDP, 6–8
  geography and, 434, 507
  hard work and, 403
  in Hong Kong, 197
  in Japan, 9–13, 16
  latitude and, 38–39
  life expectancy and, 154
  natural capital and, 451–452
  pollution and, 488–489
  in poor countries, 503
  population age and, 140
  population growth and, 39
  resource intensity and, 472
  for Singapore, 40
  social capability and, 413
  student test scores and, 175
  in U.S., 8–13, 246, 341
  in wealthy countries, 503
GDP per worker, 64–65
  latitude and, 445
  population age and, 140

predicted *versus* actual, 173
saving and, 313–314
General Agreement on Tariffs and Trade (GATT), 306
General-purpose technologies, 249
Genesis 11, 417
Geographic concentration, 438
Geographic isolation
  as barrier to mobility, 285
  trade and, 310–311
Geography, 433–442. *See also* Latitude
  climate and, 442–450
  economic growth and, 434–437, 507
  GDP per capita and, 434, 507
  government and, 438–442
  natural resources and, 450–458
  trade and, 434–437
George, Henry, 298, 310n
George II (King), 401
Georges Bank, 469
Germany
  division of, 330–331
  fertility in, 126
  patents in, 255
  R&D in, 203, 248
  textiles and, 275
Germ of laziness, 158
Gini coefficient, 365–368, 383
Glaeser, Edward L., 281n
Glasnost (political openness), 353
Globalization. *See also* Economic openness
  causes of, 302–306
  environment and, 463–497
  facts about, 300–302
  in future, 512–513
  information transmission and, 304
  natural resources and, 463–497
  trade policy and, 304–306
  transport costs and, 302–304
Global warming, 492–496
  agriculture and, 495
  population and, 121
GMB. *See* Grain Marketing Board
GNP. *See* Gross national product
Goldman, Dana, 259n
Gollin, Douglas, 54n, 287n
Goods
  final, 25
  intermediate, 25

normal, 110
public, 334
relative prices of, 256
technology and, 258–259
traded, 26
Google, 210
Gorbachev, Mikhail, 273, 353
Gordon, Robert, 246, 247n
Gottleib, 278n
Government, 330–360
  in China, 331–332, 439–442
  civil conflict and, 346–348
  colonialism and, 358–359
  cultural change and, 425–427
  doing bad things for growth,
    348–353
  economic growth and, 337–348
  as economic intervention,
    333–337
  economic mobility and, 395
  economic planning by, 343–346
  efficiency and, 505–506
  in Europe, 439–442
  factor accumulation and, 333, 506
  GDP and, 340
  geography and, 438–442
  income and, 358–359
  natural resources and, 455–458
  normative approach to, 333
  in poor countries, 353–359
  population density in, 420
  positive approach to, 333
  property rights and, 470
  resource curse and, 455–458
  rule of law by, 337–339
  saving and, 72
  self-preservation of, 350–353
  size of, 339–342
  social capital and, 410
  in Soviet Union, 336
  toward birth control, 106
  trade and, 343
Government failure, 335
Grabbing hand, 352
Grain Marketing Board (GMB), 346
Gray, Elisha, 253
Great Britain. See Britain
Great Depression
  fertility in, 101
  GDP in, 282
  inefficiency in, 281

Great Leap Forward, in China,
  331–332
Great spike, in population, 133–136
Greece
  infanticide in, 105
  malaria in, 447
Green GDP, 476–478
  natural resource prices and, 481
Greenhouse gases, 492
Greenspan, Alan, 303
Griswold v. Connecticut, 106
Gross domestic product (GDP), 3–4,
  300. *See also* GDP per capita;
    GDP per worker; Green GDP
  in Africa, 127
  banking and, 290
  capital and, 163
  capital per worker and, 48–49
  CPI and, 25
  education and, 160
  food and, 152–153
  versus GDP per capita, 6–8
  government and, 340
  in Great Depression, 282
  malaria in, 160
  measurement of, 25–27
  of Nigeria, 132
  PPP and, 25–27
  saving rate and, 314
  of U.S., 25
  value/weight ratio of, 304
  working age fraction in, 142–143
Gross national product (GNP), 300
  saving rate and, 314
Groupism, 414
Growth. *See* Economic growth
Growth accounting
  for Europe, 242
  for Hong Kong, 197
  for productivity, 193–194
Growth rate, 59
  before 1820, 17–22
  in Canada, 14
  capital per worker and, 68
  differences in, 8–22
  income levels and, 36–37
  of Nicaragua, 14
  of output, 213
  of Philippines, 14
  of population, 82, 93, 93n
  of productivity, 192–196, 242

saving and, 37
since 1820, 14–17
Solow model and, 66–68
of Somalia, 14
of South Korea, 14
steady state and, 80
of technology, 221, 235–237
of Zimbabwe, 14
Growth rate of income, 4, 8–22
  investment and, 68
Gucci Gulch, 281
Guinea-Bissau, natural resources
  of, 452
Guner, Nezih, 396n
*Guns, Germs, and Steel: The Fates of
  Human Societies* (Diamond), 436
Gürkaynak, Refet S., 54n, 55
Gutenberg, Johannes, 44, 240
Gylfason, Thorvaldur, 453n

Haber, Fritz, 486
Haiti, before 1820, 19
Hall, Robert, 162n, 187n
Hall-Heroult process, 479
Haltiwanger, John, 289n
Happiness
  economic growth and, 508–510
  income and, 510
Hardin, Garret, 470n
Hard work
  climate and, 449–450
  culture and, 402–403
  efficiency and, 505
  in Soviet Union, 426
Harley, C. Knick, 243n
Hasidic Jews, 409
Health
  exogenous variables with,
    156–158
  food and, 153
  human capital and, 151–158
  income and, 151–158
  income per capita and, 156–157
  pollution and, 491
  in poor countries, 156–157
  sanitation and, 177
  vaccinations and, 177
Health care, in U.S., 278
Height
  in Britain, 2, 151
  food and, 151

Height (*Continued*)
  income and, 151
  in South Korea, 151
Hellmich, Nanci, 259n
Henderson, Vernon, 21n
Henrich, Joseph, 423n
Heston, Alan, 4n, 7, 12, 15, 16, 16n,
      48n, 49, 65, 83, 131, 153, 186,
      308, 309, 363n, 370, 391, 408,
      413, 433, 452, 494
Higgins, Matthew, 370n
Hill, Roger Brian, 402n
Historical data, 44–45
HIV. *See* AIDS
Hochschild, Adam, 358n
Hogan, Dennis P., 108n
Hong Kong
  economic growth in, 197
  GDP per capita in, 197
  growth accounting for, 197
  patents in, 255
  saving in, 403
Hookworm, 156–157
Horioka, Charles, 315, 316
Hotelling, Harold, 479n
Howitt, Peter, 206n
Hsieh, Chang-Tai, 286n, 289n
HTC, 210
Huber, Richard J., 309n, 317
Hufbauer, Gary Clyde, 323n
Human capital, 58, 150–177
  depreciation of, 150
  in developed countries, 168
  in developing countries, 167
  education and, 158–176, 390
  externalities and, 175–176
  health and, 151–158
  income and, 163–169
  income inequality and,
      381–384
  national income and, 163
  in poor countries, 504
  productivity and, 150
  return from, 150
  in wealthy countries, 504
Human effort. *See* Hard work
Human genome sequencing, 252
Humblet, Catherine, 421, 422n
Hungary, from outer space, 21
Hurst, Erik, 286n
Hutterites, fertility of, 85

Iceland
  fishing in, 470
  patents in, 255
Idle resources, inefficiency and,
      281–282
Imitation, 215, 217–218
Incas, 19
Income. *See also specific income topics*
  anti-globalization and, 324
  capital and, 48–76
  in China, 2
  composition effect and, 144, 146
  differences in, 4–8
  economic growth and, 67
  education and, 161–163, 373–378
  energy and, 471
  exogenous variables with, 158
  fertility and, 110–111
  government and, 358–359
  happiness and, 510
  health and, 151–158
  height and, 151
  human capital and, 163–169
  marginal product and, 285–286
  modernization and, 424–425
  under $1 per day, 1
  population and, 90
  saving and, 70–74
  in sub-Saharan Africa, 23
  substitution effects and, 110–111
Income differences. *See* Theory of
      income differences
Income effects, 111
Income inequality, 363–396, 503
  agriculture and, 391
  in Canada, 390–392
  capital and, 380–381
  between and within countries,
      18–19
  economic growth and, 380–392
  education and, 373–378, 390
  efficiency and, 384–388
  empirical evidence on, 389–392
  factor accumulation and, 384, 506
  Gini coefficient and, 365–368
  human capital and, 381–384
  income per capita and, 370
  income redistribution and, 384–388
  in Latin America, 390–392
  productivity and, 187–191
  rise of, 378–380

  saving and, 380–381
  sociopolitical unrest and, 388–389,
      390, 391
  sources of, 373–380
  superstar dynamic and, 380
  taxation and, 386–387, 388
  technology and, 378–379
  trade and, 379–380
  in U.S., 379, 390–392
Income levels
  growth rate and, 36–37
  saving rate and, 71–73
  Solow model and, 64, 73
  zero population growth and, 136
Income per capita. *See also* GDP
      per capita
  country averages of, 364
  disease and, 156–157
  health and, 156–157
  income inequality and, 370
  in India, 99
  latitude and, 433
  Malthusian model and, 86–88
  in Nigeria, 132
  Olympic medals and, 145
  population and, 82, 83, 86–88,
      90–92
  proximate cause of, 506
  saving and, 69–70
  Solow model and, 72
  in South and North Korea, 330
  steady state of, 74, 88
  sustainable development and, 473
  TFR and, 131
Income redistribution, 335
  crime and, 389
  economic mobility and, 394–395
  government and, 349
  income inequality and, 384–388
  through taxation, 385–386
Index of ethnic fractionalization, 418
India
  capital in, 48
  cell phones in, 272
  China and, 356–357
  computers in, 272
  demographics for, 104–105
  development accounting for, 186
  efficiency in, 270–272
  forcible sterilization in, 108
  GDP per capita in, 16

GDP per worker in, 65
income per capita in, 99
life expectancy in, 99, 125
malaria in, 161
marginal product in, 289
misallocation among firms in, 289
tacit knowledge in, 227
technology in, 254
television in, 427–428
textiles and, 275
tool industry in, 322
Indonesia
breast-feeding in, 106
corruption in, 355
family-planning programs
in, 108
forests in, 470
life expectancy in, 2
national language for, 425
social capital and, 411
TFR in, 101
Industrialization
resource curse and, 454–455
of South Korea, 3
of Sweden, 417
Industrial Revolution
coal and, 460
England in, 244–245
international technology transfer
in, 217
technological change in, 243–246
technological change since, 246–248
Inefficiency
barriers to mobility and, 285
idle resources and, 281–282
marginal product and, 285–286
misallocation among firms and,
288–289
misallocation among sectors and,
282–285
monopoly and, 320
rule of law and, 338
from taxation, 342
technology blocking and,
289–294
types of, 280–294
unproductive activities and, 280–281
Inequality. See Income inequality
Infanticide, in Greece, 105
Inflation, 25, 247, 371
of GMB, 346

Information technology, 247–248,
259–262
Information transmission
declining cost of, 304
globalization and, 304
Ingram, James C., 319n
In-ground price, 476
current price and, 479
for oil, 477
Ink jet printer, invention of, 251
Innovation, 215
*An Inquiry into the Nature and
Causes of Wealth of Nations*
(Smith, A.), 22, 285, 389, 434
Intel Corporation, 260, 261
Intellectual property, technology
and, 206–211
Intergenerational mobility, 393
Intergovernmental Panel on Climate
Change (IPCC), 492n, 494,
495n, 496n
Intermediate goods, 25
International aid, 75
International Labour Organization,
444n
International Monetary Fund, 303n
International technology transfer,
216–229
barriers to, 223
Internet, globalization and, 304
Intrauterine device (IUD), 106
Investment, 30
banking and, 291
by Britain, 301–302
capital and, 49–50
capital per worker and, 94
in computers, 263
consumption and, 50
depreciation and, 57, 60
in developing countries, 75
economic growth and, 67
education as, 158
growth rate of income and, 68
by industrialized countries, 316
in natural capital, 476
in poor countries, 179
productivity and, 75
research and development
as, 50
saving and, 50, 68–74
Solow model and, 57, 70, 95

in Soviet Union, 75
steady state and, 60, 62, 66
trust and, 408
in U.S., 50
Invisible hand, 285
IPCC. *See* Intergovernmental Panel
on Climate Change
Iran
GDP per capita in, 7
GDP per worker in, 65
Ireland
patents in, 255
potatoes in, 88–89
Iron, in England, 244
Irwin, Douglas A., 309n, 326n
Isaacs, Julia B., 393, 395n
Ishihara, Shintaroi, 13
Islam
cultural change and, 422–423
culture and, 416
openness to new ideas in, 401–402
Israel, patents in, 255
Italy
fertility in, 126
patents in, 255
textiles and, 275
ITU, 427n
IUD. *See* Intrauterine device

Jaffe, Adam B., 208n
James, Estelle, 72n
Japan
automobiles from, 321
capital per worker in, 186
culture of, 414, 426
development accounting for, 186
exchange rates and, 27
fertility in, 126
GDP per capita in, 9–13, 16
government in, 351
happiness in, 510
hard work in, 403
international technology transfer
in, 217
life expectancy in, 2
natural resources of, 452
openness to new ideas in, 401
patents in, 255
population of, 82
population aging in, 142
R&D in, 203, 248

Japan (*Continued*)
  saving in, 403, 426
  tacit knowledge in, 227
  textiles and, 275
  TFR in, 128
  trade by, 308–309, 317
A Japan That Can Say No (Ishihara),
  11–13
Jardin, A., 425n
Java, 293
Jayaratne, Jith, 291n
Jefferson, Thomas, 204n, 309
Jenkins, Gilbert, 465
Jensen, Robert, 428n
Jevons, Stanley, 474, 475n
J.M. Smucker Company, 207
John Paul II (Pope), 326
Johnson, Paul A., 412n, 413
Johnson, Simon, 157n, 161n, 457n
Jones, Arthur F., 378n, 389
Jones, Charles I., 162n, 177n, 187n,
  248n, 266n, 286n
Jones, Eric L., 438n
Joshi, Shareen, 107n
Judicial system, corruption and, 350

Kahn, Herman, 260
Kahun Medical Papyrus, 105
Kalemli-Ozcan, Sebnem, 99
Kaneko, Ryuichi, 126n
Karl, Terry Lynn, 456n
Katz, Lawrence F., 164, 165, 378n
Kaufmann, Daniel, 338, 339, 351, 391
Kearney, Melissa S., 164, 165
Keefer, Philip, 408n
Kehoe, Patrick J., 249n
Kelley, William, 252
Kelly, Morgan, 20n
Kelvin, Lord, 261
Kendrick, John, 160n
Kenya, development accounting
  for, 186
Kertzer, David I., 105n
Keyfitz, Nathan, 103, 107n, 108n, 118
Keynes, John Maynard, 17, 381,
  381n, 429, 508, 510
Khama, Seretse, 457
Khwaja, Asim Ijaz, 346n
Kim Il Sung, 330
Kim Jong-il, 330
Kim Jong-un, 330

King, Robert, 75n
Kiszewski, Anthony, 448
Klenow, Peter, 187n, 286n, 289n
Kleptocracy, 349–350
Knack, Stephen, 406n 408n
Knight, John, 175n
Knowles, John, 396n 403n
Kolbert, Elizabeth, 355n
Koppen-Geiger system, 442–443
Korea. *See* North Korea; South Korea
Kortum, Samuel, 320n
Kraay, Aart, 338, 339, 351, 371,
  372, 391
Kremer, Michael, 43n, 84, 242n
Krueger, Alan B., 164, 165, 346n
  378n
Krugman, Paul, 197, 229n, 261
Kuznets, Simon, 368, 368n, 476
Kuznets curve, 368–370
  for environment, 488–492
Kyoto Protocol, 495–496

Labor force, growth of, 253–255
La Ferrara, Eliana, 427n
Land
  capital and, 58
  as natural resource, 450–451
  population and, 86, 88, 90
  production and, 75
  as production factor, 58
  technology and, 58
  as wealth, 58, 75
Landes, David, 217n, 353n, 399, 407n
La Porta, Rafael, 343n, 345n
Larsen, Ulla, 85n
Latin America. *See also specific*
  countries
  Catholic Church in, 416
  culture in, 416
  GDP per capita in, 16
  income inequality in, 390–392
Latitude
  agricultural productivity and, 445
  GDP per capita and, 38–39
  GDP per worker and, 445
  income per capita and, 433
Law of one price, 26, 299
Lawyers, social capital and, 411
Laziness, germ of, 158
Leapfrogging, 228
Lee, Jong-Wha, 166

Lee, Ronald D., 122n
Leeuwenhoek, Antoni van, 134
Leisure
  economic growth and, 508
  hard work and, 402
  television and, 411
  in U.S., 2
Leonardi, Robert, 410n
Lerner, Josh, 208n
Levine, Ross, 75n, 291n, 343n
Levinsohn, James, 305n
Lewis, W. Arthur, 75n
Lewis, William W., 322n
Life expectancy, 117–119
  in Brazil, 2
  in developing countries, 99
  in Egypt, 2
  GDP per capita and, 154
  in India, 99, 125
  in Indonesia, 2
  in Japan, 2
  medicine and, 100
  mortality forecasting and, 124–125
  in U.S., 125, 177
Life expectancy at birth, 98
  equation for, 117
The Limits to Growth, 474–475
Lin, Merle, 318–319
Lindbeck, Assar, 427n
Linear scale, 9
Linguistic fractionalization, 420
Linux, 210
Lipset, Seymour Martin, 402n
Livi-Bacci, Massimo, 85n, 98, 103, 143
Living standard. *See* Standard of living
Lloyd, William Forster, 470n
Loayza, Norman, 291n
Lobbying, 281
Logarithmic scale. *See* Ratio scale
Lomborg, Bjørn, 492n
London, environmental Kuznets
  curve for, 490–491
Lopez-De Silanes, Florencio, 343n,
  345n
Lorenz curve, 367–368
Lucas, Adrienne, 161n
Lucas, Robert, 14n, 23, 23n, 211n
Luddites, 206, 292, 294
Lump-sum transfer, 385
Luther, Martin, 416
Luxembourg, patents in, 255

Maddison, Angus, 8n, 9n, 12, 16, 16,n 17, 273n, 301, 301n, 303n

Malaria, 158, 446, 447–449
economic effects of, 160–161

Malaria ecology index, 447–448

Malawi, development accounting for, 186

Malaysia, population aging in, 142

Malthus, Thomas, 75, 85, 86n, 90n, 475n

Malthusian model, 127, 136
breakdown of, 90–93
income per capita and, 86–88
living standard and, 90
moral restraint in, 90–91
population and, 84–93
resource disasters and, 474
in Western Europe, 92

Manchus, 439

Mankiw, N. Gregory, 68n, 130n, 211n

Mao Zedong, 331

Maquiladora, 438

Margarine, 293

Marginal product, 52, 52n
in China, 289
income and, 285–286
in India, 289
inefficiency and, 285–286

Marginal product of capital (MPK), 56
diminishing marginal product and, 79

Marginal product of labor (MPL), 54–55
misallocation among sectors and, 284

Market failure, 333

Marketing boards, 343, 346

Marriage, fertility and, 106

Marshall, Alfred, 201, 202

Marx, Karl, 381

Mass production of automobiles, invention of, 240

Masters, William A., 446n

Mastruzzi, Massimo, 338, 339, 351, 391

Mauritius, malaria in, 449

Maximum sustainable yield, 468–469
for fishing, 471

McArthur, John W., 157n

McDermott, C.J., 480

McDermott, Darren, 197n

McGlynn, Elizabeth, 259n

McKinsey Global Institute, 274n

McLaren, Angus, 105n, 106n

Mcleod, Christine, 207n

McMillan, Margaret S., 446n

McNeill, William H., 447n

Meadows, Donella H., 474, 475n

Mean logarithmic deviation, 18

Mechanical clock, invention of, 240

Media, cultural change and, 427–428

Median, 365

Median voter, 387

Medicine
life expectancy and, 100
mortality transition and, 100

Mege-Mouiries, Hippolyte, 293

Mellinger, Andrew D., 433, 434n, 436n

Mercedes-Benz, 331

Messerlin, 323n

Metallurgy, in Industrial Revolution, 244

Mexico
capital in, 48
development accounting for, 186
family-planning programs in, 108
GDP of, 6
GDP per worker in, 65
hard work in, 403
malaria in, 161
maquiladora in, 438
old-age pension fund in, 72
population aging in, 142
privatization in, 345

Mian, Atif, 346n

Microprocessors, 260, 261

Microscope, invention of, 251

Microsoft, 206
technology blocking by, 293

Middle class, 508

Miguel, Edward, 43n, 347n, 405

Mill, John Stuart, 406, 406n

Minimum wage, as barrier to mobility, 205

Misallocation among firms, inefficiency and, 288–289

Misallocation among sectors, inefficiency and, 282–285

Moav, Omer, 168n, 384n

Mode, 365

Modernization, income and, 424–425

Mokyr, Joel, 206n, 246n, 263, 263n, 292n, 320n, 401n

Moldova
GDP per capita in, 8
from outer space, 21

Mongols, 439

Monopoly
in banking, 291
government and, 334
inefficiency and, 320
misallocation among firms and, 288
natural, 334

Monsanto Corporation, 210

Montesquieu, Charles de Secondat, Baron de, 449, 449n

Moore, Gordon, 260

Moore's law, 260, 261, 511

Moral restraint, in Malthusian model, 90–91

Morris, Cynthia Taft, 412–413

Morrison, Christian, 19

Mortality
in developing countries, 104
fertility and, 102–105, 110
forecasting of, 124–125
NRR and, 110
in Sweden, 103, 110

Mortality transition
in developing countries, 100
disease and, 100
drinking water and, 100
food and, 100
medicine and, 100
population and, 97, 98–100
sewage and, 100
standard of living and, 100

Motorola, 210

Movable type, 44
invention of, 240

Mowry, David C., 487n

Mozambique
civil conflict in, 347
education in, 174

MPK. *See* Marginal product of capital

MPL. *See* Marginal product of labor

Muhammad (Prophet), 416

Multiple regression, 41

Multiple steady state, 74

Multiplier effect, in productivity, 156

Music, technology and, 259

Muslims. *See* Islam

Nanetti, Raffaella Y., 410n
Napoleon Bonaparte, 432
Napoleon III (emperor), 293
Narayan, Deepa, 410n
Nast, Thomas, 355
National income, 3
    capital and, 54
    human capital and, 163
    natural resources and, 478
Nationalism, 302
National languages, 425
National Science Foundation, 226n
National sovereignty, anti-
        globalization and, 325
NATO. *See* North Atlantic Treaty
        Organization
Natural capital
    GDP per capita and, 451–452
    investment in, 476
    renewable resource and, 477–478
Natural monopoly, 334
Natural resources
    of Angola, 280–281
    civil conflict and, 347–348
    culture and, 416–417
    economic growth and, 450–453,
        473–486
    environment and, 463–497
    future and, 478–482, 513
    geography and, 450–458
    globalization and, 463–497
    government and, 455–458
    national income and, 478
    as nonrenewable, 464–467, 475, 487
    population and, 82
    price for, 478–482
    production and, 471–473
    property rights and, 464, 469–471
    as renewable, 467–469, 477–478
    resource curse and, 453–458
    substitution effects and, 483–485
    technology and, 464, 479,
        485–486, 500–502
Natural selection, 252
Navasky, Victor, 261
Neary, J. Peter, 305n
Negative externalities, 334
Nelson, Richard R., 210n, 254n
Netherlands, patents in, 255
Net rate of reproduction (NRR),
        102–105, 117–119

equation for, 119
    mortality and, 110
    mortality forecasting and, 124–125
    in Sweden, 103
Netscape, 293
Network electricity, invention of, 240
Neutral technology, 224–226
Newton, Isaac, 250
New York City, 353–355
New Zealand, patents in, 255
NGOs. *See* Nongovernmental
        organizations
Nicaragua, growth rate of, 14
Niger, natural resources of, 452
Nigeria
    age-specific fertility rate in, 119
    demographics for, 104–105
    GDP of, 132
    income per capita in, 132
    malaria in, 160
Nitrogen, 486
Nonexcludability, 229–230
Nongovernmental organizations
        (NGOs)
    anti-globalization and, 324
    rule of law and, 338
Nonrenewable resource, 464–467
    pollution and, 487
    resource disasters and, 475
    time until resource runs out, 465n
Nonrival technology, 204, 230, 252
Nontariff barriers, 305
Nordhaus, William, 247n, 495n
Normal goods, 110
Normative approach,
        to government, 333
North, Douglass, 337n
North Atlantic Treaty Organization
        (NATO), 330
North Korea
    autarky in, 299
    South Korea and, 330
Norway
    development accounting for, 186
    GDP per worker in, 65
    natural resources in, 457
    patents in, 255
NRR. *See* Net rate of reproduction
NTP, 209
Nuclear fusion, 486–487
Nutrition. *See* Food

Observational data, 38
Observer bias, 407
Obstfeld, Maurice, 316n
Oceans
    property rights and, 470–471
    trade and, 434–435
OECD. *See* Organisation for
        Economic Co-operation and
        Development
Oil, 464–467
    in-ground price for, 477
    price of, 480–481
    wealthy countries and, 465
Ok, Efe, 394n
Old-age pension plans, saving and, 72
Olken, Benjamin A., 411, 411n
Olympic medals, 145
Omitted variable, 41
One-child policy, of China, 108
OPEC. *See* Organization of the
        Petroleum Exporting Countries
Opportunity cost, in education, 160
Organisation for Economic
        Co-operation and Development
        (OECD), 126, 154, 306, 340
    R&D and, 203
    wealthy countries in, 465
Organization of the Petroleum
        Exporting Countries (OPEC),
        480
O'Rourke, Kevin H., 303n, 451n
Orwell, George, 71
Oster, Emily, 428n
Ottoman Empire, 19
Outliers, 38, 172, 448
Output, 3
    capital and, 93–94
    efficiency and, 505
    factors of production and, 180
    growth rate of, 213
    population and, 84–93
    productivity and, 182
    R&D and, 213
    rule of law and, 338
    in textiles, 275
    in U.S., 246
Output per capita, 51n
    productivity and, 504
Output per worker, 51–52, 51n
    climate and, 444
    differences in, 181

factor accumulation and, 195
factors of production and, 189
population and, 96
productivity and, 190, 195
R&D and, 214
Solow model and, 95
steady state for, 96, 235
Overconsumption, resource curse
and, 453
The Overeducated American
(Freeman), 164
*The Overworked American: The
Unexpected Decline of Leisure*
(Schorr), 508
Oxfam, anti-globalization and, 324

Pack, Howard, 217n
Padded horse collar, invention of, 240
Pakes, Ariel, 305n, 313n
Pakistan, 346
Palm Inc., 209
Parente, Stephen, 278n, 279, 287n
Parking tickets, culture and, 405
Pasteur, Louis, 251
Patents, 337
    alternatives to, 210–211
    for pharmaceuticals, 254
    population and, 254
    problems with, 208–210
    technology and, 206–211
    in U.S., 254, 255
Patent races, 252–253
Patent troll, 209
Peak oil, 467
Perestroika (restructuring), 353
Perotti, Roberto, 390n, 398n
Persson, Torsten, 385n, 392n
Peru, 344
    old-age pension fund in, 72
Peter the Great, 217
Petronius, 290–291
Pharmaceuticals, patents for, 254
Philippines, growth rate of, 14
Phosphorus, 474
Photography, invention of, 260
Photovoltaic cells, 487
Physical capital. *See* Capital
PISA, 175
Planning. *See* Economic planning
Plants, as renewable resource, 467–469
Plato, 29

Pliny the Elder, 290–291
Plutarch, 363
Poincaré, Henri, 1
Poland, from outer space, 21
Polanyi, Michael, 227n
Political openness, 353
Pollan, Michael, 210n
Pollard, Sidney, 243n
Pollution
    environment and, 487–488
    GDP per capita and, 488–489
    government and, 349
    Green GDP and, 478
    health and, 491
    as negative externality, 334
    poor countries and, 490
    wealthy countries and, 490
Polo, Marco, 17
Polymerase chain reaction, 241
Pomeranz, Kenneth, 20n, 460n
Ponting, Clive, 475n
Poor countries
    anti-globalization and, 324
    capital in, 75, 504
    cell phones in, 268
    civil conflict in, 347
    convergence toward the steady
        state in, 67
    demographic momentum in, 147
    environmental Kuznets curve
        for, 489
    factor accumulation in, 194,
        503–504
    factors of production in, 191
    fertility in, 130–132
    food in, 152–153
    GDP per capita in, 503
    government in, 353–359
    hard work in, 403
    health in, 156–157
    human capital in, 504
    investment in, 179
    pollution and, 490
    population in, 82, 94, 144, 146
    population density in, 420
    productivity in, 194
    saving in, 71
    technology and, 204
    technology in, 505
Population. *See also* Malthusian
        model; Zero population growth

aging of, 138–143
agricultural productivity and, 475
capital dilution and, 93–95
capital per worker and, 93–95
capital stock and, 94
of Chad, 82
of China, 88
consumption and, 82
demographic transition and, 97
distribution of, 143–146
with drinking water, 1
of Easter Island, 475
economic growth and, 82–114, 93,
    146–147
in 18th century, 243
energy use and, 471
fertility transition and, 97, 100–101
food and, 1, 91
forecasting of, 122–136
future and, 121–147
global warming and, 121
great spike in, 133–136
income and, 91
income per capita and, 82, 83,
    86–88, 91–92
of Japan, 82
land and, 86, 88, 91
Malthusian model and, 84–93
mortality transition and, 97,
    98–100
natural resources and, 82
Olympic medals and, 145
output and, 84–93
output per worker and, 96
over long run, 84–85
patents and, 254
in poor countries, 82, 94, 144, 146
production and, 82
productivity and, 88–89
with sanitation, 1
Solow model and, 93–97
standard of living and, 86, 88, 127
steady state of, 88, 90, 94
supportable by earth, 134, 135
technology and, 88, 135
in very long run, 133–136
in wealthy countries, 179
in Western Europe, 92
worldwide, 123
The Population Bomb (Ehrlich),
    134, 482

Population density
  economic growth and, 421–422
  social capability and, 420–422
  of world, 433
Population growth
  GDP per capita and, 39
  rate of, 82, 93, 93n, 136–138
  slowdown of, 136–138
Portfolio investment, 312
Portugal, textiles and, 275
Positive approach, to government, 333
Positive check, 86
Positive externalities, 334
Potatoes, in Ireland, 88–89
Pounds, Norman J.G., 440n, 441n
Poverty. See also Poor countries
  distribution of income and, 363
  economic growth and, 371–372
  future and, 71
PPP. See Purchasing power parity
Prescott, Edward, 278n, 279
Pretax income, 385, 388
Preventive check, 86
Price. See also In-ground price
  environment and, 488
  law of one, 26, 299
  for natural resources, 478–482
  of oil, 480–481
  relative, of goods, 256
Price elasticity of demand, 484–485
Price index, 25
  for computers, 262
Pritchett, Lant, 107n, 166n, 188, 410n
Private property, 337
Private saving, 72
Privatization, 335
  in Mexico, 345
Proctor, Bernadette D., 364n, 366,
  367, 378n
Production. See also Factors of
  production
  capital and, 51–56
  land and, 75
  mass production of automobiles, 240
  natural resources and, 471–473
  population and, 82
  resource intensity of, 472
Production function, 34. See also
  Cobb-Douglas production
  function; Technology production function

capital and, 51–54
  productivity in, 180–182
Productivity, 31, 33
  in automobiles, 276–278
  Cobb-Douglas production
    function and, 95
  computers and, 249
  development accounting and,
    185–186
  differences among countries,
    182–191, 194–196
  economic growth and, 196
  in education, 259
  efficiency and, 268, 269–272,
    504–505
  factor accumulation and, 191–192
  in food, 276–278
  growth accounting for, 193–194
  growth rate of, 192–196, 242
  human capital and, 150
  income inequality and, 187–191
  investment and, 75
  measurement of, 179–198
  multiplier effect in, 156
  output and, 182
  output per capita and, 504
  output per worker and, 190, 195
  in poor countries, 194
  population and, 88–89
  in production function, 180–182
  quantitative analysis of, 183–187
  R&D and, 214
  relative importance of, 191–192
  rule of law and, 339
  in services, 259
  in Soviet Union, 75
  in steel, 276–278
  in subsurface coal mining,
    278–279
  technology and, 45, 504, 505
  in telecommunications, 276–278
  in U.S., 190–191, 246
  in wealthy countries, 194
Productivity slowdown, 247
Profit, R&D and, 205, 320
Property rights, 337
  environment and, 488
  fishing and, 470–471
  government and, 470
  natural resources and, 464, 469–471
  oceans and, 470–471

Protectionism, in wealthy
  countries, 326
Protestant ethic, 399, 402. See also
  Hard work
Proximate cause
  of economic growth, 33
  of income per capita, 506
Public goods, 334
Purchasing power parity (PPP), 4
  errors in, 20
  exchange rates, 27
  GDP and, 25–27
Putnam, Robert, 410–411
Putterman, Louis, 420n, 421, 422n

Qian Long, 401
Quadrini, Vincenzo, 383n
Quah, Danny T., 304n
Quantitative analysis, 38
  of education, 169–176
  of productivity, 183–187
  of Solow model, 95–97
Quotas, 305, 343

Race to the bottom, 325
Railroads, 303
  in Britain, 292
  economic growth and, 44
  steam engine for, 244
  in U.S., 44
Rainfall, in tropical regions, 445–446
Rajan, Raghuram, 291n
Randomized controlled trials
  (RCTs), 42–43
Ratio scale, 10, 11
  for U.S., 12
RCTs. See Randomized controlled
  trials
R&D. See Research and development
Reagan, Ronald, 381
Recreation. See Leisure
Redistribution. See Income
  redistribution
Relative growth rates, Solow model
  and, 66–68
Relative prices, of goods, 256
Relative wages, of women, 111
Religious fractionalization, 420
Renewable resource, 467–469
  natural capital and, 477–478
Rent seeking, 281

Replacement fertility, 125
  in future, 512
Research and development (R&D)
  creative destruction and, 206
  growth rate of output and, 213
  as investment, 50
  output and, 213
  output per worker and, 214
  patents and, 208–209
  as positive externality, 334
  productivity and, 214
  profit and, 205, 320
  Solow model for, 213–214
  spending determinants for, 204–206
  technology and, 511
  technology production function
    and, 248
  in U.S., 202–203
Research in Motion (RIM), 209
Resources. *See also* Natural resources
  idle, 281–282
  technology and, 505
Resource curse, 453–458
Resource disasters, 474–475
Resource intensity, of production, 472
Restructuring, 353
Retirement, in U.S., 2
Return
  from capital, 50, 54–56
  constant to scale, 51–52, 252–253
  to education, 162, 373
  from human capital, 150
Reuters, 457n, 477n
Revell, Jack, 58n
Reverse causation, 40–41
Rhee, Byung-Kun, 404n
Rhee, Changyong, 404n
Ricardo, David, 75
Riddle, John M., 105n
Riden, Philip, 244, 244n
Rijsberman, Frank R., 495n
RIM. *See* Research in Motion
Ríos-Rull, José-Victor, 383n
Rising Sun (Crichton), 13
Rivalry
  with capital, 50
  in technology, 204
Robinson, James A., 157n, 353n, 457n
Robots, 260
Rodriguez, Francisco, 187n, 454n
Rodriguez-Clare, Andres, 187n

Rodrik, Dani, 385n
Rogerson, Richard, 287n
Rogoff, Kenneth, 316n
Romania
  Kuznets curve and, 370
  from outer space, 21
Romer, David, 68n, 204n, 217n, 310,
    310n, 436n
Romer, Paul, 345n
Roos, Daniel, 217n
Roosevelt, Franklin, 281
Roosevelt, Theodore, 106
Rosen, Sherwin, 153n, 380n
Rosenberg, Nathan, 487n
Rostow, W.W., 75, 133, 134n
Roumasse, James, 487n
Rubber, 486
Rules, theory of, 207
Rule of law, 337–339
  corruption and, 350
  factor accumulation and, 338
  productivity and, 339
Rule of 72, 11
Russia. *See also* Soviet Union
  government in, 351–353
Ruttan, Vernon, 229n

Sachs, Jeffrey, 157n, 160, 161n, 306n,
    307, 308, 309, 433, 434n, 436n,
    453n
Sadik, Nafis, 107n
Sali-i-Martin, Xavier, 215n
Samuelson, Paul, 75
Sanger, Margaret, 106
Sanitation
  health and, 177
  population with, 1
Sarnoff, David, 260
Satyanath, Shanker, 347n
Saving
  capital and, 73
  convergence toward the steady
    state and, 74
  culture and, 403–404
  fundamentals and, 70
  GDP per worker and, 313–314
  by government, 72
  growth rate and, 37
  income and, 70–74
  income inequality and, 380–381
  income per capita and, 69–70

investment and, 50, 68–74
  in Japan, 426
  old-age pension plans and, 72
  in poor countries, 71
  private, 72
  in Singapore, 72
  Solow model and, 69, 70
  supply and demand and, 70
  in Uganda, 71
  in wealthy countries, 70
Saving rate
  economic openness and, 314
  endogenous variables with, 70–71
  exogenous variables with, 70–71
  GDP and, 314
  GNP and, 314
  income levels and, 71–73
  of industrialized countries, 315
  Solow model and, 72, 73
  steady state and, 73, 313–314
Savings retention coefficient, 316
Scarcity, 508
Scatter plots, 38–41
Schistosomiasis, 446
Schorr, Juliet, 508
Schultz, T. Paul, 107n, 111n
Schuman, Michael, 259n
Schumpeter, Joseph, 206, 294
Science, technology and, 251
Seas. *See* Oceans
Second Industrial Revolution, 245
Secrecy
  in food, 254
  versus patents, 210
  in textiles, 254
Sectoral reallocation, efficiency from,
    287–288
Seko, Mobutu Sese, 353
Self-preservation, of government,
    350–353
Self-sufficiency, 423
Semiconductors, 249
Sergenti, Ernest, 347n
Serialized drama, 127
Services
  productivity in, 259
  technology and, 258–259
Sewage, mortality transition and, 100
Shafik, Nemat, 489
The Shame of Cities (Steffens), 355
Sharing, culture and, 414

Shastry, Gauri Kartini, 153n
Shleifer, Andrei, 343n
Shop-floor R&D, 205
Simon, Julian, 482
Singapore
  Campaign to Encourage Diligence
    and Thrift in, 72
  Central Council for Savings
    Promotion in, 72
  economic growth in, 197
  GDP per capita for, 39–40
  GDP per worker in, 65
  old-age pension fund in, 72
  patents in, 255
  saving in, 72, 403
Skewed, 365
Skill differential, 323
Slater, Samuel, 216
Sleeping sickness, 446
Smith, Adam, 22, 285, 330, 389, 434
Smith, Jessica, 364n, 366, 367,
    378n, 379
Smoot-Hawley tariff, 309
Sobel, Dava, 203n
Social capability
  culture and, 411–416
  economic growth and, 415
  population density and, 420–422
Social capital
  cultural homogeneity and, 417–420
  culture and, 408–411
Social Security, 72
Sociopolitical unrest, income
    inequality and, 388–389, 390, 391
Sohn, Byungdoo, 151n
Sokoloff, Kenneth L., 392n
Solar energy, 487
Solow, Robert, 56, 249, 276n
Solow model
  capital and, 56–68
  capital per worker and, 56–63, 94
  deficiencies in, 74–76
  depreciation and, 57, 95
  growth rate and, 66–68
  human capital and, 168
  income levels and, 64, 73
  investment and, 57, 70, 95
  output per worker and, 95
  population and, 93–97
  quantitative analysis of, 95–97
  for R&D, 213–214

relative growth rates and, 66–68
saving and, 69, 70
saving rate and, 72, 73
steady state and, 59–63
technology and, 233–237
theory of income differences and,
    63–66
Somalia, growth rate of, 14
South Africa
  AIDS in, 126
  GDP per worker in, 65
South Korea
  development accounting for, 186
  economic planning in, 345
  fertility in, 126
  growth rate of, 14
  height in, 151
  industrialization of, 2
  North Korea and, 330
  patents in, 255
  R&D in, 203
  saving in, 403
Sovereignty, national, 325
Soviet Union
  capital in, 75
  central planning in, 273–274
  efficiency in, 273–274
  GDP per capita in, 16
  government in, 336, 353
  hard work in, 426
  international technology transfer
    in, 217
  investment in, 75
  productivity in, 75
  rule of law in, 338
Spain
  fertility in, 126
  TFR in, 102
Spillovers, 438
Squire, Lyn, 372n
Stalin, Joseph, 273
Standards, as trade barrier, 305
Standard of living, 1–3
  before 1820, 18
  Malthusian model and, 90
  mortality transition and, 100
  population and, 86, 88, 127
  technology and, 201
State enterprises, 343
Steady state. See also Convergence
    toward the steady state

capital and, 80
for capital per worker, 63
of capital per worker, 95, 234–235
capital stock and, 66–67, 80
Cobb-Douglas production
    function and, 63
convergence toward, 67–68, 74
depreciation and, 60
food and, 61
growth rate and, 80
of income per capita, 74, 88
investment and, 60, 62, 66
multiple, 74
for output per worker, 96, 235
of population, 88, 90, 94
saving rate and, 73, 313–314
Solow model and, 59–63, 234–235
for technology growth, 219
theory of income differences and, 66
Steamboats, 244
Steam engine
  invention of, 240–241, 243
  thermodynamics and, 251
Steamships, 303
Steel, 252
  productivity in, 276–278
Steffens, Lincoln, 355
Sterilization, in India, 108
Stern, Bernhard, 292n
Stern, Robert M., 318n
Stevenson, Betsey, 510n
Stiglitz, Joseph E., 224n
Stokey, Nancy, 224n
Storeygard, Adam, 21n
Stout, Donald, 209
Stover, Leon E., 441
Strahan, Philip E., 291n
Strahler, Alan, 442n
Strahler, Arthur, 442n
Strauss, Lewis L., 260
Struck, Douglas, 414n
Student test scores, GDP per capita
    and, 175
Student-to-teacher ratio, 174
Stutzer, Alois, 509, 510n
Sub-Saharan Africa
  AIDS in, 126
  education in, 174
  electricity in, 1
  fertility in, 130
  income in, 23

Substitution effects
  environment and, 488
  income and, 110–111
  natural resources and, 483–485
Subsurface coal mining, in U.S.,
    278–279
Sudan, civil conflict in, 347
Suez Canal, 303, 311
Sumerians, 475
Summers, Lawrence, 489–492
Summers, Robert, 4n, 7, 12, 15, 16,
    16n, 65, 131, 153, 154, 170, 186,
    363, 413, 433, 452, 494
Superstar dynamic, income
    inequality and, 380
Supply and demand, 37–38
  college premium and, 164–165
  saving and, 70
  taxation and, 341–342
Survivorship function, 117
  age-specific, 123
  in Sweden, 118
  for women, 118
Sushi, 469
Sustainable development, 473
  technology and, 500
Sweden
  fertility in, 103
  industrialization of, 417
  mortality in, 103, 110
  NRR in, 103
  patents in, 255
  survivorship function in, 118
Switzerland
  natural resources of, 452
  patents in, 255

Tabellini, Guido, 385n
Tacit knowledge, technology and,
    227–228
Taiwan
  economic planning in, 345
  patents in, 255
  saving in, 403
  tool industry in, 322
Tanzania, national language
    for, 425
Tariffs, 305, 343
  on automobiles, 321–322
  GATT, 306
  Smoot-Hawley tariff, 309

Taxation, 339–342
  income inequality and, 388
  income redistribution through,
    385–386
Tax base, 342
Taylor, Alan M., 323n
Taylor, M. Scott, 475n
Technology, 31, 33. See also specific
    technologies
  appropriate, 224–226
  for birth control, 106
  change and, 235–237
  in China, 88
  climate and, 449–450
  constant returns to scale for,
    252–253
  creation of, 202–203
  cutting edge of, 238–264
  differential progress in, 256–262
  economic growth and, 201–230
  economic openness and, 319–320
  efficiency and, 269–272
  18th century changes in, 239–243
  embodied progress in, 228
  environment and, 488
  factors of production and, 202
  fiberoptic, 479
  food and, 240
  future of, 253–256, 511
  goods versus services and, 258–259
  growth rate of, 221, 235–237
  income inequality and, 378–379
  information, 247–248, 259–262
  intellectual property and, 206–211
  international transfer of, 216–229
  land and, 58
  leapfrogging with, 228
  milestones of progress in, 240–241
  music and, 259
  natural resources and, 464, 479,
    485–486, 500–502
  nature of progress with, 202–206
  neutral, 224–226
  nonrival, 204, 230, 252
  pace of change for, 239–248
  patents and, 206–211
  in poor countries, 204, 505
  population and, 88, 135
  predicting progress of, 260–261
  productivity and, 45, 504, 505
  R&D and, 511

  resources and, 505
  rivalry in, 204
  science and, 251
  Solow model and, 233–237
  speed of progress of, 250–252
  standard of living and, 201
  sustainable development and, 500
  tacit knowledge and, 227–228
  in textiles, 275
  trade as, 317–318
  transfer of, 203–204
  in wealthy countries, 505
Technology blocking, inefficiency
    and, 289–294
Technology followers, 254
Technology leaders, 254
Technology production function,
    248–256
  improved version of, 266–267
Telecommunications.
    See also specific media
  productivity in, 276–278
Telegraph, 304
Telenovela (serialized drama), 427
Telephone. See also Cell phones
  globalization and, 304
  invention of, 252–253
Telescope, invention of, 251
Television
  in Brazil, 427
  in India, 427–428
  social capital and, 411
Temple, Jonathan, 412n, 413
Tempo effect, TFR and, 129
Terminator gene, 210
Tertullianus, Quintus Septimus
    Florens, 121
Textiles
  efficiency in, 274–276
  in Industrial Revolution, 242
  invention of manufacturing
    for, 240
  in 1910, 274–276
  output in, 275
  secrecy in, 254
  technology in, 275
TFR. See Total fertility rate
Thailand, population aging in, 142
Theory of income differences
  Solow model and, 63–66
  steady state and, 66

Theory of rules, 207
Thermodynamics, steam engine
    and, 251
Third Industrial Revolution, 247–248
Thomas, Vinod, 383n
Thring, M.W., 260
Tiberius (emperor), 290
Tocqueville, Alexis de, 396
Tool industry
    in India, 322
    in Taiwan, 322
Total fertility rate (TFR), 100–101,
    117–119
    demographic momentum and, 132
    desired fertility and, 109
    in developing countries, 109, 130
    in England, 102
    equation for, 118
    in France, 102
    income per capita and, 131
    in Indonesia, 101
    in Japan, 128
    in Spain, 102
    tempo effect and, 129
    in U.S., 101, 126
    for zero population growth, 125
Toyoda, Eiji, 216
Trabant, 331
Trade, 299. *See also* Economic
    openness
    barriers to, 305
    China and, 436–437
    GATT, 306
    geographic isolation and, 310–311
    geography and, 434–437
    of goods, 26
    government and, 343
    income inequality and, 379–380
    by Japan, 308–309, 317
    oceans and, 434–435
    as technology, 317–318
    in world, growth of, 301
    WTO, 305, 306
Traded goods, 26
Trade policy, globalization and,
    304–306
Tragedy of the commons, 470
Transatlantic telegraph cable, 304
Transistors, invention of, 240
Transitional growth, 66

Transition matrix, 393
Transport costs
    decline of, 302–304
    globalization and, 302–304
    natural resources and, 455
Trefler, Daniel, 322n
Treisman, Daniel, 357
Tropical regions
    agricultural productivity
      in, 444
    disease in, 446–449
    rainfall in, 445–446
Trust
    culture and, 404–408
    investment and, 408
    social capital and, 409, 411
Tse, Kinping, 487n
Tsiddon, Daniel, 229n, 379n
Turkey
    culture of, 426
    development accounting for, 186
    population aging in, 142
Turnover ratio, 290
Tweed, William Marcy "Boss,"
    354–355
Typhoid fever, 100

Uganda
    economic openness in, 309
    GDP per worker in, 65
    saving in, 71
Ukraine, from outer space, 21
Ultimate cause, of economic
    growth, 33
The Ultimate Resource (Simon), 482
UNAIDS, 126n
Underemployment, 280–281
Unemployment, 280–281
UNESCO, 174n
United Kingdom. *See* Britain
United Nations Commission
    on Environment and
    Development, 473
United Nations Development
    Program, 402n
United Nations Environmental
    Program, 469n
United Nations Food and
    Agriculture Organization,
    445, 471n

United Nations Population Division,
    104, 122n, 123, 131n, 138n, 143,
    145
United States (U.S.)
    age-specific fertility rate in, 119
    college premium in, 164–165
    development accounting for, 186
    distribution of income in,
      364–365, 366
    education level changes in, 159
    efficiency in, 270–272
    food in, 2
    GDP of, 25
    GDP per capita in, 7, 8–13,
      246, 341
    GDP per worker in, 65
    geographic mobility in, 287
    health care in, 278
    income inequality in, 379, 390–392
    intergenerational mobility in, 393
    investment in, 50
    leisure in, 2
    life expectancy in, 125, 177
    Lorenz curve for, 367
    output in, 246
    patents in, 254, 255
    population density in, 433
    productivity in, 190–191, 246
    railroads in, 44
    ratio scale for, 12
    R&D in, 202–203, 248
    retirement in, 2
    saving in, 404
    subsurface coal mining in, 278–279
    tacit knowledge in, 227
    textiles and, 275
    TFR in, 101, 126
    working age fraction in, 140–141
    workweek in, 2
Unproductive activities, inefficiency
    and, 280–281
Uruguay, old-age pension fund in, 72
Uruguay Round, 317–318
U.S. *See* United States

Vaccinations, health and, 177
Value/weight ratio, of GDP, 304
van Velzen, Andre, 495n
Variables, 38
Vaupel, James W., 85n

Venezuela, 389
  natural resources of, 452
  resource curse in, 456
VERs. *See* Voluntary export
  restraints
Vietnam, economic openness in, 309
Voluntary export restraints
  (VERs), 305

Wacziarg, Romain, 306n, 307,
  308, 309
Wade, Alice H., 101
Wagner, Adolph, 340
Wagner's law, 340
Wallace, Alfred, 252
Walsh, John P., 210n, 254n
Wang, Michael, 332n
Wang, Yan, 391n
Warner, Andrew, 306n, 307, 308,
  309, 453n
Water, 1
  mortality transition and, 100
  as renewable resource, 469
Watson, Thomas, 261
Watt, James, 320
Wealth, land as, 58, 75
*Wealth of Nations. See An Inquiry
  into the Nature and Causes of
  Wealth of Nations* (Smith, A.)
Wealthy countries
  anti-globalization and, 326
  capital in, 504
  convergence toward the steady
    state in, 67
  environmental Kuznets curve
    for, 489
  factor accumulation in, 194,
    503–504
  fertility in, 83, 126–130
  food in, 152–153
  GDP per capita in, 503
  in OECD, 465
  oil and, 465

pollution and, 490
population in, 179
productivity in, 194
protectionism in, 326
saving in, 70
technology in, 505
Weber, Max, 399, 402
Wehrwein, Peter, 127n
Weil, David N., 21n, 68n, 92n, 111n,
  130n, 153n, 224n
Weinberg, Daniel H., 378n, 379
Weiner, Anthony J., 260
Weir, Shandra, 175n
Weitzman, Martin, 477
Welch, Karen Horn, 306n, 307,
  308, 309
Wells, H.G., 134, 135n
  resource disasters and, 474
Western Europe
  GDP per capita in, 16
  Malthusian model in, 92
  population in, 92
West Germany, East Germany and,
  330–331
Westinghouse, George, 292–293
Westphal, Lawrence, 217n, 345n
Wheel, invention of, 240
Williamson, Jeffrey G., 143n, 303n,
  369, 370n, 451n
Wilson, Erasmus, 261
Windhexe, invention of, 251
Within-country income inequality,
  18–19
Wolfers, Justin, 510n
Womack, James P., 217n
Women
  demographic momentum and,
    132–133
  relative wages of, 111
  survivorship function for, 118
Workers. *See also* Capital per worker;
  GDP per worker; Output per
  worker

effective, 233
exploitation of, 324
Work ethic. *See* Hard work;
  Protestant ethic
Working age fraction, 140–143
Workweek, in U.S., 2
World Bank, 2n, 127, 174n, 301,
  306n, 312, 347n, 348n, 350,
  451n, 452, 471, 489–492
  on corruption, 350
World Health Organization, 447n,
  449n
World trade, growth of, 301
World Trade Organization (WTO),
  305, 306
Worldwatch Institute, 135n
Writing, invention of, 240
WTO. *See* World Trade
  Organization

Xu, David, 332n

Yashiro, Naohiro, 128
Yellow fever, 446
Young, Alwyn, 127, 197, 287n
Young, Jeffrey, 259n

Zaire, 353
Zak, Paul J., 406n
Zambia, AIDS in, 126
Zeira, Joseph, 382n
Zeldes, Stephen P., 381
Zelnik, Melvin, 101
Zero population growth, 88
  income levels and, 136
  TFR for, 125
Zheng He, 21–22
Zilibotti, Fabrizio, 227n
Zimbabwe
  AIDS in, 126
  growth rate of, 14
  marketing board in, 346
Zingales, Luigi, 291n

CREDITS

TEXT CREDITS

Chapter 2   p. 45: Map from RAILROADS AND AMERICAN ECONOMIC GROWTH: ESSAYS IN ECONOMETRIC HISTORY, 1st Edition, by Robert W. Fogel. Copyright © 1964 by Johns Hopkins University Press. Reprinted by permission of the author.

Chapter 16   p. 474: Meadows, et al., Figure 35, 'World Model Standard Run,' p 124 in *The Limits to Growth*, Universe Books, NY, 1972. Revised as, Meadows, et al., Figure 4-11, 'Scenario 1: A Reference Point,' p 168 in *Limits to Growth   The 30 Year Update*, Chelsea Green Press, VT, 2004. Reprinted with permission.

IMAGE CREDITS

Preface   p. xx: Courtesy of the author.

Chapter 1   p. 4: A typical Malian family with their possessions: the Natomo family on the roof of their home in Kouakourou, Mali. Published in *Material World,* page 14. © 1994 Peter Menzel/menzelphoto.com; p. 5: A typical English family with their possessions: Hodson Family, Godalming, England, *Material World.* David Reed; p. 20: Eastern Europe in 1992 as seen from Orbit. Image and data processing by NOAA's National Geophysical Data Center. DMSP data collected by US Air Force Weather Agency; p. 21: Eastern Europe in 2002 as seen from Orbit. Image and data processing by NOAA's National Geophysical Data Center. DMSP data collected by US Air Force Weather Agency; p. 22: Illustration of one of Zheng He's ships compared to a ship like Columbus's caravel Nina or Pinta. Jan Adkins.

Chapter 9   p. 243 (top) *Steam Engine* (1832), J. Yeager. Engraving. Plate DVIII from the Edinburgh Encyclopedia First American Edition, Science and the Arts, Volume XVII. Philadelphia: Joseph Parker/Pearson Education; p. 243 (bottom): ARPANET logical map, April 1971. Courtesy of the Computer History Museum.

Chapter 12   p. 331: The Korean peninsula at night as seen from space. Image and data processing by NOAA's National Geophysical Data Center. DMSP data collected by US Air Force Weather Agency; p. 355: The Brains, a caricature of "Boss" Tweed drawn by Thomas Nast, 1870s. Woodcut. North Wind Picture Archives.

Chapter 14   p. 426: Soviet Union propaganda poster. Depicts male worker stoking a furnace. Caption reads "In four years we'll achieve a five year plan!" Lebrecht Music and Arts Photo Library/Alamy.

Calculator   Icon used in the preface and in the end-of-chapter problems. Volkova/Shutterstock.

The World: Population Density, 2000

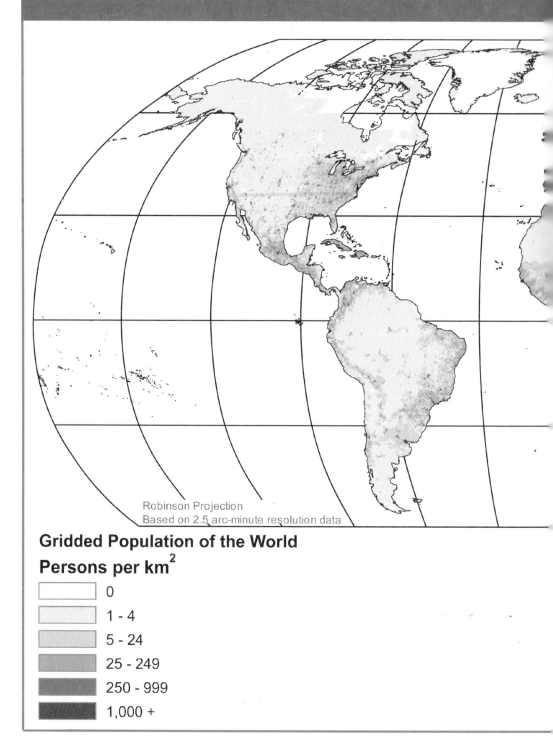

Robinson Projection
Based on 2.5 arc-minute resolution data

Gridded Population of the World

Persons per km^2

	0
	1 - 4
	5 - 24
	25 - 249
	250 - 999
	1,000 +